THE NATURE OF
PREJUDICE

THE NATURE OF
PREJUDICE

UNABRIDGED

GORDON W. ALLPORT

25th ANNIVERSARY EDITION

INTRODUCTION BY
KENNETH CLARK

FOREWORD BY
THOMAS PETTIGREW

PERSEUS BOOKS
Cambridge, Massachusetts

ISBN 0-201-00179-9

30   31   03   02

GORDON W. ALLPORT

One of the leading social psychologists of this century, Gordon W. Allport was born in 1897 in Montezuma, Indiana. He attended Harvard University, where he received his A.B. in 1919, his A.M. in 1921, and his Ph.D. in psychology in 1922. After graduate work at Cambridge, the University of Berlin, and the University of Hamburg, he taught in Istanbul, Turkey, and at Dartmouth College. From 1930 on, he was a professor of psychology at Harvard. Dr. Allport also served as president of both the American and Eastern Psychological associations, director of the National Opinion Research Center, and editor of the *Journal of Abnormal and Social Psychology*. He was author of a number of books, including *The Psychology of Rumor, The Individual and His Religion, Personality: A Psychological Interpretation,* and *Becoming: Basic Considerations for a Psychology of Personality*. Dr. Allport died in 1967.

INTRODUCTION

As one who was fortunate enough to know Gordon Allport not only as one of America's preeminent social psychologists, but also as a warm and compassionate friend, it is not easy for me to discuss his legacy in *The Nature of Prejudice* in isolation from his other contributions to social-psychological theory, research, and insights. And certainly one cannot understand Gordon Allport the social psychologist without understanding him as a social philosopher and as an empathic and warm human being.

Gordon Allport revealed a great deal about himself as a human being in the first edition of *The Nature of Prejudice*, published in 1954. But the clues to the quality of this person who dared to discuss the emotionally laden problem—the pathos and dilemmas of human prejudices—from the perspective of a social scientist are found as early as 1937. In the first edition of his classic book *Personality: A Psychological Interpretation,* Allport revealed much of himself in his discussion of the mature personality. In describing the attributes of a truly mature personality—the extension of the self; self-objectification, insight, and humor; and the unifying philosophy of life—Allport was inadvertently quite accurately describing himself, as those of us who know him could detect. His rather balanced reserve, his ego control, would make it difficult, if not unthinkable, to discuss this point with him. Nonetheless, he remains an outstanding example of the fact that a unifying philosophy of life dominated by human values permeated all aspects of and gave meaning to his life and work.

As is generally recognized, *The Nature of Prejudice* is a classic. Its table of contents establishes the parameters for a scholarly social science approach to the discussion and understanding of this complex human problem. Although changes in emphasis on particular aspects and dimensions of the dynamics and control of racial prejudices have been brought about by social, legal, and political activities within the past 25 years, the basic outline for the understanding of this overall problem remains essentially the same as presented by Allport.

What is not generally recognized or sufficiently stated for the audience of younger students of social problems is that in *The Nature of Prejudice* and in his other contributions, Allport, like Gunnar Myrdal, remains an outstanding model of a major social scientist who was not at all apologetic in his insistence that social science must be value-oriented. Allport and Myrdal demonstrated that it is possible for social science to contribute to the understanding and resolution of social problems and at the same time be value-oriented and socially sensitive. What is more important, Allport and Myrdal personify the insistence that thoughtful, moral, rationalistic social scientists must be the contemporary custodians of such enduring human values as justice—and that trained human intelligence is an important weapon in the ongoing struggle against ignorance, superstition, and injustice.

These are important lessons which must be reemphasized, particularly in the light of developments within the past 25 years wherein it has again become fashionable for some well-publicized social scientists to retreat behind the protective pose of valuelessness, moral relativism, and mere quantification as the inviolable requirements of social science. It may not be a mere coincidence that the neoconservative trends among some contemporary social scientists have come in the wake of the backlash against racial progress sparked by the *Brown* v. *Board of Education* decision of 1954. This convenient escape, whereby some social scientists can avoid involvement in the struggle for social justice or can offer their services to those who seek to use their power to maintain the status quo, may be personally protective and "realistic." But it is not social science in the Allport and Myrdal tradition. It is a subjectivity—a timidity or bias using the traditions, the methods, and the terminology of social science as a transparent cloak.

As early as 1937, Allport argued against the then early indications that the basic problems and potential truths of social science were likely to be obscured or distorted by the worship of statistics. He stated:

> In any event, mere arrays of statistics are never capable of self-interpretation. . . . If the argument is sound, statistics can do no more than symbolize the fact; if the argument is unsound, statistical elaboration can never make it sound and may increase the confusion.

Many examples of Allport's concern for the socially responsible use of social science, its reason for being, are to be found in his writings. In the foreword to the 1958 Anchor Edition of *The Nature of Prejudice,* Allport was prophetic in his critical analysis of the Supreme Court's May 1955 "deliberate speed" directive for the implementation of the 1954 historic *Brown* v. *Board of Education* public school desegregation decision. He cited the evidence which showed that desegregation "comes about most easily in response to a firmly enforced executive order" and that "most citizens accept a forthright *fait accompli* with little protest or disorder. In part they do so because integrationist policies are usually in line with their own consciences (even though countering their prejudices)."

He then concluded:

> Following this line of reasoning, it probably would have been psychologically sounder for the Supreme Court to have insisted upon prompt acquiescence with its ruling of 1954. "Deliberate speed" does not fix an early and inescapable date for compliance. . . . No firm and consistent course of action is agreed upon; leadership falters; countermovement flourish.

If one of the important indices of an objective scientific approach in the attempt to understand and control natural phenomena is the ability to make accurate predictions, then again Gordon Allport demonstrated by the prediction above that it is possible for social concern to be compatible with and reinforce the solidity and relevance of social science.

This point is made very directly when Allport, in his discussion of the roots and manifestations of human hostility, asserts that we must "employ our intelligence effectively in controlling its destructiveness."

Those of us who have been influenced by Gordon Allport and who admired his intellectual grade and his quiet, self-assured belief that the rational, cognitive, and moral potentials of human beings would eventually be antidotes to self-destructive ignorance and superstitions, are reassured by his faith that eventually humans will develop effective techniques to control their prejudices. Allport's prophetic optimism that science can be the positive answer to the struggle for human survival is ironically implicit in the following quote:

> It required years of labor and billions of dollars to gain the secret of the atom. It will take a still greater investment to gain the secrets of man's irrational nature.

In the tradition of Gordon Allport, and as a tribute to his memory, it is the obligation of concerned social scientists to see that this imperative investment is made.

New York City   KENNETH B. CLARK
January 1979

FOREWORD

Gordon Allport was a modest man. Yet in his reserved, even shy, manner, he was justly proud of *The Nature of Prejudice*. His honored place in psychology had been achieved years prior to his undertaking the writing of this volume; *Personality: A Psychological Interpretation,* published in 1937, had firmly established him as one of the world's leading personality theorists. But it was Allport's book on intergroup prejudice that most directly expressed his deepest concerns and values, that translated his more abstract work into concrete ideas for reform and social change.

Allport died in 1967 at the age of 70. Were he alive today, he would undoubtedly be especially pleased by this reissuance of *The Nature of Prejudice* on its twenty-fifth anniversary. And he would also be pleased at the judgments of the book's intellectual content now being rendered a generation later.

The table of contents you will soon inspect has in fact organized the scholarly study of the important concept of prejudice. *The Nature of Prejudice* delineated the area of study, set up its basic categories and problems, and cast it in a broad, eclectic framework that remains today. The book continues to be cited as the definitive theoretical statement of the field, and it remains unchallenged in social science as *the* book on prejudice.

Recent assessments emphasize this lasting value of the volume. Kenneth Clark's views are contained in the preceding Introduction. He is joined in his positive evaluation by two additional social psychologists, M. Brewster Smith and Elliot Aronson, in their recent reconsiderations of the book. Smith, President of the American Psychological Association, as Allport once was, writes in the Winter 1978 *New York University Education Quarterly:*

> Allport's compendious book still invites reading and defies summary. What seemed wise and judicious in 1954 mostly still seems so today. . . . His pervasive fairmindedness, his democratic values, and his concern for evidence continues to set a model for humane, problem-focused social science. . . . [F]rom Allport, we can still get wise guidance in our attempts to give more human substance to our democratic aspirations.

Aronson, writing in the July 1978 issue of *Human Nature,* concurs:

> Gordon Allport's book was both a harbinger and a reflection

of the thinking that went into the Supreme Court decision [*Brown* v. *Board of Education,* 1954]. *The Nature of Prejudice* is a remarkable mixture of careful scholarship and humane values. Allport marshalled an impressive array of data and organized these data clearly and passionately. The book has influenced an entire generation of social psychologists, and deservedly so. . . . What is modern about the book is Allport's perspective; he carefully chose among existing theories and data to come up with a brilliant and accurate statement of the eclectic causes and possible cures of prejudice. . . . This is a tribute to the wisdom, scholarship, and judgment of a graceful mind. Allport avoided the twin pitfalls of championing one position to the exclusion of all others, or of giving each position equal status.

Allport realized that *The Nature of Prejudice* would require a revised edition because the specific examples he tellingly applies throughout the book would become dated. After all, the book and its author were products of their time. The problem of prejudice is largely cast in these pages as one of Protestant whites against the targets of traditional American discrimination— blacks, Jews, and Roman Catholics. The rapid, sweeping events of the last 25 years have broadened the perspective on prejudice, and two of Allport's students—Professor Bernard Kramer of the University of Massachusetts at Boston and I—have been hard at work incorporating these complex developments into a new edition of the book. The end is not in sight, though we hope to publish the revised edition in the next few years. We have found that it is not easy to rewrite a classic. But our problem is the reader's good fortune. That special quality which makes this book so difficult to revise is precisely what also makes it a rewarding experience to read as it was originally written. As a lasting paradigm for the study of prejudice and as a broad, accurate summary of what is known on the subject, *The Nature of Prejudice* is a landmark book and deserves your careful study.

Harvard University   THOMAS FRASER PETTIGREW
January 1979

PREFACE TO THE 1954 EDITION

Civilized men have gained notable mastery over energy, matter, and inanimate nature generally, and are rapidly learning to control physical suffering and premature death. But, by contrast, we appear to be living in the Stone Age so far as our handling of human relationships is concerned. Our deficit in social knowledge seems to void at every step our progress in physical knowledge. The surplus in wealth accumulating to the human race through applied natural science is virtually canceled by the costs of armaments and war. Gains in medical science are widely negated by the poverty that results from war and from trade barriers erected largely by hatred and fear.

At a time when the world as a whole suffers from panic induced by the rival ideologies of east and west, each corner of the earth has its own special burdens of animosity. Moslems distrust non-Moslems. Jews who escaped extermination in Central Europe find themselves in the new State of Israel surrounded by anti-Semitism. Refugees roam in inhospitable lands. Many of the colored people of the world suffer indignities at the hands of whites who invent a fanciful racist doctrine to justify their condescension. The checkerboard of prejudice in the United States is perhaps the most intricate of all. While some of this endless antagonism seems based upon a realistic conflict of interests, most of it, we suspect, is a product of the fears of the imagination. Yet imaginary fears can cause real suffering.

Rivalries and hatreds between groups are nothing new. What is new is the fact that technology has brought these groups too close together for comfort. Russia is no longer a distant land of the steppes; it is over *here*. The United States is no longer remote from the Old World; it is over *there,* with its Point IV, movies, Coca-Cola, and political influence. Nations once safely separated by barricades of water or mountains are exposed to each other by air. Radio, jets, television, paratroopers, international loans, postwar migrations, atomic blasts, moving pictures, *tourism*—all products of the modern age—have thrown human groups into each others' laps. We have not yet learned how to adjust to our new mental and moral proximity.

Yet the situation is not without its hopeful features. Chief among these is the simple fact that human nature seems, on the whole, to prefer the sight of kindness and friendliness to the sight of cruelty. Normal men everywhere reject, in principle and by preference, the path of war and destruction. They like to live in peace and friendship with their neighbors; they prefer to love and be loved rather than to hate and be hated. Cruelty is not a favored human trait. Even the top Nazi officials who were tried at Nürnberg pretended that they knew nothing about the inhuman practices in the concentration camps. They shrank from admitting their part because they too wished to be thought of as human beings. While wars rage, yet our desire is for peace, and while animosity prevails, the weight of mankind's approval is on the side of affiliation. So long as there is this sense of moral dilemma there is hope that it may somehow be resolved and that hate-free values may be brought to prevail.

Especially encouraging is the fact that in recent years men in large numbers have become convinced that scientific intelligence may help us solve the conflict. Theology has always viewed the clash between man's destructive nature and his ideals as a matter of original sin resisting the redemptive process. Valid and expressive as this diagnosis may be, there has been added recently the conviction that man can and should employ his intelligence to assist in his redemption. Men are saying, "Let us make an objective study of conflict in culture and industry, between people of different color and race; let us seek out the roots of prejudice and find concrete means for implementing men's affiliative values." Since the end of the Second World War universities in many lands have given new prominence to this approach under various academic names: *social science, human development, social psychology, human relations, social relations.* Though not yet securely christened, the infant science is thriving. It has found considerable welcome not only in universities, but likewise in public schools, in churches, in progressive industries and government agencies, as well as in international bodies.

Within the past decade or two there has been more solid and enlightening study in this area than in all previous centuries combined. To be sure, the ethical guidelines for human conduct were stated millennia ago in the great creedal systems of mankind—all of them establishing the need and rationale for brotherhood among the earth's inhabitants. But the creeds were formulated in the days of pastoral or nomadic living, in the time of shepherds and petty kingdoms. To implement them in a technical, atomic age requires an improved understanding of the factors making for hatred and tolerance. Science, it has been falsely assumed, should concern itself with material progress and leave human nature and social relationships to an unguided moral sense. We now know that technical advance by itself creates more problems than it solves.

Social science cannot catch up overnight, nor swiftly repair the ravages of undirected technology. It required years of labor and billions of dollars to gain the secret of the atom. It will take a still greater investment to gain the secrets of man's irrational nature. It is easier, someone has said, to smash an atom than a prejudice. The subject of human relations is exceedingly broad. Work necessarily proceeds from a variety of starting points and is concerned with many areas of human association: family life, mental health, industrial relations, international negotiations, training for citizenship—to mention only a few.

The present volume does not pretend to deal with the science of human relations as a whole. It aims merely to clarify one underlying issue—the nature of human prejudice. But this issue is basic, for without knowledge of the roots of hostility we cannot hope to employ our intelligence effectively in controlling its destructiveness.

When we speak of prejudice we are likely to think of "race prejudice." This is an unfortunate association of ideas, for throughout history human prejudice has had little to do with race. The conception of race is recent, scarcely a century old. For the most part prejudice and persecution have rested on other grounds, often on religion. Until the recent past Jews have been persecuted chiefly for their religion, not for their race. Negroes were enslaved primarily because they were economic assets, but the rationale took a religious form: they were pagans by nature, the presumed descendants of Noah's son Ham, and cursed by Noah to be forever "the servants of servants." The concept of race so popular today is in reality an anachronism. Even if it were once applicable, it is scarcely so any longer, owing to the endless dilution of human stocks through cross-mating.

Why then did the race concept become so popular? For one thing, religion lost much of its zeal for proselytizing and therewith its value for designating group membership. Moreover, the simplicity of "race" gave an immediate and visible mark, so it was thought, by which to designate victims of dislike. And the fiction of racial inferiority became, so it seemed, an irrefutable justification for prejudice. It had the stamp of biological finality, and spared people the pains of examining the complex economic, cultural, political, and psychological conditions that enter into group relations.

For most purposes the term "ethnic" is preferable to the term "race." Ethnic refers to characteristics of groups that may be, in different proportions, physical, national, cultural, linguistic, religious, or ideological in character. Unlike "race," the term does not imply biological unity, a condition which in reality seldom marks the groups that are the targets of prejudice. It is true that "ethnic" does not easily cover occupational, class, caste, and political group-ings, nor the two sexes—clusters that are also the victims of prej-udice.

Unfortunately the lexicon of human groups is poor. Until social science offers an improved taxonomy we cannot speak with the pre-cision we should like. It is possible, however, to avoid the error of referring to "race" when the term does not apply. It is, as Ashley-Montagu insists, a mischievous and retardative term in social science. We shall take pains to use it, when we do, in a properly limited manner. For groups marked by any form of cultural cohesion we shall employ "ethnic," but at times may be guilty of overextending the meaning of this already broad term.

It is a serious error to ascribe prejudice and discrimination to any single taproot, reaching into economic exploitation, social structure, the mores, fear, aggression, sex conflict, or any other favored soil. Prejudice and discrimination, as we shall see, may draw nourishment from all these conditions, and many others.

While plural causation is the primary lesson we wish to teach, the reader may reasonably ask whether the author himself does not betray a psychological bias. Does he do justice to the complex eco-nomic, cultural, historical, and situational factors involved? Is he not, by professional habit, disposed to emphasize the role of learn-ing, of cognitive processes, and of personality formation?

It is true that I believe it is only within the nexus of personality that we find the effective operation of historical, cultural, and eco-nomic factors. Unless mores somehow enter the fibre of individual lives they are not effective agents, for it is only *individuals* who can feel antagonism and practice discrimination. Yet "causation" is a broad term, and we can (and should) acknowledge long-range socio-cultural etiology as well as the immediate causation that lies in atti-tudes held by the individual. I have tried (especially in Chapter 13) to present a balanced view of the several levels of causation, even though I place a heavy and convergent emphasis upon psychological factors. If, in spite of my efforts, the result still seems one-sided, I rely on critics to point out the failing.

While the researches and illustrations of this volume are drawn chiefly from the United States, I believe that our analysis of the dy-namics of prejudice has universal validity. To be sure, the ways in which prejudice is manifested vary considerably from country to country: the selected victims are not the same; attitudes toward physical contact with disparaged groups differ; accusations and stereotypes vary.   Yet such evidence as we have from other countries indicates that the basic causes and correlates are essentially identical. Gardner Murphy reaches this conclusion on the basis of his investigation of group tensions in India.   His book *In the Minds of Men* is pertinent in this connection.   Likewise, other studies conducted by agencies of the United Nations support this view.   And anthropological literature, whether devoted to the practices of witchcraft, clan loyalty, or to warfare, suggests that while the targets of prejudice and its expression differ greatly, the underlying dynamics are much the same in all lands.   While this guiding assumption seems safe, we should not yet regard it as conclusive.   Future cross-cultural research will certainly show that the weighting and patterning of causal factors vary greatly in different regions, and that perhaps additional important causes must be added to our present account.

In writing this book I have had in mind two groups of readers, both of which I know to be deeply interested in its subject matter. One group comprises college and university students in all countries who are increasingly concerned with the social and psychological foundations of human behavior, seeking scientific guidance in the improvement of group relations.   The second group consists of the growing population of older citizens and general readers who are of the same mind, although their interests on the whole may be less theoretical and more immediately practical.   With these two groups in mind I have written my exposition in a fairly elementary fashion. Inevitably I have simplified some of the points at issue, but not, I hope, to a point that is in any respect scientifically misleading.

So great is the ferment of investigation and theory in this area that in one sense our account will soon be dated.   New experiments will supersede old, and formulations of various theories will be improved.   Yet there is one feature of the book that I believe will be of lasting value, namely, its principle of organization.   I have tried to offer a framework into which future developments may readily fit.

While my purpose is primarily to clarify the field as a whole, I have also tried, especially in Part VIII, to show how our growing knowledge can be applied to the reduction of group tensions.   A few years ago a census conducted by the American Council on Race Relations discovered 1350 organizations in the United States devoted explicitly to the improvement of group relations.   With what degree of success they are operating is itself a problem requiring scientific evaluation, and is considered in some detail in Chapter 30.   It is fallacious to take exclusively an academic point of view without checking what we say against practical action.   At the same time it is wasteful for practical people to invest time and money in remedial programs that have little scientific support. The successful development of a science of human relations requires bridging basic research and active operation.

The volume gradually took shape under the kindly stimulus of two helpful agencies—one a continuing seminar in the Department of Social Relations at Harvard; the other, certain organizations that gave financial support and encouragement in the preparation of the volume. Valued assistance came from the Moses Kimball Fund of Boston, from the Commission on Community Interrelations of the American Jewish Congress and other friendly members of the Congress, from the National Conference of Christians and Jews, from the Laboratory of Social Relations at Harvard, and from the Research Center directed by my colleague, Professor P. A. Sorokin. These donors made possible several of the investigations reported in these pages, as well as the sifting of the growing literature in this field of study. For their generosity and encouragement I am deeply grateful.

It was the interested and arduous labor of my students in the continuing seminar on Group Conflict and Prejudice that finally determined the content and form of the exposition. In teaching the seminar I was at various times associated with my colleagues Talcott Parsons, Oscar Handlin, and Daniel J. Levinson. Their influence, I believe, is evident. I have also had the benefit of research assistance from Bernard M. Kramer, Jacqueline Y. Sutton, Herbert S. Caron, Leon J. Kamin, and Nathan Altshuler. They have provided helpful material and important suggestions. For reading portions of the manuscript and giving valued criticism I am indebted to Stuart W. Cook, an American authority in the field, and to George V. Coelho and Hugh W. S. Philp who brought to the task the perspective of distant lands. To all these generous helpers I express my gratitude, and especially to Mrs. Eleanor D. Sprague who skillfully helped pilot the project at each successive stage.

September, 1953   G. W. A.

PREFACE TO THE 1958 EDITION

Not long after this book was first printed the United States Supreme Court ruled, in May 1954, that segregation in the nation's public schools is unconstitutional. Its directive of May 1955 ordered that desegregation should be instituted "with all deliberate speed."

This historic action was greeted by world acclaim but displeased many elements in our own Deep South. At the present time at least seven states seem inconsolable and have declared massive resistance against the order. The 1957 crisis in Little Rock dramatized the federal-state deadlock. Domestic and international repercussions of this constitutional crisis cause us grave concern.

In the perspective of this volume I venture two comments on the situation. Chapters 16, 29, and 31 make clear that in this country an integrated racial situation (in employment, in the armed services, in schools) comes about most easily in response to a firmly enforced executive order. Experience shows that most citizens accept a forthright *fait accompli* with little protest or disorder. In part they do so because integrationist policies are usually in line with their own consciences (even though countering their prejudices). In part the swift change is accepted because opposing forces have no time to mobilize and launch a countermovement.

Following this line of reasoning, it probably would have been psychologically sounder for the Supreme Court to have insisted upon prompt acquiescence with its ruling of 1954. "Deliberate speed" does not fix an early and inescapable date for compliance. As subsequent events have shown, the delay has given time for the formation of Citizens' Councils, for the crusades of agitators, and, worst of all, for fierce disagreement to arise among authorities occupying strategic roles in the hierarchy of law enforcement (school boards, mayors, district courts, legislatures, state governors, and Washington officials). No firm and consistent course of action is agreed upon; leadership falters; countermovements flourish. Whether or not it would have been possible, because of the sheer administrative complexity of the step, to achieve school integration throughout the South within a year or two after the original decision, we cannot say. But we can at least explain the sorrowful results that have come from indecisiveness and delay.

Now that a gradualist policy has been adopted, we may point to the desirability of starting integrated education with younger children. In Part V of this volume we trace the development of prejudice in childhood. Young children are wholly free from racial bias and easily adjust to one another if brought together in the early elementary grades. By the time they reach high school young people have formed their teenage cliques and resent the intrusion of strangers; they have taken on the prejudices of their elders; and, worst of all, the most stubborn complex in prejudice—the fear of miscegenation—is aroused. If, therefore, gradualism is permitted, it would seem wiser to start the process of integrating with elementary schools rather than with high schools.

And so our present unhappy state may be viewed in part as a failure of psychological strategy. But in part it is simply the unavoidable reflex of re-aroused prejudice. The segregationist way of life has, of course, been weakening in the South, but to force legal acceleration upon the process compels lingering prejudices to fight a final battle for their self-preservation. Lest the reader conclude that segregation in the schools would in time naturally disappear without Court orders, we must remind him that the trend toward desegregation during the past three decades has required a long array of constitutional decisions—pertaining to transportation facilities, voting, higher education, and other areas of citizens' rights. Legal prods are necessary.

Two factors point to a hopeful outcome of the present impasse. First, we note that many border states and communities have achieved integrated schools with little inconvenience or disorder. Second, even the more resistant areas seem reluctant to employ devices of violence or to argue openly for "white supremacy." It is respectable to plead for "states' rights" but not for "keeping niggers in their place." The mores are changing. Lynchings are now virtually unknown. Recent research shows that many people living in the Deep South are not at heart bigoted. Rather they tend to conform to an established folkway. As the folkway changes they will as readily give their allegiance to the newer pattern.

Recently I had the opportunity to study racial problems at first hand in South Africa. In that country governmental policies are solidly in favor of intensified segregation (*apartheid*). The official morality is thus precisely opposite to the official morality of the United States. The people of Africa and Asia know this fact and intently watch the outcome of the two contrasting policies. In spite of the moral and legal differences, it seems to me that the general substance of this volume applies equally well to the situation in both lands. If anything, I would, on the basis of my experience in South Africa, give extra weight to the portions of this book dealing with conformity and with sociocultural factors in prejudice (Part IV).

G. W. A.

CONTENTS

PART III. PERCEIVING AND THINKING ABOUT GROUP DIFFERENCES

CHAPTER 10. THE COGNITIVE PROCESS 165

CHAPTER 11. LINGUISTIC FACTORS 178

CHAPTER 12. STEREOTYPES IN OUR CULTURE 189

CHAPTER 13. THEORIES OF PREJUDICE 206

PART IV.   SOCIOCULTURAL FACTORS

CHAPTER 14.   SOCIAL STRUCTURE AND CULTURAL PATTERN 221

CHAPTER 15.   CHOICE OF SCAPEGOATS 243

CHAPTER 16.   THE EFFECT OF CONTACT 261

PART V. ACQUIRING PREJUDICE

PART VI. THE DYNAMICS OF PREJUDICE

PART VII. CHARACTER STRUCTURE

PART VIII.   REDUCING GROUP TENSIONS

THE NATURE OF
PREJUDICE

Part I

PREFERENTIAL THINKING

CHAPTER 1

WHAT IS THE PROBLEM?

TWO CASES—DEFINITION—IS PREJUDICE A VALUE CONCEPT?—
FUNCTIONAL SIGNIFICANCE—ATTITUDES AND BELIEFS—
ACTING OUT PREJUDICE

*For myself, earth-bound and fettered to the scene of my ac-
tivities, I confess that I do feel the differences of mankind,
national and individual. . . . I am, in plainer words, a bundle
of prejudices—made up of likings and dislikings—the veriest
thrall to sympathies, apathies, antipathies.*

CHARLES LAMB

In Rhodesia a white truck driver passed a group of idle natives
and muttered, "They're lazy brutes." A few hours later he saw
natives heaving two-hundred pound sacks of grain onto a truck,
singing in rhythm to their work. "Savages," he grumbled. "What
do you expect?"

In one of the West Indies it was customary at one time for natives
to hold their noses conspicuously whenever they passed an American
on the street. And in England, during the war, it was said, "The
only trouble with the Yanks is that they are over-paid, over-sexed,
and over here."

Polish people often called the Ukrainians "reptiles" to express
their contempt for a group they regarded as ungrateful, revengeful,
wily, and treacherous. At the same time Germans called their
neighbors to the east "Polish cattle." The Poles retaliated with
"Prussian swine"—a jibe at the presumed uncouthness and lack of
honor of the Germans.

In South Africa, the English, it is said, are against the Afrikaner;
both are against the Jews; all three are opposed to the Indians;
while all four conspire against the native black.

In Boston, a dignitary of the Roman Catholic Church was driving
along a lonesome road on the outskirts of the city. Seeing a small
Negro boy trudging along, the dignitary told his chauffeur to stop
and give the boy a lift. Seated together in the back of the limou-
sine, the cleric, to make conversation, asked, "Little Boy, are you a
Catholic?" Wide-eyed with alarm, the boy replied, "No sir, it's
bad enough being colored without being one of those things."

3

Pressed to tell what Chinese people really think of Americans, a Chinese student reluctantly replied, "Well, we think they are the best of the foreign devils." This incident occurred before the Communist revolution in China. Today's youth in China are trained to think of Americans as the *worst* of the foreign devils.

In Hungary, the saying is, "An anti-Semite is a person who hates the Jews more than is absolutely necessary."

No corner of the world is free from group scorn. Being fettered to our respective cultures, we, like Charles Lamb, are bundles of prejudice.

Two Cases

An anthropologist in his middle thirties had two young children, Susan and Tom. His work required him to live for a year with a tribe of American Indians in the home of a hospitable Indian family. He insisted, however, that his own family live in a community of white people several miles distant from the Indian reservation. Seldom would he allow Tom and Susan to come to the tribal village, though they pleaded for the privilege. And on rare occasions when they made the visit, he sternly refused to allow them to play with the friendly Indian children.

Some people, including a few of the Indians, complained that the anthropologist was untrue to the code of his profession—that he was displaying race prejudice.

The truth is otherwise. This scientist knew that tuberculosis was rife in the tribal village, and that four of the children in the household where he lived had already died of the disease. The probability of infection for his own children, if they came much in contact with the natives, was high. His better judgment told him that he should not take the risk. In this case, his ethnic avoidance was based on rational and realistic grounds. There was no feeling of antagonism involved. The anthropologist had no generally negative attitude toward the Indians. In fact he liked them very much.

Since this case fails to illustrate what we mean by racial or ethnic prejudice, let us turn to another.

In the early summer season two Toronto newspapers carried between them holiday advertisements from approximately 100 different resorts. A Canadian social scientist, S. L. Wax, undertook an interesting experiment.[1] To each of these hotels and resorts he wrote two letters, mailing them at the same time, and asking for room reservations for exactly the same dates. One letter he signed

---

[1] See references at ends of the chapters.

with the name "Mr. Greenberg," the other with the name "Mr. Lockwood." Here are the results:

To "Mr. Greenberg":
  52 percent of the resorts replied;
  36 percent offered him accommodations.
To "Mr. Lockwood":
  95 percent of the resorts replied;
  93 percent offered him accommodations.

Thus, nearly all of the resorts in question welcomed Mr. Lockwood as a correspondent and as a guest; but nearly half of them failed to give Mr. Greenberg the courtesy of a reply, and only slightly more than a third were willing to receive him as a guest.

None of the hotels knew "Mr. Lockwood" or "Mr. Greenberg." For all they knew "Mr. Greenberg" might be a quiet, orderly gentleman, and "Mr. Lockwood" rowdy and drunk. The decision was obviously made not on the merits of the individual, but on "Mr. Greenberg's" supposed membership in a group. He suffered discourtesy and exclusion *solely* because of his name, which aroused a prejudgment of his desirability in the eyes of the hotel managers.

Unlike our first case, this incident contains the two essential ingredients of ethnic prejudice. (1) There is definite hostility and rejection. The majority of the hotels wanted nothing to do with "Mr. Greenberg." (2) The basis of the rejection was categorical. "Mr. Greenberg" was not evaluated as an individual. Rather, he was condemned on the basis of his presumed group membership.

A close reasoner might at this point ask the question: What basic difference exists between the cases of the anthropologist and the hotels in the matter of "categorical rejection"? Did not the anthropologist reason from the high probability of infection that it would be safer not to risk contact between his children and the Indians? And did not the hotelkeepers reason from a high probability that Mr. Greenberg's ethnic membership would in fact bring them an undesirable guest? The anthropologist knew that tubercular contagion was rampant; did not the innkeepers know that "Jewish vices" were rampant and not to be risked?

This question is legitimate. If the innkeepers were basing their rejection on facts (more accurately, on a high probability that a given Jew will have undesirable traits), their action would be as rational and defensible as the anthropologist's. But we can be sure that such is not the case.

Some managers may never have had any unpleasant experiences with Jewish guests—a situation that seems likely in view of the fact that in many cases Jewish guests had never been admitted to the hotels.   Or, if they have had such experiences, they have not kept a record of their frequency in comparison with objectionable non-Jewish guests.   Certainly they have not consulted scientific studies concerning the relative frequency of desirable and undesirable traits in Jews and non-Jews.   If they sought such evidence, they would, as we shall learn in Chapter 6, find no support for their policy of rejection.

It is, of course, possible that the manager himself was free from personal prejudice, but, if so, he was reflecting the anti-Semitism of his gentile guests.   In either event our point is made.

Definition

The word *prejudice,* derived from the Latin noun *praejudicium,* has, like most words, undergone a change of meaning since classical times.   There are three stages in the transformation.[2]

(1) To the ancients, *praejudicium* meant a *precedent*—a judgment based on previous decisions and experiences.

(2) Later, the term, in English, acquired the meaning of a judgment formed before due examination and consideration of the facts—a premature or hasty judgment.

(3) Finally the term acquired also its present emotional flavor of favorableness or unfavorableness that accompanies such a prior and unsupported judgment.

Perhaps the briefest of all definitions of prejudice is: *thinking ill of others without sufficient warrant.*[3]   This crisp phrasing contains the two essential ingredients of all definitions—reference to unfounded judgment and to a feeling-tone.   It is, however, too brief for complete clarity.

In the first place, it refers only to *negative* prejudice.   People may be prejudiced in favor of others; they may think *well* of them without sufficient warrant.   The wording offered by the New English Dictionary recognizes positive as well as negative prejudice:

A feeling, favorable or unfavorable, toward a person or thing, prior to, or not based on, actual experience.

While it is important to bear in mind that biases may be *pro* as well as *con,* it is none the less true that *ethnic* prejudice is mostly negative.   A group of students was asked to describe their attitudes toward ethnic groups.   No suggestion was made that might lead them toward negative reports.   Even so, they reported eight times as many antagonistic attitudes as favorable attitudes. In this volume, accordingly, we shall be concerned chiefly with prejudice *against*, not with prejudice *in favor of*, ethnic groups.

The phrase "thinking ill of others" is obviously an elliptical expression that must be understood to include feelings of scorn or dislike, of fear and aversion, as well as various forms of antipathetic conduct: such as talking against people, discriminating against them, or attacking them with violence.

Similarly, we need to expand the phrase "without sufficient warrant." A judgment is unwarranted whenever it lacks basis in fact. A wit defined prejudice as "being down on something you're not up on."

It is not easy to say how much fact is required in order to justify a judgment. A prejudiced person will almost certainly claim that he has sufficient warrant for his views. He will tell of bitter experiences he has had with refugees, Catholics, or Orientals. But, in most cases, it is evident that his facts are scanty and strained. He resorts to a selective sorting of his own few memories, mixes them up with hearsay, and overgeneralizes. No one can possibly know *all* refugees, Catholics, or Orientals. Hence any negative judgment of these groups *as a whole* is, strictly speaking, an instance of thinking ill without sufficient warrant.

Sometimes, the ill-thinker has no first-hand experience on which to base his judgment. A few years ago most Americans thought exceedingly ill of Turks—but very few had ever seen a Turk nor did they know any person who had seen one. Their warrant lay exclusively in what they had heard of the Armenian massacres and of the legendary crusades. On such evidence they presumed to condemn all members of a nation.

Ordinarily, prejudice manifests itself in dealing with individual members of rejected groups. But in avoiding a Negro neighbor, or in answering "Mr. Greenberg's" application for a room, we frame our action to accord with our categorical generalization of the group as a whole. We pay little or no attention to individual differences, and overlook the important fact that Negro X, our neighbor, is not Negro Y, whom we dislike for good and sufficient reason; that Mr. Greenberg, who may be a fine gentleman, is not Mr. Bloom, whom we have good reason to dislike.

So common is this process that we might define prejudice as:

> an avertive or hostile attitude toward a person who belongs to a group, simply because he belongs to that group, and is therefore presumed to have the objectionable qualities ascribed to the group.

This definition stresses the fact that while ethnic prejudice in daily life is ordinarily a matter of dealing with individual people it also entails an unwarranted idea concerning a group as a whole.

Returning to the question of "sufficient warrant," we must grant that few if any human judgments are based on absolute certainty. We can be reasonably, but not absolutely, sure that the sun will rise tomorrow, and that death and taxes will finally overtake us. The sufficient warrant for any judgment is always a matter of probabilities. Ordinarily our judgments of natural happenings are based on firmer and higher probabilities than our judgments of people. Only rarely do our categorical judgments of nations or ethnic groups have a foundation in high probability.

Take the hostile view of Nazi leaders held by most Americans during World War II. Was it prejudiced? The answer is No, because there was abundant available evidence regarding the evil policies and practices accepted as the official code of the party. True, there may have been good individuals in the party who at heart rejected the abominable program; but the probability was so high that the Nazi group constituted an actual menace to world peace and to humane values that a realistic and justified conflict resulted. The high probability of danger removes an antagonism from the domain of prejudice into that of realistic social conflict.

In the case of gangsters, our antagonism is not a matter of prejudice, for the evidence of their antisocial conduct is conclusive. But soon the line becomes hard to draw. How about an ex-convict? It is notoriously difficult for an ex-convict to obtain a steady job where he can be self-supporting and self-respecting. Employers naturally are suspicious if they know the man's past record. But often they are more suspicious than the facts warrant. If they looked further they might find evidence that the man who stands before them is genuinely reformed, or even that he was unjustly accused in the first place. To shut the door merely because a man has a criminal record has *some* probability in its favor, for many prisoners are never reformed; but there is also an element of unwarranted prejudgment involved. We have here a true borderline instance.

We can never hope to draw a hard and fast line between "sufficient" and "insufficient" warrant. For this reason we cannot always be sure whether we are dealing with a case of prejudice or nonprejudice. Yet no one will deny that often we form judgments on the basis of scant, even nonexistent, probabilities.

Overcategorization is perhaps the commonest trick of the human mind. Given a thimbleful of facts we rush to make generalizations as large as a tub. One young boy developed the idea that all Norwegians were giants because he was impressed by the gigantic stature of Ymir in the saga, and for years was fearful lest he meet a living Norwegian. A certain man happened to know three Englishmen personally and proceeded to declare that the whole English race had the common attributes that he observed in these three.

There is a natural basis for this tendency. Life is so short, and the demands upon us for practical adjustments so great, that we cannot let our ignorance detain us in our daily transactions. We have to decide whether objects are good or bad by classes. We cannot weigh each object in the world by itself. Rough and ready rubrics, however coarse and broad, have to suffice.

Not every overblown generalization is a prejudice. Some are simply *misconceptions,* wherein we organize wrong information. One child had the idea that all people living in Minneapolis were "monopolists." And from his father he had learned that monopolists were evil folk. When in later years he discovered the confusion, his dislike of dwellers in Minneapolis vanished.

Here we have the test to help us distinguish between ordinary errors of prejudgment and prejudice. If a person is capable of rectifying his erroneous judgments in the light of new evidence he is not prejudiced. *Prejudgments become prejudices only if they are not reversible when exposed to new knowledge.* A prejudice, unlike a simple misconception, is actively resistant to all evidence that would unseat it. We tend to grow emotional when a prejudice is threatened with contradiction. Thus the difference between ordinary prejudgments and prejudice is that one can discuss and rectify a prejudgment without emotional resistance.

Taking these various considerations into account, we may now attempt a final definition of negative ethnic prejudice—one that will serve us throughout this book. Each phrase in the definition represents a considerable condensation of the points we have been discussing:

> Ethnic prejudice is an antipathy based upon a faulty and inflexible generalization. It may be felt or expressed. It may be directed toward a group as a whole, or toward an individual because he is a member of that group.

The net effect of prejudice, thus defined, is to place the object of prejudice at some disadvantage not merited by his own misconduct.

Is Prejudice a Value Concept?

Some authors have introduced an additional ingredient into their definitions of prejudice. They claim that attitudes are prejudiced only if they violate some important norms or values accepted in a culture.[4] They insist that prejudice is only that type of pre-judgment that is ethically disapproved in a society.

One experiment shows that common usage of the term has this flavor. Several adult judges were asked to take statements made by ninth-grade children and sort them into piles according to the degree of "prejudice" represented. It turned out that whatever a boy may have said against girls as a group was not judged to be prejudice, for it is regarded as normal for an early adolescent to heap scorn on the opposite sex. Nor were statements made against teachers considered examples of prejudice. This antagonism, too, seemed natural to this age, and socially unimportant. But when the children expressed animosity toward labor unions, toward social classes, races or nationalities, more judgments of "prejudice" were given.[5]

In brief, the social importance of an unfair attitude entered into the judges' view of its prejudiced character. A fifteen-year-old boy who is "off" girls is not considered as biased as one who is "off" nationalities other than his own.

If we use the term in this sense we should have to say that the older caste system in India—which is now breaking down—involved no prejudice. It was simply a convenient stratification in the social structure, acceptable to nearly all citizens because it clarified the division of labor and defined social prerogatives. It was for centuries acceptable even to the untouchables because the religious doctrine of reincarnation made the arrangement seem entirely just. An untouchable was ostracized because in previous existences he failed to merit promotions to a higher caste or to a supermortal existence. He now has his just desserts and likewise an opportunity through an obedient and spiritually directed life to win advancement in future reincarnations. Assuming that this account of a happy caste system really marked Hindu society at one time, was there then no question of prejudice?

Or take the Ghetto system. Through long stretches of history Jews have been segregated in certain residential zones, sometimes with a chain around the region. Only inside were they allowed to move freely. The method had the merit of preventing unpleasant conflict, and the Jew, knowing his place, could plan his life with a certain definiteness and comfort. It could be argued that his lot was much more secure and predictable than in the modern world. There were periods in history when neither the Jew nor gentile felt particularly outraged by the system. Was prejudice then absent?

Were the ancient Greeks (or early American plantation owners) prejudiced against their hereditary class of slaves? To be sure they looked down upon them, and undoubtedly held fallacious theories concerning their inherent inferiority and "animal-like" mentality; but so natural did it all seem, so good, so proper, that there was no moral dilemma.

Even today, in certain states, a *modus vivendi* has been worked out between white and colored people. A ritual of relations is established, and most people abide unthinkingly by the realities of social structure. Since they merely follow the folkways they deny that they are prejudiced. The Negro simply knows his place, and white people know theirs. Shall we then say, as some writers have, that prejudice exists only when actions are *more* condescending, *more* negative, than the accepted culture itself prescribes? Is prejudice to be regarded merely as deviance from common practice? [6]

Among Navaho Indians, as in many societies on earth, there is belief in witchcraft. Whoever is accused of being a witch is earnestly avoided or soundly punished on the basis of the prevailing erroneous conceptions concerning the dark powers of witches. Here, as in our preceding illustrations, all the terms of our definition of prejudice are met—but few members of the Navaho society make a moral issue of the matter. Since the rejection of witches is an accepted custom, not socially disapproved, can it be called prejudice?

What shall we say about this line of argument? It has impressed some critics so much that they hold the whole problem of prejudice to be nothing more than a value-judgment invented by "liberal intellectuals." When liberals do not approve of a folkway *they* arbitrarily call it prejudice. What they should do is to follow not their own sense of moral outrage, but consult the ethos of a culture. If the culture itself is in conflict, holding up a higher standard of conduct than many of its members practice, then we may speak of prejudice existing within the culture. Prejudice is the *moral evaluation* placed by a culture on some of its own practices. It is a designation of attitudes that are disapproved.

These critics, it would seem, confuse two separate and distinct problems. Prejudice in the simple psychological sense of negative, overgeneralized judgment exists just as surely in caste societies, slave societies, or countries believing in witchcraft as in ethically more sensitive societies. The second problem—whether prejudice is or is not attended by a sense of moral outrage—is a separate issue altogether.

To be sure, countries with a Christian and democratic tradition

view ethnic prejudice with disfavor more often than do countries
without this ethical tradition. And it is also probably true that
"liberal intellectuals" are more likely than most people to become
emotionally aroused by the problem.

Even so, there is not the slightest justification for confusing the
objective facts of prejudice with cultural or ethical judgment of
these facts. The unpleasant flavor of a word should not mislead us
into believing that it stands only for a value-judgment. Take the
word *epidemic*. It suggests something disagreeable. No doubt
Pasteur, the great conqueror of epidemics, hated them. But his
value-judgment did not affect in the slightest degree the objective
facts with which he dealt so successfully. *Syphilis* is a term flavored
with opprobrium in our culture. But the emotional tinge has no
bearing whatever upon the operations of the spirochete within the
human frame.

Some cultures, like our own, abjure prejudice; some do not; but
the fundamental psychological analysis of prejudice is the same
whether we are talking about Hindus, Navahos, the Greeks of
antiquity, or Middletown, U.S.A. Whenever a negative attitude toward persons is sustained by a spurious overgeneralization we encounter the syndrome of prejudice. It is not essential that people
deplore this syndrome. It has existed in all ages in every country.
It constitutes a bona fide psychological problem. The degree of
moral indignation engendered is irrelevant.

Functional Significance

Certain definitions of prejudice include one additional ingredient.
The following is an example:

> Prejudice is a pattern of hostility in interpersonal relations
> which is directed against an entire group, or against its individual
> members; it fulfills a specific irrational function for its bearer.[7]

The final phrase of this definition implies that negative attitudes
are not prejudices unless they serve a private, self-gratifying purpose
for the person who has them.

It will become abundantly clear in later chapters that much prejudice is indeed fashioned and sustained by self-gratifying considerations. In most cases prejudice seems to have some "functional significance" for the bearer. Yet this is not always the case. Much
prejudice is a matter of blind conformity with prevailing folkways.
Some of it, as Chapter 17 will show, has no important relation to
the life-economy of the individual. For this reason it seems unwise
to insist that the "irrational function" of prejudice be included in
our basic definition.

Attitudes and Beliefs

We have said that an adequate definition of prejudice contains two essential ingredients. There must be an *attitude* of favor or disfavor; and it must be related to an overgeneralized (and therefore erroneous) *belief*. Prejudiced statements sometimes express the attitudinal factor, sometimes the belief factor. In the following series the first item expresses attitude, the second, belief:

I can't abide Negroes.
Negroes are smelly.

I wouldn't live in an apartment house with Jews.
There are a few exceptions, but in general all Jews are pretty much alike.

I don't want Japanese-Americans in my town.
Japanese-Americans are sly and tricky.

Is it important to distinguish between the attitudinal and belief aspects of prejudice? For some purposes, no. When we find one, we usually find the other. Without some generalized beliefs concerning a group as a whole, a hostile attitude could not long be sustained. In modern researches it turns out that people who express a high degree of antagonistic attitudes on a test for prejudice, also show that they believe to a high degree that the groups they are prejudiced against have a large number of objectionable qualities.[8]

But for some purposes it is useful to distinguish attitude from belief. For example, we shall see in Chapter 30 that certain programs designed to reduce prejudice succeed in altering beliefs but not in changing attitudes. Beliefs, to some extent, can be rationally attacked and altered. Usually, however, they have the slippery propensity of accommodating themselves somehow to the negative attitude which is much harder to change. The following dialogue illustrates the point:

Mr. X: The trouble with the Jews is that they only take care of their own group.

Mr. Y: But the record of the Community Chest campaign shows that they give more generously, in proportion to their numbers, to the general charities of the community, than do non-Jews.

Mr. X: That shows they are always trying to buy favor and intrude into Christian affairs. They think of nothing but money; that is why there are so many Jewish bankers.

Mr. Y: But a recent study shows that the percentage of Jews in the banking business is negligible, far smaller than the percentage of non-Jews.

Mr. X: That's just it; they don't go in for respectable business; they are only in the movie business or run night clubs.

Thus the belief system has a way of slithering around to justify the more permanent attitude. The process is one of *rationalization*—of the accommodation of beliefs to attitudes.

It is well to keep these two aspects of prejudice in mind, for in our subsequent discussions we shall have occasion to make use of the distinction. But wherever the term *prejudice* is used without specifying these aspects, the reader may assume that both attitude and belief are intended.

Acting Out Prejudice

What people actually do in relation to groups they dislike is not always directly related to what they think or feel about them. Two employers, for example, may dislike Jews to an equal degree. One may keep his feelings to himself and may hire Jews on the same basis as any workers—perhaps because he wants to gain goodwill for his factory or store in the Jewish community. The other may translate his dislike into his employment policy, and refuse to hire Jews. Both men are prejudiced, but only one of them practices *discrimination*. As a rule discrimination has more immediate and serious social consequences than has prejudice.

It is true that any negative attitude tends somehow, somewhere, to express itself in action. Few people keep their antipathies entirely to themselves. The more intense the attitude, the more likely it is to result in vigorously hostile action.

We may venture to distinguish certain degrees of negative action from the least energetic to the most.

1. *Antilocution.* Most people who have prejudices talk about them. With like-minded friends, occasionally with strangers, they may express their antagonism freely. But many people never go beyond this mild degree of antipathetic action.

2. *Avoidance.* If the prejudice is more intense, it leads the individual to avoid members of the disliked group, even perhaps at the cost of considerable inconvenience. In this case, the bearer of prejudice does not directly inflict harm upon the group he dislikes. He takes the burden of accommodation and withdrawal entirely upon himself.

3. *Discrimination.* Here the prejudiced person makes detrimental distinctions of an active sort. He undertakes to ex-

clude all members of the group in question from certain types of employment, from residential housing, political rights, educational or recreational opportunities, churches, hospitals, or from some other social privileges. Segregation is an institutionalized form of discrimination, enforced legally or by common custom.[9]

4. *Physical attack.* Under conditions of heightened emotion prejudice may lead to acts of violence or semiviolence. An unwanted Negro family may be forcibly ejected from a neighborhood, or so severely threatened that it leaves in fear. Gravestones in Jewish cemeteries may be desecrated. The Northside's Italian gang may lie in wait for the Southside's Irish gang.

5. *Extermination.* Lynchings, pogroms, massacres, and the Hitlerian program of genocide mark the ultimate degree of violent expression of prejudice.

This five-point scale is not mathematically constructed, but it serves to call attention to the enormous range of activities that may issue from prejudiced attitudes and beliefs. While many people would never move from antilocution to avoidance; or from avoidance to active discrimination, or higher on the scale, still it is true that activity on one level makes transition to a more intense level easier. It was Hitler's antilocution that led Germans to avoid their Jewish neighbors and erstwhile friends. This preparation made it easier to enact the Nürnberg laws of discrimination which, in turn, made the subsequent burning of synagogues and street attacks upon Jews seem natural. The final step in the macabre progression was the ovens at Auschwitz.

From the point of view of social consequences much "polite prejudice" is harmless enough—being confined to idle chatter. But unfortunately, the fateful progression is, in this century, growing in frequency. The resulting disruption in the human family is menacing. And as the peoples of the earth grow ever more interdependent, they can tolerate less well the mounting friction.

NOTES AND REFERENCES

1. S. L. WAX. A survey of restrictive advertising and discrimination by summer resorts in the Province of Ontario. Canadian Jewish Congress: *Information and comment,* 1948, **7**, 10-13.

2. Cf. *A New English Dictionary.* (SIR JAMES A. H. MURRAY, ED.) Oxford: Clarendon Press, 1909, Vol. VII, Pt. II, 1275.

3. This definition is derived from the Thomistic moralists who regard prejudice as "rash judgment." The author is indebted to the Rev.

J. H. Fichter, S. J., for calling this treatment to his attention. The definition is more fully discussed by the REV. JOHN LAFARGE, S. J., in *The Race Question and the Negro,* New York: Longmans, Green, 1945, 174 ff.

4. Cf. R. M. WILLIAMS, JR. The reduction of intergroup tensions. New York: *Social Science Research Council,* 1947, Bulletin 57, 37.

5. H. S. DYER. The usability of the concept of "Prejudice." *Psychometrika,* 1945, 10, 219-224.

6. The following definition is written from this relativistic point of view: "A prejudice is a generalized anti-attitude, and/or an anti-action toward any distinct category or group of people, when either the attitude or the action or both are judged by the community in which they are found to be less favorable to the given people than the normally accepted standard of that community." P. BLACK AND R. D. ATKINS. Conformity versus prejudice as exemplified in white-Negro relations in the South: some methodological considerations. *Journal of Psychology,* 1950, 30, 109-121.

7. N. W. ACKERMAN AND MARIE JAHODA. *Anti-Semitism and Emotional Disorder.* New York: Harper, 1950, 4.

8. Not all scales for measuring prejudice include items that reflect both attitudes and beliefs. Those that do so report correlations between the two types of items of the order of .80. Cf. BABETTE SAMELSON. *The patterning of attitudes and beliefs regarding the American Negro.* (Unpublished.) Radcliffe College Library, 1945. Also, A. ROSE, *Studies in reduction of prejudice.* (Mimeograph.) Chicago: American Council on Race Relations, 1947, 11-14.

9. Aware of the world-wide problem of discrimination, the Commission on Human Rights of the United Nations has prepared a thorough analysis of *The main types and causes of discrimination.* United Nations Publications, 1949, XIV, 3.

CHAPTER 2

THE NORMALITY OF PREJUDGMENT

SEPARATION OF HUMAN GROUPS—PROCESS OF CATEGORIZATION—
WHEN CATEGORIES CONFLICT WITH EVIDENCE—PERSONAL VALUES
AS CATEGORIES—PERSONAL VALUES AND PREJUDICE—SUMMARY

Why do human beings slip so easily into ethnic prejudice? They
do so because the two essential ingredients that we have discussed
—*erroneous generalization* and *hostility*—are natural and common
capacities of the human mind. For the time being we shall leave
hostility and its related problems out of account. Let us consider
only those basic conditions of human living and thinking that lead
naturally to the formation of erroneous and categorical prejudgment
—and which therefore deposit us on the very threshold of ethnic
and group antagonism.

The reader is warned that the full story of prejudice cannot be
told in this—or in any other—single chapter of this book. Each
chapter, taken by itself, is one-sided. This is the inevitable defect
of any *analytical* treatment of the subject. The problem as a whole
is many-sided, and the reader is asked, while examining one facet,
to hold in mind the simultaneous existence of many other facets.
Thus, the present chapter presents a somewhat "cognitive" view
of prejudgment. For the time being, many ego-involved, emotional,
cultural, and personal factors that are simultaneously operating are,
of necessity, held in suspense.

The Separation of Human Groups

Everywhere on earth we find a condition of separateness among
groups. People mate with their own kind. They eat, play, reside
in homogeneous clusters. They visit with their own kind, and
prefer to worship together. Much of this automatic cohesion is
due to nothing more than convenience. There is no need to turn
to out-groups for companionship. With plenty of people at hand to
choose from, why create for ourselves the trouble of adjusting to
new languages, new foods, new cultures, or to people of a different
educational level? It requires less effort to deal with people who
have similar presuppositions. One reason for the gaiety and joy
of college class reunions is that all members are the same age, have

the same cultural reminiscences (even to the old popular songs they all love), and have essentially the same educational history.

Thus most of the business of life can go on with less effort if we stick together with our own kind.   Foreigners are a strain.   So too are people of a higher or lower social and economic class than our own.   We don't play bridge with the janitor.   Why?   Perhaps he prefers poker; almost certainly he would not grasp the type of jests and chatter that we and our friends enjoy; there would be a certain awkwardness in blending our differing manners.   It is not that we have class prejudice, but only that we find comfort and ease in our own class.   And normally there are plenty of people of our own class, or race, or religion to play, live, and eat with, and to marry.

In occupational situations we are much more likely to have to deal with members of out-groups.   In a stratified industry or business, management must deal with workers, executives with janitors, and salesmen with clerks.   At machines, differing ethnic clusters may work side by side, though they almost certainly take their recreation in their own more comfortable groups.   Contact at work is seldom sufficient to overcome psychological separateness.   Sometimes the contact is so stratified that the sense of separateness is intensified.   The Mexican worker may grow jealous of the greater ease of life enjoyed by his Anglo employer.   The white workman may fear that the Negro helper stands ready and eager to advance and take the white man's job.   Foreign groups have been imported into an industrial level to do menial work, only to arouse fear and jealousy in the majority group when they start to rise in the occupational and social ladder.

It is not always the dominant majority that forces minority groups to remain separate.   They often prefer to keep their identity, so that they need not strain to speak a foreign language or to watch their manners.   Like the old grads at a college reunion, they can "let down" with those who share their traditions and presuppositions.

One enlightening study shows that high school students representing American minorities display even greater ethnocentrism than do native white Americans.   Negro, Chinese, and Japanese young people, for example, are much more insistent upon choosing their friends, their work companions, and their "dates" from their own group than are white students.   It is true that they do not select "leaders" from their own group, but prefer the non-Jewish white majority.   But while agreeing that class leaders should come from the dominant group, they then seek the greater comfort of confining their intimate relations to their own kind.[1]

The initial fact, therefore, is that human groups tend to stay apart. We need not ascribe this tendency to a gregarious instinct, to a "consciousness of kind," or to prejudice. The fact is adequately explained by the principles of ease, least effort, congeniality, and pride in one's own culture.

Once this separatism exists, however, the ground is laid for all sorts of psychological elaboration. People who stay separate have few channels of communication. They easily exaggerate the degree of difference between groups, and readily misunderstand the grounds for it. And, perhaps most important of all, the separateness may lead to genuine conflicts of interests, as well as to many imaginary conflicts.

Let us take one example. The Mexican worker in Texas is sharply set off from the Anglo employer. He lives apart, speaks a different language, has a totally different tradition, and attends a different church. His children, very likely, do not attend the same school as do the employer's children; nor do they play together. All the employer knows is that Juan comes to work, takes his money, and departs. He notes that Juan is irregular in his work, seems indolent and uncommunicative. Nothing is easier than for the employer to assume that this behavior is characteristic of Juan's entire group. He develops a stereotype concerning the laziness, improvidence, and undependability of the Mexicans. Then if the employer finds himself inconvenienced economically by Juan's irregularity, he has grounds for hostility—especially if he believes that his high taxes or financial troubles are due to the Mexican population.

Juan's employer now thinks "all Mexicans are lazy." When he meets a new Mexican he will have this conviction in mind. The prejudgment is erroneous because (1) not all Mexicans are alike; (2) Juan was not really lazy but had many private values that caused him to behave the way he did. He liked to be with his children; he observed religious holy days; he had repairs to make on his own house. The employer is ignorant of all these facts. Instead of saying, as he logically ought, "I do not know the reasons for Juan's behavior because I do not know either him as a person or his culture," the employer disposed of a complex problem in an oversimplified way, attributing to Juan and his nation an attribute of "laziness."

Yet the employer's stereotype grew up out of a "kernel of truth." It was a fact that Juan was a Mexican and was irregular at his work. It may also have been a fact that the employer had had similar experience with other Mexican workmen.

The distinction between a well-founded generalization and an erroneous generalization is very hard to draw, particularly by the individual who himself harbors the generalization.   Let us examine this issue more closely.

The Process of Categorization

The human mind must think with the aid of categories (the term is equivalent here to *generalizations*).   Once formed, categories are the basis for normal prejudgment.   We cannot possibly avoid this process.   Orderly living depends upon it.

We may say that the process of categorization has five important characteristics.

(1) **It forms large classes and clusters for guiding our daily adjustments.**   We spend most of our waking life calling upon preformed categories for this purpose.   When the sky darkens and the barometer falls we prejudge that rain will fall.   We adjust to this cluster of happenings by taking along an umbrella.   When an angry looking dog charges down the street, we categorize him as a "mad dog" and avoid him.   When we go to a physician with an ailment we expect him to behave in a certain way toward us.   On these, and countless other occasions, we "type" a single event, place it within a familiar rubric, and act accordingly.   Sometimes we are mistaken: the event does not fit the category.   It does not rain; the dog is not mad; the physician behaves unprofessionally.   Yet our behavior was rational.   It was based on high probability.   Though we used the wrong category, we did the best we could.

What all this means is that our experience in life tends to form itself into clusters (concepts, categories), and while we may call on the right cluster at the wrong time, or the wrong cluster at the right time, still the process in question dominates our entire mental life.   A million events befall us every day.   We cannot handle so many events.   If we think of them at all, we type them.

Open-mindedness is considered to be a virtue. But, strictly speaking, it cannot occur.   A new experience *must* be redacted into old categories.   We cannot handle each event freshly in its own right.   If we did so, of what use would past experience be?   Bertrand Russell, the philosopher, has summed up the matter in a phrase, "a mind perpetually open will be a mind perpetually vacant."

(2) **Categorization assimilates as much as it can to the cluster.** There is a curious inertia in our thinking.   We like to solve problems easily.   We can do so best if we can fit them rapidly into a satisfactory category and use this category as a means of prejudging the solution.   The story is told of the pharmacist's mate in the Navy who had only two categories into which he fitted every ailment

that came to his attention on sick call: if you can *see* it put iodine on it; if you *can't*, give the patient a dose of salts. Life was simple for this pharmacist's mate; he ran his whole professional life with the aid of only two categories.

The point may be stated in this way: the mind tends to categorize environmental events in the "grossest" manner compatible with the need for action. If the pharmacist's mate in our story were called to task for his overcrude practice of medicine, he might then mend his ways and learn to employ more discriminated categories. But so long as we can "get away" with coarse overgeneralizations we tend to do so. (Why? Well, it takes less effort, and effort, except in the area of our most intense interests, is disagreeable.)

The bearing of this tendency on our problem is clear. It costs the Anglo employer less effort to guide his daily behavior by the generalization "Mexicans are lazy," than to individualize his workmen and learn the real reasons for their conduct. If I can lump thirteen million of my fellow citizens under a simple formula, "Negroes are stupid, dirty, and inferior," I simplify my life enormously. I simply avoid them one and all. What could be easier?

(3) **The category enables us quickly to identify a related object.** Every event has certain marks that serve as a cue to bring the category of prejudgment into action. When we see a red-breasted bird, we say to ourselves "robin." When we see a crazily swaying automobile, we think, "drunken driver," and act accordingly. A person with dark brown skin will activate whatever concept of Negro is dominant in our mind. If the dominant category is one composed of negative attitudes and beliefs we will automatically avoid him, or adopt whichever habit of rejection (Chapter 1) is most available to us.

Thus categories have a close and immediate tie with what we see, how we judge, and what we do. In fact, their whole purpose seems to be to facilitate perception and conduct—in other words, to make our adjustment to life speedy, smooth, and consistent. This principle holds even though we often make mistakes in fitting events to categories and thus get ourselves into trouble.

(4) **The category saturates all that it contains with the same ideational and emotional flavor.** Some categories are almost purely intellectual. Such categories we call concepts. *Tree* is a concept made up of our experience with hundreds of kinds of trees and with thousands of individual trees, and yet it has essentially one ideational meaning. But many of our concepts (even *tree*) have in addition to a "meaning" also a characteristic "feeling." We not only know what *tree* is but we *like* trees. And so it is with ethnic categories. Not only do we know what Chinese, Mexican, Lon-

doner mean, but we may have a feeling tone of favor or disfavor accompanying the concept.

(5) **Categories may be more or less rational.** We have said that generally a category starts to grow up from a "kernel of truth." A rational category does so, and enlarges and solidifies itself through the increment of relevant experience. Scientific laws are examples of rational categories. They are backed up by experience. Every event to which they pertain turns out in a certain way. Even if the laws are not 100 percent perfect, we consider them rational if they have a high probability of predicting a happening.

Some of our ethnic categories are quite rational. It is probable a Negro will have dark skin (though this is not always true). It is probable that a Frenchman will speak French better than German (though here, too, are exceptions). But is it true that the Negro will be superstitious, or that the Frenchman will be morally lax? Here the probability is much less, perhaps even zero in significance if we compare these groups with other ethnic groups. Yet our minds seem to make no distinction in category formation: irrational categories are formed as easily as rational.

To make a rational prejudgment of members of a group requires considerable knowledge of the characteristics of the group. It is unlikely that anyone has sound evidence that Scots are more penurious than Norwegians, or that Orientals are more wily than Caucasians, yet these beliefs grow as readily as do more rational beliefs.

> In a certain Guatemalan community there is fierce hatred of the Jews. No resident has ever seen a Jew. How did the Jew-is-to-be-hated category grow up? In the first place, the community was strongly Catholic. Teachers had told the residents that the Jews were Christ-killers. It also so happened that in the local culture was an old pagan myth about a devil who killed a god. Thus two powerfully emotional ideas converged and created a hostile prejudgment of Jews.

We have said that irrational categories are formed as easily as rational categories. Probably they are formed *more* easily, for intense emotional feelings have a property of acting like sponges. Ideas, engulfed by an overpowering emotion, are more likely to conform to the emotion than to objective evidence.

An irrational category is one formed without adequate evidence. It may be that the person is simply *ignorant* of the evidence, in which case a misconception is formed, as defined in Chapter 1. Many concepts depend on hearsay, on second-hand accounts, and for this reason category-misinformation is often inevitable. A child in school is required to form some general conception of, say, the

Tibetan people. He can take into consideration only what his teacher and textbook tell him. The resultant picture may be erroneous, but the child has done the best he can.

Much deeper and more baffling is the type of irrational prejudgment that *disregards* the evidence. There is the story of an Oxford student who once remarked, "I despise all Americans, but have never met one I didn't like." In this case the categorization went against even his first-hand experience. Holding to a prejudgment when we know better is one of the strangest features of prejudice. Theologians tell us that in prejudgments based on ignorance there is no question of sin; but that in prejudgments held in deliberate disregard of evidence, sin is involved.

When Categories Conflict with Evidence

For our purposes it is important to understand what happens when categories conflict with evidence. It is a striking fact that in most instances categories are stubborn and resist change. After all, we have fashioned our generalizations as we have because they have worked fairly well. Why change them to accommodate every new bit of evidence? If we are accustomed to one make of automobile and are satisfied, why admit the merits of another make? To do so would only disturb our satisfactory set of habits.

We selectively admit new evidence to a category if it confirms us in our previous belief. A Scotsman who is penurious delights us because he vindicates our prejudgment. It is pleasant to say, "I told you so." But if we find evidence that is contradictory to our preconception, we are likely to grow resistant.

There is a common mental device that permits people to hold to prejudgments even in the face of much contradictory evidence. It is the device of admitting exceptions. "There are nice Negroes but . . ." or "Some of my best friends are Jews but. . . ." This is a disarming device. By excluding a few favored cases, the negative rubric is kept intact for all other cases. In short, contrary evidence is not admitted and allowed to modify the generalization; rather it is perfunctorily acknowledged but excluded.

Let us call this the "re-fencing" device. When a fact cannot fit into a mental field, the exception is acknowledged, but the field is hastily fenced in again and not allowed to remain dangerously open.

A curious instance of re-fencing takes place in many discussions concerning the Negro. When a person with a strong anti-Negro bias is confronted with evidence favorable to the Negro he frequently pops up with the well-known matrimonial question: "Would you want your sister to marry a Negro?" This re-fencing is adroit. As soon as the interlocutor says, "No," or hesitates in his reply, the biased person can say in effect, "See, there just *is* something different and impossible about the Negro," or, "I was right all along—for the Negro has an objectionable essence in his nature."

There are two conditions under which a person will not strive to re-fence his mental field in such a way as to maintain the generalization. The first of these is the somewhat rare condition of *habitual open-mindedness*. There are people who seem to go through life with relatively little of the rubricizing tendency. They are suspicious of all labels, of categories, of sweeping statements. They habitually insist on knowing the evidence for each and every broad generalization. Realizing the complexity and variety in human nature, they are especially chary of ethnic generalizations. If they hold to any at all it is in a highly tentative way, and every contrary experience is allowed to modify the pre-existing ethnic concept.

The other occasion that makes for modification of concepts is plain *self-interest*. A person may learn from bitter failure that his categories are erroneous and must be revised. For example, he may not have known the right classification for edible mushrooms and thus find himself poisoned by toadstools. He will not make the same mistake again: his category will be corrected. Or he may think that Italians are primitive, ignorant, and loud until he falls in love with an Italian girl of a cultured family. Then he finds it greatly to his self-interest to modify his previous generalization and act thereafter on the more correct assumption that there are many, many kinds of Italians.

Usually, however, there are good reasons for maintaining the grounds of prejudgment intact. It takes less effort to do so. What is more, we find our prejudgments approved and supported by our friends and associates. It would not be polite for a suburbanite to disagree with his neighbors about admitting Jews to the local country club. It is comforting to find that our categories are similar to those of our neighbors, upon whose goodwill our own sense of status depends. How pointless for me to be perpetually reconsidering all my convictions, especially those that form the groundwork of my life, so long as that groundwork is satisfactory to me and to my neighbors.

Personal Values as Categories

We have been arguing that rubrics are essential to mental life, and that their operation results inevitably in prejudgments which in turn may shade into prejudice.

The most important categories a man has are his own personal set of values. He lives by and for his values. Seldom does he think about them or weigh them; rather he feels, affirms, and defends them. So important are the value categories that evidence and reason are ordinarily forced to conform to them. A farmer in a dusty area of the country listened to a visitor complain against the dust-bowl character of the region. The farmer evaded this attack on the place he loved by saying, "You know I like the dust; it sort of purifies the air." His reasoning was poor, but it served to defend his values.

As partisans of our own way of life we cannot help thinking in a partisan manner. Only a small portion of our reasoning is what psychologists have called "directed thinking," that is, controlled exclusively by outer evidence and focused upon the solution of objective problems. Whenever feeling, sentiment, values enter we are prone to engage in "free," "wishful," or "fantasy" thinking.[2] Such partisan thinking is entirely natural, for our job in this world is to live in an integrated way as value-seekers. Prejudgments stemming from these values enable us to do so.

Personal Values and Prejudice

It is obvious, then, that the very act of affirming our way of life often leads us to the brink of prejudice. The philosopher Spinoza has defined what he calls "love-prejudice." It consists, he says, "in feeling about anyone through love more than is right." The lover overgeneralizes the virtues of his beloved. Her every act is seen as perfect. The partisan of a church, a club, a nation may also feel about these objects "through love more than is right."

Now there is a good reason to believe that this love-prejudice is far more basic to human life than is its opposite, hate-prejudice (which Spinoza says "consists in feeling about anyone through hate less than is right"). One must first overestimate the things one loves before one can underestimate their contraries. Fences are built primarily for the protection of what we cherish.

Positive attachments are essential to life. The young child could not exist without his dependent relationship on a nurturant person. He must love and identify himself with someone or something before he can learn what to hate. Young children must have family and friendship circles before they can define the "out-groups" which are a menace to them.[3]

Why is it that we hear so little about love-prejudice—the tendency to overgeneralize our categories of attachment and affection? One reason is that prejudices of this sort create no social problem. If I am grossly partisan toward my own children, no one will object— unless at the same time it leads me, as it sometimes does, to manifest antagonism toward the neighbor's children. When a person is defending a categorical value of his own, he may do so at the expense of other people's interests or safety. If so, then we note his hate-prejudice, not realizing that it springs from a reciprocal love-prejudice underneath.

Take an example from anti-American prejudice. It has been a long-standing condition among many cultivated Europeans. As long ago as 1854 one of them described the United States with contempt as "a grand bedlam, a rendezvous of European scamps and vagabonds." [4] The abuse was so common that in 1869 James Russell Lowell was moved to chide the European critics in an essay entitled "On a certain condescension in foreigners." But the same type of criticism is still current.

What lies at its root? In the first place, we can be sure that before there was criticism there was self-love—a patriotism, a pride of ancestry and culture, representing the positive values by which the European critics live. Coming to this country they sense a vague threat to their own position. By disparaging America they can feel more secure. It is not that initially they hate America, but that they initially love themselves and their way of life. The formula holds equally well for Americans traveling abroad.

A student in Massachusetts, an avowed apostle of tolerance—so he thought—wrote, "The Negro question will never be solved until those dumb white Southerners get something through their ivory skulls." The student's positive values were idealistic. But ironically enough, his militant "tolerance" brought about a prejudiced condemnation of a portion of the population which he perceived as a threat to his tolerance-value.

Somewhat similar is the case of the lady who said, "Of course I have no prejudice. I had a dear old colored mammy for a nurse. Having grown up in the South and having lived here all my life I understand the problem. The Negroes are much happier if they are just allowed to stay in their place. Northern troublemakers just don't understand the Negro." This lady in her little speech was (psychologically speaking) defending her own privileges, her position, and her cosy way of life. It was not so much that she disliked Negroes or northerners, but she loved the status quo.

It is convenient to believe, if one can, that all of one category is good, all of the other evil. A popular workman in a factory was offered a job in the office by the management of the company. A union official said to him, "Don't take a management job or you'll become a bastard like all the rest of them." Only two classes existed in this official's mind: the workmen and the "bastards."

These instances argue that negative prejudice is a reflex of one's own system of values. We prize our own mode of existence and correspondingly underprize (or actively attack) what seems to us to threaten it.   The thought has been expressed by Sigmund Freud: "In the undisguised antipathies and aversion which people feel towards strangers with whom they have to do, we recognize the expression of self-love, of narcissism."

The process is especially clear in time of war.   When an enemy threatens all or nearly all of our positive values we stiffen our resistance and exaggerate the merits of our cause.   We feel—and this is an instance of overgeneralization—that we are wholly right.   (If we did not believe this we could not marshall all our energies for our defense.)   And if we are wholly right then the enemy must be wholly wrong.   Since he is wholly wrong, we should not hesitate to exterminate him.   But even in this wartime example it is clear that our basic love-prejudice is primary and that the hate-prejudice is a derivative phenomenon.

While there may be such things as "just wars," in the sense that threats to one's values are genuine and must be resisted, yet war always entails some degree of prejudice.   The very existence of a severe threat causes one to perceive the enemy country as wholly evil, and every citizen therein as a menace.   Balance and discrimination become impossible.[5]

Summary

This chapter has argued that man has a propensity to prejudice. This propensity lies in his normal and natural tendency to form generalizations, concepts, categories, whose content represents an oversimplification of his world of experience.   His rational categories keep close to first-hand experience, but he is able to form irrational categories just as readily.   In these even a kernel of truth may be lacking, for they can be composed wholly of hearsay evidence, emotional projections, and fantasy.

One type of categorization that predisposes us especially to make unwarranted prejudgments is our personal values.   These values, the basis of all human existence, lead easily to love-prejudices. Hate-prejudices are secondary developments, but they may, and often do, arise as a reflex of positive values.

In order to understand better the nature of love-prejudice, which at bottom is responsible for hate-prejudice, we turn our attention next to the formation of in-group loyalties.

NOTES AND REFERENCES

1. A. Lundberg and Leonore Dickson.   Selective association among ethnic groups in a high school population.   *American Sociological Review,* 1952, **17,** 23-34.

2. In the science of psychology the processes of "directed thinking" and "free thinking" have in the past been kept quite separate. The "experimentalists," traditionally so-called, have studied the former, and the "dynamic psychologists" (e.g., the Freudians) the latter. A readable book in the former tradition is GEORGE HUMPHREY, *Directed Thinking*, New York: Dodd, Mead, 1948; in the latter tradition, SIGMUND FREUD, *The Psychopathology of Everyday Life*. New York: Macmillan, transl. 1914.

In recent years there is a tendency for "experimentalists" and "dynamicists" to draw together in their research and in their theory. (See Chapter 10 of this volume.) It is a good sign, for prejudiced thinking is not, after all, something abnormal and disordered. Directed thinking and wishful thinking fuse.

3. See G. W. ALLPORT, A psychological approach to love and hate. Chapter 5 in P. A. SOROKIN (ED.), *Explorations in Altruistic Love and Behavior*. Boston: Beacon Press, 1950. Also, M. F. ASHLEY-MONTAGU, *On Being Human*. New York: Henry Schumann, 1950.

4. MERLE CURTI. The reputation of America overseas (1776-1860). *American Quarterly*, 1949, 1, 58-82.

5. Important relations between war and prejudice are discussed in H. CANTRIL (ED.), *Tensions That Cause Wars*. Urbana: Univ. of Illinois Press, 1950.

CHAPTER 3

FORMATION OF IN-GROUPS

The proverb *familiarity breeds contempt* contains considerably less than a half-truth. While we sometimes do become bored with our daily routine of living and with some of our customary companions, yet the very values that sustain our lives depend for their force upon their familiarity. What is more, what is familiar tends to *become* a value. We come to like the style of cooking, the customs, the people, we have grown up with.

Psychologically, the crux of the matter is that the familiar provides the indispensable basis of our existence. Since existence is good, its accompanying groundwork seems good and desirable. A child's parents, neighborhood, region, nation are given to him—so too his religion, race, and social traditions. To him all these affiliations are taken for granted. Since he is part of them, and they are part of him, they are *good*.

As early as the age of five, a child is capable of understanding that he is a member of various groups. He is capable, for example, of a sense of ethnic identification. Until he is nine or ten he will not be able to understand just what his membership signifies—how, for example, Jews differ from gentiles, or Quakers from Methodists, but he does not wait for this understanding before he develops fierce in-group loyalties.

Some psychologists say that the child is "rewarded" by virtue of his memberships, and that this reward creates the loyalty. That is to say, his family feeds and cares for him, he obtains pleasure from the gifts and attentions received from neighbors and compatriots. Hence he learns to love them. His loyalties are acquired on the basis of such rewards. We may doubt that this explanation is sufficient. A colored child is seldom or never rewarded for being a Negro—usually just the opposite, and yet he normally grows up with a loyalty to his racial group. Thoughts of Indiana arouse a glow in the breast of a native Hoosier—not necessarily because he passed a happy childhood there, but simply because he *came* from there. It is still, in part, the ground of his existence.

Rewards may, of course, help the process. A child who has plenty of fun at a family reunion may be more attached thereafter to his own clan because of the experience. But normally he would be attached to his clan anyway, simply because it is an inescapable part of his life.

Happiness (i.e., "reward") is not then the only reason for our loyalties. Few of our group memberships seem to be sustained by the pleasures they provide—an exception perhaps being our recreational memberships. And it takes a major unhappiness, a prolonged and bitter experience, to drive us away from loyalties once formed. And sometimes no amount of punishment can make us repudiate our loyalty.

This principle of the *ground* in human learning is important. We do not need to postulate a "gregarious instinct" to explain why people like to be with people: they have simply found people lock-stitched into the very fabric of their existence. Since they affirm their own existence as good, they will affirm social living as good. Nor do we need to postulate a "consciousness of kind" to explain why people adhere to their own families, clans, ethnic groups. The self could not be itself without them.

Scarcely anyone ever wants to be anybody else. However handicapped or unhappy he feels himself, he would not change places with other more fortunate mortals. He grumbles over his misfortunes and wants his lot improved; but it is *his* lot and *his* personality that he wants bettered. This attachment to one's own being is basic to human life. I may say that I envy *you*. But I do not want to *be* you; I only want to have for myself some of your attributes or possessions. And along with this beloved self go all of the person's basic memberships. Since he cannot alter his family stock, its traditions, his nationality, or his native language, he does well to accept them. Their accent dwells in the heart as well as on the tongue.

Oddly enough, it is not necessary for the individual to have direct acquaintance with all his in-groups. To be sure, he usually knows the members of his immediate family. (An orphan, however, may be passionately attached to parents he has never seen.) Some groups, such as clubs, schools, neighborhoods, are known through personal contacts. But others depend largely on symbols or hearsay. No one can have direct acquaintance with his race as a whole, nor with all his lodge brothers or co-religionists. The young child may sit enthralled while he hears of the exploits of the great-grandfather whose role as a sea-captain, a frontiersman, or nobleman sets a tradition with which the child identifies himself. The words he hears provide him just as authentic a ground for his life as do his daily experiences. By symbols one learns family traditions, patriotism, and racial pride. Thus in-groups that are only verbally defined may be nonetheless firmly knit.

What Is an In-group?

In a static society it would be fairly easy to predict just what loyalties the individual will form—to what region, to what phratry, or to what social class. In such a static society kinship, status, even place of residence, may be rigidly prescribed.

In ancient China at one time residential arrangements actually coincided with social distance. Where one lived indicated all of one's memberships. The inner circle of a region was the Tribute Holding where government officials only were permitted to reside. A second circle contained the nobility. Beyond this an outer but defended area, known as the Peaceful Tenures, contained literary workers and other citizens of repute. Farther out lay the Prohibited territory divided between foreigners and transported convicts. Finally came the Unstrained territory, where only barbarians and ostracized felons were allowed to dwell.[1]

In a more mobile, technological society such as ours no such rigidity exists.

There is one law—universal in all human societies—that assists us in making an important prediction. *In every society on earth the child is regarded as a member of his parents' groups.* He belongs to the same race, stock, family tradition, religion, caste, and occupational status. To be sure, in our society, he may when he grows older escape certain of these memberships, but not all. The child is ordinarily expected to acquire his parents' loyalties and prejudices; and if the parent because of his group-membership is an object of prejudice, the child too is automatically victimized.

Although this rule holds in our society, it is less infallible than in more "familistic" regions of the world. While the American child normally acquires a strong sense of family membership and a certain loyalty to his parents' country of origin, race, and religion, he has considerable latitude respecting his attachments. Each individual pattern will be somewhat different. An American child is free to accept some of his parents' memberships and to reject others.

It is difficult to define an in-group precisely. Perhaps the best that can be done is to say that members of an in-group all use the term *we* with the same essential significance. Members of a family do so, likewise schoolmates, members of a lodge, labor union, club, city, state, nation. In a vaguer way members of international bodies may do the same. Some we-organizations are transitory (e.g., an evening party), some are permanent (e.g., a family or clan).

Sam, a middle-aged man of only average sociability, listed his own in-group memberships as follows:

his paternal relatives
his maternal relatives
family of orientation (in which he grew up)
family of procreation (his wife and children)
his boyhood circle (now a dim memory)
his grammar school (in memory only)
his high school (in memory only)
his college as a whole (sometimes revisited)
his college class (reinforced by reunions)
his present church membership (shifted when he was 20)
his profession (strongly organized and firmly knit)
his firm (but especially the department in which he works)
a "bunch" (group of four couples who take a good deal of
    recreation together)
surviving members of a World War I company of infantry
    (growing dim)
state where he was born (a fairly trivial membership)
town where he now lives (a lively civic spirit)
New England (a regional loyalty)
United States (an average amount of patriotism)
United Nations (in principle firmly believed in but psycho-
    logically loose because he is not clear concerning the "we"
    in this case)
Scotch-Irish stock (a vague feeling of kinship with others who
    have this lineage)
Republican party (he registers Republican in the primaries
    but has little additional sense of belonging)

Sam's list is probably not complete—but from it we can reconstruct fairly well the membership ground on which he lives.

In his list Sam referred to a boyhood circle. He recalls that at one time this in-group was of desperate importance to him. When he moved to a new neighborhood at the age of 10 he had no one of his own age to pal with, and he much desired companionship. The other boys were curious and suspicious. Would they admit him? Was Sam's style compatible with the gang's style? There was the usual ordeal by fistfight, set in motion at some slight pretext. This ritual—as is customary in boys' gangs—is designed to provide a swift and acceptable test of the stranger's manners and morale. Will he keep within the limits set by the gang, and show just enough boldness, toughness, and self-control to suit the other boys? Sam was fortunate in this ordeal, and was forthwith admitted to the coveted in-group. Probably he was lucky that he had no additional handicaps in terms of his racial, religious, or status memberships. Otherwise the probation would have been longer and the tests more exacting; and perhaps the gang would have excluded him forever.

Thus some in-group memberships have to be fought for. But many are conferred automatically by birth and by family tradition. In terms of modern social science the former memberships reflect *achieved* status; the latter, *ascribed* status.

Sex as an In-group

Sam did not mention his membership (ascribed status) in the male sex. Probably at one time it was consciously important to him—and may still be so.

The in-group of sex makes an interesting case study. A child of two normally makes no distinction in his companionships: a little girl or a little boy is all the same to him. Even in the first grade the awareness of sex-groups is relatively slight. Asked whom they would choose to play with, first-grade children on the average choose opposite-sexed children at least a quarter of the time. By the time the fourth grade is reached these cross-sexed choices virtually disappear: only two percent of the children want to play with someone of the opposite sex. When the eighth grade is reached friendships between boys and girls begin to re-emerge, but even then only eight percent extend their choices across the sex boundary.[2]

For some people—misogynists among them—the sex-grouping remains important throughout their lives. Women are viewed as a wholly different species from men, usually an inferior species. Such primary and secondary sex differences as exist are greatly exaggerated and are inflated into imaginary distinctions that justify discrimination. With half of mankind (his own sex) the male may feel an in-group solidarity, with the other half, an irreconcilable conflict.

Lord Chesterfield, who in his letters often admonished his son to guide his life by reason rather than by prejudice, nevertheless has this to say about women:

"Women, then, are only children of a larger growth; they have an entertaining tattle, and sometimes wit; but for solid reasoning, good sense, I never knew in my life one that had it, or who reasoned or acted consequentially for four and twenty hours together. . . .

"A man of sense only trifles with them, plays with them, humors and flatters them, as he does a sprightly, forward child; but he neither consults them about, nor trusts them with serious matters; though he often makes them believe that he does both; which is the thing in the world that they are most proud of. . . .³

"Women are much more like each other than men; they have in truth but two passions, vanity and love: these are their universal characteristics." ⁴

Schopenhauer's views were much like Chesterfield's. Women, he wrote, are big children all their life long. A fundamental fault of the female character is that it has no sense of justice. This is mainly due to the fact, Schopenhauer insisted, that women are defective in the powers of reasoning and deliberation.⁵

Such antifeminism reflects the two basic ingredients of prejudice—denigration and gross overgeneralization. Neither of these famous men of intellect allows for individual differences among women, nor asks whether their alleged attributes are in fact more common in the female than in the male sex.

What is instructive about this antifeminism is the fact that it implies security and contentment with one's own sex-membership. To Chesterfield and to Schopenhauer the cleavage between male and female was a cleavage between accepted in-group and rejected out-group. But for many people this "war of the sexes" seems totally unreal. They do not find in it a ground for prejudice.

The Shifting Nature of In-groups

Although each individual has his own conception of in-groups important to himself, he is not unaffected by the temper of the times. During the past century, national and racial memberships have risen in importance, while family and religious memberships have declined (though they are still exceedingly prominent). The fierce loyalties and rivalries between Scottish clans is almost a thing of the past—but the conception of a "master race" has grown to threatening proportions. The fact that women in Western countries have assumed roles once reserved for men makes the antifeminism of Chesterfield and Schopenhauer seem old-fashioned indeed.

A change in the conception of the national in-group is seen in the shifting American attitude toward immigration. The native American nowadays seldom takes an idealistic view of immigration. He does not feel it a duty and privilege to offer a home to oppressed people—to include them in his in-group. The legend on the Statue of Liberty, engraved eighty years ago, already seems out of date:

Give me your tired, your poor,
Your huddled masses yearning to breathe free,
The wretched refuse of your teeming shore.
Send these, the homeless, the tempest-tossed to me.
I lift my lamp beside the golden door.

The lamp was virtually extinguished by the anti-immigration laws passed in the period 1918-1924. The lingering sentiment was not strong enough to relax the bars appreciably following the Second World War when there were more homeless and tempest-tost than ever before crying for admission. From the standpoint of both economics and humanitarianism there were strong arguments for relaxing the restrictions; but people had grown fearful. Many conservatives feared the importation of radical ideas; many Protestants felt their own precarious majority might be further reduced; some Catholics dreaded the arrival of Communists; anti-Semites wanted no more Jews; some labor-union members feared that jobs would not be created to absorb the newcomers and that their own security would suffer.

During the 124 years for which data are available, approximately 40,000,000 immigrants came to America, as many as 1,000,000 in a single year. Of the total immigration 85 percent came from Europe. Until a generation ago, few objections were heard. But today nearly all applicants are refused admission, and few champions of "displaced persons" are heard. Times have changed, and whenever they change for the worse, as they have, in-group boundaries tend to tighten. The stranger is suspect and excluded.

Not only do the strength and definition of in-groups change over the years in a given culture, but a single individual, too, may have occasion at one time to affirm one group-loyalty and at a different time another. The following amusing passage from H. G. Well's *A Modern Utopia* illustrates this elasticity. The passage depicts a snob—a person whose group loyalties are narrow. But even a snob, it appears, must have a certain flexibility, for he finds it convenient to identify himself sometimes with one in-group and sometimes with another.

The passage illustrates an important point: in-group memberships are not permanently fixed. For certain purposes an individual may affirm one category of membership, for other purposes a slightly larger category. It depends on his need for self-enhancement.

Wells is describing the loyalties of a certain botanist:

He has a strong feeling for systematic botanists as against plant physiologists, whom he regards as lewd and evil scoundrels in this relation; but he has a strong feeling for all botanists and indeed all biologists, as against physicists, and those who profess the exact sciences, all of whom he regards as dull, mechanical, ugly-minded scoundrels in this relation; but he has a strong feeling for all who profess what he calls Science, as against psychologists, sociologists, philosophers, and literary men, whom he regards as wild, foolish, immoral scoundrels in this relation; but he has a strong feeling for all educated men as against the working man, whom he regards as a cheating, lying, loafing, drunken, thievish, dirty scoundrel in this relation; but as soon as the working man is comprehended together with these others, as *Englishmen* . . . he holds them superior to all sorts of Europeans, whom he regards. . . .[6]

Thus the sense of belonging is a highly personal matter. Even two members of the same actual in-group may view its composition

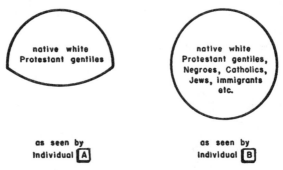

FIG. 1. The national in-group as perceived by two Americans.

in widely divergent ways. Take, for instance, the definition that two Americans might give to their own national in-group.

The narrowed perception of Individual A is the product of an arbitrary categorization, one that he finds convenient (functionally significant) to hold. The larger range of perception on the part of Individual B creates a wholly different conception of the national in-group. It is misleading to say that both belong to the same in-group. Psychologically, they do not.

Each individual tends to see in his in-group the precise pattern of security that he himself requires. An instructive example comes from a recent resolution of the convention of the Democratic Party in South Carolina. To the gentlemen assembled the Party was an important in-group. But the definition of Party (as stated in its national platform) was unacceptable. Hence in order to re-fence the in-group so that each member could feel secure, the category "Democrat" was redefined to "include those who believe in local self-government as against the idea of a strong centralized, paternalistic government; and exclude those whose ideas or leadership are inspired by foreign influences, Communism, Nazism, Fascism, statism, totalitarianism, or the Fair Employment Practices Commission."

Thus in-groups are often recreated to fit the needs of individuals, and when the needs are strongly aggressive—as in this case—the redefinition of the in-group may be primarily in terms of the hated out-groups.

In-groups and Reference Groups

We have broadly defined an in-group as any cluster of people who can use the term "we" with the same significance. But the reader has noted that individuals may hold all manner of views concerning their membership in in-groups. A first-generation American may regard his Italian background and culture as more important than do his children, who are second-generation Italian-Americans. Adolescents may view their neighborhood gang as a far more important in-group than their school. In some instances an individual may actively repudiate an in-group, even though he cannot escape membership in it.

In order to clarify this situation, modern social science has introduced the concept of reference group. Sherif and Sherif have defined reference groups as "those groups to which the individual relates himself as a part, or to which he aspires to relate himself psychologically." [7] Thus a reference group is an in-group that is warmly accepted, or a group in which the individual wishes to be included.

Now usually an in-group is also a reference group, but not always. A Negro may wish to relate himself to the white majority in his community. He would like to partake of the privileges of this majority, and be considered one of its members. He may feel so intensely about the matter that he repudiates his own in-group. He develops a condition that Kurt Lewin has called "self-hate" (i.e., hatred for his own in-group). Yet the customs of the community force him to live with, work with, and be classified with the Negro group. In such a case his in-group membership is not the same as his reference group.

Or take the case of a clergyman of Armenian descent ministering in a small New England town. His name is foreign. Townsmen classify him as an Armenian. Yet he himself seldom thinks of his ancestry, though he does not actively reject his background. His reference groups (his main interests) are his church, his family, and the community in which he lives. Unfortunately for him, his fellow townsmen persist in regarding him as an Armenian; they regard this ethnic in-group as far more important than he himself does.

The Negro and the Armenian cleric occupy *marginal* roles in the community. They have difficulty relating themselves to their reference groups because the pressures of the community force them always to tie to in-groups of small psychological importance to them.

To a considerable degree all minority groups suffer from the same state of marginality, with its haunting consequences of insecurity, conflict, and irritation. Every minority group finds itself in a larger society where many customs, many values, many practices are prescribed. The minority group member is thus to some degree forced to make the dominant majority his reference group in respect to language, manners, morals, and law. He may be entirely loyal to his minority in-group, but he is at the same time always under the necessity of relating himself to the standards and expectations of the majority. The situation is particularly clear in the case of the Negro. Negro culture is almost entirely the same as white American culture. The Negro must relate himself to it. Yet whenever he tries to achieve this relatedness he is likely to suffer rebuff. Hence there is in his case an almost inevitable conflict between his biologically defined in-group and his culturally defined reference group. If we follow this line of thinking we see why all minority groups, to some degree, occupy a marginal position in society with its unhappy consequents of apprehension and resentment.

The concepts of in-group and reference group help us to distinguish two levels of belongingness. The former indicates the sheer fact of membership; the latter tells us whether the individual prizes that membership or whether he seeks to relate himself with another group. In many cases, as we have said, there is a virtual identity between in-groups and reference groups; but it is not always so. Some individuals, through necessity or by choice, continually compare themselves with groups which for them are not in-groups.

Social Distance

The distinction between in-group and reference group is well brought out in studies of social distance. This familiar technique, invented by E. S. Bogardus, asks respondents to indicate to which steps on the following scale they would admit members of various ethnic and national groups:

1. to close kinship by marriage
2. to my club as personal chums
3. to my street as neighbors
4. to employment in my occupation
5. to citizenship in my country
6. as visitors only to my country
7. would exclude from my country

Now the most striking finding from this procedure is that a similar pattern of preference is found across the country, varying little with income, region, education, occupation, or even with ethnic group. Most people, whoever they are, find the English and Canadians acceptable as citizens, as neighbors, as social equals, and as kinsmen. These ethnic stocks have the least social distance. At the other extreme come Hindus, Turks, Negroes. The ordering—with a few minor shifts—stays substantially constant.[8]

While members of the unfavored groups tend to put their own groups high in the list, yet in all other respects they choose the prevailing order of acceptability. In one study of Jewish children, for example, it was found that the standard pattern of social distance existed excepting only that most Jewish children place Jews high in acceptability.[9] In similar investigations it turns out that on the average the Negro places the Jew at about the same distance as does the white gentile; and the Jew ordinarily places the Negro low on his list.

From such results we are forced to conclude that the member of an ethnic minority tends to fashion his attitudes as does the dominant majority. In other words, the dominant majority is for him a *reference group*. It exerts a strong pull upon him, forcing attitudinal conformity. The conformity, however, rarely extends to the point of repudiating his own in-group. A Negro, or Jew, or Mexican will ordinarily assert the acceptability of his own in-group, but in other respects he will decide as does his larger reference group. Thus, both in-group and reference group are important in the formation of attitudes.

The Group-Norm Theory of Prejudice

We are now in a position to understand and appreciate a major theory of prejudice. It holds that all groups (whether in-groups or reference groups) develop a way of living with characteristic codes and beliefs, standards and "enemies" to suit their own adaptive needs. The theory holds also that both gross and subtle pressures keep every individual member in line. The in-group's preferences must be his preference, its enemies his enemies. The Sherifs, who advance this theory, write:

> Ordinarily the factors leading individuals to form attitudes of prejudice are not piecemeal. Rather, their formation is functionally related to becoming a group member—to adopting the group and its values (norms) as the main anchorage in regulating experience and behavior.[10]

A strong argument in favor of this view is the relative ineffectiveness of attempts to change attitudes through influencing individuals. Suppose the child attends a lesson in intercultural education in the classroom. The chances are this lesson will be smothered by the more embracing norms of his family, gang, or neighborhood. To change the child's attitudes it would be necessary to alter the cultural equilibrium of these, to him, more important groups. It would be necessary for the family, the gang, or the neighborhood to sanction tolerance before he as an individual could practice it.

This line of thought has led to the dictum, "It is easier to change group attitudes than individual attitudes." Recent research lends some support to the view. In certain studies whole communities, whole housing projects, whole factories, or whole school systems have been made the target of change. By involving the leaders, the policies, the rank and file, new norms are created, and when this is accomplished, it is found that individual attitudes tend to conform to the new group norm.[11]

While we cannot doubt the results, there is something unnecessarily "collectivistic" about the theory. Prejudice is by no means exclusively a mass phenomenon. Let the reader ask himself whether his own social attitudes do in fact conform closely to those of his family, social class, occupational group, or church associates. Perhaps the answer is yes; but more likely the reader may reply that the prevailing prejudices of his various reference groups are so contradictory that he cannot, and does not, "share" them all. He may also decide that his pattern of prejudice is unique, conforming to none of his membership groups.

Realizing this individual play of attitudes, the proponents of the theory speak of a "range of tolerable behavior," admitting thereby that only approximate conformity is demanded within any system of group norms. People may deviate in their attitudes to some extent, but not too much.

As soon as we allow, however, for a "range of tolerable behavior" we are moving toward a more individualistic point of view. We do not need to deny the existence of group norms and group pressure in order to insist that each person is uniquely organized. Some of us are avid conformists to what we believe the group requirement to be. Others of us are passive conformists. Still others are nonconformists. Such conformism as we show is the product of individual learning, individual needs, and individual style of life.

In dealing with problems of attitude formation it is always difficult to strike a proper balance between the collective approach and the individual approach. This volume maintains that prejudice is ultimately a problem of personality formation and development; no two cases of prejudice are precisely the same. No individual would mirror his group's attitude unless he had a personal need, or personal habit, that leads him to do so. But it likewise maintains that one of the frequent sources, perhaps the most frequent source, of prejudice lies in the needs and habits that reflect the influence of in-group memberships upon the development of the individual personality. It is possible to hold the individualistic type of theory without denying that the major influences upon the individual may be collective.

Can there Be an In-group without an Out-group?

Every line, fence, or boundary marks off an inside from an outside. Therefore, in strict logic, an in-group always implies the existence of some corresponding out-group. But this logical statement by itself is of little significance. What we need to know is whether one's loyalty to the in-group automatically implies disloyalty, or hostility, or other forms of negativism, toward out-groups.

The French biologist, Felix le Dantec, insisted that every social unit from the family to the nation could exist only by virtue of having some "common enemy." The family unit fights many threatening forces that menace each person who belongs to the unit. The exclusive club, the American Legion, the nation itself, exists to defeat the common enemies of its members. In favor of Le Dantec's view is the well-known Machiavellian trick of creating a common enemy in order to cement an in-group. Hitler created the Jewish menace not so much to demolish the Jews as to cement the Nazi hold over Germany. At the turn of the century the Workingmen's Party in California whipped up an anti-Oriental sentiment to consolidate its own ranks which, without a common enemy, were indifferent and wavering. School spirit is never so strong as when the time for an athletic contest with the traditional "enemy" approaches. Instances are so numerous that one is tempted to accept the doctrine. Studying the effect of strangers entering a group of nursery school children, Susan Isaacs reports, "The existence of an outsider is in the beginning an essential condition of any warmth or togetherness within the group." [12]

So deeply was William James impressed by the fact that social cohesiveness seems to require a common enemy that he wrote a famous essay on the subject. In *The Moral Equivalent for War* he recognized the adventuresomeness, the aggression, and the competitiveness that marked human relationships, especially among young people of military age. In order that they themselves might live at peace he recommended that they find an enemy that would not violate man's growing sense of loyalty to humanity. His advice was: fight nature, fight disease, fight poverty.

Now there is no denying that the presence of a threatening common enemy will cement the in-group sense of any organized aggregate of people. A family (if it is not already badly disrupted) will grow cohesive in the face of adversity, and a nation is never so unified as in time of war. But the psychological emphasis must be placed primarily on the desire for security, not on hostility itself.

One's own family is an in-group; and by definition all other families on the street are out-groups; but seldom do they clash. A hundred ethnic groups compose America, and while serious conflict occasionally occurs, the majority rub along in peace. One knows that one's lodge has distinctive characteristics that mark it off from all others, but one does not necessarily despise the others.

The situation, it seems, can best be stated as follows: although we could not perceive our own in-groups excepting as they contrast to out-groups, still the in-groups are psychologically primary. We live in them, by them, and, sometimes, for them. Hostility toward out-groups helps strengthen our sense of belonging, but it is not required.

Because of their basic importance to our own survival and self-esteem we tend to develop a partisanship and ethnocentrism in respect to our in-groups. Seven-year-old children in one town were asked, "Which are better, the children in this town or in Smithfield (a neighboring town)?" Almost all replied, "The children in this town." When asked why, the children usually replied, "I don't know the kids in Smithfield." This incident puts the initial in-group and out-group situation in perspective. The familiar is *preferred*. What is alien is regarded as somehow inferior, less "good," but there is not necessarily hostility against it.

Thus while a certain amount of predilection is inevitable in all in-group memberships, the reciprocal attitude toward out-groups may range widely. At one extreme they may be viewed as a common enemy to be defeated in order to protect the in-group and strengthen its inner loyalties. At the other extreme the out-group may be appreciated, tolerated, even liked for its diversity. Commenting on this matter in his Encyclical entitled *Unity of the*

People, Pope Pius XII recognized value in the existing variety of cultural groups. Let this diversity remain, he urged, but let it not be marked by hostility. The unity of people, he said, is a unity of attitude—of tolerance and love—not a unity of uniformity.

Can Humanity Constitute an In-group?

One's family ordinarily constitutes the smallest and the firmest of one's in-groups. It is probably for this reason that we usually think of in-groups growing weaker and weaker the larger their circle of inclusion. Figure 2 expresses the common feeling that the potency of the membership becomes less as the distance from personal contact grows larger. Only a few sample memberships are included in the diagram in order not to complicate the point at issue.

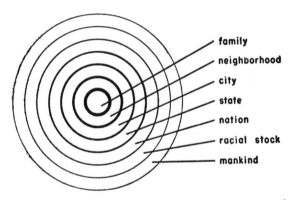

family
neighborhood
city
state
nation
racial stock
mankind

FIG. 2. Hypothetical lessening of in-group potency as membership becomes more inclusive.

Such an image implies that a world-loyalty is the most difficult to achieve. In part the implication is correct. There seems to be special difficulty in fashioning an in-group out of an entity as embracing as mankind. Even the ardent believer in One World has trouble. Suppose a diplomat is dealing at a conference table with representatives of other countries whose language, manners, and ideology differ from his own. Even if this diplomat believes ardently in One World, still he cannot escape a sense of strangeness in his encounters. His own model of propriety and rightness is his own culture. Other languages and customs inevitably seem outlandish and, if not inferior, at least slightly absurd and unnecessary.

Suppose the delegate is so broadminded that he can see many defects in his own nation, and suppose he sincerely wants to build an ideal society, where the good features of many cultures are blended. Even such an extreme idealism is likely to wring from him only minor concessions. With utmost sincerity he finds himself fighting for his own language, religion, ideology, law, forms of etiquette. After all, his nation's way of life is *his* way of life—and he cannot lightly abrogate the ground of his whole existence.

Such almost reflex preference for the familiar grips us all. To be sure, a well-traveled person, or one who is endowed with cosmopolitan tastes, is relatively more hospitable to other nations. He can see that differences in culture do not necessarily mean inferiority. But for persons neither imaginative nor well-traveled artificial props are needed. They require *symbols*—today almost lacking—in order to make the human in-group seem real. Nations have flags, parks, schools, capitol buildings, currency, newspapers, holidays, armies, historical documents. Only gradually and with small publicity are a few of these symbols of unity evolving on an international scale. They are greatly needed in order to provide mental anchorage points around which the idea of world-loyalty may develop.

There is no intrinsic reason why the outermost circle of membership needs to be the weakest. In fact, race itself has become the dominant loyalty among many people, especially among fanatic advocates of "Aryanism" and among certain members of oppressed races. It seems today that the clash between the idea of race and of One World (the two outermost circles) is shaping into an issue that may well be the most decisive in human history. The important question is, Can a loyalty to mankind be fashioned before interracial warfare breaks out?

Theoretically it can, for there is a saving psychological principle that may be invoked if we can learn how to do so in time. The principle states that *concentric loyalties need not clash*. To be devoted to a large circle does not imply the destruction of one's attachment to a smaller circle.[13] *The loyalties that clash are almost invariably those of identical scope.* A bigamist who has founded two families of procreation is in fatal trouble with himself and with society. A traitor who serves two nations (one nominally and one actually) is mentally a mess and socially a felon. Few people can acknowledge more than one alma mater, one religion, or one fraternity. On the other hand, a world-federalist can be a devoted family man, an ardent alumnus, and a sincere patriot. The fact that some fanatic nationalists would challenge the compatibility of world-loyalty with patriotism does not change the psychological law. Wendell Willkie and Franklin Roosevelt were no less patriots because they envisioned a United Nations in One World.

Concentric loyalties take time to develop, and often, of course, they fail completely to do so. In an interesting study of Swiss children Piaget and Weil discovered the resistance of young children to the idea that one loyalty can be included within another. The following record of a seven-year-old is typical of that age:

> Have you heard of Switzerland? *Yes.* What is it? *A canton.* And what is Geneva? *A town.* Where is Geneva? *In Switzerland.* (But the child draws two circles side by side.) Are you Swiss? *No, I'm Genevese.*

At a later stage (eight to ten) children grasp the idea that Geneva is enclosed spatially in Switzerland and draw their relationship as one circle enclosing the other. But the idea of concentric loyalty is still elusive.

> What is your nationality? *I'm Swiss.* How is that? *Because I live in Switzerland.* You're Genevese too? *No, I can't be.* Why not? *I'm Swiss now and can't be Genevese as well.*

By the age of ten or eleven the child can straighten the matter out.

> What is your nationality? *I'm Swiss.* How is that? *Because my parents are Swiss.* Are you Genevese as well? *Naturally, because Geneva is in Switzerland.*

Likewise by the age of ten or eleven the child has an emotional evaluation of his national circle.

> *I like Switzerland because it's a free country.*
> *I like Switzerland because it's the Red Cross country.*
> *In Switzerland our neutrality makes us charitable.*

It is evident that these emotional valuations are learned from teachers and parents, and are adopted ready-made. The mode of teaching ordinarily stops the process of enlargement at this point. Beyond the borders of the native land there is only the domain of "foreigners"—not of fellow men. Michel, aged nine and one-half, answered the interviewer as follows:

> Have you ever heard of such people as foreigners? *Yes, the French, the Americans, the Russians, the English.* Quite right. Are there differences between all these people? *Oh yes, they don't speak the same language.* And what else? Try to tell me as much as possible. *The French are not very serious, they don't worry about anything, and it's dirty there.* And what do you think of the Americans? *They're ever so rich and clever. They've discovered the atom bomb.* And what do you think of the Russians? *They're bad, they're always wanting to make*

war.   Now look, how did you come to know all you've told me?
I don't know . . . I've heard it . . . that's what people say.

Most children never enlarge their sense of belonging beyond the ties of family, city, nation.   The reason seems to be that those with whom the child lives, and whose judgment he mirrors, do not do so. Piaget and Weil write, "Everything suggests that, on discovering the values accepted in his immediate circle, the child feels bound to accept the circle's opinions of all other national groups." [14]

While the national orbit is the largest circle of loyalty that most children learn, there is no necessity for the process to stop there.   In some children of twelve and thirteen years of age these investigators found a high sense of "reciprocity," i.e., a willingness to admit that all peoples have equal value and merit, although each prefers its own mode of life.   When such a sense of reciprocity is firmly established, the way is prepared for the integrated conception ol larger and larger units of mankind, to all of which the young person can be loyal without losing his earlier attachments.   Until he learns this attitude of reciprocity, he is unlikely to accept other countries as lying within the orbit of his loyalty.

In summary, in-group memberships are vitally important to individual survival.   These memberships constitute a web of habits. When we encounter an outsider who follows different customs we unconsciously say, "He breaks my habits."   Habit-breaking is unpleasant.   We prefer the familiar.   We cannot help but feel a bit on guard when other people seem to threaten or even question our habits.   Attitudes partial to the in-group, or to the reference group, do not necessarily require that attitudes toward other groups be antagonistic—even though hostility often helps to intensify the in-group cohesion.   Narrow circles can, without conflict, be supplemented by larger circles of loyalty.   This happy condition is not often achieved, but it remains from the psychological point of view a hopeful possibility.

NOTES AND REFERENCES

1. W. G. OLD. *The Shu King, or the Chinese Historical Classic.* New York: J. Lane, 1904, 50-51.   See also J. LEGGE (Transl.), Texts of Confucianism, in *The Sacred Books of the East.*   Oxford: Clarendon Press, 1879, Vol. III, 75-76.

2. J. L. MORENO. *Who shall survive?*   Washington: Nervous & Mental Disease Pub. Co., 1934, **24.**   These data are somewhat old.   At the present time there are grounds for believing that the sex boundary is not so important among children as formerly.

3. C. STRACHEY (ED.). *The Letters of the Earl of Chesterfield to his Son.* New York: G. P. Putnam's Sons, 1925, Vol. I, 261.

4. *Ibid.*, Vol. II, 5.

5. E. B. BAX (ED.). *Selected Essays of Schopenhauer.* London: G. Bell & Sons, 1914, 340.

6. Reprinted by permission of Chapman & Hall, Ltd., from *A Modern Utopia.* London, 1905, 322.

7. M. AND CAROLYN W. SHERIF. *Groups in Harmony and Tension.* New York: Harper, 1953, 161.

8. The order found by Bogardus in 1928 (E. S. BOGARDUS, *Immigration and Race Attitudes,* Boston: D. C. HEATH, 1928) was found essentially unchanged by HARTLEY in 1946, and again by SPOERL in 1951. (Cf. E. L. HARTLEY, *Problems in Prejudice,* New York: Kings Crown Press, 1946; and DOROTHY T. SPOERL, Some aspects of prejudice as affected by religion and education, *Journal of Social Psychology,* 1951, **33,** 69-76).

9. ROSE ZELIGS. Racial attitudes of Jewish children. *Jewish Education,* 1937, **9,** 148-152.

10. M. AND CAROLYN W. SHERIF. *Op. cit.,* 218.

11. Among the studies of this type we may refer especially to: A. MORROW AND J. FRENCH, Changing a stereotype in industry, *Journal of Social Issues,* 1945, **1,** 33-37; R. LIPPITT, *Training in Community Relations,* New York: Harper, 1949; MARGOT H. WORMSER AND CLAIRE SELLTIZ, *How to Conduct a Community Self-survey of Civil Rights,* New York: Association Press, 1951; K. LEWIN, Group decision and social change in T. M. NEWCOMB AND E. L. HARTLEY (EDS.), *Readings in Social Psychology,* New York: Holt, 1947.

12. SUSAN ISAACS. *Social Development in Young Children.* New York: Harcourt, Brace, 1933, 250.

13. This spatial metaphor has its limitations. The reader may ask, What really is the innermost circle of loyalty? It is by no means always the family, as Fig. 2 implies. May not the core be the primordial self-love we discussed in Chapter 2? If we regard self as the central circle, then the broadening loyalties are, psychologically speaking, simply extensions of the self. But as the self widens, it may also *re-center* itself, so that what is at first an outer circle may become psychologically the focus. Thus a religious person, for example, may believe that man is made in God's image: therefore his own love of God and man may, for him, lie in the innermost circle. Both loyalties and prejudices are features of personality organization, and in the last analysis each organization is unique. While this criticism is entirely valid, still for our present purposes Fig. 2 can stand as an approximate representation of the fact that for many people the larger the social system the less easily do they encompass it in their span of understanding and affection.

14. J. PIAGET AND ANNE-MARIE WEIL. The development in children of the idea of the homeland and of relations with other countries. *International Social Science Bulletin,* 1951, **3,** 570.

CHAPTER 4

REJECTION OF OUT-GROUPS

We have seen that in-group loyalty does not necessarily imply hostility toward out-groups. It may not even imply any awareness of the existence of corresponding out-groups.

In one unpublished study a large number of adults were interviewed. They were asked to name all the groups they could think of to which they belonged. There resulted for each adult a long list of memberships. Family came first in frequency and intensity of mention. Then followed the specification of geographical region, occupational groups, social (club and friendship) groups, religious, ethnic, and ideological memberships.

When the list was complete the subjects were asked to name "any groups which you feel appear in direct contrast to, or as a threat to, one of the groups you are identified with." In response to this direct invitation only 21 percent of the subjects responded by mentioning out-groups. Seventy-nine percent were unable to name any. Those who did identify out-groups named chiefly ethnic, religious, and ideological groups.

The out-groups mentioned took a diversity of forms. One woman from the South named New Englanders, non-university people, colored people, foreigners, midwesterners, and Catholics as uncongenial out-groups. A general librarian declared that specialty librarians were an out-group. An employee of a nutritional laboratory felt that the hematologists in the upstairs laboratory were alien and unwelcome.

Thus it is apparent that our loyalties may, but do not necessarily, involve hostile attitudes toward contrasting groups. In Chapter 2 we argued that love-prejudice (especially when frustrated) prepares the way for reciprocal hate-prejudice. But though this line of reasoning is sound, it is evident that positive partisanship does not necessarily breed negative prejudice.

Yet many people do define their loyalties in terms of the other side of the fence. They think a great deal about out-groups, worry about them, and feel under strain. To reject out-groups is for them

48

a salient need. For them an ethnocentric orientation is important.

People with salient attitudes toward out-groups may express them with all degrees of intensity. In Chapter 1 we suggested a scale of intensity resulting in five types of rejective behavior:

1. Antilocution
2. Avoidance
3. Discrimination
4. Physical Attack
5. Extermination

In the present chapter we shall examine the gradations of rejection of out-groups in some detail, simplifying the five steps into three:

1. Verbal rejection (antilocution)
2. Discrimination (including segregation)
3. Physical attack (of all degrees of intensity)

From our earlier list we omit avoidance and withdrawal behavior, for these are the least damaging expressions of prejudice so far as the victims are concerned. We also combine sporadic physical threats and attacks with organized violence and extermination. As we pointed out in Chapter 1, most people are content to express their hostility verbally to their own friends and never go further. Some, however, reach the stage of active discrimination. A few take part in vandalism, riots, lynchings.[1]

Verbal Rejection

Words betraying antagonism come easily.

Two cultivated middle-aged women were discussing the high cost of cut flowers. One spoke of a lavish floral display at a certain Jewish wedding, and added, "I don't see how they afford it. They must doctor their income tax returns." The other replied, "Yes, they must."

In this snatch of trivial gossip three important psychological facts are present. (1) The first speaker made a spontaneous reference to Jews not called for by the topic of conversation. Her prejudice was so salient that it intruded itself into the discussion. Her dislike of this out-group was pressing for release. Probably she obtained a somewhat pleasant catharsis from speaking her mind. (2) The conversation itself was wholly secondary to the maintenance of good relations between the ladies. They were trying to sustain a friendly acquaintanceship. To do so their agreement on every topic was desirable. To cement this two-person in-group it helped for the members to name and disparage an out-group. As we have just seen, hostility to out-groups, though not necessary for in-group solidarity, can serve to strengthen it. (3) Both speakers reflected the attitudes of their class. They were thus showing a certain class-solidarity. It was as though each admonished the other to be a good upper middle-class gentile and adhere to the outlook and ways of the class. Needless to say, none of these psychological functions was consciously present in their minds. What is more, neither lady was intensely anti-Semitic. Both had many Jewish friends. Neither would countenance active discrimination, certainly not violence. Theirs was the lowest degree of prejudice (antilocution). But even the lowest degree betrays some of the complexities of the problem.

Mild animosity often underlies antilocution of the joking or derisive kind. Some of it is so gentle that it merges into friendly humor. When I tell a joke about the tight-fisted Scot I am not necessarily expressing hostility toward Scots (they are fond of the same stories). But even when jokes seem friendly they can sometimes mask genuine hostility, by providing a disarming method of telling off the out-group and exalting the in-group. One laughs at tales of the stupidity of a Negro servant, of Jewish shrewdness, or of Irish bellicosity. The incident may indeed be intrinsically funny, but the fact that the incident is typed (implied as typical of Negro, Jewish, or Irish nature) shows that it serves an added function of proving the inferiority of out-group standards to our own.

More intense hostility is reflected in the antilocution of name-calling. Epithets like "kike," "nigger," "wop" generally issue from deep and long-standing hostility. There are two marked exceptions. Children often use these pert terms innocently, realizing vaguely that they have "power," but not knowing clearly to what they apply. Also such epithets may mean much less when used by people in the "lower" classes than when used by people in the "higher" classes whose vocabulary is flexible enough to avoid them— if they wish to do so.

As noted previously, the more spontaneous and irrelevant the antilocution, the stronger the hostility that lies behind it.

A visitor to a Maine village was chatting with his barber about the local poultry industry. Wishing to learn something about this type of farming, the visitor innocently asked how long, on the average, the farmers kept their hens for laying purposes. Gesturing with a vicious jab of the scissors, the barber replied, "Until the Jews get them."

The barber's emotional outburst was sudden, irrelevant, and intense. The only rational connection lay in the fact that some Jewish dealers came into the vicinity to buy poultry for the market. No farmer needed to sell to a Jewish dealer unless he wanted to. The reply had little bearing on the question asked.

A similar instance of high-salience in hostility is the following.

> A devout Roman Catholic in Massachusetts was passing out literature designed to persuade voters to defeat a pending bill that would liberalize the birth control laws. A passing stranger took a leaflet, threw it down with the remark, "I won't vote against birth control. If I did it would only mean more and more work for those kike doctors."

Such sudden inruptions of prejudice into irrelevant contexts is a measure of the intensity and salience of a hostile attitude. In such cases it appears that a complex against out-groups presses hard upon the individual's mental life. He does not wait for some relevant occasion to express his hostility. The attitude is so dynamically charged that it explodes even under the influence of remote associations.

When antilocution reaches a high degree of intensity, the chances are considerable that it will be positively related to open and active discrimination, possibly to violence. A certain senator spoke on the floor of Congress against a federal bill to subsidize school lunches. In the course of his remarks he shouted, "Of course we will starve to death before we will strike down the bars and let whites and blacks go to school together." [2] Strong antilocution of this order is almost certain to be backed up by discriminatory action.

Discrimination

We often separate ourselves from people whom we find uncongenial. It is not discrimination when we do so, so long as it is *we* who move away from them. *Discrimination comes about only when we deny to individuals or groups of people equality of treatment which they may wish.* [3] It occurs when we take steps to exclude members of an out-group from our neighborhood, school, occupation, or country. Restrictive covenants, boycotts, neighborhood pressure, legal segregation in certain states, "gentlemen's agreements," are all devices for discrimination.

Our definition of discrimination must be further amplified. A criminal, a psychotic, a filthy person may desire "equality of treatment" and we may without compunction deny it to him. Differential treatment based on *individual* qualities probably should not be classed as discrimination. Here we are interested only in differential treatment that is based on ethnic categorization. An official memorandum of the United Nations defines the issue: "Discrimination includes any conduct based on a distinction made on grounds of natural or social categories, which have no relation either to individual capacities or merits, or to the concrete behavior of the individual person." [4] It is a detrimental distinction which does not take account of the particular characteristics of an individual as such.

Among the forms of discrimination *officially* practiced in various parts of the world, the United Nations lists the following:

> unequal recognition before the law (general denial of rights to particular groups)
> inequality of personal security (interference, arrest, disparagement because of group membership)
> inequality in freedom of movement and residence (ghettoes, forbidden travel, prohibited areas, curfew restrictions)
> inequality in protection of freedom of thought, conscience, religion
> inequality in the enjoyment of free communication
> inequality in the right of peaceful association
> inequality in treatment of those born out of wedlock
> inequality in the enjoyment of the right to marry and found a family
> inequality in the enjoyment of free choice of employment
> inequality in the regulation and treatment of ownership
> inequality in the protection of authorship
> inequality of opportunity for education or the development of ability or talent
> inequality of opportunity for sharing the benefits of culture
> inequality in services rendered (health protection, recreational facilities, housing)
> inequality in the enjoyment of the right to nationality
> inequality in the right to participate in government
> inequality in access to public office
> forced labor, slavery, special taxes, the forced wearing of distinguishing marks, sumptuary laws, and public libel of groups

In addition to these public and official indignities the list of acts that may be indulged in by private individuals is long. Opportunities for employment, promotion, or credit may be discriminative. Denial of residence opportunities or equal housing facilities is common, likewise exclusion from hotels, cafes, restaurants, theaters, or other places of entertainment. In the media of communication differential treatment of news concerning groups sometimes occurs. Refusal to offer equal educational opportunities or to associate with members of an out-group in churches, clubs, or social organizations is common. The catalogue could be greatly extended.[5]

Segregation is a form of discrimination that sets up spatial boundaries of some sort to accentuate the disadvantage of members of an out-group.

A certain Negro girl applied for a job in a federal office in Washington. At each stage in the process she encountered attempts to discriminate against her: she was told by one officer that the job had been filled, by another that she would not be happy in a white office. But by persistence she finally "landed" the job. When she went to work the supervisor placed her in a corner of the office and placed a screen around her desk. She had won out over various attempts to *discriminate* against her, but had run headfirst into *segregation*.[6]

Discrimination in housing is especially widespread. It is the rule in American cities to find Negroes living in segregated regions. The reason is not that they wish to or that rents are cheaper where they live. Customarily people in "white districts" pay less rent for equal or better accommodations. The social pressures that keep Negroes from spreading are reflected in restrictive covenants. Nor are Negroes the only people affected. Deeds sometimes contain such phrases as the following:

. . . And furthermore, no lot shall be sold or leased to, or occupied by, any person excepting of the Caucasian race.

. . . Provided further, that the grantee shall not sell to Negroes or permit use or occupation by them, except as domestic servants.

. . . shall not permit occupation by Negroes, Hindus, Syrians, Greeks, or any corporations controlled by same.

. . . No part of the area may be owned or occupied by any person of Negro blood or by any person who is more than one-fourth of the Semitic race . . . including Armenians, Jews, Hebrews, Turks, Persians, Syrians and Arabians. . . .[7]

In a historic decision of 1948 the Supreme Court of the United States ruled that such covenants may not be enforced by the courts of the land. But there is nothing to prevent their being adhered to by "gentlemen's agreement." They often are. Various studies by public opinion polling methods indicate that roughly three-quarters of the white population would object to having Negroes live in their immediate neighborhoods.   Hence there is widespread discrimination by common consent.

Discrimination in education is, like many forms of discrimination, usually a clandestine affair.   This is not true, of course, in certain southern states where most schools and colleges (the number is decreasing) openly practice 100 percent segregation.   In northern states, the process is more subtle and variable.   A great many institutions, especially those that are tax supported, admit students without regard to race, color, religion, or national origin.   Others sometimes limit the admission of certain groups to a stated fraction of the total enrollment, and still others exclude them altogether. Statistics in this matter are hard to come by, but we may cite one illustrative study that indicates the situation in one state.

1300 recent high school graduates in the state of Connecticut returned questionnaires concerning their experiences in applying for admission to college.

We shall consider only the cases of superior students—those standing in the top 30 percent of their graduating class in high school.

Privately endowed colleges (nondenominational) accepted over 70 percent of the Protestant and Catholic applicants (excluding Italians).   From among the Jewish applicants they accepted only 41 percent; from among Italians only 30 percent.   (Negroes and immigrant groups other than Italian were not counted because there were not enough cases.)

What do the rejected applicants do?   (1) By applying to *many* institutions their chances are increased, and generally they are admitted somewhere.   Italians do not seem to know this, but Jews do.   The latter apply on the average to 2.8 institutions; whereas Catholics and Protestants apply on the average to about 1.8 institutions.   The Italians are content with 1.5 applications— and thus many fail to achieve admission to private institutions. (2) They can go to tax-supported institutions where discrimination is virtually unknown (at least in Connecticut).   One reason why so many Jewish and immigrant students are found in city and state colleges is because they are not admitted in fair proportion to applications to private institutions.[8]

Occupational discrimination is also a subtle matter.   One method of studying the practice is to count the number of out-group exclusions in "Help Wanted" advertisements in daily newspapers: "Gentiles only," "Protestant preferred," "Opening for Christians," "no colored," and the like.   One study of this sort suggests that over a period of 65 years the trend is for discriminative advertisements to rise with the increased proportion of a minority group in the total population. Other studies indicate that this barometer is a sensitive reflection of the times: rising in periods of depression with general fear of outsiders, subsiding when the general state of tension is less.[9] It is unlikely, however, that this ingenious barometer can be used by social science analysts in the future. Some newspapers voluntarily ban discriminatory advertising, and an increasing number of states are passing laws against it.

It is not necessary to summarize here the story of occupational discrimination in America. It has been told by Myrdal, Davie, Saenger, and others.[10] The uneconomic aspects of discrimination have many times been disclosed. For example, Southern railroads have been known to put on an extra Pullman car to carry a single Negro passenger so that white passengers will not have to spend a few hours of consciousness or unconsciousness in proximity to a Negro. Many firms will not hire the best man for a job if his skin is dark, or if he happens to be Jewish, Catholic, foreign born. Sometimes such a person is twice as efficient and productive as his white competitor for the job, but he is not hired. It is equally uneconomical to maintain two sets of schools, waiting rooms, hospitals, when one would serve; or to keep whole groups of the population so economically depressed that they cannot buy goods and thus stimulate production. It is probably not an accident that the states with the greatest discrimination have the lowest standards of living, and the states of greatest tolerance the highest standards.[11]

Discrimination leads to all sorts of curious patterns. As a traveler I may sit willingly next to a Jew and, if I am a Northerner, next to a Negro; but I may draw the line on living next door to either one. As an employer I may admit the Jew but not the Negro to my office; but at home I may welcome a Negro to work in my kitchen, but not a Jew. However, a Jew but not a Negro may sit in my parlor. At school I may welcome all groups, but try to prevent some from attending school dances.

The Red Cross is an organization oriented to humanitarian service with the aid of scientific knowledge. Yet during World War II the Red Cross in many places segregated the blood given by Negro donors from that given by white donors. Science could not tell the blood apart, but social mythology could. Rightly or wrongly, certain offices of the Red Cross felt it better in wartime to respect the mythology and to shelve science and efficiency in deference to prejudice.[12]

As common as discrimination is in its many forms, it is not as common as antilocution. Two examples will show how people's bark (antilocution) is often sharper than their bite (actual discrimination). One common instance is the experience of many employers who fear to introduce Negroes or other minority members into their factory, store, or office—because the employees protest bitterly. But when, perhaps through legal necessity (Fair Employment Practices legislation), they do so—opposition evaporates. Over and over again it has been predicted that if discrimination is stopped dire consequences will follow—perhaps strikes or riots. Very seldom do they follow. What happens is that the verbal protest is greater than the demand for actual discrimination.

One instance of low discrimination but high verbal rejection comes from the cleverly conceived study of La Piere. This American investigator traveled widely in the United States with a Chinese couple. Together they stopped at 66 sleeping places and 184 eating places and were refused service only once. Afterwards, the proprietors of these places received through the mail questionnaires asking whether they would take "members of the Chinese race as guests in your establishment." Ninety-three percent of the restaurants and 92 percent of the hotels said they would *not* serve Chinese people. A control group of places which had not been visited gave similar questionnaire results. To raise the question which of these two sets of behavior was an expression of their "true" attitude is, of course, foolish. The outstanding contribution of La Piere's study design consists in showing that both are "true" attitudes, fitted to two different situations. The "verbal" situation aroused more hostility than the actual situation. People who threaten to discriminate may not do so.[13]

La Piere's findings have been confirmed by Kutner, Wilkins, and Yarrow.[14] These investigators arranged for visits to eleven restaurants and taverns in a fashionable suburb of New York. Two white girls entered first and obtained a table for three. Shortly afterward a colored girl entered and said she was joining the party. In no case was service refused and in no case was it unsatisfactory. At a later date the proprietors of each eating place received a letter asking for reservations for dinner; the letter included the phrase "since some guests are colored, I wonder whether you would object to their coming." None of the proprietors answered the letter. When follow-up phone calls were made eight denied receiving the letter, and all temporized in such a way as to avoid making the desired reservations.

We are dealing here with a situation that seems fairly common. The authors of the second study conclude that, "Discriminatory treatment is minimized when challenged in a direct face-to-face situation." Apparently proprietors (and many other people) will not practice discrimination when an immediate challenge is laid before them, but will attempt to practice it if they can do so without creating a scene or without insulting people to their faces. These two experiments, we note, were conducted in northern and western states, where discrimination is not legally sanctioned. Hence we may venture the following generalization: Where clear conflict exists, with law and conscience on the one side, and with custom and prejudice on the other, discrimination is practiced chiefly in covert and indirect ways, and not primarily in face-to-face situations where embarrassment would result.

Conditions of Physical Attack

Violence is always an outgrowth of milder states of mind. Although most barking (antilocution) does not lead to biting, yet there is never a bite without previous barking. Fully seventy years of political anti-Semitism of the verbal order preceded the discriminatory Nürnberg Laws passed by the Hitler regime. Soon after these Laws were passed the violent program of extermination began.[15] Here we see the not infrequent progression: antilocution → discrimination → physical violence. Verbal attacks in the time of Bismark were relatively mild. Under Hitler they had become ferocious: the Jews were loudly and officially blamed for every conceivable crime from sex perversion to world conspiracy.

But even the sponsors of verbal aggression in Germany were apparently astonished at the final consequences of their campaign. At the Nürnberg trials both Rosenberg and Streicher (the philosophers and publicists of the Nazi movement) disclaimed responsibility for the extermination of two and a half million Jews at Auschwitz because they "had no idea" that their preachment could issue into such action. Yet the Nazi officer in charge of the mass murders at Auschwitz, Colonel Hoess, made it clear that it was precisely this incessant verbal indoctrination that convinced him and his fellow executioners that the Jews were in fact to blame for everything and that they ought to be exterminated.[16] It is apparent, therefore, that under certain circumstances there will be stepwise progression from verbal aggression to violence, from rumor to riot, from gossip to genocide.

In cases where violence breaks out we can be fairly certain that the following steps have prepared the way.

(1) There has been a long period of categorical prejudgment. The victim group has long been typed. People have begun to lose the power to think of the members of an out-group as individuals.

(2) There has been a long period of verbal complaint against the

victimized minority. The habits of suspicion and blaming have become firmly rooted.

(3) There has been growing discrimination (e.g., the Nürnberg Laws).

(4) There has been some outside strain upon members of the in-group. They have for a long time suffered from economic privation, a sense of low-status, irritation due to political developments—such as wartime restrictions, or fear of unemployment.

(5) People have grown tired of their own inhibitions, and are reaching a state of explosion. They no longer feel that they can or should put up with unemployment, rising prices, humiliations, and bewilderment. Irrationalism comes to have a strong appeal. People distrust science, democracy, freedom. They agree that "he who increaseth knowledge increaseth sorrow." Down with intellectuals! Down with the minorities!

(6) Organized movements have attracted these discontented individuals. They join the Nazi party, the Ku Klux Klan, or Black Shirts. Or a less formal organization—a mob—may serve their purpose in case no formal organization exists.

(7) From such a formal or informal social organization the individual derives courage and support. He sees that his irritation and his wrath are socially sanctioned. His impulses to violence are thus justified by the standards of his group—or so he thinks.

(8) Some precipitating incident occurs. What previously might have been passed over as a trivial provocation now causes an explosion. The incident may be wholly imaginary, or it may be exaggerated through rumor. (For many people who participated in the Detroit race riot, the precipitating incident seems to have been a wildly circulating rumor to the effect that a Negro had seized a white woman's baby and tossed it into the Detroit River.)

(9) When violence actually breaks out, the operation of "social facilitation" becomes important in sustaining the destructive activity. To see other equally excited persons in a condition of mob frenzy augments one's own level of excitement and behavior. One ordinarily finds his personal impulses heightened and his private inhibitions lessened.

These are the conditions required to remove the normal brakes that exist between verbal aggression and overt violence. They are likely to be fulfilled in regions where the two opposing groups are thrown into close contact: for example, at bathing beaches, in public parks, or at boundaries of residential districts. At such meeting points the precipitating incident is most likely to occur.

Hot weather favors violence, both because it increases bodily discomfort and irritability, and because it brings people out of doors where contact and conflict can occur.   Add the idleness of a Sunday afternoon, and the stage is well set.   Disastrous riots do, in fact, seem to start most frequently on Sunday afternoons in hot weather. The peak of lynchings is in the summer months.[17]

The fact that verbal hostility may, in the above circumstances, lead to violence raises an issue concerning freedom of speech. Where freedom of speech is highly prized, as in the United States, it is commonly agreed by legal authorities that it is unwise and impracticable to attempt to control spoken or even printed slander against any out-group.   To do so would imply a restriction of people's right to criticize.   The American principle is to allow complete freedom of speech up to the point where there is a "clear and present" danger to public safety through an actual incitement to violence.   But this legal line is hard to draw.   If conditions are ripe, then even a relatively mild verbal attack may start an unimpeded progression toward violence.   In "normal" times a good deal more antilocution can be tolerated, for its aggressive thrusts meet with counter-arguments and with inner inhibitions to action. Most people normally pay little attention to slanderous remarks about out-groups.   Normally too, as we have seen, persons who make them would usually stop short of active discrimination, certainly of violence.   But in strained circumstances the principle of progression operates.   This fact has led a few states, for example New Jersey and Massachusetts, to enact laws against "racial libel"— but to date they have been found hard to apply, and their constitutionality is not clearly established.[18]

The participants in fist fights, gang fights, vandalism, riots, lynchings, pogroms, it has been noted, are predominantly youthful.[19] It seems unlikely that young people are more frustrated in their lives than older people, but presumably they do have a thinner layer of socialized habit between impulses and their release.   It is relatively easier for a youth to regress to the tantrum stage of infant wrath and, lacking long years of social inhibition, to find a fierce joy in this release.   Youth too has the agility, the energy, and the risk-taking proclivity required for violence.

In America the two most serious forms of ethnic conflict are riots and lynching.   The chief difference between them is that in a riot the victims of attack fight back; in a lynching the victim cannot do so.

Riots and Lynching

Most riots occur where there has been some rapid change in the prevailing social situation.   There has been an "invasion" of a residential district by Negroes, or members of a certain ethnic group

have been imported as strikebreakers in a region of industrial unrest, or there has been a rapid rise in immigrant population in an
unstable region. None of these conditions alone produces riots.
There must also be a prepared ground of previous hostility and
well-formed ideas concerning the "menace" of the particular group
that is attacked. And, as we have said, prolonged and intense
verbal hostility always precedes a riot.

It has been noted that rioters are usually drawn from lower
socio-economic classes, as well as from the youthful age level. To
some extent this fact may be due to the lesser degree of discipline
(self-control) taught in families of these classes. To some extent
it may be due to the lower educational level which prevents people
from perceiving correctly the true causes of their miserable conditions of living. Certainly the crowdedness, insecurity, and deprivations of existence act as direct irritants. In general, rioters are
marginal men.

A riot—like any form of ethnic conflict—may conceivably be
based on a realistic clash of interest. When a large number of
impoverished Negroes and equally impoverished whites are competing for a limited number of jobs, it is easy to see that rivalry is
genuine. Insecurity and fear make the individuals both irritable
and angry. But even in so realistic a situation we note the essential illogicality of regarding only the man of the *other* race as a
threat. One white man takes a job away from another white man as
surely as does a Negro. The chances are, therefore, that the conflict
of interests between ethnic groups in the same vicinity is not wholly
realistic. There must be also a previous sense of in-group and out-
group rivalry before the lines of competition can be perceived as
ethnic, rather than individual, rivalry.

The origins of a riot, therefore, lie in the prior existence of prej
udice strengthened and released by the chain of circumstances reviewed in this chapter.[20] After a riot has broken out the resulting
pandemonium has no logic. In the Harlem riot of 1943 the precipitating incident was apparently an "unfair" arrest of a Negro by
a white policeman. The racial protest, however, took a nonracial
form. Hot, tense, rebellious Negroes went wild. They looted,
burned, destroyed stores owned by Negroes, and damaged Negro
property as well as property owned by whites. Of all the forms
of physical hostility a riot is the least directed, the least consistent,
and therefore least logical. It can be likened only to the blind
temper tantrum of an angry child.

Rioting is a pattern of violence encountered chiefly in northern
and western areas of America, lynching primarily in southern states.

This fact is of considerable significance. It means, above all else, that in the South the Negro does not ordinarily attempt to fight back. When trouble brews he can only seek shelter until the storm passes by. The pattern is clearly due to the stringent insistence upon "white supremacy." The Negro is expected to accept an inferior role and never to retaliate, whatever indignities he is subjected to. Either because he himself accepts this caste role, or because he lives in fear, the Negro abstains from striking back in the face of provocation. Thus when conditions are too oppressive rioting is unlikely to occur.

By contrast we take an incident reported in several London newspapers in October 1943.

> In a town in Cornwall a group of United States Negro soldiers had been visiting "pubs." White MP's circumscribed their activities in an arbitrary manner. The Negroes returned to camp, obtained guns and marched back to town and asked the MP's why they were not allowed the same privileges as white soldiers. After some argument and shooting they were overpowered by the MP's, two of whom had been wounded.

This rather special instance of rioting is perhaps better called a *rebellion*. In it we note the following circumstances. (1) The Negroes felt keenly the discrimination against them, especially since they were in England where they knew equalitarian standards prevail. (2) Unlike most race rioting the minority group itself started the violence. (3) The precipitating incident was relatively trivial compared with the immense background of discrimination and ill-treatment that came to a focus in the rebellion. (4) The circumstance of being in the Army enhanced the Negroes' consciousness of their rights to impartial, nondiscriminative treatment. (5) The white soldiers were reacting to a long-established prejudgment that Negroes were not to be treated as social equals even in a foreign land. (6) The military indoctrination of the Negroes made them bold, fearless, and gave them a belief that force of arms is a proper means of settling disputes. Once again we see that the occurrence of any single riot can be understood only in terms of the background of both parties in the dispute.

Lynchings, as we have said, occur chiefly when discrimination and segregation are firmly entrenched and where they are customarily enforced by severe intimidation. There is an additional essential condition—a low level of law enforcement in the community. The fact that lynchings are not prevented, that lynchers, even when known, are seldom apprehended, and almost never punished, reflects the silent acquiescence of police officials and courts. The entire process, therefore, partakes of a "social norm"—and cannot be explained entirely in terms of the mental life of the lynchers.

Two types of lynching have been distinguished. The first is the so-called Bourbon, or *vigilante* lynching. A Negro who commits, or supposedly commits, a crime may be apprehended by a small, well-ordered band of important and influential citizens, and lynched quietly. This type of lynching is interpreted as a reaffirmation of existing barriers between Negro and white, a reminder that the Negro must be obedient, well-behaved, docile, and live in dreadful respect of his white superiors. It has been found that this brand of "polite lynching" takes place mainly in Black Belt counties that have been settled a long time, and where there are firmly entrenched caste and class distinctions.

Contrasting is the *mob lynching*, which takes place more often in localities that are unstable in their social structure, where, for example, rivalry between whites and Negroes for the same job is possible. Perhaps both groups are tenant farmers and suffer the same precariousness of livelihood. Instead of joining together to solve mutual problems, the situation is perceived as one of bitter competition, and the Negro is somehow blamed by the white man for his low status and insecurity. Granted a hostile outlook of this order—and a low grade of law enforcement—it is not hard to understand how lynchings occur even on slight pretext. Sex crimes, or alleged sex crimes, against white women are often thought to be the principal pretext for lynching, but a study of a period of sixty-five years indicates that in only one-fourth of all southern lynchings was this accusation involved.[21] Mob lynchings are generally marked by ferocity and bestiality. When many lynchers gather, each one wishing to "take a lick" at the accused, the resultant torture of the victim and mutilation of the corpse are excessive and revolting.

This whole macabre practice, as we have said, depends to a considerable extent upon cultural custom. Among marginal and uneducated men of certain localities there has existed the tradition of a man hunt (not unlike the tradition of the coon hunt). To "get your nigger" has been a permissible sport, virtually a duty. Toward this tradition law-enforcement authorities, as we have said, sometimes show a lenient or permissive attitude. When excitement grows high in the course of a lynching it is taken for granted that there will be looting and destruction of Negro homes and businesses. Not infrequently furniture from Negro homes is used as firewood for burning the victim's body. It seems like a sound idea to teach *all* the niggers a lesson at the same time.

The frequency of lynching has markedly declined. During the

decade of the 1890's there was an annual average of 154 lynchings; during the 1920's an annual average of 31; during the 1940's only two or three per year.[22] The decline may be due in part to the force of public opinion that has placed new pressure upon law-enforcement officials. For the past 30 years there have been persistent efforts in Congress to pass a federal antilynching law. Southern congressmen have resisted the legislation as unwarranted interference by Northerners in the affairs of the South. They have argued that the state authorities themselves can handle the problem—and it seems as though they are, in fact, succeeding. The decline must be viewed also as an instance of historical change. In the early American colonies courthouses were few. Social stability was often secured by vigilante pursuits of offenders and by summary punishments. Judge Lynch (whose name is so unhappily immortalized) was a Virginia Quaker. During the revolution Tories were caught stealing horses. As magistrate he set up court in his own home, and rapidly sentenced the thieves to forty lashes. His own religious scruples forbade him taking human life. In the course of history in the United States more whites have been lynched than Negroes. But in recent years the instances that have revolted the nation have been cases of Negro lynchings.

The Essential Role of Rumor

We may state as a dependable law that no riot or lynching ever occurs without the aid of rumor. Rumor is found to enter into the pattern of violence at one or all of four stages.[23]

(1) The gradual building up of animosity preceding a violent outbreak is assisted by stories of the misdeeds of the hated out-group. One hears particularly that the minority in question is itself conspiring, plotting, saving up guns and ammunition. Also the customary run of ethnic rumors takes a spurt, thus reflecting the mounting strain. One of the best barometers of tension is the collection and analysis of ethnic rumors in a community.

(2) After preliminary rumors have done their work, new rumors may serve as a call to rioting or lynching parties. They act like a bugle to assemble the forces. "Something is going to happen tonight by the river." "They'll catch that nigger tonight and whale the life out of him." If alert to the situation the police may use these "marshalling rumors" to forestall violence. During the summer of 1943 in Washington, D. C., rumor had it that large numbers of Negroes were planning an organized uprising on the occasion of their parade scheduled for a certain day. Such a rumor was almost certain to bring out an opposing army of hostile whites. But by taking a firm public stand in advance of the event, and by providing

adequate protection for the Negro marchers, the police were able to forestall the threatened clash.

(3) Not infrequently a rumor is the spark that ignites the powder keg. Some inflammatory story flies down the street, becoming sharpened and distorted at each telling. The Harlem riot was spread by means of an exaggerated story to the effect that a white policeman had shot a Negro in the back (the truth of the episode was much milder). A dozen wild rumors bruited around Detroit were the immediate touch on the trigger of overcharged passions. But for months before the fateful Sunday, Detroit had been fed on racial rumors. One tale to the effect that carloads of armed Negroes were heading for Detroit from Chicago had even been broadcast over the radio.[24]

(4) During the heat of the riot rumors sustain the excitement. Particularly puzzling are the stories that appear based on hallucination. Lee and Humphrey tell how at the peak of the violence in Detroit, police received a telephone report from a woman who claimed to have witnessed with her own eyes the killing of a white man by a mob of Negroes. When the squad car reached the scene the police found a group of girls playing hopscotch and could find no trace of violence nor any support for the woman's story. Other citizens, as excited as she, no doubt believed the tale and spread it.

Let us turn back for a moment to the suggestion that rumor provides a good barometer of group tension. In themselves, of course, rumors are mere antilocutions, expressions of verbal hostility. One hears them directed against Catholics, Negroes, refugees, government officials, big business, labor unions, the armed services, Jews, radicals, various foreign governments, and many other out-groups. The rumors without exception express hostility and give a reason for the hostility by featuring some objectionable trait. Here is a typical example:

> In a cafeteria belonging to a prosperous chain of restaurants (so the story goes) a customer standing at the counter ordered a bowl of beef stew and a cup of coffee. The clerk placed the beef stew on his tray and went to draw the coffee. When she returned she noticed a dead mouse in the stew. At the same instant the customer saw the unappetizing ingredient and created an uproar. He left the restaurant and soon brought suit against the prosperous company. Unluckily for him, evidence was brought to the trial that the mouse had not been cooked, and that another customer had seen him take the dead animal from his pocket and put it in the stew while the clerk's back was turned. The story ends, "Of course that man was a Jew."

Similar anti-Semitic rumors were collected in great quantities during the war. Many of them took some such form as the following:

> West Coast draft boards have refused to draft any more men until the Jewish boys in New York, Philadelphia, and Washington, deferred by Jewish draft boards, are drafted.

> All the officers at Westover are Jews. It is almost impossible for gentiles to get any of the higher offices in that air field.

> The Associated Press and the United Press are both controlled by Jews and therefore we cannot believe anything pertaining to Germany or Hitler who really knows what ought to be done to the Jews.

Stories derogatory to Negroes are somewhat less numerous. Of 1000 rumors collected and analyzed in the war year 1942, 10 percent were anti-Semitic, 3 percent anti-Negro, 7 percent anti-British, and about 2 percent each against business and against labor. The armed forces accounted for 20 percent, and the administration for 20 per cent. About two-thirds of all rumors were directed against some out-group. Most of the others expressed deep-seated fears concerning the course of the war.[25]

Thus rumor seems to offer a sensitive index for the state of group hostility. The discrediting of rumors may provide one means—probably a minor one—of controlling group hostility. During the war "rumor clinics" in newspapers attempted this service, and probably did succeed in making people aware of some of the dangers involved in rumor-mongering. It is doubtful, however, that the exposure of a rumor changes any deeply rooted prejudices. What it does at most is to warn those of mild or negligible prejudice that wedge-driving rumors in wartime or in peacetime are not in the best interests of the nation.

NOTES AND REFERENCES

1. Without doubt, this simple three-step scale would have a high "coefficient of reproducibility," according to Guttman's criterion for an acceptable attitude scale (scalogram). No person would take part in physical attack without also manifesting discriminatory and verbal rejection. The higher steps in the scale presuppose the lower. *Cf.* S. A. STOUFFER, Scaling concepts and scaling theory, Chapter 21 in MARIE JAHODA, M. DEUTSCH AND S. W. COOK (EDS.), *Research Methods in Social Relations,* New York: Dryden, 1951, Vol. 2.

2. Quoted from the Congressional Record as reported in the *New Republic,* March 4, 1946.

3. *The main types and causes of discrimination.* United Nations Publication, 1949, XIV, 3, 2.

4. *Ibid.,* 9.

5. *Ibid.,* 28-42.

6. This episode is reported in J. D. LOHMAN, *Segregation in the Nation's Capital.* Chicago: National Committee on Segregation in the Nation's Capital, 1949. The report is a complete account of segregation in the city of Washington in respect to housing, jobs, health services, education, and access to public places.

7. ELMER GERTZ. American Ghettos. *Jewish Affairs,* 1947, Vol. II, No. 1.

8. H. G. STETLER. *Summary and Conclusions of College Admission Practices with Respect to Race, Religion and National Origin of Connecticut High School Graduates.* Hartford: Connecticut State Interracial Commission, 1949.

9. A. L. SEVERSON, Nationality and religious preferences as reflected in newspaper advertisements, *American Journal of Sociology,* 1939, 44, 540-545; J. X. COHEN, *Toward Fair Play for Jewish Workers,* New York: American Jewish Congress, 1938; D. STRONG, *Organized Anti-Semitism in America: the Rise of Group Prejudice During the Decade 1930-40,* Washington: American Council on Public Affairs, 1941.

10. See especially: G. MYRDAL, *An American Dilemma: the Negro Problem and Modern Democracy,* New York: Harper, 1944, 2 vols.; M. R. DAVIE, *Negroes in American Society,* New York: McGraw-Hill, 1949; G. SAENGER, *The Social Psychology of Prejudice,* New York: Harper, 1953.

11. The economic costs of prejudice are discussed by FELIX S. COHEN, The people *vs.* discrimination, *Commentary,* 1946, 1, 17-22. In the boom year of 1940, the average income of states with the most serious discrimination in employment was $300 (Mississippi, Arkansas, Alabama, Louisiana, Georgia, Tennessee, and the Carolinas). States with the greatest measure of tolerance, judged by the extent to which they attract migrants of diversified races and faiths and by the record of their legislatures and Congressmen, had an average income in 1940 of $800 (Rhode Island, Connecticut, New York, New Jersey, Delaware, Illinois, Utah, Washington).

It is not clear in this statistical report whether the uneconomic practice of discrimination is actually a cause of low per capita income, or whether states which are relatively poor for other reasons engage in discrimination as a kind of vent for the frustrations of poverty. A third possibility is that discrimination in employment and poverty are both due to some deeper-lying condition.

12. Actions lie louder than words—Red-Cross's policy in regard to the blood bank. *Commonweal,* 1942, 35, 404-405.

13. R. T. LA PIERE. Attitudes versus actions. *Social Forces,* 1934, 13, 230-237.

14. B. KUTNER, CAROL WILKINS, PENNY R. YARROW. Verbal attitudes

and overt behavior involving racial prejudice. *Journal of Abnormal and Social Psychology*, 1952, **47**, 649-652.

15. P. E. MASSING. *Rehearsal for Destruction: a Study of Political Anti-Semitism in Imperial Germany.* New York: Harper, 1949.

16. G. M. GILBERT. *Nüremberg Diary.* New York: Farrar, Straus, 1947, 72, 259, 305.

17. *Lynchings and What They Mean.* Atlanta: Southern Commission on the Study of Lynching, 1931. See also M. R. DAVIE, *op. cit.,* 344.

18. The President's Committee on Civil Rights decided that this remedy was too dangerous to endorse, since censorship, once started, might threaten the expression of all disapproved opinion. See the Committee's report, *To secure these rights.* Washington: Govt. Printing Office, 1947.

19. See L. W. DOOB, *Social Psychology.* New York: Henry Holt, 1952, 266, 291.

20. A comparable list of circumstances leading to riots, with a somewhat more historical and sociological emphasis, is given by O. H. DAHLKE, Race and minority riots—a study in the typology of violence, *Social Forces*, 1952, **30**, 419-425.

21. M. R. DAVIE. *Op. cit.,* 346.

22. A good brief summary of the facts concerning lynching may be found in B. BERRY, *Race Relations: the Interaction of Ethnic and Racial Groups.* Boston: Houghton Mifflin, 1951, 166-171.

23. The account here is condensed from G. W. ALLPORT AND L. POSTMAN, *The Psychology of Rumor.* New York: Henry Holt, 1947, 193-198.

24. A. M. LEE AND N. D. HUMPHREY. *Race Riot.* New York: Dryden, 1943, 38.

25. G. W. ALLPORT AND L. POSTMAN. *Op. cit.,* 12.

CHAPTER 5

PATTERNING AND EXTENT OF PREJUDICE

One of the facts of which we are most certain is that people who reject one out-group will tend to reject other out-groups. If a person is anti-Jewish, he is likely to be anti-Catholic, anti-Negro, anti any out-group.

Prejudice as a Generalized Attitude

An ingenious demonstration of this point was made by E. L. Hartley in an investigation of college students.[1] He ascertained their attitudes toward 32 nations and races, asking them to judge each in respect to the items on the Bogardus Social Distance Scale, described in Chapter 3. In addition to 32 familiar nations and races he included three fictitious ethnic groups—the "Daniereans," "Pireneans," and the "Wallonians." The students were fooled, and thought these "nonesuch" groups were real. It turned out that students prejudiced against familiar ethnic groups were also preju-diced against the nonesuch peoples. The correlation between their social distance scores for the 32 real groups and these three none-such groups was around +.80, a high correlation indeed.[2]

One student, intolerant of many real groups, wrote on his paper regarding the nonesuch peoples, "I don't know anything about them; therefore I would exclude them from my country." At the same time, another student, generally unprejudiced, wrote, "I don't know anything about them; therefore I have no prejudices against them."

The comments of these two students are revealing. To the first any strange group represented a vague menace, and he therefore rejected it in advance of experience or evidence. The second, lack-ing apprehensiveness in his nature, would suspend judgment until the facts are known. He would give "Daniereans," for example, the benefit of a doubt and regard them innocent (and welcome) until they are proved guilty. Obviously there is a pervasive quality of mind in a student that disposes him to be prejudiced in general, or tolerant in general.

Looking at some additional results from Hartley's study, we find correlations between various specific negative attitudes as follows:

Negro	—Jew	.68
Negro	—Catholic	.53
Catholic	—Jew	.52
Nonesuch	—Jew	.63
Nonesuch	—Communist	.68
Nonesuch	—labor union member	.58

Why a person who is distrustful of labor unions should also distrust, say, "Pireneans" is a psychological puzzle indeed.

The same tendency is seen in the tirades of agitators. One delivered himself of the following composite blast. "When will the plain, ordinary, sincere, sheeplike people of America awaken to the fact that their common affairs are being arranged and run for them by aliens, communists, crackpots, refugees, renegades, socialists, termites, and traitors?" [3]

A similar example came to light in the German elections of 1952. The fascistic Socialist Reich party issued a pamphlet urging the electorate to abstain from voting, declaring

> The Jew, as dictator of democracy, Bolshevism, and the Vatican rule over all of you. Have you not realized that? Stand fast. Remain German. Do not vote but wait. We shall return.

To these fanatic Germans all out-groups comprise one undifferentiated menace.

People who dislike both Negroes and the federal administration sometimes condense their hostilities into the phrase "nigger-loving bureaucrats." The familiar expression, "Jewish international banker" reflects two fused negative attitudes—in defiance of the simple truth that few Jews are international bankers and few such bankers are Jews. In Latin America, where Catholicism is the dominant religion, one hears of a "Jewish-Protestant alliance" that threatens the world. But in lands where both anti-Catholicism and anti-Semitism are common, the result is condemnation in a single breath for the "Vatican and the Jews." The fact that scapegoats of different breeds are so often harnessed together shows that it is the *totality* of prejudice that is important rather than specific accusations against single groups.

Many other studies show that prejudice tends to be a general trait in personality.[4] Here we shall cite only one additional illustration drawn from the extensive research of a group of investigators at the University of California, whose data come both from college students and from various groups of noncollege adults.[5]

The subjects were given extensive questionnaires and asked to indicate the degree of their agreement or disagreement with a large number of stated propositions. They were allowed to use a six-point scale: +1: slight support or agreement; +2: moderate support; +3: strong support. Disagreement was expressed in the same way: −1: slight opposition; −2: moderate opposition; −3: strong opposition.

Among the questions asked were those listed in the following scale.

ETHNOCENTRISM SCALE

(slightly adapted from *The Authoritarian Personality*, p. 142)

A. JEWS

1. One trouble with Jewish businessmen is that they stick together and prevent people from having a fair chance in competition.
2. I can hardly imagine myself marrying a Jew.
3. There may be a few exceptions, but in general Jews are pretty much alike.
4. The trouble with letting Jews into a nice neighborhood is that they gradually give it a typical Jewish atmosphere.
5. To end prejudice against Jews, the first step is for the Jews to try sincerely to get rid of their harmful and irritating faults.
6. There is something different and strange about Jews; it's hard to tell what they are thinking and planning, and what makes them tick.

B. NEGROES

1. Negroes have their rights, but it is best to keep them in their own districts and schools and to prevent too much contact with whites.
2. It would be a mistake ever to have Negroes for foremen and leaders over whites.
3. Negro musicians may sometimes be as good as white musicians, but it is a mistake to have mixed Negro-white bands.
4. Manual labor and unskilled jobs seem to fit the Negro mentality and ability better than more skilled or responsible work.
5. The people who raise all the talk about putting Negroes on the same level as whites are mostly radical agitators trying to stir up conflict.
6. Most Negroes would become overbearing and disagreeable if not kept in their place.

C. Other Minorities

1. Zootsuiters prove that when people of their type have too much money and freedom, they just take advantage and cause trouble.
2. Certain religious sects who refuse to salute the flag should be forced to conform to such a patriotic action, or else be abolished.
3. Filipinos are all right in their place, but they carry it too far when they dress lavishly and go around with white girls.
4. It is only natural and right for each person to think that his family is better than any other.

D. Patriotism

1. The worst danger to real Americanism during the last 50 years has come from foreign ideas and agitators.
2. Now that a new world organization is set up, America must be sure that she loses none of her independence and complete power as a sovereign nation.
3. America may not be perfect, but the American Way has brought us about as close as human beings can get to a perfect society.
4. The best guarantee of our national security is for America to have the biggest army and navy in the world and the secret of the atom bomb.

We note that this form of the California Ethnocentrism Scale has four subscales. For our purposes what is important is the array of high correlations that exist among the different groups of items. Table 1 shows the approximate results.[6]

Table 1

CORRELATIONS OF THE E SUBSCALES WITH EACH OTHER AND WITH THE TOTAL E SCALE

(Data from *The Authoritarian Personality*, pp. 113 and 122)

	Negroes	Minorities	Patriotism	Total E
Jews	.74	.76	.69	.80
Negroes		.74	.76	.90
Other minorities			.83	.91
Patriotism				.92

The first thing that strikes us in the table is, once more, the generality of out-group rejection. It may seem odd that people who say that zootsuiters "cause trouble" (item C-1) should also usually agree that Jews are "strange and different" (A-6), or that Negroes should not be "foremen and leaders over whites" (B-2).

Still more odd—and most revealing—is the high correlation between "patriotism" and out-group rejection. A person who, for example, believes the Negro to be fit chiefly for manual jobs (B-4) is likely to hold that America should have the biggest army and navy in the world and guard the secret of the atom bomb (D-4).

Offhand, there seems to be little logic in these high correlations, particularly between those of "patriotism" and out-group rejection. Yet there must be a psychological unity that explains these mental bonds. "Patriotism" as tested by these particular items obviously does not refer to loyalty to the American creed. It has rather a flavor of "isolationism" (perhaps this label would be more accurate than "patriotism"). The person who rejects out-groups is very likely to have a narrowly conceived idea of his national in-group (Figure 1, p. 36). The "island of safety" mentality is at work. One's whole outlook calls for building defenses against threats. The "safety-islander" perceives menace on all sides—from foreigners, Jews, Negroes, Filipinos, zootsuiters, "certain religious sects"; and in his family relationships he insists it "only natural and right for each person to think that his family is better than any other" (C-4).

The California research finds further, as we might now expect, a tendency for these "safety-islanders" to be vigorously loyal to their churches, sororities, families, and other in-groups. All who live outside the ethnocentric circle of safety are viewed with suspicion. The same restrictiveness is seen in correlations between ethnocentrism and social and political "conservatism," which run in the neighborhood of +.50. The authors prefer to define the political outlook in question as "pseudoconservative" because there is no disposition on the part of out-group rejectors to preserve what is the vital core of the American tradition. Rather they are selective traditionalists.

> They emphasize competitiveness as a value, yet they support the concentration of economic power in big business—the greatest single threat at present to the individual competing businessman. They emphasize economic mobility and the "Horatio Alger" myth, yet they support numerous forms of discrimination that put severe limitations on the mobility of large sections of the population. They may also believe in extending the economic functions of government, not for humanitarian reasons, but as a means of limiting the power of labor and other groups.[7]

Other studies have found the reciprocal tendency: for liberals—those dissatisfied with the status quo—to be more tolerant.[8] One investigation, concluded during World War II, reported "that the more favorable the attitude toward labor unions, the more liberal is the attitude toward the Negro, toward religion, and toward Soviet Russia." [9]

The evidence we have reviewed constitutes a very strong argument for saying that prejudice is basically a *trait of personality*. When it takes root in a life it grows like a unit. The specific object of prejudice is more or less immaterial. What happens is that the whole inner life is affected; the hostility and fear are systematic. While many chapters in this volume elaborate and agree with this point of view (especially Chapters 25 and 27), it would be wrong to imply that deep-lying character-structure is the only factor that needs to be considered.

What Imperfect Correlations Mean

For example, let us note the contradictory evidence in the data we have just surveyed. Table 1 has shown that the agreement between anti-Semitism and anti-Negro feeling is +.74. This coefficient, though high, still leaves room for appreciable independence of the two forms of prejudice. At least some people must be anti-Semitic without being anti-Negro, and vice versa.[10]

Therefore, we must not assume that a general psychodynamic trait of prejudice tells the whole story, though it tells a lot. Special reasons may exist for special forms of ethnocentrism in special localities.

A study by Prothro reports the correlation between attitude toward the Negro and attitude toward the Jew among nearly 400 Louisiana adults. The correlation is +.49.[11] Now, as we have seen, a comparable correlation obtained in California runs to +.74, and in many studies, outside the South, the coefficient runs equally high.

Thus in the Louisiana sample only a portion of the pronounced anti-Negro feeling can be ascribed to an over-all trait of ethnocentrism (generalized dislike of minorities). In this sample, fully a third of the cases showed favorable attitudes toward Jews but unfavorable attitudes toward Negroes. In these instances we must conclude that prejudice cannot be explained entirely by approaching it at the level of generalized personality structure and dynamics. Situational, historical, and cultural factors are also important.

This important fact complicates the picture of ethnic hostility. If all prejudices correlated perfectly (i.e., +1.00) we should not need to look for any specific factors in our search for explanations. There would be just one homogeneous matrix of prejudice in the personality. People would always be tolerant of, or prejudiced against, all out-groups to a uniform degree. The explanation would, therefore, lie exclusively within the structure and functioning of personality.

Another extra-personality factor enters at this point. Even a person with a highly prejudiced nature is much more likely to direct his animosity toward the Jews than toward the Quakers—though both are minority groups exerting perhaps more than their proportional share of influence in the business world and in government. The bigot does *not* hate all out-groups equally. He will, for example, show much less prejudice against Canadian neighbors to the north than toward Mexican neighbors to the south. Such selective prejudice cannot be explained by fixing our attention exclusively upon the dynamics of personality.

Even though the mental make-up of the person may be the core of our problem, a full understanding requires also a social analysis —to which we shall turn in Chapters 6-9.

How Widespread Is Prejudice?

There can be, of course, no categorical answer to this question; but there are various instructive indications that lie before us.

The problem is to know where to draw the line between prejudice and no-prejudice. From what was said in Chapter 2 it is possible to argue that all of us are inevitably prejudiced. We all incline to prejudge in favor of our own way of life. Since in a deep sense we *are* the values that we hold, we cannot help but defend them with pride and affection, rejecting every group that opposes them.

But it is not helpful to conclude "everybody is prejudiced." Nor is it strictly true if we take a count only of people in whose lives categorical rejection plays a prominent part. Is it possible to take such a count?

One procedure is to comb the results of public opinion polls. Embarrassing as the topic of prejudice is to most people, intrepid pollsters have succeeded remarkably well in gathering illuminating data.[12]

Various types of questions have been asked. Take this example:

Do you think the Jews have too much power and influence in the United States?

This question has been used repeatedly with a representative cross section of the American population, and fairly consistently fetches a 50 percent affirmative reply.   Shall we say, therefore, that half the people are anti-Semites?

Since this is clearly a leading question, putting into the respondent's mind a thought that might not otherwise be there, a less suggestive question might be asked, viz.,

> In your opinion, what religious, national, or racial groups are a menace to America?

In this case the word "menace" is, of course, strong and forbidding, and furthermore the respondent is not reminded of the Jewish group directly.   Under these circumstances only 10 percent of the respondents spontaneously mention the Jews.   Is then the extent of anti-Semitism one-tenth of the population?

Try a third method.   This time give the interviewee a card with the names of the following groups on it: Protestants, Catholics, Jews, Negroes.   Then ask:

> Do you think any of these groups are getting more economic power anywhere in the United States than is good for the country?

This time you will find that about 35 percent select the Jews (and about 12 percent the Catholics).

Once again use the card method, with the question:

> Do you think any of these groups are getting more political power anywhere in the United States than is good for the country?

This time about 20 percent single out the Jews.

Thus we find estimates of anti-Semitism ranging between 10 and 50 percent.   Still greater extremes might have been obtained if stronger or milder questions had been used.

We learn from this approach that when a negative statement concerning Jews is *suggested* to people—as in the first question cited above—a large number agree with it; whereas when Jews are mentioned as only one of several groups the anti-response is not so frequently met; and when it is left to the individual himself to think *spontaneously* of the group, few people do so.   In this latter group, however, we can certainly say that the hostility is a definitely salient factor in their emotional lives.   Their antagonism has a dynamic quality; it presses for expression.   This estimate of virulent and spontaneous anti-Semitism in 10 percent of the population finds support from other studies.   In one, for example, the same percentage of the population during the war approved of Hitler's treatment of the Jews.   Among American soldiers stationed in Germany after World War II, 22 percent thought that Germans had some good reasons "for being down on the Jews."   An additional 10 percent were undecided.[13]

Estimates of anti-Negro feeling vary likewise with the type of question asked and with the region of the country where the interviewing takes place.   In most polls sentiment in favor of some type of segregation is high.   About four-fifths of the white soldiers in the American Army during World War II felt that white and Negro soldiers should have separate post exchanges.   Similarly large proportions favored separate service clubs, also segregated military units.[14]

Civilian judgments are similar in type and magnitude.[15]

> 1942: Do you think there should be separate sections in towns and cities for Negroes to live in?   Yes, 84 percent.
> 1944: Would it make any difference to you if a Negro family moved in next door to you?   Yes, 69 percent.

Sentiments in favor of occupational discrimination are not quite so harsh:

> 1942: Do you think your employers should hire Negroes?   No, 31 percent.
> 1946: Do you think Negroes should have as good a chance as white people to get any kind of job, or do you think white people should have the first chance at any kind of job?   White people first, 46 percent.

Regarding educational opportunities the attitude is distinctly favorable:

> 1944: Do you think the Negroes in this town should have the same chance as white people to get a good education? Yes, 89 percent.

Turning from attitudes to beliefs, and from adults to high school youth, we see in Table 2 that approximately a third of the latter group have distinctly unfavorable beliefs.[16]

While poll data are instructive, we see clearly that results will vary according to the precise question asked.

A more illuminating estimate of the extent of prejudice comes from an intensive study of 150 veterans living in Chicago.   The investigators, Bettelheim and Janowitz, held prolonged interviews with the men.   Before probing into their ethnic attitudes directly, plenty of opportunity was given for the veterans to express spon-

Table 2

PERCENTAGE OF 3,300 HIGH SCHOOL
STUDENTS FROM ALL REGIONS
OF THE UNITED STATES

"Is the Negro a member of an inferior race?"

	Yes	No
Boys	31	69
Girls	27	73

"Do you think that Negroes can contribute as much to society as other groups?"

	Yes	No
Boys	65	35
Girls	72	28

taneously their opinions. This procedure allowed the investigators to make careful estimates of the intensity of antagonism. The attitudes toward both Jews and Negroes were explored. Table 3 shows the results.[17]

Table 3

TYPES OF ATTITUDES TOWARD TWO MINORITY GROUPS

Types of Attitude Expressed	Percentage of Respondents (N = 150)	
	Toward Jews	Toward Negroes
Intensely anti- (spontaneous)	4	16
Outspokenly anti- (when questioned)	27	49
Stereotyped	28	27
Tolerant	41	8
Total	100	100

Here it is apparent that hostility toward Negroes is much greater than toward Jews. Four gradations of out-group hostility are distinguished. The men rated *intense* were those who spoke spontaneously against the minority group. They brought up the "Jewish question" or the "Negro problem" of their own accord, and also advocated severely hostile action ("send them out of the country," "use Hitler's solution"). We note that by this criterion Bettelheim and Janowitz did not discover as many virulent anti-Semites as other studies, cited earlier in this chapter, have indicated.

Outspoken prejudice was listed when the respondent showed genuine hostility toward the minority group and advocated restrictive action after being directly questioned concerning the group. *Stereotyped* cases were those who, when asked or given suitable opportunity, expressed the usual beliefs (prejudgments) concerning the minority. Jews were said to be clannish or money-minded—though no hostility was directly expressed. Negroes were said to be dirty or superstitious—but no restrictive policy was suggested. *Tolerant* individuals were those who failed in the course of the interview to express any stereotyped or hostile views whatsoever.

Our evidence up to this point has concerned only Negroes and Jews. Earlier in this chapter we proved that a person prejudiced against these groups would most likely be prejudiced against other groups as well, and vice versa. Yet, it is quite possible that the prejudices of some persons would not be tapped at all by the questions thus far asked. To include them within our "census of the prejudiced" we should have to ask questions concerning Catholics, Poles, British, political parties, labor, capital, etc. Such additional inquiry would raise our estimate of the number of prejudiced people in our society.

In one unpublished study several hundred essays were written by college students on the topic, "My experience with, and attitudes toward, minority groups." When analyzed it turned out that these documents contained clear admissions of group prejudice in *eighty* percent of the cases.

In a somewhat similar investigation over four hundred college students were asked to report the names of groups toward which they felt "uncongenial." Only 22 percent failed to mention any minority group at all. In the array of uncongenial groups were Wall Street, labor, farmers, capitalists, Negroes, Jews, Irish, Mexicans, Nisei, Italians, Catholics, Protestants, Christian Scientists, communists, New Dealers, army officers, conservatives, radicals, Swedes, Hindus, Greenwich Villagers, Southerners, Northerners, professors, and Texans. While "uncongeniality" is not identical with prejudice, it is a first cousin. By this method, therefore, about 78 percent of the subjects betray rejective attitudes.[18]

These latter studies tempt us to estimate that four-fifths of the American population harbors enough antagonism toward minority groups to influence their daily conduct. The estimate is similar to the percentage reported earlier in this chapter as favoring segregation for Negroes.

The very diversity of targets has an important social implication. With animosity widely distributed there may conceivably be less probability of "ganging up" against one particular minority. It is true that this chapter has demonstrated a generality of prejudice —those hostile toward one group are likely to be hostile toward others. Even so, there are so many cross-interests involved that an *organized* persecution of one minority seems unlikely. For example, anti-Catholic Negroes could not join with the Ku Klux Klan which is anti-Catholic, for it is *also* anti-Negro. Suburbanites of Anglo-Saxon stock may tolerate Italians in the neighborhood for fear that if they do not, Jewish residents may replace them. And so, all in all, an uneasy truce among groups is maintained.

If group prejudice plays a part in the mental lives of eighty percent of the public (or even a smaller percentage) we have reason to marvel at the relative smoothness of our social life. Undoubtedly the over-all American creed of equality and the tradition of the melting pot serve to hold rejective attitudes in check (cf. Chapter 20). The crosscurrents of hostility to some extent neutralize one another; and an ultimate obedience to the democratic creed serves as a further restraint.

Demographic Variations in Prejudice

We have been talking in broad averages. We have given virtually no breakdowns regarding the extent of prejudice in terms of geographical regions of the United States, education, religion, age, or social class.

A very large number of studies bear on this matter, but they tend to contradict each other. One will assure us that women are more prejudiced than men. Another, with equally good evidence— though on a different sample—will assert that men are more prejudiced than women. One discovers that Catholics are more prejudiced than Protestants, another discovers the opposite. It seems safest at the present time to conclude that while claims of this order may hold for single studies, they do not form a firm basis for generalization.

Perhaps we may venture three generalizations that seem to be most widely supported by evidence. The first is that, on the average, attitudes toward Negroes are less favorable in southern than in northern and western states. Also, less secure, is the evidence that anti-Semitism is greater in the northeast and midwest regions of the country than in the South or West.

Regarding *education*, it generally but not always appears from researches that people with college education are slightly less intolerant than people with grade school or high school education (at least they answer questions in a more tolerant way).

Finally, it seems fairly well established that white people in the lower socio-economic levels are, on the average, more bitterly anti-Negro than white people at the higher levels. The reverse situation holds for anti-Semitism, which seems relatively more pronounced at the higher socio-economic levels than at the lower.

Beyond these tentative assertions it seems unsafe to estimate the relation of religion, sex, age, region, or economic status to prejudice. We shall see in later chapters that each variable, under specific conditions, may be associated with higher or lower degrees of bias. But for the present it seems best to conclude that there is in this country no proof-positive of invariant relationships between demographic groupings and prejudice.

NOTES AND REFERENCES

1. E. L. HARTLEY. *Problems in Prejudice.* New York: Kings Crown Press, 1946.

2. Occasionally in this volume we shall express a degree of relationship with the aid of coefficients of correlation. For those who are not familiar with this simple statistical device, it is necessary only to know that the coefficients range between +1.00 and −1.00. The first figure represents a perfect positive relationship; the latter a perfect negative relationship. The closer the decimal figure comes to either extreme the more significant is the relationship indicated. Zero (or coefficients in that neighborhood) tell us that no significant relationship obtains.

3. This agitator is quoted by LEO LOWENTHAL and NORMAN GUTERMAN in *Prophets of Deceit,* New York: Harper, 1949, 1.

4. Among the many published studies that contain conclusive evidence that prejudices are positively correlated are the following: G. W. ALLPORT and B. M. KRAMER, Some roots of prejudice, *Journal of Psychology,* 1946, **22**, 9-39; E. L. THORNDIKE, On the strength of certain beliefs and the nature of credulity, *Character and Personality,* 1943, **12**, 1-14; G. MURPHY and R. LIKERT, *Public Opinion and the Individual,* New York: Harper, 1938; G. RAZRAN, Ethnic dislikes and stereotypes: a laboratory study, *Journal of Abnormal and Social Psychology,* 1950, **45**, 7-27.

5. T. W. ADORNO, E. FRENKEL-BRUNSWIK, D. J. LEVINSON and R. N. SANFORD. *The Authoritarian Personality.* New York: Harper, 1950.

6. The results are "approximate" because they are based on earlier forms of the Ethnocentrism and an anti-Semitic scale. The items published here are suggested by the authors for a shorter "final form," but intercorrelations of the parts are not known. They are unlikely to differ greatly from the earlier correlations.

7. *Ibid.,* 182.

8. G. MURPHY and R. LIKERT. *Public Opinion and the Individual.* New York: Harper, 1938.

9. F. L. MARCUSE. Attitudes and their relationships—a demonstrational technique. *Journal of Abnormal and Social Psychology*, 1945, **40**, 408-410.

10. There is, for example, some evidence that Jewish people who are themselves anti-Semitic (a not uncommon phenomenon) are surprisingly seldom prejudiced against other groups. Their psychological problem is quite specific to their own membership group. *Cf.* N. ACKERMAN and M. JAHODA, *Anti-Semitism and Emotional Disorder*, New York: Harper, 1950.

11. E. T. PROTHRO. Ethnocentrism and anti-Negro attitudes in the deep south. *Journal of Abnormal and Social Psychology*, 1952, **47**, 105-108.

12. The poll data cited here may be traced in the studies of E. ROPER published in *Fortune*, February 1946, October 1947, September Supplement 1949; also B. M. KRAMER, Dimensions of prejudice, *Journal of Psychology*, 1949, **27**, 389-451; also G. SAENGER, *Social Psychology of Prejudice*, New York: Harper, 1953.

13. S. A. STOUFFER et al. *The American Soldier.* Princeton: Princeton Univ. Press, Vol. II, 571.

14. *Ibid.,* Vol. I, 566.

15. These poll results are taken from H. CANTRIL (ED.), *Public Opinion, 1935-1946.* Princeton: Princeton Univ. Press, 1951.

16. World Opinion. *International Journal of Opinion and Attitude Research*, 1950, **4**, 462.

17. B. BETTELHEIM and M. JANOWITZ. *Dynamics of Prejudice.* New York: Harper, 1950, 16 and 26.

18. G. W. ALLPORT and B. M. KRAMER. *Op. cit.,* 9-39.

Part II

GROUP DIFFERENCES

CHAPTER 6

THE SCIENTIFIC STUDY OF GROUP DIFFERENCES

WOULD DIFFERENCES, IF DISCOVERED, JUSTIFY REJECTION?—
THE WELL-DESERVED REPUTATION THEORY—METHODS OF
STUDYING GROUP DIFFERENCES—TYPES AND DEGREES OF DIF-
FERENCES—INTERPRETATION OF DIFFERENCES

*Sir: . . . No one wishes more than I do to see such proofs
as you exhibit, that Nature has given to our black brethren
talents equal to those of other colors of men, and that the
appearance of a want of them is owing only to the degraded
condition of their existence, both in Africa and America. . . .*

THOMAS JEFFERSON TO BENJAMIN BANNEKER
LETTER OF AUGUST, 1791

The prejudiced person almost invariably explains his negative
attitude in terms of some objectionable quality that marks the
despised group. The group as a whole is alleged to have a bad
odor, an inferior brain, a sly, aggressive, or lazy nature. By contrast, the tolerant person (Thomas Jefferson, for example) *wishes*
to see proof that group differences are negligible or wholly lacking.
It would be well if both bigot and nonbigot could suspend judgment, and shelve their desires, until they learn such scientific facts
as are available.

Even for the scholar, strict objectivity in the study of national and
racial differences is hard to achieve. He has his own prejudices,
both for and against, to contend with. He does not know to what
degree they are affecting his own interpretation of the evidence.
Yet it is a hopeful sign that social scientists nowadays are far more
aware of the danger than they were formerly.

Not many years ago even a highly reputable sociologist could, with
impunity, make statements that abounded in careless generalizations
and in unrecognized prejudice. One of them, in a volume printed
in 1898, described the Negro population of Boston as follows:

Some have the instincts of gentlemen. . . . The majority, however, exhibit the usual characteristics of the Negro race: loud and
coarse, revealing much more of the animal qualities than of the

spiritual.   Yet even they are good-natured and obliging people, and are often, of course, very religious in their crude way.[1]

Although the author recognizes exceptions, he nevertheless pontificates on "the usual characteristics of the Negro race" in a manner that no present-day sociologist would dare employ.

Likewise, at the turn of the century James Bryce, the eminent political scientist, delivered a lecture at Oxford on "The Relations of the Advanced and Backward Race of Mankind."   In it he invoked the Darwinian theory of evolution in such a way as to justify the aggressions of the "fit" and strong races of mankind against the weaker.   He chides the American Indians for their stubborn refusal to conform to the white man's standards.   Massacres became the inevitable (and, he implies, justifiable) result.   Negroes, he is glad to perceive, are innately submissive.   The black man "survives because he submits."   They know their place as an inferior race.   To be sure they should be given good jobs and educational opportunities, but only such as are consistent with their "lesser intelligence."   Menial jobs are thus the right jobs for Negroes.   Most Negroes are unfit to vote, he argues, not only because of their ignorance, but because they have "sudden and unreasoning impulses" which make them an easy prey to bribery.   Intermarriage he views with horror.   Besides innate repulsion against the practice he finds strong arguments in the unproved assertion that racial hybrids are weak, if not physically, at least in character.

Bryce is sincere enough in wishing a better accommodation between the "superior" and "inferior" races of mankind; but his diagnosis of the situation contributes nothing at all to this end. The diagnosis, though he does not know it, is based on his own prejudgments, and at no point on proven fact.[2]

It is not necessary to turn back even a half-century to see how science may decompose under prejudice.   The "discoveries" and "laws" put forth by German psychologists and sociologists under Hitlerism are recent examples.   In all seriousness they declared, "Every line of human investigation is based on race."   In the course of their investigations they discovered, for example, that 14-year-old children in German schools in the year 1940 were better physical specimens than in 1926.   This finding they attributed entirely to the "application of principles received from the Führer."   They made no mention of the fact that in all civilized countries where modern standards of nourishment and hygiene were in effect, there was a corresponding improvement in the physical condition of children—regardless of the Führer.   These same "scientists" ascribed delinquency to racial inheritance, and declared, "Delinquent inhabitants are the cause of slums, not *vice versa*." [3]   Social scientists in nonracialist countries were for the most part convinced of the opposite point of view.

By contrast, we find social scientists who overhastily reject the very possibility of racial, national, or group differences of any appreciable or fundamental order.   Some of them do so on the basis of charitable motives, but the evidence they offer is usually fragmentary.

Would Differences, If Discovered, Justify Rejection?

The answer to this question is *Not necessarily*.   Within a family there are often marked differences of appearance, talent, temperament.   Ted is bright and handsome; his brother Jim, dull and homely; his sister May is extroverted but lazy; and his sister Deborah is "peculiar."   But each of these oddly assorted sibs may accept their differences and love one another.   Difference alone does not make for hostility.

And yet the prejudiced person almost always *claims* that some alleged difference is the cause of his attitude.   He seems never to consider the possibility of tolerating, let alone loving, people in out-groups who are (he thinks) dull, sly, aggressive, or even smelly— not even though he may feel affection for similarly ill-favored members of his family or circle of friends.

At the same time there *is* such a thing as a realistic conflict of interests.   One group may actually plot to attack or outstrip another, to restrict its freedom, or otherwise do it damage.   Furthermore, it is conceivable that a given group may have such a preponderance of offensive or dangerous traits that only a saint would consider it unwarranted to avoid and criticize the group.   To put the matter more precisely, it is conceivable that a given group may have such a preponderance of offensive or dangerous traits that a *high probability* exists that a given member of that group may possess these traits.

The Well-Deserved Reputation Theory

The average person with prejudice, when asked the grounds for his negative attitudes, will reply somewhat as follows: "Just *look* at them.   Don't you *see* that they are different in an objectionable way?   I am not prejudiced.   Their unpopularity rests on a *well-deserved reputation*." [4]

While, as we have said, the "well-deserved reputation" theory may conceivably be correct, its weakness consists in its failure to answer two questions: (1) Does the reputation rest on indisputable fact (or at least high probability)?   (2) If so, should the trait in question arouse feelings of aversion or hostility rather than feelings of, say, indifference, sympathy, or beneficent interest? Unless these two questions can be answered satisfactorily and rationally we may be sure that the "well-deserved" theory is, in fact, a mask for prejudice.

Take anti-Semitism as an example. The anti-Semite always claims that the Jews possess certain distinctive traits which merit the hostility they attract. To test this assertion one must (1) establish the fact that there are significant differences in the alleged traits when Jews and non-Jews are compared, and (2) show that such differences as are found offer reasonable grounds for rejecting the Jews.

If this proof is forthcoming then we must conclude that anti-Semitism represents a realistic social conflict, and does not fit our definition of prejudice. In Chapter 1 we argued that the antagonism felt for the Nazi clique in Germany, for gangsters and criminals in any country, and for other clearly antisocial elements in society should be regarded not as prejudice, but as cases of a realistic clash of values. We also pointed out that instances may occur where we are dealing partly with well-deserved reputation and partly with prejudice. Ex-convicts are a case in point. So, too, are many of the situations that arise in wartime. While a realistic clash of values may precipitate a war, the attendant array of rumors, atrocity stories, book burning, violent hatred for the whole enemy nation, and vindictive behavior toward Americans descended from the opposing nation show how prejudice may be added to a core of rationality.

The world scene today provides a good example. Without shadow of doubt there is a realistic opposition between many of the values held by communism and by western democracy. How this conflict can be resolved is the most serious problem of our times. But around this realistic core there is an enormous accretion of prejudice. Behind the iron curtain it is taught, and widely believed, that America is the aggressor nation, that American professors read lectures prepared for them in Wall Street. In the United States it is often believed that liberals and intellectuals, especially those who are working for international understanding or for racial equality, are communists and therefore traitors. Such irrationality stains the whole process to such an extent that it is difficult to hold in perspective the core problem that cries for solution.

Methods of Studying Group Differences

Since people almost invariably explain and justify their hostilities on the ground of group differences, it becomes absolutely vital to know which differences are *real* and which are merely *imaginary*. To state the matter more technically, unless the properties of the stimulus field (group traits) are known it is not possible to estimate the nature or extent of the irrational distortion that occurs.[5]

Now it is well to be candid at the start: differential social psychology is backward. It cannot at the present time give us a positive answer to the question we ask. There are, to be sure, literally thousands of studies dealing with differences between groups—but the findings leave much to be desired.[6] One difficulty lies in the enormous number of groups that might be compared with one another. Effort thus far has been spread thin. Another difficulty is that present methods of study are not satisfactory. In many instances different investigators working with the same populations come up with contradictory results. Finally the task of interpreting results when they are in hand is peculiarly difficult, for one seldom knows whether the difference he discovers can be attributed to native (inborn) factors, to early training, to cultural pressure, or to all these causes.

One way to start the search would be to ask what kinds of groups might be profitably compared. The possibilities seem endless. Looking at the types of groups against which prejudice is known to exist we find that they break down into at least a dozen classes:

race	social classes
sex	occupations
age levels	educational levels
ethnic groups	innumerable forms of
linguistic groups	interest groups (e.g.,
region	United Mine Workers,
religions	American Medical
nations	Association, Rotary
ideologies	Clubs, fraternities, etc.)
castes	

Under each heading an immense number of comparative studies might be made: how do law students differ from medical students, how do Buddhists differ from Baptists, men who speak French from those who speak Finnish?

But this form of sociological listing is not satisfactory. For one thing we note that people against whom prejudice is most commonly directed tend to cross-cut this classification. For example: Jews may be regarded as an ethnic, linguistic, or religious group; Negroes are conceivably marked by racial, caste, class, and occupational differences; communists cut across ideological, class, national, linguistic, religious, and special interest lines.

Hardly any group that is the object of prejudice can be tagged solely as racial, ethnic, ideological, or anything else. It is still common to speak of "race prejudice"—but as we come to realize that the Jews, for example, are not a race, and that mulattoes are as much Caucasian as Negro, the phrase falls into scientific disrepute. "Ethnic" is a looser word—covering well enough differences in culture, language, and tradition, but applying badly to sex, occupation, and interest groups.

Leaving this dilemma unsolved, let us ask what *methods* are actually employed in the study of group differences. Obviously they must be of a *comparative* type. The nature of the problem requires that at least two groups be studied by the same method. Some of the methods that have been profitably employed are the following.

1. **Travelers' reports** (including accounts by anthropologists, journalists, missionaries). Throughout history this has been the most common source of information. The traveler *against the background of his own culture* perceives, interprets, and reports what strikes him as noteworthy in the land he has visited. The observer may be highly trained, astute, and subtle. Or he may be a naive and gullible person, given to "imagining things." Good reporting is now, and perhaps always will be, the source of most of our knowledge of out-groups. Although some work of this order is deliberately comparative,[7] much of it is comparative only in the sense that the reporter has held in mind his own culture as an implicit frame of reference. The shortcoming of the traveler's impressions are obvious: the differences that he reports are not quantified nor are they necessarily typical of the whole population or group where he visited. His own interests, moral standards, and training influence his impressions. What strikes him as an important trait may strike others as minor or nonexistent.

2. **Vital (and other) statistics.** In recent years international organizations (e.g., the League of Nations, International Labor Office, the United Nations and its specialized agencies) have collected much data from member countries. But they have no figures on the relative intelligence of nations, nor on the temperament of racial groups, nor directly on the problem of national character. Some of their compilations, however, are serviceable in a limited way for our problem. It is useful to know, for example, the average educational level attained by Swedes, Dutch, Italians, and not merely to *imagine* which is the most highly educated nation. One of the services of UNESCO (the United Nations Educational, Scientific, and Cultural Organization) is to present factual accounts of various national ways

of life. Comparative statistics issued by the United Nations are helpful.[8] Relevant aid comes likewise from national sources. The United States census and the Department of Internal Revenue make many useful breakdowns. A person who has a prejudgment, for example, concerning the average income of physicians as a group, may receive a salutary correction to his idea by consulting official reports.

3. **Tests.** Every American student is familiar with mental tests. Ideally they could be used to solve some of our most puzzling problems. They could be used to compare the sensory acuity of primitive and civilized groups; to compare the intelligence of any and all groups; to discover the capacity of people in different occupations to do abstract thinking; in short, to provide "all the answers." Although we shall at times lean on the results of various tests administered to different groups, it is important at the outset to call attention to their limitations.

1. Some people are test-wise (e.g., American college students); others never saw a test. The performance will differ greatly according to the degree of familiarity with test situations.

2. Tests often require a competitive mental set. In some cultures such competitiveness is unknown. The person who takes the test is unable to understand why he should not let his family or friends work on the test in cooperative group fashion. Or he is unable to comprehend the need for speed.

3. It is easy to motivate the people in some groups to work hard at the test; in others interest lapses.

4. Testing conditions are often not comparable. The pandemonium that reigns around children in a Navaho village is unlike the quiet testing conditions that can be secured with children in some cultures.

5. Groups of people seldom have comparable degrees of literacy. They can neither read nor comprehend the questions with equal ease.

6. The items in a test are almost always "culture bound." Even rural American children may not be able to answer questions in a test that favors the experience and contacts of an urban child.

7. Most tests are devised and standardized by American psychologists. The entire pattern of American culture converges in the instruments they fashion. Everything about the test may be alien, unfair, and misleading to people who are unaffected by the same presuppositions and influences.

The psychologist himself would rightly complain if he were to be judged by an intelligence, personality, or attitude test devised by Bantus.

These limitations, fortunately, are well recognized by social scientists, and in recent years at least, results obtained from tests with different groups have been interpreted with great caution—with so much caution, we might add, that no one is quite sure what the results mean.   Perhaps the chief finding concerning intelligence tests is this: *the more culture-free a test is, the smaller the group differences appear to be.*   For example, a simple test asking children to draw a picture of a man is far more fair for cross-cultural comparison than is a straight verbal intelligence test—and the results of the Draw-a-man Test used with groups of white and Indian children reveal rather slight differences between them, sometimes favoring Indian groups over white.[9]   This finding does not prove that there are no differences in intellectual capacity between human groups; it means that it will require an *absolutely* culture-free test to discover them.

4. **Opinion and attitude studies.**   Within recent years the method of public opinion polling has become extended across national boundaries.   By this reasonably precise technique one can compare the views of representative samples of different nations on a number of matters: political issues, religious views, proposed roads to peace.[10]

This method is limited, of course, to use in countries having reliable organizations devoted to polling, and requires cooperation between such organizations.   There is also—as in the case of tests— a danger that people of different cultural backgrounds will not perceive the questions asked in the same light.   Translations of questions from one language to another often change their nuance, and therefore the meaning of the replies.

A freer variant on this method is illustrated in the research of James M. Gillespie.[11]

This investigator collected two documents from a large sample of youth in ten nations.   One called for an autobiography of the future, "My Life from now until the year 2000 A.D."   The other was a uniform questionnaire asking for answers to fifty or more direct questions.

The results show that there are clear national differences. American youth, for example, are far more preoccupied with their own personal lives, and less interested in politics and social developments, than the youth of other nations.   Closest to the Americans (among the countries studied) stand the New Zealanders.   Yet, unlike Americans, these youth see their own destiny as bound up with careers in civil service, as probable employees of the state.   American youth, by and large, seem oblivious of their dependence on, and possible contributions to, the national life.   Public and international affairs concern them relatively little.

This "privatism" of American youth is a characteristic not easily recognized unless international comparative methods are used. How may it be explained?   Youth in America has been reared in a tradition of individualism, each man for himself.   The huge size, wealth, and strength of the nation allow the youth to take his future security for granted.   The emphasis on material goods leads him to plan his competitive career with a view to maximizing his own standard of living, rather than sacrificing for the common good. Hence a kind of detachment or "privatism" dominates his outlook on the future.

Yet we cannot argue that in times of national crisis American youth would fall short in patriotism or in willingness to sacrifice their private goods.   The peculiar self-centeredness reflected in their documents will be offset in times of crisis by deep-lying ideological convictions that *also* mark the "national character" of Americans.

5. **Comparative study of official ideologies.**   In the case of doctrinal groups (national, religious, philosophical, political) there is always a creedal literature.   From the writings of Marx, Lenin, Stalin are distilled the principal mental attributes of communism, and these may be compared against the doctrinal literature, say of the United States (its Constitution, its Declaration of Independence and accumulated State papers).   If this is done, one might conclude in part that:

Communists officially believe in a naturalistic universe materially grounded; in a spiral of progress that evolves through a conflict of opposing forces (dialectical materialism); in the virtues of unanimous action as reflected in an authoritarian one-party government; that ends justify the means; that moral spontaneity of the individual is undesirable; that production and practice are themselves identical with theory.

Americans officially believe in the fundamental values set forth in the Judeo-Christian religious tradition and in English law; in a unilinear evolution directed by the common ideals of a society; in the efficacy of reason (so that truth will ultimately win out); in the desirability of many points of view interacting and freely expressed in voting under a two (or more) party system; that government is an arbitrator among divergent interests; that ethical spontaneity of the individual should be safeguarded.

Studies of ideology are perhaps even more clearly pursued in the field of comparative religion, where the volume of authoritative and sacred literature, both revered and binding upon the believer, is large.

As useful as this exegetic method is one must never forget that *official doctrines* do not always correspond to the actual views or practices of the adherents. Often they express ideals rather than attainments. Yet they are psychologically important, for where they exist they inevitably point the minds of group members in a common direction, and present norms for their behavior which from childhood onward leave their impress.

6. **Content analysis.** In keeping with the modern demand for precision in social science a new quantitative technique has evolved. It may be applied not only to official documents, but to any stream of communication within a society. Radio programs, for example, may be recorded and analyzed to discover just what messages are being conveyed. Films, newspapers, magazines, drama, advertisements, humor, and novels, can be studied in the same way. The recurrence of a given theme may be noted. Independent analysis by other investigators can check the accuracy of the record and thus establish the reliability of a single investigator's work. The principal difficulty in employing this method comes in making the initial decision: what kinds of units shall be counted? Shall we classify the subjct matter talked about, or merely count the emotionally toned words that are used in handling a given subject? Shall we take the communication at its face value, or look for the intent behind the words? Shall we consider the entire communication as one unit, or shall we use each phrase, sentence, or thought as a unit? These diverse possibilities have given rise to different forms of content analysis.[12] All of them have their uses. On p. 117 the application of one method of analyzing the problem of national character is described.

7. **Other methods.** We do not pretend that these six methods exhaust the devices for gaining dependable knowledge of group differences. They are illustrative only. Special problems call for special techniques. For example, in his laboratory a physical anthropologist might compare the bones of different races of mankind. The physiologist might study blood types. The psychopathologist working in mental hospitals might classify the forms of mental disturbance that occur with differential frequency among people of different racial stocks, national groups, or socio-economic levels.

Types and Degrees of Differences

There are, as we have said, literally thousands of studies on group differences of one sort or another. Sometimes the findings are classified according to some such scheme as the following:

> anatomical differences
> physiological differences
> differences in abilities
> "basic personality" of members of a given group
> cultural practices and beliefs

Such a listing is not particularly rewarding, for while it yields unrelated fragments of information, it does not follow a theoretically sound scheme for understanding the problem of group differences.

We shall follow a different model. This scheme has the merit of containing within four divisions all the types of group differences that have been established. It likewise enables us to grasp the fundamental logic of group differences. The scheme holds that every known difference between human groups fits into one of the four following types:

1. A *J*-curve of conformity behavior
2. A rare-zero differential
3. Overlapping "normal" curves of distribution
4. A categorical differential

Each type requires explanation.

1. **J-curve of conformity behavior.** Many groups are marked primarily by the prescription that every member (because he is a member) engage in some particular form of conduct. The prescribed language of America is English, and nearly every member of the nation accepts the precription. A very few do not (keeping perhaps to their ancestral languages). The distribution of people who conform to this distinctive group attribute may be plotted as in Fig. 3. Actually the percentages inserted in the boxes are mere estimates, but serve adequately for purposes of illustration. A frequency curve drawn to the histograms looks approximately like the letter "J."

We immediately think of many group differences that seem to be of this order. The Catholic is supposed to attend Mass every Sunday, and most Catholics do so. A few do not. American motorists are supposed to stop when they see a red traffic light; most do so; a small number merely slow down their rate of speed; a very few do not stop at all. If much pressure towards conformity exists (a red light, plus a stop sign, plus a traffic policeman at the

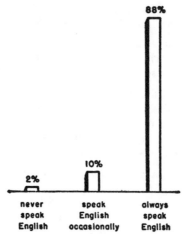

FIG. 3. Hypothetical percentage of Americans who speak English—a conformity attribute.

intersection) the conformity rate is higher (the *J*-curve is steeper). Employees in our culture are supposed to arrive at work on time. Punctuality is an American trait.   Let's look at this example with data drawn from an actual study.[18]

FIG. 4.   Number of employees punching time clock at 10-minute intervals. A variant on the *J*-curve (adapted from F. H. Allport, *Journal of Social Psychology,* 1934, **5,** 141-183).

Americans are said to be a punctual nation, which means that a larger proportion of people conform to the J-curve demanded by their engagements than is to be found in other countries.

A German visitor to the United States was asked what feature of American life impressed him most. He replied, "The fact that if a hostess invites twelve people to dinner at seven o'clock, all of them will arrive between five minutes before seven and five minutes after."

In this country theatres and concerts nearly always commence their programs on time, trains and planes conform closely to schedule, and dentist appointments are rigidly kept. The high value placed on punctuality is probably found in no other culture (even Western Europe) to such a degree.

Figure 4 shows not only conformity to the requirement of punctuality, but also the phenomenon of overconformity. Many people arrive early. They overconform. But the mode (high peak) of the distribution falls at the point prescribed by the culture (arriving on time).

The characteristic thing about the J-curve is that only the members of a given group can be fitted to it. It is simply not applicable to nonmembers. The employees of a given factory will conform to the group-ways in the manner shown, but not the wives of the employees who are, of course, not members of that factory group. Catholics will fit the J-curve of attendance at Mass, but not non-Catholics. Most American gentlemen will allow a lady to precede them when entering a door; men of certain other cultures will not.

The logic of the J-curve, then, may be stated as follows: Whenever there is a strongly prescribed action for members of an in-group they will, by virtue of their membership, tend to conform.

The outstanding and obvious differences that mark off one group from another are of this order. Hollanders speak Dutch; the western man wears trousers and the western woman skirts (with few exceptions); Jews for the most part observe Jewish holidays (no one else does so); school children attend school, most of them every day. Examples are endless. The law is: *the essential attributes of a group—those characteristics that define the group—tend to follow a J-curve type of distribution.*

There are differences that seem in principle to fit the J-distribution, but may do so less clearly than the examples given. Americans are supposed to obey all the laws of their land. Many do not. This disregard for a prescribed conformity is rightly regarded as an ominous sign. A group whose members are in the process of departing from the essential conformity that their group membership implies is in the process of weakening. By their religion Jews are expected to gather in the synagogue for worship once a week. Insofar as they fail to do so (and many Jews are apostates), the solidarity of the group weakens, or at least its nature changes. *J*-curves of conformity can *decay*. When fewer and fewer members perform the prescribed actions the distinctive character of the group gradually disappears.

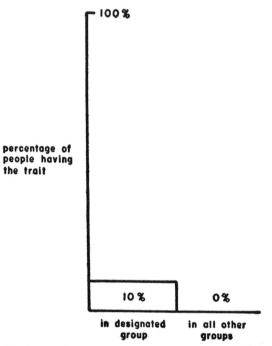

Fɪɢ. 5. Approximate situation in a rare-zero differential.

2. **Rare-zero differentials.** Some traits that are ascribed to a group are actually rare within the group, but they never exist within other groups. We speak of Turks as polygynous, but actually even in old Turkey it was rare for a man to have more than one wife. Yet legal polygyny existed *nowhere* else in Europe. There is a dialect of speech we call a "down Maine" accent. A *few* natives of Maine do talk in the indicated manner, and nowhere else in this country is this accent encountered (unless Mainers have migrated). Some (but not all) Quakers use "thee" for "you" in their form of in-group address. Since no other group of people does so, this custom is called a "Quaker trait." A few Americans are billionaires.

People in other countries sometimes mistakenly assume that "America is a land of billionaires." Other countries have none.

It is obvious that the danger of speaking of rare-zero differential traits lies in the assumption that what is in fact a rare characteristic is actually universal among members of the out-group under consideration. Few Dutch children wear wooden shoes; few Scottish Highlanders wear kilts. Few Indians hunt with bows and arrows; few people in Borneo are head-hunters. Few Esquimaux lend their wives, few Chinese wear pigtails, and few Hungarian peasants wear gay regional costumes. And yet in each case we are dealing with a veridical group characteristic, but it is *rare*.

In some of these cases we may be dealing with a decayed *J*-curve. There may have been a time when there was strong institutional and cultural pressure for all highland Scotsmen to wear kilts or for

FIG. 6. Distribution of intelligence test scores among children of Irish, Russian-Jewish, and Negro descent. (From data provided by Hirsch.[14])

all Chinese men to braid their hair. A hypothetical distribution of such traits today might appear as in Fig. 5. It would not be safe, however, to consider this type of group difference in all cases as a special case of *J*-curve distribution, for there are certainly instances (e.g., polygyny among Turks, the "down Maine accent") where it is unlikely that the practice is a mere vestige of what was once a universal trait within the group.

3. **Overlapping normal curves.** Some differences between groups can best be represented in terms of two overlapping curves of the familiar type of "bell-shaped distribution." These are the cases where we know the incidence of a given trait throughout two populations. To take an example from the field of intelligence measurement, Hirsch administered an identical test to various groups of Massachusetts school children of foreign parentage and to a group of Negro school children in Tennessee.[14] The distribution of

scores for three selected groups is shown in Fig. 6.   From Fig. 6 we
learn that in this particular investigation children of Russian-Jewish
descent had on the average slightly higher scores than children of
Irish descent; and that both stood higher than the average of Tennessee colored children.   The actual mean (average) scores are:

Russian-Jewish	99.5
Irish	95.9
Negro	84.6

Immediately, of course, the question arises as to what the differences in scores are due to: inborn ability? opportunity for learning?
incentive and motivation to do well on the tests?   Earlier in this
chapter we pointed out the dangers that lie in testing as a means
of ascertaining group differences, and while the dangers are greatest

A

B

C

Fig. 7.   Varying degrees of overlap in curves of normal distribution.

across national and linguistic lines, they exist even in testing subgroups within the American population.
Disregarding for a moment the meaning of these differences, we
can at least say that the method employed does reveal average group
differences.   Overlapping normal curves can be plotted for any
characteristic that can be measured on a continuum from low to
high in two or more groups of people.
We speak of the curves as "normal" for the reason that a great
many human characteristics are found to occur in this symmetrical
pattern of distribution.   Few people stand extremely low and few
extremely high; most are moderate in the trait in question.   This
"bell-shaped distribution" is particularly common for biological
qualities (height, weight, strength) and for most measures of ability
(intellectual capacity, learning ability, musical ability, and the
like).   It holds also for most personality traits.   Within a group
few people will be exceedingly ascendant (dominant); few will be

exceedingly submissive (yielding); and most will be moderate or "average." [15]

Many types of overlapping normal curves can be plotted. In Fig. 7 three varieties are indicated. The overlap may be considerable as in (a), slight as in (b), or moderate as in (c). Figure 7 (a) is very much like the curves many investigators find when they measure "intelligence" of two racial or cultural groups; (b) indicates the presence of definite group-correlated traits. For example, it might depict the stature of pygmies and Englishmen. Figure 7 (c) might be the curves for the width of nostrils of Negroes and whites.

If overlapping curves are plotted as one single distribution we have a bimodal curve. Whenever bimodality is encountered in a

FIG. 8. A bimodal distribution obtained by combining extreme groups: alpha scores of approximately 2770 soldiers with 4th grade education, and approximately 4000 officers with 4 years of college. (Adapted from Anastasi and Foley, *Differential Psychology*, p. 69.)

curve of distribution it is likely to be concealing a group difference. For example, in the distribution of intelligence test scores in Fig. 8, we are at first confused by two modes, until we learn that two very distinct populations are measured (plotted) together.[16]

Now in Fig. 7 (a) we see a condition where there is only slight overlap in measure. Only about 51 percent of the people in one group stand above the average measure of the other group. An example of this type of slight difference is actually represented in Fig. 6, comparing the intelligence test scores of Russian-Jewish and Irish descendants.

In Fig. 7 (c) the difference is greater, although even here we note an almost universal principle in respect to overlapping group differences: *the differences within the same group are greater (i.e., the range is wider) than the differences between the averages of the two groups.* In Fig. 6, for example, we notice that there are many Jewish children who stand lower than the average Negro child, and some Negro children who stand higher than the average Jewish child. We cannot then possibly conclude that all Jews are bright and all Negroes dull. It is even wrong to say that the Jews "as a group" are bright, and Negroes "as a group" are dull.

Categorical differentials. There is one remaining type of quantitative difference. It exists when some single attribute is found with differential frequency in various groups. Take, for example, alcoholism. It is known to be far more common among Irish-Americans than among Jewish-Americans. It is a genuine group difference, although it certainly does not mean that Irish-Americans as a whole are alcoholic. Like the rare-zero differential, the attribute in question is uncommon in either group; but unlike the rare-zero differential, it is actually present in both groups to some extent.

In studying causes of rejection from military service during World War II, it turned out that psychoneurosis was relatively high among Jewish draftees, relatively low among Negroes. As grounds for discharge from the Army psychoneurosis was mentioned among Negroes in only 7 percent of the cases, but among whites in 22 percent.[17]

In studying the extent of virginity among unmarried men in the age range from 21-28, Hohman and Schaffner[18] reported it to be:

among Protestants	27 percent
among Catholics	19 percent
among Jews	16 percent
among Negroes	1 percent

Suicide is also a discontinuous variable.[19] It cannot be measured by means of overlapping normal curves. In the year 1930, per 100,000 deaths, the suicide rate was:

in Japan	21.6
in U.S.A.	15.6
in Eire	2.8

Taking deaths only in the United States, the corresponding rate was:

for Whites	15.0
for Chinese	54.6
for Japanese	27.2
for Negroes	4.1

In this particular case we are dealing with group tendencies that are exceedingly rare. They cannot, however, be classified under our rare-zero differentials, for there are some suicidal deaths in all the groups cited.

Let us take our final example from the field of national character.[20] A number of American and English insurance clerks were asked to write a completion of the following sentence, "The qualities I admire most in a person are. . . ." The replies were diverse, and many of them showed no national difference whatsoever; for example, a sense of humor was mentioned with equal frequency in both countries. But qualities having to do with ability to control and exploit the environment ("go-getting") were mentioned by 31 percent of the Americans, and by only 7 percent of the English. On the other hand, the ability to control one's own impulses was mentioned by 30 percent of the English, and only 8 percent of the Americans. Here we seem to have a bit of evidence for the *assertiveness* of the American and the *reticence* of the English. What is equally important, however, is that the differences are less than 25 percent, and we take warning not to indulge in overcategorization. By no means do all English prize reticence, nor do all Americans value assertiveness.

The Interpretation of Differences

How great does a group difference have to be to be a *true* difference? In most of the sample results presented we notice on the whole rather small differentials. *Probably in no case can it ever be said that a group difference marks off every single member of a group from every single nonmember.* Even if we say, "White persons are white and Negroes are black," this generalization is faulty. Many Caucasians are darker than some people who are classified as Negro—furthermore there are *albino* Negroes, entirely without pigmentation. You say, "Surely every Catholic believes the same things." They don't, and we find many non-Catholics who subscribe to a Catholic theology. You say, "Well, at least primary sexual functions distinguish without exception male from female." But even this all-or-none statement does not always hold: there are hermaphrodites. There is probably not a single instance where every member of a group has all the characteristics ascribed to his group, nor is there a single characteristic that is typical of every single member of one group and of no other group.

In the case of *J*-curve differences, to be sure, we are dealing with highly *probable* characteristics. In the case of overlapping normal curves the differences are less striking, as a rule. Rare-zero differentials and categorical differentials yield appreciable differences, but their order of magnitude is seldom very great. Strictly speaking, therefore, every statement concerning a "group difference" (unless suitably qualified) is an exaggeration.

Probably the chief source of error in everyday discussions of the matter is the tendency for people to imply that all group differences follow a J-curve tendency. Thus one says that Americans are aggressive, competitive, materialistic, rich, and overvalue romantic love. Some of these alleged attributes may be entirely fanciful (i.e., no more frequent in America than elsewhere); some may be rare-zero, or categorical, differentials. But the implication is that they fall high on a J-curve. These traits are thought to be the essence of Americanism, distinctive of the group as a whole. Any stereotype concerning any people is usually thought to mark the entire group, somewhat in the manner of the J-curve, but the ascription is an exaggeration, and may be wholly false.

Facts are one thing; the significance people place upon them is something else. A person who favors cultural pluralism will ordinarily welcome demonstrated differences as adding spice to life. A person who distrusts out-groups will see the differences as a menace. At a meeting of the Prussian Diet in 1890 a member made much of the fact that whereas 1.29 percent of the males in Prussia were Jews, 9.58 percent of the students at the University were Jews.[21] The group difference was authentic, but its significance depended entirely upon its interpretation.

The reader may have noted that few of the actual differences we have discussed have dealt with vicious traits (of the sort that might justify hostility). The reason is that data are not available. It is harder to determine personality and moral differences than other types of differences. Researches upon these differences should, however, continue, for we need all the facts we can get to evaluate the alleged claim that a hated group merits hostility—that its evil reputation is well deserved.

It is exceedingly important that science continue to search for the truth about group differences. Only when we know the facts shall we be in a position to distinguish false overgeneralizations from rational judgments, and "well-deserved reputation" from prejudice. This chapter has set forth certain principles that should assist in carrying out the scientific task.

NOTES AND REFERENCES

1. R. A. Wood. *The City Wilderness*. Boston: Houghton Mifflin, 1898, 44 ff.

2. *The Relations of the Advanced and Backward Races of Mankind.* Oxford: Clarendon Press, 1903.

3. E. Lerner. Pathological Nazi stereotypes found in recent German technical journals. *Journal of Psychology,* 1942, **13,** 179-192.

4. Cf. B. Zawadski. Limitations of the scapegoat theory of prejudice. *Journal of Abnormal and Social Psychology,* 1948, **43,** 127-141.

5. Some psychologists are reluctant to speak of the *distortion* of perception or of belief. They are equally hesitant to speak of *illusions.* If a man perceives something he *perceives* it. To say that he is in error, that he *misperceives,* is to pass judgment on what is real and what is unreal. Yet in at least two large areas of applied psychology it becomes essential for the psychologist to judge the truth or falsity of a person's views. In psychopathology, for example, it is vital to know whether the patient really hears his neighbors talking against him, or whether he is suffering a hallucination. So, too, in the field of group prejudice it is essential to know whether the person who is hostile against a group is so because of its "well-deserved reputation" or for more subtle functional reasons of his own that he himself does not understand.

6. Among the sources that give compendious reviews of researches dealing with group differences are the following: L. E. Tyler, *The Psychology of Human Differences,* New York: D. Appleton-Century, 1947; Anne Anastasi and J. P. Foley, *Differential Psychology,* New York: Macmillan, 1949; T. R. Garth, *Race Psychology,* New York: McGraw-Hill, 1931; O. Klineberg, *Race Differences,* New York: Harper, 1935; G. Murphy, Lois Murphy, and T. Newcomb, *Experimental Social Psychology,* New York: Harper, 1937.

7. Cf. A. Inkeles and D. J. Levinson. National character: a study of modal personality and sociocultural systems. In G. Lindzey (Ed.), *Handbook of Social Psychology.* Cambridge: Addison-Wesley, 1954.

8. *Preliminary report on the world situation.* New York: United Nations, Department of Social Affairs, 1952.

9. Cf. C. Kluckhohn and Dorothea Leighton. *Children of the People.* Cambridge: Harvard Univ. Press, 1947.

10. See H. Cantril (Ed.). *Public Opinion 1935-1946.* Princeton: Princeton Univ. Press, 1951.

11. J. M. Gillespie, unpublished investigation.

12. Cf. B. Berelson. *Content analysis.* In G. Lindzey (Ed.), *op. cit.*

13. F. H. Allport. The *J*-curve hypothesis of conforming behavior. *Journal of Social Psychology,* 1934, **5,** 141-183.

14. N. D. M. Hirsch. A study of natio-racial mental differences. *Genetic Psychological Monographs,* 1926, **1,** 231-406. Data from p. 290 f.

15. Cf. G. W. Allport. *Personality: A Psychological Interpretation.* New York: Henry Holt, 1937, 332-337.

16. Anne Anastasi and J. P. Foley. *Op. cit.,* 69.

17. W. A. Hunt. The relative incidence of psychoneuroses among Negroes. *Journal of Consulting Psychology,* 1947, **11,** 133-136.

18. L. B. HOHMAN AND B. SCHAFFNER. The sex lives of unmarried men. *American Journal of Sociology,* 1947, **52,** 501-507.

19. L. I. DUBLIN AND B. BUNZEL. *To Be or Not to Be—A Study of Suicide.* New York: Harrison Smith & Robert Haas, 1933.

20. M. L. FARBER. English and Americans: a study in national character. *Journal of Psychology,* 1951, **32,** 241-249.

21. P. W. MASSING. *Rehearsal for Destruction.* New York: Harper, 1949, 293.

CHAPTER 7

RACIAL AND ETHNIC DIFFERENCES

The anthropologist, Clyde Kluckhohn writes:

> *Though the concept of race is genuine enough, there is per-
> haps no field of science in which the misunderstandings among
> educated people are so frequent and so serious.*

One of the misunderstandings to which Kluckhohn refers is the
confusion between *racial* and *ethnic* groupings of mankind. The
former term, of course, refers to hereditary ties, the latter to social
and cultural ties.

Why should such confusion be a matter of serious consequence?
Because there is a curious air of finality in the term "racial." One
thinks of heredity as inexorable, as conferring an *essence* upon a
group from which there is no escape. There results a distorted
series of ideas such as the following: the Oriental race is by ineradicable inheritance sly and treacherous; the Jews, being a race, are
from the beginning to the end of time endowed with gene-linked
Jewish traits; the Negro race is, through the implacable forces of
evolution, still close to its ape-ancestry. A descendant of these races
carries with him the racial propensities, even if his heredity is
mixed; thus a male with only a little Negro "blood" may, if married
to a white woman, beget a child who will turn out coal black and
be endowed with Negroid "mentality." All these alarming possibilities result directly from confusing racial and ethnic groupings.

Why Race Is Emphasized

There are several reasons why—especially in the past hundred
years—"race" has become the core for the categorization of ideas
about human differences.

1. Darwinism gave the picture of a species (e.g., dogs, cows, men)
divided into distinct varieties or races. Though there are mongrel
dogs and cows and mongrel men, the appealing idea that pure
races are best took hold on popular imagination.

Some writers profess to see in Darwinism a kind of divine law, a cosmic and ultimate sanction for racial antagonism. Sir Arthur Keith, for example, argues that the preference for our own kind is inborn in the "tribal spirit . . . come down to us from the womb of time." Nature went to great length to provide against race mixture: "To make certain that they would play the great game of life as she intended . . . she put them [races] into colors." Keith continues:

> Nature planted love and hate side by side in the tribal heart—but for what purpose? Suppose, for a moment, she had given the tribal heart only a capacity to love, what would have happened? Why, mankind throughout the world would have regarded each other as brothers, clung together, and mingled together. There could have been no separation of mankind into tribes, which are Nature's evolutionary cradles . . . no evolutionary progress—no ascent of man.[1]

These statements show how Darwinism has been constructed as an argument for racism and as a justification for prejudice. While Keith's reasoning is certainly not endorsed by most social scientists, it still appeals to a few.

2. Family inheritance is deeply impressive. If physical, physiological, mental, and temperamental traits run in families, why not in races—which are also groups characterized by common descent? This line of thinking overlooks the fact that certain family resemblances are the product not of inheritance but of learning. It also overlooks the fact that while a direct continuity of genes can be assumed in a biological family (changing, of course, through intermarriage in each generation), a race is a composite of so many families that it is far less unified in genetic composition.

3. There is proof of race in the very appearance of members of certain primary stocks, viz., the Negro, Mongolian, and Caucasian. It is not an accident that children's textbooks carry a list of supposed races as white, brown, yellow, red, and black. Color *seems* basic.

Yet expert opinion holds that very few genes are involved in the transmission of pigmentation, and that while color and a few other physical indications of race may run fairly true within a racial stock, they do not indicate the total inheritance of any given individual. It is said that not more than one percent of the genes involved in producing a person's inheritance are racially linked.[2] Color is so linked, but there is no evidence that the genes determining skin color are tied to genes determining mental capacity or moral qualities.

4. Even a fragment of visibility, however, focuses people's minds

on the possibility that everything may be related to this fragment. A person's character is thought to tie in with his slant eyes, or a menacing aggressiveness is thought to be linked to dark color. Here is an instance of our common tendency to sharpen and exaggerate a feature that captures attention and to assimilate as much as possible to the visual category thus created (Chapter 2).

The same tendency is found in the case of sex categorization. Only a small part of our human nature is differentiated by sex. There are, of course, the primary and secondary characteristics of male and female given by genes. But the vast proportion of human physical, physiological, psychological traits are not sex linked. Nonetheless, in most cultures the position of women is demarcated in an exaggerated way from that of man. They are regarded as inferior, kept in the home, dressed differently, denied many of the rights and privileges of men. The special roles assigned to them are far in excess of what sexual genetic difference would justify. So it is with race. A few genetic indicators may exist, but the social differentiations are far in excess. The visible point of physical difference is made the magnet for all sorts of imaginary ascriptions.

5. Most people do not know the difference between race and ethnic group, between race and social caste, between nurture and nature. It makes for an economy of thought to ascribe peculiarities of appearance, custom, values, to race. It is simpler to attribute differences to heredity than to juggle all the complex social grounds for differences that exist.

The error becomes clear if we consider the case of the American Negro. Nothing seems plainer than the fact that he is a member of the black race. Yet one anthropologist estimates that probably less than one-fourth of the Negroes in America are of unmixed descent, and that in respect to alleged Negro physical traits, the average American Negro is as far from the pure Negroid type as he is from the average Caucasoid type.[3] In short, the average American Negro is as much a white man as he is a black man. The label that we give is thus at least half purely social invention. Many times we apply it to people whose *race* is mostly white.

Similar is the case of the Jew. It is convenient, but fallacious, to simplify the enormously complex set of ethnic, religious, historical, and psychological influences that characterize this group with the label "race." Yet anthropologists agree that the Jews are not a race.

6. A subtle and attractive mystery surrounds the concept of "blood." There is a definiteness, an intimacy, a symbolic importance hovering around this shibboleth. Both family and racial

pride focus on "blood." This symbolism has no support from science. Strictly speaking, all blood types are found in all races. Yet people who exalt "blood" do not know they are speaking in a metaphor; they think they are talking about scientific reality. Gunnar Myrdal, in writing about Negro-white relations in America, correctly saw that this mythical symbol had stark and solid consequences.[4]

7. Race is a fashionable focus for the propaganda of alarmists and demagogues. It is the favorite bogey used by those who have something to gain, or who themselves are suffering from some nameless dread. Racists seem to be people who, out of their own anxieties, have manufactured the demon of race. One thinks of Gobineau, Chamberlain, Grant, Lothrop in this connection. These writers among others succeeded in alarming people and directing their attention to a fanciful diagnosis of the world's ills. Others, like Hitler, have found racism useful in distracting people from their own troubles, and providing them with an easy scapegoat. Demagogues who wish to unite their followers ordinarily conjure up some "common enemy" (cf. p. 41). An "enemy race," being vague, is especially serviceable.

An imaginative person can twist the concept of race in almost any way he wishes, and cause it to configurate and "explain" his prejudices. At the outbreak of the Civil War, for example, a Kentucky editor in the heat of partisanship clarified the whole situation to his satisfaction by arguing that it was now war to the death between two incompatible *races:* the pure rational Angles (the Southerners) and the decadent romantic Normans (the Northerners).

True Racial Differences

To argue that the concept of race is badly abused and exaggerated does not, of course, alter the fact that some racial differences exist. Scientific research is backward in telling us precisely what they are. The difficulties of investigation and interpretation are great. We saw on p. 91 that mental tests cannot solve the problem of hereditary racial traits until equality in social and economic opportunities exist; until differences in language are overcome; until segregation is abolished; until an equal educational level exists; until rapport is good; until motivation to do well in a test is equated; until fear of the examiner is overcome; and until other conditions are rendered constant. Hence at the present time tests are of little value.

Perhaps the best method would be *experimental.* If we could take a few (perhaps ten) newborn infants from Mongolia (from parents of pure Mongolian racial stock), transport them in an incubator by plane to America and leave them with ten well-disposed American homes to be brought up as nearly as possible like white American children, then we might learn something valuable about racial differences. Or let 10 simon-pure "Nordics" from Norway be exchanged at birth with 10 full-blooded African Bantus. Continue the experimental design in this general way, until several major racial stocks were exposed to different ethnic environments for their upbringing. Finally, let psychological measures be taken to determine whether a solid and ineradicable vestige of racial traits remained; whether the mental ability of the transplanted individuals is on the average significantly higher or lower than that prevailing among his foster contemporaries. True, the experiment is not perfect, for a child with a "foreign" physical appearance would never be treated just like a native of the adoptive country. But, imperfect as it would be, such an investigation would tell us considerably more than we now know about the matter.

Before we can hope to establish just what racial differences exist there must be agreement on the number and identity of the races of mankind. Unfortunately, anthropologists are not of one mind about the matter. Their classifications range from two to two hundred races. Ordinarily at least three are named: the Mongoloid, the Caucasoid, the Negroid. Coon, Garn, and Birdsell prefer to call these "basic stocks" and view them as groupings in terms of climatic conditions. The Mongol physique is adapted to live in extreme cold; the Negroid to extreme heat; and the Caucasoid physique is adapted to neither extreme of temperature.[5]

These authors then add three stocks to their list as very ancient and quite distinctive: the Australoid, American Indian, Polynesian. They go on to speculate that on the basis of regional separation approximately 30 "races" were created who possessed physical features that when viewed as a pattern are visibly distinctive. Among the races so defined, they list Alpine, Mediterranean, Hindu, North American Colored, South African Colored, Northern Chinese, Thiketo-Indonesian Mongoloid, Ladino (an emerging Latin-American physique). We note that even in this attenuated conception of race, the Jews are not included. They exist in nearly every known racial class.

Linton prefers to call the subdivisions of stock not "races" but "types." Thus within the Caucasian stock one might distinguish, as is commonly done, the Nordics, Alpines, Mediterraneans, and others, depending upon how fine distinctions are desired. Linton also suggests a third hereditary grouping—much more pure than the others: the breed, "a homogeneous human group, usually small, whose members resemble one another so closely that it can be assumed that all of them have a common ancestry in the not too distant past."[6] Breeds have been studied even less than stocks or types. The degree of purity here required could be expected to exist only in isolated parts of the world. A certain Esquimaux tribe, for example, might constitute a breed.

Now the characteristics by which anthropologists distinguish stocks, types, races, or breeds are exclusively physical—such features as pigmentation, hair texture, the degree of flatness of the shinbone. They virtually never claim that temperamental, mental, or moral characteristics inhere in "race," however it is defined.

In one research among American college males, an anthropologist carefully measured and classified the students according to the following "types": Nordic, Alpine, Mediterranean, Keltic, Dinaric. The men were then studied with the aid of a large battery of tests and rating scales for ability and for personality characteristics. Nearly all the findings were negative. One "type" had about the same range of abilities and traits as another. The few spasmodic statistical differences that appeared were neither consistent nor intelligible.[7]

Anthropologists have found nothing conclusive to support the view that the white race is more "evolved" than any other. If cranial capacity were any indicator of "brain power" (which it is not) several groups on the average would exceed the white man, among them the Japanese, the Polynesians, and even the Neanderthal man.[8] Although at first glance the facial features of the Negro and the ape may seem similar, actually the thin lips and plentiful body hair of the white are much closer to the ape than the corresponding features of Negroes. And underneath their fur most monkeys have white skin; even the great apes have a skin color lighter than the Negro, more resembling the white.[9]

Some investigators have tried to approach the problem of innate "racial" differences by the comparative study of newborn infants, thus attempting to rule out environmental and culture influences.

Pasamanick employed the Yale Developmental Schedule with half a hundred Negro infants in the city of New Haven and with an equal number of white infants. He found that "the average New Haven Negro infant of this study is fully equal in behavioral development to the average New Haven white baby." If any significant difference at all existed (and it is questionable), the Negro children displayed greater acceleration in gross motor behavior than did the white children.[10]

Working with somewhat older children but still in the preschool years, other investigators have made an interesting finding: that in language development Negro children living in segregated districts were more retarded than white children. But Negroes living in mixed neighborhoods were almost equal in language development. The same study shows that IQ based on the Goodenough Draw-a-Man Test was equal for Negroes and whites. Apparently in nonverbal intelligence preschool children show no differences, but verbal ability is early influenced by social factors: children in segregated districts may be offspring of less educated Negroes, or they may lack the sense of freedom in social intercourse without which language cannot develop flexibility and fully.[11]

Taking Negro and white children in a mixed nursery school, Goodman found that the average Negro child displayed as high a level of general activity as did the average white child. She also found that the Negro children were already race conscious— more so than the white children. They were vaguely troubled by their first awareness of handicap. Although they were too young to understand the nature of the trouble, some of them were already in various ways defensive, over-reactive, and tense as a consequence of their vague feeling of disadvantage.[12]

In any case it is clear that young Negro children are not apathetic, inert, or lazy. If older Negroes are proportionately more apathetic than whites the reason cannot be sought in race. It is more likely to lie in poorer health, discouragement, or in a supine defensiveness against discrimination.

When people confuse racial with ethnic traits they are confusing what is given by nature and what is acquired through learning. The confusion, as we have said, has serious consequences, for it leads to an exaggerated belief in the fixity of human characteristics. What is given by heredity can be changed only gradually. What is learned can, theoretically at least, be completely altered in one generation.

Two points stand out above all others from anthropological work on race. (1) Except in remote parts of the earth very few human beings belong to a pure stock; most men are mongrels (racially speaking); hence the concept has little utility. (2) Most human characteristics ascribed to race are undoubtedly due to cultural diversity and should, therefore, be regarded as ethnic, not racial.

Negroes, even if not of mixed heredity, belong to many different ethnic groups. Poles and Czechs are of the same stock and type, but belong to markedly contrasting ethnic (including linguistic) groups. On the other hand, different types are found in one and the same ethnic group (Switzerland). Different ethnic groups may belong to the same nation (United States).

An ethnic trait is always learned, usually so firmly learned in childhood that it remains fixed throughout one's lifetime (e.g., the accent acquired in one's native speech that prevents proper learning of another language in later years). Its possessor can hardly help passing it along, teaching his children in the manner he himself was taught.

Now some anthropologists (especially those influenced by Freud) have developed the theory of "basic personality structure" to account for ethnic group differences.[13] This theory places much emphasis upon the way in which the young child learns to meet the basic requirements of life. If he is rigidly swaddled as an infant his mental habits may be permanently influenced by this fact. If excessive emphasis is placed upon toilet training, as among some Orientals, he may grow exceedingly fastidious, aesthetic, but cruel as a result. If he is teased by his mother and made to feel jealous of his younger brothers and sisters, as among the Balinese, he may develop a high degree of "frustration tolerance" and learn not to show his anger or true feelings. Although the ethnic similarities between American and British society are great, one difference has attracted much attention. Americans, it is said, are given to overstatement, often to bragging; by contrast the British are known for reticence and understatement. According to the basic personality theory the difference might be traced to the fact that the American child is encouraged to speak out, is praised for his accomplishments, and is rewarded by his parents for expressing himself; British family training, on the other hand, subdues the child, stresses the maxim that the child should be seen and not heard, and rewards understatement rather than overstatement.

"Basic personality" then is considered to be what is common in an ethnic group due to nearly uniform practices in child rearing. That there is value in this concept no one can deny. The only danger lies in overestimating the universality of a pattern within a given group, and in overemphasizing its hold upon the child throughout his lifetime.

Many ethnic traits are in reality surprisingly flexible. In visiting a foreign country one quickly learns the customs and varies his behavior in many respects to conform to new ethnic requirements. A well-known study of ethnic patterns of gesture and gesticulation illustrates the transiency of certain habitual traits:

> Efron studied both Italians and Jews in the region of New York City. He found that when members of these groups lived closely

packed in a ghetto-type of living, there was marked uniformity in their arm movements while talking. But members of these same groups, when they moved out of the homogeneous area and began to mix with other Americans, lost their gestural habits—and used their arms in a manner indistinguishable from that of other Americans.[14]

Whether fixed or flexible, ethnic patterns of custom and value are often too subtle to be studied in any quantitative way.

Social workers in the United States frequently encounter such ethnic values. For example, with a Greek client the concept of *philotimo* looms large—a concept of personal integrity that prevents the Greek from appealing for help to those outside his own group. Spanish-speaking groups in New Mexico are likely to think much of present goods and less about tomorrow's goods. The young Mexican in the Southwest is not easily persuaded to remain in school after the legal requirement is met. To him "preparation for the future" seems to have relatively little value. Other groups reject the idea of rewarding their children for good behavior. To them—especially the Chinese and the Eastern European Jews—such conduct suggests bribery. A child should be good for the sake of being good. Virtue has its own reward.[15]

Cultural Relativity

Ethnic differences are so numerous and so elusive that some people have concluded that there are no uniformities among the cultures of the world. The claim for "cultural relativity" may go even further. The saying "mores making anything right" implies that all standards of conduct are entirely a matter of habit. Right is what you have been taught. Conscience is only the voice of the herd. In one culture it is proper to kill your grandmother; in another one may torture animals if one likes. Yet anthropologists warn against this loose interpretation of group differences. Actually, all human groups have developed activities that are "functionally equivalent." Whereas details may differ, the members of every society agree in many of their purposes and practices.

According to Murdock there are certain human practices found in every culture known to history or to ethnography. These human universals he lists as follows.

Age-grading, athletic sports, bodily adornment, calendar, cleanliness training, community organization, cooking, cooperative labor, cosmology, courtship, dancing, decorative art, divination, dream interpretation, education, eschatology, ethics, ethnobotany, etiquette, faith healing, family feasting, fire making, folklore, food taboos, funeral rites, games, gestures, gift giving, government, greetings, hair styles, hospitality, housing, hygiene, incest taboos, inheritance rules, joking, kin groups, kinship, nomenclature, language, law, luck superstitions, magic, marriage, mealtimes, medicine, modesty concerning natural functions, mourning, music, mythology, numerals, obstetrics, penal sanctions, personal names, population policy, postnatal care, pregnancy usages, property rights, propitiation of supernatural beings, puberty customs, religious ritual, residence rules, sexual restrictions, soul concepts, status differentiation, surgery, toolmaking, trade, visiting, weaning, and weather control.[16]

Such a list is too miscellaneous to be very helpful. Yet it serves to indicate that social scientists will do well at the present juncture in the world's history to study uniformities, as well as differences, among the ethnic groups. Emphasis upon differences divides. Emphasis upon similarities serves to call attention to the common ground upon which cooperation between the various branches of the human family may proceed.

National Character

National groups are by no means coextensive with ethnic groups, although in certain cases (Finland, Greece, France) the correspondence may be fairly close. Usually a given language (which creates one kind of ethnic group) is spoken by several nations; but, conversely, many nations employ more than one language (Russia, Switzerland).

Although nations and ethnic groups do not often correspond, still it is possible to slice mankind by nations, as well as by ethnic groups, and ask what differences exist among them. The concept of "national character" implies that members of a nation, despite ethnic, racial, religious, or individual differences among them, do resemble one another in certain fundamental patterns of belief and conduct, more than they resemble members of other nations.

There is, for example, an image of American national character. We find, according to Riesman, that outside observers tend to agree that it is marked by friendliness, generosity, shallowness, and by an uncertainty regarding values that leads Americans to seek and demand approval.[17]

Whether this particular image is correct or not, it is fairly typical. Especially in recent years when there has been a great upsurge of nationalism in the world, there has grown up a corresponding definiteness of images that one nation has of another, and at the same time a mounting interest in the problem among social scientists.[18]

All of the methods described in the previous chapter are applicable to the scientific study of national character. We shall cite only one illustrative investigation employing the method of content analysis (p. 94).

McGranahan and Wayne analyzed one small aspect of national artistic output, viz., successful dramas played on the German and American stages during the middle years of the decade 1920-30.[19] It turns out that the typical hero of the German plays (nearly always a man, seldom a woman) is an individual who stands above or outside normal society; a visionary pursuing a cause, maybe a prince more far-seeing and liberal than his subjects, perhaps a social outcast. American heroes (and often heroines) are ordinary people taken from society's midst.

German plays consider philosophical, ideological, and historical themes far more often than do the American plays, which favor problems of private life (chiefly love).

German plays have tragic endings three times as often as do American plays. Good wins out in American plays usually because some one character in a crucial position changes his mind. He undergoes a change of heart or "comes to his senses." Often a trivial occurrence like a slap, or a wife leaving her husband, the coming of a baby, a stroke of luck, changes the fortunes of the play. Americans believe in individual effort, character change, luck. German plays assume, by contrast, that human beings are inflexible, uncompromising, that they don't change. The only way open to them to achieve their goals is through power and even ruthlessness.

The plays of both countries deal with rebels against society, but American rebels are individualistic, deviating in the name of personal right to happiness. The German rebel is not self-interested (presumably) but dedicated to an ideal, a cause, which is in turn strongly opposed by the power of some authority. Since the individual cannot win out under such circumstances and since he will not bend, the hero in the German plots often goes to the ground. Some twist in his outlook or in circumstances generally rescues the American rebel for a happy ending when the curtain comes down.

Though based on limited material this study is revealing. It suggests that more extensive analyses of the contents of newspapers, radio programs, humor, advertisements, and other forms of communication would be a fruitful technique for discovering still further differences in national character on a wider scale.

The realities of national character should be determined by some objective technique (content analysis, public opinion polls, tests cautiously used, etc.). The kinds of difference between nations that emerge will fit the scheme suggested in the previous chapter. There will be certain *J*-curve differences (loyalty to a king, a flag, a set of traditions); there will be rare-zero differentials (royal titles, peasant costumes, polygynous practice); probably many overlapping distributions of traits will be found if adequate measures exist (competitiveness, interest in music, morality); finally there will be categorical differentials (suicide rate, percentage replies to identical questions on public opinion polls, the proportion of youth attending institutions of higher learning, etc.).

Objective findings are one thing. The "images" that people have of national character may be quite another.

During World War II it was noted that American soldiers *liked* the British people for their friendliness, hospitality, courage, and "ability to take it." They *disliked* them for their reserve, conceit, backwardness in standards of living, immorality, and their caste system.

The first thing to notice about this particular diagnosis of British character is that it is manifestly colored by the soldiers' own frame of reference. They were judging largely in terms of American standards. For example, accustomed to bathrooms and central heating, they perceived England as a "backward land" in these respects. It is doubtful whether Italian or Chinese soldiers would make the same judgment.

The Japanese, it is known, often think of Americans as hypocrites (using fine phrases but not living up to them), as materialistic and coarse, as self-indulgent and luxury loving. These unflattering judgments must be understood in terms of the high value placed by Japanese people upon "sincerity"—total self-commitment to one and only one cause for which one must die if necessary. The conception that a person may live in conflict with himself (and thus seem to be more of a hypocrite than he really is) appears alien to the Japanese training and usual mode of thinking. And the relative informality and spontaneity of Americans seem coarse and self-indulgent to members of a society where formalism, self-effacement, obligation, and a keen fear of being "shamed" are prominent.

In summary, interest has recently been growing in the problem of national character. This slicing overlaps, but is not identical with, slicing in terms of ethnic differences. The same techniques of study apply to both; the discovered differences can be classified in the same way. Objective studies to date are few in number, but rapid progress is likely to be made in the near future. It is vital not to confuse the truth about national character with people's images concerning it. The images are, like all perceptual and memory phenomena, a blend of fact and previously held frames of reference and value. Images are important to study because people act in terms of them. An urgent problem is to discover ways for correcting false images. There are plenty of clashes growing out of genuine differences in national character without aggravating them through additional misunderstanding.

Who Are the Jews?

Many groups that are the object of prejudice cannot be classified exclusively as racial, ethnic, national, religious, or as any other single sociological type. The Jews offer an excellent case in point. In the world there are approximately eleven million Jews. While they are to be found in nearly every land, seventy percent live in Russia, Israel, and the United States. While they comprise a group of stubborn antiquity, yet it is difficult to define their nature. Ichheiser has made the following attempt.

> A Jew is a person who, by and large (with many exceptions), can be socially identified by certain physical or quasi-physical characteristics (gestures, speech, manners, postures, expression of face, etc.); who has grown up in a Jewish family, characterized by a specific "Jewish atmosphere"; who consequently possesses, in the majority of cases, certain specific, even if often elusive, emotional and intellectual characteristics; who is considered by others as being a "Jew" and whose personality is significantly shaped by the fact that he is considered to be a Jew (with all that implies); who, strangely enough, is not clear himself whether his being Jewish means a religious, national, racial, or cultural classification. . . .[20]

This complex definition leans heavily toward the *social* conception of Jewishness. A small core of "physical or quasi-physical" traits exist in *some* individuals, also usually a family tradition; people meeting either or both of these conditions are *called* Jews, and it is this *label* that proceeds to configurate the group and give it such identity as it possesses. When people are called Jews and treated accordingly they often develop, according to Ichheiser, additional traits as a consequence of differential treatment.

A simpler definition is historical: A Jew is a person who is descended from people who have espoused the religion of Judaism. Originally, the group was a religious sect, but since it was also a firmly knit pastoral people, it had simultaneously a cultural (ethnic) homogeneity. It is certainly wrong to think of Jews as a "race." They do not even constitute a "type" within the Caucasoid stock. Such physical identifiability as they have is due to the fact that in the region of the world where Judaism began an Armenoid type was common. But this type included many peoples who were not Jews. The early Christians (converts from Judaism) were of course fully as Armenoid in appearance as the Jews themselves. And even today (if manners and customs of dress are disregarded) it would not be possible to distinguish Armenians and other Armenoids from Jews on the basis of physique alone.

People of other physical types (Negroid included) embraced the religion of Judaism, and throughout the centuries marriage between Jews and non-Jews was fairly common. As a result of extensive mixtures it has become difficult to pick out Jews accurately from their physical appearance alone. The fact that it can still be done in many cases (see Chapter 8) is due to the fact that in-group marriages of Jews with Armenoid features have been more common. When one sees a face with these features one makes a guess, "Jew." If the person is not in fact Armenian or Syrian, he is likely to be Jewish, and so the judgment is sometimes successful.

Besides having a common religious origin, an ethnic tradition associated chiefly with the religion, and an occasional tendency to run to a physical type, Jews have also been to some extent a linguistic group. Hebrew was, and is, their language; but relatively few Jews in modern times know this language, and probably none uses it exclusively. Yiddish, a derivative of Hebrew, is mixed with German and is spoken by only a fraction of the world's Jews.

Finally, Jews once were, and now again to some extent are, a national group. Nationhood requires a homeland. The great tragedy in Jewish history was the loss of nationhood—the dispersion (diaspora) which began with the captivity in Babylon and led eventually to the "wandering Jew" who made his home where he could in almost any country of the world. Some theories of anti-Semitism hold that since Jews were for centuries a homeless nation, they were felt to be "foreign bodies" within other nations. Zionistic Jews longed to re-establish themselves as a bona fide national state, with a separate government. Finally in recent years—after centuries of desire—they realized their dream in Palestine, their original homeland. But not all of the world's Jews wish to move to Israel. Most of them do not regard themselves as a nation, but rather as citizens of the countries in which they now reside.

Psychologically speaking, few of these historical considerations have compelling power in the lives of most individual Jews. The religion is weakened, and it is questionable whether any but the relatively few orthodox Jews feel that their identity consists *primarily* in religious observances. Zionism—though often approved in principle—does not appeal in practice to the majority of Jews. Linguistic unity is no longer present.

As the religious core of Judaism weakened the Biblical tradition that Jews are God's "chosen people" receded. One theory of anti-Semitism holds that this historic claim is the foundation of Jewish in-group feeling, and that it necessarily led to a clannish pride, bringing with it a "spoiled child" complex. To regard oneself as being a favorite of the Almighty fostered resentment in other groups. As one representative of this theory says, "An only child who first refuses to associate with others because he thinks of himself as superior, will end up by being excluded from pleasant social contacts because he gets himself disliked." [21] The theory—though it may have some applicability—has two weaknesses. (1) It disregards the common tendency of many groups of people to think of themselves as "chosen" or as being possessed of the one and only true revelation of religion. There is no necessary prejudice against these groups. (2) It disregards the fact that few modern Jews make a special issue of their claims to such divine favoritism.

With this short and inadequate discussion of the complex nature of the Jewish group, let us come to our principal problem—the nature of Jewish traits. Here, too, a bewildering complexity of evidence and opinion prevails.

There are many alleged qualities that in some way are supposed to mark off Jewish from non-Jewish groups. Our problem is to indicate, as well as possible, just what *evidence* is available concerning some of these alleged group differences. For sake of simplicity, and because data are more available, we shall confine ourselves to Jews in the United States.

1. **Jews are an urban people.** This claim is easy to substantiate by the method of categorical differential (p. 102). Jews constitute approximately 3.5 percent of the total population of the United States, but about 8.5 percent of those living in cities of more than 25,000 population. Forty percent of all the Jews in the United States live in New York City, and most of the remainder in other large cities.[22] Many factors contribute to this urban trend, such for example as the following. (a) Most immigrants from central

and eastern Europe came to work in factories, and still live in
cities, although Jews seem to show this urban-centering to a larger
extent than other groups.   (b) Rarely in the countries where Jews
came from were they permitted to own land, and their traditions
and skills were therefore not often agricultural.   (c) Orthodox
Jewish immigrants were not allowed by their religion to travel on
the Sabbath and so had to live in the vicinity of the synagogues.

2. **Jews tend to concentrate in certain occupations.** Again the
method of categorical differential may be employed.   In 1900, 60
percent of the Jews in cities were engaged in manufacturing
(mostly factory workers—chiefly in the garment trades); but in
1934 only about 12 percent were so employed.   Meanwhile the
percentage engaged in trade (including storekeepers) jumped from
about 20 to about 43 percent.   Many families that had been engaged as factory workers later opened their own businesses (often
tailoring or retail clothing).[23]

As matters stand today Jews seem to be over-represented in trade
and in clerical positions, and under-represented in manufacture and
in transportation and communications.   In the professions one
finds about 14 percent of the Jewish population, but only about
6 percent of the general population.   In New York City, whose
population is about 28 percent Jewish, almost 56 percent of the
physicians are Jewish, likewise 64 percent of the dentists, and 66
percent of the lawyers.   Contrary to common opinion, Jews seem
to be greatly under-represented in finance.   While the Jews constitute 3.5 percent of the American population, only six-tenths of one
percent of the bankers are Jewish.   The extent of their financial
control is relatively slight; they are under-represented in Wall Street
and in the stock exchange, and as "international bankers" they are
virtually nonexistent.

Trends change in Jewish employment.   Some of these are too
recent to document accurately.   It seems probable, however, that
there is a rise in recent decades in the proportion of Jews in government service (due, in part, to discrimination in private businesses),
and also in the various lines of entertainment enterprise (theaters,
movies, radio).

It is sometimes remarked that a disproportionately high percentage of Jews are found in private risk-taking ventures (trade, entertainment, professions).   This fact brings them into public view.
To a less than proportional degree are they found in the hidden,
plodding, conservative occupations (farming, finance).

One theory of anti-Semitism is based on this apparent tendency
for Jews to collect in the upwardly mobile and conspicuous occupations.   It holds that these occupations represent the "fringe of

conservative values." Cautious people do not quite approve of so much risk-taking, especially in newfangled enterprises. This "fringe-of-values" theory holds further that all through the course of history Jews have occupied an analogous position. They were at one time forced to be moneylenders (since Christians considered usury a sin); always they have been on the fringe of religious values; and still today—so the theory goes—are conspicuous deviants from sound conservatism, and accordingly distrusted.

3. **Jews are ambitious and work hard.** There are no direct measures to employ in this connection. Tests for over-all ambitiousness are lacking; and it would not be easy to prove that man for man, or hour for hour, or job for job, Jews are more hardworking than gentiles. Nor have we any sure evidence that the accomplishments of Jews are any more outstanding than those of non-Jews, although it is certainly not difficult to point to an array of Jewish geniuses.

4. **Jews have high intelligence.** Using mental tests as a criterion we can say that some Jews *do,* and some Jews *do not* have high intelligence. We can also say that fairly often the *average* score of Jewish children is slightly above that of non-Jewish children (cf. p. 99 f). The differences, however, are neither large enough nor consistent enough to permit a conclusion that there is any inborn difference in ability. Such slight differences as exist can be explained in terms of incentive and the value placed on learning and good performance within the Jewish cultural tradition.

5. **Jews have great love of, and respect for, learning.** Common observation seems to confirm this claim, although many immigrant families of other ethnic groups are also intense in their zeal for their children's education. The most relevant statistics in this area come from college attendance. Even though there is some evidence of discrimination against Jewish students in certain private institutions, the trend of enrollments for Jews is high.[24] On p. 104 we cited the fact that the same trend was evident in Prussia in 1890. Those who know Jewish culture best agree that for many centuries study and learning have been values greatly stressed in the training of Jewish children.

6. **Jews have marked family devotion.** On this point there is some slight evidence that Jewish families possess more solidarity than other families, although the weakening of family ties today is felt among both Jews and gentiles.[25] It has been said that feeding problems brought into clinics are more common among Jewish children than non-Jewish. This fact suggests oversolicitousness on the part of Jewish mothers—presumably a form of family devotion.

7. Closely related is the claim that **Jews are clannish.** This charge may mean many things. If it refers to the fact that Jewish charity is well organized and that needy Jews both in America and abroad receive generous aid from Jewish groups, it can be substantiated. If it refers to a tendency for Jews not to mingle with gentiles, the evidence is not good.[26]

One sociometric study conducted in a well-known preparatory school for boys asked the boys to indicate their choices of roommates. It was found that more Jewish boys than gentiles preferred to room alone. They did not select other Jews to room with, though this possibility was open. So far as it goes, this finding does not indicate clannishness among the Jews, but rather a fear of rebuff from the gentiles who appeared to the Jewish boys to be clannish.[27]

8. **Jews have sympathy with the oppressed.** The overlapping distribution for Jews and non-Jews on prejudice attitude scales can be used as evidence of group differences in tolerance. A scale of prejudice against Negroes was given to about four hundred college students. Among these were 63 Jewish students. In the *more* anti-Negro half of the scores were found only 22 percent of the Jews; in the *less* anti-Negro half, 78 percent of the Jews.[28] Similarly, other studies of prejudice show that the average Jewish attitude seems to be significantly more tolerant than the average attitude in Catholic or Protestant groups.

9. **Jews are money-minded.** This allegation is difficult to test, especially in a nation where competition and money are high values for most citizens. One study, however, reports that Jewish students show no more prominent "economic value" than do students of Protestant or Catholic background.[29] A single study, to be sure, is insufficient to test this, or any hypothesis.

10. **Other differences.** The list of alleged Jewish traits could be prolonged. If we did so, however, we should probably find the evidence growing poorer.[30] But in principle there is no reason why direct investigations could not be made to test further alleged qualities, such as those represented in common allegations:

Jews are highly emotional and impulsive.
They are ostentatious and conspicuous in consumption.
They are touchy and hypersensitive to discrimination.
They engage in sharp business practices and dishonesty.

But until reliable evidence is adduced we can only hold that these charges are unproved.

We have dwelt at some length upon the Jewish group in order

to show complexities that exist both in defining a minority and in discovering its objective characteristics (apart from the images that other groups may have of it). We have chosen the Jewish group because it is one that throughout the ages has met with hostility and prejudice. Our findings thus far fall far short in establishing objective grounds to justify the hostility. Even when slight ethnic differences appear, they are never large enough to warrant the prediction that any given Jew will possess the qualities in question.

Conclusions

Group differences, as we have argued in Chapters 6 and 7, can and should be more intensively studied. The results of investigations to date supply us with certain few facts about "the nature of the stimulus object." A few authentic differences do enter into our perceptions and thinking about these groups. In short, there is sometimes a kernel of truth in the categorical ideas we form about groups.

At the same time we have also discovered that, with the exception of a few *J*-curve differences, we can never predict with any high degree of probability that members of a given group will have qualities alleged to mark the group as a whole. Neither do we find that the *J*-curve or any other type of difference is intrinsically objectionable.

Moral and personal qualities are hardest to measure, but from what we now know, it seems most unlikely that our frequently strong antagonisms to groups-as-a-whole can be justified by evidence that the qualities we say we dislike are in fact distinctive attributes of all (or even most) members of the group.

In other words, the study of groups, so far as it has gone, does not permit us to say that hostility toward a group is to any appreciable extent based on "well-deserved reputation." If it were, as explained in Chapter 1, we should be dealing with a realistic conflict of values. But as matters stand, the facts we have about group differences largely fail to account for our prejudices. Our images and our feelings overreach the evidence.

Our next step must be to evaluate the psychological effects of visibility and strangeness upon the perceiver. For we now see that prejudice is a complex subjective state in which *feelings* of difference play the leading part, even if the differences are imaginary.

Following this step we shall return to the problem of group differences in a new way. The victims of prejudice also behave; they too have thoughts, feelings, and responses. Every human relationship is reciprocal. For every aggressor there is someone aggrieved; for every snob there is someone who resents his condescension; for every oppressor there is someone who strives against the oppression. Therefore, it is reasonable to expect that certain traits may develop as a response to victimization.

NOTES AND REFERENCES

1. SIR ARTHUR KEITH. *The Place of Prejudice in Modern Civilization.* New York: John Day, 1931, 41.
Realizing the great danger that lies in the adoption of superficial racist views, whether as urbane as Keith's or as vulgar as Hitler's, UNESCO recently summoned an international group of competent anthropologists to consider the matter. Their deliberations—finding no scientific support for racist reasoning—have been widely published. Cf. A. M. ROSE, *Race Prejudice and Discrimination,* New York: Knopf, 1951, Chapter 41 (Race: What it is and what it is not). A more popular analysis of the problem is to be found in the UNESCO pamphlet: *What is race? evidence from scientists,* Paris: UNESCO House, 1952.

2. C. M. KLUCKHOHN. *Mirror for Man.* New York: McGraw-Hill, 1949, 122 and 125.

3. M. J. HERSKOVITZ. *Anthropometry of the American Negro.* New York: Columbia Univ. Press, 1930.

4. G. MYRDAL. *An American Dilemma.* New York: Harper, 1944, Vol. I, Chapter 4.

5. C. S. COON, S. M. GARN, J. B. BIRDSELL. *Races: A Study of the Problems of Race Formation in Man.* Springfield, Ill.: Charles C. Thomas, 1950.

6. R. LINTON. The personality of peoples. *Scientific American,* 1949, **181**, 11.

7. C. C. SELTZER. Phenotype patterns of racial reference and outstanding personality traits. *Journal of Genetic Psychology,* 1948, **72**, 221-245.

8. M. F. ASHLEY-MONTAGU. *Race: Man's Most Dangerous Myth.* New York: Columbia Univ. Press, 1942.

9. The question of the relative primitiveness of different stocks is examined by O. KLINEBERG in *Race Differences,* New York: Harper, 1935, 32-36.

10. B. PASAMANICK. A comparative study of the behavorial development of Negro infants. *Journal of Genetic Psychology,* 1946, **69**, 3-44.

11. ANNE ANASTASI AND RITA D'ANGELO. A comparison of Negro and white preschool children in language development and Goodenough Draw-a-man IQ. *Journal of Genetic Psychology,* 1952, **81**, 147-165.

12. MARY E. GOODMAN. *Race Awareness in Young Children.* Cambridge: Addison-Wesley, 1952.

13. A. KARDINER. The concept of basic personality structure as an operational tool in the social sciences. In R. LINTON (ED.), *The Science of Man in the World Crisis.* New York: Columbia Univ. Press, 1945. See also A. INKELES AND D. J. LEVINSON, National character, in G.

LINDZEY (ED.), *Handbook of Social Psychology*. Cambridge: Addison-Wesley, 1954.

14. D. EFRON. *Gesture and Environment*. New York: Kings Crown Press, 1941.

15. DOROTHY LEE. Some implications of culture for interpersonal relations. *Social Casework*, 1950, **31**, 355-360.

16. G. P. MURDOCK. The common denominator of cultures. In R. LINTON (ED.), *op. cit.*, 124. For a particularly valuable discussion of the problem of the universals in cultures see C. M. KLUCKHOHN, Universal categories of culture, in A. L. KROEBER (ED.), *Anthropology Today*, Chicago: Chicago Univ. Press, 1953, 507-523.

17. D. RIESMAN. *The Lonely Crowd*. New Haven: Yale Univ. Press, 1950, 19.

18. See O. KLINEBERG. *Tensions affecting international understanding*. Social Science Research Council, Bulletin No. 62, 1950; also W. Buchanan and H. Cantril. *How Nations See Each Other*. Urbana: University Press, 1953.

19. D. V. McGRANAHAN AND I. WAYNE. German and American traits reflected in popular drama. *Human Relations*, 1948, **1**, 429-455.

20. G. ICHHEISER. Diagnosis of anti-Semitism: two essays. *Sociometry Monographs*, 1946, **8**, 21.

21. A. A. BRILL. The adjustment of the Jew to the American environment. *Mental Hygiene*, 1918, **2**, 219-231.
A theological variant of this theory of the cause of anti-Semitism is held by certain Roman Catholic scholars. They grant—as the Bible explicitly states—that the Jews are God's chosen people. It is for this reason that their punishment for rejecting the promised Messiah when He appeared is heavy. Until they accept the newer revelation of God's plan for Israel they are doomed to unrest and inner misery. This interpretation, the theologians add, does not justify individual acts of anti-Semitism on the part of Christians.

22. F. J. BROWN AND J. S. ROUCEK. *One America*. New York: Prentice-Hall, rev. ed., 1945, 282.

23. N. GOLDBERG. Economic trends among American Jews. *Jewish Affairs*, 1946, **1**, No. 9. See also W. M. KEPHART, What is known about the occupations of Jews, Chapter 13 in A. M. ROSE (ED.), *Race Prejudice and Discrimination*, New York: A. A. Knopf, 1951.

24. *Cf.* E. C. McDONAGH AND E. S. RICHARDS, *Ethnic Relations in the United States*, New York: Appleton-Century-Crofts, 1953, 162-167.

25. *Cf.* G. E. SIMPSON AND J. M. YINGER, *Racial and Cultural Minorities: An Analysis of Prejudice and Discrimination*, New York: Harper, 1953, 478 ff.

26. A. HARRIS AND G. WATSON. Are Jewish or gentile children more clannish? *Journal of Social Psychology*, 1946, **24**, 71-76.

27. R. E. GOODNOW AND R. TAGIURI. Religious ethnocentrism and its recognition among adolescent boys. *Journal of Abnormal and Social Psychology*, 1952, **47**, 316-320.

28. G. W. ALLPORT AND B. M. KRAMER. Some roots of prejudice. *Journal of Psychology*, 1946, **22**, 9-39.

29. DOROTHY T. SPOERL. The Jewish stereotype, the Jewish personality, and Jewish prejudice. *Yivo Annual of Jewish Social Science*, 1952, **7**, 268-276. This study contains, likewise, helpful evidence on other alleged Jewish traits.

30. A survey of literature on alleged Jewish traits has been made by H. ORLANSKY, Jewish personality traits, *Commentary*, 1946, **2**, 377-383. This writer, too, finds so little unambiguous evidence that he concludes, "Perhaps Jewish character is not such a clear-cut entity as to be immediately distinguishable from the character of non-Jews—especially of other urban dwellers."

CHAPTER 8

VISIBILITY AND STRANGENESS

The Young Child—Visible Differences Imply Real Differences—Degrees of Visibility—Condensation of Attitudes around Visible Cues—Sensory Aversion—Discussion

We have been considering the problem of genuine group differences—whether racial, national, or ethnic. We now shift our ground to consider the way in which these differences are perceived and brought into focus. The images men have of ethnic differences, we have noted, seldom correspond completely to veridical differences.

One reason why this is so lies in the strikingly visible character of some (not many) group differences. A Negro, an Oriental, a woman, a policeman in uniform, are readily fitted into a category of prejudgment because some visible mark is present to activate the category in question.

To state the point somewhat differently: Unless there is some visible and conspicuous feature present in a group we have difficulty in forming categories concerning it, also in calling upon the category when we encounter a new member of this group. Visibility and identifiability aid categorization.

When we first meet a stranger we do not know into what category to fit him, unless he happens to have such visible markings. Therefore we are often guarded and tentative in our response to him.

The story is told of a group of farmers who were gathered in a country store when a young stranger walked in. "Looks like a little rain," the stranger ventured affably. No one spoke. After a time one farmer queried, "What may your name be?" "Jim Goodwin, my grandfather used to live just a mile up the road." "Oh, Ezra Goodwin.—Ye-es, it does look like a little rain." In a sense strangeness is itself a mark of visibility. It signifies, "Go slow until the stranger can be fitted to a category."

There seems to be one general law concerning the acceptance of a stranger: his treatment depends on the degree to which he is adjudged an asset or a liability for the realization of the values of the in-group.[1] Sometimes his function is no more than to provide passing good company. In the hills of Tennessee a code grew up to regulate the conduct of the stranger. He was expected to holler before reaching the house, unless the dog gave warning. He was expected to lay his gun on the porch. If he did so, he was then welcomed with warm hospitality, for the hill dwellers liked strangers who could relieve life's boredom.

If new recruits are desired by the in-group, and if a stranger has the requisite qualities, he may be welcomed permanently. But a period of probation and accommodation is usually practiced. In some close-knit communities it may take years, even a whole generation or more, for a latecomer to be fully accepted.

The Young Child

If there is any instinctive foundation for group prejudice it lies in this hesitant response that human beings have to strangeness. We note the startled reaction infants often display to strangers. By the age of six or eight months, babies usually cry when a strange person picks them up or approaches close to them. Even a child of two or three will usually withdraw and cry if a stranger makes a friendly advance too abruptly. Shyness toward strangers often lasts into puberty. In a sense the reaction is never outgrown. Since our very safety depends on noticing changed conditions in our environment, we are sensitized to the appearance of strangers. Entering our own house we may not even notice a member of the family sitting there; but if a stranger is present we become alertly conscious of the fact, and feel on guard.

But even this "instinctive" basis for fear or suspicion of strangeness does not carry us far. The reaction is normally short-lived.

An experiment was performed with young infants, ranging in age between 11 and 21 months. Each was separated from the familiar environment of the institutional nursery and placed alone in a strange room. They were observed through a one-way screen. Although they were surrounded by all manner of easily accessible toys, all of them cried at first, apparently from fear at the change in their surroundings. They were left alone for five minutes and then returned to the nursery. On alternate days they were again placed in the new room alone. The crying rapidly decreased, and after a few repeated trials the strangeness wore off and all of them played contentedly with the toys and without protest.[2]

In Chapter 3 we saw that familiarity breeds a sense of "goodness." If the familiar is good, then strangeness must be bad. Yet with time all that is strange automatically becomes familiar. And, therefore, as acquaintance grows the stranger tends, other things being equal, to move from "bad" to "good." Since this is so, we cannot lean too heavily upon "instinctive fear of strangers" as an explanation of prejudice. Even a few minutes of habituation lessens the young child's fearful response toward newcomers.

Visible Differences Imply Real Differences

Returning to the problem of visibility, we note first that all our experience teaches us that when things look different they usually are different. A black cloud in the sky has very different significance from a white cloud. A skunk is not a cat. Our comfort and sometimes our lives depend on learning to act differently in the face of unlike objects.

All human beings show differences in appearance. One expects certain kinds of behavior from a child but not from an adult, from a woman but not from a man, from a foreigner but not from a native. Hence there is nothing abnormal or prejudiced in the sheer *expectation* that black men will be significantly different from white men, or that people with slant eyes and yellow skin will be different from people with horizontal eyes and white skin.[3]

During World War II, Negro troops sometimes complained that the American white troops which preceded them into Europe had spread anti-Negro propaganda against them. Asked why they believed this, the reply was that when they landed the European people stared at them and regarded them strangely. The more likely truth is that the white Europeans had seen few or no Negroes previously and hence watched them carefully to see whether they were as different as their skin color would suggest.

While some visible differences between people are personal and unique (each face has its own peculiar shape and expression), many of the differences can be typed. Sex and age differences are obvious examples. So, too, are many of the differences that mark outgroups. Among them we might list:

> skin color
> cast of features
> gestures
> prevalent facial expression
> speech or accent
> dress
> mannerisms
> religious practices
> food habits
> names

> place of residence
> insignia (e.g., uniforms or buttons
>   in lapels signifying memberships)

While some of these differences are physical and inborn, others are learned or even affected as tokens of group membership. No one has to wear his veteran's insignia in his lapel, or his fraternal pin or ring. While members of groups sometimes try to diminish their "visibility" (some Negroes resort to blonde face powder or to hair straighteners), others by contrast seek to highlight their membership (through using distinctive costumes and wearing insignia). In any case the important point is that groups that look (or sound) different will seem to *be* different, often more different than they are.

This law has a curious corollary: groups that seem to *be* different will be thought (or made) to look different. In Nazi Germany it was found that the visibility of the Jews was not a perfect guide to their identity. Hence the Jews were made to wear yellow arm bands. Pope Innocent III, troubled because he could not distinguish Christians from heretics, decreed that all unbelievers should dress in a distinctive manner. Similarly, many white people try to enhance the "visibility" of the Negro by claiming that he has a distinctive smell, as well as appearance.

To sum up: perceptible differences are of basic importance in distinguishing between out-group and in-group members. A category needs a visible sign. So urgent is this requirement that visibility is sometimes imagined to exist where it is actually absent. Many Orientals who know the white man by his skin color also *think* he is distinguished by his common body odor. For many years Americans *imagined* that all Bolsheviks wore whiskers. But in recent times the lack of visibility among communists (a much feared out-group) has so troubled state and national legislatures that large sums of money have been spent to "ferret them out," i.e., to make them more visible through identifying them by name.

Where visibility does exist, it is almost always thought to be linked with deeper lying traits than is in fact the case.

Degrees of Visibility

The anthropologist Keith has suggested a scheme for classifying the grades of visibility among races (stocks, types, breeds) according to the proportion of its members who are readily identifiable.[4]

Pandiacritic   = every individual recognizable
Macrodiacritic = 80 percent or more recognizable

Mesodiacritic   = 30-80 percent recognizable
Microdiacritic = less than 30 percent recognizable

Using this scheme, we might say that Jews are a mesodiacritic type. Experiments (using photographs) indicate that about 55 percent of Jewish individuals can be identified as such from appearance alone.[5] Judges are aided by visible traces of Armenoid ancestry or by ethnic habits of facial expression to select Jews from non-Jews with fair accuracy. It is undoubtedly true that the ratio of success would not be so high if the judges were required to separate, let us say, Jewish from Syrian faces.

It is a striking fact that prejudiced people are better able to identify members of the disliked out-group than are nonprejudiced people. The research just cited establishes this point. Psychologically the fact is not hard to explain. It is *important* to the prejudiced person to learn the cues whereby he may identify his "enemy." He grows observant and suspicious, and since every Jew he meets is, he thinks, a potential threat to him, he develops a sensitivity to all the signs that may indicate Jewishness. Conversely, the question of group identity is of small concern to a person free from prejudice. Asked whether a particular friend of his is or is not Jewish, he may reply in all sincerity, "Why, I don't know. I never thought about the matter." Unless one thinks about the matter one is not likely to observe or to learn distinguishing cues.

While most people with Oriental or Negro ancestry are recognizable, not all of them are. These stocks, therefore, should probably be called macrodiacritic and not pandiacritic. The Negro who "passes" as white (meaning of course a person who has mostly white, but some Negro, ancestry) has been the subject of much concern among those who have anti-Negro prejudice. They seem to think it matters. A light-skinned Negro may be taken for Spanish or Italian or even for a brunet Anglo-Saxon, and may lose altogether his identification with the Negro group. It has been variously estimated that between 2,000 and 30,000 former members of the Negro group each year slip from the ranks of the Negro group and are thereafter considered as whites.[6] The former estimate is probably more correct.

The task of distinguishing between two out-groups of the same stock is usually difficult, although experience and acquaintance will aid in the task. One investigator asked Caucasian students at Stanford University and at the University of Chicago to separate the photographs of Chinese and Japanese students who had attended an American college. The results were, on the whole, poor—scarcely better than chance, although the Stanford students who had more familiarity with students from the Orient slightly exceeded the scores of the Chicago judges.[7]

So overpowering is the impact of color upon our perceptions that we frequently go no further in our judgment of the face. An Oriental is an Oriental—whether Chinese or Japanese we fail to determine. Nor do we perceive the *individuality* of each face. While we are usually frank in admitting that all Orientals look alike to us we are scandalized to learn that a common complaint on the part of Orientals is that "Americans all look alike." One experiment dealing with memory for Negro and white faces shows that people with a high anti-Negro bias fail to recognize the faces of as many *individual* Negroes whose photographs they have seen, as well as they recognize the individual faces of whites.[8]

Although it is usually true that our perceptions of individual differences do not penetrate beneath the gross impression of skin color or ethnic type, this tendency may be reversed in the case of people who stand *near* to us in the range of visibility. While Caucasians may not be able to distinguish Chinese from Japanese in appearance, members of these two groups, needless to say, learn all the cues by which such a distinction might be made. Freud speaks of the "narcissism of small differences." We compare ourselves carefully with those who are like us—yet in some way different. According to Freud, small differences are an implied or potential criticism of ourselves. Therefore we note carefully what the difference is (the way two suburban ladies at a bridge party will scrutinize each other's grooming) and evaluate the situation, usually in such a way that it comes out in our favor. We decide that our apparent "twin" is after all not quite so slick as we are. Schisms within religious bodies seem to illustrate the "narcissism of small differences." To an outsider a Lutheran is a Lutheran, but to an insider it makes a difference whether he is a member of one Synod or another.

A Hindu woman traveling in a southern state was denied a hotel room by a clerk who noticed her dark skin. The woman thereupon took off her headdress and showed that she had straight hair—and obtained accommodations. To the clerk it was color that cued his first behavior. The Hindu lady, with her keener sense of "small differences," forced the clerk to alter his perception, and reclassify her.

Skin color, hair texture, and facial features are, of course, only a few of the forms of visibility—as we are here using the term. Jews, for example, occasionally have other attributes of visibility—attendance at the synagogue, observance of holidays and dietary laws, the practice of circumcision, and family names. As we pointed out in Chapter 1, a Jewish name alone may be the visible cue that brings an avalanche of consequences. Whether cues are few or many, dependable or undependable, they rivet attention and arouse the tendency to make categorical judgments.

Puritan settlers in America were especially distressed by visible signs of "Popery." They were alarmed and offended by the Mass, by a cross on the church steeple. Even in recent times some strict Protestants have forbidden candles on Christmas trees because they looked "Popish." In these cases the visible sign is confused with the thing-in-itself. That is to say, the sign must not be used because it activates the whole category of which it is a cue. It was in reality authoritarian ecclesiasticism that the Puritans hated. Yet mere symbols attracted their wrath and avoidance.

The Condensation of Attitudes around Visible Cues

This tendency to amalgamate the symbol and the thing it stands for may be called *condensation*. It takes various forms and has many consequences. Take skin color. Especially within the past century alarms have been sounded concerning the "yellow peril." At the same time the "white man's burden" has been a matter of pious concern. One theory has it that the exploitation and frequent cruelty practiced by European entrepreneurs and officials in China, India, Malay, Africa, have left them with a bad conscience. Half-fearing a well-merited revenge on the part of dark-skinned peoples, the white man has grown fearful, and being fearful has grown oppressive.

Whatever the reason, skin color to a white person is a salient feature, as visible as a shooting star, and symbolically important. On the whole, the colored people of the world make less of the matter. Skin color to them in general seems more or less irrelevant to the basic problems of life. A Negro woman was plaintiff in a case involving a restrictive covenant. The lawyer for the defense questioned her, "What is your race?" "The human race," she replied. "And what is your skin color?" "Natural color," she answered.

Dark skins in and of themselves are not objectionable. Many white people are really fond of deep pigmentation. The lower layers of the epidermis of all normal people contains melanin, which term in Greek means *black*. With the aid of vacations and sun-tan lotions millions of dwellers in northern countries try their best to capitalize on such melanin as they have. To be "brown as a nut," "red as an Indian," or even "black as a Negro" is a tribute to a successful summer vacation. Sun-bathers aspire to a Negroid complexion.

Why then should people favored by nature with dark skin be regarded with repugnance rather than with admiration? It is not because of their color but because of their lower status. Their skin implies more than pigmentation, it implies social inferiority. Some Negroes, realizing this fact, strive for superficial redress. They think that by resorting to blonde cosmetics they can escape from the stigma, and perhaps from the actual handicaps it signifies. They are objecting not to their natural color but to the social abasement it brings. They, too, are victims of condensation (confusing the cue with the thing it signifies). Thus on both sides of the fence visibility operates as a vastly important symbol, activating categories that have little to do with the visibility itself.

Sensory Aversion

The visual cue, then, acts as an anchorage point to which all manner of associations are tied. Among these associations are an additional array of sensory ideas. We slip quickly from the visual perception to the thought that the "blood" of people with differing skin colors must be different; also their odor and their impulses. We thus develop sensory, instinctive, "zoological" explanations of our negative attitudes.

The process is natural enough because sensory aversions and annoyances are in fact common experiences. All of us have some almost reflex feelings of dislike or repugnance—perhaps to the feel of peaches, to the odor of garlic, the sound of chalk squeaking on a blackboard, to people with oily hair, bad breath, to streaky dishes, the taste of marshmallows, or to women who talk baby talk to their lap dogs. One investigator asked over a thousand people to name their antipathies, and found that on the average each person mentioned 21 such sensory—or pseudosensory—dislikes. Furthermore, about two-fifths of the antipathies had to do with human physical traits, mannerisms, clothing.[9]

A few of these sensory aversions may be inborn, though most are learned. However acquired, they bring a shudder and lead us to move away or otherwise protect ourselves from the stimulus. They are not themselves prejudices, but they provide a ready rationalization for prejudice. Here again there results *condensation* of the symbol and the attitude. Disliking out-groups for other reasons, we *say* we dislike them for sensory reasons.

Most people have an aversion to the odor of sweat. Now suppose one *hears* that Negroes (or Orientals or Outlanders) have a peculiar odor. This verbal "information" (which he almost certainly has never verified) connects his sensory aversion with his prejudice. He thinks of Negroes when he thinks of sweat, or of sweat when he thinks of Negroes. The associated ideas form a category. Soon he comes up with the zoological diagnosis that he can't stand Negroes because of their body odor—it is, he says, a natural and instinctive aversion, and therefore nothing can ever be done to solve the Negro problem excepting to enforce segregation.

The "argument by odor" is so very common that it merits further examination.[10] Psychologists tell us three important facts about our sense of smell.

(1) It is highly affective—odors are seldom neutral. Foul odors arouse repugnance and disgust. Perfumes are sold because they invite romance. It is therefore quite possible that distinctive body odors emanating from a distinctive group of people might arouse feelings of attraction or revulsion. Orientals sometimes say that the white man's foul and distinctive odor comes from his addiction to meat eating.

Before we can accept this nasal theory of prejudice, we shall have to prove that the foul odor is real and not merely imagined, and that the odor is *distinctive,* i.e., that it is more prominent in the out-group (which revolts us) than among members of our own in-group (who attract us). It is difficult to do research on the elusive flavor of body odors, although one preliminary and instructive attempt will be described below.

(2) The associative power of odors is high—a certain fragrance may suddenly arouse an image of an old-fashioned flower garden that we visited in our childhood. A musky odor may call to mind grandmother's front parlor. Similarly, if we have once associated the odor of garlic with Italians we have met, or cheap perfume with immigrants, or fetid odors with crowded tenements, these odors newly encountered will cause us to think of Italians, immigrants, tenement dwellers. Meeting an Italian may cause us to think of the odor of garlic and even to "smell" it. Olfactory hallucinations (caused by such associations) are common. It is for this reason that people who have formed olfactory associations may declare with conviction that all Negroes or all immigrants smell.

(3) The accommodation to odors is rapid. Even when strong odors are unquestionably present (in a gymnasium, a tenement, a chemical factory) habituation is rapid. Within a few minutes we can no longer smell them. This fact by itself would greatly weaken the argument that a natural revulsive odor is the basis for our dislike of human groups. As in the case of the infant's fear of a stranger the accommodation is too rapid to permit us to build a theory of prejudice on so ephemeral a base. It is, however, true

that the rapidity of habituation is offset, as we have said, by the enormous power odors have of forming lasting associations with the *idea* of an object.

Now, what are the facts? Do Negroes, for example, have a distinctive odor or not? We cannot yet answer the question conclusively. Some slight experimental evidence, however, comes from an investigation by G. K. Morlan.

This investigator asked over fifty judges to make differentiating judgments of the body odor of two white and two Negro male students whose identity was completely disguised. During the first half of the experiment, the four boys had just come from a shower; during the second, they were perspiring profusely from 15 minutes of vigorous exercise. The overwhelming majority of the judges were unable to tell any difference in body odor, or else made incorrect identifications. It seems unlikely that the few correct identifications that were made exceeded a pure chance level.[11]

Such an experiment is highly unpleasant for the judges, but the offensiveness seems to come *equally* from the sweaty bodies of the two races.

Odor is a curious psychological shibboleth. It is made to bear the brunt of intimate subjective feelings (and prejudices), but its role seems primarily to be that of an "objective" excuse or rationalizer for affective states that are too personal and private to be understood or analyzed in their own right.

Discussion

We see now why "visibility" (real in the case of skin color, often imaginary in the case of odor and other "sensory" qualities) becomes a central symbol. If members of a group can be thought to have any distinctive sensory characteristics, these may serve as a "condensing rod" for all manner of thoughts and feelings about this group. The very existence of such a condensing rod enables us to think of the out-group as a solidary unit. In Chapter 2 we pointed out that a category assimilates all it can to itself.

We refer once again to the question of sex differences. These are, of course, high in visibility. But in all cultures they make for a distortion in human thinking about sex differences. Women are not only different in appearance, but they are accordingly thought to be, by biological nature, less intelligent, less rational, less honest, less creative—and in some cultures are thought to lack souls. A genuine physical difference comes to be regarded as a total (categorical) difference in *kind*. Thus too, the Negro is seen not only as black skinned but as black hearted, inferior, and sluggish—though none of the qualities is gene-linked to skin color.

To sum up: visible differences aid greatly the development of ethnocentrism. But they *aid* it rather than account for it. The repugnance we feel is only slightly, if at all, traceable to the visible difference—our rationalizations to the contrary notwithstanding.

Especially in times of catastrophe can the fact of visibility be of critical importance. An economic setback has sent both Russians and Poles racing into the ghetto to attack the visible and accessible Jewish "enemy." In times of racial unrest any Negro may be instantly identified as a target for abuse. During the earthquake of 1923 Japanese in a frenzy of fear and hysteria attacked unoffending Koreans.

A clear differentiation of groups in conflict is necessary. Unless we can identify our enemy we cannot attack him. The consequence of low visibility is confusion. We may refer once more to the civil chaos created in America in recent years by the relative invisibility of "communists." Because there is no clear test of membership in this hated group, Congress and state legislatures have spent much money and time in an effort to smoke them out. Professors, clergy, government employees, liberals, and artists were sucked into the maelstrom of McCarthyism in an attempt to make "communists" visible.

One subtle psychological consequence of visibility remains to be noted. Its nature is indicated in the following episode described by an acute self-observer.

> Recently while walking on a street in New York City, I passed an old colored woman. She was badly pockmarked about the face, and at the same time was spitting. I have seen white people in a similar situation and have felt only sympathy or pity since I myself have suffered for years from a severe acne infection. But the sight of a *colored* woman in the same condition seemed repulsive and disgusting to me. . . . Let a Jew or Negro commit a violation of social convention and he is immediately censured far more severely than a member of a less distinctive minority group in a similar situation.

What we see in this case is the subtle tendency even in "tolerant" people to amalgamate a *real* cause of disgust with an *irrelevant* visible characteristic. A minor offense, overlooked in a member of our own group, seems intolerable when committed by a member of an out-group. Here too is an example of *condensation*. Genuine provocation is linked to an irrelevant visual cue, and the two forces summate.

It would be a fortunate situation indeed if visibility always corresponded to realistic menace. Certain individuals in society are parasites, leeches, a danger to their fellow men. But they are seldom visible. From appearance alone it is not possible to tell who are these enemies of society. If they all had green skins or red eyes or flat noses it would be convenient. For then our hatred could rationally correspond to visible cues. At present it does not.

NOTES AND REFERENCES

1. MARGARET M. WOOD. *The Stranger: A Study in Social Relationships.* New York: Columbia Univ. Press, 1934.

2. JEAN M. ARSENIAN. Young children in an insecure situation. *Journal of Abnormal and Social Psychology,* 1943, **38**, 225-249.

3. G. ICHHEISER. Sociopsychological and cultural factors in race relations. *American Journal of Sociology,* 1949, **54**, 395-401.

4. A. KEITH. The evolution of the human races. *Journal of the Royal Anthropological Institute,* 1928, **58**, 305-321.

5. G. W. ALLPORT AND B. M. KRAMER. Some roots of prejudice. *Journal of Psychology,* 1946, **22**, 16 ff.
Since results of experiments in identifying faces will inevitably vary depending upon how many and what kind of Jewish faces are included in the group, it is desirable to draw one's evidence from diverse series of experiments. The findings stated in the text have been challenged by L. F. CARTER on the basis of his own investigations (The identification of "racial" membership, *Journal of Abnormal and Social Psychology,* 1948, **43**, 279-286). The same findings, however, have been verified by G. LINDZEY AND S. ROGOLSKY (Prejudice and identification of minority group membership, *Journal of Abnormal and Social Psychology,* 1950, **45**, 37-53). The precise percentage given (viz., 55 percent) may not stand up in subsequent experiments, but it seems very probable that within the range proposed by Keith, Jews can be considered a "mesodiacritic" group.

6. J. H. BURMA. The measurement of Negro "passing." *American Journal of Sociology,* 1946-47, **52**, 18-22; E. W. ECKARD, How many Negroes "pass"? *American Journal of Sociology,* 1946-47, **52**, 498-500.

7. P. R. FARNSWORTH. Attempts to distinguish Chinese from Japanese college students through observations of face-photographs. *Journal of Psychology,* 1943, **16**, 99-106.

8. V. SEELEMAN. The influence of attitude upon the remembering of pictorial material. *Archives of Psychology,* 1940, No. 258.

9. C. ALEXANDER. Antipathy and social behavior. *American Journal of Sociology,* 1946, **51**, 288-298.

10. Two centuries ago SIR THOMAS BROWNE felt obliged to combat the

current belief that Jews have a distinct odor. He adds the wise warning that it is improper "to annex a constant property unto any nation." *Pseudoxia Epidemica*, Book IV, Chapter 10.

11. G. K. MORLAN. An experiment on the identification of body odor. *Journal of Genetic Psychology*, 1950, **77**, 257-265.

CHAPTER 9

TRAITS DUE TO VICTIMIZATION

EGO DEFENSES—OBSESSIVE CONCERN—DENIAL OF MEMBERSHIP
—WITHDRAWAL AND PASSIVITY—CLOWNING—STRENGTHENING
IN-GROUP TIES—SLYNESS AND CUNNING—IDENTIFICATION WITH
DOMINANT GROUP: SELF-HATE—AGGRESSION AGAINST OWN
GROUP—PREJUDICE AGAINST OUT-GROUPS—SYMPATHY—FIGHT-
ING BACK: MILITANCY—ENHANCED STRIVING—SYMBOLIC STATUS
STRIVING—NEUROTICISM—THE SELF-FULFILLING PROPHECY—
SUMMARY

*Suffering which falls to our lot in the course of nature, or by
chance, or fate, does not seem so painful as suffering which is
inflicted on us by the arbitrary will of another.*

SCHOPENHAUER

Ask yourself what would happen to your own personality if you
heard it said over and over again that you were lazy, a simple child
of nature, expected to steal, and had inferior blood. Suppose this
opinion were forced on you by the majority of your fellow-citizens.
And suppose nothing that you could do would change this opinion
—because you happen to have black skin.

Or suppose you heard daily that you were expected to be shrewd,
sharp, and successful in business, that you were not wanted in clubs
and hotels, that you were expected to mingle only with Jews and
then, if you did so, were roundly blamed for it. And suppose nothing that you could do would change this opinion—because you
happened to be a Jew.

One's reputation, whether false or true, cannot be hammered,
hammered, hammered, into one's head without doing something to
one's character.

A child who finds himself rejected and attacked on all sides is not
likely to develop dignity and poise as his outstanding traits. On
the contrary, he develops defenses. Like a dwarf in a world of
menacing giants, he cannot fight on equal terms. He is forced to
listen to their derision and laughter and submit to their abuse.

There are a great many things such a dwarf-child may do, all of
them serving as his ego defenses. He may withdraw into himself,
speaking little to the giants and never honestly. He may band

together with other dwarfs, sticking close to them for comfort and for self-respect. He may try to cheat the giants when he can and thus have a taste of sweet revenge. He may in desperation occasionally push some giant off the sidewalk or throw a rock at him when it is safe to do so. Or he may out of despair find himself acting the part that the giant expects, and gradually grow to share his master's own uncomplimentary view of dwarfs. His natural self-love may, under the persistent blows of contempt, turn his spirit to cringing and self-hate.

Ego Defenses

Tolerant people, with a passion for justice, often deny that any distinctive traits exist among minority-group members. They find them "just like" everybody else. And in a broad sense this judgment is sound: for group differences, as we have seen, are certainly less marked than they are ordinarily supposed to be. Differences within groups are almost always greater than differences between groups.

But since no one can be indifferent to the *abuse* and *expectations* of others we must anticipate that ego defensiveness will frequently be found among members of groups that are set off for ridicule, disparagement, and discrimination. It could not be otherwise.

There are, however, two vitally important considerations to bear in mind concerning persecution-produced traits. (1) They are not all unpleasant traits—some of them are socially pleasing and constructive. (2) Just what ego defenses will develop is largely an individual matter. Every form of ego defense may be found among members of every persecuted group. Some will handle their minority-group membership easily, with surprisingly little evidence in their personalities that this membership is of any concern to them. Others will show a mixture of desirable and undesirable compensations. Some will be so rebellious at their handicap that they will develop many ugly defenses. These unfortunates continually provoke the snubs that they continually resent.

The way an individual reacts to his membership will depend on his own life-circumstances: how he was trained, how severe his suffering from persecution, how detached his own philosophy of life. Only to a slight extent can we say that certain types of ego defense will be more common in one disliked group than in another. In the following discussion we shall point out a few cases where because of special circumstances we may expect certain forms of ego defense more frequently within one victimized group than within others.

Obsessive Concern

Scarcely anywhere in the United States can a Negro citizen enter a store, restaurant, movie, hotel, amusement park, school, train, plane, or boat, to say nothing of a white person's home, without wondering uneasily whether he will suffer insult and humiliation. This haunting anxiety is, of course, greater if he is traveling and thus unfamiliar with local pathways where people of his color may feel safe. From night until morning the racial frame of thought is present in his mind. He cannot escape it.

How constantly the racial frame of thought is present in the Negro is nicely illustrated by a question asked of both Negroes and whites by the Research Branch of the Army during World War II. The question was, "If you could talk with the President of the United States, what are the three most important questions you would want to ask him about the war and your part in it?" Half of the Negroes, but virtually none of the whites, said they would ask about racial discrimination. The questions took various forms but all had a single theme: "Will I as a Negro share this so called democracy after the war?"—"Will the South treat Negroes like human beings?"—"Why aren't Negro troops allowed to fight in combat as much as white troops?"—"If the white and colored soldiers are fighting and dying for the same thing, why can't they train together?" [1]

The basic feeling of members of minority groups who are the object of prejudice is one of insecurity. Statements made by three Jewish students express the same point in different ways:

I wait in fear for an anti-Jewish remark; there is a definite physiological disturbance: a feeling of helplessness at all times, an anxiety, a dread.

Anti-Semitism is a constant force in the Jew's life. . . .

I have encountered at first hand very few overt expressions of anti-Semitism. Nevertheless, I am always aware of its presence off-stage, as it were, ready to come into the act, and I never know what will be the cue for its entrance. I am never quite free of this foreboding of a dim sense of some vaguely impending doom.

In the same series of personal essays written by Jewish students in an eastern university over half mentioned this vague sense of "impending doom" hovering over themselves as members of their particular ethnic group.

Thus alertness is the first step the ego takes for self defense. It must be on guard. Sometimes the sensitiveness develops to an unreal pitch of suspicion; even the smallest cues may be loaded with feeling. It is not uncommon among Jews to report a special sensitization to the sound "eu."

One day in the late 30's a recently arrived refugee couple went shopping in a village grocery store in New England. The husband ordered some oranges.

"For juice?" inquired the clerk.

"Did you hear that," the woman whispered to her husband, "tor Jews? You see, it's beginning here, too."

A minority group member has to make many times as many adjustments to his status as does the majority group member. If Mexican-Americans, let us say, make up one-twentieth of the population in a certain city, they will in the normal course of events encounter "Anglos" twenty times as often as an "Anglo" will encounter them. This ratio is, of course, altered considerably by the tendency to keep to one's own kind. But the basic phenomenon remains: the awareness, the strain, the accommodation all fall more heavily and more frequently on the minority group members.

Preoccupation with the problem may, of course, go to excessive lengths, so that every contact with members of the dominant group is viewed with deep suspicion. The result is a "chip on the shoulder." The attitude may be: "We've been hurt so often that we have learned to protect ourselves in advance by trusting no member of the group that so frequently inflicts injury. We distrust them all." Thus both vigilance and hypersensitiveness may be among the ego defenses of the minority group.

Denial of Membership

Perhaps the simplest response a victim can make is to deny his membership in a disparaged group. This device comes easy for those who have no distinctive color, appearance, or accent, and who do not in fact feel any loyalty or attachments to their group. Perhaps they are, figured by ancestry, only a half, a quarter, or an eighth inheritors of the group tradition. A Negro may be so light complected that he can "pass" as a white man. Logically he has every reason to do so, since in his case his white ancestry numerically outweighs his colored ancestry. People who deny their group membership may, by conviction, be "assimilationists" and regard it as desirable for all distinctive minorities to lose their identities as fast as they can. But often, too, the member who denies his allegiance suffers considerable conflict. He may feel like a traitor to his kind.

A Jewish student confessed with remorse that in order not to be known as Jewish he would sometimes "insert in my conversation delicate witticisms pertaining to Jewishness which, while not actually vicious, conveyed a total impression of gentile malice."

Another student wrote:

When I am with anti-Semites I "clam up" and leave as soon as possible. I don't ordinarily have the courage to confront them with the fact of my Jewishness. I have often felt guilty about not identifying myself as a Jew.

Denial of one's membership may be permanent, as when one is baptized into a different faith, or succeeds in passing as a member of the dominant group. It may be opportunistic and temporary, as it was in the case of Peter, who under emotional stress denied that he was one of Christ's followers. The denial may be partial, as in the case of an immigrant who finds it expedient to Anglicize his foreign-sounding name. A Negro may try to remove the kinkiness from his hair, not because he really expects to "pass"—but because a token escape from his handicapping characteristics is somehow symbolically satisfying.

Deliberate denials of one's membership are not always easy to distinguish from the normal adaptations that one must make to the practices of the dominant majority. A Polish immigrant who learns to speak English is not necessarily denying his Polishness, but he is certainly diminishing its relative importance in his life. He is moving away from one group membership toward another. Even when there is no intention to discard one's earlier allegiances still every step toward assimilation is, in effect, a type of "denial."

Withdrawal and Passivity

From time immemorial slaves, prisoners, outcasts have hidden their true feelings behind a facade of passive acquiescence. So well may they hide their resentment that to the superficial eye they appear completely satisfied with their lot. The mask of contentment is their means of survival.

During World War II soldiers were interviewed on many subjects by a Research Branch of the Army. One question asked of white soldiers was: "Do you think that most Negroes in this country are pretty well satisfied or do you think most of them are dissatisfied?" Only one-tenth of the Southerners and one-seventh of the Northerners said, "Most were dissatisfied." [2]

This finding is a tribute to the Negro's protective concealment behind a mask, and also a revelation of the comforting complacency of the dominant white group. The truth is that most Negroes are dissatisfied. Fully three-quarters are convinced that "white people try to keep the Negroes down." [3]

Passive acquiescence is sometimes the only way in which seriously threatened minority groups can survive. Rebellion and aggression would certainly be met by fierce punishment, and the individual himself might succumb to mental illness induced by constant anxiety and anger. By agreeing with his adversary he escapes being conspicuous, has no cause for fear, and quietly leads his life in two compartments: one (more active) among his own kind, one (more passive) in the outer world. In spite of their conflicts, most Negroes are mentally healthy—perhaps because acquiescence is a salutary mode of ego defense. One who develops a withdrawn and supine manner may be actually rewarded with a certain degree of protection.

There are all grades of passivity and withdrawal. Reticence and dignity create the impression of quiet poise. Many people have admired this pattern, found fairly often among Negro and Oriental groups in this country.

Yet another type of withdrawal is found in fantasy. In real life the despised person may not find the gratification of status. But he may imagine, and possibly talk with his equals about, a better state of life than he enjoys. Like a cripple, he pictures himself as free from physical defects. In his dreams he is strong, handsome, wealthy. He has grand clothes, social position, influence, and the cars he drives are powerful. Daydreams are a common response to deprivation.

Withdrawal may also take the less pleasing form of cringing and sycophancy. In the presence of members of the dominant group some victims of prejudice try, as it were, to eradicate their own egos. If the master jokes, the slave laughs; if the master storms, the slave quails; if the master wants flattery, the slave gives it.

Clowning

And if the master wants to be amused, the slave sometimes obligingly plays the clown. A Jewish, Negro, Irish, or Scottish comedian on the stage may caricature his own group to the delight of the audience. The actor is gratified by the applause. Richard Wright in *Black Boy* describes the colored elevator man who wins his way by exaggerating his Negro accent, and affecting the traits ascribed to his racial group: begging, laziness, and tall tales. His passengers give him coins and make him a pet. Negro children sometimes learn to behave like silly beggars because in this way they receive good-natured (if patronizing) attention and a few pennies.

Protective clowning extends into the in-group itself. Negro soldiers among themselves sometimes affected an extreme "Negro speech"—the more ungrammatical the better. To murder grammar seemed to them a pleasure, a symbolic vent for feelings of frustration. They called themselves "spooks," a term with more than humorous significance. A spook can't be hurt; he can't be downed; he doesn't talk back, but he can't be coerced. He will come right through doors and walls whatever you do; he has a sassy if silent invulnerability. There is often a flavor of pathos in the self-directed humor of minority groups. They seem to be saying, with Byron, "if I laugh at any mortal thing, it is that I may not weep."

Strengthening In-group Ties

As we saw in Chapter 3, the threat from a common enemy is not the only basis of human association, but it is a strong cement. A nation is never so cohesive as in wartime. Studies of the families of unemployed men during economic depression show that frequently a higher degree of *esprit de corps* develops within the group. True, some families already shaky are disrupted by the crisis, just as some feeble minority groups are entirely disrupted by persecution. One thinks in this connection of some of the idealistic, radical, or religious communities in American history that could not withstand the attacks of unfriendly forces around them. It may also be that certain ethnic groups—for example, certain Indian tribes—lack the strength to resist persecution. Under it they disintegrate.

But normally we may say that misery finds balm through the closer association of people who are miserable for the same reason. Threats drive them to seek protective unity within their common membership. The prevailing belief on the west coast during World War II that "a Jap is a Jap" created a strong tie among Issei (foreign born) and Nisei (American born), although before the persecution set in these groups were frequently at odds with each other.

Thus "clannishness" may be a result of persecution, although by the persecutors it is likely to be regarded as its *cause*. Few people in California blamed discriminatory laws and practices for the cohesiveness of Japanese communities. They did not see that these communities were bound to cohere in the face of alien land laws, laws against intermarriage, exclusion from citizenship, from many occupations, from many neighborhoods. Rather, the clannishness was ascribed to the "nature" of the Japanese, just as it is to "Jewish nature." But when members of minority groups are systematically excluded from occupations, residential areas, hotels, vacation resorts, it is fair to ask, Who is being clannish?

There probably is no such thing as an instinctive "consciousness of kind." Children have their tribal membership taught them. It is not uncommon for a Negro child of five to deny that he is a Negro—although he knows that others belong to this despised group. A young Jewish child may use the epithet "dirty Jew," unaware of the irony involved. Parents in minority groups often debate whether it is well to explain to the child early in life what suffering his involuntary membership will entail, or whether it is better for the child to enjoy a few years of innocent unawareness at the risk of a later shock—which often comes around the age of eight.

Whether or not the child has been prepared for the shock, he soon learns to find what consolation he can in the membership he cannot escape. Parents assist by teaching him all the glories of his group tradition. Comforting legends help to cancel out the accusations of "inferiority" made against his group. "We, not you," says the child to himself, "are the really superior people." Rationalizations increase: the dominant group may come to be regarded as coarse, vulgar, barbarian, or as filled with "sick" (i.e., prejudiced) people. Again, those who suffer discrimination may derive some inner gratification from their lot: to be singled out thus is to have one's *importance* recognized. Smugness and self-righteousness may come to mark the victim no less than the victimizer, for no person really thinks that he is of less worth than another.

Thus minority groups may develop special solidarity. Within their in-group they can laugh and deride their persecutors, celebrate their own heroes and holidays, and live quite comfortably together. As long as they cohere they need not feel too much haunted by their problem. On p. 18 we reported that ethnocentrism may be higher among minority groups than among the dominant majority. We now sense the reason why.

It is only a short step to giving favored treatment to one's own kind. Since one's safety lies in the in-group one grows *prejudiced* in favor of its members. A Jew may tend to favor his ethnic fellows; if so, the accusation of clannishness takes on meaning. The Negro slogan, "Don't buy where you can't work," is a phenomenon of the same order—easy to understand. Many Negroes have been asked why they do not attend "white" churches where they would be sincerely welcomed. Often they reply, "We are perfectly willing to do so, but will these churches give a Negro minister a fair chance to be employed?" To be prejudiced *in favor* of one's own kind is a natural reflex of out-group prejudice against one's kind.

Slyness and Cunning

Throughout history and all over the world one of the commonest accusations against out-groups is that they are dishonest, tricky, sneaky. The Egyptian Moslems so accuse the Christian Copts, the Europeans so accuse the Jews; the Turk points at the Armenian, and the Armenian at the Turk.

The root of this accusation lies in the double standard of ethics that has marked human associations from the beginning of time. One is *expected* to deal more fairly with one's own kind than with out-groups. Among primitive people sanctions against dishonesty ordinarily apply only to members of one's own tribe. It is fair and praiseworthy to cheat an outsider. Even among civilized people the double standard is still detectable. Tourists are overcharged; exporters think it fair to send merchandise of inferior quality overseas.

The tendency becomes aggravated if survival depends upon cunning. At various times in history many Jews could not possibly have survived expropriation and pogroms unless they developed cunning in misleading their persecutors. In Czarist Russia, in Hitler's Germany, and in all countries overrun by the Nazis, this fact held true. Plenty of instances can be found in the history of the Armenians, of American Indians, of many other persecuted ethnic and religious groups.

"Sneaky" traits may also develop as a means of gaining petty revenge. The weaker makes forays against the stronger: the Negro cook who "totes" from her white mistress's kitchen may do so for symbolic as well as gastronomic reasons. Cunning is not confined to forms of stealing. It entails all sorts of pretense. One ingratiates oneself, flatters, gains favors, plays the clown, and generally cheapens the ethics of human relations in the interests of both survival and revenge.

So logical is this form of response among victims of prejudice that one wonders why, in fact, it is not oftener encountered.

Identification with Dominant Group: Self-hate

A more subtle mechanism is involved in cases where the victim instead of pretending to agree with his "betters" actually *does* agree with them, and sees his own group through their eyes. This process may underlie assimilationist strivings and be the factor that leads the individual to lose himself totally in the dominant group as soon as his level of possessions, customs, and speech makes him indistinguishable from the majority. But more mysterious are the cases where the individual is hopelessly barred from assimilation and yet mentally identifies himself with the practices, outlook, and prejudices of the dominant group. He accepts his state.

The case of certain unemployed men may help explain the situation. During the great depression of the 30's, studies disclosed that these men felt a profound shame. They took the blame for their penurious situation upon themselves. In most of these cases, by no stretch of the imagination could the men be considered at fault. Yet shame was felt. The primary reason is that in our western culture we hold to the doctrine of individual responsibility. It is the individual who shapes his world, or so we believe. When things go wrong the individual is to blame. Hence the immigrant grows *ashamed* of his faulty accent, his lack of ease and social grace, his defective education.

A Jew may hate his historic religion (for if it did not exist he would not be marked out for persecution). Or he may blame some one class of Jews (the orthodox, or those who are dirty, or the merchants). Or he may hate the Yiddish language. Since he cannot escape his own group, he thus in a real sense hates himself— or at least the part of himself that is Jewish. To make matters worse he may hate himself for feeling this way. He is badly torn. His divided mind may make for furtive and self-conscious behavior, for "nervousness" and a lasting sense of insecurity. Since these are unpleasant traits they augment his hatred for his own Jewishness and then aggravate the conflict. The circle is vicious and never-ending.[4]

Over a century ago de Tocqueville described self-hatred among Negro slaves. Although the passage is poignant it commits the fallacy of ascribing this state of mind to *all* Negroes. Actually this form of ego defense was probably not common, certainly not universal, among slaves; nor is it common among Negroes today.

> The Negro makes a thousand fruitless efforts to insinuate himself among men who repulse him; he conforms to the tastes of his oppressors, adopts their opinions, and hopes by imitating them to form a part of their community. Having been told from the beginning that his race is naturally inferior to that of the whites, he assents to the proposition, and is ashamed of his own nature. In each of his features he discovers a trace of slavery, and if it were in his power, he would willingly rid himself of everything that makes him what he is.[5]

Studies of Nazi concentration camps show that identification with one's oppressors was a form of adjustment that came only when all other methods of ego defense had failed. At first prisoners tried to keep their self-respect intact, to feel inward contempt for their persecutors, to try by stealth and cunning to preserve their lives and their health. But after two or three years of extreme suffering many of them found that their efforts to please the guards led to a mental surrender. They imitated the guards, wore bits of their clothing (symbolic power), turned against new prisoners, became anti-Semites, and in general took over the dark mentality of the oppressor.[6]

Every personality has its breaking point. The slaves to whom de Tocqueville refers and the long-term concentration camp prisoners show that group oppression may destroy the integrity of the ego entirely, and reverse its normal pride, and create a groveling self-image.

Not all cases of identification or of self-hate are so extreme. In a half-joking, half-serious manner northern Negro soldiers teased southern blacks respecting their "inferiority." The standards of judgment prevailing among white people are not uncommonly applied by Negroes to themselves. They have heard so frequently that they are lazy, ignorant, dirty, and superstitious that they may half believe the accusations, and since the traits are commonly despised in our western culture—which, of course, Negroes share—some degree of in-group hate seems almost inevitable. For example, in unconsciously accepting the white man's evaluation of pigmentation, the light-skinned Negro may look down upon his darker-skinned brother.

Aggression against Own Group

We have applied the term self-hate to one's sense of shame for possessing the despised qualities of one's group—whether these qualities be real or imaginary. We have applied it also to repugnance for other members of one's group because they "possess" these qualities. Both meanings of self-hate are possible.

When the hatred is clearly limited to other members of one's group we may expect all manner of intragroup troubles to ensue. Some Jews refer to other Jews as "kikes"—blaming them exclusively for the anti-Semitism from which all alike suffer. Class distinctions within groups is often a result of trying to free oneself from responsibility for the handicap which the group as a whole suffers. "Lace curtain" Irish look down on "shanty Irish." Wealthy Spanish and Portuguese Jews have long regarded themselves as the top of the pyramid of Hebraic peoples. But Jews of German origin, having a rich culture, view themselves as the aristocrats, often looking down on Austrian, Hungarian, and Balkan Jews, and regarding Polish and Russian Jews at the very bottom. Needless to say, not all Jews would accept this ordering, especially those from Poland and Russia.

Class distinctions among the Negroes are particularly sharp. Color, occupation, and degree of education help mark the strata. And it is not hard for the uppers to shift much of the blame for their disadvantaged position upon the lowers. Living in the close and frustrating conditions of army service it was observed that dark-skinned Negro troops often took out their aggression against lighter-skinned companions who to them resembled the master race; while those of lighter complexion were hard on the "spooks" of darker hue because they were "shiftless" and "ignorant."

Thus relations are often strained between members of an in-group grown irritable over their handicapped status. Those who have adopted one mode of defense may be annoyed by those who have adopted a different mode. The ingratiating Negro is despised as an "Uncle Tom." The orthodox Jew, with his long tunic and curls, may be rejected by the modern Jew whose feelings are sometimes indistinguishable from those of the anti-Semitic gentile. Members of almost any group who wish to lose their identity and assimilate with the dominant culture are viewed with hostility by their fellow-members. They are regarded as "stuck up," as "apple-polishers," or even as traitors.

It is true, as we have seen, that acute and lethal persecution may drive all in-group members together, so that local animosities are dropped. But whenever prejudice is merely at a "normal" level, we can expect to find the in-group bickering as one additional mode of ego defense.

Prejudice against Out-groups

Victims of prejudice may, of course, inflict on others what they themselves receive. Deprived of power and status one craves to feel power and status. Pecked at by those higher in the pecking order, one may, like a fowl in the barnyard, peck at those seen as weaker and lower than oneself, or as threatening.

An investigation compared the prejudices of white and Negro students in two colleges in the State of Georgia, using the Bogardus Social Distance Scale with both. Negro students turned out on the average to be less friendly toward *all* the 25 national and ethnic groups listed than were white students (excepting only toward the Negro group).[7]

Several additional studies have supported this discovery of greater average ethnic prejudice among Negroes than among white people. But it is not only the Negro who responds to prejudice with prejudice. Other minority members do so likewise, especially those who have felt themselves to be victimized for their membership.[8]

Their state of mind is expressed by a Jewish student who wrote:

> I am intolerant because I have been a victim of intolerance during my early formative years. The hatreds and prejudices I have developed are reactions used as a defense mechanism. If Joe Doakes hates me I naturally will return the compliment.[9]

While the victim's personal frustration and anger are the principal reasons for both his direct and displaced hostility to other groups, there are other reasons why he develops prejudice. Through it he may find a comforting if frail bond with the majority. A white gentile may say, or imply, to a Negro that after all neither of them is a Jew. One anti-Semite remarked in a patronizing way to a Negro, "Well, Sam, anyhow you are more like us whites than those damned Jews are." Feeling flattered, Sam agreed and proceeded to look down on the Jews as a lower breed than himself. Or, an insecure Jew may join his gentile neighbors in fighting to keep Negro homes out of the suburbs where they live. Common prejudices create common bonds.

Finally, a curious arithmetical possibility arises. The Jew who resents the gentile may doubly resent the Negro, who is both Negro and gentile. The Negro who resents the white man may doubly resent the Jew for being both Jewish and white. It is not politic for the Negro to express anti-white sentiments, but he can with double force condemn the "dirty Jew" (meaning, in part, "dirty white").[10] Similarly the Jew, when he says "dirty nigger" may be getting rid of some of his venom against the *goyim*.

Sympathy

The mechanism of defense just described is entirely absent in the case of many victims of prejudice. Just the reverse happens. A Jewish student wrote:

> I sympathize easily with the Negro who is even more likely to have people against him than the Jew. I know what it is like to be discriminated against. How could I be prejudiced?

The philanthropies of Julius Rosenwald were directed chiefly toward benefiting the Negro. Enlightened Jews say that compassion is the natural response of their group toward the plight of all sufferers from oppression. Their own trials and suffering (as well as the universalism of their religion) make for understanding and sympathy.

It is interesting to note that Sigmund Freud himself credits his membership in the Jewish group with his objectivity of mind and his freedom to pioneer. He writes, "Because I was a Jew I found myself free from many prejudices that hampered others in the use of their intellects; and as a Jew I was prepared to take my place on the side of the opposition and renounce being on good terms with the 'compact majority.'" [11]

Evidence bears out the logic here expressed. In most large-scale studies that have been made, Jews in fact are on the average *less prejudiced* toward other minorities than are Protestants or Catholics. But, here is the important point: not only Jews but others who feel that they have been victims of discrimination are usually either very high in prejudice (as reported in the previous pages) or else very low in prejudice. They are seldom "average." In short, being a victim oneself disposes one either to develop aggression toward *or* sympathy with other out-groups.[12]

This is a point of considerable importance. *Victimization can scarcely leave an individual with a merely normal amount of prejudice.* Broadly speaking, he will take one of two paths. Either he will join the pecking order and treat others in the way he has been treated, or else he will consciously and deliberately avoid this temptation. With insight he will say, "These people are victims exactly as I am a victim. Better stand with them, not against them."

Fighting Back: Militancy

As yet we have scarcely mentioned the simple possibility that minority group members will refuse to "take it." They may fight back whenever they can. Psychologically this is the simplest response of all. "He who conceives himself hated by another," wrote Spinoza, "and believes that he has given him no cause for hatred, will hate that other in return." In psychoanalytic parlance, frustration breeds aggression.

A study following the Harlem riot in the summer of 1943 asked a large number of Negro residents what they thought of the riot. It turned out that nearly a third *approved* of it. They said, "I'm in favor of it—hope it happens again. Let my people go." "It's the only way Negroes get the government to pay attention to them." "It was revenge for Detroit." On the other hand, 60 percent of the population, who had presumably suffered the same discriminations, said it was "shameful," "it only set us back," "it was terrible and degrading." It was not possible in this study to determine just why some victims of race prejudice should condone and some condemn this violent outbreak. There was some indication that the disapproval came from those who were better read, attended church more regularly, and were younger (perhaps not having suffered so long). But these indications are not too certain.[13]

It is not hard to comprehend the ceaseless protests voiced by some members of minority groups. Their style of response is counter-aggression. Occasionally they are so compulsively militant that even members of their own group will not thank them. Yet genuine reforms often follow from the efforts of these zealots.

It should be observed that it is no easier for a victim of discrimination to make fine distinctions than it is for members of the dominant group to do so. "A Jap is a Jap." "Although there may be a few exceptions all Negroes are pretty much alike." "All Catholics are fascists at heart." Returning the compliment, militants may damn all whites, all goyim, all Protestants. They express truculent reprisals against the entire dominant group.

Realizing the futility of violence, some victims of prejudice join political or actionist organizations pledged to improve the existing situation. For this reason immigrant groups have been prominently represented in left-wing political parties. Recently Negroes have sensed possible improvement through political action, and have widely shifted their votes from the Republican (Lincoln's) party to the Democratic (Roosevelt's) party. A few have become communists. The fact that minority groups often embrace liberal or radical political action means that they will be accused of being troublemakers and agitators. Jews sometimes feel driven into the forefront of social change, and may become leaders of liberal causes. When such an event occurs they appear to anti-Semites more than ever as "value-violators," at "the fringe of conservative values" (p. 123).

Enhanced Striving

To redouble one's efforts is a healthy response to an obstacle. People admire the cripple who has persevered and overcome his handicap. Such direct compensation for an inferiority is the type of response most highly approved in our culture. Accordingly, some members of minority groups view their handicap as an obstacle to be surmounted by an extra spurt of effort. After working all day, some immigrants attend night school to learn American ways of speech and thought. In every minority group there are many individuals who adopt this direct and successful mode of compensation.

This seems to be the style of life of many Jewish people. Feeling that all Jews suffer a handicap, they sometimes urge their children to study harder and to work harder than their competitors in order to run an equal race. To be successful, they may point out, a Jew must be better prepared, must have higher academic records, and more experience than a gentile. Without doubt the Jewish tradition of scholarship and study reinforces this particular response to prejudice.

Those who adopt this mode of adjustment often evoke grudging admiration. They may also evoke abuse for being *too* industrious and clever. But in any case, they have taken the road of open competition, saying, "I'll play the game and accept the handicap you give me. Here goes."

Symbolic Status Striving

Contrasted with this direct and successful striving, we find a variety of off-center efforts that victims of prejudice may make to gain status. Sometimes minority group members are especially fond of pomp and circumstance. In the army some Negro troops seemed especially devoted to parades, to well-shined shoes, well-pressed clothes, and other signs of good soldiering. These were all status symbols—and status for Negroes is a scarce commodity. One sometimes notes similar pride and polish in the processions, rituals, even in the funerals, of immigrant groups. And the flashy display of jewels and expensive autos on the part of the *nouveau arrivé* may be a way of saying, "You held me in contempt, now look at me. Am I so contemptible?"

A similar "compensation by substitution" may lead to obsessive interest in sexual conquests. The despised member of a minority group may find potency, pride, self-respect in such activities. He is the equal of—nay a better man than—the snob who patronizes him. It seems probable that the Negro does not resent his reputation for sexual vigor. He takes it as a tribute, since in many other ways he feels emasculated. Whether sexual libertinism does in fact characterize some Negroes or some members of other minority groups is not at issue. The point is that even one's reputation may constitute a symbolic status gratification.

A curious instance of symbolic status striving may be found in the pretentious use of language. Big words may seem to the person deprived of status to lift him higher in the social scale. Elegant diction and a fullsome vocabulary (even if sprinkled with malapropisms) are found among certain individuals who all too plainly betray their craving for an educational status they do not in fact possess.

Neuroticism

With so much inner conflict to contend with one wonders about the statistics of mental health among victims of discrimination. There is some evidence that the psychoneurotic rate is relatively high among Jews. Hypertension is common among Negroes.[14] But, on the whole, mental health in minority groups is not greatly different from the run-of-the-mill in society at large.

If any generalization can be made it might be to the effect that victims of prejudice learn to lead their lives under a condition of mild dissociation. So long as they can move freely and act naturally within their own in-group they manage to put up with (and discount) rebuffs received outside. And they grow habituated to this slight split in their mode of living.

It would be well, however, for the victims of prejudice to be on guard. Because of the constant bombardment of stimuli upon them they are *likely* to take on one or more of the defensive modes of behavior described in this chapter. Some of these modes are both agreeable and successful, others are troublemaking and verge toward the neurotic type of defense mechanism. To recognize the pitfalls is one way of steering a more successful course of life.

Correspondingly, members of the favored dominant group do well to learn the same lesson. Ego-defensive traits are likely to be found wherever an individual's self-esteem is threatened, and some such traits will be disagreeable. They should be regarded as the consequence of, rather than a justification for, discriminative treatment.

A twelve-year-old boy came home from school sharply criticizing a classmate whom he called a "jerk." The "jerk" seemed to be disliked for his boasting, lying, and cringing. When asked, "What do you suppose made him like that?" the lad suddenly grew thoughtful and slowly formulated what in all probability was a sound diagnosis: "Well he looks funny, isn't good at sports, and gets left out of everything; no one gives him a break; so I think he acts mean and tries to buck himself up."

Following this exercise in clinical diagnosis the lad grew more interested in the "jerk," at first viewing him objectively and gradually becoming friendly with him. To comprehend is to excuse— or at least to tolerate more easily.

It would have been well if the "jerk" himself had been able to make the diagnosis. He might have sought less objectionable modes of compensating for his defects if he knew the deeper reasons for his behavior. Even a neurotic defense mechanism may be controlled, or at least kept off parade, if its nature and source are fully understood. Occasionally a member of a victimized group may need to learn the same lesson.

But to think of victims in terms of neurotic compensations is usually less appropriate than to think of them as living in a marginal state—sometimes accepted and sometimes not. Lewin likens their lot to the condition of adolescents who are never quite certain whether they will be admitted to the world of dominant adults. Storm and stress result, tension and strain, and occasional irrational outbreaks. To make a mature adjustment one has to belong to a *definite* world. Many minority group members are never permitted to belong fully, to participate normally, or to feel at home. Like the adolescent, they belong neither here nor there. They are marginal beings.[15]

The Self-fulfilling Prophecy

Let us return to the point made at the beginning of this chapter: What people think of us is bound to some degree to fashion what we are. If a child is said to be a "natural clown" and is petted and praised for being one, he will learn the tricks and become a jester. If a man enters a group believing that all those present feel aggressive toward him, he will probably behave in such a defensive and insulting manner that true aggression will be evoked. If we expect the new maid in our family to steal, and if we betray this fact, she may be goaded into doing so if only to avenge the insult.

To the countless subtle ways in which expectancy of certain behavior in others evokes that very behavior, Robert Merton has given the term "self-fulfilling prophecy." [16] It serves to call attention to the reciprocal conduct of human beings when in interaction. Too often we think of out-groups as simply possessing certain qualities (Chapter 7) and in-groups as having certain false images of these qualities (Chapter 12). The truth of the matter is that these two conditions interact. The way we perceive qualities in others cannot help but have an effect on what qualities others will display. It is not true, of course, that every grim image we have of hated groups results in the development of hateful traits to confirm our worst expectations. Yet there is likely to be some kind of unpleasant reflex of our unpleasant opinions. And thus a vicious circle is established that tends, unless specifically halted, to augment social distance and enhance the grounds of prejudice.

A self-fulfilling prophecy may lead to a benign circle as well as to a vicious circle. Tolerance, appreciation, praise, beget good behavior.   An outsider welcomed into our group is likely to make a solid contribution because he responds from the core of his personality and not from the defensive layers alone.   In all human relations—familial, ethnic, international—the engendering power of expectancy is enormous.[17]   If we foresee evil in our fellow man, we tend to provoke it; if good, we elicit it.

Summary

Not all minority group members—even those of the most persecuted groups—display visible ego defenses.   If they do so, an interesting question arises as to why an individual takes one rather than another means to protect himself and advance his interests. The many devices described in this chapter seem to fall into two types.[18]   The first includes mechanisms that are essentially aggressive, outgoing, indicating attacks on the source of the difficulty. The second includes more introverted modes.   In the first instance the victim *blames* the outer causes of his handicap; in the second he tends, if not actually to blame himself, at least to take the responsibility upon himself for adjusting to the situation.   The first we might designate (following Rosenzweig) as *extropunitive* individuals; the latter groups as *intropunitive*.   Using this scheme, we might summarize our chapter with the aid of Fig. 9.

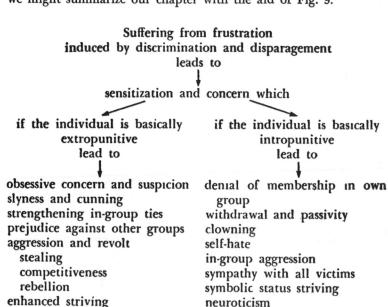

Fig. 9. Possible types of compensatory behavior among victims of discrimination.

The shortcoming of this analysis is that it may leave in our minds a disorderly array of "mechanisms." Every personality is, in fact, a pattern. A single victim of prejudice may display several traits, frequently blending some on the extropunitive side with some on the intropunitive.

To illustrate the point, let us depict a pattern characteristic of many sufferers from discrimination. First of all, they do not regard their marginality as fatal in their pursuit of a wholesome and enjoyable life. Their basic values are human and universal, and they know that many human beings in all groups are fundamentally in agreement with them concerning these values. Therefore, they seek their friends and associates not exclusively from their own minority group, but in many groups where these same values are to be found. When, in other less central regions of that activity, they encounter discrimination and prejudice they react with dignity and broad understanding. They say in effect, "Everyone has hardships; everyone suffers injustice; my lot, like theirs, calls for courage and perseverance." There develops then a measured competitiveness, an intelligent pursuit of one's goals, including efforts to reduce discrimination in society and to increase the practice of democracy. There develops a broad compassion for oppressed people whoever they are. In short, sympathy, courage, persistence, and dignity mark such a personality. Some patterns, to be sure, are far less socialized and less mature. But it has been well said that a fully developed personality is one that can handle its suffering without inflicting suffering in return. Since many victims of prejudice have learned to do so, we admire them for having characters notably rich and mature.

NOTES AND REFERENCES

1. S. A. STOUFFER, et al. The American Soldier: Adjustment During Army Life. Princeton: Princeton Univ. Press, 1949, Vol. I, Chapter 10.

2. Ibid. P. 506.

3. T. C. COTHRAN. Negro conceptions of white people. American Journal of Sociology, 1951, 56, 458-467.

4. Cf. K. LEWIN. Self-hatred among Jews. Contemporary Jewish Record, 1941, 4, 219-232.

5. A. DE TOCQUEVILLE. Democracy in America. New York: George Dearborn, 1838, I, 334.

6. B. BETTELHEIM. Individual and mass behavior in extreme situations. Journal of Abnormal and Social Psychology, 1943, 38, 417-452.

7. J. S. GRAY AND A. H. THOMPSON. The ethnic prejudices of white and Negro college students. Journal of Abnormal and Social Psychology, 1953, 48, 311-313.

8. G. W. ALLPORT AND B. M. KRAMER. Some roots of prejudice. *Journal of Psychology*, 1946, **22**, 28.

9. DOROTHY T. SPOERL. The Jewish stereotype, the Jewish personality and Jewish prejudice. *Yivo Annual of Jewish Social Science*, 1952, **7**, 276.

10. For a discussion of anti-Semitism among Negroes see: K. B. CLARK, Candor about Negro-Jewish relations, *Commentary*, 1946, **1**, 8-14.

11. S. FREUD. On being of the B'nai B'rith. *Commentary*, 1946, **1**, 23.

12. G. W. ALLPORT AND B. M. KRAMER. *Op. cit.*, 29.

13. K. B. CLARK. Group violence: a preliminary study of the attitudinal pattern of its acceptance and rejection: a study of the 1943 Harlem riot. *Journal of Social Psychology*, 1944, **19**, 319-337.

14. HELEN V. McLEAN. Psychodynamic factors in racial relations. *The Annals of the American Academy of Political and Social Science*, 1946, **244**, 159-166.

15. K. LEWIN. *Resolving Social Conflict*. New York: Harper, 1948, Chapter 11.

The importance of self-esteem and pride in one's own group—as a means of avoiding the devastating effects of marginality—is stressed by G. SAENGER, Minority personality and adjustment, *Transactions of the New York Academy of Sciences*, 1952, Series 2, **14**, 204-208.

16. R. K. MERTON. The self-fulfilling prophecy. *The Antioch Review*, 1948, **8**, 193-210. See also: R. STAGNER, Homeostasis as a unifying concept in personality theory, *Psychological Review*, 1951, **58**, 5-17.

17. G. W. ALLPORT. The role of expectancy. Chapter 2 in H. CANTRIL (ED.), *Tensions that Cause Wars*. Urbana: Univ. of Illinois Press, 1950.

18. A somewhat different way of summarizing the types of behavior found in minority group members is suggested by I. L. CHILD in his book, *Italian or American?* New Haven: Yale Univ. Press, 1943. Child discovers that some second-generation youth of Italian extraction strongly *rebel* against their own in-group. Others *consolidate in-group ties,* even to the extent of hating the enveloping American culture. Still others are *apathetic,* choosing to de-emphasize and disregard ethnic conflict as much as possible. All of these forms of response find a place in our classification which differs from Child's, chiefly in its breadth. We list a wider variety of adjustments than Child finds in his more limited study of a single ethnic group.

Part III

PERCEIVING AND THINKING ABOUT
GROUP DIFFERENCES

CHAPTER 10

THE COGNITIVE PROCESS

SELECTION, ACCENTUATION, INTERPRETATION—DIRECTED AND
AUTISTIC THINKING—CAUSE AND EFFECT THINKING—THE
NATURE OF CATEGORIES—THE PRINCIPLE OF LEAST EFFORT—
THE DYNAMICS OF COGNITION IN THE PREJUDICED PERSONALITY
—CONCLUSIONS

The light within meets the light without.

PLATO

As we have said, group differences are one thing; how we perceive them and think about them is quite another. In Part II we have examined the *stimulus object* itself—the characteristics of outgroups. Now we turn to mental processes on our part that *meet* the stimulus object—and with what results.

Nothing that strikes our eyes or ears conveys its message directly to us. We always *select* and *interpret* our impressions of the surrounding world. Some message is brought to us by the "light without" but the meaning and significance we give to it are largely added by the "light within."

As I look out of my window I see a wild cherry bush swaying in the breeze. The underside of its leaves show. This much of the message is conveyed through my sense organs excited by the light waves reflected by the bush itself. But I find myself saying, "It will probably rain tonight," for somewhere I have heard that it is a sign of rain when bushes or trees blow in such a way that the underside of their leaves is clearly exposed.

What I sense, what I perceive, and what I think become blended into one single act of cognition. When I meet a Negro, his blackness is conveyed to me by sensation, but the fact that he is a man, also a member of a certain race, and that he may accordingly have other attributes of the group (which I think I know about) are all added by past experience. The whole complex process takes place as one knowledgeful act of cognition.

It is important that we never fall into the error of supposing that we perceive group characteristics directly. As Alfred Adler wrote:

A perception is never to be compared with a photographic image because something of the peculiar and individual quality

165

of the person who perceives is inextricably bound up with it. . . . Perception is more than a simple physical phenomenon; it is a psychic function from which we may draw the most far-going conclusions concerning the inner life.[1]

Selection, Accentuation, Interpretation

The process of perception-cognition is distinguished for three operations that it performs on "the light without." It selects, accentuates, and interprets the sensory data.[2] The following example illustrates the course of events:

> I have had, let us say, ten encounters with student X. On all these occasions he has turned in work or made comments that seemed to me of poor quality. I therefore judge that his ability is substandard and that he cannot continue his studies with profit and should therefore leave college at the end of the academic year.

I have *selected* my evidence, focusing my attention upon certain signs of ineptitude to which a teacher is sensitive. I have also *accentuated* these signs, deliberately overlooking X's many personal virtues and his charm, and placing great weight upon my ten intellectual encounters with him. Finally, I have *interpreted* the evidence by generalizing it into a judgment of "academic incompetence." The process seems rational enough—about as rational as any judgment can be. The teacher in this case, we might say, "did not go beyond the evidence." Actually he did so. Who knows but on the eleventh or twelfth occasion different evidence would come to light? But on the whole he selected as best he could, accentuated in terms of his own experienced standards, and interpreted the situation as wisely as possible.

Let us consider another example:

> In South Africa on a Public Service Examination, candidates were instructed to "underline the percentage that you think Jews constitute of the whole population in South Africa: 1 percent, 5 . . . , 10 . . . , 15 . . . , 20 . . . , 25 . . . , 30 percent." When tabulated, the modal estimate turned out to be 20 percent. The true answer is just a little over 1 percent.[3]

In this case, while thinking about the problem presented them, most of the candidates apparently selected from their memories, recalling Jews they knew or had seen. They then clearly accentuated (exaggerated) this past experience, and interpreted it in a manner that led to their false judgment. The error must have been induced by some hypersensitiveness to the "Jewish question." Quite likely fear of a Jewish "menace" underlay the inflated estimate.

The next illustration shows a still more marked effect of the "light within" upon the "light without."

> At a session of summer school an irate lady of middle age approached the instructor saying, "I think there is a girl of Negro blood in this class." To the instructor's noncommittal reply, the lady persisted, "But you wouldn't want a nigger in the class, would you?" Next day she returned and firmly insisted, "I know she's a nigger because I dropped a paper on the floor and said to her, 'Pick that up.' She did so, and that proves she's just a darky servant trying to get above her station."

This lady had only a slight sensory cue to start with. The student she singled out was brunet, but to most people's eyes she was certainly not Negroid. Yet her accuser *selected* cues that she thought existed, *accentuated* them in her mind, and *interpreted* the total situation to accord with her prejudices. Note, for example, her highly arbitrary interpretation of the fact that the girl picked up the sheet of fallen paper.

A final example is still more extreme. During 1942 there was a dimout in New York City. Even the illumination in the round red and green traffic lights was reduced by covering them in part. In order to retain maximum visibility with minimum illumination, only two slits, appearing in this form ⊰⊱, were allowed to show. Such was the objective situation. Following is the way in which one man perceived it.

> What a shock it must be to the descendants of the Star of David to see all traffic signal lights in the Five Boroughs of Greater New York being changed, for the duration, from the dull red and green circular light, about 6 inches in diameter, now to show a red or green cross, for or against traffic. This change is made in the dimout idea, but the use of the Cross is the work of our Engineering Department of the New York police, so the Jews can be reminded that this is a Christian nation.[4]

In this case the processes of selection, accentuation, misinterpretation go wild.

Directed and Autistic Thinking

Thinking is basically an endeavor to anticipate reality. By thinking we try to foresee consequences and plan actions that will avoid whatever threatens us and will bring our hopes and dreams to pass. There is nothing passive about thinking. It is, from the ground up, an active function of remembering-perceiving-judging-planning.

When thinking is used efficiently to anticipate reality we speak of *reasoning*. If it genuinely advances the person along his way to important and fundamental goals in life, squaring so far as possible with the objectively known properties of the stimulus-object, we say the person is reasoning. He may, of course, make errors in his reasoning, but still if the total direction is realistically oriented, we affirm the basically rational character of his thought. This normal, problem-solving process is usually called "directed" thinking.[5]

To it we may contrast fantasied, autistic, or "free" thinking. Often our minds run on, turning up one idea after another, making no progress whatsoever toward a given goal. Daydreams, for example, may picture a goal and bring an imaginary success in fantasy; but they normally do not advance us. The term *autistic thinking* is a good one to adopt for this less rational form of mental activity. Autistic means "referring to self." The lady who "perceived" the Negro and the man who "perceived" the Christian cross in the traffic lights were both engaged in autistic rather than directed thinking—because their private obsessions completely colored the situation. Neither was correct in his interpretations—and neither was "getting anywhere." The whole process was squashy and self-serving.

We may cite an experiment. S. B. Sells wished to study people's ability to reason from syllogisms. A syllogism is a brief problem in directed thinking. The subject matter of one of his series of syllogisms dealt with Negroes. Two examples are given:

> If many Negroes are famous athletes; and if many famous athletes are national heroes; then many Negroes are national heroes.

> If many Negroes are sex offenders; and if many sex offenders are infected with syphilis; then many Negroes are infected with syphilis.

Sells' subjects, all college students, were asked to judge the syllogisms as to the truth or falsity of the logic involved. In the case of the above examples both syllogisms are *false* (one cannot reach a valid conclusion when the premises contain the word "many"). Whether or not he is trained in logic, an unbiassed judge should certainly judge both of these syllogisms as equally valid or invalid, for they are stated in identical forms.

It turned out that while the majority of the students did, in fact, reason consistently—stating both syllogisms in a given pair to be either valid or invalid—yet a number of them declared the first item to be valid and the second invalid. It was found that the majority of these students had *pro-Negro* attitudes as measured by an attitude test. Others declared the first item to be invalid and the second valid. The majority of these students had *anti-Negro* attitudes.[6]

This experiment shows how a purely objective problem in reasoning may be approached in an autistic manner. The outcome is resonant with one's self-interest, with one's preconceptions. The experiment shows likewise that pro-Negro bias may distort one's reasoning just as much as may anti-Negro bias.

An important accompaniment of autistic thinking is *rationalization*. People do not like to admit that their thinking is autistic. In fact, they usually do not *know* that it is. Especially do people resist any imputation that their thinking is due to prejudice. They generally have a more respectable reason to offer. A prejudiced white man would be unlikely to admit that his refusal to drink from the same cup as a Negro is due to his dislike of Negroes; hence he claims that Negroes are "diseased." It is a *plausible* reason, even though he does not hesitate to drink from the same cup as whites who also may be diseased. Many people did not vote for Al Smith in the presidential election of 1928 because he was a Catholic. Yet the reason they gave was that he was "uncouth." Again, a plausible reason, but not the real reason.

It is not possible always to distinguish between reasoning and rationalization, especially between *errors* in reasoning and rationalization. The term rationalization should be used cautiously and applied only to cases where there is palpably false justification given for what is in reality an autistic course of thinking.

One reason why rationalizations are so hard to detect is that they generally obey the following rules. (1) They tend to conform to some accepted social canons. It is *all right* to reject an "uncouth" candidate for president—even if this is not the real reason for rejecting him. (2) They tend to approximate as closely as possible the canons of accepted logic. Though not real reasons, they are at least *good* reasons. It *sounds* sensible not to drink from a cup because of fear of disease, even though this is not the basic reason for refusing to do so.

Cause and Effect Thinking

Whether we use directed or autistic thinking all of us are continually trying to build up a world-picture that is orderly, manageable, and reasonably simple. Outer reality is in itself chaotic—full of too many potential meanings. We have to *simplify* in order to live; we need stability in our perceptions. At the same time we have an insatiable hunger for *explanations.* We like nothing left dangling; everything should have its place in the scheme of things. Even the young child asks, "Why, why, why?"

As if in response to this basic hunger for meaning, every culture in the world supplies an answer to every question that can be asked. No culture ends up by saying, "We don't know the answer." There are myths of creation, legends of the origin of the people, encyclopaedias of knowledge. At the end of the road there is always some guiding religion adequate to all perplexities.

This basic need has an important bearing upon group relations. For one thing, we tend to regard *causation* as something *people* are responsible for. Ultimately it is a Deity who created the world and tidied it up. It is the devil who brings evil and disorder. It is the President,of the country who brings on a depression. The conflict in Korea was called "Truman's war." It is the *Jew,* said Hitler, who caused the war. This anthropomorphic tendency is exceedingly marked. It is the "House of Morgan" that brought on the stock market crash in 1929. It is "the monopolists" who cause inflation. It is "communists" who are responsible for fires, explosions, or flying saucers. High prices are a result of Jewish conspiracy.[7] If evils are personally caused, what could be more logical than to attack the persons who are causing them? To do so seems to us to indicate neither discrimination nor aggression, but merely self-defense.

Thus we continually seek an outer explanation for our frustrations and ills, and are particularly prone to look for a human agency. This quirk, unless it is strenuously disciplined, predisposes us to prejudice. While in reality our frustrations and ills are frequently due to impersonal causes—to altered economic conditions, to the tides of social and historical change—unless we fully realize this fact we tend to slip into the habit of blaming our lot upon identifiable human agents (scapegoats).

The Nature of Categories

Frequently we have spoken of categories. In Chapter 2 we introduced the concept and pointed to some of its salient characteristics. We said that categories assimilate as much old and new experience as possible to themselves; that they enable us quickly to identify any object that belongs to the category; that whatever belongs to a category tends to be saturated with a common emotional flavor. Finally we pointed out that categorical thinking is a natural and inevitable tendency of the human mind, and that irrational categories are formed quite as easily as rational categories.

But we have not yet defined *category*. We mean by the term an *accessible cluster of associated ideas which as a whole has the property of guiding daily adjustments*. Categories, of course, overlap. We have one category for dogs, another for wolves. There are subsidiary categories: a smaller for spaniels, a larger for dogs. All nouns in my vocabulary point to categories (we may call them concepts, if we prefer), but nouns do not exhaust the possibilities. There are combinational categories, overlapping, superordinate, and qualified. I have categories for "watch dog," for "modern music," for "uncouth social behavior." A category, in short, is whatever organizational unit underlies cognitive operations.

No one quite knows why related ideas in our minds tend to cohere and form categories. Since the time of Aristotle various "laws of association" have been proposed to account for this important property of the mind. The clusters formed do not need to correspond to outer reality as found in nature. For example, there are no such things as elves, but I have a firm category in my mind concerning them. Similarly, I have firm categories concerning groups of mankind, although there is no guarantee that my categories correspond to fact.

To be rational a category must be built primarily around the *essential* attributes of all objects that can be correctly included within the category. Thus all houses are structures marked by some degree of habitability (past or present). Each house will also have some nonessential attributes. Some are large, some small, some wooden, brick, cheap or expensive, old or new, painted white or gray. These are not the essential or "defining attributes" of a house.

Similarly, to be a Jew, a person must possess a certain defining attribute. It is somewhat difficult, as we saw in Chapter 7, to tell just what this attribute is, but it has to do with a person's connection by descent (or conversion) to people having a Judaic religious tradition. There is no other essential (defining) attribute of a Jew.

Nature unfortunately has given us no sure means of making certain that our categories are composed exclusively, or even primarily, of the defining attributes. Thus a child many think falsely that all houses must have, as his house has, two floors, a gas refrigerator, and a television set. Such occasional attributes are not at all necessary. In fact, so confusing are they to the formation of a dependable category that psychologists sometimes call them "noisy" attributes.

Returning to the concept of Jew. There is, as we have said, probably only one central defining attribute. But there are many other ascribed attributes that may for various reasons enter into our category, making it more or less "noisy." A few of these attributes may have some degree of probability. The chances are appreciably greater than zero that a given Jew will have an Armenoid appearance, be in trade or a profession, and be relatively well educated. These attributes, as we saw in Chapter 7, constitute true (but by no means essential) group characteristics. Still other attributes that we find in our category may be completely false and noisy, e.g., Jews are bankers, conspirators, and warmongers.

But unfortunately nature does not tell us which attributes are defining, which merely probable, and which totally fallacious. To our minds one attribute may be as valid as another. To put the matter differently, we ordinarily fail to detect which group qualities that compose our category fall on a J-curve distribution, which constitute a rare-zero differential, and which are purely imaginary. Psychologically, though not logically, they are to us equivalent.

Now obviously some categories are more flexible (differentiated) than others. When they are inflexible we may, following Postman, call them "monopolistic." [8] They are so powerful and so rigid, and the attributes included so invariant, that all contradictory evidence is rejected. The mind, in respect to this particular category, is closed. Furthermore, the category is "confirmed" by small or imaginary bits of evidence. The individual selects and interprets whatever he sees or hears in such a way as to fit and to strengthen the monopolistic category. A confirmed anti-Semite will reject or discount (as "an exception") every particle of evidence friendly to Jews, and welcome every particle that confirms his hostile view.

Not all categories have such a granitic character. Some are flexible and discriminated. Many people find, for example, that the more they know about a group the less likely they are to form monopolistic categories. For example, most Americans know that any fixed hypotheses about "Americans" are likely to be a poor guide to conduct. We know, for example, that not all Americans are dollar-worshippers, breezy, or vulgar. Nor are they all friendly and hospitable. On the other hand, Europeans, who know us less well, often view us as one big monolithic unit having all these qualities.

When we hold to a category tentatively and make allowance for variation and subdivision, we may speak of a *differentiated category*.

A differentiated category is the opposite of a stereotype. An example of a differentiated category is indicated by the following bit of rumination.

> I've known many Catholics. At first, when I was a child, I thought of them all as ignorant and superstitious people much below me in social standing and intelligence. I used to run past their church and never would play with Catholic children or buy at a "Catholic" store. I know now that there are only a few traits that Catholics have in common. They conform to certain beliefs and practices. But apart from this limited uniformity I have learned through subsequent acquaintance that there are so many kinds of Catholic people that I cannot include in my concept any attributes excepting only religious adherence. There is, I realize, some probability that there will be proportionately more poor people, urban ·dwellers, and foreign born among Catholics than among Protestants. Also I know that many will have attended parochial rather than public schools. But as for virtually all other qualities I cannot see that they differ from any other group that I can name. Therefore in only a few respects can I regard Catholics as a group.

The Principle of Least Effort

As a rule monopolistic categories are easier to form and to hold than are differentiated categories. While most of us have learned to be critical and open-minded in *certain* regions of experience we obey the law of least effort in others.[9] A doctor will not be swept away by folk generalizations concerning arthritis, snake bite, or the efficacy of aspirin. But he may be content with overgeneralizations concerning politics, social insurance, or Mexicans. Life is just too short to have differentiated concepts about everything. A *few* pathways are enough for us to walk in. Having learned that a given make of automobile is good enough for me, I then class all others as outside the pale, and my life is accordingly simplified and more efficient. The principle clearly applies to group relations.

It is not necessary for all simplifications to be malign. I may think the Swedes are all clean, honest, diligent. I can regulate my dealings with them by this favorable view (and some of the attributes may, of course, have some probability of being accurate). Our point is merely that life becomes easier when the category is not differentiated. To consider every member of a group as endowed with the same traits saves us the pains of dealing with them as individuals.

One consequence of least effort in group categorizing is that a *belief in essence* develops. There is an inherent "Jewishness" in every Jew. The "soul of the Oriental," "Negro blood," Hitler's "Aryanism," "the peculiar genius of America," "the logical Frenchman," "the passionate Latin"—all represent a belief in essence. A mysterious mana (for good or ill) resides in a group, all of its members partaking thereof. In the following lines Kipling was indulging in a belief in essences concerning the Asiatic and African people whose lands and labor Britain found it convenient to appropriate.

> Your new-caught, sullen peoples,
> Half-devil and half-child.

Kipling's way of thinking made life momentarily easy for him and for many Britishers who, adopting it, did not have to adjust to the individual differences among their colonial subjects, nor to the complex ethics involved. The disintegration of the British Empire in recent years is due in large part to the Kipling error of regarding great populations in an undifferentiated fashion. A monopolistic category may be successful for the time being. But in the long run it may bring disaster.

The ultimate manifestation of the principle of least effort is found in *two-valued* judgments.

A young boy, from approximately the age of four until ten, had the habit of asking his father many times a day, e.g., after every radio report of news, "Is that good or bad?" Lacking his own standards of judgment the child wished the parent to simplify this confusing world by putting every happening into one of two value categories.

Not everyone outgrows the little boy's stage. It is tempting to fit all categories into the superordinates of "good" or "bad." To do so simplifies greatly our adjustment to life. Simplification comes likewise if we can subscribe to other kinds of two-valued propositions: that there is a right way and a wrong way to do everything; that all women are either pure or bad; that black is black, white is white, and there are no shades of gray.

In Chapter 5 we reported that people who dislike one out-group tend to dislike all other out-groups. Here is a crowning example of two-valued logic. In-groups are good; out-groups are bad. It is as simple as that.

The Dynamics of Cognition in the Prejudiced Personality

We come now to what is perhaps the most momentous discovery of psychological research in the field of prejudice. To state it broadly: the cognitive processes of prejudiced people are *in general* different from the cognitive processes of tolerant people.   In other words, a person's prejudice is unlikely to be merely a specific attitude toward a specific group; it is more likely to be a reflection of his whole habit of thinking about the world he lives in.

For one thing, research shows that the prejudiced person is given to two-valued judgments *in general*.   He dichotomizes when he thinks of nature, of law, of morals, of men and women, as well as when he thinks of ethnic groups.

For another, he is uncomfortable with differentiated categories; he prefers them to be monopolistic.   Thus his habits of thought are rigid.   He does not change his mental set easily, but persists in old ways of reasoning—whether or not this reasoning has anything to do with human groups.   He has a marked need for definiteness; he cannot tolerate ambiguity in his plans.   When he forms categories he does not seek out and emphasize the true "defining" attribute, but admits many "noisy" attributes to equal prominence.

In Chapter 25 we shall discuss "The Prejudiced Personality," and shall there set forth these findings in greater detail.   We shall see how the dynamics of prejudice, the dynamics of cognition, and the dynamics of emotion are woven into a single and unitary style of life.

The opposite pattern is equally valid.   In Chapter 27 we shall examine "The Tolerant Personality," and shall there see also that the cognitive process is marked by greater differentiation of categories, by greater tolerance for ambiguity, by a greater readiness to admit ignorance, and by a habitual skepticism concerning monopolistic categories.

We are not, of course, implying that there are only two types of people (to do so would be unjustified dichotomization).   There are all degrees and shadings of the prejudice-syndrome and of the tolerance-syndrome.   What we are saying is not that mixed types of personality do not occur, but rather that whenever prejudice is found it is unlikely to stand isolated from the process of cognition in general, or from the dynamics of the person's whole style of life.

Conclusions

This chapter, together with Chapter 2, presents an elementary psychology of cognitive processes.   We have established the following propositions:

Impressions that are similar, or that occur together, or that are spoken of together, especially if a label is attached (see the following chapter), tend to cohere into categories (generalizations, concepts).

All categories engender meaning upon the world. Like paths in a forest, they give order to our life-space.

While they are often modified through experience when they no longer serve our purposes, still the principle of least effort inclines us to hold to coarse and early-formed generalizations as long as they can possibly be made to serve our purposes.

Categories normally assimilate as much as possible into their unitary structure.

They tend to resist change. The device of admitting "exceptions" serves to preserve the category (refencing).

Categories help us to identify a new object or person, and to expect from it (him) a certain kind of behavior to accord with our preconceptions.

Since categories may comprise a blend of knowledge (kernel of truth) as well as false ideas and emotional tone, they may reflect both directed and autistic thinking.

When evidence conflicts with categories, it may be distorted (through selection, accentuation, interpretation) so as to seem to confirm the category.

A rational category is built around the essential or defining attributes of the object. But nonessential and "noisy" attributes often enter into the category, lessening its correspondence to outer reality.

An ethnic prejudice is a category concerning a group of people, not based on defining attributes primarily, but including various "noisy" attributes, and leading to disparagement of the group as a whole.

When we think about causation, especially about causes for our own frustrations and ills, we tend to think anthropomorphically; i.e., we blame a human agency, often minority groups.

Categories that are two-valued, especially those that declare objects within a category to be all good or all bad, are easily formed, and readily control our thinking about ethnic groups.

It is characteristic of the prejudiced mentality that it forms in all areas of experience categories that are monopolistic, undifferentiated, two-valued, and rigid. In general, the opposite tendencies seem to mark the cognitive processes of tolerant people.

NOTES AND REFERENCES

1. A. ADLER. *Understanding Human Nature.* New York: Permabooks, 1949, 46.

2. J. S. BRUNER AND L. POSTMAN. An approach to social perception.

Chapter 10 in W. DENNIS (ED.), *Current Trends in Social Psychology*. Pittsburgh: Univ. of Pittsburgh Press, 1948.

3. E. G. MALHERBE. *Race Attitudes and Education*. Hornlé Lecture, 1946. Johannesburg: Institute of Race Relations.

4. From a letter published in *America in Danger*, June 15, 1942.

5. G. HUMPHREY. *Directed Thinking*. New York: Dodd, Mead, 1948. See also: Chapter 2, Footnote 2.

6. S. B. SELLS. *Unpublished research*. See also "The atmosphere effect," *Archives of Psychology*, 1936, No. 200.

7. The extent to which we tend to anthropomorphize even such an impersonal pattern as the movement of lines is shown in an experiment by FRITZ HEIDER, Social perception and phenomenal causality, *Psychological Review*, 1944, **51**, 358-374. Watching lines move in a brief motion picture presentation, nearly all subjects told a *human story* of some type that the mechanically moving lines seemed to them to represent. To the watchers the moving lines and geometrical figures seemed to stand for persons with motives, doing things to one another.

8. L. POSTMAN. Toward a general theory of cognition. In J. H. ROHRER AND M. SHERIF (EDS.), *Social Psychology at the Crossroads*, New York: Harper, 1951.

9. For an extended treatment of the law of least effort see G. K. ZIPF, *Human Behavior and the Principle of Least Effort*. Cambridge: Addison-Wesley, 1949.

CHAPTER 11

LINGUISTIC FACTORS

NOUNS THAT CUT SLICES—EMOTIONALLY TONED LABELS—
THE COMMUNIST LABEL—VERBAL REALISM AND SYMBOL PHOBIA

Without words we should scarcely be able to form categories at all. A dog perhaps forms rudimentary generalizations, such as small-boys-are-to-be-avoided—but this concept runs its course on the conditioned reflex level, and does not become the object of thought as such. In order to hold a generalization in mind for reflection and recall, for identification and for action, we need to fix it in words. Without words our world would be, as William James said, an "empirical sand-heap."

Nouns That Cut Slices

In the empirical world of human beings there are some two and a half billion grains of sand corresponding to our category "the human race." We cannot possibly deal with so many separate entities in our thought, nor can we individualize even among the hundreds whom we encounter in our daily round. We must group them, form clusters. We welcome, therefore, the names that help us to perform the clustering.

The most important property of a noun is that it brings many grains of sand into a single pail, disregarding the fact that the same grains might have fitted just as appropriately into another pail. To state the matter technically, a noun *abstracts* from a concrete reality some one feature and assembles different concrete realities only with respect to this one feature. The very act of classifying forces us to overlook all other features, many of which might offer a sounder basis than the rubric we select. Irving Lee gives the following example:

> I knew a man who had lost the use of both eyes. He was called a "blind man." He could also be called an expert typist, a conscientious worker, a good student, a careful listener, a man who wanted a job. But he couldn't get a job in the department store order room where employees sat and typed orders which came over the telephone. The personnel man was impatient to get the interview over. "But you're a blind man," he kept saying, and one could almost feel his silent assumption that somehow

178

the incapacity in one aspect made the man incapable in every other. So blinded by the label was the interviewer that he could not be persuaded to look beyond it.[1]

Some labels, such as "blind man," are exceedingly salient and powerful. They tend to prevent alternative classification, or even cross-classification. Ethnic labels are often of this type, particularly if they refer to some highly visible feature, e.g., Negro, Oriental. They resemble the labels that point to some outstanding incapacity—*feeble-minded, cripple, blind man.* Let us call such symbols "labels of primary potency." These symbols act like shrieking sirens, deafening us to all finer discriminations that we might otherwise perceive. Even though the blindness of one man and the darkness of pigmentation of another may be defining attributes for some purposes, they are irrelevant and "noisy" for others.

LABELS OF PRIMARY POTENCY

FIG. 10. The effect of linguistic symbols upon perception and thinking about individuals.

Most people are unaware of this basic law of language—that every label applied to a given person refers properly only to one aspect of his nature. You may correctly say that a certain man is *human, a philanthropist, a Chinese, a physician, an athlete.* A given person may be all of these; but the chances are that *Chinese* stands out in your mind as the symbol of primary potency. Yet neither this nor any other classificatory label can refer to the whole of a man's nature. (Only his proper name can do so.)

Thus each label we use, especially those of primary potency, distracts our attention from concrete reality. The living, breathing, complex individual—the ultimate unit of human nature—is lost to sight. As in Fig. 10, the label magnifies one attribute out of all proportion to its true significance, and masks other important attributes of the individual.

As pointed out in Chapters 2 and 10, a category, once formed with the aid of a symbol of primary potency, tends to attract more attributes than it should. The category labeled *Chinese* comes to signify not only ethnic membership but also reticence, impassivity, poverty, treachery. To be sure, as shown in Chapter 7, there may be genuine ethnic-linked traits, making for a certain *probability* that the member of an ethnic stock may have these attributes. But our cognitive process is not cautious. The labeled category, as we have seen, includes indiscriminately the defining attribute, probable attributes, and wholly fanciful, nonexistent attributes.

Even proper names—which ought to invite us to look at the individual person—may act like symbols of primary potency, especially if they arouse ethnic associations. Mr. Greenberg is a person, but since his name is Jewish, it activates in the hearer his entire category of Jews-as-a-whole. An ingenious experiment performed by Razran shows this point clearly, and at the same time demonstrates how a proper name, acting like an ethnic symbol, may bring with it an avalanche of stereotypes.[2]

Thirty photographs of college girls were shown on a screen to 150 students. The subjects rated the girls on a scale from one to five for *beauty, intelligence, character, ambition, general likability*. Two months later the same subjects were asked to rate the same photographs and fifteen additional ones (introduced to complicate the memory factor). This time five of the original photographs were given Jewish surnames (Cohen, Kantor, etc.), five Italian (Valenti, etc.), and five Irish (O'Brien, etc.); and the remaining girls were given names chosen from the signers of the Declaration of Independence and from the Social Register (Davis, Adams, Clark, etc.).

When Jewish names were attached to photographs there occurred the following changes in ratings:

> decrease in liking
> decrease in character
> decrease in beauty
> increase in intelligence
> increase in ambition

For those photographs given Italian names there occurred:

> decrease in liking
> decrease in character
> decrease in beauty
> decrease in intelligence

Thus a mere proper name leads to prejudgments of personal attributes. The individual is fitted to the prejudiced ethnic category, and not judged in his own right.

While the Irish names also brought about depreciated judgment, the depreciation was not as great as in the case of the Jews and Italians. The falling of likability of the "Jewish girls" was twice as great as for "Italians" and five times as great as for "Irish." We note, however, that the "Jewish" photographs caused higher ratings in *intelligence* and in *ambition*. Not all stereotypes of out-groups are unfavorable.

The anthropologist, Margaret Mead, has suggested that labels of primary potency lose some of their force when they are changed from nouns into adjectives. To speak of a Negro soldier, a Catholic teacher, or a Jewish artist calls attention to the fact that some other group classifications are just as legitimate as the racial or religious. If George Johnson is spoken of not only as a Negro but also as a *soldier,* we have at least two attributes to know him by, and two are more accurate than one. To depict him truly as an individual, of course, we should have to name many more attributes. It is a useful suggestion that we designate ethnic and religious membership where possible with *adjectives* rather than with *nouns.*

Emotionally Toned Labels

Many categories have two kinds of labels—one less emotional and one more emotional. Ask yourself how you feel, and what thoughts you have, when you read the words *school teacher,* and then *school marm.* Certainly the second phrase calls up something more strict, more ridiculous, more disagreeable than the former. Here are four innocent letters: m-a-r-m. But they make us shudder a bit, laugh a bit, and scorn a bit. They call up an image of a spare, humorless, irritable old maid. They do not tell us that she is an individual human being with sorrows and troubles of her own. They force her instantly into a rejective category.

In the ethnic sphere even plain labels such as Negro, Italian, Jew, Catholic, Irish-American, French-Canadian may have emotional tone for a reason that we shall soon explain. But they all have their higher key equivalents: nigger, wop, kike, papist, harp, cannuck. When these labels are employed we can be almost certain that the speaker *intends* not only to characterize the person's membership, but also to disparage and reject him.

Quite apart from the insulting intent that lies behind the use of certain labels, there is also an inherent ("physiognomic") handicap in many terms designating ethnic membership. For example, the proper names characteristic of certain ethnic memberships strike us as absurd. (We compare them, of course, with what is familiar and therefore "right.") Chinese names are short and silly; Polish names intrinsically difficult and outlandish. Unfamiliar dialects strike us as ludicrous. Foreign dress (which, of course, is a visual ethnic symbol) seems unnecessarily queer.

But of all these "physiognomic" handicaps the reference to color, clearly implied in certain symbols, is the greatest. The word Negro comes from the Latin *niger*, meaning black. In point of fact, no Negro has a black complexion, but by comparison with other blonder stocks, he has come to be known as a "black man." Unfortunately *black* in the English language is a word having a preponderance of sinister connotations: the outlook is black, blackball, blackguard, blackhearted, black death, blacklist, blackmail, Black Hand. In his novel *Moby Dick*, Herman Melville considers at length the remarkably morbid connotations of black and the remarkably virtuous connotations of white.

Nor is the ominous flavor of black confined to the English language. A cross-cultural study reveals that the semantic significance of black is more or less universally the same. Among certain Siberian tribes, members of a privileged clan call themselves "white bones," and refer to all others as "black bones." Even among Uganda Negroes there is some evidence for a white god at the apex of the theocratic hierarchy; certain it is that a white cloth, signifying purity, is used to ward off evil spirits and disease.[3]

There is thus an implied value-judgment in the very concept of *white race* and *black race*. One might also study the numerous unpleasant connotations of *yellow*, and their possible bearing on our conception of the people of the Orient.

Such reasoning should not be carried too far, since there are undoubtedly, in various contexts, pleasant associations with both black and yellow. Black velvet is agreeable, so too are chocolate and coffee. Yellow tulips are well liked; the sun and moon are radiantly yellow. Yet it is true that "color" words are used with chauvinistic overtones more than most people realize. There is certainly condescension indicated in many familiar phrases: dark as a nigger's pocket, darktown strutters, white hope (a term originated when a white contender was sought against the Negro heavyweight champion, Jack Johnson), the white man's burden, the yellow peril, black boy. Scores of everyday phrases are stamped with the flavor of prejudice, whether the user knows it or not.[4]

We spoke of the fact that even the most proper and sedate labels for minority groups sometimes seem to exude a negative flavor. In many contexts and situations the very terms *French-Canadian, Mexican,* or *Jew*, correct and nonmalicious though they are, sound a bit opprobrious. The reason is that they are labels of social deviants. Especially in a culture where uniformity is prized, the name of *any* deviant carries with it *ipso facto* a negative value-judgment. Words like *insane, alcoholic, pervert* are presumably neutral designations of a human condition, but they are more: they are finger-pointings at deviance. Minority groups are deviants, and for this reason, from the very outset, the most innocent labels in many situations imply a shading of disrepute. When we wish to highlight the deviance and denigrate it still further we use words of a higher emotional key: crackpot, soak, pansy, greaser, Okie, nigger, harp, kike.

Members of minority groups are often understandably sensitive to names given them. Not only do they object to deliberately insulting epithets, but sometimes see evil intent where none exists. Often the word Negro is spelled with a small *n*, occasionally as a studied insult, more often from ignorance. (The term is not cognate with white, which is not capitalized, but rather with Caucasian, which is.) Terms like "mulatto" or "octoroon" cause hard feeling because of the condescension with which they have often been used in the past. Sex differentiations are objectionable, since they seem doubly to emphasize ethnic difference: why speak of Jewess and not of Protestantess, or of Negress and not of whitess? Similar overemphasis is implied in terms like Chinaman or Scotchman; why not American man? Grounds for misunderstanding lie in the fact that minority group members are sensitive to such shadings, while majority members may employ them unthinkingly.

The Communist Label

Until we label an out-group it does not clearly exist in our minds. Take the curiously vague situation that we often meet when a person wishes to locate responsibility on the shoulders of some out-group whose nature he cannot specify. In such a case he usually employs the pronoun "they" without an antecedent. "Why don't they make these sidewalks wider?" "I hear they are going to build a factory in this town and hire a lot of foreigners." "I won't pay this tax bill; they can just whistle for their money." If asked "who?" the speaker is likely to grow confused and embarrassed. The common use of the orphaned pronoun *they* teaches us that people often want and need to designate out-groups (usually for the purpose of venting hostility) even when they have no clear conception of the out-group in question. And so long as the target of wrath remains vague and ill-defined specific prejudice cannot crystallize around it. To have enemies we need labels.

Until relatively recently—strange as it may seem—there was no agreed-upon symbol for *communist*. The word, of course, existed but it had no special emotional connotation, and did not designate a public enemy. Even when, after World War I, there was a growing feeling of economic and social menace in this country, there was no agreement as to the actual source of the menace.

A content analysis of the *Boston Herald* for the year 1920 turned up the following list of labels. Each was used in a context implying some threat. Hysteria had overspread the country, as it did after World War II. Someone must be responsible for the postwar malaise, rising prices, uncertainty. There must be a villain. But in 1920 the villain was impartially designated by reporters and editorial writers with the following symbols:

> alien, agitator, anarchist, apostle of bomb and torch, Bolshevik, communist, communist laborite, conspirator, emissary of false promise, extremist, foreigner, hyphenated-American, incendiary, IWW, parlor anarchist, parlor pink, parlor socialist, plotter, radical, red, revolutionary, Russian agitator, socialist, Soviet, syndicalist, traitor, undesirable.

From this excited array we note that the *need* for an enemy (someone to serve as a focus for discontent and jitters) was considerably more apparent than the precise *identity* of the enemy. At any rate, there was no clearly agreed upon label. Perhaps partly for this reason the hysteria abated. Since no clear category of "communism" existed there was no true focus for the hostility.

But following World War II this collection of vaguely interchangeable labels became fewer in number and more commonly agreed upon. The out-group menace came to be designated almost always as *communist* or *red*. In 1920 the threat, lacking a clear label, was vague; after 1945 both symbol and thing became more definite. Not that people knew precisely what they meant when they said "communist," but with the aid of the term they were at least able to point consistently to *something* that inspired fear. The term developed the power of signifying menace and led to various repressive measures against anyone to whom the label was rightly or wrongly attached.

Logically, the label should apply to specifiable defining attributes, such as members of the Communist Party, or people whose allegiance is with the Russian system, or followers, historically, of Karl Marx. But the label came in for far more extensive use.

What seems to have happened is approximately as follows. Having suffered through a period of war and being acutely aware of devastating revolutions abroad, it is natural that most people should be upset, dreading to lose their possessions, annoyed by high taxes, seeing customary moral and religious values threatened, and dreading worse disasters to come. Seeking an explanation for this unrest, a single identifiable enemy is wanted. It is not enough to designate "Russia" or some other distant land. Nor is it satisfactory to fix blame on "changing social conditions." What is needed is a human agent (cf. Chapter 10) near at hand: someone in Washington, someone in our schools, in our factories, in our neighborhood. If we *feel* an immediate threat, we reason, there must be a near-lying danger. It is, we conclude, communism, not only in Russia but also in America, at our doorstep, in our government, in our churches, in our colleges, in our neighborhood.

Are we saying that hostility toward communism is prejudice? Not necessarily. There are certainly phases of the dispute wherein realistic social conflict is involved. American values (e.g., respect for the person) and totalitarian values as represented in Soviet practice are intrinsically at odds. A realistic opposition in some form will occur. Prejudice enters only when the defining attributes of "communist" grow imprecise, when anyone who favors any form of social change is called a communist. People who fear social change are the ones most likely to affix the label to any persons or practices that seem to them threatening.

For them the category is undifferentiated. It includes books, movies, preachers, teachers who utter what for them are uncongenial thoughts. If evil befalls—perhaps forest fires or a factory explosion —it is due to communist saboteurs. The category becomes monopolistic, covering almost anything that is uncongenial. On the floor of the House of Representatives in 1946, Representative Rankin called James Roosevelt a communist. Congressman Outland replied with psychological acumen, "Apparently everyone who disagrees with Mr. Rankin is a communist."

When differentiated thinking is at a low ebb—as it is in times of social crises—there is a magnification of two-valued logic. Things are perceived as either inside or outside a moral order. What is outside is likely to be called "communist." Correspondingly— and here is where damage is done—whatever is called communist (however erroneously) is immediately cast outside the moral order.

This associative mechanism places enormous power in the hands of a demagogue. For several years Senator McCarthy managed to discredit many citizens who thought differently from himself by the simple device of calling them communists. Few people were able to see through this trick and many reputations were ruined. But the famous senator has no monopoly on the device. As reported in the *Boston Herald* on November 1, 1946, Representative Joseph Martin, Republican leader in the House, ended his election campaign against his Democratic opponent by saying, "The people will vote tomorrow between chaos, confusion, bankruptcy, state socialism or communism, and the preservation of our American life, with all its freedom and its opportunities." Such an array of emotional labels placed his opponent outside the accepted moral order. Martin was re-elected.

In Chapter 14 we shall consider further the distinction between realistic social conflict and prejudice, and in Chapter 26 shall examine additional devices used by demagogues who for their own ends endeavor to confuse the distinctions.

Not everyone, of course, is taken in. Demagogy, when it goes too far, meets with ridicule. Elizabeth Dilling's book, *The Red Network*, was so exaggerated in its two-valued logic that it· was shrugged off by many people with a smile. One reader remarked, "Apparently if you step off the sidewalk with your left foot you're a communist." But it is not easy in times of social strain and hysteria to keep one's balance, and to resist the tendency of a verbal symbol to manufacture large and fanciful categories of prejudiced thinking.

Verbal Realism and Symbol Phobia

Most individuals rebel at being labeled, especially if the label is uncomplimentary. Very few are willing to be called *fascistic, socialistic,* or *anti-Semitic.* Unsavory labels may apply to others; but not to us.

An illustration of the craving that people have to attach favorable symbols to themselves is seen in the community where white people banded together to force out a Negro family that had moved in. They called themselves "Neighborly Endeavor" and chose as their motto the Golden Rule. One of the first acts of this symbol-sanctified band was to sue the man who sold property to Negroes. They then flooded the house which another Negro couple planned to occupy. Such were the acts performed under the banner of the Golden Rule.

Studies made by Stagner[5] and by Hartmann[6] show that a person's political attitudes may in fact entitle him to be called a fascist or a socialist, and yet he will emphatically repudiate the unsavory label, and fail to endorse any movement or candidate that overtly accepts them. In short, there is a *symbol phobia* that corresponds to *symbol realism.* We are more inclined to the former when we ourselves are concerned, though we are much less critical when epithets of "fascist," "communist," "blind man," "school marm" are applied to others.

When symbols provoke strong emotions they are sometimes regarded no longer as symbols, but as actual things. The expressions "son of a bitch" and "liar" are in our culture frequently regarded as "fighting words." Softer and more subtle expressions of contempt may be accepted. But in these particular cases, the epithet itself must be "taken back." We certainly do not change our opponent's attitude by making him take back a word, but it seems somehow important that the word itself be eradicated.

Such verbal realism may reach extreme lengths.

The City Council of Cambridge, Massachusetts, unanimously passed a resolution (December, 1939) making it illegal "to possess, harbor, sequester, introduce or transport, within the city limits, any book, map, magazine, newspaper, pamphlet, handbill or circular containing the words Lenin or Leningrad.[7]

Such naiveté in confusing language with reality is hard to comprehend unless we recall that word-magic plays an appreciable part in human thinking. The following examples, like the one preceding, are taken from Hayakawa.

The Malagasy soldier must eschew kidneys, because in the Malagasy language the word for kidney is the same as that for "shot"; so shot he would certainly be if he ate a kidney.

In May, 1937, a state senator of New York bitterly opposed a bill for the control of syphilis because "the innocence of children might be corrupted by a widespread use of the term. . . . This particular word creates a shudder in every decent woman and decent man."

This tendency to reify words underscores the close cohesion that exists between category and symbol. Just the mention of "communist," "Negro," "Jew," "England," "Democrats," will send some people into a panic of fear or a frenzy of anger. Who can say whether it is the word or the thing that annoys them? The label is an intrinsic part of any monopolistic category. Hence to liberate a person from ethnic or political prejudice it is necessary at the same time to liberate him from word fetishism. This fact is well known to students of general semantics who tell us that prejudice is due in large part to verbal realism and to symbol phobia. Therefore any program for the reduction of prejudice must include a large measure of semantic therapy.

NOTES AND REFERENCES

1. I. J. Lee. How do you talk about people? *Freedom Pamphlet.* New York: Anti-Defamation League, 1950, 15.

2. G. RAZRAN. Ethnic dislikes and stereotypes: a laboratory study. *Journal of Abnormal and Social Psychology*, 1950, **45**, 7-27.

3. C. E. OSGOOD. The nature and measurement of meaning. *Psychological Bulletin*, 1952, **49**, 226.

4. L. L. BROWN. Words and white chauvinism. *Masses and Mainstream*, 1950, **3**, 3-11. See also: *Prejudice Won't Hide! A Guide for Developing a Language of Equality.* San Francisco: California Federation for Civic Unity, 1950.

5. R. STAGNER. Fascist attitudes: an exploratory study. *Journal of Social Psychology*, 1936, **7**, 309-319; Fascist attitudes: their determining conditions, *ibid.*, 438-454.

6. G. HARTMANN. The contradiction between the feeling-tone of political party names and public response to their platforms. *Journal of Social Psychology*, 1936, **7**, 336-357.

7. S. I. HAYAKAWA. *Language in Action.* New York: Harcourt, Brace, 1941, 29.

CHAPTER 12

STEREOTYPES IN OUR CULTURE

Why do so many people admire Abraham Lincoln? They may
tell you it is because he was thrifty, hardworking, eager for knowledge, ambitious, devoted to the rights of the average man, and emi
nently successful in climbing the ladder of opportunity.

Why do so many people dislike the Jews? They may tell you it
is because they are thrifty, hardworking, eager for knowledge, ambitious, devoted to the rights of the average man, and eminently
successful in climbing the ladder of opportunity.

Of course, the *terms* used may be less laudatory in the case of the
Jews: one may say they are tight-fisted, overambitious, pushing, and
radical. But the fact remains that, essentially, the personality qualities admired in Abraham Lincoln are deplored in Jews.

What we learn from this example (suggested by Robert K. Merton) is that stereotypes are not in themselves a full explanation
for rejection. They are primarily images within a category invoked
by the individual to justify either love-prejudice or hate-prejudice.
They play an important part in prejudice but are not the whole
story.

Stereotypes versus Group Traits

Now an image manifestly comes from *somewhere*. It may, and
normally should, come from repeated experience with some class
of objects. If it is a generalized judgment based on a certain probability that an object of the class will possess a given attribute, we
would not call the judgment a stereotype. As shown in Chapter 7,
not all estimates of probable ethnic or national character are fictitious. A verifiable assessment of a group is not the same as the
selecting, sharpening, and fictionizing of a stereotype.

It is possible for a stereotype to grow in defiance of *all* evidence.

For example, in Fresno County, California, at one time the
prevailing stereotype of Armenians held them to be "dishonest,
lying, deceitful." La Piere made a study to determine whether

189

there was objective evidence to justify this belief. He found that the records of the Merchant's Association gave Armenians as good credit ratings as those received by the other groups. Moreover, Armenians applied less often for charity and appeared less frequently in legal cases.[1]

One wonders how, with all evidence so contradictory, the stereotype of "dishonest, lying, deceitful" could have arisen. Although we cannot say for certain, it may be that the physical Armenoid features resembled those of some Jews, and the attributes commonly attributed to the Jew were transferred to the Armenian. Or it may be that a few people once had disagreeable experiences with the early Armenian peddlers in the vicinity. Through selective memory and sharpening these encounters were overgeneralized. In any case, here seems to be a stereotype with *no* ascertainable basis in fact.

Other stereotypes may, of course, have a kernel of truth. It is historically true that certain Jews favored the crucifixion of Christ. The stereotype sharpens this fact until the entire Jewish group in modern times becomes known as "Christ killers." Again, it seems to be true, as we saw in Chapter 7, that according to overlapping normal curves, the average intelligence (as determined by culture-bound intelligence tests) is slightly higher for Jewish than for gentile children, and slightly lower for Negro than for white children. But this verifiable difference is not great enough to sustain the stereotype that "Jews are clever" or that "Negroes are stupid."

Thus some stereotypes are totally unsupported by facts; others develop from a sharpening and overgeneralization of facts. Once formed, they cause their possessor to view future evidence in terms of the available categories (Chapter 2). Furnished with suitable stereotypes, I shall be sensitized to signs of cleverness in Jews and of stupidity in Negroes, to signs of communism in labor unions, and to signs of fascism in Roman Catholics.

The possession of stereotypes may interfere with even the simplest rational judgments. Lasker cites the case of an item in a silent reading test for children.

> Aladdin was the son of a poor tailor. He lived in Peking, the capital city of China. He was always idle and lazy and liked to play better than to work. What kind of a boy was he: Indian; Negro; Chinese; French; or Dutch?

The majority of the children in a class replied *Negro*.[2]
In this case it is quite likely that the children were expressing no

animosity against Negroes. They were simply disclosing, at the expense of their reasoning ability, a highly available stereotype.

Stereotypes are by no means always negative. They may exist together with a favorable attitude.

> A veteran was telling about his excellent lieutenant, a Jew. No words of praise were too warm. "He took pictures of me and a buddy of mine the day before he was killed. . . . He was really white. . . . He took good care of his men. He saw to it they had the things they needed. They had cigarettes all the time when there weren't many around. *That's the Jew in him*—he was good at getting things like that. He'd do anything for his men and they'd do anything for him."

> Another veteran said, "I take off my hat to the Jews. They know how to do things and get things, despite handicaps. I certainly would be happy if my daughter married a Jew. They are good providers, loyal to their wife and children, and don't drink."[3]

These cases are interesting in their stereotyped belief in a Jewish "essence" without at the same time betokening the animosity that so often accompanies such belief.

Stereotype Defined

Whether favorable or unfavorable, *a stereotype is an exaggerated belief associated with a category. Its function is to justify (rationalize) our conduct in relation to that category.*

In Chapter 2 we examined the nature of categories; in Chapter 10 we explored the cognitive organization that builds itself around categories. In the preceding chapter we stressed the importance of the linguistic tag that designates our categories. At the present time we are completing the story by talking about the ideational content (the image) that is bound in with the category. Thus category, cognitive organization, linguistic label, and stereotype are all aspects of a complex mental process.

More than a generation ago Walter Lippmann wrote of stereotypes, calling them simply "pictures in our heads." To Mr. Lippmann goes credit for establishing the conception in modern social psychology.[4] His treatment, however excellent on the descriptive side, was somewhat loose in theory. For one thing he tends to confuse stereotype with category.

A stereotype is not identical with a category; it is rather a fixed idea that accompanies the category. For example, the category "Negro" can be held in mind simply as a neutral, factual, nonevaluative concept, pertaining merely to a racial stock. Stereotype enters when, and if, the initial category is freighted with "pictures" and judgments of the Negro as musical, lazy, superstitious, or what not.

A stereotype, then, is not a category, but often exists as a fixed mark upon the category. If I say, "All lawyers are crooked," I am expressing a stereotyped generalization about a category. The stereotype is not in itself the core of the concept. It operates, however, in such a way as to prevent differentiated thinking about the concept.

The stereotype acts both as a justificatory device for categorical acceptance or rejection of a group, and as a screening or selective device to maintain simplicity in perception and in thinking.

Once again we point to the complicating issue of true group characteristics. A stereotype need not be altogether false. If we think of the Irish as more prone to alcoholism than, say, Jews, we are making a correct judgment in terms of probability. Yet if, as some say, "Jews don't drink," or "the Irish are whiskey-soaked" we are manifestly exaggerating the facts, and building up an unjustified stereotype. We can distinguish between a valid generalization and a stereotype only if we have solid data concerning the existence of (the probability of) true group differences.

Stereotypes concerning the Jew

Many studies have been made of the "pictures" that non-Jews have of Jews. In 1932 Katz and Braly found that college students ascribed the folowing traits to Jews:[5]

> shrewd
> mercenary
> industrious
> grasping
> intelligent
> ambitious
> sly

With somewhat less agreement, the following traits were also mentioned:

> loyal to family ties
> persistent
> talkative
> aggressive
> very religious

This study conducted in 1932 was repeated in 1950. The change in stereotypes over time is discussed in a later section of this chapter. Interviewing 150 veterans in Chicago, Bettelheim and Janowitz discovered the following accusations against Jews approximately in this order of frequency:[6]

They are clannish.
Money is their God.
They control everything.
   "Everybody blames the Jews.   They control it all.   They are in the right places—in the offices and in politics.   They're the ones running things . . .   They have power all over the world —in all the industries.   They own the radio, banks, movies, and stores.   Marshall Field and all the big stores are Jewish."
They use underhanded business methods.
   "They're too tight.   If they owe you money, you have to fight to get paid."
They don't do manual work.
   "They own the factories and get white people to work for them."

Somewhat less frequently mentioned:

They are overbearing.
They are dirty, sloppy, filthy.
They are energetic and smart.
They are loud, noisy, and cause commotions.

A survey conducted in 1939 by *Fortune Magazine* asked, "What do you feel is the reason for hostility toward Jewish people here or abroad?" [7]   The leading reasons mentioned were:

They control finances and business.
They are grasping and covetous.
They are too smart or successful.
They are not good mixers.

Attempting to summarize these and other studies, and give due weighting to the frequency with which various traits are mentioned, Forster presents the following list.[8]

Clannishness (refusal to intermarry, setting up of barriers to assimilation).
Love of money coupled with shady financial ethics.
Pushy, aggressive, uncouth social behavior.
Intelligence, ambition, ability to get ahead.

One notes that in these lists the factor of religion plays little or no part.   Originally, of course, this difference (the only *J*-curve difference characterizing the Jewish group) was all-important.   Accusations based on religion, e.g., "ritual murder," were formerly more common than now. Today in our secularized society the category of Jew appears to be losing its one real defining attribute. Other attributes have taken its place—attributes that at best rest on slight probability, or are wholly irrelevant and noisy.

The preceding lists of stereotypes seem to be roughly in agreement with one another. That is to say, the same accusations crop up time and again. Technically speaking, there is considerable "reliability" (i.e., uniformity) in people's images of what Jewish character is like.

But closer analysis reveals a curious situation. Some of the stereotypes are inherently contradictory. Two opposing images are held, and it is unlikely that both could be equally true. We gain considerable light on this matter through the research of Adorno, Frenkel-Brunswik, Levinson, and Sanford.[9] These investigators devised a comprehensive scale to measure attitudes toward Jews, and inserted various propositions that were essentially opposite in type. Thus the subject was asked whether he did or did not agree with each of the following statements:

(a) Much resentment against Jews stems from their tending to keep apart and to exclude gentiles from Jewish social life.

(b) The Jews should not pry so much into Christian activities and organizations, nor seek so much recognition and prestige from Christians.

An additional pair of statements:

(a) Jews tend to remain a foreign element in American society, to preserve their old social standards and to resist the American way of life.

(b) Jews go too far in hiding their Jewishness, especially such extremes as changing their names, straightening noses, and imitating Christian manners and customs.

Several items of type (a) comprised a subscale of "seclusiveness"; several of type (b) a subscale of "intrusiveness."

The important finding is that these subscales correlated to the extent of +.74. That is to say, the *same* people who accused the Jews of being seclusive also tended to accuse them of being intrusive.

It is, of course, conceivable that an individual might in some sense be both seclusive and intrusive (likewise both generous and self-advertising, both miserly and ostentatious, both slovenly and showy, both cowardly and threatening, both ruthless and helpless);

but it is unlikely.   At least it is unlikely to occur to the extent to which we find these contrary accusations coexisting.

One conversation ran as follows:

Mr. *A*.   I say the Jews are too much alone; they stick together, and are clannish.

Mr. *B*.   But look; in our community there are Cohen and Morris on the Community Chest, several Jews in the Rotary Club and Chamber of Commerce.   Many support our community projects. . . .

Mr. *A*.   That's just what I was saying, they're always pushing and elbowing their way into Christian groups.

What plainly happens is that people who dislike Jews (for deeper reasons) subscribe to any and all stereotypes that would justify this dislike, whether or not the stereotypes are compatible.   Whatever Jews are like, are not like, do, or don't do, the prejudice finds its rationalization in some presumed aspect of "Jewish essence."

The case of the essayist, Charles Lamb, is instructive in this regard.   In his essay "Imperfect Sympathies" he admits that he has a prejudice against Jews.   In the course of easy and mellifluous discourse he writes: "I boldly confess that I do not relish the approximation of Jew and Christian, which has become so fashionable.   The reciprocal endearments have, to me, something hypocritical and unnatural in them.   I do not like to see the Church and Synagogue kissing and congeeing in awkward postures of an affected civility.   If *they* are converted, why do they not come over to us altogether?"

Seven sentences later, perceiving no contradiction, he comments on the case of a converted Jew who did in fact "come over to us altogether":

"*B*—— would have been more in keeping if he had abided by the faith of his forefathers."

Lamb's self-contradictory standards betray even more than his open confession.   He damns Jews if they do, and if they don't.

The fact that prejudiced people so readily subscribe to self-contradictory stereotypes is one proof that genuine group traits are not the point at issue.   The point at issue is rather that a dislike requires justification, and that any justification that fits the immediate conversational situation will do.

It will help to understand the mental process involved if we leave the field of prejudice for a moment, and consider the case of everyday proverbs.   Compare the following pairs of contradictions:

> It is never too late to mend.
> No use crying over spilled milk.
>
> Birds of a feather flock together.
> Familiarity breeds contempt.
>
> A young monk makes an old devil.
> As the twig inclines the tree is bent.

If one state of affairs exists we can call on one proverb to "explain" it. If the opposite state prevails, we can call on the reverse proverb. And so it is with ethnic stereotypes. If one accusation at a given time seems to explain and justify our dislike, we call upon it; if an opposite accusation at another time seems more appropriate, we invoke it. The need for sequential and uniform logic does not trouble us.

A stereotype is sustained by selective perception and selective forgetting. When a Jew of our acquaintance achieves a goal, we may say quite automatically—"The Jews are so clever." If he fails to achieve the goal we say nothing—not thinking to amend our stereotype. In the same way we may overlook nine neat Negro householders, but triumphantly exclaim when we encounter the slovenly tenth, "they do depreciate property." Or, take the case of "Christ killer." In this cliché we find selective forgetting of many relevant facts; that it was Pilate who permitted the Crucifixion, and that the soldiers who executed it were Romans, that the mob was only in part composed of Jews, that Christianity was established and preserved in its precarious early days entirely by men who were ethnically and religiously Jews.

While the scientific problem remains of finding out just what the ethnic and psychological characteristics of a group may be, the fancifulness of many stereotypes is apparent. We therefore conclude that the rationalizing and justifying function of a stereotype exceeds its function as a reflector of group attributes.

Stereotypes concerning the Negro

Surveying stereotyped beliefs concerning the Negro, Kimball Young reports the following array:[11]

> inferior mentality
> primitive morality
> emotional instability
> over-assertiveness
> lazy and boisterous
> religious fanaticism
> fondness for gambling

gaudy and flashy in dress
close to anthropoid ancestors
given to crimes of violence with razors and knives
high birthrate threatening to white majority
susceptible to bribery by politicians
occupationally unstable

Katz and Braly in the study previously cited find:

superstitious
lazy
happy-go-lucky
ignorant
musical

These investigators, employing a method of measuring the *definiteness* of stereotyped ideas concerning various groups, discovered that the agreement of people regarding traits to be assigned to Negroes was greater on the whole than for any other group. Thus 84 percent of all the judges ascribed "superstitiousness" to the Negro. The Katz-Braly study used the method of a checklist. Respondents had before them a large number of traits from which they were to pick those that seemed most appropriate. The fact that the 84 percent chose "superstitious" means that when *forced* to pick out some trait-names, people selected this particular association in a large majority of the cases.

Using a more open method, letting respondents characterize Negroes as they wished, Bettelheim and Janowitz found a list of stereotypes quite unlike their list for the Jew.[12] Arranged in order of frequency of mention:

sloppy, dirty, filthy
depreciate property
taking over; forcing out the whites
lazy, and slackers at work
low character; immoral and dishonest
lower standards; lower class
ignorant; low intelligence
troublesome and cause disturbances
smell bad; have a body odor
carry diseases
spend their money on a good front; don't save

A study by Blake and Dennis asked youthful judges to check traits that were characteristic of Negro and of white.[13] Among the qualities regarded as predominantly Negroid were:

    superstitious
    slow-moving
    ignorant
    happy-go-lucky
    flashy dressing

An interesting feature of this research was the discovery that children in the fourth and fifth grades were far less differentiated in their stereotypes than children in the seventh and eighth grades. The younger children ascribed all "bad" traits to the Negro. For example, white people were judged to be more "cheerful" by the younger children. But by the older children the stereotypes accorded with those of adults—and not all were unfavorable. Thus the Negro was thought to be more cheerful and more humorous. Younger children had negative attitudes towards Negroes, but did not yet have the more complex pattern of stereotypes that would sustain a slightly more differentiated view of this out-group. Meltzer also reports that younger children show much less stereotyping of out-groups than do college students.[14]

There seems to be somewhat less self-contradiction in stereotypes concerning Negroes than concerning Jews, but contradiction is by no means absent. We hear that they are lazy and inert, but also aggressive and pushing. In the South one sometimes hears that there is "no race problem" because the Negro knows his place and stays in it; but in the next breath, that force is needed in order to keep the Negro there.

Minority groups also have stereotypes regarding each other—and regarding themselves. We pointed out in Chapter 9 that so heavy is the prevailing cultural pressure that members of minority groups sometimes look at themselves through the same lens as other groups. Anti-Semitic Jews see other Jews (not themselves) as having objectionable Jewish traits. Some Negroes accuse other Negroes of having precisely the qualities that anti-Negro whites say they have.

Likewise, one minority group may have particularly vivid stereotypes concerning a closely related minority group. Such images may result from what Freud called the "narcissism of slight differences." The German Jew has a keen sense of what the Polish Jew is like. American Negroes have a set of stereotypes to characterize the immigrant West Indian Negro. Ira Reid lists these as follows.[15] Compared with the native Negro, the West Indian is:

very "smart" and better educated than the native American
craftier than the Jews and not to be trusted in financial matters
oversensitive and quick to defend his dignity
hot-tempered

pro-British or pro-French
feels superior to the native-born Negro
either too proud or too lazy to work
clannish
beats his wife and treats women as chattel
a troublemaker with white people
seeks to make an impression
lacks race pride
talks incessantly

Comparison of Jewish and Negro Stereotypes

There seems to be a reciprocal character in anti-Negro and anti-Semitic stereotypes. The former, as noted by Bettelheim and Janowitz, tend to accuse Negroes of lecherous, lazy, filthy, and aggressive traits. The latter accuse Jews of cleverness, deceit, overambition, and sly achievement. These authors next ask us to think of ourselves. What sins do we find in our nature? On the one hand, sins of the flesh. We have to fight against lechery, laziness, aggression, and slovenliness. Hence we personify these evils in the *Negro*. On the other hand, we have to fight also against the sins of pride, deceit, unsocialized egotism, and grasping ambition. We personify these evils in the *Jew*. The Negro reflects our own "id" impulses; the Jew reflects our own violations of our "superego" (conscience). Thus our accusations and feelings of revulsion against both groups symbolize our dissatisfaction with the evil in our own nature. As Bettelheim and Janowitz state the matter:

> According to psychoanalytical interpretation, ethnic hostility is a projection of unacceptable inner strivings onto a minority group.[16]

Support is offered for this theory by the observation that in Europe, where there is no Negro minority, it is the *Jew* who is blamed for the lechery, filth, and violence. Americans, having the Negro to personify these traits, do not *need* the Jew for this purpose. The American, therefore, can build up a more specialized stereotype for the Jew, embracing only the "superego" qualities of ambition, pride, adroitness.

Thus there is some plausibility in regarding the Negro and Jew as complementary objects. Between them they take care of the two major kinds of evil—the more "physical" and the more "mental." The Jews can be hated because they are few and clever; the Negroes because they are numerous and stupid. Although there are many other varieties of prejudice in our society, it is true that anti-Negro and anti-Jewish feeling are the predominant forms.

Investigations show that the extent of prejudice against the Negro is the greater. Can it be because the sins of the flesh are so common?

This type of explanation will receive further attention in Chapters 23 and 24. For the moment it is sufficient to note that for some people stereotypes may indeed have an unconscious self-reference. One may imagine qualities in a group and hate the group for them because one is in conflict over the same qualities in oneself. The Negro and the Jew thus become alter egos. In them we may perceive our own shortcomings.

Mass Media and Stereotypes

We have seen that stereotypes may or may not originate in a kernel of truth; they aid people in simplifying their categories; they justify hostility; sometimes they serve as projection screens for our personal conflict. But there is an additional, and exceedingly important, reason for their existence. They are socially supported, continually revived and hammered in, by our media of mass communication—by novels, short stories, newspaper items, movies, stage, radio, and television.

During the war year 1944 the Writers' War Board, with the assistance of the Bureau of Applied Social Research at Columbia University, made an extensive study of the "stock characters" portrayed in the mass media.[17]

Popular light fiction was found to be perhaps the most striking offender. Analyzing 185 short stories, it was found that over 90 percent of the characters—nearly all the reputable ones—were Anglo-Saxon (or "Nordics"). But when characters were "menials, racketeers, thieves, gamblers, shady night club proprietors, crooked prize fight managers, such nonsympathetic characters were seldom Anglo-Saxon." And, in general, "the behavior of these fictional characters could easily be used to 'prove' that Negroes are lazy, the Jews wily, the Irish superstitious, and the Italians criminal."

In the analysis of 100 motion pictures involving Negro characters, it was found that in 75 cases the portrayal was disparaging and stereotyped. In only 12 cases was the Negro presented in a favorable light as an individual human being.

The reason for the preference given to Anglo-Saxons as heroes is indicated by the comments of two hard-headed businessmen, the first in the comic book field, the second in advertising:

We are interested in circulation primarily. Can you imagine a hero named Cohen?

You'd lose your audience if a colored man appeared in the ad.

However, in a picture of the Old South, whiskey ads and so forth, one puts in an Uncle Tom for atmosphere.

So far as radio is concerned the report says:

The broadcasting fraternity has been arguing for years as to whether "Amos 'n' Andy" helps or hurts the Negro race. Some Negroes do, some don't, object to the series. Another continuing argument revolves around "Rochester" on the Jack Benny program. This presentation is good-natured and pictures "Rochester" as quick-witted and wise, yet it is stereotyped on all the usual counts—addiction to drink, dice, wenching, and razors.

Several surveys have disclosed a common trend in the handling of the Negro in American daily newspapers—a heavy concentration upon crime news and slight attention to achievement.[18] It is sometimes argued that to say, "John Brown, a Negro, was caught breaking and entering" can be justified on the ground that it helps the reader form a mental image, makes for ease of reading, and gives a considerable amount of information in a small space. From the reporter's point of view this practice may have no deeper basis in prejudice. His motives are harmless. Yet so frequently to associate Negro with crime is bound to leave a lasting effect on readers, particularly if this association is not offset by news items favorable to the colored group. And there are, no doubt, certain newspapers that have a deliberate policy of disparaging Negroes. Some Southern newspapers make it a practice, for example, never to capitalize the word *Negro*. Spelled with a small *n* it seems, through some verbal magic, to help hold the race "where it belongs."

All recent studies agree in noting a marked improvement in the policies of mass media in recent years, partly perhaps because minority groups, hitherto silent, have entered complaints. So marked is the protest that one Hollywood director complained that he dare not cast anyone in the role of villain excepting a pure Yankee type.

The growing protests against stereotypes in mass media sometimes go to extremes. In 1949 a controversy arose over a British film *Oliver Twist*. In this popular story by Dickens the Jew, Fagin, is the embodiment of a stereotype. Owing to protests in advance the film was withdrawn from showing in various parts of the United States. Some people have objected to the study of *The Merchant of Venice* in schools—fearing that the portrayal of Shylock, if not studied in its full depth, would lead to stereotyped impressions on young people. The children's story, *Little Black Sambo*, is disfavored because the silly Negro lad loses his clothes and eats too many pancakes. *Pinocchio* is considered harmful because it features Italians and "assassins" in close association. And so it goes. It is probably a poor policy to try to protect everyone's mind from all encounter with stereotypes. Better to strengthen one's ability to differentiate among them, and handle their impact with critical power.

Textbooks used in schools have come in for close scrutiny and criticism. An unusually thorough analysis reports that the treatment given minority groups in over three hundred textbooks reveals that many of them perpetuate negative stereotypes. The fault seems to lie not in any malicious intent, but in the culture-bound traditions which the authors of the textbooks unwittingly adopted.[19]

Stereotypes Change in Time

We have given some evidence to indicate that stereotypes are weakening in mass media. It seems probable likewise that the upswing in intercultural education in the schools may also be having an effect on ethnic clichés in the minds of today's students. All in all, the younger generation may be less stereotype-ridden than the parent generation.

Revealing, if limited, evidence for this statement comes from two pieces of research conducted at Princeton College, separated by an interval of 18 years. We have already reported how in 1932 Katz and Braly asked undergraduates in that college to select five out of a list of 84 attributes that they thought most characteristic of Germans, English, Jews, Negroes, Turks, Japanese, Italians, Chinese, Americans, and Irish.

Teaching at the same college in 1950, G. M. Gilbert repeated the experiment with the same procedure.[20] His subjects were born about the time that the first study was conducted. They grew up in a different social atmosphere even though their economic and social class did not differ greatly from that of their predecessors. A fairly large percentage in both groups came from the South.

The most striking result of this comparative study was what Gilbert calls the "fading effect." Stereotypes for the 10 national and ethnic groups, while similar to those in 1932, were much, much weaker. Take the case of Italians. Table 4 shows the percentage of students assigning a given trait to this national group. The reduction all down the line (excepting in "very religious") is due to the fact that students (who were forced to make five choices) scattered their selections among the 84 traits more than in 1932. In the earlier study they agreed to a greater extent as to what the Italian was like. Gilbert comments as follows:

Table 4

TRAITS ASCRIBED TO ITALIANS BY VARIOUS PERCENTAGES OF STUDENTS

	1932	1950	Difference
Artistic	53	28	−25
Impulsive	44	19	−25
Passionate	37	25	−12
Quick-tempered	35	15	−20
Musical	32	22	−10
Imaginative	30	20	−10
Very religious	21	33	+12

The artistic and hot-tempered Italian, representing a cross between the temperamental maestro and the cheerful organ grinder, is still with us; but . . . he is only a faded image of his former self. There is considerable reduction in the artistic cluster—*artistic, musical, imaginative*—as well as in the temperamental one—*passionate, impulsive,* and *quick-tempered.*

The increase in "very religious" is probably due to the focusing of interest on the Catholic pilgrimages to Rome during the Holy Year of 1950. This fact in itself shows how transitory events can shape the images people have of nations.

In the case of the Turk in 1932, 47 percent ticketed him as "cruel"; in 1950 only 12 percent did so. The stereotype of the terrible Turk had manifestly weakened. In the case of Negroes, the chief stereotypes in both years were *superstitious* and *lazy;* but these traits were checked by *less than half* as many students in the later study compared with the earlier.

Americans as a group were much less adulated. The favorable stereotypes of *industrious, intelligent, ambitious, efficient* had shrunk considerably. Judgments of *materialistic* and *pleasure-loving* increased slightly. It appears that time has brought a more critical view of the in-group.

Perhaps the most important finding of all concerns the extreme reluctance of the 1950 students to take part in the experiment at all. How unreasonable, they said in effect, to force us to make generalizations about people—especially those we have hardly ever met. The project was regarded as insulting to the students' intelligence. One wrote:

I refuse to be a part of a childish game like this. . . . I can think of no distinguishing characteristics which will apply to any group as a whole.

The "childish game" in 1932 met with no such mutiny.

Gilbert points out that the "fading effect" and protest may be due to various factors. One of these may be the gradual disappearance of stereotyping in our entertainment and communications media. Another may be the increase of study of the social sciences among postwar college students. Another may be the wider use of intercultural education in the schools. Whatever the reason, it seems to be a fact that the "pictures in our heads" of ethnic and national groups are today less uniform and less cocksure than they were in former years.

From the point of view of the theory of prejudice the changeability of stereotypes is important. They wax and wane with the intensity and direction of prejudice. They also, as we have seen, obediently follow the conversational situation. The Russian, judged at a time when the Soviet government and the United States were wartime allies, was seen as rugged, brave, and patriotic. Within a few years the picture changed so that he appeared fierce, aggressive, and fanatic. Meanwhile the unfavorable images of the Japanese (and Japanese-Americans) altered and softened.

Here we have further evidence for the point made at the beginning of this chapter. Stereotypes are not identical with prejudice. They are primarily rationalizers. They adapt to the prevailing temper of prejudice or the needs of the situation. While it does no harm (and may do some good) to combat them in schools and colleges, and to reduce them in mass media of communication, it must not be thought that this attack alone will eradicate the roots of prejudice.[21]

NOTES AND REFERENCES

1. R. T. LA PIERE. Type-rationalizations of group antipathy. *Social Forces,* 1936, **15**, 232-237.

2. B. LASKER. *Race Attitudes in Children.* New York: Henry Holt, 1929, 237.

3. B. BETTELHEIM AND M. JANOWITZ. *Dynamics of Prejudice: A Psychological and Sociological Study of Veterans.* New York: Harper, 1950, 45.

4. W. LIPPMANN. *Public Opinion.* New York: Harcourt, Brace, 1922.

5. D. KATZ AND K. W. BRALY. Racial stereotypes of 100 college students. *Journal of Abnormal and Social Psychology,* 1933, **28**, 280-290.

6. B. BETTELHEIM AND M. JANOWITZ. *Op. cit.,* Chapter 3.

7. *Fortune,* 1939, **19**, 104.

8. A. FORSTER. *A Measure of Freedom.* New York: Doubleday, 1950, 101.

9. T. W. ADORNO, et al. *The Authoritarian Personality.* New York: Harper, 1950, 66 and 75.

10. C. LAMB. Imperfect sympathies. *The Essays of Elia.* New York: Wiley and Putnam, 1845.

11. K. YOUNG. *An Introductory Sociology.* New York: American Book, 1934, 158-163, 424 ff.

12. *Ibid.*

13. R. BLAKE AND W. DENNIS. The development of stereotypes concerning the Negro. *Journal of Abnormal and Social Psychology,* 1943, **38,** 525-531.

14. H. MELTZER. Children's thinking about nations and races. *Journal of Genetic Psychology,* 1941, **58,** 181-199.

15. I. REID. *The Negro Immigrant.* New York: Columbia Univ. Press, 1939, 107 ff.

16. B. BETTELHEIM AND M. JANOWITZ. *Op. cit.,* 42.

17. *How Writers Perpetuate Stereotypes.* New York: Writers' War Board, 1945.

18. A. McC. LEE. The press in the control of intergroup tensions. *The Annals of the American Academy of Political and Social Science,* 1946, **244,** 144-151.

19. Committee on the Study of Teaching Materials in Intergroup Relations (H. E. WILSON, DIRECTOR). *Intergroup Relations in Teaching Materials.* Washington: American Council on Education, 1949.

20. G. M. GILBERT. Stereotype persistence and change among college students. *Journal of Abnormal and Social Psychology,* 1951, **46,** 245-254.

21. For an excellent account of national stereotypes as they exist today, see W. BUCHANAN and H. CANTRIL. *How Nations See Each Other.* Urbana: University of Illinois Press, 1953. This study represents one of UNESCO's efforts to bring about an objective understanding of the images people in one nation hold of others. When we know the stereotypes that prevail, we may more intelligently set about our attempt to rectify them.

CHAPTER 13

THEORIES OF PREJUDICE

HISTORICAL EMPHASIS—SOCIOCULTURAL EMPHASIS—SITUATIONAL
EMPHASIS—PSYCHODYNAMIC EMPHASIS—PHENOMENOLOGICAL
EMPHASIS—EMPHASIS ON EARNED REPUTATION—FINAL WORD

The time has come for us to seek an over-all theoretical orientation to the problem of prejudice.

In previous chapters we have had a good deal to say about the *stimulus object*. (Chapters 6-9 dealt with group differences, visibility, and the development of ego-defensive traits.) We have likewise discussed at considerable length the process of perceiving and cognizing group differences. (Chapters 1, 2, 5, 10, 11, 12 dealt with categorization and the nature of prejudgment as determined by normal mental operation, aided by language and stereotype formation.) This focusing of cognition upon the stimulus object is sometimes called the *phenomenological* level of study. The prejudiced *act* (Chapter 4) depends upon the way the stimulus object is perceived (i.e., its phenomenology).

Now if the reader will look at Fig. 11 he will see that all these preceding chapters have dealt chiefly with two of the principal approaches to the study of prejudice: the stimulus object approach and the phenomenological approach. At times, especially in Chapters 3, 5, 7, we have also approached the subject from a sociocultural and, occasionally, historical point of view. It was necessary to do so, since group norms, group values, group membership play a continuous and interlocking part in the development of the individual's mental life. In the chapters immediately following, Chapters 14-16, we shall have more to say about the social and historical determinants of prejudice.

We shall reserve for Chapters 17-28 our discussion of the role of personality factors and of social learning. The fact that we shall devote so much time to these approaches perhaps indicates the author's psychological bias. If so, he pleads with the reader to recognize his attempt to give considerable emphasis likewise to historical, sociocultural, and situational determinants. The author hopes the present volume may be regarded as a reflection of the present tendency for specialists to cross boundaries and to borrow methods and insights from neighboring disciplines in the interests of a more adequate understanding of a concrete social problem. But even a specialist with a broad intention is likely to over-emphasize his own professional field.

Figure 11, then, represents a diagrammatic view of various existing approaches to prejudice. We do not wish to slight any one of them, for none alone gives a complete picture. Quarrels among them are unprofitable.

What do we mean when we speak of a "theory" of prejudice?

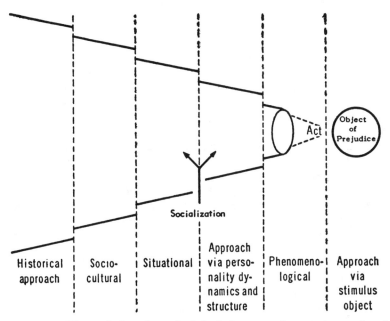

FIG. 11. Theoretical and methodological approaches to the study of the causes of prejudice. (From G. W. Allport, Prejudice: a problem in psychological and social causation. *Journal of Social Issues*, Supplement Series, No. 4, 1950.)

Do we imply that the theory in question is offered as a complete and sovereign explanation for all human prejudice? Seldom is this the case, even though when we read enthusiastic exponents of the Marxian view, or of the scapegoat theory, or of some other, we sometimes gain the impression that the author feels that he has buttoned up the subject completely. Yet as a rule most "theories" are advanced by their authors to call attention to some one important causal factor, without implying that no other factors are operating. Usually an author selects for emphasis one of the six approaches in our diagram; he then develops his ideas concerning certain forces that operate within this approach to create prejudice. To take an example, we discussed in Chapter 3 the theory of "group norms." Proponents of this theory are so deeply impressed by the existence of prejudice in a group's mode of life that they "explain" an individual's prejudiced attitudes as a mere reflection of his group's values. Supporters of this view would no doubt say that this is the most important factor in prejudice, but they probably would not deny the simultaneous operation of other, less central etiological influences.

Our own approach to the problem is eclectic. There seems to be value in all of the six main approaches, and some truth in virtually all of the resulting theories. It is not possible at the present time to reduce them to a single theory of human action. Nevertheless, as we proceed, we hope that the principal points of view will fall into a clear perspective. There is no master key. Rather, what we have at our disposal is a ring of keys, each of which opens one gate of understanding.

It will help the reader to note that causal influences lying toward the right side of Fig. 11 tend to be more immediate in time and more specifiable in operation. A person acts with prejudice in the first instance because he perceives the object of prejudice in a certain way. But he perceives it in a certain way partly because his personality is what it is. And his personality is what it is chiefly because of the way he was socialized (training in family, school, neighborhood). The existing social situation is also a factor in his socialization and may also be a determinant of his perceptions. Behind these forces lie other valid but more remote causal influences. They involve the structure of society in which one lives, long-standing economic and cultural traditions, as well as national and historical influences of long duration. While these factors seem so remote as to be alien to the immediate psychological analysis of prejudiced acts, they are, nonetheless, important causal influences.

Let us look now more closely at some of the characteristic features of each of the six major approaches indicated in Fig. 11.[1]

Historical Emphasis

Impressed by the long history that lies behind each and every present-day ethnic conflict, historians insist that only the total background of a conflict can lead to its understanding. Anti-Negro prejudice in America, for example, is a historical matter, having its roots in slavery, in carpetbagging, and in the failure of reconstruction in the South following the Civil War. If it also has psychological causes these are affected, if not created, by the intricate impact of historical circumstance.

Commenting on recent efforts to establish a purely psychological view of the subject, one historian objects:

> Such studies are enlightening only within narrow limits. For personality is itself conditioned by social forces; in the last analysis, the search for understanding must reach into the broad social context within which personality is shaped.[2]

While admitting the force of this criticism, we may point out that while history provides "the broad social context" it cannot tell why within this context one personality develops prejudice and another does not. And this is precisely the question that the psychologist most wants to answer. Here, then, is an instance of an unprofitable quarrel. Both specialists are indispensable, for they are seeking to answer not identical, but complementary, questions.

Historical studies are markedly diverse in type. Some, but not all, stress the importance of economic determinants. An example of this treatment is the *exploitation theory* of prejudice held by Marxists and others. A brief summary of its argument is given by Cox.

> Race prejudice is a social attitude propagated among the public by an exploiting class for the purpose of stigmatizing some group as inferior so that the exploitation of either the group itself or its resources may both be justified.[3]

This author goes on to argue that race prejudice rose to unprecedented heights in the nineteenth century when European imperial expansion called for some justification. Therefore, poets (Kipling), racial theorists (Chamberlain), and statesmen proclaimed colonial peoples to be "inferior," "requiring protection," a "lower form of evolution," a "burden" to be borne altruistically. All this pious concern and condescension masked the financial advantage that came from exploitation. Segregation developed as a device for preventing sympathy and sentiments of equality. Sexual and social taboos placed on the colonial peoples prevented them from developing expectations of equality and freedom of choice.

It was in this process of rationalized exploitation that the theory of *race* grew up. Prior to the period of capitalist expansion it played a negligible role in world history. Native Hindus, Africans, Malayans, Indonesians were all clearly *visible*. A category was needed that would mask exploitation. The victims must not be known for what they were—involuntary slaves. Hence "race" was seized upon as a God-given, not a man-made, category to justify the discrimination practiced. Cox argues that *class* difference (i.e., the exploiter-exploited relationship) is the foundation of all prejudice; and that all talk about racial, ethnic, and cultural factors is mostly a verbal mask.

Many considerations make this theory attractive. It explains the rationalizations for economic exploitation that are frequently heard: the Orientals only "need" a handful of rice a day to live on; the Negro shouldn't receive high wages, for he will spend them unwisely trying to rise above his racial station; the Mexicans are so primitive that they would only drink and gamble away their money if they had it; so too the American Indian.

While there is obvious truth in the exploitation theory it is weak in many particulars. It fails to explain why there is not equal prejudice against all exploited people. Many of the immigrant groups coming to America have been exploited without suffering from prejudice to the extent that Negroes and Jews have suffered. Nor is it clear that Jews are, in fact, victims of economic exploitation. The Quakers and Mormons were at one time severely persecuted in America, but certainly not primarily for economic reasons.

Nor is it correct to consider bigotry against even the Negro in America as wholly an economic phenomenon, though it is here that Cox's argument is strongest. While it seems obvious that many white people derive advantage from underpaying Negro workers and rationalizing the injustice through theories concerning their "animal nature," still the story is more complex. White employees in factories, or white tenant farmers, are similarly exploited, but no ritual of discrimination has developed against them. In sociological studies of certain Southern communities, for example, it turns out that on an objective scale of "class," Negroes are no lower than the whites. Their cabins are no smaller, their income is no less, their household facilities are the same. Yet their position socially and psychologically is lower.

We conclude, therefore, that the Marxist theory of prejudice is far too simple, even though it points a sure finger at *one* of the factors involved in prejudice, viz., rationalized self-interest of the upper classes.

The contributions of history to the understanding of prejudice are by no means confined to the economic interpretation. The rise of Hitler in Germany together with his genocide policies cannot be understood except by tracing an ominous sequence of events historically. Within the past century the road leads first through a period of liberalism (in 1869 all legal restrictions on Jews were repealed), then through the Bismarck era when Jews were blamed by conservatives and monarchists for Bismarck's reformism, much as they were later blamed for Roosevelt's New Deal. Converging with this trend was the doctrine of race and purity of blood which was a reflection of Hegel's plea for a spiritual unity of the German state. All these factors became psychologically blended with the rise of labor. To many the labor movement seemed an alien growth in a military society. The Jews were blamed for labor's rise. Finally, World War I prepared the ground for personifying in the Jew all the radically disruptive forces that were troubling Germany.[4]

Whether this fateful progression can be explained fully by history without the help of psychology is not here the question. We insist only that any pattern of prejudice existing in any part of the world receives marked illumination when it is examined from the historical point of view.

Sociocultural Emphasis

The following chapters will deal with some of the multitude of sociocultural factors that help explain group conflict and prejudice. Sociologists and anthropologists place principal weight on this type of theorizing. Like the historian, they are impressed by the total social context in which prejudiced attitudes develop. Within this social context some writers emphasize the traditions that lead to conflict; some the relative upward mobility in out-groups and in-groups; some the density of the populations concerned; some the type of contacts that exist between groups.

For the present, let us cite one example from theories in this class —the phenomenon known as *urbanization* and its possible relation to ethnic prejudice. The case is argued somewhat as follows.

Although people desire peaceful and affiliative relations with others, this striving has been badly blocked by the mechanical culture of our day—especially by the culture of our cities that arouses so much insecurity and uncertainty in men's minds. In the city personal contacts are diminished. Literally or figuratively the assembly line rules us. Central government replaces local and more intimate forms of government. Advertising controls our standards of living and our desires. Giant corporations fill the landscape with monstrous factories, regulating our employment, income, and safety. No longer do personal thrift, private effort, face-to-face adjustments count for much. Fear of the Juggernaut settles upon us. Big city life expresses to us what is inhuman, impersonal, dangerous. We fear and hate our subservience to it.

What has this urban insecurity to do with prejudice? For one thing, as mass-men we follow the conventions of the times. The snob-appeals of advertising affect us deeply. We want more goods, more luxury, more status. The standards forced upon us by advertisers call for contempt of people who are poor, who do not reach the level of material existence that is prescribed. Hence we look down upon groups economically below us—upon Negroes, immigrants and rustics. (Here we note echoes of the Marxian view.)

But while we yield to the materialistic urban values, we also hate the city that engenders them. We hate the domination of finance and shady politics. We despise the traits that develop in response to urban pressures. We dislike those who are sneaky, dishonest, selfish, too clever, too ambitious, vulgar, noisy, and on the fringe of old-fashioned virtues. These urban traits have been personified in the Jew. "The Jews are hated today," writes Arnold Rose, "primarily because they serve as a symbol of city life." [5] They are symbols especially of that monster, all-dominant, much feared City of New York. The city has emasculated us. We will therefore hate the symbol of the city—the Jew.

The merit of this theory is that it has a logic that applies both to anti-Semitism and to feelings of condescension toward other minorities who have not "made the grade." It would have some difficulty, however, in explaining why Japanese-American farmers were so vehemently feared and hated during World War II. It would also be forced to concede that "city hatred" is as intense among rural dwellers as among urbanites, for ethnic prejudice is certainly as acute in the country as in the town.

Blending a historical and a sociocultural emphasis, we have the *community* pattern theory of prejudice. Here the stress is upon the basic ethnocentrism of every group. If at one time members of the Polish nobility exploited and suppressed Ukrainian peasants (as they did) a pattern of resentment was laid down that perpetuated itself in the very fabric of Ukrainian lore. And the well-known hostility of many Irish toward the English reflects a pattern having its origins in the misdeeds of some English landlords and statesmen literally centuries ago. Thomas and Znaniecki express the dynamics of the situation in the following words.

> Every cultural problem reaches the individual only through the mediacy of his group which, because of the immediate character of the relations between its members, is for each member the primary and fundamental complex of values. . . . The continual tendency of social education . . . is to have each individual appreciate every object from the standpoint of the attitude of the group toward this object.[6]

This view combines history and sociology. It tells us that individuals cannot help but adopt the judgments of their ancestors, viewing each out-group through the screen of tradition.

In Europe there is an intricate network of historic hostilities. A given city, especially in the eastern sectors, might at various times have been "owned" by Russia, Lithuania, Poland, Sweden, the Ukraine. Descendants of all these assorted conquerors might still reside in the city and with some justification regard all other claimants as pretenders or intruders. A veritable checkerboard of prejudice results. Even should the settlers of disputed territories migrate, say to America, the traditional hostilities may move with them. But unless there is a strong community pattern in the New World as well as in the Old, ancient animosities are likely to die out. Many, perhaps most, immigrants want to start a new life, and have chosen a new community pattern where (to their mind) there is an atmosphere of freedom, equal opportunity, and a sense of dignity available to all.

Situational Emphasis

If we subtract the historical background from the sociocultural approach we have left a *situational emphasis*. That is to say, emphasis upon past patterns gives way to emphasis upon current forces. Several theories of prejudice are of this order. One might, for example, speak of an *atmosphere* theory. A child grows up surrounded by immediate influences and very soon reflects them all. Lillian Smith, in *Killers of the Dream*, propounds such a theory.[7] The Southern child obviously has no knowledge of historical events, of exploitation, or of urban values as such. All he knows is that he must *conform* to the complex and inconsistent teaching that he receives. His prejudice is thus merely a mirror image of what he now sees around him.

An instance of the subtle impact of atmosphere in shaping attitudes is implied in the following incident.

An inspector of education in a British African colony wondered why so little progress was made in learning English in a certain native school. Visiting the classroom, he asked the native teacher to put on a demonstration of his method of teaching English. The teacher complied, first making, however, the following preface to the lesson in the vernacular which he did not know the inspector understood: "Come now, children, put away your things, and let us wrestle for an hour with the enemy's language."

Other situational theories may stress the present *employment situation:* and see hostility primarily in terms of prevailing economic competition.   Or they may regard prejudice primarily as a phenomenon of upward and downward *social mobility*.   Situational theories also may stress the importance of *types of contact* between groups, or the relative *density* of groups.   These situational theories are so important that they will be examined separately in subsequent chapters.

Psychodynamic Emphasis

If man is by nature quarrelsome or hostile we must expect conflict to flourish.   Theories that stress causation in human nature are inevitably psychological in type in contrast to the historical, economic, sociological, or cultural points of view mentioned above. As one example we may cite the convictions of the philosopher Hobbes, who sought the roots of prejudice in the unsavory instincts of man:

> So that in the nature of man, we find three principal causes of quarrel.   First, Competition; Secondly, Diffidence; Thirdly, Glory.
>
> The first maketh men invade for Gain; the second, for Safety; and the third, for Reputation.   The first use violence to make themselves masters of other men's persons, wives, children, and cattell; the second to defend them; the third for trifles, as a word, a smile, a different opinion, and any other sign of undervalue, either direct in their persons, or by reflection in their kindred, their friends, their nation, their profession, or their name.[8]

Hobbes is here saying that the sources of conflict lie in (1) economic advantage, (2) fear and defensiveness, (3) desire for status (pride).   To Hobbes these three desires were but aspects of man's basic power-drive.   He seeks power in these three ways.   The same essentially instinctivist view is held by the man in the street who shrugs his shoulders and says, "Prejudice is only natural; nothing can be done about it."

Psychologists today would point out the question-begging character of the argument.   How does one know that primordial pride, "the pursuit of power after power that ceases only in death" is a root instinct?   Only by pointing to the widespread existence of conflict.   But widespread conflict does not mean in itself that instinct underlies it.

Starting with the same fact of widespread conflict, one might (probably with greater validity) argue as follows: What the infant seeks at the beginning of its life is not "power after power" but a close, affiliative relationship with its surroundings, including all people who cross his path. Symbiosis and a loving relation always precede hate (Chapter 3). There can, in fact, be no hatred until there has been long-continued frustration and disappointment. Any observer of children knows that in the early years it is difficult to teach them to compete with one another; it is still more difficult to teach them prejudice, as we shall see in Chapters 17-20. Thus to say that negative attitudes toward people are more "basic" than affiliative attitudes is to reverse the factual time sequence, and to invert the order of importance of needs as they seem actually to exist in human nature.[9]

In better standing is the *frustration* theory of prejudice. It, too, is a psychological theory rooted in the "nature of man," but makes no hazardous assumptions regarding instincts. It can readily admit that affiliative needs seem as basic, or more basic, than protest and hatred, and at the same time hold that when positive and friendly advances toward the environment are thwarted, ugly consequences result.

We can clarify the theory by citing the vehement prejudice of a World War II veteran:

When asked about possible unemployment and a future depression he replied:
We'd better not have it. Chicago'll blow wide open. On South Park the niggers are gettin' so smart. We'll have a race riot that'll make Detroit look like a Sunday School picnic. So many are bitter about the part the Negro played in the war. They got all the soft jobs—the quartermasters, engineers. They're no good for anything else. The white got his ass shot off. They're pretty bitter. If both whites and niggers get laid off, that'll be bad. I'm gonna eat. I know how to use a gun.[10]

This case clearly shows the role of frustration in causing, or intensifying, prejudice. Deprivation and frustration lead to hostile impulses, which if not controlled are likely to discharge against ethnic minorities. Tolman has pointed to the "narrowing of our cognitive maps due to too strong motivations or to too intense frustration."[11] With emotional provocation, a person's view of his social world becomes constricted and distorted. He sees personal demons (minorities) at work because his normal directed thinking is blocked by the intensity of his feelings. He cannot analyze the evil; he can only personify it.

The frustration theory is sometimes known as the *scapegoat* theory (Chapters 15, 21, 22). All formulations of this theory assume that anger once engendered may be displaced upon a (logically irrelevant) victim.

It has been pointed out that the chief weakness of this theory is that it fails to tell upon what victim the hostility will be discharged. It also fails to explain why in many personalities no such displacement takes place, however great the frustration. But these complications we shall consider later.

A third type of "nature of man" theory emphasizes the *character structure* of the individual person. Only certain types of people develop prejudice as an important feature in their lives. These seem to be insecure and anxious personalities who take the authoritarian and exclusionist way of life rather than the relaxed and trusting democratic way. This theory stresses the importance of early training, pointing out that most highly prejudiced people have lacked a secure and affectionate relationship with their own parents. For this reason, or others, they grow up craving definiteness, finality, authority in all their human relationships—and this pattern leads them to exclude and fear groups that seem less familiar and safe than their own.

Like the frustration theory, the character structure theory has much evidence to back it up (see Chapters 25-27). These two theories are not, however, all-sufficient, but require supplementation from other theories we are here surveying.

Phenomenological Emphasis

A person's conduct proceeds immediately from his view of the situation confronting him. His response to the world conforms to his definition of the world. He attacks members of one group because he perceives them as repulsive, annoying, or threatening; members of another he derides because to him they are crude, dirty, and stupid. Both visibility and verbal labels, as we have seen, help define the object in perception so that it can be readily identified. Again, as we have seen, historical and cultural forces, and the person's entire character structure, may lie behind his hypotheses and perceptions. Writers who approach the study of prejudice from the phenomenological point of view assume the convergence of all these factors into a final common focus. What the man finally believes and perceives is the important thing. Obviously, the stereotype plays a prominent part in sharpening the perception prior to action.

Certain studies of prejudice employ the phenomenological approach exclusively. The Katz-Braly and Gilbert studies of ethnic stereotypes (Chapter 12) do so; so too Razaan's investigation of the effect of ethnic proper names on ratings of personality from photographs of faces (Chapter 11). Additional studies combine the phenomenological approach with some other. For example, in Chapter 10 we reported that the cognitive process is found to differ in rigidity when we compare people with two kinds of *character structure*. Another frequent combination of approaches is the phenomenological with the situational. In Chapter 16 we shall see how people who live in close contact with Negroes tend to perceive them differently from those who live in segregated situations.

The phenomenal level, as we have said, is the immediate level of causation, but it is well to combine this approach with others. If we do not do so we are likely to lose sight of the equally important determinants that are to be found in the underlying dynamics of personality as well as in the situational, cultural, and historical contexts of life.

Emphasis on Earned Reputation

Finally we come once again to the problem of the *stimulus object* itself. There may be, as Chapters 6 and 9 have indicated, bona fide differences between groups that provoke dislike and hostility. Enough has been said, however, to show that these differences are much *less* than they are imagined to be. In most cases a reputation is not earned but is gratuitously thrust upon a group.

It would be impossible to find any social scientist today who would subscribe completely to the *earned reputation* theory. At the same time, some warn against assuming that every minority group is always blameless. There may be ethnic or national traits that *are* menacing, and that therefore invite realistic hostility. Or, still more likely, hostility may feed partly on realistic estimates of the stimulus (the true nature of groups) and partly on the many unrealistic factors that comprise prejudice. Some writers, therefore, advocate an *interaction theory*.[12] Hostile attitudes are *in part* determined by the nature of the stimulus (earned reputation) and *in part* by considerations essentially irrelevant to the stimulus (e.g., scapegoating, conforming to tradition, stereotypes, guilt projection, etc.).

There is certainly no objection to such an interaction theory provided proper weight is given to each of the two sets of factors. It says little more than "Let's allow for the simultaneous operation of all scientifically established causes of hostile attitudes, not forgetting to include relevant features of the stimulus object itself." Taken in this broad sense, there can be no possible objection to the theory.

Final Word

By far the best view to take toward this multiplicity of approaches is to admit them all. Each has something to teach us. None possesses a monopoly of insight, nor is any one safe as a solitary guide. We may lay it down as a general law applying to all social phenomena that *multiple causation* is invariably at work and nowhere is the law more clearly applicable than to prejudice.

NOTES AND REFERENCES

1. The sixfold approach is developed more fully by the author in a paper entitled, "Prejudice: a problem in psychological causation," *Journal of Social Issues*, 1950, Supplement Series No. 4; likewise published in T. PARSONS AND E. SHILS, *Toward a Theory of Social Action*, Part 4, Chapter 1, Cambridge: Harvard Univ. Press, 1951.

2. O. HANDLIN. Prejudice and capitalist exploitation. *Commentary*, 1948, **6**, 79-85. See also by the same author *The Uprooted: The Epic Story of the Great Migrations that Made the American People*. Boston: Little, Brown, 1951.

3. O. C. COX. *Caste, Class, and Race*. New York: Doubleday, 1948, 393.

4. P. W. MASSING. *Rehearsal for Destruction*. New York: Harper, 1949.

5. A. ROSE. Anti-Semitism's root in city-hatred. *Commentary*, 1948, **6**, 374-378; also published in A. ROSE (ED.), *Race Prejudice and Discrimination*, New York: Alfred A. Knopf, 1951, Chapter 49.

6. W. I. THOMAS AND F. ZNANIECKI. *The Polish Peasant in Europe and America*. Boston: Badger, 1918, Vol. II, 1881.

7. LILLIAN SMITH. *Killers of the Dream*. New York: W. W. Norton, 1949.

8. T. HOBBES. *Leviathan*. First published 1651, Pt. 1, Chapter 13.

9. Cf. G. W. ALLPORT. A psychological approach to the study of love and hate. Chapter 7 in P. A. SOROKIN (ED.), *Explorations in Altruistic Love and Behavior*. Boston: Beacon Press, 1950; also M. F. ASHLEY-MONTAGU, *On Being Human*, New York: Henry Schuman, 1950.

10. B. BETTELHEIM AND M. JANOWITZ. *The Dynamics of Prejudice: A Psychological and Sociological Study of Veterans*. New York: Harper, 1950, 82.

11. E. C. TOLMAN. Cognitive maps in rats and men. *Psychological Review*, 1948, **55**, 189-208.

12. Cf. B. ZAWADSKI. Limitations of the scapegoat theory of prejudice. *Journal of Abnormal and Social Psychology*, 1948, **43**, 127-141. Also, G. ICHHEISER, Sociopsychological and cultural factors in race relations, *American Journal of Sociology*, 1949, **54**, 395-401.

Part IV

SOCIOCULTURAL FACTORS

CHAPTER 14

SOCIAL STRUCTURE AND CULTURAL PATTERN

HETEROGENEITY—VERTICAL MOBILITY—RAPID SOCIAL CHANGE—
IGNORANCE AND BARRIERS TO COMMUNICATION—SIZE AND DENSITY
OF MINORITY GROUPS—DIRECT COMPETITION AND REALISTIC
CONFLICT—EXPLOITATIVE ADVANTAGE—SOCIAL REGULATION OF
AGGRESSION—CULTURAL DEVICES TO ENSURE LOYALTY—CUL-
TURAL PLURALISM VERSUS ASSIMILATION—SUMMARY

As we have just seen, some theorists by training and preference accent *cultural causation*. Historians, anthropologists, sociologists are interested in the outside influences that shape the attitudes of the individual. Psychologists, on the other hand, want to know how these influences get tied into a living, dynamic nexus of the individual's life. Both approaches are needed. In the present chapter we confine ourselves to the former.

On the basis of what is now known, we may say that prejudiced personalities will be more numerous in times and in places where the following conditions prevail:

Where the social structure is marked by heterogeneity
Where vertical mobility is permitted
Where rapid social change is in progress
Where there are ignorance and barriers to communication
Where the size of a minority group is large or increasing
Where direct competition and realistic threats exist
Where exploitation sustains important interests in the community
Where customs regulating aggression are favorable to bigotry
Where traditional justifications for ethnocentrism are available
Where neither assimilation nor cultural pluralism is favored

Each of these ten sociocultural laws of prejudice will be considered in order. The evidence for none is complete or incontrovertible; but each represents as good an "educated guess" as can be made at the present time.

Heterogeneity

Unless there is considerable diversity in a society there are few "perceptual points for alarm." In a homogeneous society people are alike in color, religion, language, styles of clothing, and standards of living. Scarcely any group has sufficient visibility around which prejudice may be built (Chapter 8).

In a diversified civilization, by contrast, there is much differentiation (division of labor—with resulting class differences; immigration—with resulting ethnic differences; and many religious and philosophical points of view—with resulting ideological differences). Since no person can embrace all of the interests represented, his outlook grows particularistic in consequence. Over and against his interests and memberships stand other interests and memberships.

There are only two types of antagonisms available to people within a homogeneous culture. (1) They may distrust foreigners and strangers (Chapter 4), as the Chinese distrust "foreign devils." (2) They may single out individuals for ostracism, as the Navaho ostracizes "witches." Xenophobia and witchcraft are the "functional equivalents" of group prejudice in homogeneous cultures.

In the United States—probably the most heterogeneous and complex society on earth—conditions are ripe for abundant group conflict and prejudice. Differences are numerous and visible. The resulting clash of customs, tastes, ideologies cannot help but engender friction.

Occasionally a society may show a kind of frozen heterogeneity that acts, in fact, like homogeneity. Where slavery has existed, for example, active prejudice has not been especially marked. If relationships are frozen by custom, then little overt friction can occur. Fixed *modi vivendi* between servant and master, employer and employee, priest and parishioner are cases in point. There must be activity, mobility, change in a society in order to create the "live" heterogeneity that brings prejudice to the fore.

Vertical Mobility

In a homogeneous society or in a frozen caste system one does not perceive differences as actively menacing. Yet even when a caste system, such as slavery, functions smoothly, there is probably always a certain amount of anxiety connected with keeping lower classes "in their places." Sumptuary laws were enacted in Japan and elsewhere to fix upper-class privileges and deny them officially to lower classes. Thus even a frozen caste system shows traces of prejudice (Chapter 1).

But, when men are viewed as potentially equal, and by national creed are guaranteed equal rights and equal opportunity, a very different psychological condition exists. Members of even the lowest group are encouraged to put forth effort, to rise, and to demand their rights. A "circulation of the elite" sets in. By effort and good fortune families low in the social scale may climb high, and sometimes displace the previous aristocracy. Such vertical mobility brings both incentive and alarm to members of a society. Williams has pointed out that in the United States it is chiefly members of the socially most secure groups (e.g., professional people, wealthy old families) who can afford to fight vigorously for the universalistic values of the "American Creed." All others are in fact threatened by this vertical circulation—which may lead downward as well as upward.[1]

One empirical study throws considerable light on the subject. The investigators Bettelheim and Janowitz discover that it is not a person's present status in society that is important. It is rather the *shifting* of his status upward or downward that regulates his prejudice. The dynamic concept of social mobility turns out to be more important than any static demographic variable. This finding helps to explain why most investigators have failed to discover important relationships between prejudice and such variables as age, sex, religious membership, or even income (Chapter 5). It helps to explain why the covariation of tolerance with higher education is not particularly marked. Mobility seems to be a more important factor.

The veterans in this study were asked to indicate their occupational situation as it was just before they entered the Armed Services, and as it was after the war, at the time of the interview.[2] Some men after the war failed to meet their prewar status; others found jobs equal in status; others found better jobs. Dividing the cases according to these three grades of mobility, the degrees of anti-Semitism expressed are found to be strikingly different. The number of cases in this research is not large, but the trend is striking. Those who are falling on the occupational ladder are far more anti-Semitic than those who are rising. Supporting evidence comes

Table 5

ANTI-SEMITISM AND SOCIAL MOBILITY

(after Bettelheim and Janowitz, *Dynamics of Prejudice*, p. 59)

	Downward Mobility Percentage	No Mobility Percentage	Upward Mobility Percentage
Tolerant	11	37	50
Stereotyped	17	38	18
Outspoken and Intense	72	25	32
Total	100	100	100

from the investigation of Campbell, who reports that people dissatisfied with their jobs (probably to a considerable extent an indicator of downward mobility) were far more anti-Semitic than those who expressed contentment.[3]

The same trend is found in relation to anti-Negro prejudice. Because this form of hostility is more widespread than anti-Semitism the categories are arranged somewhat differently than in the preceding table.

Table 6

ANTI-NEGRO ATTITUDES AND SOCIAL MOBILITY

(after Bettelheim and Janowitz, *Dynamics of Prejudice,* p. 150)

	Downward Mobility Percentage	No Mobility Percentage	Upward Mobility Percentage
Tolerant and Stereotyped	28	26	50
Outspoken	28	59	39
Intense	44	15	11
Total	100	100	100

Rapid Social Change

Heterogeneity and the urge toward upward mobility thus make for ferment in society, and are likely to bring ethnic prejudice in their wake. But the process seems to be speeded up in times of crisis. As the Roman empire crumbled the Christians were more frequently fed to the lions. During the period of war strain in America, race riots markedly increased (especially in the year 1943). Whenever the cotton business in the South has slumped, the number of lynchings has appreciably increased.[4] One investigator writes, "Throughout the history of the United States there seems to have been a direct correlation between the peaks of nativist spirit and the valleys of exceptional economic difficulty." [5]

In times of calamities, such as flood, famine, or fire, all manner of superstitions and dread flourish, among them legends that minority groups are responsible for the disaster. For the forest fires that ravaged Maine in 1947, many citizens blamed the communists. Communists in Czechoslovakia returned the compliment in 1950 and blamed the failure of the potato crop on Americans who "released swarms of potato bugs" in that country. Whenever anxiety increases, accompanied by a loss of predictability in life, people tend to define their deteriorated situations in terms of scapegoats.

Anomie is a sociological concept representing the accelerated disruption of social structure and of social values such as mark most nations today. It is a term that calls attention to dysfunction and demoralization in social institutions.

One investigator, Leo Srole, wished to test the hypothesis that people who perceived current conditions as highly anomic would be people who displayed high prejudice against minority groups. He gave questionnaires designed to measure opinion regarding the anomic state of present-day American society to a large number of people. He likewise gave them tests to determine their minority group prejudices. The correlation was strikingly high.[6]

The same investigator wished to see whether this sociocultural hypothesis of anomie as a cause of prejudice was firmer than the *psychological* hypothesis that prejudice results from an "authoritarian" character structure (Chapter 25). Accordingly, he administered to his subjects a third questionnaire dealing with the authoritarianism of their outlook. He found that the *anomie* variable was the more important.

This finding was subsequently challenged by a team of psychologists who repeated Srole's work. While they too found anomie, as perceived by the subjects, to be an important correlate of prejudice, they did not find it to be more important than the authoritarian character structure.[7]

This research is interesting because it presumes to discover which of two causes of prejudice is the more important. While at the present time the matter is not settled, we can at least point to this work as arguing for the importance of anomie as a factor in prejudice. (The reader will note that, strictly speaking, the investigations concern only the perception of—or belief in—anomie. They do not deal with factual disruption of society but with people's belief that such disruption is occurring. Hence the variable is, strictly speaking, phenomenological rather than sociocultural.)

Before leaving the subject, it should be remarked that certain types of crisis within a nation may conceivably have the effect of lessening intergroup hostility. When a whole nation is in jeopardy, for example, antagonists may forget their hostilities and cooperate to defeat a common enemy. Wartime allies usually show a friendly mien toward one another for the duration, even if peacetime restores their rivalries. An acute national crisis is not, however, the same as anomie. The latter state is marked by an internal instability, and it is this factor (whether the nation is at war or at peace) that seems to correlate with augmented prejudice.

Ignorance and Barriers to Communication

Most programs for the eradication of prejudice proceed on the assumption that the more one knows about a person the less likely he is to feel hostility toward him. It seems self-evident that a gentile who is well informed concerning the Jewish religion will not believe tales concerning Jewish "ritual murders." A person who knows what the Catholic doctrine of transubstantiation means will not shudder at the "cannibalism" of Catholics. As soon as we understand that it is a peculiarity of the Italian language to end its nouns in vowels we cease to ridicule the efforts of an Italian immigrant who speaks English with a lilt. The larger part of the effort of intercultural education in this country is directed toward remedying ignorance so that prejudice may decrease.

Does scientific evidence on this matter justify the assumption made? Surveying studies carried out up to a decade ago, Murphy, Murphy and Newcomb incline to think so. They conclude that our rather meager evidence suggests that those who know most about other races and peoples tend to have favorable attitudes about them.[8]

More recent evidence in the main supports this conclusion, but at the same time points to an important qualification. While we tend to feel friendly to those nations about which we have most knowledge, we likewise have considerable knowledge about those nations we hate. In other words, the law of the inverse relation between knowledge and hostility fails to hold at the extreme degree of hostility. We are not wholly ignorant of our worst enemies.[9]

All in all, it seems safe to conclude that when barriers to communication are insurmountable, ignorance tends to make a person an easy prey to rumor, suspicion, and stereotype. This process is most likely to occur, of course, if the unknown is also regarded as a potential threat.

To this generalization it may properly be objected that individual differences must be taken into account. In Chapter 5 we cited the case of Americans who would not admit "Daniereans" to this country *because* they knew nothing about them. At the same time others said that *because* they knew nothing about them they had nothing against them, and therefore would gladly admit them as immigrants. Not all individuals use their knowledge (or their ignorance) in the same way. But if we can feel satisfied with an empirical generalization of a broad type we may safely conclude that *knowledge of other groups derived through free communication is as a rule correlated with lessened hostility and prejudice.*

Knowledge is of many types. For this reason, our generalization is loose and taken by itself not very helpful. For example, it seems probable that self-acquired knowledge, gained through first-hand experience, is more effective than information sprayed upon us by lectures, textbooks, or publicity campaigns (Chapter 30). And as for breaking down barriers of communication, research discloses that some conditions of intergroup *contact* are more effective than others (Chapter 16).

Size and Density of Minority Groups

A single Japanese or Mexican child in a schoolroom is likely to be a pet. But let a score move in, and they will certainly be set off from the remainder of the children, and in all probability be regarded as a threat.

Williams states this sociocultural law in the following way:

> Migration of a visibly different group into a given area increases the likelihood of conflict; the probability of conflict is the greater (a) the larger the ratio of the incoming minority to the resident population, and (b) the more rapid the influx.[10]

Only about 1,000 Hindus live in the United States, but about 13,000,000 Negroes. The former group is overlooked (excepting as individual Hindus may be mistaken for Negroes). But were the number of Hindus to rise into the tens or hundreds of thousands there is no doubt that a definite and articulate anti-Hindu prejudice would arise.

If the law is correct, we should find evidence that anti-Negro feeling is most intense where Negro density is greatest.

> One limited but well-designed investigation finds supporting data in the state of South Carolina. In 1948, a third party candidate, Governor Thurmond, ran for the office of President of the United States on a "states rights" platform. The issue was primarily one of protest against the civil rights plank of the Democratic party. The investigator, David M. Heer, tested the hypothesis that in South Carolina counties where Negro population was densest, prejudice would be more intense, and the Thurmond vote would be highest.[11] The results, well controlled for other variables that might also enhance Thurmond's vote, showed that to an appreciable degree the hypothesis was justified. The denser the Negro population the higher the Thurmond vote.

> The first part of the law that Williams proposes holds that the static composition of the population is important. Heer's study lends support. (One might say that the manifestly greater anti-Negro prejudice in southern than in northern states is also proof

of the proposition—though here we must be careful to admit that many factors other than relative density are operating.)

But the second part of Williams' statement seems even more important. Its validity is easily demonstrated.

> Before World War II it was known that color prejudice in England was slight. During the war a large number of Negroes from America, Africa, and the West Indies, also many Malayans, were introduced into the English city of Liverpool. Richmond, studying this situation, found a tremendous growth of feeling against them where little or none existed before.[12]

In America the most serious riotous conditions have coincided with the immigration of large numbers of unfavored groups. Examples are the Broad Street riot in Boston in 1832 when the Irish population was rapidly increasing, the zoot-suit riots in Los Angeles in 1943 when Mexican labor was moving in, the Detroit riot in the same year. The succession of race troubles in Chicago seem directly related to the growing density of Negro population. In that city 90,000 Negroes live in one square mile, sometimes 17 persons to a room. And the Negro population is expanding at the rate of 100,000 every ten years.[13]

To offset the operation of this law, it has been argued that if minority groups would disperse themselves as individuals (not in clusters) they would encounter less hostility. Weaver, a student of Negro housing, concludes that experience has shown that when an individual or a few individual Negro families have entered high and medium income areas, resistance to them has gradually declined.[14] And Parsons, pointing to the concentration of Jews not only in residential districts but in certain selected occupations, gives his judgment:

> If Jews could be evenly distributed through the social structure, anti-Semitism would probably be greatly reduced.[15]

But dispersion for many minorities is not easily achieved. For reasons of economy and sociability immigrants from a given country or region tend to huddle together. Negroes moving into Northern cities can obtain housing only in districts where the Negro population is already dense. As the concentration increases a parallel society is set up. The new minority group becomes a community within a community having its own churches, stores, clubs, companies of the National Guard. This separatism emphasizes the gulf and often makes a bad situation worse. Occupational specialization is likely to grow up to aggravate matters: Italians are seen only as pushcart vendors, shoe repairmen, or laborers. Jews take what local specialties are open to them: retailing, pawnshops, work in garment factories.

The tendency to concentrate in residential districts, in a subsociety, in given occupations, greatly augments the barriers to communication between majority and minority groups. It maintains ignorance which, as we have seen, is itself an important provoker of prejudice.

Like all of the other sociocultural laws we are here considering, the principles of relative size and gradient of density cannot stand alone. Let us suppose that a rapid influx of Nova Scotians occurred into a New England city. The resulting prejudice would certainly be less than if an equal number of Negroes should arrive. Some ethnic groups seem more menacing than others—either because they have more points of difference or a higher visibility. Growing density, therefore, is not in itself a sufficient principle to explain prejudice. What it seems to accomplish is the *aggravation* of whatever prejudice exists.

Direct Competition and Realistic Conflict

We have frequently spoken of the fact that some members of a minority group may *in fact* have objectionable characteristics, and have given due weight to the "earned reputation" theory of hostile attitudes. We now must examine a closely related proposition—namely, that intergroup conflict may have a realistic basis. An idealist may say, "But conflict is never absolutely necessary; one may use arbitration or find a peaceful resolution of divergent interests." So one may—ideally. All we are saying here is that clashes of interests and values do occur, and that these conflicts are not in themselves instances of prejudice.

At times in the past, mill towns in New England needed cheap labor. Agents from the mills went to Southern Europe to arrange for a large-scale immigration to supply the need. When the Italians and Greeks arrived they were not made welcome by the established Yankees in the region, for they did, in fact, temporarily debase the labor market, reduce income, and increase unemployment among former workers. Especially in slack seasons or in times of economic depression, the sense of competition was keen. After a period of time, adjustments took place, each ethnic group finding a distinctive level in the division of labor. Collins reports how in many New England factories today, management and administration are controlled exclusively by old Yankee stock, while supervisory jobs and foremanships are controlled by Irish-Americans. The workers are newer South European groups. An informal social structure is recognized and by tacit agreement maintained.[16]   But before such coordination occurs, artificial as it is, there may be a period of acutely suspicious competition.

It is often said that Negroes constitute a realistic threat to the lower classes of white people, since both are competing for lower class jobs.   Strictly speaking, of course, the rivalry is not between group and group, but between individuals.   It is never the colored *group* that prevents a white laborer from obtaining a job, but only some person (white or colored) who got there first.   To say that the conflict is "realistic" in this case means nothing more than that the contestants *view* the rivalry as an ethnic matter.   When immigrant or Negro strikebreakers are brought into a plant the hostility toward these "job snatchers" becomes structured as ethnic, although the color or national origin of the offenders is merely incidental to the economic clash involved.

A given minority group can be viewed as a realistic threat only if the bulk of its members have such attributes as the following: a reluctance to join trade unions, a willingness to work long hours for low pay under poor conditions of safety and health, an ability to undersell natives in any respect, a tendency to become public charges and pay negligible taxes, a tendency to spread disease or to commit crimes, an increasing birthrate, low standards of living, unusual resistance to assimilation.

In group disputes it is—we must admit—exceedingly difficult to distinguish realistic conflict from prejudice proper.   Let us consider a case of a clash over national interests.   On December 7, 1941, Japan's war organization bombed Pearl Harbor.   The threat to the interests and safety of Americans was utterly realistic.   The reflex of resistance was immediate; a state of war existed.   In this incident no prejudice was involved.   Soon, however, the persecution of Japanese-Americans began.   Not a single instance of sabotage was proved; the relocation program was cruel and unnecessary. At the same time, an American view of the common people of Japan took on a typical stereotyped character; they were all "rats," fit only for extermination.   Thus from a realistic core of conflict there rapidly developed an unrealistic complex of prejudice which did not contribute to the realistic handling of issues.   (It would have been far more efficient for the war effort, for example, to allow Japanese-American farmers to continue their food production, and to have avoided the expense and commitment of personnel needed for running the relocation camps.)

Difficult as the distinction is, we maintain that in any given case of national conflict, or of economic conflict between minority groups, a rational analysis of the situation is usually possible—so that the inherently competitive elements in the situation can be set off from the accompanying prejudice.

In the field of religion the analysis is still more difficult. To many individuals religious convictions are profoundly real. The Mohammedan may feel that it is his moral duty to convert the infidel by sword; whereas the Crusader of old certainly felt it to be his God-given duty to destroy the Mohammedan in order to rescue the Holy Grail.

The Christian church has been rent by many schisms, as have all the great religions of the world. The dissident minorities have broken off for what seemed to them important reasons. There are *free* Methodists, *reformed* Jews, *primitive* Baptists, *old* Catholics and *Vedantist* Hindus. While some of the schismatics may have a charitable view of the parent congregation, the very conditions of conflicting values under which the split occurred often make for intolerance. It goes without saying that if two religions (or branches of a religion) are *militantly* disposed, each claiming to be the one and only true religion, and if each is bent on converting or eliminating the rival sect, a genuinely realistic conflict will ensue.

Let us consider a situation in present-day America. Each citizen is, according to the American creed, entitled to seek the truth in his own way and to worship God as he chooses, or not to worship Him at all if he so prefers. In order that this liberty be universally respected, each citizen is expected to hold at bottom a basic ideal of relativism (one man's truth is as respectable as another's). At the same time, his religion is likely to demand a contradictory ideal of absolutism. One truth only can be final. Anyone who does not hold this truth is in error, and cannot be encouraged to follow false paths.

Thus stated, the realistic clash of intrinsically contradictory values is likely to occur in any citizen who is loyal to the democratic creed and at the same time firmly convinced that his religion is the one and only true religion. It seems unlikely that this conflict is upsetting to many individuals, for they have lived their lives according to both frames of reference, generally guiding their public acts and civic policy by the American creed, and their private lives by their religion.

But the clash, many people think, is inherent in the contradictory ideals of the state and of the church in America. They point, as the prime example, to the situation of Roman Catholicism in this country. While for two centuries the Church has lived in close affiliation with the American doctrine, both enjoying and permitting liberty, is there not, they ask, an inherent contradiction present? If Roman Catholicism represents, as it claims, the only true Church, and if Protestantism is a heresy, should or could the Church, if politically powerful enough, countenance a social system that encourages heresy?

Rightly or wrongly, many Protestant Americans fear the Roman Church—arguing that they do so not on the ground of ignorance, fear, or prejudice, but on the wholly realistic grounds that this Church may in time be in a position to wield dominant political influence. When such a time comes, will it destroy (through its own firm sense of conviction) the religious liberties enjoyed by non-Catholics? One student expressed this attitude as follows:

> I have no objections to Catholics as individuals, nor to their religion; but I mistrust the motives of the Catholic Hierarchy toward democracy, toward the public school system, and in the State Department (in its dealings with Spain, Mexico, the Vatican). I have seen its pressure on editorial policy of newspapers, and I resent that.

To this individual the issue seems wholly realistic.

Whether there are realistic grounds for the conflict is not a problem we can consider adequately here. Only a most searching study of Catholic theology and a dispassionate weighing of the Church's actual respect for the American creed, in the past and in the present, could give a satisfactory answer.

What, for our present purposes, is especially significant is the fact that the realistic issue (if it exists) seems almost impossible to disentangle from prejudice. While the student's statement of the problem just cited sounds relatively objective, the following statement written by another student is more typical.

> The Catholic religion is bigoted, reactionary, superstitious, a threat to American freedom. All Catholics know is what the priests tell them. I should like to know just what the Church teaches in respect to freedom of worship in America if the time comes when the voting majority of the people are Catholic.

This whole issue is particularly interesting, for it starts with a sensible question: can the contradiction implied in the American democratic and Roman Catholic ethos be successfully resolved in the future, as it has in the past? The issue, if one exists, is entirely realistic—for non-Catholics have a right to be vigilant concerning their own future liberties. But what for our present purposes is important is the fact that it seems virtually impossible to consider this issue objectively and in a dispassionate manner unclouded by irrelevant bias.   Certainly the most widely read current discussions of the issue fail to do so.[17]

To summarize this section: there are many economic, international, and ideological conflicts that represent a genuine clash of interests.   Most of the rivalries that result, however, take on a great amount of excess baggage.   Prejudice, by clouding the issue, retards a realistic solution of the core conflict.   In most instances the rivalry that is perceived is inflated.   In the economic sphere it is seldom true that one ethnic group directly threatens another, although this interpretation is often given.   In the international sphere, disputes are magnified through the addition of irrelevant stereotypes.   Similar confusion clouds religious disputes.

Realistic conflict is like a note on an organ.   It sets all prejudices that are attuned to it into simultaneous vibration.   The listener can scarcely distinguish the pure note from the surrounding jangle.

Exploitative Advantage

In the preceding chapter we stated briefly the Marxian view that prejudice is fostered by capitalists in order to keep control over the proletariat which they exploit.   This theory improves in credibility if we enlarge it to mean that exploitation occurs in many ways in addition to the economic, and that any form of exploitation brings prejudice in its train.

Carey McWilliams offers an exploitative theory to explain anti-Semitism.[18]   Social exclusion of Jews, he points out, commenced in the 1870's just at a time when huge fortunes were being made in industry and in railroading.   The tycoons, the theory holds, felt that their new power was not strictly in keeping with the democratic ideals of America.   Hence they sought a diversionary issue.   Jews, they argued, were the real villains, responsible for economic ills, political chicanery, and moral lapses.   It was convenient, too, to have someone to exclude from clubs and residential zones, someone to serve as a doormat for the newfound snobbery on the part of the successful and rich.   Anti-Semitism thus became a "mask for privilege," a convenient evasion and justification.   The parvenus encouraged labor to take up the myth and blame the Jews for their discomforts.   Doing so diverted attention from the factory owners, whose labor policies left much to be desired.   Active propaganda was financed by some capitalists in order to fix attention on Jewish misdeeds.   This theory asserts that prejudice brings a mixture of exploitative gains: economic advantage, social snobbery, a feeling of moral superiority.

Similarly, exploitation of the Negro takes many forms.   Being forced to work at menial jobs and for low wages, Negroes provide financial advantage to their employers (*economic gain*); the double standard that gives white men access to Negro women but denies corresponding access of white women to male Negroes provides *sexual gain*. Almost uniform agreement that Negroes are low class in mentality and manners provides all whites who hold the view with a comforting *status gain*. Intimidated or cajoled, the Negro may support a certain candidate for office, or by not voting ensure his election; in this way there is *political gain*. Thus from the exploitative point of view there is abundant practical reason for keeping Negroes in their place. Nearly every white man stands to gain from it.[19]

The agitator who makes it his business to stir up hatred and hostility toward certain ethnic groups is essentially an exploiter. He takes his tribute not from minority groups directly, but from his own followers. They may elect him to office if he pictures himself as their savior from the threat he himself has luridly depicted. A politician elected to maintain "white supremacy" is always one who has whipped up animosity toward the Negro in the course of his campaigning. Sometimes direct financial gain accrues to the agitator. Potentates of the Ku Klux Klan have made much money out of the initiation fees, hooded costumes, and "klektokens" of members. Bigotry can be a big business on the part of "prophets of deceit."[20]

To summarize: there lies at the heart of any diversified and stratified social system the tempting possibility that economic, sexual, political, and status gains may result from a deliberate (and even from unconscious) exploitation of minorities. To achieve these gains prejudice is propagated by those who stand to win the most advantage.

Social Regulation of Aggression

Anger and aggression are normal impulses. Culture, however, endeavors (just as it does in the case of sex) to reduce the intensity of the impulse, or else severely to restrict its channels of expression. Lord Chesterfield, writing in courtly England, said, "The mark of a gentleman is that he never shows his anger." Balinese society trains its children to remain relatively impassive in the face of provocations to anger. But most cultures approve of some open expressions of hostility. In our society an adult is generally permitted a good bout of swearing when he is sufficiently enraged.

But American modes of handling aggressive impulses are on the whole complex and contradictory. We encourage competitive games and strenuous competition in business, but in both a subtle infusion of good sportsmanship and generosity is expected. Children are taught at Sunday School to turn the other cheek. At home they are taught to stand up for their rights. While an exaggerated sense of personal honor is not encouraged, yet no one is supposed to tolerate humiliation beyond a certain point. School boys' fights are often approved. Traditionally the mother inculcates patience and control while the father stimulates "manly virtues"—among which competitiveness is outstanding.[21]

In some societies the institutionalization of aggressiveness is not so intricate and confusing. Among the Navaho, Kluckhohn reports, it is taken for granted that one will blame a witch for his privations or misfortune.[22] This custom provides the answer to the problem every society faces: what to do about satisfying hate so as still to keep the core of society solid. In one sense or another, Kluckhohn believes, every social structure since the Stone Age has permitted "witches"—or some functional equivalent—in order that the natural impulses of aggression may have a legitimate outlet, causing least harm to the in-group.

In European societies of the 15th century people were officially encouraged to direct hostility toward witches, just as they were in 17th century Massachusetts, and among 20th century Navahos. Nazi Germany officially offered both Jews and communists as targets of aggression, legally absolving all citizens who attacked them. In communist China today there is evidence that Americans are the official target for abuse.

It is characteristic of American democracy that in peacetime it has no *officially* approved scapegoats. The American creed is egalitarian and high in its morality. No ethnic or religious or political group can be abused or discriminated against with official approval. Yet even here customs do sanction certain forms of aggressive attack. It is proper in many clubs, neighborhoods, offices, to talk against and actively discriminate against Jews, Negroes, Catholics, liberals. There is also a tendency to wink at gang fights between ethnic groups of children. Not long ago it was a tolerated practice for boys from the North End of Boston (Italian extraction) and boys from the South End (Irish extraction) to gather at the Boston Common for an annual pitched battle in which both epithets and stones were hurled with considerable abandon. The ruction was not officially approved, but was tolerated.

Thus, either officially or informally, most societies do seem to encourage the open expression of hostility toward certain groups of "witches." Perhaps, as Kluckhohn asserts, the process may best be viewed as a safety-valve arrangement, so that aggression will do the least damage to the central organization of a society.

There is, however, one weakness in this theory as it stands. It implies too dogmatically that in persons (and therefore in each society itself) there is a certain irreducible quantity of aggression that must find an outlet. If this view is true, then some form of prejudice and hostility is inevitable. Social policy should not be concerned with reducing prejudice but only with deflecting it from certain targets onto others. The theory, then, has exceedingly important consequences for social action. Before accepting it, we must analyze much more fully the nature of aggression, and the psychological relationship that obtains between aggression and prejudice (Chapter 22).

Cultural Devices to Ensure Loyalty

Besides the channeling of aggression, every group employs other mechanisms to ensure the loyalty of its members. We have already seen in Chapter 2 that preference for one's own country or ethnic group comes from habit: we think in its language; its successes are ours; it provides the frame of personal security. But groups are not content with this "natural" identification of its members; they stimulate it in many ways—usually at the expense of out-groups.

One device is to fix attention upon the group's own glorious past. Each nation has some verbal expression that indicates that its inhabitants are *the* people, or the *chosen* people, or that they inhabit "God's country," or that God is "mit uns." The legend of a Golden Age intensifies the ethnocentrism. A modern Greek measures his worth by the ancient glory of Greece. An Englishman takes pride in his Shakespeare. An American proudly identifies himself as a Son of the American Revolution. A resident of Breslau can claim the city as belonging historically to *his* ethnic group whether he happens to be Polish, Czech, German, or Austrian. As territorial boundaries change and rechange, more and more groups pile up a claim, each thinking of its own Golden Age. In Europe especially, so many areas are claimed by so many ethnic groups that friction is intense.

School instruction magnifies the friction. Virtually no history book ever teaches that one's country was ever in the wrong. Geography is ordinarily taught with a nationalistic bias. The number of inventions that Soviet Russia claims for itself causes a smile in other countries. All these chauvinistic devices breed ethnocentrism.

In the previous chapter we spoke of the "community pattern" theory of prejudice. To some writers it seems that no other explanation is needed. The atmosphere is so saturated with in-group legend and belief that a member cannot escape their effect. A child in a Catholic school cannot help but learn the Catholic version of the Reformation and as a result probably come to regard Protestants as dupes of the sinful and heretical monk, Luther. A Protestant child cannot help but learn another version of the Reformation and consequently suspect Catholics of being under the cloud of mediaeval darkness and corruption.

There is a Machiavellian view of the usefulness of prejudice in society. It maintains that the intricate pattern of prejudice holds society in a kind of equilibrium. Prejudice maintains the status quo, and for a standpatter the status quo is a positive value. Lord Chesterfield, a conservative, frankly held this position:

> The herd of mankind can hardly be said to think; their notions are almost all adoptive; and, in general, I believe it is better that it should be so, as such common prejudices contribute more to order and quiet, than their own separate reasonings would do, uncultivated and unimproved as they are. We have many of those useful prejudices in this country, which I should be very sorry to see removed. The good Protestant conviction, that the Pope is both Anti-Christ and the Whore of Babylon, is a more effectual preservative, in this country, against popery than all the solid and unanswerable arguments of Chillingworth.[23]

Chesterfield finds the prejudices of the herd (for whom he has contempt) help to hold in check the Catholic Church (for which he also has contempt). Since the blind prejudices of the masses are useful (in supporting his own position) he approves them.

To accuse a group of holding prejudice is often an effective way of uniting that group and intensifying its convictions. Many Southerners (whatever their own attitudes toward the Negro may be) unite in resisting Northern criticism. Widespread disapproval throughout the world of the South African laws disenfranchising the Cape Coloured had the effect of strengthening the Nationalist Party of Malan and his supporters. Outside criticism is interpreted as an attack on the autonomy of the group. It usually results in greater cohesion. Hence the ethnocentrism that is under attack may become a necessary symbol of solidarity and flourish as never before.

Cultural pressure makes difficulty for the occasional individual whose private attitudes are at variance. One who presumes to resist social pressure—refusing to hate and avoid the groups proscribed—may be greeted with derision or with persecution. Friendly social relations with Negroes in some regions of the United States bring accusations of "communism" or "nigger-loving," and are likely to lead to social ostracism. This type of conflict—between social pressure and personal conviction—is illustrated in the following excerpt from an interview conducted with a white housewife who was living in an interracial housing project.

> I like it here. . . . I think the Negro people are wonderful. They should be given every opportunity, the same as whites. I want my children to grow up to be unprejudiced . . . yet I am worried about my daughter Ann. She's grown up so that she doesn't see any differences between Negro and white people. She's only 12 now—there are a lot of fine Negro boys here in the project—she's likely to just naturally fall in love with one. If she does, it would be such a mess—people are so prejudiced— she'd never be happy. I don't know what to do—it would be all right, I guess, if everybody wasn't so prejudiced against mixed marriages—I've been thinking a lot about it—I'll probably move out before Ann gets much older.[24]

Cultural Pluralism vs. Assimilation

In most minority ethnic groups members are of two minds. Some believe that in-group bonds should be strengthened by preserving all ethnic and cultural characteristics, by endogamy (marriage only within the group), and by educating the children in the language and traditions of the group. Others favor amalgamation into the dominant culture. They prefer to attend the same schools, churches, hospitals; to have one set of codes, to read the same newspapers; and perhaps through intermarriage to participate in a common melting pot. Negroes, Jews, immigrants of all types divide on this issue. So, too, do members of the dominant group, some of whom favor assimilation, and some separatism—*apartheid*, as the South Africans call it.

Like most realistic issues, the practical choice does not lie between mutually exclusive alternatives. Even those who favor segregation do not want Negroes to develop their own language or their own laws. They want them to be amalgamated *in certain respects.* And even those who argue for assimilation may wish to preserve certain pleasant cultural traits—perhaps the cuisine of the French, Negro spirituals, Polish folk dances, St. Patrick's Day.

Supporters of assimilation sincerely believe that until unity of practice, and even unity of stock are accomplished, there will be too much visibility—too many grounds for conflict, both genuine and specious.

Supporters of cultural pluralism believe that variety is the spice of life. Each culture has distinctive contributions to make, and while divergent customs and languages seem strange, they are stimulating, instructive, and beneficial to society. America, they say, should have something more colorful than the monotonous, standardized, commercialized culture that one sees along its motorized highways. They argue further, difference does not necessarily make for hostility. Open minds and hospitable attitudes are not incompatible with pluralism.

Perhaps the least effective policy to pursue is for members of a dominant group to *insist* that members of minority groups give up some cherished belief or code. Such pressure is not made in good faith and will surely be resisted by the group being attacked. In fact, it will have the reverse effect, for, as we have just seen, victimization often enhances in-group feeling and intensifies in-group traits. Such attacks are particularly futile when they concern deep values, as in the case of religion. To abuse their theology will not make Catholics less Catholic, nor devout Jews less Jewish.

One sociological author, Alfred Lee, believes that there is a tendency for diverse ethnic groups in the United States to assimilate into four principal "ethnoid segments," viz., the white Protestant, the Roman Catholic, Colored, and Jewish.[25] The labels in three of these cases are religious, but they imply a far broader basis of integration than mere religion. Thus "Roman Catholic" implies relatively recent immigrant stock and urban living in addition to church membership.

Lee believes that all four segments press toward an adjustment to the white Protestant ethos. In many cases Jews lose their identity and merge into this dominant group; some middle- and upper-class Roman Catholics do the same. The assimilation of colored strains is harder, though Orientals are said to succeed relatively more easily than Negroes.

The dominant group tends to resist the pressure toward assimilation, especially at the point where the pressure is greatest. Middle- and upper-class white Protestants are more anti-Semitic, because the pressure from Jews toward assimilation occurs in these classes. For the same reason, lower-class white Protestants are more strongly anti-Negro. On the political front a recent militant antagonism toward Roman Catholicism has appeared, since it is at the political level that Catholic pressure is most acutely felt.

Lee further suggests that we might indicate the intensity of the forces working against assimilation. There is a special potency in the Negro group making for in-group consciousness, combined with strong color prejudice in the dominant group. If this potency were estimated at a rating of 10, one might then hazard that the "cohesion-making morale" of the Jewish ethnoid group is 8; of the Roman Catholic group 6. By contrast, all special minorities, say the Ulster Irish Presbyterians, would have far less cohesion potency, on the same rating scale perhaps in the region of 1. While purely speculative, this manner of approach to the problem is suggestive.

When the dominant group has marked prejudice it is favorable neither to cultural pluralism nor to assimilation. It says in effect, "We don't want you to be like us, but you must not be different." What is the minority to do? Negroes are blamed for being ignorant and also for seeking an education to raise their status; Jews are criticized, as we saw in Chapter 12, for being seclusive and for being intrusive. The Afrikaner wants total *apartheid* but is reluctant to give the Bantu people the territory and political independence that alone would make total *apartheid* possible. Immigrants to America have found themselves abused both for maintaining their cultures and for pressing for assimilation. Minorities are damned if they seek assimilation, damned if they don't.

All in all, it seems that the solution to the problem of intergroup relations will be found neither through assimilation nor through cultural pluralism, if we regard these as categorically distinct policies. The process of accommodation is much subtler. What is needed is freedom for both assimilation and for pluralism to occur according to the needs and desires of the minority group itself. Neither policy can be forced. The evolution of societies is a slow process. It can come about with minimum friction only if we take a relaxed and permissive attitude toward the process.

Summary

We shall repeat our list of ten sociocultural conditions that seem to make for prejudice:

1. Heterogeneity in the population
2. Ease of vertical mobility
3. Rapid social change with attendant *anomie*
4. Ignorance and barriers to communication
5. The relative density of minority group population
6. The existence of realistic rivalries and conflict
7. Exploitation sustaining important interests in the community
8. Sanctions given to aggressive scapegoating
9. Legend and tradition that sustain hostility
10. Unfavorable attitudes toward both assimilation and cultural pluralism

NOTES AND REFERENCES

1. R. M. WILLIAMS, JR. *The reduction of intergroup tensions.* New York: Social Science Research Council, 1947, Bulletin 57, 59.

2. B. BETTELHEIM AND M. JANOWITZ. *Dynamics of Prejudice: A Psychological and Sociological Study of Veterans.* New York: Harper, 1950, Chapter 4.

3. A. A. CAMPBELL. Factors associated with attitudes toward Jews. In T. M. NEWCOMB AND E. L. HARTLEY (EDS.), *Readings in social psychology.* New York: Henry Holt, 1947.

4. A. MINTZ. A re-examination of correlations between lynchings and economic indices. *Journal of Abnormal and Social Psychology,* 1946, **41,** 154-160.

5. D. YOUNG. *Research memorandum on minority peoples in the depression.* New York: Social Science Research Council, 1937, Bulletin 31, 133.

6. L. SROLE. Unpublished study.

7. A. H. ROBERTS, M. ROKEACH, K. McDITRICK. Anomie, authoritarianism and prejudice: a replication of Srole's study. *American Psychologist,* 1952, **7,** 311-312.

8. G. MURPHY, LOIS B. MURPHY, T. M. NEWCOMB. *Experimental Social Psychology.* New York: Harper, 1937.

9. H. A. GRACE AND J. O. NEUHAUS. Information and social distance as predictors of hostility toward nations. *Journal of Abnormal and Social Psychology,* 1952, **47,** Supplement, 540-545.

10. R. M. WILLIAMS, JR. *Op. cit.,* 57 ff.

11. D. M. HEER. *Caste, class, and local loyalty as determining factors in South Carolina politics.* (Unpublished.) Cambridge: Harvard Univ., Social Relations Library.

12. A. M. RICHMOND. Economic insecurity and stereotypes as factors in colour prejudice. *Sociological Review* (British), 1950, **42,** 147-170.

13. H. COON. Dynamite in Chicago housing. *Negro Digest,* 1951, **9,** 3-9.

14. R. C. WEAVER. Housing in a democracy. *The Annals of the American Academy of Political and Social Science,* 1946, **244,** 95-105.

15. T. PARSONS. Racial and religious differences as factor in group tensions. In L. BRYSON, L. FINKELSTEIN AND R. M. MACIVER (EDS.), *Approaches to National Unity.* New York: Harper, 1945, 182-199.

16. O. COLLINS. Ethnic behavior in industry: sponsorship and rejection in a New England factory. *American Journal of Sociology,* 1946, **51,** 293-298.

17. For example: P. BLANSHARD, *American Freedom and Catholic Power,* Boston: Beacon Press, 1949; and J. M. O'NEILL, *Catholicism and American Freedom,* New York: Harper, 1952.

18. C. McWILLIAMS. *A Mask for Privilege.* Boston: Little, Brown, 1948.

19. Some of these factors are discussed more fully in J. DOLLARD, *Caste and Class in a Southern Town.* New Haven: Yale Univ. Press, 1937.

20. *Cf.* A. FORSTER, *A Measure of Freedom,* New York: Doubleday, 1950; also L. LOWENTHAL AND N. GUTERMAN, *Prophets of Deceit,* New York: Harper, 1949.

21. T. PARSONS. Certain primary sources and patterns of aggression

in the social structure of the Western world. *Psychiatry*, 1947, **10**, 167-181.

22. C. M. KLUCKHOHN. *Navaho Witchcraft*. Cambridge: Peabody Museum of American Archaeology and Ethnology, **22**, No. 2, 1944.

23. LORD CHESTERFIELD. *Letters to His Son*. February 7, O.S. 1749.

24. M. DEUTSCH. The directions of behavior: a field-theoretical approach to the understanding of inconsistencies. *Journal of Social Issues*, 1949, **5**, 45.

25. A. McC. LEE. Sociological insights into American culture and personality. *Journal of Social Issues*, 1951, **7**, 7-14.

CHAPTER 15

CHOICE OF SCAPEGOATS

*They take the Christians to be the cause of every disaster to
the state, of every misfortune to the people. If the Tiber
reaches the wall, if the Nile does not reach the fields, if the sky
does not move or if the earth does, if there is a famine, or if
there is a plague, the cry is at once, "The Christians to the
Lions."*

TERTULLIAN (THIRD CENTURY A.D.)

Strictly speaking, the term "minority" refers only to some group
that is smaller than some other group with which it is compared.
In this sense the Caucasian race would be a minority, so too Methodists in the United States and Democrats in Vermont. But the term
has also a *psychological* flavor. It implies that the dominant group
has stereotyped ideas about some smaller segment of the population
which bears ethnoid characteristics, that to some degree it accords
this segment discriminatory treatment, with the result that members
of this segment grow resentful and often intensify their determina-
tion to remain a distinct group.

Why some statistical minorities become psychological minorities
is the problem of this chapter. And a difficult problem it is. It
might be stated in the form of a simple diagram.

STATISTICAL MINORITIES

Mere Actuarial Minorities	*Psychological Minorities*	
Designated as minorities for certain purposes but never an object of prejudice	Mildly disparaged and discriminated against	Scapegoats

School children, registered nurses, Presbyterians, are actuarial minorities but are not the object of prejudice. Among the psychological minorities we include many immigrants and regional groups,
occupations, colored people, and adherents to certain religions.

As the diagram implies, some psychological minorities are the object of merely mild disparagement; others attract such strong hostility that we call them "scapegoats." What we have to say applies to any psychological minority, whether it is mildly or roundly abused. For the sake of simplicity we shall employ the term "scapegoat" to cover both.

This term, the reader will note, implies a specific theory of prejudice, namely the *frustration theory* described briefly in Chapter 13 and discussed more fully in later chapters. The implication is that some out-group innocently attracts the aggression engendered by frustrations suffered by members of some in-group. There is much truth in this theory, but we need not assume that it explains all of prejudice in order to discuss why certain groups and not others become targets for displaced aggression.

Meaning of Scapegoat

The term *scapegoat* originated in the famous ritual of the Hebrews, described in the Book of Leviticus (16:20-22). On the Day of Atonement a live goat was chosen by lot. The high priest, robed in linen garments, laid both his hands on the goat's head, and confessed over it the iniquities of the children of Israel. The sins of the people thus symbolically transferred to the beast, it was taken out into the wilderness and let go. The people felt purged, and for the time being, guiltless.

The type of thinking here involved is not uncommon. From earliest times the notion has persisted that guilt and misfortune can be shifted from one man's back to another. Animistic thinking confuses what is mental with what is physical. If a load of wood can be shifted, why not a load of sorrow or a load of guilt?

Nowadays we are likely to label this mental process *projection.* In other people we see the fear, anger, lust that reside primarily in ourselves. It is not we ourselves who are responsible for our misfortunes, but other people. In our common speech we recognize this failing in such phrases as "whipping-boy," "taking it out on the dog," or "scapegoat."

The psychological processes involved in scapegoating are, as we shall see in Chapters 21-24, complex. What concerns us at present are the sociocultural factors involved in the selection of scapegoats. Psychological theory alone will not tell us why certain groups are scapegoated more than others.

In each of six separate years—1905, 1906, 1907, 1910, 1913, 1914— over a million immigrants came to the United States. The resulting minority group problems were legion, but in the course of a few years most of them began to iron themselves out. The great bulk of this influx was made up of adaptable people, eager to become Americans. The melting pot commenced to swallow them up. In the second generation the assimilation was partly, though not entirely, complete. It is estimated today that there are approximately 26 million second-generation Americans. To some extent this enormous group still suffers certain (gradually diminishing) handicaps. Many, speaking a foreign language at home, find their knowledge of English less than complete. They are ashamed of their parents, who still seem foreign. The sense of social inferiority in status is haunting. Usually they lack a reassuring pride in the ethnic traditions and culture of the parent. Sociologists have discovered a relatively high crime rate and other evidences of maladjustment in second-generation Americans.

Yet most of the psychological minorities arriving from Europe have rubbed along amicably enough in the elastic social structure of America. Occasionally they have been scapegoats, but not persistently so. Yankees in a conservative Maine community may discriminate socially against the Italians or French-Canadians who live there—but the snobbery is relatively mild, and one can seldom see evidences of actual aggression (true scapegoating). On the other hand, a much more serious problem of antagonism exists in the case of other minorities (Jews, Negroes, Orientals, Mexicans) to whom the dominant majority has said, "We shall never accept you as one of us."

Just as it is impossible to tell clearly when a group is a scapegoat and when it is not, so too we cannot find a clear formula that will cover the selection of scapegoats. The essence of the matter seems to be that different groups are singled out for different reasons. We have already noted the contrast between the accusations made against Negroes and Jews (Chapter 12), and have discussed the theory which states that each of these two scapegoats "take away" different *kinds* of guilt.

There seems to be no such thing as an "all-duty scapegoat" although some groups come nearer to this objective than others. Perhaps today Jews and Negroes are blamed for the widest variety of evils. We note that these are *inclusive* social groups consisting of both sexes (and their children), which transmit social values and cultural traits. They are more or less permanent, definite, and stable. By contrast one finds many *ad hoc* scapegoats who are blamed for quite specific things. The American Medical Association or the Soft Coal Miners Union may be much hated by certain portions of society, being blamed for evils in health policy, labor policy, high prices, or some particular inconvenience for which they may or may not be partly responsible. (Scapegoats need not be lily-white in their innocence, but they always attract more blame, more animosity, more stereotyped judgment than can be rationally justified.)

The nearest to the all-duty scapegoat then is a religious, ethnic, or racial group. Having permanence and stability, they can be given a definite status and stereotyped as a group. The arbitrariness of the categorization we have already commented upon—many people being included or excluded by a kind of social fiat. A given Negro may have more white ancestry than colored—but what is wanted is a "socially supposed" race, and so he is arbitrarily included. Occasionally the process is reversed. A Vienna mayor during Nazi days wished to accord some privilege to a prominent Jew. He met the objection that his beneficiary came from a Jewish family by saying, "It is up to me whether he is a Jew or not." The fact that Nazis made certain favored Jews into "honorary Aryans" shows the importance of maintaining the persecuted minority intact. So long as this is done the evil can be viewed as proceeding from an integrated, personalized group with alien values, possessing a permanently threatening character continuing from generation to generation. It is for this reason that racial, religious, and ethnic hate is more pervasive than prejudice against occupational, age, or sex groupings. Definite and permanent categories are needed to rivet definite and permanent hate.

Historical Method

These various generalizations still do not bear on one principal question: why over a given period of time is one particular ethnic, racial, religious, or ideological group made to suffer more discrimination and persecution than can be rationally accounted for by its known traits or deserved reputation?

It is chiefly the historical method that helps us to understand why over a course of years scapegoats come and scapegoats go, and why there is a periodic lessening or intensification of the hostility they receive. Anti-Negro prejudice today is unlike what it was under slavery; anti-Semitism, the most persistent of all prejudices, takes a different form in different epochs and waxes and wanes according to circumstances (for example, those discussed in the preceding chapter).

Anti-Catholicism in the United States today exists but in a less aggravated form than sixty years ago. At that time there flourished the so-called American Protective Association, a militantly anti-Catholic organization.[1] Around the turn of the century the Association died out, and at the same time—for reasons that are not clear—anti-Catholic feeling seemed to subside. Even the great waves of immigration of European Catholics did not revive the persecutions of the 19th century. In very recent years, however, as we saw in the preceding chapter, alarm at the alleged rise in the political influence of the Roman Church seems again to be increasing. The tide of prejudice may again be on the flood. Only a careful historical analysis can give us an understanding of these waves.

During the heyday of the American Protective Association there was little or no interest among social scientists in the phenomenon it represented. Today such agitational movements are more carefully studied.[2] There was, however, a forgotten citizen who raised a protesting voice against the American Protective Association, offering an analysis and a warning that were in advance of his time. Especially interesting is his final reference to anti-Semitism which, according to his diagnosis, was in 1895 a much less virulent form of scapegoating than anti-Catholicism. Half a century has brought a reversal of emphasis in the two forms of prejudice.

> It might happen though, at some future time, that some other peaceful, law-abiding, producing and patriotic element would become the hated thing of intolerance, bigotry and fanaticism. APA-ism, if allowed now and tolerated because it has the support of persons and interests of individual power and importance, might be some time directed at any class or individual who shall fall under the displeasure of its leaders or managers. Foreigners and American Catholics having been disposed of, who knows but that the next step might be an attempt to wipe out the Jews.
>
> (signed) "An American"[3]

Since the problem of the choice of scapegoats is primarily one for the historical method, we shall work as the historian works, and focus upon concrete cases. The following analyses deal with only three selected victims: Jews, Reds, and the "occasional" scapegoat. None of the surveys pretends to be complete. Each story is exceedingly complex, and errors of interpretation or emphasis quite likely occur.

Jews as Scapegoats

Anti-Semitism is thought to reach back at least to the fall of Judea in 586 B.C. When the Jews were dispersed, they took with them their relatively rigid and unbending customs. Dietary laws prohibited them from eating with others; intermarriage was forbidden. They were even by their own prophet Jeremiah considered "stiff-necked." Wherever they went their orthodoxy presented a problem.

In Greece and Rome—to mention only two of their new home-lands—new ideas were welcomed. The Jews were received as inter-esting strangers. But the cosmopolitan cultures which they entered could not understand why Jews did not reciprocate the meals, games, and gaiety of their own pagan life. Jehovah could easily be fitted into the galaxy of gods who were worshipped. Why could not the Jews accept the pantheon? Judaism seemed too absolute in its theology, ethnic customs, and rites.

Among these rites that of circumcision probably caused much consternation. The symbolism (circumcision of the spirit) was not comprehended. The butchery seemed, rather, a barbaric prac-tice, a threat to manhood. How much unconscious fear and sexual conflict this rite has aroused in the minds of non-Jewish people throughout the centuries is impossible to say. The intimacy of the "castration threat" may play a large, if unconscious, part in the ab-horrence of things Jewish.

Yet in Ancient Rome it is fairly certain that Christians were persecuted more vigorously than Jews. Tertullian, in the passage cited at the beginning of this chapter, gives a terse record of the scapegoating of Christians. Until the 4th Century when Chris-tianity became the officially dominant religion under Constantine, it is probable that the Jews fared relatively better than the Chris-tians. But after that time the Sabbaths were separated, and the Jews became a highly visible group marked off from the Christians.[4]

Since the early Christians were themselves Jews, it took the first two or three centuries of the Christian era for this fact to be for-gotten. Then only did the accusation arise that the Jews (as a group) were responsible for the Crucifixion. Subsequently, for cen-turies it seems that to a large number of people the epithet "Christ killer" was a sufficient cause for scapegoating the Jew on any and all occasions. Certain it is that by the time of St. John Chrysostom (Fourth Century) elaborate anti-Semitic homilies were preached, accusing Jews not only of the Crucifixion but of all other conceivable crimes as well.

Some support for anti-Semitism is drawn from straight Christian theological reasoning. Since the Bible explicitly asserts that the Jews are God's chosen people, they must be hounded until they acknowledge their Messiah. God will punish them until they do so. Thus their persecution by Christians is ordained. It is true that no modern theologian would interpret this situation to mean that an individual Christian is justified in acting unfairly or un-charitably toward any individual Jew. Yet the fact remains that God acts in mysterious ways, and apparently His concern is to bring recalcitrant Jews, His chosen people, to acknowledge the New Testament as well as the Old. While modern anti-Semites are certainly not aware that they are punishing the Jews for this particular reason, from the theological point of view their conduct is understandable in terms of God's long-range design.

At this point the theological explanation invites a still subtler psychological analysis. Since the Hebrews did not accept the Messiah they were not bound by the peculiarly exacting moral teaching of the New Testament. (The fact that their own moral laws were likewise stringent is not at this point relevant.) The argument is that Christians themselves have a hidden desire to escape from the stringent morality enjoined by the Gospels and Epistles. This evil impulse may, according to psychoanalytic reasoning, create severe conflict and hatred of oneself for having such unholy desires. Symbolically, therefore, sinful Christians are also "Christ killers." But this thought is so painful that it must be repressed. Behold: here is the Jew who openly repudiates New Testament teaching. I shall therefore hate him (because I hate the same inclination in myself). My guilt is laid upon the Jew, just as the ancient Hebrew's guilt was laid upon the goat.

Freud extends this logic by pointing to the repressed desire most men have to "kill the father." The restrictions placed by parental authority are hard to bear—and there may also be an element of sexual rivalry involved. In any case, Freud argues, a strong inclination to parricide exists—and this leads even to the desire to kill God, the Father of all. Now the Jews, if they are Christ-killers, are (from the Christian point of view) also God-killers. I cannot face the impulse in myself but I can transfer it to the Jews, and hate them for it.[5]

It is necessary to stress these religious factors in anti-Semitism, for the Jews are above all else a religious group. It may be rightly objected that many (perhaps most) Jews today are not religious.[6] While orthodoxy has declined, there has been no decrease in persecution. Further, it may be objected that in present-day anti-Semitism the sins of the Jews are said to be moral, financial, social; religious deviance is seldom mentioned. All this is true—and yet the vestiges of the religious issue certainly persist. The Jewish religious holidays make for visibility; so too the imposing synagogues in Jewish residential districts.

Still, many people today are indifferent to the specifically religious quarrel between Judaism and Christianity. Many more are able in their own minds to transcend it, realizing well the essential unity of the Judeo-Christian tradition. But, according to a broader interpretation of the matter, each one of us is still affected by the epic quality of spiritual ferment in Jewish culture. Jacques Maritain, the Catholic scholar, expresses the matter thus:

> Israel . . . is to be found at the very heart of the world's structure, stimulating it, exasperating it, moving it. Like an alien body, like an activating ferment injected into the mass, it gives the world no peace . . . it teaches the world to be discontent and restless as long as the world has not God, it stimulates the movement of history.[7]

A Jewish scholar continues the argument: the Jews as a group are no larger than certain unheard of tribes in Africa. Yet they have provided continous spiritual ferment. They insist upon monotheism; upon ethics; upon moral responsibility. They insist upon high scholarship; upon closely knit home life. They themselves aspire to high ideals, are restless, and ridden by conscience. Throughout the ages they have made mankind aware of God, of ethics, of high standards of attainment. Thus—though imperfect in themselves—they have been the mentors of the world's conscience.[8]

On the one hand people admire and revere these standards. On the other hand they rebel and protest. Anti-Semitism arises because people are irritated by their own consciences. Jews are symbolically their superego, and no one likes to be ridden so hard by his superego. Ethical conduct is insisted upon by Judaism, relentlessly, immediately, hauntingly. People who dislike this insistence, along with the self-discipline and acts of charity implied, are likely to justify their rejection by discrediting the whole race that produced such high ethical ideals.

Granted that all these religious and ethical considerations may have played a more prominent part formerly than they play today, still they were decisive factors in preparing the ground for the differential treatment of the Jews throughout succeeding centuries. For one thing Jews, partly at least because of their religious deviance, were excluded in many countries for long periods of time from owning land. Only transient and fringe occupations were open to them. When the Crusaders needed money, they could not borrow from Christians (whose code did not allow usury). Jews became the moneylenders. In so doing they invited customers but also contempt. Excluded not only from land-owning but also from handicraft guilds, Jewish families were forced to develop mercantile habits. Only moneylending, trading, and other stigmatized occupations were open to them.

This pattern has to some extent persisted. Occupational traditions of the European Jews transferred to new lands when Jews emigrated. To some extent the same discrimination barred them from conservative occupations. They were again obliged to develop the fringe activities where risk, shrewdness, enterprise were required. We have seen in Chapter 7 how this factor led large numbers of Jewish people, especially in New York City, into retailing, theatrical ventures, and professions. This somewhat uneven distribution on the economic checkerboard of the nation made the Jewish group conspicuous; it also intensified the stereotype that they work too hard, make lots of money, and engage in shady dealings in the less stable occupations.

It is at this point that we recall the theory of "city-hatred" (p. 211 f). If the growing urbanization of the nation means a concomitant loss of certain values and increase of anxiety due to insecurity, and if in people's minds the Jews are a symbol of the city, then it follows that Jews will be blamed for such deterioration in life as accompanies urbanization.

Looking backward once more over the historical course of events, we find another consideration of importance. Lacking a homeland, the Jews were regarded by some as parasites upon the body politic. They had certain attributes of a nation (ethnic coherence plus a tradition of nationhood). But they were, in fact, the only nation on earth without a home. People who distrusted "bi-loyalty" accused them of being less patriotic, less honorable within their adopted land than they should be. Since many Jewish people had blood relatives in other countries, and were deeply concerned for the fate of Jewish people in all lands, they were accused of "internationalism"—of less than normal patriotic loyalty Concerning the charge of divided loyalty we have no evidence, but concerning the historical fact of "homelessness" there can be no doubt. Only in recent years has the situation been altered—with what ultimate effect so far as anti-Semitism is concerned we cannot yet say. The increase in anti-Jewish feeling in Arab lands surrounding the new state of Israel seems of ominous proportions.

A further factor to be noted is that the insistence upon scholarship and intellectual attainment is a long-standing mark of Jewish culture. One method of measuring this trait as a categorical differential (p. 102) would be to compare the proportion of Jewish students in institutions of higher learning with the proportion of non-Jewish students. Provided there is no effective discrimination, one finds customarily that it is large. Why this deference to learning should help make the Jews scapegoats again requires a "depth" interpretation. Jewish intellectualism calls to mind one's own defects of ignorance and laziness. The Jews once more symbolize our conscience, against whose pricks we protest. All of us feel relatively inferior in our intellectual attainment, in the face of the great amount to be learned. When Jews on the average (or in conspicuous cases) make us conscious of our inferiority we feel a certain jealousy. By enumerating their weaknesses and sins we again recover our equilibrium. Anti-Semitism then may in part be a "sour grapes" rationalization of inferiority feelings.

Surveying such a welter of historico-psychological factors, one naturally wonders whether there is a leading motif that would sum them all up. The nearest approach would seem to be the concept of "fringe of conservative values" (p. 122 f). The expression, however, must be understood to cover not only deviance in religion, occupation, nationhood, but likewise departure from conservative mediocrity: conscience pricking, intellectual aspiration, spiritual ferment. One might put the matter this way: the Jews are regarded as just far enough *off center* (slightly above, slightly below, slightly outside) to disturb non-Jews in many different ways. The "fringe" is perceived by conservative people to represent a threat. The differences are not great; indeed, the fact that they are relatively slight may make them all the more effectively disturbing. Again we cite "the narcissism of slight differences."

This analysis of anti-Semitism, historically considered, is far from complete. It is intended only to demonstrate that, without historical perspective, we cannot tell why one group rather than another is the object of hostility. The Jews are a scapegoat of great antiquity, and only the long arm of history, aided by psychological insights, can reconstruct the story.

There are many attempts to explain anti-Semitism. Most of them center on a few features, and do so without careful regard for evidence. As a fairly typical example of "explanations" let us look at the following statement by the British anthropologist, E. J. Dingwall:

> In the case of the Jews, we find that in some important respects their own beliefs and actions excite feelings against them which are not always wholly unjustified. A people without a home, they exist everywhere as minorities, yet are knit together by religious or traditional customs which proclaim their exclusiveness and apparent refusal to assimilate . . . abhorrent of racial prejudice when applied to themselves, they do not hesitate to regard others as their inferiors. Thus they exercise a kind of perpetual, but mild, irritant in every society into which they penetrate. Although Christianity itself arose from them, they stand apart, a constant reminder that even now the slayers of the Lord are

still unrepentant. Whilst the unambitious poor are sunk in squalor, the more impatient and energetic among them climb upwards and onwards through those commercial, competitive channels where every man is for himself and where ethics are not those common in personal relations. . . . Hardened by adversity and the dislike by which they are surrounded, they become bold and provocative. Their approach to women is often open and unrestrained, and success is not always lacking. This in itself excites the jealousy and rage of more sensitive and timid suitors. . . .[9]

Certain features of this analysis are worthy of note. On the whole it takes a "stimulus object" approach, emphasizing Jewish traits and practices that are irritating to others. While some of the statements are no doubt correct, others drift into fantasy and ambiguity. The term "they" is used loosely to imply that the entire Jewish group (not a few of the individual members) regard others as inferior, or "become bold and provocative." And it is not proved, nor provable, that in their "approach to women" Jews are more "open and unrestrained" than men in other ethnic groups. Vagueness, innuendo, and imagination mar this analysis of anti-Semitism, as they mar many others.

The problem is exceedingly complex, but it will never be solved unless there is at every stage scrupulous regard for factual evidence, concerning both the traits of the Jewish group and the psychodynamic processes of anti-Semites.

Reds as Scapegoats

Our next analysis is selected for contrast. Unlike anti-Semitism, the choice of Reds as scapegoats is of relatively recent origin. Reds are of "lower visibility" than Jews; they are hard to identify or define. Yet the realistic basis of conflict (Chapter 14) is more apparent.

The fact that Jews are often called communists, and communism is dubbed a "Jewish plot" must not be allowed to confuse us. This syncretism is explained elsewhere (Chapters 2, 10, 26). It reflects the generality of prejudice and an emotional equating of disliked objects.

The scapegoating of Reds (communists) did not commence in the United States until after the Russian Revolution, for there were no available symbols or identifiable threats. To be sure, radicals of all types in the past have been scapegoats; but a new focus started to form in the United States about 1920, and has been central ever since.

It is important to note, however, that three peaks in the persecution have occurred: in the years immediately following World War I, in the middle of the 1930's, and again in the years immediately following World War II.

Certain features were common to these three periods of intensified scapegoating. (1) All represented periods when labor was in a position to test its strength against industry—two occasions being produced by wartime prosperity and full employment, and one by the legislative favors of the New Deal that gave to labor, even in the midst of economic depression, an unusually strong position. (2) The three periods also coincided with periods of unusually rapid social change wherein both the economic and political future seemed unpredictable. An atmosphere of instability and apprehension prevailed. People with property were particularly anxious, and their anxiety spread throughout the social structure. In two cases disaffected war veterans were numerous, in the other the unemployed created a comparable group troubled by uncertainties. (3) There were active liberal movements on foot during these periods: unionism was increasing, minor political parties flourished, left-wing organizations were outspoken.

The symbol "red" is a symbol of primary potency (Chapter 11). Corresponding to the color of the Russian flag, it readily came to mean "Russian." By extension it then covered all people ideologically in agreement with the Soviet position. By still further extension it has come to mean citizens of the United States who are to any extent radical, or even liberal in their views on almost any matter. Paradoxically, it even covers liberals whose convictions are totally opposed to the position of Russian communism.

> The point is made in a current story told about a state committee investigating "subversive" activities. The inquisitor asked a suspected liberal,
>
> "Are you a communist?"
>
> "No," replied the accused, "I am an anti-communist."
>
> "That's all we want to know," said the inquisitor triumphantly, "we don't care what *kind* you are."

Although it is not possible to tell clearly just who or what is red, there is, of course, a realistic conflict at the core of the animosity. Following World War I the basis was slight, for Russia was not a military threat to the United States, and as for domestic "reds," the picture was thoroughly confused. On p. 184 we listed the overlapping epithets against the new-found domestic scapegoat. They were numerous and mixed ("wobblies," "hyphenated-Americans," "Bolsheviks," "anarchists"). But the situation gradually clarified and became sharpened. The factual conflict between American and communist ideologies came into focus, mounting as Russia grew stronger. After World War II only the symbols "red" and "communist" were employed to any appreciable extent. The ideological agreement between the American communist party (though small in numbers) and the Russian "party line" became a matter of clear record. While there was chaotic confusion regarding the fringe ("front organizations," softness in the State Department, liberals, the Progressive Party, the CIO, PAC, and the like) there was at the same time a basic and sharp realistic core of conflict.

The American Communist Party was accused—and documentary evidence seemed to prove it guilty—of (1) advocating the overthrow of American government by force; (2) standing for the nationalization of means of production and distribution; (3) substituting a proletariat dictatorship for a representative form of government and destroying civil liberties; (4) proposing the elimination of the wealthy and owning class, and much of the middle class, by expropriation and Russian-style "purges." Additional charges, less realistic, include (5) militant atheism and (6) sexual immorality. (It is an interesting fact that the legend of the Russian "nationalization of women," heard so frequently in the 1920's gradually disappeared. The reason may lie in the fact that as realistic conflict increases, there is less need for innuendo and fiction.)

When a conflict is entirely realistic we can speak neither of prejudice nor of scapegoating. Yet there is in this situation a large region where the conflict is fanciful and unrealistic, animated by borrowed emotion, distorted by rash judgment and intensified by stereotype. Though the issues are sharper the confusion today is not unlike that of 1920 when the sponsor of the repressive "Lusk Laws" in the State of New York stated the issue as follows:

> The radical movement is not a peaceable endeavor to bring better economic and social conditions. . . . The movement . . . started here . . . by paid agents of the Junker class in Germany as a part of their program of industrial and military conquest . . . threatens practically everything that by tradition we hold dear. . . . It is against the thrifty prosperous, a class which the communists particularly hate. . . . It is against the Church and the family . . . attacking the institution of marriage . . . and all American institutions.[10]

With the exception of the reference to the Junker class this indictment sounds entirely modern. What is important to note is the irrationality of fusing communism with the Junkers (who were at that time also hated); also the revealing use of the broad symbols, "the radical movement." It is not specifically *communists* who are accused of extensive misdeeds but all *radicals*. Significant too is the fact that Lusk finds it necessary not to oppose "better economic and social conditions."

The fact is that not all communist values are opposed by all Americans. On the contrary, "better economic and social conditions" are desired by most. Sensing the fact that some Russian reforms were both desirable and successful, many American intellectuals, especially during the 1920's, were enthusiastically pro-Soviet. Their ardor cooled as it became evident that civil liberties were nonexistent within what was presumably a democratic people's movement. But the temporary enthusiasm of some intellectuals, and of some labor leaders, brought them into "guilt by association." Even a college professor writing an objective expository article might be labeled pro-Soviet (for not being explicitly *anti*). If anyone found anything good to say about communism he was likely to be called "red."

Thus the striking feature of red scapegoating is its grease spot effect. Almost anyone who is disliked or suspected of holding any contrary values on almost any subject can be, and is, called a communist—especially those who advocate liberal, pro-labor, tolerant, or even analytical views of communism and its policies. College professors are suspect because whenever emotion is in control, anti-intellectualism prevails. During the witch-hunting of the Fifteenth Century, Pope Innocent VIII saw fit to denounce liberals and rationalists who "with most unblushing effrontery" contended that witchcraft was not a real thing.[11] Anyone who called for a critical and differentiated appraisal of communism and of communist phobia in the middle of the Twentieth Century similarly laid himself open to abuse from high sources (Senate committees, State legislatures, Boards of college regents).

The selection of reds as scapegoats must therefore be explained as a double phenomenon, involving first and foremost a realistic clash of values—and this conflict in itself would not be classed as prejudice. But to this clash have accrued much autistic thinking, stereotyping and diffusion of emotion—primarily of fear. The troubled times of our technological revolution, of mounting debt, of social cataclysm, of war threats, atomic bombs, and anomie make everyone apprehensive, most of all people established in positions of financial security, including middle-class property owners, and those who have vested interests in the church or endowed institutions. One writer summed up the situation in the middle 1930's as follows.   The passage is as applicable twenty years later.

It ("the Red hunt") is today (1935) as it was in 1920 a crisis phenomenon, a blind emotional nationalism intolerant of dissent and fearful of changes to come . . . their campaign results in the creation of a suspicion of everyone who thinks independently and sponsors any change in the status quo . . . it forges an easy weapon for any person or group that would prefer to call names rather than to discuss issues . . . in this country the communist scare is amply supported by the reactionary press and reactionary business leaders who seek a convenient label with which to brand all social, political, and economic change . . . to create a diversion is an absolute necessity . . . the red herring is always useful.[12]

While "reactionaries" may take the lead in scapegoating liberals and reformers, all economic classes join in.   They do so partly because of the anti-red propaganda they read and hear, partly because they both understand and oppose the essential nature of communism, and partly because of the needs for definiteness and security.   Prejudice has functional value for all levels of society. Those who are religiously inclined fear their values will be threatened; those who are worried about war now can identify the menace; those who find life generally unsatisfactory now suspect it is because of reds at home and abroad.

Finally, reds are scapegoats because of the specific exploitative advantage that can be obtained from the arrangement.   A demagogue deliberately excites rage and fear against communists in order that people may rally round the demagogue to secure safety and protection (Chapter 26).   Scapegoating was employed in this way by Hitler to solidify his followers (with anti-Jewish oratory), by Bilbo of Mississippi (with anti-Negro appeals), by Senator McCarthy of Wisconsin (with his anti-red hysteria).

Scapegoats for Special Occasions

Scapegoats may be centuries old, as are the Jews; relatively recent, as the reds; or they may be so transient and ephemeral that their existence is scarcely remarked.

In daily newspapers we note the phenomenon of the "occasional" scapegoat.   Let there be a prison outbreak, an escape of a homicidal maniac from a state hospital, or an exposure of graft in the city government, and a hue and cry go up.   There are outraged editorials and irate letters from the public.   Sometimes these voices name their own scapegoat, sometimes they merely cry for one. Anger wants a personal victim, and wants it now. As a result, some official is removed from office—not necessarily because he was guilty, but because by sacrificing him the wrath can be assuaged.

A case study was made of one such event—the disastrous Coconut Grove (night club) fire in Boston on November 28, 1942.[13]

The disaster caused the death of nearly 500 persons. Immediately after the event newspaper editorials and letters to editors began to clamor to fix the blame. The first scapegoat was the busboy who lit a match to replace an electric light bulb; by his own account his match set fire to highly inflammable paper decorations. Headlines blared, "Busboy Blamed." The enormity of the accusation created a reaction, so that public opinion strove to exonerate him (partly as a reward for his straightforward testimony). Letters to the editors proposed that he be recommended for West Point; he received fan mail and even gifts of money. The next victim was the "unknown prankster" who is said to have removed the bulb; but he was soon dropped in favor of public officials: the fire commissioner, police commissioner, fire inspector, and other officials. Scarcely any newspaper article featured the inordinate panic that was no doubt chiefly responsible for the large loss of life, although one official correctly stated that "the Boston tragedy was due in part to a psychological collapse." A more tangible culprit was desired.

Gradually attention centered upon the owner, manager, and other proprietors of the night club. The owner, being Jewish, received much of the animosity, although his racial identity was implied rather than specified in the papers. One heard, however, sharp comments about "dirty, grasping Jews." The owner and political officials were often combined as joint scapegoats under the accusation of "corruption," "political favor," etc.

All this varied scapegoating was confined largely to the first week or so following the disaster. Soon interest waned, to revive again two months later when the County Attorney General returned 10 indictments, including the owner, manager, fire commissioner, building inspector, and other officials. Another brief period of blaming occurred in the papers. All the accused pleaded "not guilty." Eventually only the owner himself was punished by imprisonment.

We note from this case the effect of emotional turmoil in directing attention on some (almost any) personalized culprit. Anger and horror demand that their instigator be identified as an individual. The blame seems readily to shift from one accused scapegoat to another. As the emotion wanes the demand lessens, and the final punishment is generally milder and more limited than the initial clamor demanded. One feels at the end of such an episode that one scapegoat is sufficient and that his punishment readily brings a closure to the brief period of distress.

Summary

While psychological principles help us to understand the process of prejudice, they cannot by themselves fully explain why cne group and not another should be selected as objects of hate.

In Chapter 14 we examined certain sociocultural laws that help to predict when a given minority group will become the focus of hostility. In the present chapter we have explored the issue more concretely. Our conclusion is that maximum understanding of the problem can be gained only by knowing the historical context of each single case. Two cases are examined in some detail: anti-Semitism, a prejudice of stubborn antiquity; and anti-red feeling, a recent development. The concrete clinical method is helpful likewise in comprehending temporary phenomena, as in the case of scapegoating public officials following a disastrous fire.

If we are right in asserting that a pattern of particular circumstances determines each object of prejudice, a long volume indeed would be needed to explain the plight of the American Negro, the South African Indian, the Mexican in the southwest, and countless other instances of scapegoating in the world today. The task lies beyond our present reach. It is sufficient if we have illustrated the method of study that must be used.

NOTES AND REFERENCES

1. R. H. Lord. *History of the Archdiocese of Boston.* New York: Sheed and Ward, 1946.

2. Cf. L. Lowenthal and N. Guterman, *Prophets of Deceit.* New York: Harper, 1949.

3. Anonymous. *A.P.A.: An Inquiry into the Objects and Purposes of the So-called American Protective Association.* Stamped: Astor Library, New York, 1895. (Now at the New York Public Library.)

4. The early roots of anti-Semitism in the Christian Church are traced by M. Hay, *The Foot of Pride.* Boston: Beacon Press, 1950.

5. S. Freud. *Moses and Monotheism.* New York: A. A. Knopf, 1939.

6. It is a fact that Jewish youth today shows more widespread rejection of their ancestral religion than do young Christians, and in

general regard the values of religion less highly. See, for example, G. W. ALLPORT, J. M. GILLESPIE, JACQUELINE YOUNG, The religion of the post-war college student, *Journal of Psychology*, 1948, **25**, 3-33; also, DOROTHY T. SPOERL, The values of the post-war college student, *Journal of Social Psychology*, 1952, **35**, 217-225.

7. J. MARITAIN. *A Christian Looks at the Jewish Question.* New York: Longmans, 1939, 29.

8. L. S. BAECK. Why Jews in the world? *Commentary*, 1947, **3**, 501-507.

9. E. J. DINGWALL. *Racial Pride and Prejudice.* London: Watt, 1946, 55.

10. C. R. LUSK. Radicalism under inquiry. *Review of Reviews*, 1920, **61**, 167-171.

11. H. KRAMER AND J. SPRENGER. *Malleus Maleficarum.* (Transl. by M. SUMMERS.) London: Pushkin Press, 1948, xx.

12. J. G. KERWIN. Red herring. *Commonweal*, 1935, **22**, 597.

13. HELEN R. VELTFORT AND G. E. LEE. The Cocoanut Grove fire: a study in scapegoating. *Journal of Abnormal and Social Psychology*, 1943, **38**, Clinical Supplement, 138-154.

CHAPTER 16

THE EFFECT OF CONTACT

It has sometimes been held that merely by assembling people without regard for race, color, religion, or national origin, we can thereby destroy stereotypes and develop friendly attitudes. The case is not so simple. Yet somewhere there must be a formula that will cover the fact reported by Lee and Humphrey in their analysis of the Detroit riot of 1943:

> People who had become neighbors did not riot against each other. The students of Wayne University—white and black—went to their classes in peace throughout Bloody Monday. And there were no disorders between white and black workers in the war plants. . . .[1]

Some sociologists hold that when groups of human beings meet they normally pass through four successive stages of relationship. At first there is *sheer contact,* leading soon to *competition,* which in turn gives way to *accommodation,* and finally to *assimilation.* This peaceful progression does, in fact, occur frequently. As instances we could point to the many immigrant groups that have finally become absorbed into new homelands.

But this progression is far from being a universal law. While many individual Jews have become completely assimilated and lost to their group, the group as a whole, in spite of countless contacts with out-groups, has persisted throughout 3000 years of its recorded history. According to one estimate, it would take 6000 years for Negro stock in America to become assimilated, assuming that the present rate of "passing" is maintained.[2]

Nor is the sequence irreversible. We know that where accommodation once existed, retrogression to the stage of competition and conflict may often occur. Race riots represent such a throw-back, so too do periodic outbreaks against Jews. In Germany, as we have noted, all existing anti-Semitic legislation was repealed in 1869. For the next sixty years a period of peaceful accommodation seemed to have set in. Then, under Hitler, the tide was reversed. The Nürnberg Laws and pogroms exceeded in ferocity any anti-Semitism that had ever previously existed in Germany.

Whether or not the law of peaceful progression will hold seems to depend on the *nature of the contact* that is established.

In an unpublished study of topical life histories (written on the subject, "My experiences with and attitudes toward minority groups") it was found that contact was frequently mentioned as a factor. But while the autobiographers reported that contact *lessened* their prejudice on 37 occasions, they also report that it *increased* their prejudice on 34 occasions. Obviously, the effect of contact will depend upon the kind of association that occurs, and upon the kinds of persons who are involved.

Kinds of Contact

In order to predict the effect of contact upon attitudes we should ideally study the consequences of each of the following variables acting both separately and in combination. The task would be of vast magnitude. Up to now only a beginning has been made—and yet the results, so far as they go, have been enlightening.[3]

Quantitative aspects of contact:
   a. Frequency
   b. Duration
   c. Number of persons involved
   d. Variety

Status aspects of contact:
   a. Minority member has inferior status
   b. Minority member has equal status
   c. Minority member has superior status
   d. Not only may the individuals encountered vary thus in status; but the group as a whole may have relatively high status (e.g., Jews) or relatively low status (e.g., Negroes).

Role aspects of contact:
   a. Is the relationship one of competitive or cooperative activity?
   b. Is there a superordinate or subordinate role relation involved; e.g., master-servant, employer-employee, teacher-pupil?

Social atmosphere surrounding the contact:
   a. Is segregation prevalent, or is egalitarianism expected?
   b. Is the contact voluntary or involuntary?
   c. Is the contact "real" or "artificial"?

    d. Is the contact perceived in terms of intergroup relations or not perceived as such?

    e. Is the contact regarded as "typical" or as "exceptional"?

    f. Is the contact regarded as important and intimate, or as trivial and transient?

Personality of the individual experiencing the contact:

    a. Is his initial prejudice level high, low, medium?

    b. Is his prejudice of a surface, conforming type, or is it deeply rooted in his character structure?

    c. Has he basic security in his own life, or is he fearful and suspicious?

    d. What is his previous experience with the group in question, and what is the strength of his present stereotypes?

    e. What are his age and general education level?

    f. Many other personality factors may influence the effect of contact.

Areas of contact:

    a. Casual

    b. Residential

    c. Occupational

    d. Recreational

    e. Religious

    f. Civic and fraternal

    g. Political

    h. Goodwill intergroup activities

Even this list of variables that enter into the problem of contact is not exhaustive. It does, however, indicate the complexity of the problem we face. Scientific knowledge is not available on *all* the variables, but we shall report such dependable generalizations as can be drawn at the present time.

Casual Contacts

People in southern states and in certain northern cities may think they know the Negro, people in New York City may think they know the Jew—because they meet so many of them. But their contacts are likely to be wholly superficial. Where segregation is the custom contacts are casual, or else firmly frozen into superordinate-subordinate relationships.

Such evidence as we have clearly indicates that such contact does *not* dispel prejudice; it seems more likely to increase it.[4] The fact reported in Chapter 14 that prejudice varies with the numerical density of a minority group supports this proposition. The more contact the more trouble.

We can understand the reason if we examine the perceptual situation in a casual contact. Suppose that on the street or in a store one sees a visible out-group member. By the association of ideas there is likely to come to mind a recollection of rumor, hearsay, tradition, or stereotype by which this out-group is known. Theoretically, every superficial contact we make with an out-group member could by the "law of frequency" strengthen the adverse mental associations that we have. What is more, we are sensitized to perceive signs that will confirm our stereotypes. From a large number of Negroes in a subway we may select the one who is misbehaving for our attention and disapproval. The dozen or more well-behaved Negroes are overlooked, simply because prejudice screens. and interprets our perceptions (Chapter 10). Casual contact, therefore, permits our thinking about out-groups to remain on an autistic level.[5] We do not effectively communicate with the outsider, nor he with us.

An imaginary instance will illustrate the process. An Irishman and a Jew encounter each other in casual contact, perhaps in a small business transaction. Neither has, in fact, any initial animosity toward the other. But the Irishman thinks, "Ah, a Jew; perhaps he'll skin me; I'll be careful." The Jew thinks, "Probably a Mick; they hate the Jews; he'd like to insult me." With such an inauspicious start both men are likely to be evasive, distrustful, and cool. Both are motivated to some extent by fear —though in fact neither has any realistic basis for distrusting the other. By the time they part the offishness each has shown has confirmed the other's suspicion. The casual contact has left matters worse than before.

Acquaintance

In contrast to casual contacts, most studies show that true acquaintance lessens prejudice. Direct demonstration of this point is contained in a research by Gray and Thompson.[6]

These investigators administered to both white and Negro students in Georgia the Bogardus Social Distance scale. The students were also asked to indicate whether they were personally acquainted with at least five individuals belonging to the groups rated. There was a uniform tendency for students to rate higher in the scale of acceptability all groups in which they had five or more acquaintances. Where there was no personal knowledge of a group it suffered in esteem.

Within recent years there has developed a vigorous movement known as intercultural education. It proceeds on the assumption that both knowledge about and acquaintance with out-groups lessen hostility toward them.

Its raison d'être lies in the parable:
See that man over there?
Yes.
Well, I hate him.
But you don't know him.
That's why I hate him.

Now there are many ways to impart knowledge about people. One of these is straight academic teaching in the schools. Anthropological facts concerning "race" can be taught, likewise the truth concerning group differences (Chapter 6), also the psychological reasons why different customs have developed in various ethnic groups to serve the same human needs.

That such teaching has an effect is indicated in a study of over 400 college students. Only 31 of these could recall that in school they had received instructions in "scientific facts about race." But of these few cases 71 percent fell in the less prejudiced half of the 400 cases tested, and only 29 percent in the more prejudiced half.[7]

The proponents of modern education think it better not to rely on imparting facts, but to give students direct experience with other groups. As a result, intercultural education has evolved many ingenious devices. One of these is the "social travel" technique.

A high school in Columbus employed the method "for the purpose of studying conditions in a given area as a means toward more realistic education."[8] On one occasion 27 students, boys and girls, visited Chicago for a week. They lived in close proximity with one another. The study is not concerned with attitudes of the young people toward out-groups but toward *each other*. Before and after the trip the students rated each member of the group (known previously to them from association in the classroom). A seven-point scale was employed as follows:

1. closest to me—would have as my best friend
2. very close to me—would like to take home for a visit
3. close to me—would enjoy talking with
4. neither close to me nor far from me—would accept on a committee

5. some distance from me—would keep only as a speaking acquaintance
6. farther away from me—would rather not sit with in class
7. farthest away from me—would rather have miles away

The findings showed that the experience of living and traveling together resulted in significantly less social distance in general. Actually 20 out of the 27 participants climbed in the scale of esteem. A few did not wear well and returned less popular than at the start of the trip. Among those who climbed in status were members of minority groups. Lillian, for example, was no longer just a person of Jewish faith, but an interesting and thoughtful individual. The fact that 7 members lost status is important. It shows that the general gain in popularity is not due merely to the glow of "having a good time." Solid acquaintance may depreciate a person's standing if it brings to light realistic defects in his nature.

An additional evaluation of "social travel" is reported by F. T. Smith.[9] Forty-six graduate students in education accepted an invitation to spend two consecutive week-ends in Harlem. They were entertained in Negro homes, meeting prominent Negro editors, doctors, writers, artists, social workers. In the course of their experience they learned a great deal about life in Harlem and about the people they met there. It happened that 23 students who originally accepted the invitation were prevented from taking part. This group served as a control. Attitudes toward Negroes were measured in both groups by means of several scales before and after the week-ends. Marked gains were evident in the experimental group, but not in the control group. Even after a year had elapsed only 8 of the 46 participants failed to show more favorable attitudes than they had before the experiment. The effect of this knowledge-giving contact was positive and apparently lasting. We note, however, one important limitation in the experiment: the Negroes who became intimately known were all of relatively *high status*—equal or superior to the social status of the participants.

This research does not prove that every visit to Chinatown, Harlem, or Little Italy will result in lessened prejudice. Many people start with stereotypes, and the tourist mode of contact is unlikely to change them.

Intercultural education may employ still more vivid methods. One is psychodrama (role playing). A miniature scene is acted out. A child is asked to play the part of an immigrant child of his own age who is spending his first day in an American school.

Or an adult, perhaps one with previous anti-Negro prejudice, is assigned the part of a Negro musician who tries to obtain a room in a hotel in the face of the desk clerk's refusal when it is known to both that rooms are available. To assume voluntarily the role of a different human being is an effective way of gaining sympathy for him.

An encouraging feature of modern intercultural education is its willingness to evaluate its programs of instruction. Do they, in fact, lessen prejudice? Do all of them do so, or only certain types? In Chapter 30 we shall examine more of these evaluative studies and see what conclusions can be drawn.

Apart from the field of intercultural education, there is evidence that the more sustained the acquaintance the less the prejudice. Table 7 gives the results of one typical study, drawn from data of the United States Army of Occupation in Germany.

Table 7

OPINION OF U. S. SOLDIERS REGARDING GERMANS AS RELATED TO THE FREQUENCY OF THEIR CONTACT WITH GERMAN CIVILIANS[10]

Among men who . . .	Percentage with very favorable or fairly favorable opinion of German people
Reported within last 3 days . . .	
Personal contact of 5 hours or more with German civilians	76
Personal contact of 2 hours or more	72
Personal contact of less than 2 hours	57
No personal contact	49
Had never been in Germany	36

It is true that the *causal* factor in studies of this type is not entirely clear. It is quite possible that soldiers with low *initial* prejudice sought out the companionship of German civilians. But it is also likely that the acquaintanceship itself had something to do with the favorable attitudes displayed following the contact.

To summarize: the trend of evidence favors the conclusion that knowledge about and acquaintance with members of minority groups make for tolerant and friendly attitudes. The relationship is by no means perfect; nor is it clear whether the knowledge causes the friendliness, or whether friendliness invites the acquiring of knowledge. But that there is some positive relationship is evident.

One important qualification must, however, be added. In Chapter 1, we noted that prejudice is reflected in both *beliefs* and in *attitudes*. It seems highly probable that increased knowledge of a minority group would lead directly to a truer set of *beliefs*. It does not follow that *attitudes* will change proportionately. One may, for example, learn that Negro blood is not different in composition from white blood without thereby learning to like Negroes. Plenty of rationalizations for prejudice are available to people who have a good deal of sound knowledge.

For the sake of caution, therefore, let us state our conclusion as follows: Contacts that bring knowledge and acquaintance are likely to engender sounder beliefs concerning minority groups, and for this reason contribute to the reduction of prejudice.

Residential Contact

In most cities of America a game of social checkers has long been in progress. It can be illustrated by the North End of Boston. When the Irish immigrants moved in the Yankees moved out; when the Jews moved in the Irish moved out; when the Italians moved in the Jews moved out. In other localities the sequence has been Anglo-Saxon, German, Russian Jew, Negro. So long as frontiers were wide, suburbs uncrowded, and horizontal mobility easy, this game went on without attracting much attention.

Now, however, for various reasons the problem of residential contact has become acute. A general shortage in housing, combined with intensive Negro migrations from southern states, has created a considerable degree of realistic competition in many areas. Further, the spread of public housing projects (supported in part by the federal government) has raised the issue whether segregation can be *legally* practiced with the support of public funds. The issue has recently been sharpened by the 1948 decision of the Supreme Court that "restricted covenants"—whereby landholders agree to bar their premises to Orientals, Negroes, Jews, or other minority groups—cannot be enforced in American courts of law.

All of these conditions have raised in pointed form the question whether integrated housing (where minority groups live side by side) does in fact increase or lessen prejudice as compared with segregated housing (regional separation of minorities). Segregated housing, whether coerced or voluntary, means segregation in much else. It means that children will go to schools attended largely or entirely by members of their own in-group. Stores, medical facilities, churches will be automatically segregated as well. Neighborhood projects will be ethnocentric, not truly civic in their scope or intent. Friendships across group boundaries will be difficult or impossible to form. And if one group (usually the Negro) is forced into overcrowded slums, disease and crime will have a high incidence. The fact of segregation into poor districts may be largely responsible for the stereotype that Negroes are intrinsically criminal, diseased, and given to depreciating property. What is due to segregation in *housing* is falsely ascribed to *race*.

Segregation markedly enhances the visibility of a group; it makes it seem larger and more menacing than it is. Negroes in Harlem comprise the largest, most solid Negro city in the world —and yet they are less than 10 percent of the total population of metropolitan New York. If they were randomly distributed throughout the city their presence could not be viewed as a dangerously expanding "black belt."

Serious conflict may occur at the boundaries of the segregated region. It is at this point of junction that ethnic riots are most likely to occur (Chapter 4). Especially is this true if the minority belt is expanding through increasing pressure of population. Focusing upon this problem at the southern edge of the "black belt" in Chicago, B. M. Kramer finds that the attitudes of white people vary with the immediacy of a Negro "invasion." [11]

This investigator marked off five zones, Number 1 being at the point of contact with the expanding Negro movement, Number 5 being more remote (two or three miles away). Table 8 shows that the closer the Negro movement the more spontaneous are the expressions of hostility.

Table 8

SPONTANEOUS EXPRESSION OF ANTI-NEGRO SENTIMENT
AMONG RESPONDENTS IN THE FIVE ZONES
(AFTER KRAMER)

	Zone 1	Zone 2	Zone 3	Zone 4	Zone 5
Percentage spontaneously expressing anti-Negro sentiment	64%	43%	27%	14%	4%
N	118	115	121	123	142

Table 9 illustrates interesting trends in "social perception." In Zone 1, where residents encounter more Negroes, we find fewer complaints that they are personally and physically unclean or diseased. In Zone 5, where there is little knowledge-giving contact, this stereotype is more common.

Table 9

PERCENTAGE OF RESPONDENTS GIVING INDICATED REASONS FOR WANTING TO EXCLUDE NEGROES FROM THEIR NEIGHBORHOOD

	Zone 1	Zone 2	Zone 3	Zone 4	Zone 5
Negroes are personally unclean, diseased, smell bad, are physically unpleasant to associate with	5	15	16	24	25
Don't want children associating with Negroes, fear social mixing and intermarriage	22	14	14	13	10

On the other hand, a more realistic problem comes to the fore in Zone 1. What will happen when the children play together? The probability of love affairs and mixed marriages is bound to increase. Granted the state of social opinion today, such an eventuality is viewed quite realistically as fraught with potential suffering for the children. (Compare the case cited on p. 238.) In Zone 5 this issue is mentioned much less often, since white and Negro children in this region have not yet met.

From this study we learn that *approaching* residential contact is viewed as a threat by the dominant group, but that the nature of the complaints and perceptions vary with the immediacy (or distance) of the threat.

Besides the segregated pattern of housing, we find in some localities an integrated pattern. Sometimes, thanks to the rapid development of public housing, we find each of these two patterns practiced in similar surroundings. The situation is one to delight the social scientist's heart. He is able to discover localities where the sociocultural, economic, populational factors are virtually identical except for the fact that in one public housing is segregated and in another integrated. Obviously such a set-up invites experimental study.   At least three important experiments of this type have been carried out.[12]

The first finding to report is that Negro and white tenants treat their property alike, provided they come from the same general economic class and are selected as tenants according to the same rules, and are given an opportunity to live in homes of similar quality.   Nor do they differ in their rent-paying habits—one group is as reliable as the other.

In one study where it seems certain that the white residents in an integrated and in a segregated housing unit had the same *initial* attitude toward Negroes, a marked difference was found when they were asked how they felt about living in the same building with Negroes.   Among those living in an all-white unit, 75 percent said they would "dislike the idea."   Among those actually living in an integrated unit only 25 percent said they disliked the idea.

Particularly interesting are the differences in social perception. Table 10 shows the responses of white people to the question, "Are they (the Negro people in the project) pretty much the same as the white people who live here or are they different?"   The question was asked of white people living in all-white buildings— Negroes in the same project being segregated in all-black buildings—as well as of white people who lived in integrated buildings.

Table 10 [13]

Are they (the Negro people in the project) pretty much the same as the white people who live here or are they different?

	Percentage of replies in	
	Integrated Housing Units	Segregated Housing Units
Same	80	57
Different	14	22
Don't Know	6	20

Those who have closer contact perceive less difference than those who are more remote.

The same research contains other evidence of phenomenological differences.   When asked to mention the chief faults they thought Negro people had, whites living in segregated units tended to name aggressive traits: troublemaking, rowdy, dangerous.   Those living in closer association mentioned predominantly an entirely different type of trait, namely, feelings of inferiority or oversensitiveness to prejudice. The shift here is from a fear-sustained perception to one sustained by a friendly, "mental hygiene" point of view.[14]

The trend of evidence clearly indicates that white people who live side by side with Negroes of the same general economic class in public housing projects are on the whole more friendly, less fearful, and less stereotyped in their views than white people who live in segregated arrangements.

Like all broad generalizations, this one, needs certain qualifications. It is not the mere fact of living together that is decisive. It is the forms of resulting *communication* that matter. Whether Negro and white neighbors are jointly active in community enterprises is what counts. Do they have parent-teacher associations; local betterment groups? Do they happen to have effective leadership that knows how to break down the reticence and remaining suspicion that may exist in the project? We must not assume that integrated housing automatically solves the problem of prejudice. At most we can say that it creates a condition where friendly contacts and accurate social perceptions can occur.

A further qualification must be made in terms of the density of the Negro population in an integrated unit. What proportion of white and Negro families make for the optimum conditions of communication? If only 5 or 10 percent of the families are Negro they can be overlooked and psychologically isolated.

The three studies we have cited agree that we cannot take a merely mechanical view of occupancy patterns. What matters is the opportunity they afford for neighborly contact. Perhaps "group work" to stimulate such contact within a housing unit or in a city block would have best effects. But, lacking evidence on this point, we can say that integrated units, where the number of Negroes is not too few, seem to make for optimum neighborliness.

It is sometimes argued that Negroes themselves prefer to live together, and reject the idea of an integrated housing unit. This belief is wholly false, as an unpublished study by S. Aronson shows.

> In a segregated project populated entirely by Negroes the question was asked, "If an apartment became vacant next to you, what kind of people would you like to have as your neighbors? Would you care if they were white families?" One hundred percent of the Negroes said that they would not care. But when the corresponding question was asked of white dwellers in a segregated project, 78 percent said they would not want a Negro neighbor.

We can lay it down for certain that it is not the Negro, but the white, who wants (or thinks he wants) segregation in housing and elsewhere. As in the study just mentioned it generally turns out that fully three-quarters of the white population say that they do not want to live in the immediate neighborhood of Negroes. If, then, integrated housing is proposed as a policy we must expect protests from whites in advance.

Yet studies show that if for any reason (perhaps housing shortage or the inducement of low rental) white people can be led to live in close association with Negroes their attitude shifts in a more favorable direction. The following incident seems fairly typical of what may happen.

One morning at the opening of school the Dean of a girls' college in the East had two angry visitors. They were students from the South who found that in the small dormitory to which they were assigned a Negro student was also assigned. They demanded that she be moved out. The Dean thought for a moment and then said, "Well, we have a rule that girls may not change their dormitory assignments when they are once made for the year; but in this case, I'll make an exception. You girls may move out if you wish and go to another house." The girls were taken aback. But they did not move, for their training told them that a Negro should get out of *their* way. Staying on, a bit grimly at first, they soon found that their feelings of hostility against their colored housemate lessened; by the end of the term they were good friends with her.

The moral seems to be that housing administrators should not pay too much attention to protests that occur in advance of inaugurating an integrated housing policy. Experience shows that such protests are likely to subside in time and that amicable results follow.

In sum: Zonal residential contact makes for increased tension, whereas integrated housing policies, through encouraging knowledge and acquaintanceship, remove barriers to effective communication. When these barriers are removed the result is the reduction of fallacious stereotypes, and the substitution of a realistic view for one of fear and autistic hostility. There is ordinarily a net gain in friendship. At the same time, whatever realistic obstacles there are to close relationships come to light. One of the studies suggests that the defensive sensitivity of the Negro is more accurately perceived in integrated living. It is also true that the mingling of adolescent boys and girls brings with it the possibility of mixed marriages which in our present culture constitute a serious problem for the couples involved.

But to perceive the real problems in race relations for what they are marks a distinct gain. While they are difficult to solve, they stand a better chance of being solved if the irrelevancies of stereotype and autistic hostility are first eliminated. And to achieve this gain the abolition of segregation helps greatly.

Occupational Contact

The jobs that most Negroes, and members of certain other minority groups, hold are at or near the bottom of the occupational ladder. They carry with them poor pay and low status. Negroes are usually servants, not masters; doormen, not executives; laborers, not foremen.[15]

Evidence is now accumulating that this differential status in occupation is an active factor in creating and maintaining prejudice.

Thus among one group of veterans MacKenzie found that men who had known Negroes only as unskilled workmen had favorable attitude scores in but 5 percent of the cases; whereas those who had encountered skilled or professional Negroes outside the armed services, or had worked with Negroes of the same skill level as themselves in these services, had favorable scores in 64 percent of the cases.[16]

The same investigator found that among college students who had held war industry jobs a similar striking differential existed. Those who knew both skilled and white-collar Negroes but had worked only with Negroes in lower status jobs than they themselves held were favorable in only 13 percent of the cases; whereas 55 percent of those who had worked with Negroes occupying the same or higher level jobs than themselves were favorable. Equally striking is MacKenzie's finding that employees who know Negroes holding *professional* positions (doctors, lawyers, teachers) are far less prejudiced than those who have never encountered Negroes of this high occupational grade.

The official task of breaking down discrimination in business and industry has in recent years been assigned chiefly to what has been called Fair Employment Practices Commissions. The federal agency set up by President Roosevelt's executive order was a wartime measure of only temporary duration. Since World War II the legislative re-establishment of a federal FEPC has been one of the controversial civil rights measures much fought over in Congress. In the meantime several states have set up FEPC's by statute, and so too have some cities.

Enacting an FEPC law does not automatically stop discrimination. On the contrary, a large amount of "psychology" is required to persuade employers that their business will not suffer, nor their organization be disrupted, by a more liberal employment policy. One lesson learned is the desirability of introducing minority group workers not only at the bottom of the occupational ladder but in the higher echelons as well. Such a policy forestalls accusations that factory and office workers are forced to accept associations that management itself will not tolerate. "The smart personnel man," write two experienced arbitrators, "will always start his nondiscrimination program with employment of a Negro in his own department or on the top management level." [17]

We have seen that impending or threatened residential contact ordinarily elicits more protest than does actual contact. The same principle holds true in occupational contact. Vocal objections, threatened strikes, and other resistance sometimes greet management's proposal to introduce minority group (especially Negro) workers. If a vote is taken in a democratic fashion whether or not to admit Negroes to work as stenographers in an office, as salespeople in stores, or as members of a union or professional organization, the vote is often negative. The officials in charge feel that they "cannot go against majority vote."

Oddly enough, when the change is introduced without raising the issue for discussion there is usually no more than a flurry of excitement of short duration. Soon the new policy is accepted as a matter of course. The newcomers are tolerated and respected as soon as their merits as individuals become apparent.[18]

A study of seamen shows that the initial resistance to shipping with Negroes was very great, likewise the resistance to having them as members in the National Maritime Union. In this particular case vigorous leadership forced the antidiscrimination policy, supporting it by educational campaigns and appeals for solidarity. Before long the *fait accompli* became accepted, and the longer the experience of equal-status association with Negroes, the more favorable was the attitude of the white seamen toward them.[19]

Without passing judgment upon the relative merits of the "democratic" versus the "fait accompli" techniques, an explanation of the psychology involved is in order. Most people, as we shall see in Chapter 20, are double-minded about their prejudices.

Their first impulse is to obey them. Why expose oneself to needless annoyance by voting to work beside a Negro, a Jew, or other member of a disliked minority? But such an attitude often arouses at least a trace of shame, more especially since the tradition of fair play and equal opportunity are authentic values to most Americans. It is for this reason that strong and forthright action from "higher up"—official FEPC, top management, Board of Directors, etc.—is, after an initial flurry of excitement, generally accepted. The *fait accompli* is often welcomed if it is in line with one's conscience. We shall discuss this important principle further in Chapter 29.

To summarize, occupational contacts with Negroes *of equal status* tend to make for lessened prejudice. It helps also if one knows Negroes of *higher* occupational status than one's own. To hire Negroes with minimum friction it seems advisable for management to lead the way in breaking down discrimination at the top level. Likewise a firm policy ruling will probably offset the initial protests that are likely to occur. Whether these same principles hold for minority groups other than Negro is not so certain, since fewer studies have been made, but in the absence of definitely contradictory evidence the logic may be assumed to be the same.

Pursuit of Common Objectives

While the net effect of occupational contact seems favorable, yet this type of contact, like many others, suffers an inherent limitation. People may come to take for granted the particular situation in which the contact occurs but fail completely to generalize their experience. They may, for example, encounter Negro sales personnel in a store, deal with them as equals, and yet still harbor their over-all anti-Negro prejudice.[20] In short, equal-status contact may lead to a dissociated, or highly specific, attitude, and may not affect the individual's customary perceptions and habits.

The nub of the matter seems to be that contact must reach below the surface in order to be effective in altering prejudice. Only the type of contact that leads people to *do* things together is likely to result in changed attitudes. The principle is clearly illustrated in the multi-ethnic athletic team. Here the goal is all-important; the ethnic composition of the team is irrelevant. It is the cooperative striving for the goal that engenders solidarity. So too, in factories, neighborhoods, housing units, schools, common participation and common interests are more effective than the bare fact of equal-status contact.

A vivid wartime illustration of this principle comes from the

Research Branch of the Information and Education Division of the United States Army.[21]

While it was a policy of the Army to have no mixed units of white and Negro soldiers, circumstances developed during a period of fierce combat that made it necessary to replace a number of white platoons with platoons of Negro soldiers, placing them *within* the companies of white soldiers. While a certain amount of segregation remained in this arrangement, still it brought the two races into close contact *on an equal footing in a common project* (of life and death importance). Following this new arrangement the Research Branch asked two questions of a widely divergent sample of white soldiers.

Question 1: Some Army divisions have companies which include Negro and white platoons. How would you feel about it if your outfit was set up something like that?

Question 2: In general, do you think it is a good idea or a poor idea to have the same company in a combat outfit include Negro platoons and white platoons?

Table 11

ATTITUDES OF WHITE SOLDIERS TOWARD ASSOCIATION WITH NEGRO SOLDIERS AS RELATED TO THEIR CONTACT EXPERIENCE IN COMBAT

Extent of Army Contact with Negroes	*Percent answering*	
	Q.1. "Would dislike it very much"	Q.2. "Good idea"
Field force units with no colored platoons in white companies	62	18
Men in same division, not in same regiment, as colored troops	24	50
Men in same regiment, not in same company, as colored troops	20	66
Men in company with a Negro platoon	7	64

Table 11 shows that those who were more closely associated with Negro soldiers under combat conditions were more favorably dis-

posed than those who had had no experience in common participation.

The investigators warn that this result may be valid only for
such extreme conditions as combat, where men live together or die
together according to the success of their joint effort. The warning is in order, although the principle that common participation
makes for lessened prejudice has been demonstrated in other
fields of joint activity as well. The investigators warn also that
in this particular research only "volunteer" platoons of Negroes
were involved, presumably made up of men anxious to make
good and to demonstrate their ability as fighters. Whether a less
selected group would have earned equally high esteem from their
white companions we do not know.

Another writer commenting on Negro-white solidarity in times
of combat says:

> Put a white man and a Negro in the same shell hole and
> they will fight together to the last breath, sharing food and
> water; if either is wounded, the other will risk his life to carry
> him out. But the shell hole must be large enough for both of
> them.[22]

This assertion warns us that intergroup solidarity may have its
limits, even when there is marked commonality of interests. No
doubt this is true. But in such extreme situations there are limits
to social solidarity *within* an ethnic group as well.

Goodwill Contacts

Following the severe riots in 1943 many states and scores of
cities in America established official commissions to combat prejudice. For the most part these groups were composed of substan-
tial citizens of the community, including representatives of the
leading minorities in the region. While some of the commissions
have done effective work, some have merited the uncomplimentary
label, "the Mayor's Do-nothing Committee." The members are
often too busy and too untrained to do much except deplore
prejudice.

Besides official groups there have been hundreds of agencies and
committees of citizens organized on unofficial lines. Most of them
have not known how to proceed, and after a short life of futility
many have disbanded. When a committee does not know what
action to take, disappointment results, recrimination may break
out within the community, and matters may be worse than they
were before.

Psychologically, the error lies in the lack of concretely defined objectives. The focus is unclear. No one can "improve community relations" in the abstract. Goodwill contact without concrete goals accomplishes nothing. Minority groups gain nothing from artificially induced mutual admiration. The story is told of a lady of goodwill who planned an interracial tea. When the guests came she insisted that they sit in alternate chairs—first a white lady then a colored lady. The tea was a failure.

We should not be too hard, however, on such neighborly endeavor. The fact that people of different groups want to come together and do something to repair the ravages of prejudice in the community is a good beginning. Our point is that sound leadership is also required. As a first step the neighborhood festival technique described by Rachel Du Bois has been successfully used.[23] It consists of reminiscences on the part of all present concerning experiences in childhood. All who compose the group —Armenians, Mexicans, Jews, Negroes, Yankees—are invited to compare their recollections of autumn days, of fresh bread, of childhood pleasures, hopes, punishments. Almost any topic will bring out the universal (or closely similar) values of all the ethnic groups. With the ground for acquaintance thus laid, an agenda for the improvement of community relationships can gradually be evolved, and common projects and cooperative endeavor will then fortify and implement what might otherwise be abortive goodwill.

Personality Differences

In none of the studies cited in this chapter do we find that contact reduces prejudice among *all* the individuals concerned. It does not do so even when the contact is of equal status in the pursuit of common goals. The reason is that certain personalities resist the influences of contact. One research, by P. H. Mussen, sheds light on this matter.[24]

This investigator studied the attitudes of approximately 100 white boys, eight to fourteen years of age, who spent 28 days in a biracial camp where Negro and white children lived, ate and played together. Before the boys left home for the camp, and again on the last day of camp, they were tested with indirect methods of assessing prejudice. For example, each was presented with 12 photographs of boys' faces, eight of them Negroes, four white. The boy then picked out the photographs of individuals he would like to go to the movie with; and in other ways indicated his preference for, or rejection of, the white and colored boys. In no part of the investigation was there any direct discussion of Negro-white relationships or of personal feeling.

At the end of the 28 days of close association these tests were repeated, and a study was made of each boy's personality—especially the amount of aggression he harbored in general, and of the way he regarded his own parents and the environment he lived in.

About a quarter of the boys showed a marked lessening of prejudice during the period of camping, but about the same number showed a marked increase in prejudice.

The boys whose prejudice *decreased* were, on the whole, marked by the following characteristics:

they had fewer aggressive needs
they held a generally favorable view of their parents
they did not perceive their home environment as hostile and threatening
they did not fear that punishment would follow expression of aggression
they were generally satisfied with the camp and fellow-campers

The boys whose prejudice *increased* were, on the other hand, marked by the following characteristics:

they had more aggressive and dominance needs
they had more hostility toward their parents
they felt their home environments to be hostile and threatening
they desired to defy authority, but feared the punishment that would result
they were more dissatisfied with the camp and with their fellow-campers

Thus, it was the anxious and the aggressive boys who failed to develop tolerance as a result of their equal-status contact with Negro boys. To them life seemed deeply threatening, and their home relationships were badly tangled. It seems that their personal disorders run too deep to permit them to benefit from equal status contact and acquaintance with Negroes. They still *need* scapegoats.

Conclusion

It would seem fair, then, to conclude that contact, as a situational variable, cannot always overcome the personal variable in prejudice. This is true whenever the inner strain within the person is too tense, too insistent, to permit him to profit from the structure of the outer situation.

At the same time, given a population of ordinary people, with a normal degree of prejudice, we are safe in making the following general prediction, which summarizes the principal findings of this chapter:

Prejudice (unless deeply rooted in the character structure of the individual) may be reduced by equal status contact between majority and minority groups in the pursuit of common goals. The effect is greatly enhanced if this contact is sanctioned by institutional supports (i.e., by law, custom or local atmosphere), and provided it is of a sort that leads to the perception of common interests and common humanity between members of the two groups.

NOTES AND REFERENCES

1. A. M. Lee and N. D. Humphrey. *Race Riot*. New York: Dryden, 1943, 130.

2. E. W. Eckard. How many Negroes "Pass"? *American Journal of Sociology*, 1947, **52**, 498-500.

3. The following analysis of types of contact is drawn from R. M. Williams, Jr., *The Reduction of Intergroup Tensions*. New York: Social Science Research Council Bulletin 57, 1947, 70; and from B. M. Kramer, *Residential Contact as a Determinant of Attitudes toward Negroes* (unpublished), Harvard College Library, 1950.

4. R. M. Williams. *Op. cit.*, 71; H. H. Harlan, Some factors affecting attitude toward Jews, *American Sociological Review*, 1942, **7**, 816-833.

5. T. M. Newcomb. Autistic hostility and social reality. *Human Relations*, 1947, **1**, 69-86.

6. J. S. Gray and A. H. Thompson. The ethnic prejudices of white and Negro college students. *Journal of Abnormal and Social Psychology*, 1953, **48**, 311-313.

7. G. W. Allport and B. M. Kramer. Some roots of prejudice. *Journal of Psychology*, 1946, **22**, 20.

8. W. van Til and L. Raths. The influence of social travel on relations among high school students. *Educational Research Bulletin*, 1944, **23**, 63-68.

9. F. T. Smith. An experiment in modifying attitudes toward the Negro. *Teachers College Contributions to Education*, 1943, No. 887.

10. S. A. Stouffer et al. *The American Soldier*. Princeton: Princeton Univ. Press, 1949, Vol. II, 570.

11. B. M. Kramer. *Op. cit.* Tables are from pp. 61, 63.

12. M. Deutsch and M. E. Collins, *Interracial Housing: A Psychological Evaluation of a Social Experiment*, Minneapolis: Univ. of Minnesota Press, 1951; Marie Jahoda and Patricia S. West, Race relations in

public housing, *Journal of Social Issues,* 1951, **7,** 132-139; D. M. WILNER, R. P. WALKLEY, S. W. COOK, Residential proximity and intergroup relations in public housing projects, *Journal of Social Issues,* 1952, **8,** 45-69.

13. M. DEUTSCH AND M. E. COLLINS. *Op. cit.,* 82.

14. M. DEUTSCH AND M. E. COLLINS. *Op. cit.,* 81.

15. For an analysis of Negro occupations, see G. MYRDAL, *The American Dilemma,* New York: Harper, 1944, Vol. 1, Part 4.

16. BARBARA K. MACKENZIE. The importance of contact in determining attitudes toward Negroes. *Journal of Abnormal and Social Psychology,* 1948, **43,** 417-441.

17. F. J. HAAS AND G. J. FLEMING. Personnel practices and wartime changes. *The Annals of the American Academy of Political and Social Science,* 1946, **244,** 48-56.

18. G. WATSON. *Action for Unity.* New York: Harper, 1947, 65.

19. I. N. BROPHY. The luxury of anti-Negro prejudice. *Public Opinion Quarterly,* 1946, **9,** 456-466.

20. Cf. G. SAENGER AND EMILY GILBERT. Customer reactions to the integration of Negro sales personnel. *International Journal of Opinion and Attitude Research,* 1950, **4,** 57-76.

21. S. A. STOUFFER *et al. Op. cit.,* Vol. I, Chapter 10. Table 11 is taken from p. 594.

22. H. A. SINGER. The veteran and race relations. *Journal of Educational Sociology,* 1948, **21,** 397-408.

23. RACHEL D. DUBOIS. *Neighbors in Action.* New York: Harper, 1950.

24. P. H. MUSSEN. Some personality and social factors related to changes in children's attitudes toward Negroes. *Journal of Abnormal and Social Psychology,* 1950, **45,** 423-441.

Part V

ACQUIRING PREJUDICE

CHAPTER 17

CONFORMING

Someone has defined culture as that which gives ready-made answers to the problems of life.

So far as life's problems have to do with group relations, the answers are likely to be ethnocentric in tone. This is natural enough. Each ethnic group tends to strengthen its inner ties, to keep bright the legend of its own golden age, and to declare (or imply) that other groups are less worthy. Such ready-made answers make for self-esteem and for group survival. This ethnocentric habit of thought is much like grandmother's furniture. Sometimes it is revered and prized, more usually just taken for granted. Occasionally it is modernized. But for the most part, it is used generation after generation. It serves a purpose. It is homelike and therefore good.

Conformity and Functional Significance

Now the important problem we face is this: Is conforming a superficial phenomenon or has it deep functional significance for the person who conforms? Is it skin-deep or marrow-deep?

The answer is that our obedience to cultural ways has all gradations of depth. Sometimes we follow customs almost unconsciously or with only a surface interest (e.g., keeping to the right side of the street); sometimes we find a cultural pattern of great significance to ourselves (for example, the right to own property); sometimes a culturally transmitted way of life is particularly precious (belonging to a certain church). Psychologically, we may say that people find all degrees of ego-involvement in their habits of conformity.

The following study illustrates nicely two different degrees of ego-involvement in conforming with an ethnocentric folkway. It is taken from *The American Soldier:*[1]

During the war a large number of Air Force enlisted men were asked two questions: (1) *Do you think white soldiers and Negro*

*soldiers in the Air Force should be in the same or in separate
ground crews?* About *four-fifths* voted for separate, i.e., segregated, ground crews. (2) *Would you have any personal objection
to working in the same ground crew with Negro soldiers?*
Roughly, *one-third* of the Northern white and *two-thirds* of the
Southern whites had "personal objections." Allowing for the
proportions of Northern and Southern soldiers in the sample,
we may safely say that apparently *half* of the soldiers who favored
the segregated policy had no personal objection to working with
Negroes. If this result is representative of ethnocentrism as a
whole, we might then guess that *about a half of all prejudiced
attitudes are based only on the need to conform to custom, to let
well enough alone, to maintain the cultural pattern.*

Fɪɢ. 12. The continuum of ego-relevance in prejudiced attitudes.[3]

But the other half are not based on conformity alone. Deeper
motives are apparently at work—motives with a functional significance for the individual. He has "personal objections" to working with Negroes. For him the status quo is more than an arbitrary custom. The sheer conformist says, in effect, "Why should I
be the one to buck the situation?" Whereas the functional bigot
says, in effect, "This custom of segregation is essential to the
economy of my life."

It would be wrong, of course, to imply that every case of prejudice can be classified clearly as "sheer conformity" or as "functionally significant." There may be a degree of mixture, as Figure 12
suggests. The situation should be regarded as a continuum. A
given case of prejudice may fall anywhere between the pole of
surface conformity and the pole of extreme functional relevance.[2]

Social Entrance Ticket

Many conformists have no deeper motive than to avoid a scene.
Finding themselves with prejudiced people, they string along.
Why be rude? Why challenge the community pattern? Only

the headstrong idealists make a nuisance of themselves. Better to parrot a folkway than to be a bore.

> An employer with a penchant for peace (and profits) refused to hire Negro sales personnel, saying, "After all, there is some risk. Why should I be the first to do it? What will my customers say?"

In their endorsement of segregation apparently many of the Air Force enlisted men had no deeper motivation than this.

Much conformity prejudice is of the "polite and harmless" order. In the course of an evening's conversation in a gentile group it is not uncommon to hear the Jews blamed once or twice for some current evil. Everyone nods a head and goes on to the next subject. A group of Republicans might find the same conversational cement in abusing the Democratic administration, or vice versa. And a dig at Irish politicians is in many cities a safe adhesive to apply to a faltering conversation. The abuse is often as hollow as that we heap upon the weather.

Such chatter—if indeed there is little behind it—can be called *phatic* discourse—the words meaning nothing excepting as a device to avoid silence and signify social solidarity.

Sometimes, of course, there is somewhat more at stake in the act of conforming.

> A girl with very little money entered a private school, attended chiefly by girls from homes of wealth. In order to become accepted by the students "who were somebody" she found herself aping their prejudiced talk concerning the one or two Jewish girls in the school. In this case, the need for greater personal security underlay the conformity.

No one, least of all an adolescent, wants to be excluded from the dominant group. Even a tone of voice may bring him into line. A college student reports a memory of his first day at prep school:

> One of the older boys remarked about a schoolmate, "Don't you know that Harry is a Jew?" I had never met a Jewish boy before, and personally didn't care whether or not Harry—who seemed likable fellow—was a Jew. But the older boy's tone of voice was enough to convince me that I had better not make Harry my friend. Thereafter I avoided Harry. And, although I could not understand why we should dislike Jews, I gradually accepted the prejudice. It seems strange that a feeling of antagonism toward Harry should grow up in me. But it did.

Personally, I had no unpleasant experience with him or with any other Jew I ever met.

This case is particularly interesting because the writer goes on to show how little personal ground (how little functional significance) the prejudice seemed to have for any of the boys at school.

The boys concerned were all secure economically. They were all seventeen or under and had few worries about social prestige. They received as good grades as did Harry. There were no marked frustrations that made them look for a scapegoat. These boys simply had a fixed, irrational prejudice which they could neither explain nor discard. Of course they brought the attitude from home, but why? What earthly good did it do them?

Why a child should take on a ready-made prejudice without its having specific functional significance for him as an individual is a subject that will soon engage our attention. First, however, let us consider a case of extreme cultural obedience with manifestly high functional significance.

The Neurosis of Extreme Conformity

It is still difficult for us to believe the story of the Auschwitz Concentration Camp. The tale is the zenith of horror. Between the summer of 1941 and the end of World War II, two and a half million men, women, and children were murdered there. The gas chambers and ovens, working 24 hours a day, exterminated as many as 10,000 human beings daily. The victims were mostly Jews, and the deliberate genocide represented what Hitler had called the "final solution" of the Jewish problem. Gold from their teeth and their rings was melted down and sent to the Reichsbank. Hair from the women's heads was salvaged for commercial purposes.

A forty-six-year-old colonel of the German Army, Rudolf Hoess, was commandant of the camp, and when testifying at the Nürnberg trials, readily admitted these facts.[4] He said he had received orders in the summer of 1941 when Himmler called for him and explained, "The Führer has ordered the final solution of the Jewish question—and we have to carry out this task. For reasons of transportation and isolation, I have picked Auschwitz for this. You now have the hard job of carrying this out."

Asked how he felt when receiving such grim orders, Hoess denied any feeling. He had answered, "Jawohl," to Himmler and set about obediently to carry through the endless murders, just because two superior officers, first Hitler and then Himmler, had

told him to do so. When pressed to say whether the Jews whom
he murdered deserved such a fate, he complained that such questions didn't mean anything. "Don't you see, we SS men were not
supposed to think about these things; it never even occurred to us."
And besides, it was something already taken for granted; he said,
"We just never heard anything else. . . . It was not only newspapers like the *Stürmer*, but it was everything we ever heard.
Even our military and ideological training took for granted that
we had to protect Germany from the Jews. . . . It only started to
occur to me after the collapse that maybe it was not quite right,
after I had heard what everybody was saying."

Hoess had put obedience to his superior officer above everything
else—above the Ten Commandments, above sympathy, above
logic. "You can be sure that it was not always a pleasure to see
those mountains of corpses and smell the continual burning. But
Himmler had ordered it and had even explained the necessity and
I really never gave much thought to whether it was wrong. It
just seemed a necessity."

The case of Hoess demonstrates a neurotic degree of conformity.
The loyalty and obedience involved were prepotent over every
rational and humane impulse. The frenzy of conformity to a Nazi
folk-belief and to the Führer's orders was a vital factor in the
personality of Hoess—a compulsive obedience. Yet, one cannot
suppose Hoess to be a madman; there were too many other SS
guards who would have done the same thing with as little remorse.
We can only learn from this case that a fanatic ideology may engender conformity of incredible tenacity.

Ethnocentric Pivots in Culture

Less extreme, but more widespread, is the deliberate attempt to
maintain a chosen ethnocentric creed as a vital part of a culture.
Anyone exposed to this creed is bound to be affected by it in some
degree. The doctrine of "white supremacy" in various parts of
the world is such a pivotal theme.

More than a century ago de Tocqueville discussed this feature
of the culture of the southern portion of the United States. He
reported that a cheaply won pride seemed characteristic of the
dominant group:

In the South there are no families so poor as not to have slaves.
The citizen of the Southern states becomes a sort of domestic
dictator from infancy; the first notion he acquires in life is that
he is born to command, and the first habit which he contracts
is that of ruling without resistance. His education tends, then,

to give him the character of a haughty and hasty man, irascible, violent, ardent in his desires, impatient of obstacles, but easily discouraged if he cannot succeed in the first attempt.[5]

Writing on this same subject more than a century later, Lillian Smith tells how child training in many Southern families is still directed toward the theme of white supremacy.

I do not remember how or when, but by the time I had learned that God is love, that Jesus is His Son and came to give us more abundant life, that all men are brothers with a common Father, I also knew that I was better than a Negro, that all black folks have their place and must be kept in it, that sex has its place and must be kept in it, that a terrifying disaster would befall the South if ever I treated a Negro as my social equal. . . .[6]

Child training is not the only focus of self-conscious ethnocentrism. The following incident shows how solidarity may be maintained even in the halls of justice:

In 1947, in the state of South Carolina, 28 white men were charged with the lynching of a Negro. The counsel for the defense faced the task of persuading the jury to disregard the confessions of several of the prisoners. It proved to be a not difficult task. Although under the stern eye of the judge the counsel was prevented from injecting the race issue directly, he contrived to appeal to white southerners to stick together in their crusade to maintain white supremacy. Leaning on the jury box, and speaking softly, he said, "I know that you are all good citizens of South Carolina." "We understand each other," he coaxed. "Not a soul in South Carolina would criticize you if you turn these boys loose. You are not expected to convict them." The jury acquitted the defendants. One more Negro was lynched with impunity.

Self-conscious maintenance of in-group superiority is by no means confined to the United States. A Chinese student indicates how parents and teachers cooperate to instil in-groupism into the children of that land:

Why can China still survive when the country has had numerous times of national crisis? It is thoroughly believed by the Chinese that the great philosophy of our ancestral teachers has saved the nation. The culture and civilization of China *were, are,* and *will be* always the light of the Orient. When the boy Sun Yat-Sen (the founder of the Chinese Republic) refused to kneel down before an ancestral wooden tablet, he was fiercely condemned by his schoolteacher, who later stirred up the whole village mob to drive Sun Yat-Sen out of that locality even though his father was one of the elders of the town.

The writer of this analysis reports that the total atmosphere of her upbringing gave her a strong prejudice against American missionaries. Why should they try to impose their ways upon an older and superior civilization?

My hatred of American missionaries has carried over, even to this country. When some American friends tell me excitedly that they had missionary relatives or acquaintances in China, my response is always a very discouraging, "Oh?"

She reports that fences are formed, not only to exclude other races or nationalities, but to exclude regions and classes:

The education of northern China, we were taught, was better than that of the southern Chinese. So we in Shanghai looked down upon Canton. Also, we learned the old Chinese saying of some educated sage, "Our people are masters of the servant class, because there is an unremovable feeling of prestige and superiority existing among educated people." Since educated people live mostly in the city, we hired our servants from the country, and looked down upon them for their rural upbringing.

Deliberate teaching thus established prejudice against other Orientals, western nations, southern Chinese, rural Chinese, and less-educated Chinese. The communist suzerainty has no doubt complicated and perhaps modified all this. But the case is instructive because it has been said that China is a land relatively free from prejudice!

Basic Psychology of Conformity

As we pointed out in Chapter 3, there is no society on earth where the children are not thought to belong to the ethnic and religious group of their parents. By virtue of kinship, the child is expected to take on the prejudices of his parents, also to become the victim of whatever prejudice is directed against his parents.

It is because of this fact that prejudice *looks* as though it were inherited, linked somehow to biological descent. Since children are identical with their parents in respect to memberships, we must expect ethnic attitudes to be handed down from parent to child. So universal and automatic is it that somehow heredity seems to be involved.

Actually, the course of transmission is one of teaching and

learning, not heredity. As we have seen, parents sometimes deliberately inculcate ethnocentrism, but more often they are unaware of doing so. The following excerpt shows how the process appears to a child:

> In my earliest childhood I recall that I felt strong antagonism toward anyone who opposed the views and feelings of my parents. They would often talk about such people at the supper table. I think it was the confident tone of voice in which my parents aired their convictions and condemned their opponents that affected me, and assured me of their omnipotent wisdom.

A young child is likely to regard his parents as omnipotent (for they seem to be able to do all the things that the child fumbles with and fails to do). Why should not their judgments be his judgments?

Sometimes the family circle includes other omnipotent and omniscient relatives:

> When I was about six, my great-grandfather lived in our home. He was especially rabid against Southerners and against Irish Catholics. After hearing him condemn both these groups repeatedly, I became convinced that they must be obnoxious indeed.

Sometimes the parental view contains mixtures of tolerance and intolerance, and both are adopted:

> My father was a minister. One of the ideas I acquired from him was that one never hates a person, but only some vice in a person, such as conceit. Yet he taught me that certain vices—superstitiousness for example—were more likely to be found in Catholics.

In the following case the teaching is less complicated:

> My prejudice against Jews arose through my parents' attitude toward Jews. In my father's business, he had encountered certain Jews with whom his transactions had been unfortunate, and he was, and still is, very bitter on the subject. I also avoided Catholic girls because I heard my parents talk of what an awful mess the world would come to if everyone turned Catholic.

Tolerance too can be learned from family and neighborhood mores:

> Every child has a need for conforming to his group in order to be accepted by the group. In the community in which I grew

up, and in our family, conformity did not involve antagonism toward other groups. Therefore, I did not acquire prejudice.

If we take a Darwinian view of the matter, we may say that all this conforming has "survival value." The young child is helpless unless, in matters of basic value, he strings along with his parents. His only possible pattern for survival is their pattern. If their design for living is tolerant, so too is his; if they are hostile toward certain groups, so too is he.

We must not imply that the young child is consciously aware of his imitativeness. Certainly he does not say to himself, "I must conform to my family ways in order to survive." Psychologically there are more subtle ways of acquiring family attitudes.

The process most often named in this connection is *identification*. The term is broad and ill-defined, but it serves to convey the sense of emotional merging of oneself with others. One form of identification is indistinguishable from love and affection. A child who loves his parents will readily become depersonalized from himself and "repersonalized" in them. Their signs of feeling are eagerly scanned and mirrored in the child, who is alert to all cues coming from them. Whether in play or in seriousness, the parental model is acted out. The young son, firmly attached to his father, mimics him from morning until night. Not only are the outer acts cues for mimicry, but so too the thoughts expressed—including the hostilities and rejections.

It is almost impossible to describe the subtlety of the process involved. Learning through identification seems basically to involve a type of muscle strain or postural imitation. Supposing the child, hypersensitive to parental cues, senses a tightness or rigidity when his parents are talking about the Italian family that has moved in next door. In the very act of perceiving these parental cues, the child himself grows tight and rigid. (His perceptions tend to take a motor form—acting out what he perceives.) This strain in the child becomes conditioned by the words his parents are speaking. After this associated experience, he may tend, ever so slightly, to feel a tenseness (an incipient anxiety) whenever he hears (or thinks) of Italians. The process is infinitely subtle.

It is not only affection for the parent that may lead to identification. Even in a family where power is dominant over love, the child has no other model for strength, for success in life, than his parents. By imitating their conduct and mirroring their attitudes, he often can gain approval and reward from the parent. Even if reward is not forthcoming, he can, as it were, gain assurance by simulating their adulthood. Strutting, scolding, hating—like his father—makes the youngster feel grown-up.

One of the areas where identification may most easily take place is that of social values and attitudes. The child has none of his own to start with. Topics that are beyond his comprehension leave him no alternative but to absorb the pronouncements of others. Sometimes a child who confronts a social issue for the first time will ask his parent what attitude he should hold. Thus he may say, "Daddy, what are we? Are we Jews or gentiles; Protestants or Catholics; Republicans or Democrats?" When told what "we" are, the child is fully satisfied. From then on, he will accept his membership and the ready-made attitudes that go with it.

Conflict and Rebellion

Although conformity with the home atmosphere is undoubtedly the most important single source of prejudice, it must not be thought that the child grows up to be a mirror image of his parents' attitudes. Nor is it true that the parents' attitudes are always in conformity with the prejudices prevailing in their community.

What the father and mother transmit to their offspring is their own personal version of cultural traditions. They may be skeptical concerning the stereotypes current in their community, and pass their skepticism on to the children. They may have a few pet prejudices of their own that are not represented in their cultural group. Unless the child picks up outside the home the standard attitudes of the community, his pattern of prejudice will reflect whatever idiosyncrasies the parents have imposed.

And the child himself is sometimes selective. While he lacks the experience and strength to counter his parents' value-attitudes in his earliest years, he sometimes develops early skepticism regarding them. The case of the six-year-old who absorbed anti-Southern and anti-Irish prejudices from his great-grandfather was even at that age complicated by conflict.

> One day I was playing with my uncle, and I said, with foolish patter, "Well, anyway, we wouldn't let you and your old Irishmen live on our street." Later, with a sick feeling, I heard that my good-natured uncle was Irish. I then and there decided that my great-grandfather must be mistaken. If anyone as nice as Uncle Bill was Irish, it must be a very fine national group.

A similar conflict occurred in a little girl, likewise six years old:

> My mother told me not to play with girls on the next street, who were of a lower social class. She said she wanted me to

grow up to be a "lady." I remember feeling distinctly guilty that I had not, up to then, been ladylike. Yet I was fond of my playmates and felt guilty ever after for avoiding them.

What we learn from such cases is that even a young child may be skeptical concerning the grounds for parental prejudice. Even while conforming, they may have their doubts. Later they may reject the parental model altogether.

Sometimes the rejection takes the form of open rebellion in adolescence:

> At the age of fifteen I revolted, not only against my parents, but against the whole system of living in our town that had led me through so much misery as a boy. If the custom was to hate Negroes, I would cultivate them as friends. I shocked my parents by bringing the janitor's son into our house to play cards and listen to the radio.

Often the process of outgrowing parental prejudice, taken over second-hand, occurs first in college years:

> My parents were much prejudiced against Roman Catholics. They told me the church was treacherous, had too much political power, kept firearms, and practised immorality in the convents. During college I rethought my religious position. I came to know Roman Catholic clergy and to understand their position. Closer contact with the group led me to see that my previous fears were groundless. Now I laugh at my parents' fixed ideas.

Another college student writes:

> Inwardly I rebelled. I finally broke loose from my chains—from my father's ideas of class prejudice that I had acquired from him. For a time I went to the other extreme and compulsively associated with all sorts of people of all races, creeds, religions, and classes.

We do not know what proportion of children grow into adulthood without modifying the second-hand ethnocentrism taken over initially from the parents. Probably for every rebel who reverses his value-attitudes, there are several conformists who merely modify slightly the parental teaching to accord with their own functional needs in later life. Certain it is that in spite of rebels ethnocentrism continues generation after generation. While it may be slightly re-tailored, it is not often discarded.

Since the home is the chief and earliest source of prejudiced attitudes. we should not expect too much from programs of inter-cultural education in the schools. For one thing, schools scarcely dare to countermand parental teachings. They would get into trouble if they did so. And not all teachers are themselves free from prejudice. Nor can the church or the state—for all their official creeds of equality—easily cancel out the earlier and more intimate influence of the family.

The primacy of the family does not mean, of course, that school, church, and state should cease practising or teaching the principles of democratic living. Together, their influence may establish at least a secondary model for the child to follow. If they succeed in making him question his system of values, the chances for a maturer resolution of the conflict are greater than if such questioning never takes place. *Some* effects from school, church, and state may be expected, and their cumulative influence may affect the next generation of parents. We recall in this connection that college students are today much more reluctant to ascribe stereotyped judgements to national out-groups than were students twenty years ago (p. 202). Why should this be so, unless extra-familial influences are gradually working upon students or upon the parents, or upon both?

NOTES AND REFERENCES

1. S. A. Stouffer, et al. *The American Soldier: Adjustment During Army Life.* Princeton: Princeton Univ. Press, 1949, Vol. 1, 579.

2. A similar conclusion is offered by Van Til and Denemark on the basis of their survey of a wide variety of investigations. These authors write, "There are two major sources of prejudice and discrimination toward minority groups: (a) frustration and (b) cultural learning." In our terms frustration is one (but not the only) important factor making for functional significance. Cultural learning refers to conformity. W. Van Til and G. W. Denemark. Intercultural education. *Review of Educational Research,* 1950, **20**, 274-286.

3. Reproduced from G. W. Allport, Prejudice: a problem in psychological and social causation. *Journal of Social Issues,* 1950, Supplement Series, No. 4, 16.

4. This account is derived from G. M. Gilbert. *Nüremberg Diary.* New York: Farrar, Straus, 1947, 250 and 259 ff.

5. A. de Tocqueville. *Democracy in America.* New York: George Dearborn, 1838, 374.

6. Lillian Smith. *Killers of the Dream.* New York: W. W. Norton, 1949, 18.

CHAPTER 18

THE YOUNG CHILD

How is prejudice learned? We have opened our discussion of this pivotal problem by pointing out that the home influence has priority, and that the child has excellent reasons for adopting his ethnic attitudes ready-made from his parents. We likewise called attention to the central role of identification in the course of early learning. In the present chapter we shall consider additional factors operating in preschool years. The first six years of life are important for the development of all social attitudes, though it is a mistake to regard early childhood as alone responsible for them. A bigoted personality may be well under way by the age of six, but by no means fully fashioned.

Our analysis will be clearer if at the outset we make a distinction between *adopting* prejudice and *developing* prejudice. A child who adopts prejudice is taking over attitudes and stereotypes from his family or cultural environment. Most of the cases cited in the previous chapter are instances in point. Parental words and gestures, along with their concomitant beliefs and antagonisms, are transferred to the child. He adopts his parents' views. Some of the principles of learning discussed in this and the following chapter will help explain further how this transfer comes about.

But there is also a type of training that does not transfer ideas and attitudes directly to the child, but rather creates an atmosphere in which he *develops* prejudice as his style of life. In this case the parents may or may not express their own prejudices (usually they do). What is crucial, however, is that their mode of handling the child (disciplining, loving, threatening) is such that the child cannot help acquire suspicions, fears, hatreds that sooner or later may fix on minority groups.

In reality, of course, these forms of learning are not distinct. Parents who *teach* the child specific prejudices are also likely to *train* the child to develop a prejudiced nature. Still it is well to

297

keep the distinction in mind, for the psychology of learning is so intricate a subject that it requires analytical aids of this type.

Child Training

We consider now the style of child training that is known to be conducive to the *development* of prejudice. (We shall disregard for the time being the learning of specific attitudes toward specific groups.)

One line of proof that a child's prejudice is related to the manner of his upbringing comes from a study of Harris, Gough, and Martin.[1] These investigators first determined the extent to which 240 fourth, fifth, and sixth grade children expressed prejudiced attitudes toward minority groups. They then sent questionnaires to the mothers of these children, asking their views on certain practices in child training. Most of these were returned with the mothers' replies. The results are highly instructive. Mothers of prejudiced children, *far more often* than the mothers of unprejudiced children, held that

Obedience is the most important thing a child can learn.
A child should never be permitted to set his will against that of his parents.
A child should never keep a secret from his parents.
"I prefer a quiet child to one who is noisy."
(In the case of temper tantrums) "Teach the child that two can play that game, by getting angry yourself."

In the case of sex-play (masturbation) the mother of the prejudiced child is much more likely to believe she should punish the child; the mother of the unprejudiced child is much more likely to ignore the practice.

All in all, the results indicate that pervasive family atmospheres do definitely slant the child. Specifically, a home that is suppressive, harsh, or critical—where the parents' word is law—is more likely to prepare the groundwork for group prejudice.

It seems a safe assumption that the mothers who expressed their philosophies of child training in this questionnaire actually carried out their ideas in practice. If so, then we have strong evidence that children are more likely to be prejudiced if they have been brought up by mothers who insist on obedience, who are suppressive of the child's impulses, and who are sharp disciplinarians.

What does such a style of child training do to a child? For one thing it puts him on guard. He has to watch his impulses carefully. Not only is he punished for them when they counter the parents' convenience and rules, as they frequently do, but he feels at such times that love is withdrawn from him. When love is withdrawn he is alone, exposed, desolate. Thus he comes to watch alertly for signs of parental approval or disapproval. It is they who have power, and they who give or withhold their conditional love. Their power and their will are the decisive agents in the child's life.

What is the result? First of all, the child learns that power and authority dominate human relationships—not trust and tolerance. The stage is thus set for a hierarchical view of society. Equality does not really prevail. The effect goes even deeper. The child mistrusts his impulses: he must not have temper tantrums, he must not disobey, he must not play with his sex organs. He must fight such evil in himself. Through a simple act of projection (Chapter 24) the child comes to fear evil impulses in others. They have dark designs; their impulses threaten the child; they are not to be trusted.

If this style of training prepares the ground for prejudice, the opposite style seems to predispose toward tolerance. The child who feels secure and loved whatever he does, and who is treated not with a display of parental power (being punished usually through shaming rather than spanking), develops basic ideas of equality and trust. Not required to repress his own impulses, he is less likely to project them upon others, and less likely to develop suspicion, fear, and a hierarchical view of human relationships.[2]

While no child is always treated according to one and only one pattern of discipline or affection, we might venture to classify prevailing home atmospheres according to the following scheme:

Permissive treatment by parents
Rejective treatment
    suppressive and cruel (harsh, fear-inspiring)
    domineering and critical (overambitious parents nagging and
      dissatisfied with the child as he is)
Neglectful
Overindulgent
Inconsistent (sometimes permissive, sometimes rejective, some-
    times overindulgent)

Although we cannot yet be dogmatic about the matter, it seems very likely that rejective, neglectful, and inconsistent styles of training tend to lead to the development of prejudice.[3] Investigators have reported how impressed they are by the frequency with which quarrelsome or broken homes have occurred in the childhood of prejudiced people.

Ackerman and Jahoda made a study of anti-Semitic patients who were undergoing psychoanalysis. Most of them had had an unhealthy homelife as children, marked by quarreling, violence, or divorce. There was little or no affection or sympathy between the parents. The rejection of the child by one or both parents was the rule rather than the exception.[4]

These investigators could not find that specific parental indoctrination in anti-Semitic attitudes was a necessary element. It is true that the parents, like the children, were anti-Semitic, but the authors explain the connection as follows:

> In those cases where parents and children are anti-Semitic, it is more reasonable to assume that the emotional predispositions of the parents created a psychological atmosphere conducive to the development of similar emotional dispositions in the child, than to maintain the simple imitation hypothesis.[5]

In other words, prejudice was not *taught* by the parent but was *caught* by the child from an infected atmosphere.

Another investigator became interested in paranoia. Among a group of 125 hospital patients suffering from fixed delusional ideas he found that the majority had a predominantly suppressive and cruel upbringing. Nearly three-quarters of the patients had parents who were either suppressive and cruel or else domineering and overcritical. Only seven percent came from homes that could be called permissive.[6] Thus may paranoia in adult years be traceable to a bad start in life. We cannot, of course, equate paranoia and prejudice. Yet the rigid categorizing indulged in by the prejudiced person, his hostility, and his inaccessibility to reason are often much like the disorder of a paranoiac.

Without stretching the evidence too far, we may at least make a guess: children who are too harshly treated, severely punished, or continually criticized are more likely to develop personalities wherein group prejudice plays a prominent part. Conversely, children from more relaxed and secure homes, treated permissively and with affection, are more likely to develop tolerance.

Fear of the Strange

Let us return again to the question whether there is an inborn source of prejudice. In Chapter 8 we reported that as soon as infants are able (perhaps at six months of age) to distinguish between familiar and unfamiliar persons, they sometimes show anxiety when strangers approach. They do so especially if the stranger moves abruptly or makes a "grab" for the child. They may show special fear if the stranger wears eyeglasses, or has skin of an unfamiliar color, or even if his expressive movements are different from what the child is accustomed to. This timidity usually continues through the preschool period—often beyond. Every visitor who has entered a home where there is a young child knows that it takes several minutes, perhaps several hours, for the child to "warm up" to him. But usually the initial fear gradually disappears.

We reported also an experiment where infants were placed alone in a strange room with toys. All of the children were at first alarmed and cried in distress. After a few repetitions they became entirely habituated to the room and played as if at home. But the biological utility of the initial fear reaction is obvious. Whatever is strange is a potential danger, and must be guarded against until one's experience assures one that no harm is lurking.

The almost universal anxiety of a child in the presence of strangers is no more striking than his rapid adaptability to their presence.

In a certain household a Negro maid came to work. The young children in the family, aged three and five, showed fear and for a few days were reluctant to accept her. The maid stayed with the family for five or six years and came to be loved by all. Several years later, when the children were young adults, the family was discussing the happy period of Anna's services in the household. She had not been seen for the past ten years, but her memory was affectionately held. In the course of the conversation it came out that she was colored. The children were utterly astonished. They insisted that they had never known this fact, or had completely forgotten it if they ever knew it.

Situations of this type are not uncommon. Their occurrence makes us doubt that instinctive fear of the strange has any necessary bearing upon the organization of permanent attitudes.

Dawn of Racial Awareness

The theory of "home atmosphere" is certainly more convincing than the theory of "instinctive roots." But neither theory tells us just when and how the child's ethnic ideas begin to crystallize. Granted that the child possesses relevant emotional equipment, and that the family supplies a constant undertone of acceptance or rejection, anxiety or security, we still need studies that will show how the child's earliest sense of group differences develops. An excellent setting for such a study is a biracial nursery school.

In investigations conducted in this setting, it appears that the earliest age at which children take any note of race is two and a half.

One white child of this age, sitting for the first time beside a Negro child, said, "Dirty face." It was an unemotional remark, prompted only by his observing a wholly dark-skinned visage—for the first time in his life.

The purely sensory observation that some skins are white, some colored, seems in many cases to be the first trace of racial awareness. Unless there is the quiver of fear of the strange along with this observation, we may say that race difference at first arouses a sense of curiosity and interest—nothing more. The child's world is full of fascinating distinctions. Facial color is simply one of them. Yet we note that even this first perception of racial difference may arouse associations with "clean" and "dirty."

The situation is more insistent by the age of three and a half or four. The sense of dirt still haunts the children. They have been thoroughly scrubbed at home to eradicate dirt. Why then does it exist so darkly on other children? One colored boy, confused concerning his membership, said to his mother, "Wash my face clean; some of the children don't wash well, especially colored children."

A first grade teacher reports that about one white child in ten refuses to hold hands during games with the solitary Negro child in the classroom. The reason apparently is not "prejudice" in any deep-seated sense. The rejective white children merely complain that Tom has dirty hands and face.

Dr. Goodman's nursery school study shows one particularly revealing result. Negro children are, by and large, "racially aware" earlier than are white children.[7] They tend to be confused, disturbed, and sometimes excited by the problem. Few of them seem to know that they are Negroes. (Even at the age of seven one little Negro girl said to a white playmate, "I'd hate to be colored, wouldn't you?")

The interest and disturbance take many forms. Negro children ask more questions about racial differences; they may fondle the blond hair of a white child; they are often rejective toward Negro dolls. When given a white and Negro doll to play with, they almost uniformly prefer the white doll; many slap the Negro doll and call it dirty or ugly. As a rule, they are more rejective of Negro dolls than are white children. They tend to behave self-consciously when tested for racial awareness. One Negro boy, being shown two baby dolls alike save for color, is asked, "Which one is most like you when you were a baby?"

Bobby's eyes move from brown to white; he hesitates, squirms, glances at us sidewise—and points to the white doll. Bobby's perceptions relevant to race, feeble and sporadic though they are, have some personal meaning—some ego-reference.

Especially interesting is Dr. Goodman's observation that Negro children tend to be fully as active as white children at the nursery school age. They are on the whole more sociable—particularly those who are rated as high on "racial awareness." A larger proportion of the Negro children are rated as "leaders" in the group. Although we cannot be certain of the meaning of this finding, it may well come from the fact that Negro children are more highly stimulated by the dawning awareness of race. They may be excited by a challenge they do not fully understand, and may seek reassurance through activity and social contacts for the vague threat that hangs over them. The threat comes not from nursery school, where they are secure enough, but from their first contacts with the world outside and from discussions at home, where their Negro parents cannot fail to talk about the matter.

What is so interesting about this full-scale activity at the nursery school age is its contrast to the adult demeanor of many Negroes who are noted for their poise, passivity, apathy, laziness—or whatever the withdrawing reaction may be called. In Chapter 9 we noted that the Negro's conflicts sometimes engender a quietism, a passivity. Many people hold that this "laziness" is a biological trait of Negroes—but in the nursery school we find flatly contradictory evidence. Passivity, when it exists as a Negro attribute, is apparently a learned mode of adjustment. The assertive reaching out of the four-year-old for security and acceptance is ordinarily doomed to failure. After a period of struggle and suffering the passive mode of adjustment may set in.

Why is there, even in the dawning race-awareness of four-year-olds, a nebulous sense of inferiority associated with dark skin? A significant part of the answer lies in the similarity between dark pigmentation and dirt. A third of Dr. Goodman's children (both Negro and white) spoke of this matter. Many others no doubt had it in their minds, but did not happen to mention it to the investigators. An additional part of the answer may lie in those subtle forms of learning—not yet fully understood—whereby value-judgments are conveyed to the child. Some parents of white children may, by word or act, have conveyed to their children a vague sense of their rejection of Negroes. If so, the rejection is still only nascent in the four-year-old, for in virtually no case could the investigators find anything they were willing to label "prejudice" at this age level. Some of the Negro parents, too, may have conveyed to their children a sense of the handicaps of people with black skin, even before the children themselves knew their own skin was black.

The initial damage of associated ideas seems inescapable in our culture. Dark skin suggests dirt—even to a four-year-old. To some it may suggest feces. Brown is not the aesthetic norm in our culture (in spite of the popularity of chocolate). But this initial disadvantage is by no means insuperable. Discriminations in the realm of color are not hard to learn: a scarlet rose is not rejected because it is the color of blood, nor a yellow tulip because it is the color of urine.

To sum up: four-year-olds are normally interested, curious, and appreciative of differences in racial groups. A slight sense of white superiority seems to be growing, largely because of the association of white with cleanness—cleanliness being a value learned very early in life. But contrary associations can be, and sometimes are, easily built up.

One four-year-old boy was taken by train from Boston to San Francisco. He was enchanted by the friendly Negro porter. For fully two years thereafter he fantasied that he was a porter, and complained bitterly that he was not colored so that he could qualify for the position.

Linguistic Tags: Symbols of Power and Rejection

In Chapter 11 we discussed the immensely important role of language in building fences for our mental categories and our emotional responses. This factor is so crucial that we return to it again—as it bears on childhood learning.

In Goodman's study it turned out that fully half the nursery school children knew the word "nigger." Few of them understood what the epithet culturally implies. But they knew that the word was potent. It was forbidden, taboo, and always fetched some type of strong response from the teachers. It was therefore a "power word." Not infrequently in a temper tantrum a child would call his teacher (whether white or colored) a "nigger" or a "dirty nigger." The term expressed an emotion—nothing more. Nor did it always express anger—sometimes merely excitement. Children wildly racing around, shrieking at play might, in order to enhance their orgies, yell "nigger, nigger, nigger." As a strong word it seemed fit to vocalize the violent expenditure of energy under way.

One observer gives an interesting example of aggressive verbalization during wartime play:

> Recently, in a waiting room, I watched three youngsters who sat at a table looking at magazines. Suddenly the smaller boy said: "Here's a soldier and an airplane. He's a Jap." The girl said: "No, he's an American." The little fellow said: "Get him, soldier. Get the Jap." The older boy added, "And Hitler too." "And Mussolini," said the girl. "And the Jews," said the big boy. Then the little fellow started a chant, the others joining in: "The Japs, Hitler, Mussolini, and the Jews! The Japs, Hitler, Mussolini, and the Jews!" [8] It is certain that these children had very little understanding of their bellicose chant. The names of their enemies had an expressive but not a denotative significance.

One little boy was agreeing with his mother, who was warning him never to play with niggers. He said, "No, Mother, I never play with niggers. I only play with white and black children." This child was developing aversion to the term "nigger," without having the slightest idea what the term meant. In other words, the aversion is being set up prior to acquiring a referent.

Other examples could be given of instances where words appear strong and emotionally laden to the child (goy, kike, dago). Only later does he attach the word to a group of people upon whom he can visit the emotions suggested by the word.

We call this process "linguistic precedence in learning." The emotional word has an effect prior to the learning of the referent. Later, the emotional effect becomes attached to the referent.

Before a firm sense of the referent is acquired, the child may go through stages of puzzlement and confusion. This is particularly true because emotional epithets are most likely to be learned when some exciting or traumatic experience is under way. Lasker gives the following example:

> Walking across the playground, a settlement worker found a little Italian boy crying bitterly. She asked him what was the matter. "Hit by Polish boy," the little man repeated several times. Inquiry among the bystanders showed that the offender was not Polish at all. Turning again to her little friend, she said, "You mean, hit by a big naughty boy." But he would not have it thus and went on repeating that he had been hit by

a Polish boy. This struck the worker as so curious that she made inquiries of the little fellow's family. She learned that it lived in the same house with a Polish family and that the Italian mother, by constantly quarreling with her Polish neighbor, had put into the heads of her children the notion that "Polish" and "bad" were synonymous terms.[9]

When this lad finally learns who Poles are, he already will have a strong prejudice against them. Here is a clear case of linguistic precedence in learning.

Children sometimes confess their perplexity concerning emotional tags. They seem to be groping for proper referents. Trager and Radke, from their work with kindergarten, first and second grade children, give several examples:[10]

> Anna: When I was coming out of the dressing room, Peter called me a dirty Jew.
> Teacher: Why did you say that, Peter?
> Peter (earnestly): I didn't say it for spite. I was only playing.

> Johnny (helping Louis pull off his leggings): A man called my father a goy.
> Louis: What's a goy?
> Johnny: I think everybody around here is a goy. But not me. I'm Jewish.

> On being called a "white cracker" by a Negro boy in the class, the teacher said to her class, "I am puzzled by the meaning of two words. Do you know what 'white cracker' means?"
> A number of vague answers were received from the children, one being "You're supposed to say it when you're mad."

Even while the child is having difficulty with words, they have a great power over him. To him they are often a type of magic, of verbal realism (Chapter 11).

> A little boy in the South was playing with the child of the washerwoman. Everything was going smoothly until a neighbor white child called over the fence, "Look out, you'll catch it."
> "Catch what?" asked the first white child.
> "Catch the black. You'll get colored too."
> Just this assertion (reminding the child, no doubt, of expressions such as "catch the measles") frightened him. He deserted his colored companion then and there, and never played with him again.

Children often cry if they are called names. Their self-esteem is wounded by any epithet: naughty, dirty, harum-scarum, nigger, dago, Jap, or what not. To escape this verbal realism of early childhood, they often reassure themselves, when they are a little older, with the self-restorative jingle: Sticks and stones may break my bones, but names can never hurt me. But it takes a few years for them to learn that a name is not a thing-in-itself. As we saw in Chapter 11, verbal realism may never be fully shaken off. The rigidity of linguistic categories may continue in adult thinking. To some adults "communist" or "Jew" is a dirty word—and a dirty thing—an indissoluble unity, as it may be to a child.

The First Stage in Learning Prejudice

Janet, six years of age, was trying hard to integrate her obedience to her mother with her daily social contacts. One day she came running home and asked, "Mother, what is the name of the children I am supposed to hate?"

Janet's wistful question leads us into a theoretical summary of the present chapter.

Janet is stumbling at the threshold of some abstraction. She wishes to form the right category. She intends to oblige her mother by hating the right people when she can find out who they are.

In this situation we suspect the preceding stages in Janet's developmental history:

1. She identifies with the mother, or at least she strongly craves the mother's affection and approval. We may imagine that the home is not "permissive" in atmosphere, but somewhat stern and critical. Janet may have found that she must be on her toes to please her parent. Otherwise she will suffer rejection or punishment. In any event, she has developed a habit of obedience.

2. While she has apparently no strong fear of strangers at the present time, she has learned to be circumspect. Experiences of insecurity with people outside the family circle may be a factor in her present effort to define her circle of loyalties.

3. She undoubtedly has gone through the initial period of curiosity and interest in racial and ethnic differences. She knows now that human beings are clustered into groups—that there are important distinctions if only she can identify them. In the case of Negro and white the visibility factor has helped her. But then she discovered that subtler differences were also important; Jews somehow differed from gentiles; wops from Americans; doctors from salesmen. She is now aware of group differences, though not yet clear concerning all the relevant cues.

4. She has encountered the stage of linguistic precedence in learning. In fact, she is now in this stage. She knows that group X (she knows neither its name nor its identity) is somehow hate-worthy. She already has the emotional meaning but lacks the referential meaning. She seeks now to integrate the proper content with the emotion. She wishes to define her category so as to make her future behavior conform to her mother's desires. As soon as she has the linguistic tag at her command, she will be like the little Italian boy for whom "Polish" and "bad" were synonymous terms.

Up to the present, Janet's development marks what we might call the first stage of ethnocentric learning. Let us christen it the period of *pregeneralized* learning. This label is not altogether satisfactory, but none better describes the potpourri of factors listed above. The term draws attention primarily to the fact that the child has not yet generalized after the fashion of adults. He does not quite understand what a Jew is, what a Negro is, or what his own attitude toward them should be. He does not know even what *he* is—in any consistent sense. He may think he is an American only when he is playing with his toy soldiers (this type of categorizing was not uncommon in wartime). It is not only in ethnic matters that thoughts are prelogical from an adult point of view. A little girl may not think that her mother is her mother when the latter is working at the office; and may not regard her mother as an officeworker when she is at home tending the family.[11]

The child seems to live his mental life in specific contexts. What exists here and now makes up the only reality. The strange-man-who-knocks-at-the-door is something to be feared. It does not matter if he is a delivery man. The Negro boy at school is dirty. He is not a member of a race.

Such independent experiences in concrete procession seem to furnish the child's mind. His pregeneralized thinking (from the adult's point of view) has sometimes been labeled "global," or "syncretistic," or "prelogical." [12]

Now the place of linguistic tags in the course of mental development is crucial. They stand for adult abstractions, for logical generalizations of the sort that mature adults accept. The child learns the tags before he is fully ready to apply them to the adult categories. They prepare him for prejudice. But the process takes time. Only after much fumbling—in the manner of Janet and other children described in this chapter—will the proper categorizing take place.

The Second Stage in Learning Prejudice

As soon as Janet's mother gives a clear answer to Janet, she will in all probability enter a second period of prejudice—one that we may call the period of *total rejection*. Suppose the mother answers, "I told you not to play with Negro children. They are dirty; they have diseases; and they will hurt you. Now don't let me catch you at it." If Janet by now has learned to distinguish Negroes from other groups, even from the dark-skinned Mexican children, or Italians—in other words, if she now has the adult category in mind—she will undoubtedly reject all Negroes, in all circumstances, and with considerable feeling.

The research of Blake and Dennis well illustrates the point.[13] It will be recalled that these investigators studied Southern white children in the fourth and fifth grades (ten- and eleven-year-olds). They asked such questions as, "Which are more musical—Negroes or white people?" "Which are more clean?"—and many questions of a similar type. These children had, by the age of ten, learned to reject the Negro category *totally*. No favorable quality was ascribed to Negroes more often than to whites. In effect, whites had all the virtues; Negroes, none.

While this totalized rejection certainly starts earlier (in many children it will be found by the age of seven or eight), it seems to reach its ethnocentric peak in early puberty. First- and second-grade children often elect to play with, or sit beside, a child of different race or ethnic membership. This friendliness usually disappears in the fifth grade. At that time children choose their own group almost exclusively. Negroes select Negroes, Italians select Italians, and so on.[14]

As children grow older, they normally lose this tendency to total rejection and overgeneralization. Blake and Dennis found that in the 12th grade the white youth ascribed several favorable stereotypes to Negroes. They considered them more musical, more easygoing, better dancers.

Thus, after a period of *total rejection,* a stage of *differentiation* sets in. The prejudices grow less totalized. Escape clauses are written into the attitude in order to make it more rational and more acceptable to the individual. One says, "Some of my best friends are Jews." Or, "I am not prejudiced against Negroes—I always loved my black Mammy." The child who is first learning adult categories of rejection is not able to make such gracious exceptions. It takes him the first six to eight years of his life to learn total rejection, and another six years or so to modify it. The actual adult creed in his culture is complex indeed. It allows for (and in many ways encourages) ethnocentrism. At the same time, one must give lip service to democracy and equality, or at least ascribe some good qualities to the minority group and somehow plausibly justify the remaining disapproval that one expresses. It takes the child well into adolescence to learn the peculiar double-talk appropriate to prejudice in a democracy.

Around the age of eight, children often *talk* in a highly prejudiced manner. They have learned their categories and their totalized rejection. But the rejection is chiefly verbal. While they may damn the Jews, the wops, the Catholics, they may still *behave* in a relatively democratic manner. They may play with them even while they talk against them. The "total rejection" is chiefly a verbal matter.

Now when the teaching of the school takes effect, the child learns a new verbal norm: he must talk democratically. He must profess to regard all races and creeds as equal. Hence, by the age of 12, we may find *verbal* acceptance, but *behavioral* rejection. By this age the prejudices have finally affected conduct, even while the verbal, democratic norms are beginning to take effect.

The paradox, then, is that younger children may talk undemocratically, but behave democratically, whereas children in puberty may talk (at least in school) democratically but behave with true prejudice. By the age of 15, considerable skill is shown in imitating the adult pattern. Prejudiced talk and democratic talk are reserved for appropriate occasions, and rationalizations are ready for whatever occasions require them. Even conduct is varied according to circumstances. One may be friendly with a Negro in the kitchen, but hostile to a Negro who comes to the front door. Double-dealing, like double-talk, is hard to learn. It takes the entire period of childhood and much of adolescence to master the art of ethnocentrism.

NOTES AND REFERENCES

1. D. B. Harris, H. G. Gough, W. E. Martin. Children's ethnic attitudes: II, Relationship to parental beliefs concerning child training. *Child Development*, 1950, **21**, 169-181.

2. These two contrasting styles of child training are described more fully by D. P. Ausubel in *Ego Development and the Personality Disorders*. New York: Grune & Stratton, 1952.

3. The most extensive evidence is contained in researches conducted at the University of California. See: T. W. Adorno, Else Frenkel-Brunswik, D. J. Levinson, R. N. Sanford, *The Authoritarian Personality*, New York: Harper, 1950; also, Else Frenkel-Brunswik, Patterns of

social and cognitive outlook in children and parents, *American Journal of Orthopsychiatry*, 1951, **21**, 543-558.

4. N. W. ACKERMAN AND MARIE JAHODA. *Anti-Semitism and Emotional Disorder.* New York: Harper, 1950, 45.

5. *Ibid.*, 85.

6. H. BONNER. Sociological aspects of paranoia. *American Journal of Sociology*, 1950, **56**, 255-262.

7. MARY E. GOODMAN. *Race Awareness in Young Children.* Cambridge: Addison-Wesley, 1952. Other studies have confirmed the fact that Negro children are race-aware before white children: e.g., RUTH HOROWITZ, Racial aspects of self-identification in nursery school children, *Journal of Psychology*, 1939, **7**, 91-99.

8. MILDRED M. EAKIN. *Getting Acquainted with Jewish Neighbors.* New York: Macmillan, 1944.

9. B. LASKER. *Race Attitudes in Children.* New York: Henry Holt, 1929, 98.

10. HELEN G. TRAGER AND MARIAN RADKE. Early childhood airs its views. *Educational Leadership*, 1947, **5**, 16-23.

11. E. L. HARTLEY, M. ROSENBAUM, AND S. SCHWARTZ. Children's perceptions of ethnic group membership. *Journal of Psychology*, 1948, **26**, 387-398.

12. *Cf.* H. WERNER. *Comparative Psychology of Mental Development.* Chicago: FOLLETT, 1948. J. PIAGET. *The Child's Conception of the World.* New York: Harcourt, Brace, 1929, 236. G. MURPHY. *Personality.* New York: Harper, 1947, 336.

13. R. BLAKE AND W. DENNIS. The development of stereotypes concerning the Negro. *Journal of Abnormal and Social Psychology*, 1943, **38**, 525-531.

14. J. H. CRISWELL. A sociometric study of race cleavage in the classroom. *Archives of Psychology*, 1939, No. 235.

CHAPTER 19

LATER LEARNING

Social learning is an exceedingly complex process. Up to now we have told only part of the story. Among the fundamental factors operating in the earlier years of life we have called attention to the central process of identification that helps the child establish a sense of his own membership and sensitizes him to his parents' ethnic attitudes. We have stressed the atmosphere of child training, particularly as concerns punishment and affection. We have dealt with the confusions that mark the child's first perceptions of ethnic differences, and with his struggle to form adult categories. Language labels play an important part in category formation, and often lead to emotional attitudes even before the idea-system itself is formed. We have suggested that three roughly chronological stages can be distinguished in the formation of prejudiced attitudes: pregeneralization, total rejection, differentiation. It is not until adolescence that the child is able to handle ethnic categories in a culturally approved way, and only then that his prejudices can be said to be fashioned in the adult form.

What is missing from this account is an adequate picture of the continual integrating and organizing activity that occurs from the very outset of the learning process. Above all else the human mind is an organizing agent. A child's ethnic attitudes gradually form coherent units within his personality, and become integrated into its very texture.

Although integrating and organizing are continuously present, it seems that these activities are particularly important in puberty. The reason is that up to this time a child's prejudices are mostly secondhand. He has learned to parrot the view of his parents, or to reflect the ethnocentrism of his immediate culture. Gradually, as the poignant period of adolescence approaches, he finds that his prejudices, like his religion or political views, must become a firsthand fitting to his personality. In order to become an adult, with status and privileges, he fashions his social attitudes into their mature form—appropriate to his own ego.

312

The present chapter will deal with the integration and organization of prejudiced attitudes, chiefly in puberty and adolescence.

Conditioning

The simplest example of integration and organization occurs in cases of trauma or shock. One young woman writes:

> For years I have been much afraid of Negroes. The reason is that when I was very small, a coal man (covered with coal dust) came suddenly around the corner of the house and startled me violently. I soon associated his black face with colored people as a whole.

Here the mechanism of simple conditioning is at work:

sudden appearance ——————————▸ startled response
black face ——————
all black faces ——

The sudden appearance of a strange man was a "biologically adequate" cause of a violent startle and fear. The black face was an integral part of the frightening stimulus situation. Any black face thereafter is a sufficient cue to reactivate the fear response.

Simple conditioned response-learning of this type does not have to be emotionally colored. If it is not, then a large number of repetitions may be required in order to "set" the associative connection. But in the case of traumatic conditioning, the emotional response is so violent that only a single contiguous connection between the "biologically adequate" stimulus and the "conditioned stimulus" is needed. The following case illustrates the same principle:

> When I was a young girl, a Filipino houseboy tried to make love to me. I reacted violently and negatively both to the lovemaking and to him. I now actually shudder when I am in the presence of an Oriental.

While such instances may occur in early childhood, many of them are dated later. And they may involve other than ethnic group experiences. Thus—

> When I was thirteen years old, my family was forced to leave our town and sell our beloved home because of labor trouble in my father's firm. I have never forgiven labor.

In all these cases we note the element of overgeneralization (total rejection) that follows a traumatic experience. It is not against a specific person (the houseboy, the coal man, or a specific laborer) that one is prejudiced, but against the category *as a whole*.

Sometimes a trauma is not based on personal experience at all (although usually it is). There are cases where an intense moving picture, or a horrible story, or a vivid recital, seems to crystallize an attitude that may endure for years. One girl writes:

> My prejudice against Turks I can trace to a vivid account by a playmate who told that Turkish men all have handlebar mustaches to hide their knife scars, and are drunken and vicious.

Traumatic learning is, then, a matter of vivid one-time conditioning. It tends to establish an attitude at once, and this attitude overgeneralizes to include all members of a class of objects associated with the original stimulus. Many years ago, the philosopher Spinoza expressed the principle in the following words:

> If a man has been affected pleasurably or painfully by anyone . . . and if the pleasure or pain has been accompanied by the idea of the said stranger as cause . . . the man will feel love or hatred not only to the individual stranger, but also to the whole class or nation whereto he belongs.[1]

We need not, of course, go back to Spinoza to find discussions of conditioning and generalization in the learning of ethnic attitudes. Recent experiments have shown that it is possible in the setting of a psychological laboratory both to create and to diminish ethnic hostility.[2]

An instance of pleasurable and favorable conditioning is given by a college student:

> I used to join with my gang in chasing Negro kids whom we called "dirty niggers." But after our church organization produced a minstrel show (the first I had ever seen) I decided I liked Negroes very much—and I have never changed my mind.

In the following case we note another instance of traumatic conversion away from prejudice:

> In my sophomore year, a Jewish girl was assigned a room on our corridor. She remained largely an outsider for some time. One day in her presence I told how I had gone to a train with a Jewish girl and then walked off leaving her when I saw an Aryan friend. I said to the group to whom I was telling the story, "It probably wasn't nice, but after all . . ." The Jewish girl quietly got up and left the room. It quickly dawned on

me that I had said almost the worst possible thing I could have said. For the first time in my life I really tried to appraise my attitude toward the Jewish people and to weigh it in the scales of reason.

While traumatic learning may sometimes be an important factor in the establishment and organization of prejudiced attitudes —and occasionally in destroying them—certain cautions are in order.

1. In many cases the trauma merely intensifies or accelerates a process already under way. Thus in the last-mentioned case, unless the narrator had a latent sensitivity and remorse at her own anti-Semitism, she would not have been so shocked at hurting the feelings of her Jewish dormitory-mate. The experience merely intensified shame that was already present.

2. People tend to look for simple childhood traumatic experiences in order to explain their own attitudes. They tend to recall (or invent) experiences to conform to their present prejudices. One study, for example, found that anti-Semites reported a far larger proportion of unpleasant experiences with Jews than tolerant people did, but the result seemed best explained in terms of the selectivity or inventiveness of memory in order to rationalize and justify current hostility.[3]

3. A hundred college students were asked to write topical life histories on the subject of "My experience with, and attitudes toward, minority groups in America." When analyzed, it turned out that only about ten percent had recounted traumatic incidents of sufficient weight to be considered even partial generators of prejudice.

4. Trauma must not be confused with the normal integration of successive experiences. If, over and over again, a person has a certain kind of experience with members of a certain group, there is no question of trauma. There may even be no question of prejudice. For a well-founded generalization is not a prejudice (Chapter 1).

Selective Perception and Closure

It may help to think of the principles we have discussed as providing a scaffolding for learning. The style of child training prevailing in a home, the process of identification and imitative conformity, the phenomenon of linguistic precedence whereby emotional labels are prepared for attachment to later categories, the process of conditioning, especially of a traumatic order, the early formation and later differentiation of stereotyped generalizations—all these are conditions for the formation of attitudes. Still missing is an explanation how these conditions lead to the *structure* of prejudice as it exists in any given individual's mind.

To cover this step in learning theory it is necessary to assume that the child lives under constant pressure to obtain definite meanings from his welter of experience; that he is himself intent upon the task of organization.

Take the case of an authoritarian family atmosphere. The child who is harshly disciplined, never allowed to pit his will against his parents', can scarcely help perceive existence as a threatening thing. Life, he is forced to assume, is based not on tolerant acceptance, but on a power relationship. Only a hierarchical view of human relationships will satisfy this root quality of his experience. As a result he is likely to perceive all his acquaintanceships in terms of a pecking order. He sees that he stands higher than some, lower than others. How can he help but arrange his life according to the only model he knows?

Or suppose the seed-form of prejudice is traumatic; here too the individual will order his perception and reasoning to accord with the directional set he has received. The following excerpt, although written by a young adult, shows the selective and rationalizing process that we find prevailing even in childhood. The author is an American schoolteacher in the Near East:

> In my first contacts with Greek students, a few unhappy cases of cheating in examinations occurred, and, without my realizing what was happening, my attitude toward the Greeks as a people became biased by this. This bias was increased, no doubt, by the fact that the relations between the Greeks and the Turks were somewhat strained at that time and my sympathies were drawn toward the Turks. A conflict existed, however, between the new attitude that I was forming toward the Greeks and my deep admiration for the ancient Greek culture. It was difficult to reconcile the two, but I found a way out. I looked up all the evidence that I could find to substantiate the claim that the modern Greeks are not the lineal descendants of the Greeks of the Classical Period and hence have no rightful pride in that glorious tradition. This was purely a biased process on my part, since I made no effort to weigh this evidence critically or to seek out the counterarguments.[4]

What seems to be happening in this, and in similar instances, is that some precondition (home atmosphere, conditioning, linguistic tag) gives a slant, a directional set, a posture, to the mind. This set in turn starts up the process of selective perception and logical closure that are needed to fashion concrete idea-systems. (In Chapter 2 we pointed out how a category attracts all possible support to itself.) We cannot help but strive to put flesh and clothes upon the skeleton of an attitude. We demand that it be concrete, viable, justified, and reasonable—or at least, that it appear so to ourselves.

Learning by Subsidiation

The principle of closure, just described, is a somewhat intellectualistic principle. It states that a mental structure not yet complete will tend to complete itself—to grow more meaningful, more self-consistent. But we do not live our lives exclusively on an intellectualistic plane.

The principle needs to be broadened. It is not only specific meanings that are rounded out and justified, but likewise the whole complex value-pattern and system of interest. Take the following case report:

> I wanted to join the Congregational church when I was eleven years old because all my friends went to that church and seemed to have such a good time. But I didn't. Why? Well, because in some subtle way, which I've never been able to figure out, the family made it clear to me that there was a certain dignity in belonging to the Episcopal Church. Also, it was the old story of grandfather and great-grandfathers having sat in those same pews.

Here we see that the girl's family had established for her a value frame of reference. It would be well for her to maintain dignity, status, and a prideful design for living. Within this directional set she gradually develops her specific attitudes—pro-Episcopalian, anti-Congregational. First she begins to take a certain view of herself—one of subtle superiority. Her prejudices, such as they are, will be merely incidents in the maintenance of this self-image. Her broad values (the scheme she lives by) will form her view of out-groups. In this instance, there probably will never be hatred or unkind discrimination. Rather there will be just the slightest sense of superiority over groups that are less "dignified."

The law of subsidiation might be stated as follows: *there will be a tendency to acquire ethnic attitudes to conform to whatever dominant frames of value the individual has.* Since values are a personal matter, lying at the center of one's ego-structure, we might also state the law as follows: *there will be a tendency to acquire ethnic attitudes to conform to whatever self-image the individual has.*

The law asserts that the process of learning prejudice is not exclusively (nor primarily) a product of external influence. Prejudice is not merely a matter of propaganda, of handing the young person a ready-made attitude, of the impact of movies, comic books, or radio. It is not merely a matter of specific parental teaching, nor of rationalizing any and all occurrences through "closure." It is not a matter of blind imitation or mirroring the culture. It is all these things, *provided* their influence is "subsidiated" to the child's growing philosophy of life. If they seem to fit his own image of himself, to confer status upon him, to have "functional significance" for him, he will then be more likely to learn the lesson.

Let us take one final example. It happens to be a case free from prejudice.

As a child, William was always sympathetic. There may have been a tenderhearted core in his inborn temperament that slanted his outlook on life from the very beginning. His home was secure and permissive. He was also praised for his sympathetic deeds. He particularly liked to take care of sick people or sick animals, and took as his ego-ideal the kindly family physician. He thought of himself as a healer. His concern for suffering later transferred itself to people handicapped by deformities, social ostracism, or minority-group status.

Now it must not be thought that his environment was free from prejudice. Even his parents, who gave him ample security and affection, often spoke against Jews and Catholics. The community itself was prejudice-ridden. William could scarcely help picking up the epithets and using them in a superficial manner. But these seeds of prejudice never took root. His image of himself as a healer, as a friend to man, was too dominant. After adolescence he made an objective appraisal of the situation. He decided that he was unusually sensitive about the matter, but also that ethnic prejudice was counter to the values most central in his life. After this stocktaking, he deliberately reaffirmed his own values, and devoted himself professionally to the improvement of intergroup relations.

William was selectively perceiving his world in terms of his own frame of values. His specific attitudes grew in a fashion subsidiary to this frame. The original slanting in this case is not absolutely clear. Perhaps it was the temperamental disposition he speaks of, perhaps the permissive home atmosphere. But once under way the major influence in the development seems to be his own conception of himself.

The Need for Status

Now, William's case seems to be noteworthy in two respects. In the first place, he establishes his own sense of worth, not at the expense of "inferior" people but by identifying with them in a sympathetic manner. (Many, perhaps most, people do not do this: a personal sense of worth is maintained by virtue of *looking down* on other people.) In the second place, William seems to have grown up relatively unaffected by the competitive values of American culture. Being "on top" means little to him. He resists the invitation of his family and his community to feel personal status at the expense of the Jews and Catholics in the neighborhood.

Let us now examine the more usual situation. There seems to be every reason why a child, especially in western culture, should come to regard himself as better than other people. (Hobbes and other philosophers have insisted that this is an absolutely universal trait in human nature. They would say that William is really a fraud; that he simply gets egoistic pleasure from his sympathies—just as other people get the same pleasure from snobbery.)

Nature requires that every individual be a self-sufficient biological organism. He must devote his life cycle to maintaining his physical and mental integrity. Thus, in a sense, everything he does has to be self-centered. If he did not live and work for his own maintenance, he would perish—unless someone else assumed the burden. In the process he cannot fail to develop a strong, clamorous sense of his own ego. It is the pivot of his existence. When his sense of integrity and self-direction are interfered with, he has the capacity for rage. He has the capacity, likewise, for aggression, resentment, hate, envy, and other forms of self-righteousness. These self-restorative mechanisms are likely to be called into play whenever the ego-esteem is threatened.

If he has the capacity for anger and hostility, he also has considerable susceptibility to praise and flattery. To have one's virtues acknowledged, and one's self-love thus vindicated, is to experience *status*. Such elation has survival-value, for it indicates to the person that he is, for the time being at least, secure and successful—not only in his dealings with the physical world, but, what is harder to achieve, in his dealings with the social world where other egos, too, are clamoring for recognition. Egoism in human nature is, then, a *sine qua non* of existence. Its social manifestation is the *need for status*.

For the moment we shall overlook the other side of the coin of human nature. There are also capacities that can cancel, or greatly modify, the egoistic need for status. Life starts as a loving, symbiotic relationship between mother and child. The child is infinitely trustful, and develops normally a markedly affiliative relation with his environment—with things and with people. It is because of this affectional equipment that the constructive values of human cooperation are realizable. And it is because of them that prejudice (though natural from the egoist side) is not an inevitable development in personality.

But for the present it is enough to admit that there is in most people a strong need for a sense of personal status. We shall see later (especially in Chapter 27) how this need can be socialized and its teeth pulled in the development of authentically tolerant personalities.

Caste and Class

If culture gives us ready-made answers to the problems of living, we may expect it to provide a ready-made solution to the problem of status-craving. It does so in ample fashion.

To people who crave status, culture offers the formula of "caste." If for any reason this formula proves inadequate, it offers the alternative formula of "class." The total, unwieldy, heterogeneous population of a country is normally subdivided into layers, and this stratification makes for clear distinctions of status.

One author defines caste as "an endogamous status group which places culturally defined limits upon the individual member in terms of mobility and interaction, and on his nature as a person." [5] Between castes intermarriage is usually forbidden. It is so in the Brahmanic-Indian caste system. In the United States, in all Southern and some Northern states intermarriage between white people and Negroes is legally prohibited.

The Negro in America is socially a better example of caste than he is of race. Since many Negroes are more Caucasian in their racial descent than they are African, it makes poor sense to assign them to the Negro race. The handicaps they suffer (even those individuals with only a trace of "Negro blood") are typically the socially imposed handicaps peculiar to lower caste—not natural handicaps engendered by racial inheritance. Discrimination in employment, segregation in housing, and all other stigmata are marks of caste alone. The fact that the Negro is expected to "know his place" is also a caste requirement—a folkway intended to enforce ascribed lower status.[6] Legal sanctions enforce the caste system in Southern states today, but informal sanctions are even more powerful.

The formal change in the Negroes' condition from slavery to freedom has only moderately altered the total situation up to now. As Golightly describes it:

> Each individual is born into the Negro or white group and he can neither earn nor work himself out. These characteristic features of a caste system are enforced in the South by laws requiring segregation in all major areas of intergroup life. In the North, caste lines are not legally sanctioned; nevertheless, they are effectively held intact by personal prejudices.[7]

The same writer shows the undoubted utility of this arrangement from the point of view of the white people. It is, in essence, a cultural device for enhancing self-esteem. From the point of view of status-craving a caste system makes good sense.

The question arises as to what cultural devices are available to members of the lower caste for enhancing *their* self-esteem. The answer is, of course, that they create their own layers. Skin color is one criterion; the lighter skins rate higher than the darker. There also are what seem to be frivolous distinctions, in terms of straightness of hair, possession of a washing machine, or whom one knows among the white neighbors. With a small amount of contriving, anyone can find valid reasons for feeling superior to someone else. In an audience of lower-class Negroes there was great gaiety at the expense of an English nobleman caricatured on the stage. The audience thought that his "silly ass" manner of speaking was ridiculous. They felt superior to *him*.

Status distinctions that cannot be put in terms of caste can be classified as manifestations of *social class*. Roughly, a social class is a group of people who participate socially with one another on equal terms, or who would be willing to do so. They tend to have similar manners, modes of speech, moral attitudes, educational levels, and comparable amounts of material property. Unlike castes, social classes are not separated by impassable barriers. In a mobile society, as in America, people frequently move from one social class to another.

Sociologists tell us that there are two kinds of social status: that which is *achieved* and that which is *ascribed*. In the first type, the individual may by his own efforts (or the efforts of his parents) attain a certain location in the hierarchy. On the other hand, ascribed status is hereditary in its force. The scion of the British ruling family is, and always will be, a member of the aristocracy. Nothing he does can change this fact. Caste, then, is a matter of ascribed status. Class, on the other hand, at least in America, is largely an achieved status.

It would be difficult to say how many classes there are in American society. Everyone, it is true, seems vaguely aware of the existence of an *upper* class, a *middle* class, and a *lower* class; and without too much difficulty could locate himself within this layering. Actually, however, this cleavage is too coarse to serve the individual's need for a sense of status superiority. He wishes to look down on concretely defined groups in his community. He can, of course, regard all colored peoples—especially all Negroes —as a lower caste and thus feel a categorical superiority. But he craves a more discriminating system.

One fairly definite basis for layering exists in ethnic groups. We have seen in Chapter 3 how remarkably uniform is the judgment among Americans concerning the relative acceptability of various ethnic stocks: Germans, Italians, Armenians, and the like. Each of these can in sequence look down upon all groups lower in the series. Another uniform principle of layering lies in occupation. Physicians have high status, mechanics and mailmen intermediate, day laborers low.

Another fairly uniform indicator of social class is place of residence. Every community has regions that are known as "better neighborhoods" and regions where only "lower class" people live. Since everyone knows the approximate boundaries of these districts, a person's address instantly tickets his social status. The residential earmark of status is so insistent that we find in almost every city a continuous effort to escape this stigma. When a family succeeds in moving to a higher-rent district, its place is taken by a family next lower in the social hierarchy.

Now it must not be thought that class distinction, or even caste distinctions, automatically engender prejudice in the individual who knows these distinctions. To be sure, they are, in a sense, cultural *invitations* to prejudice. An individual who wishes to exploit his own class or caste superiority, and to look down on one and all lower groups, is free to do so. And around this core of superiority he may build the negative, overgeneralized attitudes that we call prejudice.

But it is also possible for a person to know the social hierarchy and to be unaffected by it, so far as his own feelings and conduct toward other groups are concerned. Or he may feel a mild sense of superiority without actually organizing prejudiced attitudes around it.

Subsidiation of Attitudes to Caste and Class

Caste and class do, however, offer culturally provided opportunities for building prejudices if the individual has personal reasons for doing so. And so far as conformity is a factor in learning prejudice (Chapter 17), it invites the individual to take advantage of the cultural strata.

Now young children early learn the facts of caste and class. In one experiment, both white and Negro children in kindergarten and in the first and second grades were given different types of doll clothing and houses, and asked to assign them to dolls representing Negro and white men and women. A great majority of the children of both races gave the white doll good clothes and housing, and the Negro doll poor clothes and housing.[8]

The young child seems to develop an urgent sense of his own ego by the age of three. The age of negativism (saying "I won't" and "No" to almost every request) coincides with this development. Not more than two additional years are needed for the idea of *social* status to become connected with this self-esteem. One little girl, five years of age, cried when she saw the Negro family next door moving away. "Now," she wailed, "there is no one that we are better than."

At a somewhat older age, children are inclined to ascribe all sorts of virtues to upper-class individuals and all sorts of defects to members of the lower classes. An experiment with fifth- and sixth-grade children, for example, asked them to give the names of schoolmates whom they considered "clean," "dirty," "good-looking," "not good-looking," "always having a good time," and the like. For every desirable quality the children of higher social classes in the school were given high ratings. Children from lower social classes were given lower ratings. It seems that the youngsters were not able to perceive their classmates as individuals, but only as representatives of class. To them children from the upper classes seem to be good-in-general; from the lower classes, bad-in-general. Since these fifth and sixth graders are "thinking ill without sufficient warrant" we conclude that they are manifesting class prejudice.

Neugarten, the author of this study, rightly notes the serious strain that is placed upon the lower-class child. Realizing his predicament, he often loses interest in going to school and drops out at the first opportunity. While in school he joins with others of his level; together they lead their lives entirely separated from the more privileged children.[9]

The implication of these facts for later learning is considerable. They show that many young people take the social distinction of caste and class as *major* guides in their way of life, and subsume their social attitudes under these guides. The cultural invitation to status-enhancement has been accepted.

Returning to the law of "subsidiation," we conclude that for these children the social model has become their model. The cultural pattern has for them prescribed where layers of fraternity may develop. To disregard this guide would be merely confusing. To be sure, our American culture tells us, too, to prize individuality, to choose our associates for themselves alone—not for their membership. But this democratic guideline is contradictory and is more difficult to follow. It is easier to take the cleavages as offered.[10]

Conclusion

It must not be thought that learning by subsidiation takes place only under the dominance of cultural guidelines. There are many personal reasons why prejudice develops to support an individual's style of life. The self-image that he needs may be determined by his insecurity, fear, guilt; by an initial trauma or by the family pattern; by his level of frustration tolerance or even by his inborn temperament. In all these cases specific ethnic attitudes develop to round out, to bring closure to, the pattern of personality that is developing.

We have, however, stressed "subsidiation to stratification" in order to reinforce the importance of the social-norm theory of prejudice (Chapter 3) and likewise the importance of conformity (Chapter 17). Our purpose has been to acknowledge the immense part that sociocultural norms play in the acquisition of prejudice while stating this truth in its proper relation to the development of personality.

No child is born prejudiced. His prejudices are always acquired. They are acquired chiefly in fulfilment of his own needs. Yet the context of his learning is always the social structure in which his personality develops.

NOTES AND REFERENCES

1. B. SPINOZA. *Ethics.* Proposition XLVI. New York: Scribner, 1930, 249.

2. *Cf.* R. STAGNER AND R. H. BRITTON, JR. The conditioning tech-

nique applied to a public opinion problem. *Journal of Social Psychology*, 1949, **29**, 103-111. Also, G. RAZRAN. Conditioning away social bias by the luncheon technique. *Psychological Bulletin*, 1938, **35**, 693. For a brief discussion of the subject see G. MURPHY, *In the Minds of Men*. New York: Basic Books, 1953, 219 ff.

3. G. W. ALLPORT AND B. M. KRAMER. Some roots of prejudice. *Journal of Psychology*, 1946, **22**, 9-39.

4. MARGARET M. WOOD. *The Stranger: A Study in Social Relationships*. New York: Columbia Univ. Press, 1934, 268.

5. N. D. HUMPHREY. American race and caste. *Psychiatry*, 1941, **4**, 159.

6. After making a comprehensive study of the position of Negroes in American life, GUNNAR MYRDAL concludes that no concept so aptly defines this position as "caste." He considers the concepts of "race," "class," "minority group," and "minority status" as inadequate. *Cf. An American Dilemma*. New York: Harper, 1944, Vol. 1, 667.

7. C. L. GOLIGHTLY. Race, values, and guilt. *Social Forces*, 1947, **26**, 125-139.

8. MARIAN J. RADKE AND HELEN G. TRAGER. Children's perception of the social roles of Negroes and whites. *Journal of Psychology*, 1950, **29**, 3-33.

9. B. L. NEUGARTEN. Social class and friendship among school children. *American Journal of Sociology*, 1946, **51**, 305-313.

10. The enormous power of social class in determining the attitudes and conduct of adolescents in an American community is demonstrated in an intensive study by A. B. HOLLINGSHEAD. *Elmtown's Youth*. New York: John Wiley, 1949.

CHAPTER 20

INNER CONFLICT

The course of prejudice in a life seldom runs smoothly. For prejudice attitudes are almost certain to collide with deep-seated values that are often equally or more central to the personality. The influence of the school may contradict the influence of the home. The teachings of religion may challenge social stratification. Integration of such opposing forces within a single life is hard to achieve.

Prejudice with and without Compunction

There are many cases, of course, where bias clearly and emphatically dominates. The bigot may be so sure of himself that he never for a moment allows his prejudice to be gnawed at by feelings of doubt or guilt. A good example of such prejudice without compunction is contained in a telegram sent by Governor Bilbo of Mississippi to the Mayor of Chicago in 1920. The city was faced with a surplus of Negro migrants who had come to Chicago looking for work during the First World War. The Mayor had inquired whether some of them might be repatriated in their native state. Governor Bilbo replied:

> Your telegram, asking how many Negroes Mississippi can absorb, received. In reply, I desire to state that we have all the room in the world for what we know as N-i-g-g-e-r-s, but none whatever for "colored ladies and gentlemen." If these Negroes have been contaminated with Northern social and political dreams of equality, we cannot use them, nor do we want them. The Negro who understands his proper relation to the white man in this country will be gladly received by the people of Mississippi, as we are very much in need of labor.[1]

The Bilbo mentality will not concern us in this present chapter. We shall consider it in Chapters 25 and 26.

More common seems to be prejudice with compunction. Anti-attitudes alternate with pro-attitudes. Often the see-saw and zig-zag are almost painful to follow, as in the case given below:

I have no contacts with Jews except at school, where I avoid them as much as possible. I was openly pleased when a Christian was elected class president. My father feels quite strongly against them. What I dislike most is the way they always seem to stick together. They are clannish and when one moves into a neighborhood, they all move in. I do not hate individuals because some of the nicest people I know are Jewish. I have met and enjoyed the company of Jewish girls, but sometimes when I see a group of them quibbling over something, my temper flares. I hate to see any group maltreated for their religious beliefs. It is not their beliefs I condemn. I just don't like the way they behave. Of course I know that all men are created equal and that no one is really better than anyone else.

Such inconsistency is bewildering to read; it must be awkward to live with.

In a group of one hundred college essays on "My Experience with, and Attitudes toward, Minority Groups in America" (from which the above excerpt was taken), only about ten percent of the students who expressed prejudice did so without betraying feelings of guilt and conflict—only one-tenth held their prejudices without compunction. Far more typical are such statements as the following:

Every rational voice within me says the Negro is as good, as decent, sincere, and manly as the white, but I cannot help noticing a split between my reason and prejudice.

I try to see only the good points in Jewish people, but even though I try hard to overcome my prejudice, I know it always will be there—thanks to my parents' early influence.

Although prejudice is unethical, I know I shall always have prejudices. I believe in goodwill toward the Negro, but I shall never invite him to my house for dinner. Yes, I know I'm a hypocrite.

Intellectually, I am firmly convinced that this prejudice against Italians is unjustified. And in my present behavior to Italian friends I try to lean over backwards to counteract the attitude. But it is remarkable how strong a hold it has on me.

These prejudices make me feel narrow-minded and intolerant and therefore I try to be as pleasant as possible. I get so angry with myself for having such feelings, but somehow I do not seem to be able to quench them.

The more I try to treat Jews as individuals, the more conscious I seem to become of them as a group. My compulsive prejudice is putting up a fight against its own elimination.

Defeated intellectually, prejudice lingers emotionally.

In the particular group of students from whom these comments are borrowed, half stated clearly that they had examined their grounds for prejudice and found them irrational and false. One-third of the students affirmed their desire to be rid of their ethnic and class biases. And, as stated previously, only one-tenth held and defended their attitudes without some show of guilt.

Perhaps these autobiographies are not typical. Being students of psychology, the writers were fairly sophisticated regarding the point at issue. It is even possible that some of them were trying to "please the teacher." (But anyone familiar with the critical candor of college students in writing autobiographical papers will, however, doubt this explanation of the results.)

What the results seem to mean is that college students (who usually come from privileged homes and have prolonged exposure to schools and other civic institutions) are keenly aware of the American creed and of the Judeo-Christian ethic. They are genuinely in conflict concerning their failure to conform to the virtues they admire.

But it would be wrong to assume that compunction is felt only in "upper-class" college students. In a study of anti-Semitism among suburban women—some but not all of whom were college graduates—it was found that

> a quarter regarded their feelings as "just due to my own prejudice"; a half regarded them as due to their own prejudice in part, and in part to the misdeeds of Jews themselves; a quarter regarded them as wholly the fault of the Jews (prejudice without compunction).[2]

This study does not report what proportion of the women felt shame in connection with their "own prejudice." But it is probable that feelings of guilt were not uncommon. At the very least, we can say that three-quarters of the women manifested some degree of insight—that is, they knew their attitudes to be, at least in part, not founded on objective fact.

Self-insight, however, does not automatically cure prejudice. At best it starts the individual wondering. And unless one questions the truth of his convictions, he certainly is unlikely to alter them. If he begins to suspect that they are not in conformity with facts, he may then enter a period of conflict. If the dissatisfaction is great enough, he may be driven to a reorganization of beliefs and attitudes. Self-insight is ordinarily the first, but not in itself a sufficient, step. What we note in the students' reports cited above is a hesitation, a weakening, and an increased self-discipline, but not a total abandonment of the avertive attitudes.

What about people who flatly deny that they have any prejudices? In some instances, of course, they may be telling the truth (showing good self-insight). In Chapter 5 we estimated that perhaps 20 percent of the population could accurately deny having prejudice. We have just seen that a fairly large number (most of the students) own up to having prejudice. These people also have good self-insight. But there remains a sizeable group who totally lack insight. They are filled with prejudices and deny this fact. They are the genuine bigots.

Now, even in genuine bigots there probably are, at times, traces of guilt, of compunction. Even the ferocious Governor Bilbo may have had qualms. None of the top Nazis caught and tried would condone the atrocities committed against the Jews. None would admit responsibility. Goering, second to Hitler in command, tried to deny their existence, declaring the documentary films forgeries and fakes. But even he added, "If only five percent of it were true, still it would be horrible." [3] It appears that even the most depraved of mortals, leading lives dominated by hostility and inhumanity, cannot in their consciences condone the ultimate consequences of their own outlook.

All in all, we are forced to conclude that prejudice in a life is more likely than not to arouse some compunction, at least some of the time. It is almost impossible to integrate it consistently with affiliative needs and humane values.

Theory of "An American Dilemma"

This assumption provides the central theme of Gunnar Myrdal's monumental study of Negro-white relations in America. To him the crux of the whole issue is the inner "moral uneasiness" white Americans suffer at failing to make their practice conform to the American creed. The dilemma is:

. . . the ever-raging conflict between, on the one hand, the valuations preserved on the general plane which we shall call the "American creed," where the American thinks, talks, and acts under the influence of high national and Christian precepts, and, on the other hand, the valuations on specific planes of individual and group living, where personal and local interests; economic, social, and sexual jealousies; consideration of community prestige and conformity; group prejudice against particular persons or types of people; and all sorts of miscellaneous wants, impulses, and habits dominate his outlook.[4]

In short, Americans cannot escape the values represented by democratic and Christian teaching. Under this aegis, many habits and beliefs are learned by subsidiation. But at the same time, there are opposing postures engendered by infantile egoism, needs for status and security, material and sexual advantage, and sheer conformity—all leading to subsidiary learning of many contrary habits and beliefs. The average American, therefore, experiences moral uneasiness and "a feeling of individual and collective guilt." He lives in a state of conflict.

The sense of guilt, especially in recent years, has been sharply enhanced by the international situation. The United States is learning that its greatest handicap in dealing with the colored nations and colonial peoples of the world is its treatment of American Negroes. Foreign visitors and the foreign press often seem to enjoy our discomfiture over this. No doubt their accusations are extreme and one-sided, and may even be a cover-up for the domestic shortcomings of the accusing nation.

The story is told of an American visiting Moscow. His Russian guide was proudly displaying the city's subway system. After admiring the station and tracks, the American remarked, "But where are the trains? I see no trains running." The guide retorted, "And what about your lynchings in the Southern states?"

Irrelevant and inexact as many of the accusations are, it is generally admitted that only an early and striking improvement in the status of Negroes in the United States will win for the United States the position of moral leadership to which it aspires.[5] So long as we do not seem to other peoples to practise what we preach, our preachments sound hollow. Unless the promises of our civilization are soon fulfilled, the civilization will die. Mechanical cleverness will not save it.

Yet, with or without rapid progress in the solution of the "Negro problem," the United States holds a unique position among the nations of the world in its high *official* morality. No other country has such ringing expressions of the creed of equality in its historic papers of State. The laws, the executive orders, and the Supreme Court decisions have not often departed from this creed. It would be impossible for any child in America to grow up without knowing, and in some degree respecting, this guideline for national conduct. In many countries of the world, by contrast, we find official discrimination against minority groups practised by the government itself. But in the United States, discrimination is *unofficial*, illegal, and, in a profound sense, regarded as un-American. The founding fathers took a strong stand on the matter. And the common people, from the earliest days of the Republic, knew what that stand was.

When the United States Constitution was adopted on July 4, 1788, Raphael Jacob Cohen, minister of Mickve Israel, marched in the procession in honor of the occasion. A contemporary writer wrote:—"The Clergy formed a very agreeable part of the procession. They manifested by their attendance, their sense of the connection between religion and good government. They amounted to seventeen in number. Four and five of them marched arm in arm with each other, to exemplify the Union. Pains were taken to connect Ministers of the most dissimilar religious principles together, thereby to show the influence of a *free* government in promoting Christian charity. The Rabbi of the Jews, locked in the arms of two ministers of the gospel, was a most delightful sight. There could not have been a more happy emblem contrived of that section of the new constitution, which opens all its powers and offices alike, not only to every sect of Christians, but to worthy men of *every* religion.[6]

The American creed has not lost its potency for forming and for changing attitudes. In a recent experiment, Citron, Chein, and Harding set themselves the problem of discovering what type of reply would best offset anti-minority remarks of the sort one hears in public places such as bakery shops, waiting rooms, crowded buses. With the help of skilled actors they created situations where one of the participants would make insulting remarks concerning "wops" or "kikes." They then tried out, with the aid of another actor, various sorts of replies that might put the bigot in his place. (The purpose was not to reform the bigot, but to affect the attitudes of bystanders.) Hot and angry replies were tested; so, too, calm and reasoned retorts. Out of the series of trials came the most effective formula, as judged by bystanders themselves. It was, in essence, an appeal to the American creed. Whenever it is pointed out, preferably in a calm tone of voice, that prejudiced remarks are not in the American tradition, the bigot is most effectively defeated.[7]

National history seems to confirm the point. Whenever an agitator goes too far, someone is sure to slap him down in the

name of the American creed. Much rope is allowed a racist demagogue in this country, but sooner or later he hangs himself. People will—in the interests of free speech—permit much abuse of
minorities. (We do not like "racial libel laws" because they
threaten to restrict freedom of speech.) But public indignation
finally silences extreme forms of demagogy. At least it has done
so up to the present time. The tenets of the American creed—
as Myrdal rightly says—still have dynamic force.

Yet there is justified criticism to be made of Myrdal's theory
of "an American dilemma." It exaggerates the truth it contains.
Critics point out that since social tradition is responsible for
caste and for its attendant discriminations, the individual living
within a caste system may feel no grounds for guilt over his
infinitesimal role. He did not create the system. The blame is
not his. Since he has little or no choice in the matter, he feels
no real "moral uneasiness." [8]

A different type of criticism, somewhat less convincing, comes
from economic determinists. They insist that the material self-
interest of whites is solely responsible for keeping the Negro "in
his place." White men have no moral problem, because morality
is a mere "ideology" rationalizing economic advantage.[9] This
essentially Marxist argument, as we saw in Chapter 14, is not
so much wrong as one-sided. Granted that there are exploitative
advantages to be gained from discrimination, there is still room
for troublesome inner conflict over the enjoyment of these advantages.

While these criticisms should be heeded, they amount merely to
saying that not *every* American experiences the dilemma as Myrdal
defines it. But many do. The theory, therefore, is valid enough
if we take it to mean that often (but not always) prejudice is
attended by mental conflict.

The Inner Check

Especially when inner conflict is present, people put brakes
upon their prejudices. They do not act them out—or they act
them out only up to a certain point. Something stops the logical
progression somewhere. In New York City, as E. B. White has
pointed out, there smolders every ethnic problem there is; yet the
noticeable thing is not the problem, but the remarkable control.

To be sure, the inner check operates differently in different circumstances. One may feel quite free to damn a minority group
within his family, club, or neighborhood gathering, but will inhibit the tendency when a member of that group is present. Or
he may criticize the group verbally to its face, as it were, but not

engage in any other discriminative action. Or he may try to bar minority group members from teaching in the community schools or from entering his own profession, but draw the line at street fights and riots. Brakes may be applied anywhere, according to the strength of counterforces (inner and outer). Only occasionally does prejudice issue into violent, destructive, homicidal action. This possibility is, however, always theoretically present, should external controls disintegrate and should mob incentives be present to throw their weight upon the side of hatred.

An interesting experiment showing the subtlety of situational brakes is reported by Festinger.[10] Groups of young women were formed, each of them consisting of half Jewish and half Catholic members. They were placed in situations where they had to vote for a group leader. In all cases the candidate's religion was known. But in some situations the voters were anonymous and no one knew the religion of whoever cast a ballot. In other situations, it was known who cast the ballot, and what her religion was. When all the girls were anonymous, it was found that in both religious groups most of the girls voted for a member of their ingroup. When the voters were identified, however, Jews chose Jews less frequently. Catholic girls, on the other hand, openly continued to vote for Catholics.

Just how to explain this particular result is not altogether clear. It may be that Catholic girls, standing somewhat higher in the status hierarchy, felt more secure and dared maintain their ingroupishness more openly. It may be that Jewish girls, more sensitized to prejudice, had a general habit of braking and adapting their behavior according to its probable impression on others. But for our purposes, the important point is that checks do exist upon the expression of in-group and out-group preferences.

We have already called attention to the phenomenon of braking prejudice, so that it stops short of overt incident. In Chapter 4 we described experiments where both Chinese and Negro guests were in fact admitted to restaurants and lodgings without discrimination, although the proprietors tried, in the safe medium of correspondence, to prevent guests of these ethnic groups from arriving. No doubt the case of "Mr. Greenberg," described in Chapter 1, is similar. It is questionable whether such a large percentage of proprietors among the Canadian resort hotels would have denied him accommodations if instead of writing in advance he had appeared in person at the registration desk.

It seems a safe generalization to say that an ethnic label arouses a stereotype which in turn leads to rejective behavior. But this is especially true if the process runs its course at an abstract and impersonal level. When a concrete human being is involved, and when unpleasantness would surely result from face-to-face rejection, then most people follow their "better instincts," and inhibit their prejudiced impulses. But such marked contrast in *situational* behavior would not occur unless there were *inner conflict* in the person harboring prejudice.

How the Conflict Is Handled

Let us generalize the problem, and ask how, by and large, people handle their contrary impulses. Psychologically speaking, there seem to be four modes. We may label them as follows: (1) *repression* (denial); (2) *defense* (rationalization); (3) *compromise* (partial resolution); (4) *integration* (true resolution). Each requires some explanation.

1. **Repression.** In almost every community where the subject of prejudice or discrimination is brought up the first response is, "Here we have no problem." [11] The mayor's office will make this assertion, so will the man in the street—in villages and cities, in North and in South. No problem! It may be, of course, that the citizens think of "problem" in terms of violence only. They may be saying, in effect, "We have no riots here." Or it may be that they are so accustomed to the familiar caste and class lines that they regard them as normal.

The assertion is also a device for keeping unwelcome issues successfully repressed. To deny that a problem exists is to forestall the turmoil it could cause, both in the community and in the individual, if it were faced.

Let us take the point of view of the individual. To admit prejudice is to accuse oneself of being both irrational and unethical. No one wants to be at odds with his own conscience. Man has to live with himself. He finds it uncomfortable to admit that malintegration exists within his character. It is not surprising, then, to hear the statement, "I have no prejudices," even when an outsider sees them bristling.

In most instances the repressers do not recognize their prejudices, and do not view their frame of mind as antidemocratic (and therefore in conflict with their own values). Proof comes from the fact that most antidemocratic movements are dressed up with wholly democratic symbolism: The Cross and the Flag; Social Justice; Golden Rule; Liberation; and the like. By affirming verbally the American creed the inconsistency of one's actual conduct is more successfully repressed.

Often a prejudiced remark starts with the disarming prelude, "I am not prejudiced, but. . . ." or, "Jews have as much right as anybody, but. . . ." Such initial lip-service to the democratic creed seems to atone for all the bias that follows. Psychologically, the mechanism is one of affirming virtue so that the subsequent lapses will pass unnoticed.

Repression is a protective device. With its aid no one needs to be troubled by inner conflict—or so he thinks. Actually, however, repression seldom stands alone. It needs the support of ego defense and rationalization.

2. **Defensive Rationalizations.** The most obvious way to buttress one's prejudices, and therefore to preserve them from conflict with ethical values, is to marshal "evidence" in their favor. Here, selective perception helps. The person narrates incident after incident of Negro dishonesty or Jewish vulgarity. He names a whole list of Italian gangsters, or cites a whole array of undemocratic pronouncements by Roman Catholic clergy. He may persuade himself that this evidence is conclusive. (If by scientific and logical standards the evidence *is* conclusive, then there is, as shown in Chapter 1, no question of prejudice. Rationalization is at work only so long as the individual selects his evidence to bolster a categorical overgeneralization.) Perceptual selectivity to confirm a hypothesis already formed is the commonest form of defensive rationalization.

Who today wishes to hear good things about Russia or about communism? It is more economical (and safer) to reject these disturbing virtues, lock, stock, and barrel. In order to do so, one assembles all the unfavorable evidence—of which there is plenty. Newspapers help by selective reporting and editorializing. Rationalization and support for an animosity are available through selective perception. The fact that there are realistic grounds for conflict does not alter the fact that these grounds are strengthened through selective perception and selective forgetting.

The "impression of universality" often comes to the rescue of a prejudice. A student wrote, "There seems to be a unanimous feeling against the Jews, not only in this country, but throughout the world." The writer herself was, according to an attitude test, the most anti-Semitic individual in a group of one hundred students. She *needed* to feel that her views had unanimous backing —which, of course, they didn't. The Southern lawyer who told the jury in the lynching case that "No one would blame you if you let these men go free," was playing upon the "impression of universality." Social support for one's views (whether the support is real or imaginary) validates these views and protects the individual from harassing doubt and conflict.

Another defensive trick is to shift the blame back onto the

accuser. When the scandal of lynchings in Southern states is pointed out, it not infrequently happens that Southern newspapers retaliate with the statement that gang killings are a form of lynching that occurs more often in the North than in the South. When top Nazi leaders, after the war, were accused of crimes against humanity, they retorted that the Allies had dropped bombs on women and children in German cities. Such *tu quoque* accusations are an easy defense against guilt feelings. Why should you blame me; you are guilty of the same thing! Hence I do not need to listen to your charges.

Then there is the defense by *bifurcation*. "I am not prejudiced against Negroes; some are good. It is only bad niggers that I dislike." "I don't hate Jews, but only the kikes among the Jews." Such distinctions seem, on the surface, to represent differentiation within categories. Do they not come close to discriminating individuals as individuals, and thus to avoiding prejudice altogether? Not really. If we look more closely, the line between "good" and "bad," between "Jews" and "kikes," is not a line based on objective evidence so much as on subjective feeling. The sycophantic Negro sustains the white man's self-esteem. He is therefore "good." All others are "niggers." The bifurcation is based on what does and what does not seem to threaten one, not on the merit of individuals. Bifurcators still believe that there is an evil Negro or Jewish or Catholic "essence," even if this essence permeates only part of the group.

A somewhat similar defense is represented in the familiar phrase, "Some of my best friends are Jews, but. . . ." or, "I know some educated and liberal Catholics, but. . . ." This device we may call rationalization by making exceptions. If one makes a few exceptions, then one can justify holding the remaining portion of the category intact. The "exceptions" are sops to reason, to the demand for fair-mindedness, and to the American creed. If one has good friends within a group, then one's adverse opinion of the remainder of the group cannot possibly be due to prejudice. It appears to be a carefully considered and discriminated judgment. The device usually fools both speaker and listener. But the fact is that the phrase "Some of my best friends are. . . ." is almost invariably a cover-up to protect the remainder of the prejudiced category intact.

Identical in significance is the defense which says, "I have no quarrel with the Jew as an individual but only with what his race represents in the mass." This device is popular with demagogues. It has an oratorical flavor. But it is an extreme instance of confusion—the "group fallacy" at its worst. How could the Jewish population, if composed wholly of meritorious individuals (with whom one has no quarrel), still be evil in the mass? Masses are composed of individuals—nothing else. This particular line of double-talk is interesting for the theory of prejudice. It admits that one cannot dislike the individual, but maintains notwithstanding that one can and should somehow dislike the group. This is the essence of unfounded generalization.

3. **Compromise Solutions.** An outstanding fact of social life is that the multiplicity of roles a man has to play forces him into inconsistent behavior.

We are not only permitted to contradict ourselves but are actually expected to do so—depending on the situation. A politician is virtually required to pay tribute to equal rights for all in his campaign speeches, and to favor special interests when he is in office. A white banker in the South should not hire Negroes in his office, but should contribute generously to a campaign to build a Negro hospital.

We cannot say that such inconsistency in behavior is abnormal. Indeed, it is the rigid consistency of the fanatic (whether of a bigot or a crusader for equal rights) that is regarded as pathological in our society. One is expected to bend with the wind, to conform on occasion to the American creed and on occasion to prevailing prejudice.

This handling of conflict might be called technically an "alternation." When one frame of reference is invoked, one set of subsidiary attitudes and habits comes into play; when a contrary frame is invoked, a quite opposite set of dispositions is activated. If we were consistently avertive, hostile, unkind towards members of a minority group, most of us would suffer from conflict, for we cannot forever repress the contrary value-system (American and Christian creed). But if we often give expression to our ethical impulses (in our pledge of allegiance to the flag, in kindness to Negro employees, or in giving money for the relief of the underdog), we can more easily excuse our prejudices which other occasions call into play.

Such alternation makes certain rationalizations plausible. We can say, for example, "Things are getting better all the time, we must be patient." "You can't change human nature overnight." "You can't legislate against prejudice; it is a long, hard educational road." While there may be truth in the arguments of such "gradualists," the point is that gradualism may itself be a compromise-mode of handling conflict. One is willing to overcome discrimination—but not too fast.

The phenomenon of inconsistency in people's ethnic attitudes and behavior has caused speculation and concern among psychologists.[12] The situation is not hard to understand if we keep in mind two basic facts:

(1) Alternation is one of the commonest of all methods of handling inner conflict. We feast on feast days, and fast on fast days—thus expressing in turn both our fleshly and spiritual desires.

In sport, we seek the thrills of skiing or hunting, and at night return to our cabin to rest. The need for activity and for passivity are thus satisfied—seriatim, and serious conflict is avoided. Similarly, since most people have both prejudiced attitudes and a humane creed, they avoid too disruptive a conflict by expressing them at various times according to circumstances.

(2) Most important is the factor of multiple roles that we play. Hymns in church and lessons in school bring out and reinforce one set of values; a club meeting or a Pullman smoking car elicits and reinforces an opposing set. The more diversified the structure of our environments, the greater is the pressure on us to conform in contradictory ways. In certain situations we are habitually one thing, in other situations, something else. To be a conformist under diverse sets of conditions is almost unavoidably to compromise one's integrity as a person.

4. **Integration (true resolution).** Some people, however, are not satisfied with the inconsistency of their role behavior. They regard alternation as a threat to their integrity. One should be oneself under any and all circumstances, they feel; such role adaptation as is necessary should be only superficial. It should not be so serious as to split the basic value system that one holds. This striving for wholeness and maturity requires a consistency that is extremely hard to achieve.

People who are well along in this course of development are likely to be troubled by the truly fundamental conflict that prejudice arouses. Earlier in the chapter we encountered several instances of distress and shame. These individuals have examined their defenses and found them wanting. They can neither repress, rationalize, nor compromise with any comfort. They wish to face the whole issue and get it settled so that their daily conduct will be under the dominance of a wholly consistent philosophy of human relationships.

Such people are well on the way to getting rid of all hostilities based on stereotyped categories. They are gradually coming to discriminate between fanciful sources of evil (prejudice) and genuine sources. A given individual may for good reason be regarded as an enemy; certain vices or unlikable qualities in people may be hated; occasionally a corporate entity, such as an antisocial organization or foreign government, may for good reasons be declared insupportable. There are such things as realistic opponents in our quest for our values. But what vanishes in an integrated personality are the racial bogies and traditional scapegoats who have nothing, really, to do with life's woes.

Perhaps few people achieve integration of this type; but many are fairly far along the road. They acquire a humane outlook because they know that most mortals are not their enemies, and that most of the designated villains in society are neither dangerous nor designing. Such resentments and hatred as they may have are reserved strictly for those who actually threaten basic value systems. Only a personality organized in such a manner can be fully integrated.

NOTES AND REFERENCES

1. Quoted in K. Young, *Source Book for Social Psychology.* New York: F. S. Crofts, 1933, 506.

2. Nancy C. Morse and F. H. Allport. The causation of anti-Semitism: an investigation of seven hypotheses. *Journal of Psychology,* 1952, **34,** 197-233.

3. G. M. Gilbert. *Nüremberg Diary.* New York: Farrar, Straus, 1947.

4. G. Myrdal. *An American Dilemma.* New York: Harper, 1944, Vol. 1, xliii.

5. This point of view has been strongly presented by John LaFarge, S. J., *No Postponement.* New York: Longmans, Green, 1950.

6. J. R. Marcus. *Jews in American Life.* New York: The American Jewish Committee, 1946.

7. A. F. Citron, I. Chein, and J. Harding. Anti-minority remarks: a problem for action research. *Journal of Abnormal and Social Psychology,* 1950, **45,** 99-126.

8. C. L. Golightly. Race, values and guilt. *Social Forces,* 1947, **26,** 125-139.

9. O. C. Cox. *Caste, Class, and Race: A Study in Social Dynamics.* New York: Doubleday, 1948.

10. L. Festinger. The role of group belongingness in a voting situation. *Human Relations,* 1947, **1,** 154-180.

11. This was the finding of Goodwin Watson, who reports the results of a tour of investigation into many communities to study the problem of group relations: *Action for Unity.* New York: Harper, 1947, 76.

12. *Cf.* I. Chein, M. Deutsch, H. Hyman, and Marie Jahoda (Eds.). Consistency and inconsistency in intergroup relations. *Journal of Social Issues,* 1949, **5,** No. 3.

Part VI

THE DYNAMICS OF PREJUDICE

CHAPTER 21

FRUSTRATION

The rich take to opium and hashish. Those who cannot afford them become anti-Semites. Anti-Semitism is the morphine of the small people. . . . Since they cannot attain the ecstasy of love they seek the ecstasy of hatred. . . . It matters little who it is they hate. The Jew is just convenient. . . . If there were no Jews the anti-Semites would have to invent them.

The author of this passage, written more than forty years before Hitler came into power, was Herman Bahr, a German Social Democrat.[1] He calls attention to the escapist function of aggressiveness, to its druglike capacity to soften the disappointments and frustrations of life.

It seems to be undeniably true that man's instinctive response to frustration is aggressive assertiveness in some form. An infant when balked will kick and scream. Under anger it certainly shows no sign of love or affiliation; its reaction is random and wild. The infant attacks not the true source of the frustration, but any object or person who crosses its path.

Throughout life the same tendency persists for anger to center upon available rather than upon logical objects. Everyday speech recognizes this *displacement* in a variety of phrases: to take it out on the dog; Don't take it out on me; whipping boy; scapegoat. While the full sequence is frustration-aggression-displacement, current psychology speaks more simply of the "frustration-aggression hypothesis." [2] The scapegoat theory of prejudice—probably the most popular theory—rests exclusively upon this hypothesis.

Sources of Frustration

On the chance that prejudice may be more closely related to certain sources of frustration than to others, it will help us if we classify roughly those regions of life in which thwarting and insecurity may arise.

1. **Constitutional and personal.** A short stature—particularly among males in western culture—is a handicap and often a life-long cause for irritation. Poor health, a poor memory, or slow intelligence may be so likewise. But these sources of frustration, so far as we now know, do not seem particularly conducive to ethnic prejudice. Short people seem to be no more anti-Semitic than tall people; nor are sick people, by and large, more prejudiced than well people. Handicaps of this order seem on the whole to lead to more personal compensations, to ego defenses that do not involve projection upon out-groups. How about thwarted drives? If a person were trapped in a coal mine and needed more oxygen, his way of meeting this emergency would be immediate. He would not blame this acute frustration upon an out-group. Similarly, acute hunger, thirst, and other immediate bodily needs do not induce displacement. But the story may be different if the thwarting of needs is chronic. If continually frustrated, the sex need may get mixed up with attitudes toward out-groups (Chapter 23). Likewise, if we include self-esteem (status need) among the drives, it too is manifestly involved (Chapters 19 and 23). But, in general, constitutional defects, acute organic needs, illness, do not seem to be demonstrably associated with prejudice—unless or until they are knit in with the social life of the individual. Prejudice is a social fact, and seems to require a social context. If frustrations are involved, they must have a social flavor.

2. **Frustrations within the family.** One's "family of orientation" consists of parents, siblings, and sometimes grandparents, uncles, and aunts. The "family of procreation" consists of wife, husband, children. In both sets of intimate relationships many frustrations and resentments occur.

The evidence tells us that prejudice is frequently associated with family disorders. In Chapter 18 we saw how a rejective atmosphere in the home and harsh treatment (with emphasis upon obedience and power-relationships) are likely to lead to prejudice in the children.

During World War II it was reported that certain seriously maladjusted children, whose difficulties stemmed from insecure home life, showed open sympathy with enemy countries (Germany and Japan) and turned against America and against minority groups in America—especially the Jews.[3]

Bixler describes the case of a white workman who for a time had entirely friendly relations with a Negro fellow-employee. When, however, relations with his wife became strained and divorce threatened, he suddenly developed a marked race prejudice.[4]

It would be easy to marshal much evidence on this point, but it would be wrong to assume that family conflict invariably leads to hostility toward out-groups. Most family squabbles are handled in ways that have no bearing whatever upon ethnic prejudice. Yet the relationship in some cases manifestly exists.

3. **Near-lying community.** Most men and many women spend less time within the family group than in outside groups: in school, factory, office, or the armed services. Life in educational, business, military environments may be—and usually is—even more frustrating than at home.

The following case shows how a blend of home and school frustration may lead to prejudice. A college student writes:

> I had honors all the way through school and one double promotion, but I did not have a straight "A" record. I was not happy. My father boasted that he had had only an A and A-plus record when he was in college, and at the same time held down a full-time job. He never let me forget it, and berated me for doing less well than he. I felt utterly frustrated. I wanted to please him but could not succeed. Finally I found comfort in telling myself and other people that it was only the Jewish grinds and cheats who did me out of the top position. (In thinking the matter over I realize that I do not know for a fact that the boys who excelled me in scholarship were Jews, or that they cheated.)

This case is interesting for bringing to light the importance of *felt* frustration and the negligible importance of *objective* frustration. Actually, the boy had an outstanding record. Yet, owing largely to his father's criticisms, this excellence was *perceived* as failure and induced a feeling not of satisfaction but of frustration.

In a study of veterans, previously cited, Bettelheim and Janowitz found that among veterans who claimed to have had a "bad break" in the Army, almost five times as many were intolerant as tolerant; whereas among those who claimed to have had a "good break" the majority were tolerant.[5] We cannot check the objective facts, but it seems likely that the *feeling* of frustration bears a more significant relation to prejudice than the actual occurrence of good and bad "breaks" during Army life. But in either event, a relationship between frustration and prejudice is established.

That economic frustration engenders prejudice we have already seen in several studies cited in Chapter 14. The reader will recall Campbell's demonstration that anti-Semitism is high when job satisfaction is low, also the evidence given by Bettelheim and Janowitz pertaining to the correlation between downward mobility and anti-Negro bias.

The frustration-aggression-displacement sequence has even been demonstrated experimentally. Boys 18 to 20 years of age attending a summer camp were asked to indicate their attitudes toward Japanese and Mexicans before and after a situation involving severe frustration. (Instead of being allowed to attend bank night at a local theatre they were required to stay at camp and take a series of hard tests.) After the frustration they attributed a smaller number of desirable traits to Japanese and to Mexicans than before. They also, to a slighter extent, attributed more undesirable qualities to these two nationalities.[6] While this experiment merely induces a *mood* and measures its short-run effect, still it does demonstrate the diffuse spread of a negative emotion to judgments of minority groups.

4. **Remoter community.** Many frustrations arise in connection with wider conditions of living. The intensely competitive culture of the United States, for example, must be expected to engender irritation in the individual who fails to reach the high level of attainment that is set for him: in school, in popularity, in occupational achievement, in social status.

This competitiveness may well account in part for the feeling that each newcomer diminishes one's own chance of success. The current antagonism of many people toward admitting refugees to this country is an example.

Immigration restriction is a recent phenomenon. In the earlier stages of the country's development, each person's success clearly depended upon enlarging the population. Slaves were needed, and the more slaves one possessed, the higher his status. Immigrants were needed and were imported to work in factories and on farms. Orientals were welcomed in California, since everyone needed many hands, white or yellow, to develop the resources. Gradually the situation shifted. It was felt that these immigrants, once so warmly welcomed, had improved themselves too much. They became free men, landowners, and often rose to positions of eminence and wealth. Fearing there would not be enough goods or prestige to go around, a change in public opinion resulted. Its first expression was the Oriental Exclusion Act of 1908. In 1924 the quota system froze all immigration at a low level. Recent emergency legislation, admitting a few of Europe's millions of displaced persons, has been hedged with restrictions, but even so its meagre provisions cause alarm and resistance. Economists tell us that more liberal immigration would be a good thing for the country. But it is not economic advice that rules immigration policy, but rather the *felt frustrations* of citizens who rightly or wrongly think an immigration iron curtain will protect them in their search for status.[7]

It is a well-established fact that anti-Semitism tends to rise in periods of widespread frustration and insecurity attendant upon major social change. More specifically, it seems to thrive whenever there is a period of postwar readjustment, especially following defeat; whenever there is instability in the government; and in times of economic depression.[8]

Wartime is also a breeding time for domestic hostilities. This is an ironical fact. One might think that in times of national peril, with an outside enemy to defeat, all groups would pull together. A common enemy tends to consolidate a nation. And in a sense this is true. Yet, at the same time, wars saddle the populace with all manner of new frustrations: rationing, taxes, apprehension, casualties. The net result is increased domestic friction. In the year 1943, the most serious period of the war for the United States, four of the six largest cities in the United States had disastrous race riots. Anti-Semitic incidents in the Nazi pattern occurred. Among a thousand wartime rumors collected and analyzed, two-thirds attacked some group of Americans—Jews, Negroes, Labor, the Administration, the Red Cross or the Armed Forces.[9]

Frustration Tolerance

That some relationship exists between frustration and prejudice we have now abundantly proved. Yet not everyone who is frustrated is prejudiced. People handle their frustrations in different ways; some have more frustration tolerance than others.

In an experimental study of frustration, Lindzey made a pertinent discovery. He selected ten students known from previous tests to be very high in ethnic prejudice, and ten known to be extremely low. These twenty subjects were invited, one at a time, to take part in a group experiment. The situation was so arranged that the subject worked with four strange students (all stooges) on a cooperative card-sorting task. The experiment was rigged so that he, and he alone, caused the group to fail to reach its objective and so to lose a monetary reward. The stooges were polite, but yet obviously aggrieved by his failures. Try as he would, he could not redeem himself. No subject in the series "saw through" the deception, and all were manifestly disturbed and uncomfortable. But—and this is the important finding— those who were high in prejudice seemed, to a statistically significant degree, even more frustrated than those who were low in prejudice. This fact was determined both by hidden observers during the course of the experiment, and by subsequent interviews with the subjects—to whom the experiment was eventually explained.[10]

This finding may be accounted for in various ways. For example, it may be that people high in prejudice are always, in all situations, more susceptible to frustration; there may even be a constitutional irritability in their nature. Or, highly prejudiced people may especially need status, and crave the good regard of their associates; when the situation thwarts this affiliative need (as this one did) these people betray great distress. It is their intense craving for status that underlies both the present frustration and, ultimately, their high prejudice. Finally, it may be that some sort of inner control is the differentiating factor. Those who are high in prejudice lack the resignation or "philosophical" attitude that is possessed by people who are low in prejudice. For our present purposes it does not greatly matter which of these explanations is true. It is sufficient to note that the evidence, so far as it goes, indicates that prejudiced individuals have more *frustration susceptibility* than do tolerant individuals.

Responses to Frustration

The issue we are here discussing lies at the heart of the whole problem of prejudice. On the one hand, evidence is overwhelming that frustrations may beget out-group hostility, via the displacement of aggression. On the other hand, we must be careful not to give this process, important as it is, undue weight. It is simply not true, as some enthusiasts have said, that "frustration always leads to some sort of aggression." If it were, then all of us (for we are all frustrated) would harbor vast stores of aggression, and would be prejudice-prone.

The commonest reaction to frustration is not aggression at all, but a simple and direct attempt to surmount the obstacle in our path.[11] True, the young infant's response to frustration is usually anger. But in the process of learning, the child, and later the adult, acquires a considerable degree of frustration tolerance, and learns to substitute perseverance, planning, and intelligent solutions for the initial tendency to rage.

Taking Lindzey's experiment as a cue, we may say that prejudiced people are those who have developed less frustration tolerance and therefore less skill in meeting their frustrations head on, rather than through infantile anger and displacement.

In addition to the variable factor of frustration tolerance, and to the differential tendency to take either an aggressive (angry) or planful (overcoming) approach to our frustrations, there is a further distinction that characterizes individuals. Granted that at times we all do feel irritation and aggressive impulses, how do we direct them? To accord with our discussion in Chapters 9 and 20 we may say that some frustrated people tend to blame themselves for the frustrating experience; these individuals are *intropunitive* in type. Some are so detached and philosophical about life's frustrations that they blame no one; they are *impunitive*. But others characteristically see (and seek) outside agencies to blame. This *extropunitive* type of reaction may be realistic (if the true source of frustration is identified) or it may be unrealistic, if the blame is displaced.[12]

It is, of course, only in the extropunitive type of response that we find scapegoating at work. The following is a clear example:

A steelworker was unhappy in his job. The heat and the noise were intense; his job was not too secure; he had failed to become an engineer as he once had hoped. In the course of his bitter complaint he railed against "the goddam Jews who run this place." The place was not, in fact, run by Jews; not a single Jew was connected with either the ownership or management of the plant.

Our conclusion is that some people sometimes respond with aggression to frustrating circumstances; that some take an extropunitive attitude and place the blame not upon themselves but upon outer conditions; and that some do not blame the true source of the frustration but displace the blame upon other objects, specifically upon available out-groups. The process, while common, certainly is not universal. Whether a person adopts it or not probably depends upon his own innate temperament, also upon the habits he has built up in handling frustration, and upon the total situation that prevails (for example, whether his culture encourages him to blame witches as the Navahoes do, or to blame the Jews, as Hitler urged the German people to do).

Further Discussion of the Scapegoat Theory

One reason for the popularity of the scapegoat theory is that it is easy to understand. Probably this fact is also an argument for its validity, for the ease of understanding must be related in some way to the commonness of the experience. A storybook for seven-year-olds contains a clear example of the scapegoating theme. The tale runs as follows:

An enterprising pig with some ducks as companions is aloft in a rudderless balloon. A farmer with evil intentions is trying to capture the balloon, but the alert piglet pelts the farmer with cans of tomato soup. The farmer is spattered by the soup and thoroughly angry. A dirty-faced boy comes out of the barn to help him wipe off the soup. But the farmer cuffs the little boy good. He does this for three reasons: first, because the balloon had got away; and second, because he would now have to take a bath to get the sticky soup off him; and, third, because it seemed like a pretty good thing to do anyway. The author adds, "I don't say they were good reasons, but that is what they were."

A more complete example of scapegoating could scarcely be found. Even young children can grasp the point.

There are, in reality, two versions of the scapegoat theory. In Chapter 15 the Biblical version was summarized. There the sequence is

personal misconduct → guilt → displacement.

This version will again engage our attention in Chapter 24. The version considered in the present chapter is somewhat different:

frustration → aggression → displacement.

All of the examples in the present chapter deal only with the second form of scapegoating.

The theory in this version assumes three stages: (1) frustration generates aggression; (2) aggression becomes displaced upon relatively defenseless "goats"; (3) this displaced hostility is rationalized and justified by blaming, projecting, stereotyping.

The proper attitude to take toward this sequence is to accept it, provided certain important qualifications are kept in mind.[13]

1. **Frustration does not always lead to aggression.** The theory tells nothing at all concerning the social conditions, or types of temperament, or types of personality that tend to seek aggressive outlets when thwarted. Nor does it tell what sources of frustration tempt one to seek scapegoats. Earlier in this chapter it was suggested that certain areas of frustration seem more likely than others to invite displacement.

2. **Aggression is not always displaced.** Anger may be directed toward oneself, intropunitively. If so, scapegoating does not occur. The theory itself tells nothing concerning the personal or social factors that make for extropunitive *vs.* intropunitive response. Nor does it tell under what circumstances the individual will be aggressive toward the *real* source of his frustration, and under what circumstances he will *displace* his aggression. We must study individual personalities to find the answer.

3. Displacement does not, as the theory seems to imply, actually relieve the feeling of frustration. Since the displaced object is not, in fact, related to the frustration, the feeling continues. Germany was not better off economically nor happier in its family life for having killed the Jews. Nor did a single one of its national problems become solved. The Southern poor white does not raise his standard of living by blaming Negroes. Displacement never removes the frustration. It is not a successful drainage of aggression because the continuing frustration constantly builds new aggression. Nature never created a less adaptive mechanism than displacement.

4. The theory says nothing concerning the choice of scapegoats. Why some minorities are liked or overlooked while others are hated remains wholly unexplained; so, too, does the fact that there are different degrees and kinds of dislike. As we saw in Chapter 15, the *selection* of scapegoats has nothing intrinsically to do with the displacement process itself.

5. It is not true that a defenseless minority is always chosen for displacement purposes. Individuals may become scapegoats. So, too, majorities. Jews may have prejudice against gentiles (goyim) and Negroes may hate the entire white race. Displacement (or at least overgeneralization) is here at work, but the scapegoat is not always a "safe goat" as the theory tends to imply.

6. Available evidence does not indicate that the displacement tendency is any more common among people high in prejudice than among those low in prejudice. We cannot pin the scapegoating tendency only upon the habitual disposition of a prejudiced person to displace aggression. In Lindzey's experiment, cited earlier, subjects markedly high in prejudice were no more prone in general to displace hostility after frustration than were subjects low in prejudice. The high in prejudice (those who in real life did apparently scapegoat minority groups) were distinguished, not for their displacement tendency, but for other characteristics. They seemed to be, in general, somewhat more aggressive; they were, as we have seen, more "frustratable"; and they seemed on the whole to be conventional in adhering to social customs. Not all of these elements are intrinsic to the frustration-aggression-displacement theory. In other words, the theory taken by itself will not fully explain why some personalities are prejudiced, others not.

7. Finally, the theory itself overlooks the possibility of realistic social conflict. What seems like displacement may, in some instances, be an aggression directed toward the true source of the frustration. It may be, for example, that many members of Group

X are in fact trying to obstruct members of Group Y. In such a case the hostility felt by Group Y would be, in part, realistic. Their antagonism to Group X would, to a degree, rest on a "well-deserved reputation." The scapegoat theory, like all other theories of prejudice, should make certain that it is not misapplied to cases of realistic social conflict.

Meaning of Psychodynamics

These strictures upon the scapegoat theory are not meant to invalidate it. They are intended only to convey two lines of caution: (1) No single theory of prejudice is adequate. A number of essential phenomena are not touched at all by the scapegoat theory. (2) The theory is stated too broadly. It fails to supply the many differentials needed: why some people respond to frustration in an aggressive manner; why some types of frustration are more likely to induce displacements upon out-groups; why some people persist in displacement in spite of its complete failure as a mode of adaptation; or why, on the other hand, some people hold the displacement tendency in check, and never allow it to affect their ethnic attitudes.

We have not yet called attention to one important feature of the scapegoat theory. It assumes a large amount of *unconscious* mental operation in the individual. The steelworker who blamed the Jews "who run the place" did not know that he was inventing a wholly mythical villain to account for his plight. The souped-up farmer did not know why it was "a good idea anyway" to cuff the dirty-faced boy. Most Germans did not see the connection between their humiliating defeat in World War I and their subsequent anti-Semitism.

Few people know the real reason for their hatred of minority groups. The reasons they invent are merely rationalizations. This is the central thesis of all *psychodynamic* theories of prejudice. The scapegoat theory is one of this type. But there are others. When we say that prejudice covers up severe inferiority feelings; or that it gives security; or that it is bound up with repressed sexuality; or helps to relieve personal guilt feelings—we are in all cases talking in the realm of psychodynamics. In all these cases the sufferer is not aware of the psychological function that prejudice serves in his life.

The following chapters are a continuation of our discussion of the psychodynamics of prejudice. The major insights they contain are in many instances derived from psychoanalytic work. Occasionally, we shall have to place strictures upon the exuberance of the theorizing, as we have in the case of the frustration-aggression-displacement sequence. Yet this criticalness will not in the least diminish our indebtedness to Freud and to psychoanalysis.

NOTES AND REFERENCES

1. Quoted by P. W. Massing. *Rehearsal for Destruction.* New York: Harper, 1949, 99.

2. J. Dollard, L. Doob, N. E. Miller, O. H. Mowrer, R. R. Sears. *Frustration and Aggression.* New Haven: Yale Univ. Press, 1939.

3. Sibylle K. Escalona. Overt sympathy with the enemy in maladjusted children. *American Journal of Orthopsychiatry,* 1946, **16**, 333-340.

4. R. H. Bixler. How G. S. became a scapegoater. *Journal of Abnormal and Social Psychology,* 1948, **43**, 230-232.

5. B. Bettelheim and M. Janowitz. *Dynamics of Prejudice: A Psychological and Sociological Study of Veterans.* New York: Harper, 1950, 64.

6. N. E. Miller and R. Bugelski. Minor studies of aggression: II. The influence of frustrations imposed by the in-group on attitudes expressed toward out-groups. *Journal of Psychology,* 1948, **25**, 437-442.

7. *Cf.* E. S. Bogardus. A race-relations cycle. *American Journal of Sociology,* 1930, **35**, 612-617.

8. *Cf.* K. S. Pinson. Anti-Semitism. In *Encyclopedia Britannica,* Vol. 2, 74-78. Chicago: Encyclopedia Britannica, 1946. Also: *Universal Jewish Encyclopedia* (I. Landman, Ed.), Vol. 1, 341-409. New York: Universal Jewish Encyclopedia, 1939.

9. G. W. Allport and L. Postman. *The Psychology of Rumor.* New York: Henry Holt, 1947, 12.

10. G. Lindzey. Differences between the high and low in prejudice and their implications for a theory of prejudice. *Journal of Personality,* 1950, **19**, 16-40.

11. *Cf.* R. S. Woodworth. *Psychology: A Study of Mental Life.* New York: Henry Holt, 1921, 163. Also, G. W. Allport, J. S. Bruner, and E. M. Jandorf. Personality under social catastrophe. *Character and Personality,* 1941, **10**, 1-22.

12. These distinctions were first made explicit in the work of S. Rosenzweig, who also has developed a test to determine the degree to which people are extropunitive, intropunitive, and impunitive in dealing with frustrating situations. *Cf.* S. Rosenzweig. The picture-association method and its application in a study of reactions to frustration. *Journal of Personality,* 1945, **14**, 3-23.

13. A general critique of the subject is contained in B. Zawadski, Limitations of the scapegoat theory of prejudice. *Journal of Abnormal and Social Psychology,* 1948, **43**, 127-141.

CHAPTER 22

AGGRESSION AND HATRED

In the preceding chapter we considered aggression in its relation
to frustration and to displacement. But more needs to be said,
for aggression is often held to be central in explaining the origin
of most social ills. In a century of unparalleled bloodshed, the
attention of social scientists has been riveted upon aggression.
It is frequently used as a basic explanatory principle. While
popularized especially by Sigmund Freud, the concept is found
serviceable by all schools of psychology.

Nature of Aggression

The tendency in Freud's own writing, and in that of many
other psychodynamicists, is to consider aggression as a global,
instinctive, steam boiler-like force. It is regarded as one of a
small number of prime movers in life. It is ubiquitous, urgent,
basically unavoidable. Freud writes:

> Men clearly do not find it easy to do without satisfaction of
> this tendency to aggression that is in them. . . . It is always
> possible to unite considerable numbers of men in love towards
> one another, so long as there are still some remaining as objects
> of aggressive manifestations.[1]

He equates the instinct with the desire to kill or destroy the
object of the aggression. In the last analysis, it makes even for
self-destruction. *Thanatos* is no less of a blind urge in our natures than is *Eros,* with which it sharply contrasts. But aggression and love often get mixed up in the course of living, so that
even our affiliative needs are contaminated by destructive impulses.

Following this line of thought, some psychoanalysts have seen
in infant behavior a predominance of aggressiveness. The act
of feeding is considered one of destructive devouring. Sucking
is a form of attack. Our primordial ancestors, writes Simmel,
were cannibals.

We all enter life with the instinctive impulse to devour not only food, but also all frustrating objects. Before the infantile individual acquires the capacity to love, it is governed by primitive hate-relationship to its environment.[2]

Now the consequence of such a theory of aggression is to make war, vandalism, criminality, personal and group conflict seem entirely natural—even unavoidable. The best that could happen would be a sublimating, a draining, a shifting of the ubiquitous aggressive impulse into acceptable or less damaging channels. Everyone would *need* a scapegoat. We would have to discover or invent victims for our aggression.

We do well to reject this monolithic conception of aggression. It is not a single devouring force. The term covers several different kinds of acts carried on for several different reasons. Let us look at some of them.[3]

1. When an animal eats a plant or another animal, or when a child helps himself to a toy, there is no intent other than to ensure the organism's desire. Others might call the act *aggressive,* but not the agent. A child of two seems "destructive," but his depredations are entirely incidental to his eager curiosity and interest. From his point of view he is not being aggressive, not even when he takes a toy away from another child.

2. The term is sometimes used as synonymous with *assertiveness.* We hear it said that Americans are aggressive. What is meant is that they (i.e., some of them) have a forthright way of attacking life's problems in general. This type of aggression is not personal in its reference. In itself it has no necessary relation to inflicting injury upon others. In a study of nursery school children, Lois Murphy found that the most sympathetic children were also more "aggressive" (coefficient of correlation $= +.44$).[4] This interesting finding seems to mean that children who are outgoing, i.e., interactive with others, are more likely to engage in all types of social contact. They are not so much "aggressive" as they are *active.*

3. Sometimes the term means more than mere assertiveness. It refers to a temperamental love of battle. There is enjoyment of a fight for fight's sake. The Irish are (rightly or wrongly) said to be aggressive in this sense. A familiar ethnic joke makes the point: Two women have been discussing their ancestry—

First Irish woman: And from what people do the McCarthys spring?

Mrs. McCarthy: I'll have you know they don't spring from any people; they spring at them.

4. Sometimes an intent to injure a rival is a by-product of the course of competitive activity. Here again the desire to reach a certain goal is uppermost; but the urgency is so great that the agent does not hesitate, if necessary, to use force or deception. The "aggressor" intends to obtain an object in spite of, and against, the resistance of others. A great deal of national aggressiveness, incident upon imperialism and expansion, falls within this category.

5. True sadism sometimes occurs, where the agent takes pleasure in giving hurt to his victim. Here aggression is not instrumental, as in the first two instances, but is an end in itself. It seems probable that the aggression of many of Hitler's storm troopers against the Jews in Germany was of this order.

6. Finally, we come to the type of anger and aggression discussed in the preceding chapter. It may be called *reactive*. A frustration has occurred. The individual does not meet it with realistic planning or perseverance, nor does he resign himself to withdrawal or self-blame. Instead, he becomes angry and aggressive against the obstacle itself—or, as we have seen, may displace the hostility upon a substitute object (scapegoat). It is this reactive aggression that is of greatest concern to an understanding of prejudice.

Whatever else this brief analysis may signify, it clearly means that an instinctivist, steam-boiler theory of aggression is untenable. There are too many different motives involved and too many resultant types of conduct. It seems absurd to classify the infant's benign sucking, the enterprise of an American businessman, the cruelties of a sadist, and the outrage of a man who loses his job—all as manifestations of one and the same instinct. What similarity they seem to have lies in the mind of the observer, not in psychodynamic identity.

The reader should note that while we are here repudiating one aspect of the Freudian theory of aggression, we are accepting another. Aggression is not a grandiose instinct that demands an outlet. Reactive aggression is, however, a capacity most people seem to have, and this capacity sometimes leads to displacement. The frustration-aggression-displacement theory is a part of the total Freudian theory. And this part, as we saw in the last chapter, is valid, provided several important qualifications are held in mind.

The difference between an "instinct" and a "capacity" is crucial. An instinct demands an outlet. A capacity is only latent—and may never be brought into play. This distinction is obviously vital for our outlook upon prejudice. If an instinct is involved—

always seeking satisfaction—the prospects for restraining or eliminating prejudice are dim. If a mere reactive capacity is involved it is probable that inner and outer conditions can be created that will avoid arousing this capacity altogether. Theoretically at least, we can create conditions in the family and in the community that are less frustrating; we can train children to meet such frustrations as occur without extropunitive aggression; or we can train them to direct such aggression as remains upon the true source of their frustration rather than upon a scapegoat.

The Problem of "Drainage"

We sometimes encounter the term "free-floating aggression." Thus the anthropologist Kluckhohn writes, "In every known human society there appears to exist a varying amount of free-floating aggression." [5] Kluckhohn goes on to explain, by the reactive hypothesis, that in most cultures restraints are placed upon children in the process of socialization, and that severe deprivations and frustrations occur throughout the adult stage of life in all societies. There must be an accumulation and a merging of aggressive impulses. Sometimes chronic irritation builds up a vast amount of vague unattached protest; sometimes, when life is smoother, there may be relatively little of such free-floating aggression.

Up to this point we may accept the concept. It seems to make sense, both for whole societies of people and for individuals. When we meet an individual who is full of complaints, resentment, and has many out-group prejudices, we can safely assume he has much unresolved reactive aggression, undoubtedly built up through a long series of chronic frustrations which he has not known how to handle.

But we cannot accept the steam-boiler and safety-valve image which Kluckhohn next offers to account for the course of this aggression:

In many societies this "free-floating aggression" has been mainly drained off by periodic (or almost continual) wars. Some cultures, at their flowering, seem to have been able to channel most of it into socially creative channels (literature and the arts, public works, invention, geographical exploration, and the like). In most societies, most of the time, the greater part of this energy is diffused into various streams: into the small angry outbursts of daily living; into constructive activities; into occasional wars. But history shows that at epochs in the careers of most nations much of this aggressive energy has been, for longer or shorter periods, concentrated against segmental or distributive minorities within the society.[6]

To say that free-floating aggression may be channeled into creative work in literature, art, public works, is too far-fetched. Normally there is no aggression in painting a picture or drafting a blueprint. This passage seems to return full force to the Freudian view that a certain quantum of aggression exists. It may "float" anywhere. It may even be sublimated into non-aggression (peaceful pursuits). In other words, it may exist even when it doesn't exist.

Equally questionable is the statement that free-floating aggression may be "drained off" by warfare. Such evidence as we have indicates that a wholly contrary process takes place. If the theory of drainage were correct, we should expect to find *less* bickering within a nation in times of warfare. When the free-floating aggression of the citizens of the United States was directed in full force against German, Italian, and Japanese enemies during World War II, we should have had tranquillity at home. But the situation was the opposite. In previous chapters we noted how violent were the hostility rumors and how serious were the race riots—much more so than in peacetime. Nor does the current hostility toward communist Russia "drain off" attacks upon liberals, intellectuals, labor, Jews, Negroes, or the Administration in Washington. It seems rather to aggravate them.

Studying manifestations of aggressive behavior in college students, Stagner reports that being aggressive in one direction does not in the least diminish the likelihood that a student will be aggressive in other directions. On the contrary, a person who "channels" aggression in one way is likely to "channel" it also in other ways. The coefficient of correlation between various avenues of expression is +.40.[7]

A comparative study of cultures shows the same tendency. Where a society is warlike there is a tendency for individuals within the society to behave aggressively toward one another, and for aggression to appear in the mythology of that society. In societies that are not warlike, these evidences of aggression are lacking. The Rif and Apache illustrate the former tendency; the Hopi and Arapesh, the latter. Using various measures of individual, group, and ideological aggression within a society, Boggs found correlations ranging from +.20 to +.54.[8] He concludes that aggressive behavior is either present in a given case or relatively lacking, and when present is highly generalized.

All this evidence is hard on the theory that free-floating aggression may be "drained off" from one object to another. It is—to a less extent—somewhat hard on the frustration-aggression sequence, for it is unlikely that the more aggressive societies (or individuals) are always the more frustrated. Life among the Hopi and Arapesh would seem not easier, on the whole, than among the Rif or Apache. But in this case we can properly argue that the Hopi and Arapesh have learned how to handle their frustration in nonaggressive ways, while Rif and Apache culture encourage extropunitive response to frustrations. There seems no way, however, of saving the drainage theory. It simply is not true that a given quantum of free-floating aggression can be used up in this, that, or the other way.

To deny "drainage" is not to deny "displacement." In two respects the concepts are utterly unlike: (1) Displacement refers only to a specific tendency sometimes found in reactive aggression. It can be demonstrated experimentally to occur. A limited impulse acquires a substitute object. "Free-floating" aggression with drainage, on the other hand, suggests vague channels of possible sublimation—even in nonaggressive ways. (2) Displacement does not in the least imply that the "release" of aggression in one channel lessens the likelihood of "release" in another. It is compatible with the finding that the more aggression is expressed the more of it there will be. The drainage theory holds the opposite.

Aggression as a Trait of Personality

While we have been critical of certain aspects of Freud's view of aggression, we can agree with him that the characteristic way in which an individual handles his aggressive impulses is an important feature of his character structure.

Unlike Freud, however, we are assuming that aggression is a capacity rather than an instinct. It is primarily a reactive matter. In some people it runs its course in relation to a specific objective stimulus and does not become a deep-set trait of personality. Normal reactive aggression has certain adaptive characteristics, listed by Bergler as follows: It

1) is used only in self-defense or in defense of other people;
2) is directed against a real enemy—the true source of the frustration;
3) is not accompanied by guilt-feelings, for the act is perceived as wholly justified;

4) is not excessive, but adequate in amount;
5) is used at the appropriate time when the enemy is vulnerable;
6) is used in such a way that the agent expects the effort to be successful;
7) is not easily provoked, but only when the offense is considerable;
8) is not confused by irrelevant frustrations arising out of the past, perhaps in early childhood.[9]

Rationally adaptive aggression of this type does not result in neurotic disorders, nor in the development of prejudice. It is only when these criteria of normality are violated that we encounter unwholesome aggressive formations within the personality. One individual may be unaware of the true source of frustration (violating Criterion 2), and thus be forced to displace his hostility upon an unreal enemy. Another person, knowing the source of his difficulty, may yet find that he cannot be successful in his direct attempts to remove it (violating Criterion 6). Another may find that each daily annoyance is greatly enhanced because of lingering childhood frustrations (violating Criteria 7 and 8).

Following this line of thought, we come to the conclusion that the handling of aggressive impulses becomes a serious problem only for individuals who for some reason cannot follow the normal course. In them aggression is more than a capacity, it becomes a trait. It is no longer rational and adaptive but habitual and compulsive. Reaction may be excessive, displaced, inappropriate. In genuinely neurotic aggression we find all of the eight criteria violated.

Disordered aggressiveness may thus become a deep-seated character disorder. It may do so because of the blocking of normal reactive aggression, because of many family and personal factors which psychoanalysis has called to our attention. And it may do so partly because of cultural pressure.

Social Patterning of Aggression

The competitive way of life in the United States puts a premium on certain kinds of aggressiveness. The little boy is expected to stand up for himself and engage in fist fights, if necessary. In certain regions, custom sanctions verbal and physical hostility against selected minority groups. But culture not only provides norms for the development of aggressive behavior, it also supplies the source of many of the characteristic frustrations individuals suffer.

Take the case of western culture. Parsons has pointed out certain features of social structure that have a marked bearing upon the evolution of aggressive traits, and thus predispose the individual to prejudice.[10] In the western home (perhaps particularly in the United States) the father is absent most of the day. The child is thrown with the mother so continuously that she alone provides the model and mentor for his conduct. An early identification with the mother usually sets in. Since the daughter in the family early learns that she too will be a housewife and mother, the identification gives her little or no trouble—at least for several years. The young son, however, is early placed in conflict. Womanish ways are not for him. While he is accustomed to them, he early senses a different set of expectations for himself. He learns that males have power, freedom of movement and strength. Women are weaker. Yet his tie to his mother is close. The love she gives him fulfills his deepest needs. This love, however, may be contingent upon his being brave, being a little man, and thus, in a sense, repudiating the very femininity with which he identifies. A large number of neurotic difficulties in older males stem from "mother fixation" and a "sissy complex" which the son is trying to escape.

As a kind of overcompensation, boys may later identify vigorously with the father, aping particularly his masculine ways. The rough, tough, and nasty behavior in boyhood culture can be explained, at least in part, as an over-reaction to mother domination. While most males make the transition somehow, and finally contrive to balance filial love toward the mother with requisite adult masculinity, there are cases that continue an overdependence on the mother, along with overaggressiveness toward the outer world. There is some evidence that among these cases will be found a large proportion of anti-Semitic males. The sufferer conceives himself to be masculine, aggressive, and tough, but underlying he has not mastered his passive and dependent attitude. The consequence is a compensatory hostility—displaced upon a socially sanctioned scapegoat.[11]

The father too often plays his part in inducing a compulsive masculinity in the son. He is a carrier of the competitive culture with its frontier tradition. He encourages the son, often beyond his age, to exploits of prowess. The standard is set higher than the youth can attain. One common response is to confuse sheer aggression with masculinity. The boy can at least talk tough, criticize loudly, and berate out-groups. This pattern of sham ferocity may in time turn into genuine hostility. The gang pattern and the "bad boy" pattern in our culture are basically signs of compulsive masculinity. So, too, to a degree, is ethnic prejudice. German culture is in many respects unlike ours, but it seems likely that the cult of compulsive masculinity among the Nazis, accompanied by ferocious persecution of the Jews, was also related to prevailing family patterns.

Daughters in the American family escape this particular conflict. But they, too, have cultural sources of frustration. Many of them harbor resentment against the inferior role assigned to women in our culture. Likewise, a woman stakes virtually everything on making a successful, romantic marriage. If it proves unsuccessful, she has fewer avenues of escape than has a man. Her frustration in marriage, therefore, can be, and often is, far more acute than a man's. Likewise she, too, has not escaped the emphasis upon masculine ideals in the culture. She too wants to be moderately "tough," but the tendency may be more firmly repressed because of her feminine role in the social order.

That this situation has something to do with the development of ethnic prejudice is indicated by research. It was found characteristic of anti-Semitic college women to have a large amount of pent-up aggression under a conventional feminine facade. This pattern did not exist to so marked a degree among women who were tolerant toward Jews.[12]

Turning to the occupational situation in America, it too seems to invite both reactive aggression and displacement. Standards of achievement are so high (every son is ordinarily expected to surpass his father in wealth and prestige) that failure and frustration frequently result. Yet the occupational situation that instigates aggression fails to provide any legitimate outlets at all.

One might say of Western society in general that aggression is sharply inhibited from direct expression within the very groups which generate it. There is, as a result, an immense amount of irritation ready for displacement. When we consider the commonness of frustration within family and occupation, and the amount of repression required to prevent inconvenient expressions of hostility, we may wonder that so many people escape developing out-group prejudice.

The type of sociological analysis here presented helps account for the uniformity in prejudice patterns within a society. It does not, however, account for the enormous range of individual differences encountered. To do so requires us to turn our attention back to the development of the personality as a selective agent.

The Nature of Hatred

Anger is a transitory emotional state, aroused by thwarting some on-going activity. Since it is aroused at a given time by an identifiable stimulus, it leads to impulses to attack the source of the frustration directly and to inflict injury upon this source.

Long ago Aristotle pointed out that anger differed from hatred in that anger is customarily felt toward individuals only, whereas hatred may be felt toward whole classes of people. He observed, too, that a person who gives way to anger is often sorry for his outburst and pities the object of his attack, but in expressing hatred, repentance seldom follows. Hatred is more deep-rooted, and constantly "desires the extinction of the object of hate." [13]

To put the matter another way, we may say that anger is an emotion, whereas hatred must be classified as a sentiment—an enduring organization of aggressive impulses toward a person or toward a class of persons. Since it is composed of habitual bitter feeling and accusatory thought, it constitutes a stubborn structure in the mental-emotional life of the individual. And since it makes for social disruption, and is condemned by religion, it has a strong ethical tinge, though the hater usually manages to avoid conflict about the matter. By its very nature hatred is extropunitive, which means that the hater is sure that the fault lies in the object of his hate. So long as he believes this he will not feel guilty for his uncharitable state of mind.

There is a good reason why out-groups are often chosen as the object of hate and aggression rather than individuals. One human being is, after all, pretty much like another—like oneself. One can scarcely help but sympathize with the victim. To attack him would be to arouse some pain in ourselves. Our own "body image" would be involved, for his body is like our own body. But there is no body image of a group. It is more abstract, more impersonal. It is especially so if there is some visibly distinguishing characteristic (cf. Chapter 8). A different-colored skin removes the person to some extent from our own circle. We are less likely to consider him an individual, and more likely to think of him only as an out-group member. But even so, he remains at least partially like ourselves.

This sympathizing tendency seems to explain a phenomenon we have frequently noted: people who hate groups in the abstract will, in actual conduct, often act fairly and even kindly toward individual members of the group.

There is another reason why it is easier to hate groups than individuals. We do not need to test our unfavorable stereotype of a group against reality. In fact, we can hold it all the more easily if we make "exceptions" for the individual members we know.

Fromm points out that it is essential to distinguish between two kinds of hate: one might be called "rational," the other, "character conditioned." [14] The former kind serves an important biological function. It arises when fundamental natural rights of persons are violated. One hates whatever threatens his own freedom, life, and values. Also, if well socialized, he hates whatever threatens the freedom, lives, and values of other human beings. During the occupation of Holland, Norway, and other countries during the Second World War, the inhabitants for the most part hated the Nazi invader with a hatred that has become legendary. It was a "cold" hatred, leading only occasionally to open aggression. It was not momentary anger, but a lasting contempt. The invader was treated, so far as possible, as nonexistent. A Nazi soldier entered a crowded railway carriage in Holland and was utterly disregarded by the occupants. Noting their hatred, but still trying to ingratiate himself, he said, "Please could you make room for a little bit of air?" They continued to ignore him.

Rational hatred does not concern us so much as "character-conditioned" hatred. Here we have, as Fromm points out, a continuing readiness to hate. The sentiment has little relation to reality, although it may be the product of a long series of bitter disappointments in life. These frustrations become fused into a kind of "free-floating hatred"—the subjective counterpart of free-floating aggression. The person carries a vague, temperamental sense of wrong which he wishes to polarize. He must hate *something*. The real roots of the hatred may baffle him, but he thinks up some convenient victim and some good reason. The Jews are conspiring against him, or the politicians are set on making things worse. Thwarted lives have the most character-conditioned hate.

Neither kind of hatred can exist unless something one values has been violated (Chapter 2). Love is a precondition of hate. Always some affiliative relationship is interrupted before the agent thought to be responsible for the interruption can be hated. This fact stands in direct contradiction to the assertion by Simmel quoted on p. 354 f., to the effect that before the individual acquires the capacity to love he is governed by a primitive hate-relationship to his environment. This is a seriously mistaken view.

What governs an individual at the beginning of his life is a dependent, affiliative relationship with the mother. There is little, if any, evidence of destructive instincts. After birth, the affiliative attachment of the child to his environment still remains dominant while nursing, resting, playing. The social smile early symbolizes contentment with people. Toward his entire environment the baby is positive, approaching nearly every type of stimulus, every type of person. His life is marked by eager outgoingness and, normally, by positive social relationships.

The initial affiliative tendencies, when threatened or frustrated, may give way to alarm and defense. Ian Suttie puts the matter picturesquely, "Earth hath no hate but love to hatred turned, and hell no fury but a baby scorned." [15] Thus, the genesis of hatred is secondary, contingent, and relatively late in the development process. It is always a matter of frustrated affiliative desire and the attendant humiliation to one's self-esteem or to one's values.

Perhaps the most perplexing problem in the entire field of human relations is this: why do so relatively few of our contacts with other people fit in with, and satisfy, our predominating affiliative needs, and why do so many find their way into sentiments of hatred and hostility? Why are loyalties and loves so few and restricted, when at bottom human beings feel that they can never love or be loved enough?

The answer to this riddle seems to lie in three directions. One concerns the amount of frustration and the hardness of living that beset people. Because of severe frustration it is easy to fuse one's recurring anger into rationalized hatreds. In order to avoid hurt and achieve at least an island of security it is safer to exclude than to include.

A second explanation has to do with the learning process. We have seen in previous chapters that children brought up in a rejective home, exposed to ready-made prejudices, will scarcely be in a position to develop a trustful or affiliative outlook upon social relationships. Having received little affection, they are not in a position to give it.

Finally, there is a kind of economy in adopting an exclusionist approach to human relations. (We spoke in Chapter 10 of "least effort.") By taking a negative view of great groups of mankind, we somehow make life simpler. For example, if I reject all foreigners as a category, I don't have to bother with them— except to keep them out of my country. If I can ticket, then, all Negroes as comprising an inferior and objectionable race, I conveniently dispose of a tenth of my fellow citizens. If I can put the Catholics into another category and reject them, my life is still further simplified. I then pare again and slice off the Jews . . . and so it goes.

Thus the prejudiced pattern, involving various degrees and kinds of hatred and aggression, takes its place in the individual's world-view. It has an economy about it that we cannot deny. Still it falls considerably short of the dreams men have for themselves. At bottom they still long for affiliation with life and peaceful and friendly relations with their fellow men.

NOTES AND REFERENCES

1. S. FREUD. *Civilization and Its Discontents.* London: Hogarth Press, (Translated) 1949, 90.

2. E. SIMMEL (ED.). *Anti-Semitism: A Social Disease.* New York: International Universities Press, 1948, 41.

3. This analysis parallels in part that offered by FRANZISKA BAUMGARTEN, Zur Psychologie der Aggression. *Gesundheit und Wohlfahrt,* 1947, 3, 1-7.

4. LOIS B. MURPHY. *Social Behavior and Child Personality.* New York: Columbia Univ. Press, 1937.

5. C. M. KLUCKHOHN, Group tensions: analysis of a case history. In L. BRYSON, L. FINKELSTEIN, AND R. MACIVER (EDS.), *Approaches to National Unity.* New York: Harper, 1945, 224.

6. *Ibid.*

7. R. STAGNER. Studies of aggressive social attitudes: I. Measurement and inter-relation of selected attitudes. *Journal of Social Psychology,* 1944, 20, 109-120.

8. S. T. BOGGS. *A Comparative Cultural Study of Aggression.* (Unpublished.) Cambridge: Harvard University, Social Relations Library, 1947.

9. E. BERGLER. *The Basic Neurosis.* New York: Grune & Stratton, 1949, 78.

10. T. PARSONS. Certain primary sources and patterns of aggression in the social structure of the western world. *Psychiatry,* 1947, 10, 167-181.

11. ELSE FRENKEL-BRUNSWIK AND R. N. SANFORD. Some personality factors in anti-Semitism. *Journal of Psychology,* 1945, 20, 271-291.

12. *Ibid.*

13. ARISTOTLE. *Rhetoric.* Book II.

14. E. FROMM. *Man for Himself.* New York: Rinehart, 1947, 214 ff.

15. I. D. SUTTIE. *The Origins of Love and Hate.* London: Kegan Paul, 1935, 23.

CHAPTER 23

ANXIETY, SEX, GUILT

*We are now in a position to understand the anti-Semite. He
is a man who is afraid. Not of the Jews, to be sure, but of
himself, of his own consciousness, of his liberty, of his instincts,
of his responsibilities, of solitariness, of change, of society, and
of the world—of everything except the Jews.*

JEAN PAUL SARTRE

What we have to say about the relation of fear, sexuality, and
guilt to prejudice is in many respects similar to our analysis of
the psychodynamics of aggression.

Fear and Anxiety

Rational and adaptive fear entails the accurate perception of
the source of danger. An illness, an approaching fire or flood, a
highwayman are among the conditions that make for realistic
fear. When we perceive the source of the threat accurately, we
ordinarily strike back at it or withdraw to safety.

Sometimes the source of the fear is correctly perceived, but the
person can do nothing to control it. A workman fearful of
losing his job or citizens living in a vague apprehension of atomic
warfare are swayed by fear, but they are powerless. Under such
circumstances, the fear becomes chronic—and we speak of *anxiety*.

Chronic anxiety puts us on the alert and predisposes us to see
all sorts of stimuli as menacing. A man who lives in constant
dread of losing his job feels surrounded by danger. He is sensitized to perceive the Negro or the foreigner as trying to take his
job away from him. Here is a displacement of a realistic fear.

Sometimes the source of the fear is not known, or has been
forgotten or repressed. The fear may be merely a mounting
residue of inner feelings of weakness in dealing with the hazards
of the outer world. Time and again the sufferer may have
failed to win in his encounters with life. He thus develops a
generalized feeling of inadequacy. He is fearful of life itself.
He is afraid of his own ineffectiveness and grows suspicious of

other people whose greater competence he regards as a threat.

Anxiety then is a diffuse, irrational fear, not directed at an appropriate target and not controlled by self-insight. Like a grease spot, it has spread throughout the life and stains the individual's social relationships. Because he is far from satisfied in his affiliative needs, he may become compulsive—overpossessive toward some people (his own children, perhaps)—and over-rejective toward others. But these compulsive social relationships create further anxieties, and the vicious circle is intensified.

Existentialists tell us that anxiety is basic in every life. It is more prominent than aggression because the very conditions of human existence are mysterious and dreadful, though they are not always frustrating. It is for this reason that fear becomes even more readily diffused and character-conditioned than does aggression.

Anxiety, however, is like aggression in that people tend to be ashamed of it. Our ethical codes place a premium on courage and self-reliance. Pride and self-respect lead us to mask our anxiety. While we repress it in part, we also give it a displaced outlet—upon socially sanctioned sources of fear. Some people suffer an almost hysterical fear of "communists" in our midst. It is a socially allowable phobia. The same people would not be respected if they admitted the real source of much of their anxiety, which lies in personal inadequacy and dread of life.

There may, of course, be elements of realistic fear mingled with displaced fear. Communists in our midst do constitute a menace, though to a lesser degree than many demagogues and phobiacs would have us believe. A remarkable shift in public opinion came after Japan was defeated. Previously, the animosity knew no bounds. Not only was the nation considered sly and sub-human, but even loyal Japanese-Americans were herded into "re-location" camps. In 1943 the Russians were loved, the Japanese feared. Five years later the situation had more or less reversed itself. This shift demonstrates that a core of realism may be present even in conditions where much displacement is also taking place. Men are rational enough to *prefer* plausible targets for their fears if they are available.

So far as our knowledge now extends, it seems probable that the principal source of character-conditioned anxiety comes from a bad start in early life. In previous chapters we have several times noted the peculiarities of child training that may arouse lasting anxiety. The male child, in particular, strives against odds to achieve a masculine role, and may carry lasting anxiety with him concerning the degree of his success. The rejective parent creates a condition of profound apprehension that we know may underlie nervous disorders, delinquency, and hostility. The following case is by no means extreme, but serves to illustrate the subtlety of the process that may be involved.

When George was four years old his mother gave birth to his baby brother. George was fearful lest his baby brother displace him in his mother's affection. He worried and fretted, and came to hate his younger brother. The baby was ailing and the mother did, in fact, give more of her attention to him than to George. The four-year-old felt increasingly resentful and insecure. He tried at times to injure his young brother but was, of course, restrained and punished. Unfortunately, the mother died before she could restore the balance. George never recovered from the double deprivation.

When he entered school he was of a suspicious nature. He particularly resented strangers coming into the neighborhood, and had a fist fight with each newcomer. This method of testing strangers is common enough in boyhood circles. They must prove themselves to be regular guys in order to be accepted. Within a few weeks the distrust of the stranger is dissolved and the old boys and the new come to terms.

But there were certain types of strangers that George could not accept, even after the initial ritual of the fist fight. They were boys who seemed to him definitely alien to the community. They were so different that (like his baby brother) they seemed unassimilable intruders. They had odd homes, odd foods, odd coloring, and observed queer holidays. The strangeness would not wear off. The newcomer stood out sharply, was everywhere visible (like the baby brother of his earlier years). George's initial suspicion and hostility just didn't dissolve. He would accept boys who were like him (self-love), but he would reject boys who were alien to his self-image (symbols of his baby brother). Difference in ethnic membership came for George to have the same functional significance as the difference between him and his sibling rival.

In the community there are many Georges not necessarily working out their sibling rivalry but, for other reasons connected with early deprivations, suffering from nameless apprehension. Like George, they perceive differences between people as menacing. Feeling anxious for no consciously ascertainable reason, they seek to discover a cause for their anxiety. It lies, they decide, in some difference that can be rationalized as a source of their dread. When all the anxious Georges in a community put their fears together and agree on an imagined cause (the Negro, the Jew, the communist), a great deal of fear-produced hostility may result.[1]

Economic Insecurity

While much anxiety has its origin in childhood, the adult years are also potent sources, especially in connection with economic insufficiency. We have already cited considerable evidence (especially in Chapter 14) to the effect that downward mobility, periods of unemployment and depression, and general economic dissatisfaction are all positively correlated with prejudice.

Sometimes, as we have likewise seen, there may be a realistic conflict involved, as when the upgrading of Negro workmen creates more competitors for certain jobs. It is not inconceivable, too, that members of one ethnic group may actually conspire to gain a monopoly of a business, a factory, or an occupation. But ordinarily, the "threat" that is felt is not geared to realities in that situation. The apprehensive and marginal man is vaguely terrified at any signs of ambition or progress on the part of any member of the out-group, whether or not it may constitute a realistic danger.

In most countries, people grow fiercely possessive of their property. It is a bastion of conservatism. Any threat, real or imagined, will invoke anxiety and anger (this blend is particularly suited to the growth of hatred). A grim reflection of this relationship is found in the experience of many Jews who were sent to concentration camps in central Europe during the Nazi control. These Jews often entrusted their property to some gentile friend. Most of the Jews were killed, and the property automatically became that of the friend. But occasionally a Jew returned, and found that he was cordially hated for claiming his property, which perhaps had been used up by the trustee, sometimes to buy food. One Jew, foreseeing this outcome, refused to ask gentile friends to guard his goods, saying, "Isn't it enough for my enemies to want me to die? I don't want my friends also to want me dead."

Outright greed is certainly a cause of prejudice. If we took a historical over-view of feelings against colonial people, Jews, and aborigines (including the American Indian), we should probably find that rationalization of greed is a principal source. The fomula is simple enough: greed → grabbing → justifying.

The role of economic apprehension in anti-Semitism has often been commented on. In the United States it seems that the well-to-do are especially prone to anti-Semitism.[2] The reason may be that the Jew is seen as a symbolic competitor. To keep him down is to avoid symbolically all potential threat. Hence he is excluded not only from occupations, but also from schools, clubs, neighborhoods. In this way a specious feeling of security and superiority results. McWilliams characterizes the total process as a "mask for privilege." [3]

Self-Esteem

Economic worries have their origins in hunger and the need to survive. But they continue to exist long after this rational function has been fulfilled. They ramify into the need for status, prestige, self-esteem. Food is no longer the issue, nor is money—excepting so far as it can buy that one thing in life that is always short in supply: *differential status.*

Not everyone can be "on top." Not everyone wants to be. But most people want to be higher on the status ladder than they are. "This hunger," writes Murphy, "operates like a vitamin deficiency." He regards it as the primary root of ethnic prejudice.[4]

The hunger for status is matched by a haunting fear that one's status may not be secure. The effort to maintain a precarious position can bring with it an almost reflex disparagement of others. Asch gives one instance:

> We observe this in the racial pride of Southerners, in the preoccupation with face-saving and self-justification, which are probably born of deep, mostly not conscious but also not bearable, doubts of their position. Sectional pride in the face of the North, the pride of a decaying landed group in the face of a newly arising industrial order, the pride of the new industrialist in the face of the old aristocracy, of the wretched poor white in the face of the precariously inferior Negro— these are the reactions of a people unsure whether their failures are not their own fault.[5]

The philosopher Hume once pointed out that envy seems to appear only when the distance between ourselves and those more fortunate than ourselves is small enough so that we can reasonably compare ourselves with them—the "narcissism of small differences." A schoolboy does not envy Aristotle, but he may envy his neighbor whose "A" in a course of study makes his own grades seem intolerably low. Slaves probably did not envy their rich masters—the gap was too great—but they may well have envied other slaves who had positions of favor. Whenever rigid class distinctions break down or mobility increases, there is much more occasion for envy. Americans are near enough to one another in education, opportunity, freedom, to feel envy for one another. That is why, paradoxically enough, augmented hatred may well accompany diminished class distance.

The easiest idea to sell anyone is that he is better than someone else. The appeal of the Ku Klux Klan and racist agitators rests on this type of salesmanship. Snobbery is a way of clutching at one's status, and it is as common, perhaps more common, among those who are low in the ladder. By turning their attention to unfavored out-groups, they are able to derive from the comparison a modicum of self-esteem. Out-groups, as status builders, have the special advantage of being near at hand, visible (or at least nameable), and occupying a lower position by common agreement, thus providing social support for one's own sense of status enhancement.

The theme of egoism (status) has run through many of our chapters. Perhaps Murphy is right in regarding it as the "primary root" of prejudice. Our purpose in the present discussion is to bring this theme into proper relation with the factors of fear and anxiety. High status, we feel, would abolish our basic apprehensions, and for this reason we struggle to achieve a secure position for ourselves—often at the expense of our fellows.

Sexuality

Sex, like anger or fear, may ramify throughout the life, and may affect social attitudes in devious ways. Like these other emotions, it is less diffuse when it is rationally and adaptively directed. But in sexual maladjustment, frustration, and conflict, a tenseness spreads outward from the erotic area of the life into many by-paths. Some maintain that it is impossible to understand group prejudice in the United States, particularly the prejudice of whites toward Negroes, without reference to sex maladjustment. Dingwall, a British anthropologist, writes:

> Sex dominates life in the United States in a manner and in a way which is found nowhere else in the world. Without a full appreciation of its influence and its results, no elucidation of the Negro problem is possible.[6]

We may overlook the unproved assertion that Americans are more sex-ridden than people in other countries, while at the same time admitting that an important issue has been raised.

A housewife in a northern city was asked whether she would object to Negroes living on the same street. She replied,

I wouldn't want to live with Negroes. They smell too much. They're of a different race. That's what creates racial hatreds. When I sleep with a Negro in the same bed, I'll live with them. But you know we can't.

Here the sexual barricade intrudes itself into a logically unrelated issue—the simple question of residence on the same street.

It is by no means only anti-Negro prejudice that reveals sex interest and sex accusations. An advertisement for an anti-Catholic pamphlet reads as follows:

See the nun bound hand and foot, gagged, lying in a dungeon because she refused to obey a priest. . . . Read about nun locked in a room stark naked with three drunken priests. . . . Poison, Murder, Rapine, Torturing and smothering babies. . . . If you want to know what goes on behind convent walls read this book *House of Death* or *Convent Brutality*.

The linking of lechery with the Roman Catholic Church (known also as "the mother of harlots") is an old and familiar trick of Catholic-haters. Dark tales of sexual debauchery were common a century ago, and were part of the whispering campaign of the Know-Nothing political party that flourished at that time.

The fierce persecution of the Mormons in the Nineteenth Century was related to their doctrine, and occasional practice, of polygamy. Granted that plural marriage, ended by law in 1896, was an unsound social policy, a prurience of interest and licentiousness of fantasies were revealed in the anti-Mormon tracts of the time. The opposition to the sect drew nourishment from the conflict that many people had within their own sex lives. Why should others be allowed a wider choice of sex partners than they? And during the 1920's perhaps the commonest accusation against communist Russia was that it "nationalized" its women.

In Europe it is common to accuse the Jews of gross sexual immorality. They are said to be given to overindulgence, rape, perversion. Hitler, whose own sex life was far from normal, contrived over and over again to accuse the Jews of perversion, of having syphilis, and of other disorders suspiciously akin to Hitler's own phobias. Streicher, the Number One Nazi Jew-baiter, at least in private conversation, mentioned circumcision about as often as he mentioned Jew.[7] Some peculiar complex seemed to be haunting him (Could it be his castration-anxiety?), which he managed to project upon the Jews.

In America one seldom hears sex accusations against the Jews. Is it because there is less anti-Semitism? Is it that American Jews are more moral than European Jews? Neither explanation seems right. The reason, more probably, as we saw in Chapter 15, is that in America we have in the Negro a preferred target for our sexual complexes.

There is a subtle psychological reason why Negroid characteristics favor an association of ideas with sex. The Negro seems dark, mysterious, distant—yet at the same time warm, human, and potentially accessible. These elements of mystery and forbiddenness are present in sex appeal in a Puritanical society. Sex is forbidden; colored people are forbidden; the ideas begin to fuse. It is no accident that prejudiced people call tolerant people "niggerlovers." The very choice of the word suggests that they are fighting the feeling of attraction in themselves.

The fact that interracial sex attraction exists is proved by the millions of mixed breeds in the country. Differences in color and social status seem to be sexually exciting rather than repelling. It has often been noted that liaisons with members of lower classes seem particularly attractive to people with higher status. The daughter of the patrician family who runs away with the coachman is almost as familiar a theme in literature as is the prodigal son who wastes his substance in riotous living with lower-class women. Both reveal the same truth.

We note that sun-bathing is for the purpose of darkening the skin—and is a pastime indulged in by male and female alike to enhance their attractiveness. There is intrigue in contrasting complexions. Moreno has reported that homosexual crushes between white and Negro adolescent girls were common in a reformatory, for difference in skin color in many instances seemed to serve as a functional substitute for difference in sex.[8]

The attraction is further enhanced by the fact (or legend) that Negroes have an open and unashamed way of looking at life. Many people with suppressed sex lives would like the same freedom. They grow jealous and irritated at the openness and directness of sex life among others. They accuse the males of extreme sexual potency, and the females of shamelessness. Even the size of the genitalia becomes a subject of jealous exaggeration. Fantasies easily get mixed with fact.

This illicit fascination may become obsessional in some localities where life is otherwise intolerably dull. In her novel *Strange Fruit*, Lillian Smith has described the emotional aridness of a small southern town. Escape is sought in religious orgies, or in the excitement of race conflict. Or people may see in the Negro the lusty qualities they lack, and may alternately ridicule, desire, and persecute them. Forbidden fruit arouses contrasting emotional reactions. Helen McLean writes:

> In calling the Negro a child of nature, simple, lovable, without ambition, a person who gives way to his every impulse, white men have made a symbol which gives a secret gratification to those who are inhibited and crippled in their instinctual satisfactions. Indeed, white men are very loath to relinquish such a symbol.[9]

Now this common cross-race sexual fascination seldom expresses itself normally. The mixed dating of adolescents is virtually a social impossibility. Legal intermarriage, where possible at all, is rare and is bedeviled by social complications that create grave problems even for the most devoted couples. Hence sexual liaisons are clandestine, illicit, and accompanied by feelings of guilt. Yet the fascination is so strong that this most rigid of taboos is frequently broken, more often by the white male, however, than by the white female.

The psychodynamic process that relates this sexual situation to prejudice may be described separately for the white female and white male. (It must, of course, be understood that not every individual is affected in the same way; but the process is probably common enough to be an important factor in the establishment and maintenance of prejudice.)

Suppose a white woman is fascinated by the taboo against the Negro male. She is unlikely to admit, even to herself, that she finds his color and lower status attractive. She may, however, "project" her feelings, and accordingly imagine that the desire exists on the *other* side—that Negro males have sexually aggressive tendencies toward her. What is an inner temptation is perceived as an outer threat. Overgeneralizing her conflict, she develops an anxiety and hostility respecting the whole Negro race.

In the case of the white male the process may be even more complex. Suppose he is anxious concerning his own sexual adequacy and attractiveness. One study of adult prisoners discovered a close relationship between this condition and high prejudice. Men who were antagonistic toward minority groups, on the whole, showed more fierce protest against their own sexual passivity, semi-impotence, or homosexual trends. The protest took the form of exaggerated toughness and hostility. These individuals committed more crimes of a sexual nature than did those who were sexually more secure. And the pseudo masculinity of the former group made them more hostile toward minorities.[10]

Again, a male who is dissatisfied with his own marriage may grow envious when he hears rumors of Negro sexual prowess and license. He may also resent and fear the approach Negroes might make to white women who are potentially his. A state of rivalry may thus result, based on the same type of reasoning that says the supply of jobs is limited and if Negroes have them, whites will be deprived.

Or suppose the white male has taken his pleasure with Negro women. Such liaisons, being illicit, give rise to guilt. A wry sense of justice forces him to see that the Negro males, in principle, should have equal access to white women. Jealousy plus guilt create a disagreeable conflict. He, too, finds a way out by "projecting." It is the lecherous Negro male that is the real menace. He would deflower white womanhood. The deflowering of Negro womanhood is conveniently forgotten in the outburst of righteous indignation. The indignation is guilt-evading and restorative of self-respect.

For this reason the penalties visited upon male Negroes for sex transgressions (with white women) are disproportionately heavy. (Although in fact, of course, the bulk of transgression is on the white side.) During the years 1938-1948, in thirteen southern states, 15 whites and 187 Negroes were executed for rape. In these same states Negroes made up only 23.8 of the population. Unless we assume that Negroes commit rape fifty-three times as often as white men (in proportion to their numbers in the population), we are forced to conclude that bias is largely responsible for the unequal number of executions for this crime.[11]

There is no doubt that lifting the sexual ban would reduce the glamor and the conflict. But the ban is a stubborn composite of several factors. It rests, in the first instance, upon a Puritanical view of sex activity of any sort. Sex itself is taboo. But since normal social intercourse and intermarriage are scarcely ever possible between Negroes and whites, any intimate relationships seem to take on an adulterous flavor.[12]

The central question allegedly is intermarriage. Since this sounds like a legal, and therefore respectable, issue, it becomes the pivot of nearly all discussion. The fact that miscegenation between two healthy people has no weakening effect on the offspring is overlooked. Intermarriage cannot rationally be opposed on biological grounds. It can, however, be rationally opposed on the grounds of the handicap and conflict it could cause both parents and offspring in the present state of society. But the opposition is seldom stated in these mild terms, for to do so would imply that the present state of society should be improved so that miscegenation can safely take place.

For the most part the marriage issue is not rational. It comprises a fierce fusion of sex attraction, sex repression, guilt, status superiority, occupational advantage, and anxiety. It is because intermarriage would symbolize the abolition of prejudice that it is so strenuously fought.

Perhaps the most interesting feature of the whole situation is the way in which the issue of intermarriage has come to dominate discussion. When a Negro obtains a good pair of shoes and learns to write a literate letter, some whites think he wants to marry their sister. Perhaps most discussions of discrimination end with the fatal question, "But would *you* want a Negro to marry your sister?" The reasoning seems to be that unless all forms of discrimination are maintained, intermarriage will result. The same argument was used to defend slavery. Nearly a hundred years ago Abraham Lincoln was forced to protest against "that counterfeit logic which presumes that, if I do not want a Negro woman for a slave, I do necessarily want her for a wife." [13]

Why the prejudiced person almost invariably hides behind the issue of marriage is itself a lesson in rationalization. He takes what is admittedly the argument most likely to confuse his opponent. Even the most tolerant person may not welcome intermarriage—because of the practical unwisdom in a prejudiced society. He may therefore say, "No, I wouldn't." The bigot then has the advantage, and replies in effect, "Now, see, there is ultimately an unbridgeable chasm, and I am therefore right in maintaining that we must look on Negroes as a different and undesirable group. All my strictures against them are justified. We had better not let down the barriers because it will raise their expectations and hopes of intermarriage." Thus, the intermarriage question (actually so irrelevant to most phases of the Negro question) is forcibly introduced to protect and justify prejudice.[14]

Guilt

A non-Catholic boy had a broken romance with a Catholic girl, and this affair was preceded by a rather free infatuation with another Catholic girl. He wrote:

> Both girls begged me to come back and marry them. They promised anything if I would do so. Their groveling disgusted me. But I realized that the Catholic Church has only an ignorant, bigoted following to draw from.

Not he, but the Church, was somehow to blame for the unpleasant situation. A gentile businessman was guilty of unethical practices that forced a Jewish competitor into bankruptcy. He, too, consoled himself, saying:

> Well, they are always trying to run Christians out of business, and so I had to get him first.

The student was a cad; the gentile a cheat. But subjectively each evaded his sense of guilt by projection; others were guilty, not he.

Somewhat more subtle is the evidence that comes from clinical studies. We spoke in Chapter 18 of the child who through repressive training is made fearful of his own impulses, and comes therefore to fear the impulses of others. The California studies, to which we alluded, show among prejudiced people a marked tendency to regard others (but not oneself) as blameworthy. Interesting confirmation comes from comparable studies in India, where the psychologist, Mitra, discovered in Hindu boys having greatest prejudice against Muslims a high tendency to unconscious guilt reactions in the Rorschach test.[15]

While nearly all people, to varying degrees, suffer from feelings of guilt, not all mix this emotional condition in with their ethnic attitudes. As in the case of anger, hatred, fear and sexuality, there are rational and adaptive responses to guilt. It is only certain personalities who allow these states to enter into the formation of character-conditioned bigotry.

Some of the ways in which people handle guilt-feelings are benign and wholesome; some lead almost unavoidably to prejudice against out-groups. Let us list the principal modes of dealing with guilt. Some of them are closely related to the methods of solving mental conflict described in Chapter 20.

1. **Remorse and Restitution.** This is the response that receives highest ethical approval. It is wholly intropunitive and avoids all temptation to shift blame to other shoulders. A person who is normally penitent and contrite for his own failings is not likely to find much in others, specifically in out-groups, to criticize.

Sometimes, though not often, we find among persecutors of out-groups converts who repent and devote themselves ever after to supporting the cause of those they at first hated. St. Paul's conversion represented such a shift. Somewhat more often we find a sensitive person who feels a *collective* guilt. It is likely that some white workers who devote themselves to the improvement of conditions for Negroes may have some such motivation. Being intropunitive to a high degree, they feel that their own group is at fault, and work hard to make amends.

2. Partial and Sporadic Restitution. Some people who themselves hold firmly the doctrine of white supremacy will, up to a point, work for the betterment of the Negro. They feel that they can hold to a basic prejudice if only they act now and then as if it were nonexistent. "We frequently do good," wrote La Rochefoucault, "to enable us with impunity to do evil." In one community the woman who was most active in keeping Negroes out of the neighborhood and "in their place," was found at the same time to be the most active in devoting herself to Negro charities. Here is a case of "alternation" and "compromise," discussed in Chapter 20.

3. Denial of Guilt. A common escape from feelings of guilt is to assert that there is no reason to have them. A familiar justification for discrimination against the Negroes is, "They are happier by themselves." A common Southern conceit is that Negroes prefer Southern to Northern employers because the former "understand" them better. During the Second World War, it was often said that Negroes, for this reason, preferred to serve under Southern rather than under Northern white officers. Also, it was maintained that they greatly preferred white to colored officers. The facts are entirely contradictory. When asked in a poll whether they would prefer to serve under white or Negro lieutenants, only four percent of the Northern and six percent of the Southern Negroes preferred white. Further, only one percent of the Northern Negroes preferred a white officer from the South, and only four percent of the Southern Negroes did so.[16]

4. Discrediting the Accuser. No one likes another person to blame him for misconduct. A common defense against facing the justice of an accusation is to declare the accuser to be somehow off base. Hamlet confronted his mother with her faithlessness in marrying her husband's murderer. Rather than face her own guilt, his mother reproves Hamlet for "the coinage" of his brain, laying his charges to his madness. Hamlet tries to show her that she is but rationalizing to escape her own conscience:

> . . . Mother, for love of grace,
> Lay not that flattering unction to your soul,
> That not your trespass, but my madness speaks;
> It will but skin and film the ulcerous place,
> Whilst rank corruption, mining all within,
> Infect unseen. Confess yourself to heaven!
> Repent what's past; avoid what is to come;
> And do not spread the compost on the weeds,
> To make them ranker.[17]

In the realm of ethnic relations those who would rouse the voice of conscience are called "agitators," "troublemakers," "communists."

5. **Justification of Conditions.** The simplest evasion of all is to say that the hated person is wholly to blame. In Chapter 20 we saw that many people who are prejudiced take this path. This is prejudice without compunction. "Who could tolerate them? Look, they are dirty, lazy, sexually libertine." The fact that these qualities may be the very ones we have to fight in ourselves, makes it all the easier to see them in others. In any case, complete extropunitiveness, with recourse to the deserved reputation theory, avoids the necessity of guilt.

6. **Projection.** The sense of guilt, by definition, means that I blame myself for some misdeed. But only Item 1 in this list (remorse and restitution) is strictly appropriate to this definition. It alone is a rationally adaptive mode of response. All others are devices for *guilt evasion*. Guilt-evading processes have one feature in common: the self-referred perception is repressed in favor of some external (extropunitive) perception. There is guilt somewhere, yes, but it is not *my* guilt.

Thus in all guilt evasion there is some projective mechanism at work. We have listed certain examples. But they do not cover all of the types of cases we find. For example, there is the device of pointing to greater sin in others in order to diminish the sense of sin in ourselves. The businessman quoted at the beginning of this section held that his cheating was excusable in view of the greater dishonesty of the Jewish group as a whole.

Whenever, and in whatever way, a correct appraisal of one's own emotional life fails and gives way to an incorrect judgment of other people, we are dealing with the psychodynamic process of *projection*. And so central is it in the understanding of prejudice that we shall devote the following chapter to it.

NOTES AND REFERENCES

1. *Cf.* A. H. KAUFMAN. The problem of human difference and prejudice. *Journal of Orthopsychiatry*, 1947, **17**, 352-356.

2. H. H. HARLAN. Some factors affecting attitudes toward Jews. *American Sociological Review*, 1942, **7**, 816-827.

3. C. MCWILLIAMS. *A Mask for Privilege*. Boston: Little, Brown, 1948.

4. G. MURPHY. Preface to E. HARTLEY, *Problems in Prejudice*. New York: King's Crown, 1946, viii.

5. S. ASCH. *Social Psychology*. New York: Prentice-Hall, 1952, 605.

6. E. J. DINGWALL. *Racial Pride and Prejudice*. London: Watts, 1946, 69.

7. G. M. GILBERT. *Nüremberg Diary*. New York: Farrar, Straus, 1947, *passim*.

8. J. L. MORENO. *Who Shall Survive?* Washington: Nervous and Mental Disease Publishing, 1934, 229.

9. HELEN V. MCLEAN. Psychodynamic factors in racial relations. *The Annals of the American Academy of Political and Social Science*, 1946, **244**, 159-166.

10. W. R. MORROW. A psychodynamic analysis of the crimes of prejudiced and unprejudiced male prisoners. *Bulletin of the Menninger Clinic*, 1949, **13**, 204-212.

11. J. A. DOMBROWSKI. Execution for rape is a race penalty. *The Southern Patriot*, 1950, **8**, 1-2.

12. Our account in these pages has said nothing about the Negro's point of view. It may be that color difference and the taboo add glamor to interracial mating for the Negro as well as for the white. It may be that hostility and resentment are released along with sex desire and occasionally lead to brutal rape. But it seems unlikely that potency and impulsiveness are greater among Negro males than among whites. In fact, certain studies suggest that fear, dependency, and broken homes create a passivity and impotence in Negro males to a surprisingly large extent. *Cf*. A. KARDINER AND L. OVESEY. *The Mark of Oppression*. New York: W. W. Norton, 1951.

13. Reply to Judge Stephen A. Douglas at Chicago, July 10, 1858.

14. How the tolerant person should respond to the fatal question, "Would you want your sister to marry a Negro?" has caused some inventive speculation. One suggestion is to reply, "Perhaps not, but I shouldn't want her to marry you either."

15. Cited by G. MURPHY. *In the Minds of Men*. New York: Basic Books, 1953, 228.

16. S. A. STOUFFER, *et al*. *The American Soldier: Adjustment During Army Life*. Princeton: Princeton Univ. Press, 1949, Vol. 1, 581.

17. *Hamlet*, Act III, Scene 4.

CHAPTER 24

PROJECTION

Projection may be defined as the tendency to attribute falsely
to other people motives or traits that are our own, or that in some
way explain or justify our own. There are at least three distinguishable types of projection. These we shall call

1) direct projection,
2) mote-beam projection,
3) complementary projection.

Before we discuss each in some detail, it is desirable to prepare the
ground, for since projection is a process hidden from consciousness,
it is not easy to understand.

Jealousy

We start with the simplest type of case. A person who is envious
of another knows that he is envious. This much of the emotional
situation is not walled off from consciousness. But simple jealousy
immediately starts up some strange attendant mental operations.

Take the attitude of front-line troops in the Second World War.
They envied troops who had less dangerous jobs—an assignment
to the quartermaster's corps, at headquarters, or elsewhere behind
the lines. Denied these privileges, they frequently developed two
outlooks that might be called incipient prejudice.[1] (1) They grew
resentful of troops who were not in combat and became critical
of all rear echelons. About half of the front-line soldiers openly
admitted this feeling of resentment, although it was perfectly obvious that no soldier in the rear was responsible for the danger or
discomfort of the men in the line. From this fact we learn that
one may feel resentment against wholly innocent people who happen to enjoy more privileges than we, and at the same time one
may give way to an illogical tendency to blame them for one's own
deprivation. They are seen as *causes* for one's discomfort even
though they are not. This tendency we shall discuss further under
complementary projection. (2) At the same time, the front-line

troops developed a feeling of superiority. Even though they wished to change places with the secure troops, they felt greatly superior to them. Intense in-group esteem became a way of compensating for a lack. Here we see the reciprocal relation between in-group loyalty and out-group scorn. They are two sides of the same coin.

Jealousy, of course, does not always lead to prejudice, although in this case we clearly have an incipient prejudice that would no doubt have become set if there had been no rotation of troops. Our point is simply that in states of jealousy we are likely to encounter in a fairly elementary form the projective mechanism at work. Envy leads one to think ill of someone else—more ill than the situation warrants.

Extropunitiveness as a Trait

We have already indicated that extropunitiveness may be a trait of personality (Chapter 21). Some people look constantly for alibis. Hitler was such a person. He blamed the bad world, a bad school, fate, for his many failures in early life. When he did not pass in school, he blamed illness. For his political reverses, he blamed others. For the defeat at Stalingrad, his generals. For starting the war, he blamed Churchill, Roosevelt, the Jews. There seems to be no record of his blaming himself for any missteps or failures.

There is something exhilarating about extropunitive indignation. To be good and angry at someone else, or even at fate, is like being on a spree. The joy is twofold. Partly it is a physical relief from pent-up tension and frustration. Partly it is restorative of one's self-esteem. Not I but others are wholly at fault. I am blameless, virtuous, more sinned against than sinning.

Studies of children show how early the tendency develops to excuse oneself from taking responsibility. A day at a nursery school is crowded with alibis. "I can't drink my orange juice from a paper cup; it makes me throw up." "I can't take my nap on my side; my mother won't let me." Gradually this tendency may give way to a habit of fixing blame on other children. It is interesting to note that scarcely ever before the age of six or seven do children blame others for their own misdeeds, although they may, previous to that age, give excuses and evade responsibility.

One psychologist made a special study of personalities having a kind of "dirty-deal complex." They are the people who grow up with the conviction that their lives are plagued by misfortune and by the misconduct of others. Of this type the investigator writes

The throwing of blame on others makes them feel angel-pure. This projection of one's own faults upon others is one of the least pleasant character traits of the person with this type of complex.[2]

The disposition to blame others can exist in any degree—from intense paranoia (Chapter 26) to the mildest type of captiousness. In either case, it represents a retreat from rational and objective thinking toward projective thinking.

Let us take a distinctly mild case of the blaming tendency and see how it leads away from a realistic analysis:

> A college president was asked to speak on the subject of prejudice to a Jewish audience. He accepted the invitation but devoted his whole time in the speech to admonishing the Jews to behave themselves better, so that it would be easy for non-Jews to like them.
>
> Some people, hearing about this, said, "That wasn't very tactful of him." Others said, "Well, maybe it was a courageous thing to do, for surely the Jews are not perfect. Many of them *are* objectionable."

The president's censorious approach was typical of the blaming tendency. Let the Jews make themselves less objectionable; let the Catholics prove they are not fascists; let the Negroes show more ambition. This approach (reasonable though it may seem) is based on false assumptions. So far as Jews are concerned, it implies that they have more objectionable traits than non-Jews (which has never been proved). It assumes, further, that simply being a member of a group has something to do with being objectionable. It also assumes that where objectionable individuals exist they are initially at fault, and not (what is often true) that the objectionable (defensive) features in their personalities might be the *result* of being disliked. The president placed the responsibility for change only on one side of the balance.

Granted that an objective discussion of group differences and their causes is a legitimate topic, we note how even a person who prides himself on fair-mindedness easily slips over into an attitude where a *preponderance* of responsibility is placed on the other fellow.

Repression

Projection cannot take place unless and until the inner (insightful) perception of the situation is somehow blocked. In some of the instances we have considered, this condition already prevails.

The sufferer from a "dirty-deal complex" simply lacks perspective upon his total situation; he does not know how much he himself may be to blame for it. By refusing to face his internal defects, he finds himself free to look for external villainy. Certainly Hitler was not blessed with self-insight. Otherwise he could not so consistently have seen "Jewish pluto-democratic warmongers" as responsible for his woes.

Repression means the exclusion of all or part of a personal conflict situation from consciousness and from adaptive response. Anything unwelcome to consciousness may be repressed, especially those elements in a conflict that would lower our self-esteem if frankly faced. Repressed material often has to do with fear and anxiety; hatred, especially of parents; sex desires of a disapproved order; past actions that would cause guilt if faced, as well as earlier feelings of guilt and shame; greed; impulses to cruelty and aggression; one's desire for infantile dependence; one's wounded pride; and all rawer manifestations of egoism. The list could be extended to include whatever antisocial or unwelcome impulses, emotions, or sentiments the individual has not handled through a successful integration with his conscious life. (It must be remarked that not all repressions are harmful, for some may be sacrifices of unwanted impulses in the interests of a greater gain. Thus one's philosophy of life may rule out tendencies toward greed or dishonesty or libertinism completely and effectively. Repression in this sense is necessary and benign. We are speaking here only of *ineffective* repression, where a troublesome residue may remain to disturb the personality and bedevil his social relations.)

When ineffective repression occurs the sufferer lives in distress. His troublesome motives are still active in a helter-skelter sort of way. He cannot act them out adaptively by gearing his unrest to an appropriate line of conduct. It is thus between his motives and his behavior that the mechanism of projection is likely to intervene. He *externalizes* the whole situation. Denied perspective on himself, he thinks entirely in terms of the outer world. If a destructive impulse in himself troubles him, he sees it *out there* in someone else.

Living Inkblots

It is far easier to project an inner state upon an outer object if the outer object lacks a firm structure of its own. In the daytime it is hard for us to see the sapling along the roadside as a highwayman. Our inner anxiety may be great, but still we do not see thugs in broad daylight if they are not there. At night, when objects are shadowy, projection of fear is easier.

So-called "projective tests" in clinical psychology always involve unstructured forms upon which the individual may readily project whatever inner state he will. Shown a somewhat ambiguous picture of an older woman and younger man, he may report that it concerns a mother and her son. And the flavor of the story he tells about this picture is *likely* to betray his own repressions (perhaps overdependence, hostility, even incestuous wishes).

The most famous projective medium is the inkblot (Rorschach test). In the formless smear of an inkblot it is extraordinary what some people will see. And it is not only the objects they see that have significance, but also their manner of handling and organizing the details and composition of the inkblot.

"For the anti-Semite," write Ackerman and Jahoda, "The Jew is a living Rorschach inkblot." [3] The meaning is clear. The Jew is mysterious, unknown. He is unstructured. He might be almost anything. Tradition says he is evil. One may use him as an outer representation of inner repressed guilt, anxiety, hatred.

There is another reason why the Jew is a good target for pro-jection. Those who suffer serious repression (perhaps to a neurotic degree) often feel alien to themselves. Swayed by unconscious turmoil, they feel strange and depersonalized. This ego-alien feeling makes them look for a projective target that is also strange and alien, for something as foreign to them as their own unconscious. What is wanted is an object that is strange and yet still human. Jews are such a group. Negroes are likewise. Social norms (stereotypes) tell the individual which qualities he should project upon one group, and which upon the other. We have already noted that sex debauchery is a more common charge against the Jews in Europe than in the United States. Here Negroes are available to absorb this particular accusation, along with charges of dirtiness and laziness. The Jew (connected historically with the founding of Christianity and with monotheism) is an especially good object for the projection of the Christian's own moral failings.

It must not be thought that the only available "projection screens" are Jews and Negroes. In many cases, Poles, Mexicans, big business, the Administration will do just as well. How often a citizen who cheats on his income tax sees Washington only as a great big bureaucratic inkblot teeming with graft and corruption! (Perhaps it is well here to repeat what we have previously said, that a "kernel of truth" in an accusation does not prove that prejudice is not involved. Most people are rational enough to seize, if they can, upon a plausible projection screen. The fact remains that a person still betrays his own guilt conflict by the type of accusation he makes, and by the alacrity and glee with which he makes it, and by the particular defects in the object that he notices and exaggerates.)

Let us consider a case of mutual accusation—of reciprocal ink-blots. Bettelheim, who was a prisoner in Nazi concentration camps, reports that Jewish prisoners and Gestapo guards in concentration camps regarded each other about the same way.

> Both believed that the members of the other group were sadistic, dirty, unintelligent, of an inferior race, and that they indulged in sexual perversion. Both groups accused each other of being interested only in material goods and of having no respect for ideals, or for moral and intellectual values.[4]

How could the same accusations be made on both sides? It would be hard to find two groups of people more different than Nazis and Jews. Their group characteristics, however computed (Chapter 6), could not be identical. We must rule out, then, the possibility that both views are accurate and realistic depictions. (And obviously not all of the traits ascribed could be true of all members of either group—the element of overgeneralization is, in any case, clearly present.)

The mutual accusation in part seems to signify: "I hate your group; I justify this hatred by declaring your group to be the antithesis of traditional German values." Since both Nazis and Jews had a common culture, and therefore a common reference group (Chapter 3), both paint the villain in the same way—as opposite to the cultural ideal.

Direct Projection

Take the Nazis' accusation that the Jews are "sadistic." Nothing could be more directly projective. Not only are the traditions of Jewish culture singularly devoid of sadism, but the circumstances of life under extreme persecution would prevent any sadistic behavior even if a member of the Jewish group had this impulse. On the other hand, the conspicuous pleasure many Nazis took in torturing Jews showed that sadism was, in fact, an approved SS policy.

Here is a clear instance of *direct projection*. An attribute that lies wholly within ourselves—and not at all in the other person— is nonetheless seen as existing in the other person. The protective significance of the device is evident: it is a conscience-soothing falsity. One can disapprove a quality that is evil—but can do so comfortably only if he perceives it as existing in others and not in himself. *Direct projection is a means of solving one's conflict by ascribing to another person (or group) emotions, motives, and be-*

*havior that actually belong to the person who projects them, and
not to the person who is blamed for them.*

It is important to understand the relation between direct projection and stereotype. Suppose there are unwanted traits in oneself
—perhaps greed, lust, laziness, and untidiness. What the sufferer
needs is a caricature of these attributes—a simon-pure incarnation
of these evils. He needs something so extreme that he need not
even suspect himself of being guilty. The Jew is therefore seen as
wholly concupiscent; the Negro as completely lazy; the Mexican
as filthy. One who holds such extreme stereotypes need not even
suspect himself of having these hated tendencies.

Direct projection can occur either in reference to quite specific
traits in oneself, or in reference to an over-all view that one has of
oneself. The specific tendency is illustrated in an experiment by
Sears, who found that certain men in a fraternity group tended to
attribute to other men the obstinacy and stinginess that they
themselves possessed to a high degree.[5]

The tendency to a generalized projection is seen in the clinical
observation that a person who has a low estimate of himself is likely
to have a low estimate of other people. This finding in therapeutic
work suggests that it may often be more effective to help an individual gain in self-esteem than to try to raise his respect for
others. Only people who are at peace with themselves in terms of
self-respect can be respectful of others. Hatred of other people
may be a mirrored reflection of self-hatred.[6]

The case of Adolf Hitler's hatred of the Jews offers as classical an
example of direct projection as we could hope to find. The following facts, pieced together from accounts of his early life, are important:

His father, an illegitimate son of a woman named Schickl-
gruber, was an intemperate retired custom's collector with whom
Adolf had many fights. His mother, hardworking, and dying
of cancer when Adolf was adolescent, was dear to him. He
was so attached to her that he may be said to have had a strong
Oedipus complex. His father and mother were second cousins
and required an episcopal dispensation for their marriage.
Later in life Hitler was strongly attached to his half-sister,
Angela. Still later he had his one great, passionate love affair
with Angela's daughter, Geli—his niece. The nature of this
relationship suggests incest. Geli was shot and killed (whether
suicide or murder, no one knows) just as she was about to break
off with Adolf. These facts are all of the unpleasant story that
needs to be told, to show that there were reasons enough for

Adolf to feel guilty (consciously or unconsciously) over the subject of incest.

Now, where does projection come in? By his own account, it was when he was 14 or 15, living alone and in great poverty and misery in Vienna, that his attention was called to the "Jewish problem." In his writings he blames the Jew in particular for sexual (including incestuous) misdeeds. In one passage in *Mein Kampf*, for example, he writes, "For hours the black-haired Jew boy, diabolic joy in his face, waits in ambush for the unsuspecting girl whom he defiles with his blood." Hitler was black-haired. His friends, in jest, called him Jewish. Writing of his leaving Vienna for Munich, he explained that he had grown to hate Vienna. "I detest the conglomeration of races . . . Jews and more Jews. To me the big city appeared as the personification of incest." Besides incest, all manner of other sexual misdeeds were attributed to Jews: prostitution and venereal disease (which was of special interest and repugnance to Adolf, judging from his writings). Though we need not go into the matter here, there is strong evidence that Hitler suffered a severe sexual perversion which must have obsessed him and made him loathe himself at times—had he not been able to loathe others for the same propensities.

From this evidence it seems clear that Hitler identified his own baser nature with the Jews, and in condemning the latter evaded the necessity of pointing the accusing finger at himself. The historical consequences of this particular instance of direct projection have been pointed out by Gertrud Kurth, who writes, "The torrent of apocalyptic horrors that engulfed six million Jews was unleashed in the futile endeavor to exterminate that incestuous, black-haired little monster that was Adolf Hitler's Mr. Hyde." [7]

Projection of this type (or of any type) solves no basic problems. It is merely a temporary, self-restorative trick. Why nature invented so maladaptive a mechanism is far from clear. It is essentially a neurotic device, and does not fundamentally relieve the sufferer's sense of guilt or establish a lasting self-respect. The hated scapegoat is merely a disguise for persistent and unrecognized self-hatred. A vicious circle is established. The more the sufferer hates himself, the more he hates the scapegoat. But the more he hates the scapegoat, the less sure he is of his logic and his innocence; hence the more guilt he has to project.[8]

The Mote-Beam Mechanism

It has been well argued by Ichheiser that to perceive qualities in others that they do not possess at all is quite pathological. At the same time, to magnify the defects (or virtues) in others that we ourselves possess, and which they too possess—perhaps only to a slight degree—is a more normal human failing.[9]

The mote-beam mechanism might be defined as *the process of exaggerating qualities in other people which both they and we possess, though we may not realize that we possess them.*

Most writers make no distinction whatever between this process and direct projection. They are indeed similar, but it is worthwhile to observe the distinction. Seldom is the "projection screen" completely devoid of the evil we attribute to it. Anyone can find certain Jews who are dishonest, certain Negroes who are lazy. Somewhere within these groups, therefore, the mote exists. What happens is that the person who views the inkblot seizes upon this detail (because it reflects his own conflict) and exaggerates its importance. By so doing he evades the necessity for beholding the beam in his own eye.

In the case of the mutual recriminations between Nazis and Jews, some of them reflect this mechanism. For example, most individuals on both sides undoubtedly had some repressed sex conflict. With special alacrity, therefore, they magnify the charge of perversion applied to the other group. Again, both sides contain individuals who are aware of their failure to live up to German intellectual ideals. They seize upon the same failure in the other side and there perceive gross lack of culture and patriotism.

Mote-beam projection, then, is a kind of "perceptual accentuation" (Chapter 10). We see more than is there. And we see it because it mirrors our own unconscious state of mind.

The difference between this and what we have called direct projection may be summarized with the aid of Pope's adage, "All looks yellow to the jaundiced eye." Taken by itself the statement refers to direct projection. But if we add the thought, "and all things that *are* yellow look more yellow to the jaundiced eye," we include also the mote-beam mechanism.

Complementary Projection

We come now to a distinctly different form of projection. It is less of a mirrored perception and more of a rationalized perception. It has to do with finding *causes* for our own troubled emotions. We might define complementary projection simply as *the process of explaining and justifying our own state of mind by reference to the imagined intentions and behavior of others.* To be a true instance of complementary projection, the description of intentions and behavior must be false. For if it is accurate, then the perception is realistic and no projection at all is involved.[10]

An experiment illustrates the operation of complementary projection. A group of children attending a party were shown photographs of strange men, and asked to tell about each—how friendly he was, how much they liked him, etc. Subsequently the children played a spine-chilling game of "murder" in the darkened house. Following this creepy experience they again characterized the photographs. Each of the strange men now took on a menacing appearance to the children. They seemed to be dangerous strangers. The children were, in effect, saying: *We* fear; therefore *they* threaten.[11]

Complementary projection has innumerable applications to the problem of prejudice, particularly to prejudice that has its roots in anxiety or low self-esteem. The timid housewife (who does not know the causes for her heavy burden of anxiety) fears tramps. She double-locks the doors against them, and regards all wayfarers with suspicion. She may also be an easy victim of bogey rumors. She can easily believe that the Negroes are hoarding ice picks with which to attack white people, or that the basement of that Catholic Church is full of guns. With so many menacing groups around, her anxiety, otherwise inexplicable, becomes to her mind rational and justified.

Returning once more to Bettelheim's report on the Nazis and Jews, both saw the other as "an inferior race." This particular rationalization can be regarded as a complementary projection. For one thing, the members of each group desired to enhance their self-esteem. To be high in status requires that somebody else be low. Hence the "inferior breed" of the other automatically supplies the need.

Conclusion

The last four chapters have been devoted to various aspects of the psychodynamics of prejudice. The processes described are the very pulse of irrationality in human nature. They represent the infantile, repressed, defensive, aggressive, and projective portions of unconscious mental life. An individual in whose character-structure these mechanisms are prominent can scarcely become a fully poised adult capable of making mature adjustments in his social relationships.

Important as these processes are in explaining prejudice, they must not be made to assume the whole weight. Cultural tradition, social norms, what the child is taught and how he is taught it, the parental model, semantic confusion, ignorance of group differences, the principle of category formation, and many other factors play a part. Most important of all is the way the individual weaves all these influences, including his unconscious conflicts and his psychodynamic reactions, into a total style of life. Our next task is to examine this *structural* aspect of the problem.

NOTES AND REFERENCES

1. The following material is drawn from S. A. STOUFFER, *et al.* *The American Soldier: Combat and Its Aftermath.* Princeton: Princeton Univ. Press, 1949, Vol. 2, Chapter 6.

2. FRANZISKA BAUMGARTEN. Der Benachteiligungskomplex. *Gesundheit und Wohlfahrt,* 1946, **9**, 463-476.

3. N. W. ACKERMAN AND MARIE JAHODA. *Anti-Semitism and Emotional Disorder.* New York: Harper, 1950, 58.

4. B. BETTELHEIM. Dynamism of anti-Semitism in Gentile and Jew. *Journal of Abnormal and Social Psychology,* 1947, **42**, 157.

5. R. R. SEARS. Experimental studies of projection, I. Attribution of traits. *Journal of Social Psychology,* 1936, **7**, 151-163.

6. ELIZABETH T. SHEERER. An analysis of the relationship between acceptance of and respect for self and acceptance and respect for others in ten counseling cases. *Journal of Consulting Psychology,* 1949, **13**, 169-175.

7. GERTRUD M. KURTH. The Jew and Adolf Hitler. *Psychoanalytic Quarterly,* 1947, **16**, 11-32.

8. The futility of projection is discussed by A. KARDINER AND L. OVESEY. *The Mark of Oppression.* New York: W. W. Norton, 1951. (See especially p. 297.)

9. G. ICHHEISER. Projection and the mote-beam mechanism. *Journal of Abnormal and Social Psychology,* 1947, **42**, 131-133.

10. The distinction between complementary and direct projection has been discussed by H. A. MURRAY. The effect of fear upon estimates of the maliciousness of other personalities. *Journal of Social Psychology,* 1933, **4**, 310-329. (Especially p. 313.)

11. *Ibid.*

Part VII

CHARACTER STRUCTURE

CHAPTER 25

THE PREJUDICED PERSONALITY

Prejudice, as we have seen, may become part of one's life tissue, suffusing character because it is essential to the economy of a life. It does not always act in this way, for some prejudices are merely conformative, mildly ethnocentric, and essentially unrelated to the personality as a whole (Chapter 17). But often it is organic, inseparable from the life process. This condition we shall now examine more closely.

Methods of Study

Two methods have proved fruitful in the study of character-conditioned prejudice, the *longitudinal* and the *cross-sectional*.

In the longitudinal approach the investigator attempts to trace back through a given life history factors that might account for the present pattern of prejudice. The technique of interviewing may be used, as in the California studies, or the technique of psychoanalysis, illustrated in the investigation by Ackerman and Jahoda. There is also the ingenious device employed by Gough, Harris, and Martin, who compared the present prejudice level of children with their mothers' ideas on child training, thus revealing situational factors presumably operating in the present prejudice. All these studies are described in Chapter 18.

The cross-sectional method attempts to find out what the contemporary prejudice pattern is like, asking especially how ethnic attitudes are related to other social attitudes and to one's outlook on life in general. Using this method, we uncover some interesting relationships. For example, Frenkel-Brunswik reports that highly prejudiced children tend to endorse the following beliefs (not one of which deals directly with ethnic matters):[1]

There is only one right way to do anything.

If a person does not watch out somebody will make a sucker out of him.

It would be better if teachers would be more strict.

Only people who are like myself have a right to be happy.

Girls should learn only things that are useful around the house.

There will always be war; it is part of human nature.

The position of the stars at the time of your birth tells your character and personality.

When the same method is applied to adults, similar results occur. Certain types of propositions are endorsed by highly prejudiced more often than by tolerant adults.[2]

The world is a hazardous place in which men are basically evil and dangerous.

We do not have enough discipline in our American way of life.

On the whole, I am more afraid of swindlers than I am of gangsters.

At first sight these propositions seem to have nothing to do with prejudice. Yet it is proved that all of them have. This finding can only mean that prejudice is frequently woven firmly into a style of life.

Functional Prejudice

In all cases of intense character-conditioned prejudice a common factor emerges which Newcomb has called "threat orientation." [3] Underlying insecurity seems to lie at the root of the personality. The individual cannot face the world unflinchingly and in a forthright manner. He seems fearful of himself, of his own instincts, of his own consciousness, of change, and of his social environment. Since he can live in comfort neither with himself nor with others, he is forced to organize his whole style of living, including his social attitudes, to fit his crippled condition. It is not his specific social attitudes that are malformed to start with; it is rather his own ego that is crippled.

The crutch he needs must perform several functions. It must give reassurance for past failures, safe guidance for present conduct, and ensure confidence in facing the future. While prejudice by itself does not do all these things, it develops as an important incident in the total protective adjustment.

To be sure, not all character-conditioned prejudice serves precisely the same purposes in every prejudiced personality, for "threat orientation" differs in nature from person to person. In some, for example, it may be particularly related to unresolved infantile conflicts with parents or siblings, in others to persistent failure in later years. But in any case, we are likely to find a picture of ego-alienation, longing for definiteness, for safety, for authority.

Personalities which for any reason feel threatened are likely to evolve similar patterns of accommodation to life in general.

An essential feature of this pattern is *repression*. Since the person cannot in his conscious life face and master the conflicts presented to him, he represses them in whole or in part. They are fragmented, forgotten, not faced. The ego simply fails to integrate the myriad of impulses that arise within the personality and the myriad of environmental presses without. This failure engenders feelings of insecurity, and these feelings engender, in turn, repression.

Thus an outstanding result of studies of bigoted personalities seems to be the discovery of a sharp cleavage between conscious and unconscious layers. In a study of anti-Semitic college girls they appeared on the surface to be charming, happy, well-adjusted, and entirely normal girls. They were polite, moral, and seemed devoted to parents and friends. This was what an ordinary observer would see. But probing deeper (with the aid of projective tests, interviews, case histories), these girls were found to be very different. Underneath the conventional exterior there lurked intense anxiety, much buried hatred toward parents, destructive and cruel impulses. For tolerant college students, however, the same cleavage did not exist. Their lives were more of a piece. Repressions were fewer and milder. The *persona* they presented to the world was not a mask but was their true personality.[4] Having few repressions, they suffered no ego-alienation, and facing their own calamities frankly, they needed no projection screen.

This study, as well as others, reveals that the consequences of such repression are likely to be the following:

Ambivalence toward parents
Moralism
Dichotomization
A need for definiteness
Externalization of conflict
Institutionalism
Authoritarianism

All of these characteristics can be regarded as devices to bolster a weak ego unable to face its conflicts squarely and unflinchingly. They are accordingly the earmarks of a personality in whom prejudice is functionally important.

Ambivalence toward Parents

In the study of anti-Semitic women students cited above, the authors found that "without exception these girls declared that they liked their parents." Yet in their interpretation of pictures (Thematic Apperception Test), a preponderance of responses to parental figures accused them of meanness and cruelty, and betrayed jealousy, suspicion, and hostility on the part of the daughter. By contrast, the unprejudiced subjects in the same test were much more critical of their parents when they discussed them openly with the interviewer, but showed less animosity in the projective tests.[5] The sentiments of these latter girls toward their parents was more *differentiated*. That is to say, they saw their parents' faults and openly criticized them, but they also saw their virtues, and on the whole got along pleasantly enough with them. The prejudiced girls were torn: on the surface all was sweetness and light, and this view was held up to public gaze; but deeper down there was often vigorous protest. The sentiment had become bifurcated. The anti-Semitic girls had more fantasies of their parents' death.

In spite of this buried animosity there seems to be less ideological friction between prejudiced youth and their parents. As children they take over the parents' views, especially their ethnic attitudes. They do so because ideological imitation is demanded and rewarded. In Chapter 18 we examined the conditions of child training that are likely to prevail in prejudiced homes. There we saw that the themes of obedience, punishment, actual or threatened rejection loom large. A relationship of power rather than love prevails. In such circumstances it is often difficult for the child to identify fully with the parent because his affectional needs are not met. He learns through imitation, coerced by reward, punishment, reproof. He cannot fully accept himself and his failings, but must be ever on guard against slips from grace. In such a family situation a child never knows just were he stands. A threat hangs over him at every step.

Moralism

This anxiety is reflected in the rigidly moralistic view that most prejudiced personalities take. Strict insistence on cleanliness, good manners, conventions is more common among them than among tolerant people. When asked the question, "What is the most embarrassing experience?" anti-Semitic girls responded in terms of violations of mores and conventions in public. Whereas nonprejudiced girls spoke more often of inadequacy in personal relations, such as failing to live up to a friend's expectation. Also, anti-Semitic girls tend to be harsh in their moral judgments of others. One said, "I would sentence any striker to 50 years in the penitentiary." Tolerant subjects, by contrast, show much greater leniency toward transgression of the mores. They are less condemnatory of social misdemeanors, including violations of sexual standards. They tolerate human weakness just as they tolerate minority groups.

Studies with children show the same tendencies. When asked what makes for a perfect boy or girl, the prejudiced children mentioned usually purity, cleanliness, good manners; the more liberal children are often content to mention merely companionship and good fun.[6]

The Nazis were noted for their emphasis upon conventional virtues. Hitler preached and in many respects practised asceticism. Overt sex perversion was violently condemned, sometimes punished with death. A rigid protocol dominated every phase of military and social life. The Jews were constantly accused of violating conventional codes—with their dirtiness, miserliness, dishonesty, immorality. But while pretentious moralism ran high, there seemed to be little integration with private conduct. It was sham propriety, illustrated by the urge to make all expropriation and torture of the Jews appear "legal."

The genetic theory underlying such scrupulosity has to do with the child's early failure to live with his own impulses. Suppose he is punished and made to feel guilty whenever he soils himself, whenever he is found handling his genitals (we recall that mothers of prejudiced children are more likely to punish the child for this offense), whenever he has a temper tantrum, whenever he strikes his parent. A child who finds his every impulse wicked—and feels that he is unloved when he gives way to it—is likely to grow up hating himself for his many transgressions. He carries a burden of infantile guilt. As a consequence, when he sees any lapses from the conventional code in others he grows anxious. He wishes to punish the transgressor, just as he himself was punished. He develops a dread of the very impulses that trouble him. When a person grows overconcerned with sin in others, the tendency may be viewed as a "reaction formation." Having had to fight unholy impulses in himself, he cannot be permissive and lenient toward others.

The tolerant individual, by contrast, seems to have learned how to accept socially tabooed impulses early in life. He is not afraid of his own instincts; he is not a prude; he views bodily functions in a natural way. He knows that anyone may fall from grace. In his own upbringing his parents were skillful in teaching him the socially correct line of conduct without withdrawing their love when he failed to toe this line. The tolerant individual, having learned to accept the evil in his nature, does not grow anxious and fearful whenever he sees (or imagines) similar evil in others. His view is humane, compassionate, understanding.

Moralism is only surface compliance; it does not solve the conflicts within. It is tense, compulsive, projective. True morality is more relaxed, integral, and congruent with the life pattern as a whole.

Dichotomization

We have reported that prejudiced children, more often than nonprejudiced, hold "there are only two kinds of people: the weak and the strong"; also, "there is only one right way to do anything." Prejudiced adults show the same tendency to bifurcation. Males with ethnic bias more often subscribe to the proposition: "There are only two kinds of women: the pure and the bad."

Those who tend to dichotomize in their cognitive operations (Chapter 10) are the very people who accentuate the distinction between in-group and out-group. They would *not* agree with the sentiment expressed in the familar bit of doggerel:

> There is so much good in the worst of us,
> So much bad in the best of us,
> That it scarcely behooves any of us
> To talk about the rest of us.

The functional significance of "two-valued logic" for the prejudiced person is not far to seek. We have noted his failure to accept the crisscross of good and bad in his own nature. He is therefore chronically sensitized to right and wrong. This inner bifurcation becomes projected upon the outer world. He gives approval or disapproval categorically.

Need for Definiteness

In Chapter 10 we asserted that one of the most important psychological discoveries of recent years is that the dynamics of prejudice tend to parallel the dynamics of cognition. That is to say, the style of thinking that is characteristic of prejudice is a reflection, by and large, of the prejudiced person's way of thinking about *anything*. We have already made the point in connection with the dichotomizing tendency. We may now underline it by citing a series of experiments related to the matter of "tolerance for ambiguity."

An experimenter placed his subjects in a dark room. Only a point of light was visible. Without any visual anchorage or habits to guide them, all subjects under such circumstances saw the light sway in various directions. (Probably internal conditions of the retina or brain are responsible.) The experimenter discovered, however, that prejudiced people soon established a norm for themselves. That is, they reported the light as moving in a constant direction from trial to trial and to a constant number of inches. They require stability, and manufacture it when it does not objectively exist. Tolerant people, by contrast, tend to take longer to establish a norm for themselves. That is, for a longer period of trials they could tolerate the ambiguity of the situation.[7]

Another experimenter studied memory traces in people with high and with low prejudice. He employed a drawing of a truncated pyramid, as shown in Figure 13.[8]

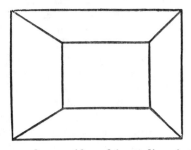

FIG. 13. Truncated pyramid used in studies of memory traces.

Immediately after looking at the design for a brief time the subjects were asked to draw it from memory.

About 40 percent of both groups tended to draw a symmetrical figure, equalizing the two margins of the drawing. This type of symmetrization is normal enough, since our memories do tend to simplify and to reach a level of "better Gestalt." But what is especially interesting is that after a four-week interval, many more of the highly prejudiced subjects equalized the margins. Sixty-two percent of the high-prejudiced and only 34 percent of the low-prejudiced group did so.

Here it seems as though the highly prejudiced could not for long tolerate the ambiguity of the design; they needed a firm, simple, categorical memory. On the other hand, those who were low in prejudice seemed to say in effect, "I know this is a truncated pyramid, but I also know it is not as simple as it might be; there is something individual and unusual about it."

In short, while the low in prejudice also tend to form simplified memory traces, they are relatively better able to hold in mind what William James called "feelings of but. . . ."

Another manifestation of the need for definiteness is encountered in the way prejudiced persons cling to past solutions. If they are shown a definite line drawing of a cat, and if in a series of subsequent brief exposures this picture gradually undergoes transformation until the line drawing of a dog appears, the more prejudiced subjects *cling* to the image of the cat for a longer time. They do not see the change so quickly; nor do they report, "I don't know what it is." [9]

From this experiment we see that prejudiced people are more given to *perseveration,* which means that old and tried solutions are considered to provide safe anchorage. The experiment also discloses an interesting related phenomenon. Prejudiced people seem afraid to say "I don't know." To do so would cast them adrift from their cognitive anchor. This finding is duplicated in widely different investigations. In one, Rokeach asked his subjects in an experiment dealing with the recognition of names and faces to tell him which name should be associated with which face. Those high in prejudice made many erroneous guesses, while those low in prejudice often admitted defeat and refused to guess. [10] Roper, studying the results of a public opinion poll, reports that individuals high in anti-Semitism give a low proportion of "Don't know" responses when asked their opinions on current events. [11] Prejudiced people, it seems, feel more secure when they "know the answers."

The need for definiteness is likely to lead to a constriction of cognitive processes. The individual fails to see all relevant sides to his problem. Rokeach labels the resulting type of solution "narrow-minded." An experiment illustrates the process.

The ten following concepts were presented in alphabetical order to college freshmen: *Buddhism, Capitalism, Catholicism, Christianity, Communism, Democracy, Fascism, Judaism, Protestantism, Socialism.* The students were asked to tell in what way any or all of these concepts were interrelated. Rokeach summarizes the results as follows:

"Analysis revealed that the cognitive organization as represented by the descriptions could be ordered along a single continuum ranging from *comprehensive* to *isolated* to *narrow.* A *comprehensive* organization is one in which all 10 concepts are organized into a single whole (e.g., 'all are beliefs'). An *isolated* organization is one in which the 10 concepts are broken down into two or more substructures with little or no inter-communication among substructures (e.g., 'Five are religions. Five are governments'). A *narrow* organization is one in which one or more of the parts objectively present is omitted from the description, the remaining parts being organized into one or more substructures (e.g., 'Only Buddhism, Catholicism, Christianity, Judaism, and Protestantism are related because they all believe in God')." [12]

It turned out to a significant degree that those high in prejudice gave *narrow* groupings, i.e., left out some of the relevant items; those low in prejudice took them all into account and gave *comprehensive* groupings; while those intermediate in prejudice inclined to favor *isolated* groupings.

The same sort of constrictedness in thinking is reported by Reichard, who notes that prejudiced subjects taking the Rorschach test tend to give responses that are more inhibited, compulsively overmeticulous, as compared with other groups who are more given to seeing wholes and are more productive of associations.[13]

All these experiments point in the same direction. Prejudiced people demand clear-cut structure in their world, even if it is a narrow and inadequate structure. Where there is no order they impose it. When new solutions are called for they cling to tried and tested habits. Wherever possible they latch onto what is familiar, safe, simple, definite.

There are at least two theories as to why this intolerance of ambiguity exists. Both may be right. One holds that the self-image of prejudiced persons is badly confused. From early life they have never been able to integrate their natures; the result is that the ego itself does not provide a fixed anchorage point. By compensation, therefore, the individual must find outer definiteness to guide him. There is no inner definiteness.

The other theory, slightly more complex, holds that when they were children prejudiced individuals suffered much deprivation. Many things were forbidden. They therefore grew apprehensive of delay and gratifications, for delay might mean deprivation. They therefore developed an urge for quick and definite answers. To think abstractly is to risk ambiguity and uncertainty. Better not hesitate; better adopt concrete, if rigid, modes of thinking. In favor of this view, we recall the evidence that prejudiced people do seem more susceptible to frustration (p. 347). Their low tolerance may well be the reason they want always to see the ground on which they stand, for only with a clearly structured perceptual field can they avoid the threat of frustration.

Externalization

In the last chapter we saw that prejudiced people are given to projection, to seeing qualities in others that they should see in themselves but do not. In fact, all along the line they seem defective in self-insight.[14]

To the prejudiced person things seem to happen "out there." He has no control over his destiny. He believes, for example, that "although many people may scoff, it may be shown that astrology can explain a lot of things." Tolerant people, by contrast, tend to believe that our fate lies not in our stars, but in ourselves.[15]

Prejudiced girls, in telling stories from pictures (Thematic Apperception Test) more often see the events transpiring without the active participation of the heroine. The action is determined by fate (for example, the heroine's fiancé is killed in battle), and not by herself. When asked the question, "what would drive a person nuts?" prejudiced subjects respond in terms of threats from *without* or else say something like, "ideas which keep running through the head." Both replies indicate uncontrolled external agencies. It is not one's own shortcomings or actions that could "drive one nuts." [16]

To explain this tendency we may again refer to ego-alienation as an underlying factor. It is easier and safer for a person in inner conflict to avoid self-reference. It is better to think of things happening *to* him rather than as caused *by* him. Extropunitiveness, as a trait, is one expression of this generalized tendency. The relation to group prejudice is obvious: it is not *I* who hates and injures others; it is *they* who hate and injure me.

Institutionalism

The person with character-conditioned prejudice likes order, but especially *social* order. In his clear-cut institutional memberships, he finds the safety and the definiteness he needs. Lodges, schools, churches, the nation, may serve as a defense against the disquiet in his personal life. To lean on them saves him from leaning on himself.

Research shows that, by and large, prejudiced people are more devoted to institutions than are the unprejudiced. Anti-Semitic college girls are more wrapped up in their sororities; they are more institutionally religious; they are more intensely "patriotic." Asked "What is the most awe-inspiring experience?" they usually answer in terms of external patriotic and religious events.[17]

Many studies have discovered a close link between prejudice

and "patriotism." As the following chapter will show, extreme bigots are almost always super-patriots. The tie between nationalism and persecution of minority groups was clearly seen in Nazi Germany. It seems to hold for other countries as well. One investigation, conducted by Nancy C. Morse and F. H. Allport in a suburban American community, among middle-class people, is particularly revealing.[18]

These investigators undertook the ambitious task of discovering which of several alleged causes of anti-Semitism was in fact most outstanding and demonstrable. The method was elaborate, requiring a 92-page booklet of tests, scales, questionnaires. The collaboration of 175 subjects was secured by paying into the treasury of their local clubs a certain amount of money for each booklet completed and returned.

First of all, the extensive instrument measured several aspects of anti-Semitism: how much aversion the subjects felt to Jews; how much they would say against them (antilocution); and how far they would actually go in hostile and discriminative behavior (antiaction).

It then tested several hypotheses, such as the following: that anti-Semitism would be associated with insecurity or fear of the future; with actual economic need or uncertainty; with feelings of frustration; with belief in a Jewish "essence"; with "national involvement."

This last variable was measured by a series of propositions asking for agreement or disagreement, one of these being, "Whereas some people feel that they are citizens of the world, that they belong to mankind and not to any one nation, I, for my part, feel that I am, first, last, and always, an American."

By the method employed the investigators discovered a high degree of anti-Semitism among their subjects. In only 10 percent did it seem wholly absent. In about 16 percent it reached an extreme, almost violent, degree.

While there was some evidence that insecurity and frustration do play a part in the nexus of anti-Semitism, the investigators find proof that the *most important single factor* is "national involvement." Only this factor stands up when all other variables are held constant. It alone meets the criterion of "unique covariation" with prejudice. Important too is the "belief in essence"—that Jews at bottom are in some way utterly unlike other people. But this belief is effectively related to prejudice only if strongly nationalistic views are likewise present. Thus "patriotism" may be a mask for bigotry.

The findings of this research are important. It will be noted that the anti-Semite is not merely a bundle of negative attitudes. Rather he is trying to *do* something: namely, to find an island of institutional safety and security. The nation is the island he selects. It is a positive anchorage; it is *his* country right or wrong; it is higher than humanity; more desirable than a world state. It has the definiteness he needs. The research establishes the fact that the higher the degree of nationalism, the higher the anti-Semitism.

Note the emphasis here is upon positive security. Anti-Semitism is not merely the shadow that fear and anxiety cast. Plenty of apprehensive and frustrated people never develop into anti-Semites. What is important is the way fear and frustration are handled. The *institutionalistic* way—especially the nationalistic —seems to be the nub of the matter.

What happens is that the prejudiced person defines "nation" to fit his needs (cf. Fig. 1, p. 36). The nation is first of all a protection (the chief protection) of *him* as an individual. It is his in-group. He sees no contradiction in ruling out of its beneficent orbit those whom he regards as threatening intruders and enemies (namely, American minorities). What is more, the nation stands for the *status quo*. It is a conservative agent; within it are all the devices for safe living that he approves. His nationalism is a form of conservatism. According to his definition, the nation is that which resists change. It follows that he distrusts liberals, reformers, supporters of the Bill of Rights, and other "commies": they threaten to change his safe conception of what the nation means.[19]

Authoritarianism

Living in a democracy is a higgledy-piggledy affair. Finding it so, prejudiced people sometimes declare that America should not be a democracy, but merely a "republic." The consequences of personal freedom they find unpredictable. Individuality makes for indefiniteness, disorderliness, and change. It is easier to live in a defined hierarchy where people are types, and where groups are not constantly shifting and dissolving.

To avoid such slipperiness the prejudiced person looks for hierarchy in society. Power arrangements are definite—something he can understand and count on. He likes authority, and says that what America needs is "more discipline." By discipline, of course, he means *outer* discipline, preferring, so to speak, to see people's backbones on the outside rather than on the inside. When students are asked to list the names of great people they most admired, prejudiced students usually gave names of leaders who had exercised power and control over others (Napoleon, Bismark) whereas the unprejudiced listed, more typically, artists, humanitarians, scientists (Lincoln, Einstein).[20]

This need for authority reflects a deep distrust of human beings. Earlier in this chapter we noted the tendency of prejudiced people to agree that "the world is a hazardous place where men are basically evil and dangerous." Now, the essential philosophy of democracy is the reverse. It tells us to trust a person until he proves himself untrustworthy. The prejudiced person does the opposite. He distrusts every person until he proves himself trustworthy.

The same suspicion is seen in responses to the following question: "If I were to express a greater fear of one of the following types of criminals I would say that I am more afraid of (a) gangsters, (b) swindlers." About half of the respondents choose one, and half the other alternative. But those who are more afraid of *swindlers* have higher prejudice scores in general. They feel more threatened by trickery than by direct physical attack. Ordinarily it might seem that fear of gangsters (physical threat) is a more natural and normal type of fear—and it is this that unprejudiced people report.[21]

To the prejudiced person the best way to control these suspicions is to have an orderly, authoritative, powerful society. Strong nationalism is a good thing. Hitler and Mussolini weren't so wrong. What America needs is a strong leader—a man on horseback!

We have evidence that the authoritarian pattern may become set at an early age. Prejudiced children are more likely than others to believe that "teachers should tell children what to do and not worry about what the children want." Even by the age of seven the same type of child is distressed and at loose ends unless the teacher gives him instructions what to do and makes his assignments definite and authoritative.[22]

Discussion

Our portrait of the prejudiced personality (called by some authors "the authoritarian personality") is based largely on the results of recent research. While the outlines of the pattern are clear, the weighting and interlocking of evidence are not yet complete. Contrasting with the authoritarian type, investigators report an opposite pattern of correlated qualities that comprise what is sometimes called a "democratic," a "mature," a "productive," or a "self-actualizing" personality.[23] This pattern will be examined more fully in Chapter 27.

Most of the research underlying this comparison is based on the study of extreme or contrasting groups of subjects—those having very high or very low prejudice scores.   Median or "average" subjects are usually discarded.   This procedure is defensible, but it has the disadvantage of overemphasizing types.   We are likely to forget that there are plenty of mixed or run-of-the-mill personalities in whom prejudice does not follow the ideal pattern here depicted.

There is a further methodological weakness in research to date. Most of it takes only one starting point.   It creates a cluster of high-prejudice and one of low-prejudice subjects, and then discovers, for example, that the former shows greater intolerance for ambiguity in perceptual or problem-solving tasks.   It does not use the desirable reverse control which would be to take a cluster of subjects who have intolerance for ambiguity and then discover whether this group has more ethnic prejudice.   There should be a two-way demonstration of the correlations claimed, before we can feel entirely sure.

But in spite of these weaknesses—due largely to the youthfulness of this area of research—we cannot possibly explain away the trends reported in this chapter.   Our picture may be . oversharp and may later need modification and supplementation, but the basic fact is firmly established—prejudice is more than an incident in many lives; it is often lockstitched into the very fabric of personality.   In such cases it cannot be extracted by tweezers.   To change it, the whole pattern of life would have to be altered.

NOTES AND REFERENCES

1. ELSE FRENKEL-BRUNSWIK. A study of prejudice in children. *Human Relations,* 1948, **1**, 295-306.

2. G. W. ALLPORT AND B. M. KRAMER. Some roots of prejudice. *Journal of Psychology,* 1946, **22**, 9-39.

3. T. M. NEWCOMB. *Social Psychology.* New York: Dryden, 1950, 588.

4. ELSE FRENKEL-BRUNSWIK AND R. N. SANFORD. Some personality factors in anti-Semitism. *Journal of Psychology,* 1945, **20**, 271-291.

5. *Ibid.*

6. See note #1 above.

7. J. BLOCK AND JEANNE BLOCK. An investigation of the relationship between intolerance of ambiguity and ethnocentrism. *Journal of Personality,* 1951, **19**, 303-311.

8. J. Fisher. The memory process and certain psychosocial attitudes, with special reference to the law of Prägnanz. *Journal of Personality,* 1951, **19**, 406-420.

9. Else Frenkel-Brunswik. Intolerance of ambiguity as an emotional and perceptual personality variable. *Journal of Personality,* 1949, **18**, 108-143.

The tendency toward useless perseveration in people with high prejudice is clearly demonstrated in the experiments on problem-solving conducted by M. Rokeach. Generalized mental rigidity as a factor in ethnocentrism. *Journal of Abnormal and Social Psychology,* 1948, **43**, 259-278.

10. M. Rokeach. Attitude as a determinant of distortions in recall. *Journal of Abnormal and Social Psychology,* 1952, **47**, Supplement, 482-488.

11. E. Roper. United States anti-Semites. *Fortune,* February 1946, 257 ff.

12. M. Rokeach. A method for studying individual differences in narrow-mindedness. *Journal of Personality,* 1951, **20**, 219-233; also, "Narrow-mindedness" and personality, *Journal of Personality,* 1951, **20**, 234-251.

13. S. Reichard. Rorschach study of prejudiced personality. *American Journal of Orthopsychiatry,* 1948, **18**, 280-286.

14. Considerable evidence is contained in T. W. Adorno, et al., *The Authoritarian Personality.* New York: Harper, 1950; also in G. W. Allport and B. M. Kramer, *op. cit.*

15. Else Frenkel-Brunswik and R. N. Sanford. The anti-Semitic personality: a research report. In E. Simmel (Ed.), *Anti-Semitism: A Social Disease.* New York: International Universities Press, 1948, 96-124.

16. *Ibid.*

17. See note #4 above.

18. Nancy C. Morse and F. H. Allport. The causation of anti-Semitism: an investigation of seven hypotheses. *Journal of Psychology,* 1952, **34**, 197-233.

19. Other studies confirm the correlation between prejudice and political-economic and religious conservatism. See, e.g., R. Stagner. Studies of aggressive social attitudes. *Journal of Social Psychology,* 1944, **20**, 109-140.

20. See note #4 above.

21. G. W. Allport and B. M. Kramer. *Op. cit.*

22. B. J. Kutner. *Patterns of Mental Functioning Associated with Prejudice in Children.* (Unpublished.) Cambridge: Harvard College Library, 1950.

23. The fullest and most standard comparison of these two basic types of personality is contained in T. W. Adorno, et al., *op. cit.* Likewise relevant are the discussions in E. Fromm, *Man for Himself,* New York: Rinehart, 1947; and in two articles by A. H. Maslow, The authoritarian character structure. *Journal of Social Psychology,* 1943, **18**, 401-411; Self-actualizing people: a study of psychological health. *Personality Symposium,* 1949, **1**, 11-34.

Demagogues play up false issues to divert public attention from true issues. Not all of them select the alleged misconduct of minority groups as their false issue—but a great many do so. What they say appeals particularly to the authoritarian type of personality described in the preceding chapter.

It has been estimated that there are ten million followers of racist demagogues in the United States. The estimate is, however, hazardous and probably too high, for not everyone who attends an agitator's meeting is a follower. However that may be, in the year 1949 there were, according to Forster, forty-nine anti-Semitic periodicals in the United States, and over sixty organizations with an anti-Semitic record.[1] Add to this array periodicals and organizations that specialize in anti-Catholicism and in anti-Negroism—and the total, in spite of overlapping, is impressive.

Sample Materials

The outpouring from the agitator's tongue and pen has a curiously constant quality, though this quality defies easy definition. The following excerpts from a "Christian Nationalist" meeting in 1948 are typical:

> We're gathered together from the corners of America for the sole purpose of taking the steps necessary to beat back the wave of materialism, the tidal waves of the evil force that threaten to engulf our beloved nation, the United States of America. We have assembled under the banner of Jesus Christ and the banner of our American Republic, the Cross and the Flag, to demonstrate to the international financiers of Wall Street, the international Communists of Moscow and the international Jewish terrorists throughout the world, that they have failed. The political party that we are creating is a monument to the fact that resistance to evil, resistance to slavery, resistance to godless Communism still lives in the world.

Why were not the American people told that 90 million dollars of Marshall Plan funds were to be paid to the international banking houses to feed and fatten the purses of the black marketeers and the socialist racketeers who are destroying Christianity throughout Europe and who would destroy it here if we give them a chance? Under the bipartisan foreign policy we were burdened with the secret deals and the secret promises of our now dead former dictator, Franklin Delano Roosevelt! Under the bipartisan foreign policy we became guilty of allowing the satanic Morgenthau policy to be imposed upon the German people. Millions of Christian women and children being deliberately starved. Now why were not the American people told that this Morgenthau policy was invented by a group of power mad sadistic, pro-Communistic Jews who wanted to destroy the German people so that the Soviet armies could occupy and enslave all of Christian Europe?

In searching the platforms of the old political parties for a solution to the problems of international Jewish conspiracy, and the problem of Communist Jewish treason, and the problem of Zionist Jewish terrorism, the only words we found was a wailing cry of sympathy because of the work that the old political parties had done in creating the so-called Jewish state in Palestine. We saw no mention of the Jewish gestapos in America that coerce and smear American citizens who stand and speak for Christian Americanism. We saw no mention of the Communist Jews who have infiltrated our government for the purpose of preparing the way for regimentation and slavery in a Communist America. We saw no condemnation of the dual allegiance practiced by the Zionist Jews who milk America to arm a foreign army. We saw no condemnation of the Jewish terror gangs that stalk the streets of America for the purpose of depriving Christian Americans of their rights of free speech and assembly.

It's the purpose of the Christian Nationalist Party to outlaw the Communist Party in America, as a crime against all that is decent, as a crime against the American government, and as a crime against all things that we Christian Nationalists hold dear. We intend to throw into the jails of the United States every member of the Communist party, every member of the communist brotherhood and every person who puts the love of Josef Stalin ahead of his love for the stars and stripes of America and the Constitution of the United States.

Now all of these people that are being exposed in Washington were students of Felix Frankfurter, I think it's about time we find out what he's teaching these fellows at Harvard University if they all turn out to be Communist spies when he gets through with them. And he sits on the Supreme Court of the United States. Now how can our government be safe when these people remain in positions of power and importance in Washington, D.C. It's time that we have a cleansing of the government in the United States and we're organizing the Christian Nationalist Party to clean out the rats who have taken over our government.

Now we're not demagogic about the Negro problem. We're going to speak the truth, we're going to speak what we believe, we're going to speak what is the only solution of the problem of black and white mixture in the United States. We advocate a Constitutional amendment making segregation of the black and white races a law of the United States of America. And we advocate making it a federal crime for intermarriage between the black and the white races!

I shall tell a little story I heard the other day when I was down in Jackson, Mississippi, meeting with some of my good friends there. A Negro had been up to St. Louis and married a white woman and he came back to Jackson, Mississippi and the boys cornered him on the street and said, "Mose, you can't stay here in this town with that white woman. We don't allow niggers to go around with white women, to marry white women, you know." And he said, "Boss, you is wrong as wrong can be, that woman is half Yankee and half Jew, she ain't got a drap of white blood in her."

Communists on the right, Communists on the left, out to liquidate Father Coughlin, Charles Lindbergh, Martin Dies, Burton Wheeler, Gerald Smith. Threaten, incite them, persecute them, ridicule them, DESTROY them, take them out of circulation, and by the Grace of God I refuse to go out of circulation. I was right on the Dies Committee, I was right on Alger Hiss, I was right on Stettinius, I was right on the United Nations, I was right . . . on Eleanor Roosevelt!

Never have business men been ruined, never have more men and women been abused, shaken down, trampled on by the presidential household, equal with what has been practised over the last fifteen years by that family of cut-throats, charlatans, Stalin appeasers, warmongers, known as the Roosevelts! God save America from the Roosevelts!

At first sight, this concoction seems to defy analysis.
The obvious motif is hatred. Mentioned as hated villains in this relatively short tirade are: materialism, international finan-

ciers, Jews, communists, black marketeers, socialists, Morgenthau, Soviet armies, Zionists, Felix Frankfurter, Harvard University, Negroes, Alger Hiss, the then Secretary of State Stettinius, former President Roosevelt, Mrs. Roosevelt, and the Roosevelt family. The leading devil seems to be the Jews, who are mentioned more often and in more combinations than any other malefactors. There is, in addition, a peculiarly fierce venom reserved for the Roosevelts. Catholics are not condemned—for in a large urban gathering there might be many Catholics in the audience, and the demagogue may be bidding for their support.

We learn from this diversified animus (as we learned from our statistical analysis in Chapter 5) that hatred for minority groups does not stand alone. The hatred is generalized. Whatever is sensed as a threat is hated.

The threat is never clearly defined. But underlying the abuse appears one fairly evident theme—namely, fear of liberalism or social change. The Roosevelts are above all else a symbol of change—threatening especially conservative patterns of economic life and race relations. Intellectualism (the symbol here being Harvard University) is hated, for it too brings about change, and at the same time intensifies the inferiority feelings of anti-intellectuals. Socialism and communism bring about change. An improvement in the condition of the Negro would do so likewise. Jews have always been associated with venture, risk, and fringe values (Chapter 15). Authoritarian personalities cannot face all this indefiniteness, unconventionality, and loss of familiar anchorage (Chapter 25).

Their symbols of security are no less interesting than their symbols of dread. Mentioned as idols are: Jesus Christ, the banner of the American Republic, the Cross and the Flag, Father Coughlin, Charles Lindbergh, Martin Dies, Burton Wheeler, Gerald K. Smith. In portions of the speech not printed here, there were favorable references to Paul Revere, Nathan Hale, Lincoln and Lee, and to George Washington—"the mightiest Christian Nationalist of all time." As perceived by the speaker and auditors, these idols are all symbols of conservatism, standing for nationalism, isolationism, anti-Semitism, or a conventional religion which serves as the ultimate island of safety for institutionalists (Chapter 28).

Having learned from this sample speech what some of the negative and positive symbols are, and how they reflect above all else the theme of dread and insecurity, let us consider the appeal in more detail. One demagogic speech is much like another. It is the pattern that is important.

The Program of the Demagogue

In their volume *Prophets of Deceit,* Lowenthal and Guterman have analyzed a large number of similar speeches and tracts. There is a sameness of protest and hatred in all of them. What the demagogue is saying seems to boil down to the following points:[2]

You've been cheated. Your social position is insecure because of the machinations of Jews, New Dealers, communists, and other agents of change. Sincere and plain folk like us are always dupes. We must do something.

There is widespread conspiracy against us. It is being engineered by devils—by Wall Street, Jewish bankers, internationalists, the State Department. We must do something.

The conspirators are sexually corrupt too. They "roll in wealth, bathe in liquor, surround themselves with the seduced daughters of America." "Oriental erotics debauch youth for the purpose of wrecking gentile morale." Aliens enjoy all the forbidden fruit.

Our present government is corrupt. The two-party system is a sham. Democracy is a "trick word." "Liberalism is anarchy." Civil liberties are "silly liberties." We cannot be universalistic in our ethics. We must look out for ourselves.

Doom is just around the corner. Look at the "Nudeal communistic confiscatory taxation," at the CIO and radical AF of L unions. They and the Jews are rapidly taking power. There will be immediate revolutionary violence. We must do something.

Capitalism and communism both threaten us. After all, atheistic communism was originally spawned in Jewish capitalism and Jewish intellectualism.

We can't trust the foreigners. Internationalism is a threat. But we can't trust our own government either. Alien termites bore within. Washington is a "Bolshevik rat's nest."

Our enemies are low animals: reptiles, insects, germs, subhuman. Extermination is called for; we must do something.

There is no middle ground. The world is divided. Those who are not for us are against us. It is a war between haves and have-nots; between true Americans and "foreigners." "The Talmudic philosophy of Europe-Asia-Africa and Nudeal is directly opposite that of Christian."

There must be no polluting of blood. We must keep racially pure and elite. Vile contamination comes from dealing at all with the moral lepers of liberalism.

But with disaster around the corner what can you do? Poor, simple, sincere people need a leader. Behold I am he. It isn't the American nation that is wrong; it is the corrupt men in office. Change the personnel. I am available. I'll change the whole smelly mess. You'll have a happier and safe life.

The situation is too urgent to permit the luxury of thought. Just give me your money, and I'll tell you later what to do.

Everybody is against me. I am your martyr. The press, the Jews, the stinking bureaucrats are trying to shut me up. Enemies plot against my life, but God will protect me. I'll lead you. And I'll ignite the public mind everywhere. And I'll liquidate millions of bureaucrats and Jews.

Maybe we'll march on Washington. . . .

Here the program trails off. For there are laws against inciting violence and advocating the overthrow of the government by force. The excitement is left dangling with a vague promise of a Utopia where milk and honey shall flow, and a hint that some legal or extra-legal way will be found to enter this New Jerusalem. In various countries of Europe this demagogy has, of course, translated itself into action. Whole governments have been swept away by the mobs that have been swayed by a similar set of appeals.

The demagogue makes a dramatic but erroneous diagnosis of the causes of the dissatisfaction and malaise that his followers suffer. That they are frustrated, bitter, on the outs with themselves and society, there can be no doubt. True issues are not stated; they would point to flaws in economic structure, to the failure of men to find a cure for war, to neglect of basic principles of human relations in schools, industries, and community life, and—above all—to inner lack of mental health and ego-firmness.

This true causation, being complex, is entirely avoided. The sufferers are assured that they are not to blame. Their precarious self-esteem is protected by comforting assurance that they are Christians, true patriots, the elite. They are even told that to hate the Jews is not a sign of anti-Semitism. At every turn their extropunitiveness is justified and their ego-defenses strengthened.

While the demagogue never offers a rational program for the relief of social anomie and personal malaise, neither does he, in a country with a firm governmental structure, offer a clear-cut program of violence. A tottering social structure, such as has existed in Germany, Spain, Italy, and in Russia, is needed before the agitator can safely incite to revolution. Prosperity and stability are poor soil for agitators.

Sometimes, however, even in an otherwise stable nation, he may gain a measure of political power on a local basis—in cities or states.

Whether successful or not, the demagogue is at bottom advocating a totalitarian revolution following the pattern of fascism. In America certain face-saving devices are required in order that the historical values of the nation shall not be too obviously violated. Demagogues usually protest that they are not anti-Semites and that they are opposed to fascism just as they are opposed to communism. It has been remarked that if fascism comes to the United States it will take the guise of an anti-fascist movement. But the earmarks are nevertheless clearly visible. The program is essentially alike in all countries.

In a memorandum entitled "How to recognize an American Pro-Fascist," the Friends of Democracy, Incorporated, has listed the following characteristics:

1. *Racism* is common to all groups. In fact, it is a cornerstone of the pro-fascist movement everywhere. In this country it takes the form of White Supremacy.
2. *Anti-Semitism* is a common denominator of all pro-fascist and "one-hundred percent Americans" groups. *Anti-Catholicism* sometimes is substituted for anti-Semitism in predominantly Protestant areas, but the demagogues have found anti-Semitism to be the most effective political weapon.
3. *Antialienism, antirefugeeism, and anti-everything foreign* is a major characteristic. Fascism all over the world professes strong "nativism" and invariably is opposed to "foreigners" and people of other nations.
4. *Nationalism* is the key. The extreme nationalist claims that his own country is "the master country," just as he asserts that his own people are "the master race." Power is the keynote.
5. *Isolationism* is a distinct part of the pattern. Isolationists take the position that this country is secure behind the impregnability of two great oceans.
6. *Anti-internationalism* is also a part of the pattern. This anti-internationalism includes opposition to the United Nations and all other efforts to arrive at international understanding and cooperation for peace.
7. *Red-baiting* indiscriminately labels all opponents as communists and bolsheviks. Communism is used as a bugaboo to frighten people into accepting fascism. Liberals and progressives, Jews, intellectuals, international bankers, and for-

eigners are described as communists or "fellow-travelers" by the pro-fascists.

8. *Antilabor,* particularly antiorganized labor, is a predominant characteristic, though often masked.

9. *Sympathy for other fascists* is common among the pro-fascists. In pre-Pearl Harbor days, this sympathy included a defense of Hitler and Mussolini as "the great bulwarks" against communism. During the war, it was directed to sympathy for Petain, and his Vichy government. Later it took the shape of sympathy and defense of the Franco and Peron regimes.

10. *Antidemocracy* is another common denominator. "Democracy is decadent," fascists everywhere declare. In the United States, the favorite theme is that our country is a "Republic," not a "democracy." A "Republic" is the rule of the elite, while democracy is virtually a synonym for communism.

11. *The glorification of war, force, and violence* is a major theme. War is regarded as creative activity, and military heroes are glorified. One of the pro-fascist slogans maintains "Life is struggle, struggle is war, war is life."

12. *The one-party system* is a distinct feature of the fascist pattern. Totalitarianism is applauded under the slogan, "One people, one party, one State."

American democracy has a remarkable resiliency, for it has withstood such demagogy for decades, in fact, since before the founding of the nation.[4] But today, the aggravating of strains, the cultural lag (i.e., the failure of social skills to keep pace with technological) have made the appeal greater than ever before. It is not a movement that is born overnight. Its seeds are always present, and its growth may be gradual and imperceptible up to a point, and then sudden and alarming. It waxes and wanes with the rise and fall of particular demagogues. But sometimes its roots gain a firm hold in congressional committees, in local and state political groups, in certain newspapers, and among certain radio commentators.

On the whole, the democratic tradition seems still in the ascendancy. Each fascistic movement generates a strong countercurrent. Yet the mounting of social strain and the acceleration of social change in our day create a precarious condition. The question is whether realistic diagnoses and policies can be evolved to ameliorate domestic and international ills and to improve men's outlook before panic and fear drive them in larger numbers to embrace demagogic nostrums.

The Followers

People who follow demagogues have no precise idea of the cause to which they are devoted. There is vagueness both about the objective and about the means for reaching the objective. The demagogue may not know them himself or, if he does, he finds it expedient to keep attention riveted only on himself. He has learned that concrete images (leaders) are more firmly held in mind than are abstractions.

Since there is no way out of the predicament (except the distant and vague possibility of unspecified violence) followers are forced to trust the demagogue for guidance and devote themselves to him blindly. He provides them with channels for protest and hate, and these pleasures of indignation are diverting and temporarily satisfying. There is comfort in the tautological assurance that Americans are Americans and that Christians are Christians and that these are the best people, the truly elite. One is a Christian because one is not a Jew, an American because not a foreigner, a simple fellow because not an intellectual. The comfort may seem thin, but it bolsters self-esteem.

We need a comprehensive, scientific study of the membership of nativist organizations. Observers have reported that members seem to be people who have obviously not succeeded in life, mostly over 40 years of age, uneducated, bewildered, grim in facial expression. The presence of many rigid-appearing women suggests that some may be loveless creatures ready to find in the demagogue a fantasied lover and protector.

It may well turn out that followers are nearly all individuals who have felt themselves to be somehow rejected. Unhappy home life, unsatisfactory marriage, may be frequent among them. Their age suggests that they have lived long enough to sense a hopelessness about their vocations and social relations. Because they have little backlog in terms of personal or financial resources, they dread the future and gladly ascribe their insecurity to the malignant forces that the demagogue singles out. Deprived of realistic gratifications and subjective safety, they have a nihilistic view of society and indulge in fantasies of fury. They need an exclusive island of security where their frustrated hopes may yet be fulfilled. All liberals, intellectuals, deviates, and other agents of change must be excluded. To be sure, they too want change of a sort, but only the change that will provide personal security and bolster their own weakness.

Every character-conditioned source of prejudice that we have examined in previous chapters helps to explain the followers of demagogues. Demagoguery invites the externalization of hatred and anxiety; it is an institutional aid to projection; it justifies and encourages tabloid thinking, stereotyping, and the conviction that the world is made up of swindlers. It bifurcates life into clear-cut choices: follow the simple fascist formula or disaster will occur. There is no middle ground, no national solution. While the ultimate objective is vague, still the need for definiteness is met by the rule, "Follow the Leader." By declaring that every social issue is the result of out-group misconduct, the demagogue consistently avoids focusing his followers' attention upon their own painful internal conflicts. Their repressions are thus safeguarded and all the mechanisms of ego defense are bolstered.

One small-scale experimental study gives us a certain amount of insight into the nature of people who are susceptible to the appeals of demagogues. The subjects of this experiment were a selected sample of war veterans in Chicago who had been previously interviewed and whose opinions and history were known. To them were mailed two pieces of anti-Semitic propaganda. Two weeks later these men were re-interviewed. It was found that some had accepted and agreed with the message; some had rejected it. The former group was composed of men who had previously shown intolerance or who had given mere lip-service to tolerance. They were not among the veterans who had strong pro-tolerance convictions. Furthermore, they perceived the tracts as coming from an authoritative, reliable, and unbiased source. Finally, they were men who found the literature reassuring; it alleviated their anxieties and aroused no new fears or conflicts. Summing up this evidence, so far as it goes, the demagogic appeal builds on previous attitudes and beliefs in harmony with the appeal; it appears to the consumer as authoritative; it reduces his anxiety. If it does all these things it is likely to be accepted.[5]

The Demagogue as a Person

Agitators flourish because the authoritarian type of personality needs them. Their motives, however, are not altruistic. They have axes of their own to grind.

In many instances, demagogism is a lucrative racket. Dues and gifts, the purchase of shirts and other insignia, may keep the leaders in clover.[6] Small fortunes have been made at the game, and by the time the movement fails—through mismanagement, legal complications, or the desire of followers for novelty—a tidy sum has been salted away.

Political motives are also common. Extravagant if vague promises (spiced with hate-appeals) have elected senators and congressmen, as well as candidates for local offices. The techniques are melodramatic enough to make good headline stories or to invite radio comment. The result is that the demagogue becomes well known by name, and this prominence he finds an asset in re-election. His technique is one of arousing hope (e.g., "share the wealth") and also of arousing fear. "Vote for me, or the Reds (Negroes, Catholics) will get control of the government." Both techniques—used with skill—lifted Hitler into power within a short time.

But the motives of demagogues are likely to be still more complex. They too have character-conditioned prejudice. Rarely does one find a completely cold and calculating politician who uses anti-Semitism and related tricks only for gain.

Consider Hitler's anti-Semitic strategy. Some of its roots probably lay in his own inferiority and sexual conflicts, as discussed on p. 388 f. But it seems unlikely that he would carry out anti-Semitism as a state policy merely to satisfy his personal feelings. Perhaps he and his henchmen wanted Jewish money and property. Straight expropriations of Jewish wealth may be a contributing factor, although here again it is questionable whether the gain actually offset the capital loss in the Reich through a disruption of business and markets. The chief motive lay in offering to the German people a scapegoat for the defeat of 1918 and for the subsequent inflation. Nationalism and unity were intensified by fixing blame in this way. All these motives probably existed, along with another. Hitler tried, not only in Germany but in the world at large, to gain favor for himself by posing as St. George slaying the dragon. Since anti-Semitism is widespread in all countries, he wished to be seen as a friend to all. In many lands one heard people say they liked Hitler for one reason only, because he was against the Jews. He counted on this bid for sympathy to carry him through his many rough dealings with foreign countries. That he gained some sympathy cannot be doubted; but in the long run he overestimated the value of this particular trump.

Demagogues who are already in power may use antiminority appeals as a diversion. Occupied with plots of their own, they keep telling people of the peril they are being saved from. They use minority groups much as the Roman emperors used bread and circuses.

Agitators cannot succeed unless there is large-scale malaise in the population. They fail if their intended followers are people with strong inner security and mature ego-development. But usually there is a sufficiently large potential population of followers (someone has called them "propageese") to reward their efforts. The masses are necessary to the demagogues. When there is no demagogue the population is not likely to become inflamed. McWilliams lays the blame for the treatment of the Japanese-Americans after Pearl Harbor upon certain professional patriots and witch-hunters.[7] Whether the violence of World War II and the persecution of the Jews in Germany would have been avoided if Hitler had never existed is a question that will never be answered. It seems likely, however, that a demagogue is essential to the occurrence of the catastrophe. But when times are ripe, if one agitator does not arise, another probably will.

All in all, the motives of demagogues are likely to be a complex mixture. But many agitators, if not all, are themselves authoritarian personality types, endowed with verbal fluency. While some seek power and money, most of them are character conditioned, especially the small-time fellows who have neither money nor political power to win by their printed tracts and soap-box oratory. Perhaps they are gratifying some exhibitionistic tendency, but they would not take this particular avenue of display unless their own bigotry was intense. Some of them—like many of the big-timers—seem close to the borderline of paranoid insanity.

Paranoid Bigotry

Kraepelin, in the course of classifying mental diseases, defined *paranoid ideas* as "erroneous judgments not subject to correction by experience." According to this rather broad definition, many ideas, including prejudice, would be paranoid.

The true paranoiac, however, has an impenetrable rigidity. His ideas are delusional, disconnected from reality and not subject to any influence.

A paranoid woman had the fixed delusion that she was a dead person. The doctor tried what he thought was a conclusive logical demonstration to her of her error. He asked her, "Do dead people bleed?" "No," she answered. "Well, if I pricked your finger, would you bleed?" "No," answered the woman, "I wouldn't bleed; I'm dead." "Let's see," said the doctor, and pricked her finger. When the patient saw the drop of blood appearing she remarked in surprise, "Oh, so dead people *do* bleed, don't they."

A peculiarity of paranoid ideas is that they are usually localized. That is to say, the sufferer may be normal in all matters excepting in the region of his disordered conviction. It is as though all the preceding misery of his life—all his conflicts—had condensed into a single limited delusional system. On p. 300 we saw that rejective home life is characteristic of most paranoiacs. It is as though all their diffused early misery were caught up and rationalized in a single set of ideas—usually to the effect that the sufferer is being persecuted, perhaps by his neighbors, or by communists, or by Jews.

Paranoid ideas are sometimes mixed up with other forms of mental disease, but often they seem to constitute an entity in themselves called "pure paranoia." And sometimes the affliction is mild enough to warrant only a diagnosis of borderline condition —a "paranoid tendency."

The theory held by most psychoanalysts and by many psychiatrists is that paranoia, of any degree or type, is a consequence of repressed homosexuality. There is some clinical evidence to support this claim.[8] The explanation goes something like this: many people, especially if they have been sternly punished for any sex activity as children, cannot face homosexual impulses in themselves. They repress them, saying to themselves in effect, "I do not love him, I hate him." (A similar "reaction formation" we encountered in the case of sexual hatred of Negroes, Chapter 23.) This conflict becomes externalized. Complementary projection comes into play. "The reason I hate him is that he hates me. He has it in for me. He is persecuting me." A final step in this tortuous series of rationalizations is displacement and generalization. "It is not only he that hates me and has designs against me, but it is the Negro, Jewish, communistic group that is after me." (These may be regarded as substitute sexual symbols, or merely as convenient, socially sanctioned scapegoats who to the sufferer account for his feeling that *someone* is persecuting him.)

Whether or not this elaborate theory is altogether sound, the formula for paranoid thinking seems always to have a history consisting of the following steps: (1) There is deprivation, frustration, inadequacy of some sort (if not sexual, then something else of a highly personal order). (2) The cause, due both to repression and projection, is seen as lying wholly outside oneself. (The paranoiac utterly lacks insight in the region of his disorder.) (3) Since the external cause is seen as an acute threat, this source is cordially hated and aggression is generated against it. In extreme cases the sufferer may attack or eliminate the "guilty" party. Some paranoiacs are homicidal.

When a true paranoiac becomes a demagogue disaster may result. The demagogue's success will, of course, be greater if he is normal and shrewd in all other phases of his leadership. If so, his delusional system will seem reasonable, and he will attract followers, especially among those who themselves have latent paranoid ideas. Combine enough paranoiacs, or enough people with paranoid tendencies, and a dangerous mob may result.[9]

The paranoid tendency explains why the compulsive drives of the anti-Semite and the communist-phobe never seem to relax. The sufferer is keyed up all the time. Even public disapproval, ridicule, exposure, or jail do not deter him. Although he may stop short of inciting his hearers to violence, he has an intensity, a humorlessness, and aggressiveness that nothing can shake. Neither argument nor experience will change his views. If contradictory evidence is offered him he will twist it to serve his previous conviction, as did the "dead" woman.

It is especially important for our purposes to note that paranoia may exist in otherwise normal individuals, also that all gradations of the paranoid tendency occur. The mechanism of projection is central in paranoia, but it is also present in normal people. It is not always possible to say where normality leaves off and pathology begins.

Paranoia represents the extreme pathology of prejudice. At present it seems impossible to prescribe a cure. Whoever invents a remedy for paranoia will be mankind's benefactor.

One approach to the problem of cancer control has been to study conditions that make for healthy organisms and that prevent the malignant growth of cells. Similarly, we may hope to learn something about the control of paranoia, projection, and prejudice from a study of tolerant personalities, where these forms of mental functioning have failed to take root. What makes for a tolerant personality?

NOTES AND REFERENCES

1. A. FORSTER. *A Measure of Freedom.* New York: Doubleday, 1950, 222-234.

2. L. LOWENTHAL AND N. GUTERMAN. *Prophets of Deceit: A Study of the Techniques of the American Agitator.* New York: Harper, 1949.

3. How to spot American pro-Fascists. *Friends of Democracy's Battle,* 1947, **5**, No. 12. Issued by Friends of Democracy Inc., 137 East 57th St., New York 22, N. Y.

4. *Cf.* L. LOWENTHAL AND N. GUTERMAN. *Op. cit.,* 111.

5. B. Bettelheim and M. Janowitz. Reactions to fascist propaganda—a pilot study. *Public Opinion Quarterly,* 1950, **14,** 53-60.

6. A. Forster. *Op. cit.*

7. C. McWilliams. *Prejudice.* Boston: Little, Brown, 1944, 112.

8. J. Page and J. Warkentin. Masculinity and paranoia. *Journal of Abnormal and Social Psychology,* 1938, **33,** 527-531.

9. It is going too far, however, to declare that a whole nation may be paranoid, as one author has done in discussing Germany under Hitler. *Cf.* R. M. Brickner. *Is Germany Incurable?* Philadelphia: J. B. Lippincott, 1943. But a handful of paranoiacs, or even one, can do quite sufficient damage.

CHAPTER 27

THE TOLERANT PERSONALITY

Tolerance may seem to be a flabby word. When we say that we tolerate a headache, or our shabby apartment, or a neighbor, we certainly do not mean that we like them, but merely that in spite of our dislike we shall endure them. To tolerate newcomers in a community is merely a negative act of decency.

Yet the term also has a more rugged meaning. We say that an individual who is on friendly terms with all sorts of people is a tolerant person. He makes no distinction of race, color, or creed. He not only endures but, in general, approves his fellow men. It is this warmer grade of tolerance that we wish to discuss. It is, however, unfortunate that the English language lacks a better term to express the friendly and trustful attitude that one person may have toward another, regardless of the groups to which either belongs.

Some writers prefer the concept of "the democratic personality," or the "productive personality." While these concepts are distinctly relevant, they cover somewhat too much ground for our purposes. They do not necessarily take their point of departure, as we must, from ethnic attitudes as such.

In our discussion of the prejudiced personality (Chapter 25) we noted that two methods of study are commonly employed. The *longitudinal* approach focuses attention upon the development of biased attitudes, starting with the earliest stages of child training. The *cross-sectional* approach seeks to study the present pattern and asks, What is the organization and the function of ethnic attitudes in the total personality today? Both methods are equally applicable to the investigation of tolerant personalities as well. But, unfortunately, research on "good neighbors" is less plentiful than on "bad neighbors." It is delinquents rather than law-abiding citizens who attract investigators. It is disease more than health that interests the medical researcher. And it is the pathology of bigotry and not the wholesome state of tolerance that, as a rule, interests social scientists.[1]   It is not surprising, therefore, that we know less about tolerance than about prejudice.

Early Life

Most of our genetic knowledge comes from the control groups that are used in studies of prejudice.   As we saw in Chapter 25, it is customary to pair a group of tolerant with a group of intolerant individuals, and then to note the background factors that differentiate the two.

Tolerant children, it seems, are likely to come from homes with a permissive atmosphere.   They feel welcome, accepted, loved, no matter what they do.   Punishment is not harsh or capricious, and the child does not have to guard every moment against impulses that might bring down parental wrath upon his head.[2]

Thus "threat orientation," so often found in the background of prejudiced children, is relatively lacking in the history of tolerant children.   The keynote in their lives is security rather than threat. As the sense of selfhood develops, the child is able to synthesize his own pleasure-seeking tendencies with the demands of the outer situation, and with his own developing conscience.   His ego finds sufficient gratification without resorting to repression, and without the guilt that leads him through projection to lay blame on others. There is, in consequence, no sharp cleavage between conscious and unconscious layers of his mental-emotional life.

The attitude toward parents is well differentiated.   That is to say, while the child accepts them on the whole he may, without fear, be critical.   Unlike the prejudiced child, he does not love them consciously and hate them unconsciously.   His attitude is patterned and public, affectionate but not hypocritical.   He accepts them for what they are, and does not live in dread of their superior power.

Since moral conflicts are, on the whole, satisfactorily handled, there is less rigidity and less disposition to be harsh with the errors other people make.   Transgressions of custom and code are tolerated.   Good companionship and fun are regarded as more essential than good manners and "proper" behavior.

The greater mental flexibility of the tolerant person (even in childhood) is shown by his rejection of two-valued logic.   He seldom agrees that "there are only two kinds of people: the weak and the strong"; or that "there is only one right way to do anything."   He does not bifurcate his environment into the wholly proper and the wholly improper.   For him there are shades of gray.   Nor does he sharply distinguish between the roles of the sexes. He does not agree that "girls should learn only things that are useful around the house."

In school (and later life) tolerant individuals, as contrasted with prejudiced, do not need precise, orderly, clear-cut instructions before they proceed with a task. They can "tolerate ambiguity" and there is no insistent demand for definiteness and structuredness. They feel it safe to say "I don't know," and to wait until time brings the needed evidence. They are less fearful of delay; they have no special need to categorize quickly, nor to persist in categorizations once made.

Their frustration tolerance seems to be relatively high. They are not thrown into a panic when threatened with deprivations. Feeling secure within their own egos, there is less of a tendency to externalize (project) conflict. When things go wrong it is not necessary to blame others: one can blame oneself without falling into a state of alarm.

Such seems to be the general groundwork for tolerant social attitudes. Undoubtedly this groundwork is in large part the product of home training, of the modes of reward and punishment used by parents, of the subtle atmosphere of family living. But it would be wrong to overlook the possibility that innate temperamental qualities may also predispose the child to develop tolerant attitudes. One student writes:

> As far back as I can remember I was trained to love living things. My parents tell of an incident when I was about five years old and came running into the house crying because a boy outside was "shaking Nature." When they looked out the window, they saw a boy shaking acorns out of a tree. Even at this age I disliked violence, a feeling which still remains. It was early in my childhood that I was taught not to stare at the lame or blind and to give generously to the needy, and this training I am sure did much to prevent formation of prejudiced attitudes toward minority groups.

This case suggests that both temperament and specific teaching may combine to produce an affiliative outlook.

Many of these factors making for the formation of tolerant attitudes come to light in an investigation of anti-Nazi Germans. (Cross-cultural evidence of this sort is always welcome, for it helps us to see to what extent we are dealing with universal principles in human nature, and to what extent culture alone seems to be operating.) David Levy reports on the backgrounds of certain German males who resisted Hitler's regime of intolerance.[3] He found that they, more than the average German, had close and friendly relations with their fathers who, on the whole, were not harsh disciplinarians. Also, their mothers were more than usually demonstrative in their affection. This sense of early and basic security was intensified in many cases because there were no siblings. These findings clearly support the American studies we have reported, and make us feel doubly sure that early training is an important agent in slanting a child toward tolerance.

Levy's study also finds that the families of these anti-Nazis often had a crossing of religious or nationality lines by intermarriage; likewise that the men through wide reading or travel had enlarged their horizons. In other words, family atmosphere is not the only factor in producing tolerance; later experience is also important.

Tolerance, we conclude, is seldom, if ever, the product of a single cause, but rather the result of several forces pressing in the same direction. The greater the number of forces that press in this one direction (temperament, family atmosphere, specific parental teaching, deversified experience, school and community influences), the more tolerant the developed personality will be.

Varieties of Tolerance

Tolerant people differ in the degree to which their ethnic attitudes are *salient* or *nonsalient*. For some the issue of fair play seems always in the forefront of consciousness and plays a vital part in their motivation. The German anti-Nazis are a case in point. They were aware all the time of Hitler's racism and of their own part in fighting it. Since the issue endangered their lives, they were forced to keep it salient.

Other tolerant people seem never to feature the issue. They are so habitually democratic in their outlook that for them there is neither gentile nor Jew, neither bond nor free. All men are equal: group membership is for most purposes irrelevant. We reported in Chapter 8 that people who lack prejudice against the Jews are more often unable to tell a Jew from a gentile by his facial appearance than are prejudiced people to whom the issue is more salient.

A case might be made for the claim that the most tolerant people are those in whom ethnic attitudes have no salience at all. They have no interest in group distinctions. To them a person is a person. But this benign lack of awareness is difficult to achieve in our society, where human relations are so largely framed in terms of caste and class. As much as one might wish to treat a Negro simply as a human being, circumstances force an awareness of race. The prevalence of social discrimination tends to make ethnic attitudes salient.

Besides salience and nonsalience it is desirable to make a further distinction between *conformity* tolerance and *character-conditioned* tolerance, just as we did in the case of prejudice (Chapter 17). In a community where ethnic issues do not arise, or where they are habitually handled according to a code of tolerance, we may expect people to take equality for granted. Swayed by the tolerant group norm, they are conformists. Character-conditioned tolerance, however, is a positive state of personality organization which, like character-conditioned prejudice, has functional significance in the economy of the whole personality.

Character-conditioned tolerance always means that the person has a positive respect for individuals—whoever they are. This respect may be tied into many styles of life. Some people seem to have a generalized state of affection, a true trait of goodwill. Others are more aesthetic in their values, and take delight in cultural differences, finding members of out-groups interesting and stimulating. Some have their tolerance embedded in a framework of political liberalism and progressive philosophy. In others a sense of justice is uppermost. In still others fair treatment of minority groups at home is conjoined with the issue of international amity. They see that peaceful relations with the colored people of the world will not be possible unless colored peoples are treated more fairly in this country.[4] In short, character-conditioned tolerance is set in a positive world view.

Militant and Pacifistic Tolerance

Some tolerant people are fighters. They will not put up with any infringement of the rights of others. They are intolerant of intolerance. Sometimes they form a group (e.g., Committee on Racial Equality) to test restaurants, hotels, and public conveyances, to see whether discrimination is practiced. They make themselves into spies to study and eventually expose agitators and intolerant pro-fascist organizations.[5] They support and carry through legal suits in order to challenge and defeat segregation. They join the more militant reformist organizations, and are heard at legislative hearings or seen in picket lines whenever a hot issue of civil rights is involved.

Can we say that such zealots are themselves prejudiced? Sometimes, yes; sometimes, no. Among them are a few "bigots in reverse," who may, for example, hate Southern whites as irrationally as some whites hate Negroes. The same overcategorizing and the same hidden psychodynamics may be operating. Reverse bigots may mistakenly type all prejudiced people as "fascists," or accuse all employers of exploiting their employees. It seems not unlikely that many communist agitators, crusading for "equality," are cases in point. Prejudice, to refer to Chapter 1 again, exists whenever there is irrational hostility toward a group of people whose evil attributes are exaggerated and overgeneralized. On the basis of this definition, some reformers turn out to be no less prejudiced than those they are trying to reform.

Other militants, however, seem capable of a finer analysis of the issue. They see that a particular act at a particular time, perhaps the passage of a particular legislative bill, will advance the interests of minority groups, and thereupon throw themselves into the battle. They do so on the basis of a realistic appraisal of their own values, and without stereotyping the opponent. Or they may deliberately choose to flaunt social custom and risk ostracism in order to demonstrate friendship for the outcast, again for the realization of personal values. In such instances there is no overtyping of the opposition. Vigor of conviction is not the same as prejudice. When asked to define the difference between *conviction* and *prejudice,* someone replied, "You can talk about your convictions without emotion." The answer is not wholly satisfactory—though it has truth behind it. Conviction is by no means devoid of emotion, but it is a disciplined and differentiated emotion, pointed to the removal of a realistic obstacle. By contrast, the emotion behind prejudice is diffused and overgeneralized, saturating unrelated objects.

Strong democratic sentiments are likely to lead to militancy. This finding emerges from the research of Dombrose and Levinson.[6] These investigators gave two tests to their subjects: one a test of ethnocentrism (*E*-scale) and one a test of "ideological militancy and pacifism" (*IMP*-scale). It was found that those who were moderately opposed to ethnocentrism tended to endorse moderate and mild methods of reform. Those who were strongly opposed to ethnocentrism were more militant in their outlook. The coefficient of correlation was +.74. For example, the militants endorsed such propositions as the following:

> Every possible means, including laws, should be used now to give equal social status and rights to Negroes and other groups.

> One can be democratic and believe in free speech, and still deny fascists the right to speak and hold meetings.

> The present difference between the Republicans and the Democrats is very minor and we need a party which will really represent the people.

There is, as the authors point out, a temperamental militancy in many people of democratic persuasion extending beyond racial and ethnic issues. They want widespread reform and they want it now.

Peaceful democrats (who also tend to be less extreme in their opposition to ethnocentrism) are milder in their methods, and endorse gradual reform movements. Particularly they endorse such propositions as

There is a middle ground for intelligent people between the conflicting ideologies of Right and Left.

"Turn the other cheek" is still a good rule for living.

It doesn't do much good opposing anti-Jewish remarks; you only get into pointless arguments.

International tension is largely the result of lack of knowledge of other people and nations.

The preferred mode of action is education, patience, gradualism —a "pacifistic" pattern.

While it is true, as this research proves, that there is a tendency for intensely anti-ethnocentric people to be militant, still the correlation is not perfect. It is entirely possible for extremely democratic individuals to be gradualists and "pacifists" in their theory of reform. The great Negro leader, Booker T. Washington, is an example.

Liberalism and Radicalism

Whether the tolerant person is militant or pacifistic, he is very likely to be liberal in his political views. Prejudiced individuals are more often conservatives. Correlations in the neighborhood of .50 persistently occur.[7] A "liberal," as measured by the scales used in such research, is a person who is critical of the status quo, who wants progressive social change. He de-emphasizes the importance of rugged individualism and business success; he would diminish the power of business by increasing the role of labor and of government in economic life. And he tends to take a somewhat optimistic view of human nature—that it can be changed for the better. Radicalism is defined by most scales as a more intense grade of this same pattern.

But, as we have pointed out, there seems to be a qualitative difference between liberals and extreme radicals (e.g., communists) who are opposed to the present social structure *in toto*. The ethnic sentiments of radicals are often embedded in a violent protest against the whole of society. Their hatred of a system is more central than is their desire to improve the condition of minorities.

It is not accurate, therefore, to say that radicalism is merely an extreme degree of liberalism. The functional significance of the two outlooks may be markedly different. The liberal-equalitarian may feel that society rubs along pretty well, all things considered, but that improvements are needed in order to reinforce respect for the person, whether the person is suffering from poverty, ill health, or the handicap of minority group membership. His goal in life is meliorism—to make things better. The radical, on the other hand, may be a person whose whole frame of existence is negativistic—charged with hate. He wants to turn things topsy-turvy, without worrying too much about the consequences.

The fact that liberalism and radicalism both correlate positively with ethnic tolerance places a strong weapon in the hands of bigots (who are likely to be political conservatives). They can make the charge, with a grain of truth, that those who believe in equal rights are "radicals." A congressman from the South argued as follows: "Everyone knows that the communists' main objective in the South is to commingle the races." Therefore, his opponent, who was pressing for some mild reform in behalf of the Negroes, was, to him, a communist. The logic is fallacious. It is like saying, all people over 75 years of age favor social security; therefore all people who favor social security are over 75. Confusion, however, accomplishes what the accuser desires. He forces reformers into the inappropriate category of "communists." In reality very few of them belong there.

Education

Besides being more liberal (or radical) than prejudiced people, are the tolerant also more intelligent? Offhand it would seem so, for are not bifurcations, overcategorization, projection, displacement, the mark of stupidity?

But the question, however, is complex. Even paranoid people may be highly intelligent outside the narrow region of their disorder. Prejudiced people are often successful people, and show none of the generalized stupidity that would go with "low intelligence."

If we appeal to studies of children we find that tolerance tends *slightly* to be associated with higher intelligence. Correlations range around .30.[8] These are not high and are affected by social class membership. Children with lower IQ's tend to come from poorer families where education and opportunity are low and where ignorance and prejudice may be high. Hence we cannot be sure that a basic correlation exists between tolerance and brightness, or whether conditions of class and family training underlie both.

We are on somewhat firmer ground if we ask, Are better educated people more tolerant than less educated? One study from South Africa gives a strongly affirmative answer.[9] Asked concerning their attitudes toward natives, white people with differing degrees of education gave the following responses:

Favoring more opportunities for jobs:
84 percent of university trained
30 percent with elementary education only

Favoring equal educational opportunities:
85 percent of university trained
39 percent with elementary education only

Favoring more political rights:
77 percent of university trained
27 percent with elementary education only

From these data it would appear that education has a marked effect. Perhaps it is because higher education lessens feelings of insecurity and anxiety. Or perhaps education enables the individual to see the social scene as a whole, and to comprehend that the welfare of one group is linked to the welfare of all groups.

Comparable studies made in America yield findings in the same direction—though not nearly so marked. Questions of the type used in the South African study generally reveal an educational difference of the order of 10-20 percent, rather than the 50 percent reported here.[10]

We call attention to a distinction (referred to in Chapter 1) between two types of questions: those pertaining to attitudes and those dealing with beliefs and knowledge. It is true that large differences are found in *knowledge* concerning minority groups when people with higher education are compared with those having only elementary schooling. For example, many more of the former know that Negro blood is not essentially different from white blood, and that most Negroes are seriously dissatisfied with their lot. Questions of knowledge often yield differences of the order of 30-40 percent. But tolerance does not keep pace with knowledge. Attitudes, on the average, are less related to educational level.

One study shows that the tolerance scores of college students vary with the educational level of their parents. Over four hundred students took a prejudice test. The scores were divided into two equal halves—the more tolerant and the less tolerant. Table 12 shows the results.[11]

Table 12

PERCENTAGE DISTRIBUTION OF PREJUDICE SCORES AS A FUNCTION OF PARENTAL EDUCATION

	More Tolerant Half	Less Tolerant Half
Both parents college graduates	60.3	39.7
One parent college graduate	53.0	47.0
Neither parent college graduate	41.2	58.8

We conclude, therefore, that general education does to an appreciable degree help raise the level of tolerance, and that the gain apparently is passed along to the next generation. Whether this educational gain in tolerance occurs because of an enhanced security, more critical habits of thought, or superior knowledge we cannot say. It is unlikely that the result could be due in any large degree to *specific* training in intercultural problems, for up to very recent years there has been little such training in schools or colleges.

Where there is such specific teaching we should expect the gain in tolerance to be greater. And there is some evidence that it is. In one study it was found that among college students who reported having had specific intercultural education, over 70 percent fell in the *more tolerant half* of the distribution of prejudice scores.[12]

These students reported—to quote their own words—that they had learned "the ground lessons of the theory of racial superiority and inferiority," or that "minority groups are the same as anyone else—some good, some bad."

While education—especially specific intercultural education—apparently helps engender tolerance, we note that it by no means invariably does so. The correlation is appreciable but not high. Therefore we cannot agree with those enthusiasts who claim that "the whole problem of prejudice is a matter of education."

Empathic Ability

One important factor in tolerance is an ability we know little about. This ability is sometimes called empathy, though we might call it "the ability to size up people," "social intelligence," "social sensitivity," or, to borrow the expressive German term, *Menschen-kenntnis.*

There is good evidence that tolerant people are more accurate in their judgments of personality than are intolerant people.

In one experiment, for example, a college student who stood high on a scale measuring authoritarianism was paired with another student of the same age and sex who stood low on the same scale. For twenty minutes these students conversed with each other informally about radio, television, or the movies, as they preferred. In this way each formed an impression of the other, as one inevitably does when thrown with a stranger for a short interval of casual conversation. The purpose of the experiment was, of course, unknown to the participants. After the termination of the conversation each student was taken to a separate room and given a questionnaire to fill out *as he thought the other student with whom he had conversed would respond to it.* This method was used with 27 pairs of students.

The results show that high authoritarians "projected" their own attitudes; that is, they thought their interlocutor would answer the test in an authoritarian manner (though, of course, their partners were all low on this scale). By contrast, the non-authoritarian students estimated the attitudes of their partners more correctly. They not only perceived them as authoritarians, which they were, but also estimated more correctly their response to certain other questions revealing other sorts of personality trends. In short, the tolerant students seemed in general to "size up" their interlocutors better than did intolerant students.[13]

Another (unpublished) study conducted by Noreen Novick makes the issue even clearer. A number of foreign students in a training school in the United States were asked to name those Americans from among their fellow students whom they thought would be most likely to succeed, and to be accepted, if they entered U. S. foreign service in the foreign student's home country. This request brought forth strikingly homogeneous agreement: certain Americans would be welcomed in any foreign country; certain others were wanted by none. Taking the extreme groups of the always chosen and never chosen, the investigator then sought for differentiating characteristics. Why were some *personae gratae,* others not?

The crucial factor turned out to be "empathic ability." Those who were chosen were students who had demonstrable ability to put themselves in other people's shoes; they had skill in sizing up other people; they were sensitive to the other's frame of mind; they were *Menschenkenner*. The unchosen lacked this social sensitivity.

Two findings in this research are particularly important. (1) Skill in human relations is not specific to a given culture; all the nations represented chose the same gifted persons. (2) The giftedness consists largely in an empathic ability, a flexible capacity to know the other person's state of mind, and adapt to it.

Let us ask why empathic ability leads to tolerance. Is it not because a person who correctly sizes up another has no need to feel apprehensive and insecure? Able to comprehend accurately the cues he perceives, he feels confident that he can sidestep unpleasant involvements if need arises. Realistic perception endows him with the ability to avoid friction and to conduct successful relationships. On the other hand, a person lacking this ability cannot trust his skill in dealing with others. He is forced to be on guard, to put strangers into categories, and to react to them *en masse*. Lacking subtle powers of discrimination, he resorts to stereotyping.

Just what the basis of empathic ability may be we cannot say. Perhaps it is a joint product of a secure home environment, aesthetic sensitivity, and high social values. For our purposes it is sufficient to note that, whatever its origins, it seems to be a prominent feature in personalities possessing ethnic tolerance.

Self-Insight

Somewhat similar is the trait of self-insight. Knowledge of oneself, research shows, tends to be associated with tolerance for others. People who are self-aware, self-critical, are not given to the ponderous habit of passing blame to others for what is their own responsibility. They know their own capabilities and shortcomings.

Various lines of evidence are available on this point. The California studies of tolerant and prejudiced groups report that the ego-ideal of tolerant people often calls for traits that they themselves lack; whereas prejudiced subjects paint as their ideal pretty much the sort of person they are now. Tolerant people, "being more basically secure, it seems, can more easily afford to see a discrepancy between ego-ideal and actual reality." [14] They know themselves and are not satisfied with what they find. Their self-awareness reduces the temptation to project their shortcomings onto others.

Another research asked both tolerant and prejudiced subjects whether they felt themselves to be more or less prejudiced than the average person. Virtually all of the tolerant people knew themselves to be less prejudiced, but only a fifth of the prejudiced subjects knew themselves to have more than an average amount of prejudice.[15]

Several investigators have called attention to a general *inwardness* in the personalities of tolerant people. There is interest in imaginative processes, in fantasies, in theoretical reflections, in artistic activities. Prejudiced people, by contrast, are *outward* in their interests, given to externalizing their conflicts, and finding their environment more absorbing than themselves. Tolerant people have a desire for personal autonomy rather than for external, institutional anchorage.[16]

Empathy, self-insight, inwardness are difficult traits to submit to laboratory, or even to clinical, investigation. It is surprising that our evidence is as good as it is. There is, however, one related trait that, up to now, has defied successful psychological study, viz., *sense of humor*. We have grounds for supposing a person's sense of humor is closely related to his degree of self-insight.[17] Yet, just what humor is it is hard to say, and its accurate measurement is beyond the present competence of psychology. But we venture to assert that humor is probably an important variable in relation to prejudice. Those who have attended the meetings of agitators where grim-visaged auditors applaud intolerant utterances often comment on their "humorlessness." The judgment is impressionistic. Yet if the syndrome of the prejudiced personality is correctly defined in Chapter 25, we can easily believe that humor is a missing ingredient; also that it is a present ingredient in the syndrome of tolerance. One who can laugh at oneself is unlikely to feel greatly superior to others.

Intropunitiveness

This inwardness and ability to know and to laugh at oneself make for the intropunitive tendency that we examined in Chapters 9 and 24. Self-blame takes the place of projected external blame.

One investigator, studying attitudes toward Russia, asked many subjects the question, "When things go wrong, are you more likely to get sore at other people or to feel bad and blame yourself for the situation?" Those who reported self-blame were discovered to be less inclined to heap excessive abuse on Soviet Russia. Thus a trait of intropunitiveness reflects itself even in international attitudes. People who blame themselves may be, and usually are, critical of communism but are not given to irrational scapegoating.[18]

This trait has another, more positive, effect: it engenders sympathy for the underdog. (Someone has called it infracaninophilia.) Such sympathy may, of course, be a mixed state of mind. It may be genuine, or it may have the flavor of patronage. It is easy to feel inflated by helping the underprivileged. And sometimes the partisanship takes on a compulsive and neurotic quality. But, whether the sympathy is selfless or self-serving, it is likely to be associated with intropunitive tendencies.

It is here that we should call attention to a fairly common socialized personality pattern. A tolerant person of this type feels genuine sympathy for the underdog; he himself has deep feelings of inferiority and unworthiness; he is given to self-blame; he empathizes quickly and keenly with the suffering of others, and finds happiness in helping improve the lot of his fellow men. Not all personalities that are intropunitive develop this complete syndrome, but the pattern is not uncommon.

Tolerance for Ambiguity

The reader will recall our several discussions of the distinctive cognitive processes that mark the mental operations of prejudiced people. We have demonstrated in various chapters (especially 10 and 25) the rigidity of their categories, their proneness to bifurcation, to selective perception, to simplification of memory traces, and their need for definite mental structure—even in processes that have nothing directly to do with prejudice. In all these instances our evidence came from studies based on contrasting groups of prejudiced and unprejudiced subjects. Therefore we can assert with confidence that the characteristic mental operations of tolerant personalities are also marked by distinctive (and opposite) attributes.

It is not easy to designate with a single phrase the flexibility, the differentiation, and the realism that, on the whole, seem to characterize the mental life of the tolerant individual. Perhaps the best single phrase is that suggested by Else Frenkel-Brunswik, "tolerance for ambiguity." [19] While the label itself is not important, it is important to bear in mind the principle involved, namely, that *tolerant thinking about ethnic groups is, no less than prejudiced thinking, a reflection of a total style of cognitive operation.*

Personal Values

But tolerant thinking is not only a reflection of the style of cognitive operation, it is also a reflection of the total style of life.

When we speak of a total style of life we have in mind the way in which all the discrete variables mentioned in this chapter are organized and integrated.   There is a tolerant *pattern,* not merely a tolerant attitude.   Temperament, emotional security, intropunitiveness, differentiated categories, self-insight, humor, tolerance for frustration, and tolerance for ambiguity—all these, and many other, ingredients may enter into the pattern.   A pattern is a synthesis, but psychologists by preference tend to work in terms of analysis.   For this reason psychology finds it difficult to deal with pattern or with "total style."

One study, however, approaches closely to the problem of pattern.   It shows how tolerance is embedded in a person's value-orientation toward life.[20]   The investigator measured college students' values in terms of the six categories proposed originally by Eduard Spranger.[21]   He also measured prejudice against the Jews with the Levinson-Sanford Anti-Semitism Scale.[22]   Taking the extreme 25 percent of the cases at high and low ends of the latter scale, the rank order of values turns out as follows:

	High in Anti-Semitism	Low in Anti-Semitism
Highest Value	Political	Aesthetic
	Economic	Social
	Religious	Religious
	Social	Theoretical
	Theoretical	Economic
Lowest Value	Aesthetic	Political

The order of values is almost precisely reversed for the two groups.   This discovery takes on considerable significance when we consider the nature of the values as defined by the scale.   The *political* value means interest in power; it means that the person customarily views the transactions of daily life in terms of hierarchy, control, domination, status.   Something is seen as higher, better, more worthy than something else.   A person who views life through this lens would naturally regard out-groups as low in status, less worthy, perhaps as contemptible; or he would see them as a threat to his own status, possibly as conniving to gain control of society.   Our confidence in this interpretation is strengthened by the finding that the most tolerant people, by contrast, have little or no tendency to view life in terms of power-hierarchies.   For them the political value is lowest of all.

Now the *aesthetic* value (highest in the tolerant and lowest in the anti-Semitic group) stands for interest in *particularity.*   It means that each event in life—whether a sunset, a garden, a symphony, or a personality—is to be appreciated in its own right. The aesthetic attitude does not categorize; each single experience is self-contained and intrinsically valuable. The aesthetic person individualizes. When he meets someone he judges him as a person, not as a group member. It is instructive to discover that prejudiced people stand low in this value, and that tolerant people have it to a high degree.

Interesting, too, are the values that fall in the second place. The *economic* value stands for interest in utility. Of what use is it?—this is the question most often asked by an economic person. This value-type is often wrapped up in the production and distribution of goods, or in banking and finance. In a competitive society the economic and political values are naturally related (they correlate about .30 on the *Study of Values*). The anti-Semite readily develops an image of the Jew as an economic threat, as money-minded (projection of his own money-mindedness?), and as a competitor. The tolerant person, having less of the economic outlook on life, is not sensitized to minority groups in terms of their economic threat.

The *social* value, second highest for the tolerant personalities, stands for love, sympathy, altruism. When this value is high, ethnic bias cannot play a prominent part in a life. This is particularly true when it is combined with *aesthetic* interest which, like the social value, draws attention to the merits of the individual, and resists categorical thinking about people.

Apparently the two values least decisively involved are the *religious* and the *theoretical*. It is easy to explain why. As we shall see in the next chapter, religion tends both to increase and to decrease prejudice, depending entirely upon how the individual conceives religion. In this research, then, its effects cancel out, and the value appears in mid-position. As for the *theoretical* value, it stands for an interest in generalized truth. It is next to the lowest for the anti-Semitic group. Prejudiced people, evidently, have little concern with truth as a value. The failure of this value to stand higher for tolerant people is no doubt due to the fact that, important though it is, aesthetic, social, and religious values are still more decisive in the formation of tolerance.

Philosophy of Life

In E. M. Forster's classic novel on prejudice, *Passage to India*, several Englishmen are planning a party. The list of invited guests is growing long. Even some Moslems and Hindus are included. One of the Englishmen remarks in consternation, "We must exclude someone from our gathering, or we shall be left with nothing."

Tolerant people take the opposite view. They feel actually stronger and more content when they invite many to their gathering. The exclusionist style of life is not for them.

The present chapter has set forth many reasons why people prefer an inclusionist style of living. Some seem tenderhearted almost by nature. Others are apparently mirroring their early training. In some the aesthetic and social values are highly developed. Educational level plays a part; so too does a general liberal outlook on political issues. Self-insight has a place, likewise the ability to size up and deal with individuals (empathy). Above all, a basic security and ego-strength are present which counteract the tendency to repress, to blame others, and to seize upon institutional and authoritarian guarantees of personal safety.

The core of the matter seems to be that every living being is trying to complete his own nature: i.e., to learn by subsidiation (Chapter 19). His quest may take one of two roads. One road calls for safety through exclusion, through a *rejective* equilibrium. The person clings to a narrow island, restricts his circle, sharply selects what reassures him and rejects what threatens him. The other road is one of relaxation, self-trust and, therefore, trust of others. There is no need to exclude strangers from one's gathering. Self-love is compatible with love of others. This tolerant orientation is possible because security has been experienced in the realistic handling of inner conflicts and social transactions. Unlike the prejudiced person, the tolerant person does not perceive the world as a jungle where men are basically evil and dangerous.

Some modern theories of love and hate, as we saw in Chapter 22, maintain that the original orientation of all men is toward a trusting and affiliative philosophy of life. This disposition grows naturally out of the early dependent relationship of mother and child, of earth and creature. Affiliation is the source of all happiness. When hatred and animosity grow in a life, they are crippling distortions of this naturally affiliative trend. Hate results from the mishandling of frustrations and deprivations that have been allowed to disintegrate the very core of the ego.[22]

If this view is correct, the development of mature and democratic personalities is largely a matter of building inner security. Only when life is free from intolerable threats, or when these threats are adequately handled with inner strength, can one be at ease with all sorts and conditions of men.

NOTES AND REFERENCES

1. A change of emphasis in social research seems to be coming about. The Grant Study at Harvard University has devoted itself entirely to the study of the physical and mental health of normal college men. *Cf.* C. L. HEATH. *What People Are: A Study of Normal Young Men.* Cambridge: Harvard Univ. Press, 1945. At the same university, P. A. Sorokin heads a research center devoted exclusively to the discovery of conditions making for "good neighbors." *Cf.* P. A. SOROKIN. *Altruistic Love: A Study of American "Good Neighbors" and Christian Saints.* Boston: Beacon Press, 1950.

2. The evidence for these assertions and others made in this section (unless otherwise specified) is presented in Chapters 18 and 25.

3. D. M. LEVY. Anti-Nazis: criteria of differentiation. *Psychiatry,* 1948, **11**, 125-167.

4. *Cf.* J. LAFARGE. *No Postponement.* New York: Longmans, Green, 1950.

5. *Cf.* J. R. CARLSON. *Under Cover.* New York: E. P. Dutton, 1943. Also the publications by Friends of Democracy, Inc.

6. L. A. DOMBROSE AND D. J. LEVINSON. Ideological "militancy" and "pacifism" in democratic individuals. *Journal of Social Psychology,* 1950, **32**, 101-113.

7. See studies by S. P. ADINARAYANIAH. A research in color prejudice. *British Journal of Psychology,* 1941, **31**, 217-229. Also, T. W. ADORNO, *et al. The Authoritarian Personality.* New York: Harper, 1950, especially 179.

8. *Cf.* R. D. MINARD. Race attitudes of Iowa children. *University of Iowa Studies in Character,* 1931, **4**, No. 2. Also, RUTH ZELIGS AND G. HENDRICKSON. Racial attitudes of 200 sixth-grade children. *Sociology and Social Research,* 1933, **18**, 26-36.

9. E. G MALHERBE. *Race Attitudes and Education.* Johannesburg, S. A.: Institute of Race Relations, 1946.

10. S. A. STOUFFER, *et al. The American Soldier: Adjustment During Army Life.* Princeton: Princeton Univ. Press, 1949; RIVA GERSTEIN. Probing Canadian prejudices: a preliminary objective survey. *Journal of Psychology,* 1947, **23**, 151-159; BABETTE SAMELSON. *The Patterning of Attitudes and Beliefs Regarding the American Negro.* (Unpublished.) Cambridge: Radcliffe College Library, 1945.

11. G. W. ALLPORT AND B. M. KRAMER. Some roots of prejudice. *Journal of Psychology,* 1946, **22**, 9-39.

12. *Ibid.*

13. A. SCODEL AND P. MUSSEN. Social perceptions of authoritarians and non-authoritarians. *Journal of Abnormal and Social Psychology,* 1953, **48**, 181-184.

14. T. W. ADORNO, *et al. Op. cit.,* 430.

15. G. W. ALLPORT AND B. M. KRAMER. *Op. cit.*

16. *Cf.* E. L. HARTLEY. *Problems in Prejudice.* New York: Kings Crown, 1946.

17. *Cf.* G. W. ALLPORT. *Personality: A Psychological Interpretation.* New York: Henry Holt, 1937, 220-225.

18. M. B. SMITH. *Functional and Descriptive Analysis of Public Opinion.* (Unpublished.) Cambridge: Harvard College Library, 1947.

19. ELSE FRENKEL-BRUNSWIK. Intolerance of ambiguity as an emotional and perceptual personality variable. *Journal of Personality,* 1949, **18,** 108-143.

20. R. I. EVANS. Personal values as factors in anti-Semitism. *Journal of Abnormal and Social Psychology,* 1952, **47,** 749-756.

21. Also G. W. ALLPORT AND P. E. VERNON. A test for personal values. *Journal of Abnormal and Social Psychology,* 1931, **26,** 231-248. In 1951 this test was revised by G. W. ALLPORT, P. E. VERNON, AND G. LINDZEY. *Study of Values.* Boston: Houghton Mifflin, 1951.

22. D. J. LEVINSON AND R. N. SANFORD. A scale for measurement of anti-Semitism. *Journal of Psychology,* 1944, **17,** 339-370.

23. For a fuller exposition of this view see E. FROMM. *Man for Himself.* New York: Rinehart, 1947; I. SUTTIE. *The Origins of Love and Hate.* London: Kegan Paul, 1935; G. W. ALLPORT. Basic principles in improving human relations. Chapter 2 in K. W. BIGELOW (ED.). *Cultural Groups and Human Relations.* New York: Columbia Univ. Press, 1951.

CHAPTER 28

RELIGION AND PREJUDICE

REALISTIC CONFLICT—DIVISIVE FACTORS IN RELIGION—DO RE-
LIGIOUS GROUPS DIFFER IN PREJUDICE?—TWO KINDS OF RELIG-
IOSITY—THE CASE OF SIMON PETER—RELIGION AND CHARACTER
STRUCTURE

God hath made of one blood all nations.

THE ACTS OF THE APOSTLES

*Religion is a curse—making for divisions in an already
divided world.*

WORLD WAR II VETERAN

The role of religion is paradoxical. It makes prejudice and it
unmakes prejudice. While the creeds of the great religions are
universalistic, all stressing brotherhood, the practice of these creeds
is frequently divisive and brutal. The sublimity of religious ideals
is offset by the horrors of persecution in the name of these same
ideals. Some people say the only cure for prejudice is more religion; some say the only cure is to abolish religion. Churchgoers
are more prejudiced than the average; they also are less prejudiced
than the average. We shall try to unravel the paradox.

Realistic Conflict

First, it is well to be clear concerning the existence of certain
natural, and perhaps unresolvable, conflicts inherent in various
aspects of religion.

Take first the claim of certain great religions—that each has absolute and final possession of Truth. People who adhere to different absolutes are not likely to find themselves in agreement. The
conflict is most acute when missionaries are actively engaged in
proselytizing divergent sets of absolutes. Moslem and Christian
missionaries in Africa, for example, have long been at odds. Each
insists that if its creed were completely realized in practice, it
would eliminate all ethnic barriers between men. So it would.
But in actuality, the absolutes of any one religion have never yet
been accepted by more than a fraction of mankind.

Catholicism by its very nature must believe that Judaism and
Protestantism are in error. And varieties of Judaism and Prot-

estantism feel keenly that other varieties of their own faith are perverse in many points of belief. Among the world's great religions Hinduism seems to be the most tolerant in principle, granting as it does, that "Truth is one—men call it many things," and that there are many valid aspects and incarnations of God. At the same time historic Hinduism has engendered the evil of caste among its own adherents, and has not been without schismatic conflict.

Since no one religion has succeeded in uniting the world, the points of difference may be real foci of conflict. When a sincere believer tries to convert an unbeliever at the point of a sword, the unbeliever (who is a believer in a different absolute) may resist persuasion to the death. Martyrs are sometimes victims of prejudice, but they may also be victims of a realistic clash of ideals. As long as there are human beings with different central values, there will be disagreement. And those who argue valiantly for their convictions, or who go to their death defending them, are not necessarily prejudiced, nor victims of prejudice.

While the grounds for realistic conflict are considerable, most religions have ameliorating doctrines that lessen the clash. They hold, for example, that while out-groups dwell in error, they too can be saved through God's mercy in His own time. Compassion is a virtue. In principle, theologies seldom sanction cruelty to infidels, even though in practice brutality has been common enough. In modern times there is less often an open clash over purely religious issues. What happens is that people desiring to express certain absolutes of faith withdraw into their own group. For the most part they allow others a similar privilege.

In the United States at the present time there is considerable discussion concerning the question whether the Catholic Church is a potential threat to democratic freedoms, whether if Catholics acquired a majority control of government they would deny freedom of worship to others. Stated in this fashion the problem is realistic, and presumably open to a factual answer. If the answer were affirmative, then a realistic clash of absolutes would certainly occur. If the answer were negative, the issue should on rational grounds be dropped. If the accusation persisted in spite of clear negative evidence, then prejudice would be at work.

But this particular issue, like many others, is seldom kept on a factual plane. Partisans on both sides arise and cloud the issue with irrelevant accusations. Anti-Catholics use the issue merely to mask their hatred. Disliking Catholics as they do, they are quick to perceive any Catholic doctrine or practice as a "threat" to democratic freedoms. Their perception and interpretation are selective. Contrariwise, embattled Catholics resent the irrelevancies to such an extent that they too are distracted from the basic issue and make countercharges.

In sum: While there are often irreconcilable differences between contrary sets of absolutes, in practice there are usually ways of accommodating these differences in a peaceful manner. In fact, some of the absolutes in religion are themselves integrative to a high degree and aid such accommodation. Militancy, however, is likely to sharpen the conflict to the point of an open clash. Most apparent of all is the tendency for religious issues to become a rallying point for all sorts of irrelevancies. And whenever irrelevancies cloud realistic conflict, prejudice is in command.

Divisive Factors in Religion

The chief reason why religion becomes the focus of prejudice is that it usually stands for more than faith—it is the pivot of the cultural tradition of a group. However sublime the origins of a religion may be, it rapidly becomes secularized by taking over cultural functions. Islam is more than a religion; it is a well-knit cluster of related cultures carried by ethnic cousins who are sharply demarcated from the non-Moslem world. Christianity is so locked with western civilization that it is hard to keep in mind its original core; and sects of Christianity have become tied into subcultural and national groups so that religious divisions march hand in hand with ethnic and national divisions. Most clear of all is the case of the Jews. While they are primarily a religious group, they are likewise viewed as a race, a nation, a people, a culture (Chapter 15). When religious distinctions are made to do double duty, the grounds for prejudice are laid. For prejudice means that inept, overinclusive categories are employed in place of differentiated thinking.

The clergy of a church may and often do become defenders of a culture. They, too, work with inept categories. In defending the absolutes of their faith, they tend to defend their in-group as a whole, finding in the absolutes of their faith justification for the secular practices of their in-group. Not infrequently they justify and sweeten ethnic prejudices with religious sanctions. An immigrant from Poland to the United States tells the following experience:

> I vividly remember a lesson in religion which I heard at school when I was twelve years old. Some pupil asked the priest whether it was all right to boycott the Jewish stores. The priest put our consciences at ease. "Although God wants us to love all

fellow men, He does not say that we should not love some of them more than others.   Therefore, it is all right to love Poles more than Jews and to patronize Polish businesses only."

The priest was a pious fraud, twisting religion to fit secular prejudice, and planting seeds of bigotry that could, and did, grow out of hand in plunder and pogroms.   Protestantism has been equally hypocritical in finding theological rationalizations for ethnic self-interest.

Piety may thus be a convenient mask for prejudices which intrinsically have nothing to do with religion.   William James makes the point in the following passage:

> The baiting of the Jews, the hunting of Albigenses and Waldenses, the stoning of Quakers and ducking of Methodists, the murdering of Mormons and the massacring of Armenians, express much rather that aboriginal human neophobia, that pugnacity of which we all share the vestiges, and that inborn hatred of the alien and of eccentric and nonconforming men as aliens, than they express the positive piety of the various perpetrators. Piety is the mask, the inner force is tribal instinct.[1]

We quote this passage because it states the irrelevance of religion to much persecution.   We need not, however, endorse James' conviction that prejudice has instinctive roots in "aboriginal human neophobia."

Abominations inevitably result when men use their religion to justify the pursuit of power, prestige, wealth, and ethnic self-interest.   It is then that religion and prejudice merge.   Often one can detect the fusion in ethnocentric slogans: "Cross and Flag," "white, Protestant, gentile, American," "the chosen people," "Gott mit uns," "God's country."

Some theologians explain this perversion of religion by saying that sinners are people who build religion around their own self-interest.   Evil comes whenever man turns to God without turning away from self.   In other words, people suffering from the sin of pride have failed to learn that the essence of religion is not self-justification, self-support, but rather humility, self-negation, and love of neighbor.

Nothing is easier than to twist one's conception of the teachings of religion to fit one's prejudice.   A particularly anti-Semitic Catholic priest declared that Christianity is not a religion of love, but one of vengeance and hate.   And to him it is.   A whole array of Protestant sects flourish by similar corruption of the Gospel.[2]

History, we cannot deny, has seen an endless array of such perversions. What is particularly striking is the ease with which spiritually minded people seem to slip from piety into prejudice. Even certain saints of the Church have shown this tendency. Take the following excerpts from a sermon:

> The synagogue is worse than a brothel . . . it is the den of scoundrels. . . . It is a criminal assembly of Jews . . . a place of meeting for the assassins of Christ . . . a den of thieves; a house of ill fame, a dwelling of iniquity. . . . I would say the same things about their souls. . . . Debauchery and drunkenness have brought them to the level of the lusty goat and the pig. . . . We should not even salute them, or have the slightest converse with them. . . . They are lustful, rapacious, greedy, perfidious robbers.[3]

This sermon, to be sure, was written in the fourth century; but it was written by one of the greatest saints of the Church, the author of the most ancient liturgy and of many exalted prayers, St. John of Chrysostom. Some personalities, we are forced to conclude, can be genuinely religious and universalistic in certain regions of their life, and inconsistently prejudiced and particularistic in others. The history of Catholic treatment of the Jews is marked by this conflict. At certain times the elements of bigotry have prevailed, at others a broad compassion, as expressed in the present-day pronouncement of Pope Pius XI, "Anti-Semitism is a movement in which we Christians can have no part whatsoever. Spiritually we are Semites."

The contamination of universalistic religion with ethnocentric attitudes is seen likewise in the Jim Crow churches in the United States. The majority of Protestant Negroes attend segregated churches.[4] Segregation is less marked in Catholic churches. Among both it is slowly declining.[5] But the criticism seems justified that through most of America's history the Church has been a preserver of the status quo in race relations rather than a crusader for improvement.

We have argued that whereas realistic conflicts between religions may occasionally occur, most of what is called religious bigotry is in fact the result of a confusion between ethnocentric self-interest and religion, with the latter called upon to rationalize and justify the former.

The extreme diversity of institutional religion helps to aggravate the situation. The 1936 U. S. census of religious bodies shows approximately 56,000,000 members. Of these, some 31,000,000 were Protestants, 20,000,000 Catholics, and 4,600,000 Jews. In all, there were 256 denominations, although 52 bodies, each having more than 50,000 members, account for 95 percent of the total. One should add small numbers of Hindus, Moslems, Buddhists, and adherents of native Indian religions. It is unlikely that anywhere in the world do so many forms of religious persuasion (and non-persuasion) exist as in this country. Many sects exist because Old World divisions were transplanted to this country by immigrants, though some, like the Latter Day Saints, Disciples of Christ, and various Pentacostal bodies, are indigenous. In spite of some recent and mild ecumenical skirmishes among Protestant bodies, there is no reason to believe that in the foreseeable future any considerable degree of unification will take place.

In its institutional organization, therefore, religion is divisive. Many of the creedal distinctions are not so sharp nor so important today as when they first were drawn. Furthermore, the movement for general religious amnesty has gained immeasurably since the early days of the American colonies. The Constitution and the Bill of Rights marked a great departure from the long-standing practice of religious intolerance in the Old World and in the colonies. But at the same time the divisions that exist make it easy to contaminate the universalistic creeds of religion with irrelevant considerations of caste, social class, national origin, cultural differences, and race. Catholics are less often disparaged for their faith, but inherit prejudice directed originally to immigrants, who are often poorly educated. Episcopalians are no longer persecuted for their doctrine but are sometimes disliked for being snobbish and upper-crust. Pentacostalists are considered primitive, less for their theology than for their emotionalism. Jehovah's Witnesses are persecuted for minor political deviations. In none of these cases is the prejudice primarily religious.

In fact, if one looks at the matter closely, it becomes doubtful whether bigotry ever is or can be exclusively religious. Differences of creed there are; realistic conflicts can occur. But bigotry enters only when religion becomes the apologist for in-group superiority and overextends itself by disparaging out-groups for reasons that extend beyond deviation in creed.

Do Religious Groups Differ in Prejudice?

A great many studies have been directed to the question whether Protestants or Catholics as a group display more prejudice. The results are entirely equivocal: some studies find Catholics more bigoted, some Protestants, and some find no difference.[6]

Where differences have been found it seems likely that the variation is not due to religious affiliation directly. Thus in regions where Catholics are less educated and of lower socio-economic status, they may show the slightly higher degree of prejudice appropriate to these nonreligious variables. In communities where Protestants are less educated and of lower status, they seem more prejudiced.

While there is no over-all difference, one study in this field is of particular interest. The investigator tested 900 incoming freshmen in an eastern college with the Bogardus Social Distance Scale.[7] On the average, there was no difference between Catholic, Protestant, and Jewish students. Each group welcomed or rejected about as many nationalities as the others. The investigator did find, however, that each of these religious groups had characteristic patterns of rejection.

> Jewish students stood highest in their rejection of Canadians, English, Finnish, French, German, Irish, Norwegian, Scottish, and Swedish (a rejection of the "majority" or "favored" groups in our country). Catholic students stood highest in rejection of Chinese, Hindus, Japanese, Negroes, and Filipinos (a rejection of the colored groups—possibly associated with the idea of "heathen"). Protestant students stood highest in rejecting Armenians, Greeks, Italians, Jews, Mexicans, Polish, Syrians (a rejection of familiar "minority" groups in our culture).

This instructive study shows that while average prejudice may be the same, special groups may yet have their own pet dislikes determined by their own values. Thus Jewish students seem to resent fair-skinned, dominant majority groups who have traditionally placed them in a lower position. Catholics seem to hold non-Christian races (the great colored masses) at greater distance. Protestants pick on the lower social status groups.

Although this study did not find a lower average prejudice among Jewish subjects, it is true that most investigators have noted this trend. In one research, for example, 78 percent of the Jewish subjects fell into the more favorable half of scores in respect to attitudes toward the Negro.[8] Findings of this order are common. In Chapter 9 we discussed the effect of persecution upon the attitudes of Jews, and discovered that identification with the underdog, with a resulting sympathy, was a common response in this particular group.

We lack data to make finer comparisons—for example, of one Protestant sect with another. From indications thus far it seems that such analyses would probably not be profitable.

We do have, however, some striking findings concerning the relation of the intensity of religious training in general to prejudice.

Over four hundred students were asked the question, "To what degree has religion been an influence in your upbringing?" Lumping together those who report that religion was a marked or moderate factor, we find the degree of prejudice far higher than among those who report that religion was a slight or nonexistent factor in their training.[9] Other studies reveal that individuals having no religious affiliation show on the average less prejudice than do church members.

Two Kinds of Religiosity

This finding, distressing as it must be to religionists, demands closer inspection. Not only does it seem to belie the universalistic import of religious teaching, but it is contradicted by other evidence. Students were asked in the same investigation to tell *how* their religious training had influenced their ethnic attitudes. Two types of report were given. Some said frankly that the impact was negative, that they were taught to despise other religious and cultural groups. But some said the influence was wholly positive:

> The Church taught me that we are all equal and that there should be no persecution, for any reason, of minority groups.

> It has helped me to understand the way these groups feel and that they are human beings also.

This double influence of religious teaching was noted also by the California investigations reported in Chapter 25. There we learned that many anti-Semites were puritanical, moralistic, devoted members of churches (in an institutional sense). The same investigators, however, report:

> Those low on the anti-Semitism scale are by no means generally irreligious, but religion takes another form. It seems to be experienced on a deeper level and infused with the character of ethics and philosophy rather than with the utilitarian tough characteristic of the highs who generally regard religion as a means rather than an end.[10]

Thus, while church membership seems, on the whole, more often associated with prejudice than not, still there are many cases where its influence is in precisely the reverse direction. Religion is a highly personal matter; it has quite different meanings in different lives. Its functional significance may range from its crutch-like ability to bolster infantile and magical forms of thinking to its support for a guiding and comprehensive view of life that turns the individual from his self-centeredness towards genuine love for his neighbor.

In an attempt to obtain more light upon this issue, an (unpublished) experiment was conducted in a university seminar. A Catholic priest and a Protestant clergyman carried through the investigation.

Two groups of laymen were selected in both a Catholic and a Protestant parish. The two groups might be called "devout" and "institutional," respectively. In the Catholic parish they were selected by a person who knew nothing about the experiment, but who was well acquainted with the parishioners. He chose 20 men to whom, in his opinion, "their faith really meant something"; and 20 "who seemed influenced more by political and social aspects of religious activities." The two Protestant (Baptist) groups were selected in a different way. One group consisted of 22 regular attendants at a Bible class, the other of 15 irregular attendants. All subjects filled out a questionnaire consisting of many items, being asked to indicate the extent of their agreement or disagreement with such statements as the following:

There are a few exceptions, but in general Jews are pretty much alike.

I can conceive of circumstances under which the lynching of a Negro might be justified.

In general, Negroes can't be trusted.

One big trouble with the Jews is that they are never contented, but always try for the best jobs and the most money.

The questions used in the two studies differed slightly, since anti-Catholic statements were included in the instrument used by the Baptists.

But in both studies, the same result occurred: those who were considered the most devout, more personally absorbed in their religion, were far less prejudiced than the others. The institutional type of attachment, external and political in nature, turns out to be associated with prejudice.

In the light of our discussions in Chapters 25 and 27, the finding is easily understood. Belonging to a church because it is a safe, powerful, superior in-group is likely to be the mark of an authoritarian character and to be linked with prejudice. Belonging to a church because its basic creed of brotherhood expresses the ideals one sincerely believes in, is associated with tolerance. Thus, the "institutionalized" religious outlook and the "interiorized" religious outlook have opposite effects in the personality.

The Case of Simon Peter

The two-way pull of religion—toward prejudice and away from it—is vividly illustrated in the classic Biblical story of the Apostle Peter.[11] In the early days of the Church there was perplexity concerning the catholicity of the Gospel. Was it merely a New Testament of Judaism? Or was it intended for out-groups as well? The lineage of Christ and the early apostles was Jewish, and the framework of Christianity was Judaism. Therefore, it was easy to think of Christianity as a doctrine of salvation reserved for Jews. What is more, there was at the time strong prejudice among Jews against all non-Jews, and it was natural for even the Christian Jews to think that salvation was not for the gentiles.

Now an Italian centurion by the name of Cornelius lived in the town of Caesarea, not far from Joppa where Peter was staying. Peter was on a missionary journey. Cornelius was a religious man who desired to hear more concerning the new Christian doctrine. Therefore he sent messages to Peter inviting him to come to Caesarea as his guest and to instruct his household in the new faith.

The invitation brought to a head the deep conflict that Peter was suffering. He knew that according to his own tribal custom, "it is an unlawful thing for a man that is a Jew to keep company, or come unto one of another nation." At the same time he knew of Christ's compassion for outcasts. Shortly before Cornelius' messenger arrived, Peter had had a vision. Being very hungry he had fallen asleep,

And saw heaven opened, and a certain vessel descending unto him, as it had been a great sheet knit at the four corners and let down to the earth:

Wherein were all manner of fourfooted beasts of the earth, and wild beasts, and creeping things, and fowls of the air.

And there came a voice to him, Rise Peter; kill and eat.

But Peter said, Not so, Lord; for I have never eaten anything that is common or unclean.

And the voice spake unto him again a second time, What God hath cleansed, that call not thou common.

The dream both reflected Peter's conflict and indicated the course that he should follow. Somewhat reluctantly, therefore, he went to the house of Cornelius, and told him frankly the conflict he was in, specifying the tribal taboos that bound him, and only then asked why Cornelius had so urgently invited him.

As Cornelius spoke Peter became impressed by his sincerity and devoutness, and said, "Of a truth I perceive that God is no respecter of persons." So Peter preached, and the zeal of Cornelius and his associates grew. So much so that Peter and his Jewish companions "were astonished, because that on the gentiles also was poured out the gift of the Holy Ghost." Finally, Peter administered baptism to the group—fully knowing the unusualness of the step.

On returning to Jerusalem he was confronted wrathfully by his Jewish associates who said, "Thou wentest into men uncircumcized, and didst eat with them." They were probably still more scandalized that he had baptized them into the new faith. The Gospel was for the in-group alone.

Peter then told them the story from start to finish and explained his own change of heart, how the manifest sincerity of Cornelius had won him from the ethnocentric view of Christianity since God had granted gentiles the same gift of faith. "What was I," Peter concluded, "that I could withstand God?"

The story ends with the persuasion of the group at Jerusalem, and therewith a change in Church policy:

When they heard these things, they held their peace, and glorified God, saying, Then hath God also to the gentiles granted repentance unto life.

This same conflict between the in-group and universalistic conceptions of religion lasts to the present day. Not everyone has resolved the matter as did Peter and his associates. Quite the contrary, we have reported the finding that on the average, Church members seem to be *more* prejudiced than nonmembers.

It is the prevalence of ethnocentric interpretations of religion that alienates many tolerant people from the church. They turn apostate because historical religions have become overburdened with the secular prejudice of in-group safety-seekers.[12] They judge religion not by its scriptural purity, but as it is perverted by a majority of its followers. As we have said, the "institutionalized" and the "interiorized" religious outlooks are worlds apart.

Religion and Character Structure

It is clear, then, that religion bears no univocal relationship to prejudice. Its influence is important, but it works in contradictory directions. The apologists for religion overlook its ethnocentric and self-exalting reference; its opponents see little else. Clarity of analysis demands a sharp distinction between the functional role of religion in a constricted and immature personality on the one hand, and in a mature and productive life on the other.[13] Some people seize upon the tribal investments of traditional religion for comfort and security; others take its universalistic teaching as an authentic guide to conduct.

Many zealous workers for the betterment of group relations are motivated by the demand of their religion that they love their neighbor. They say with Booker T. Washington, "I will not let any man reduce my soul to the level of hatred." They mark the passage in the *Book of Proverbs* which says that God abominates a man "who soweth discord among the brethren." They sincerely believe that "he that hateth his brother is in darkness." They know, too, that religion means more than their own religion—that for example, the Golden Rule is common to all great religions—to Judaism, Buddhism, Taoism, Mohammedanism, Hinduism, as well as Christianity. They know that whatever absolute differences exist, they are partially offset by common affirmations—including the doctrine of the brotherhood of man.

In their investigation of ethnic attitudes among veterans, Bettelheim and Janowitz discovered that "veterans who had stable religious convictions tended to be more tolerant." They define stability as the internalization of central teachings:

> If the moral teachings of the church are accepted by the individual not through fear of damnation or of societal disapproval but because he considers them absolute standards of behavior, independent of external threats or approval, then we say the individual has "internalized" these moral precepts.

The authors distinguish this inner sense of control and stability from external control that depends on props in the outside world, including parental domination and institutional religion.[14]

Besides conferring a stable ego-control and providing a clear standard of conduct, religion may also engender tolerance through its warning against the sin of pride. A devout person must acknowledge his own shortcomings. As we have discovered in other connections, self-blame—intropunitiveness—leads to tolerance; it makes for humility and discourages arrogance.

Many democratic personalities, to be sure, are not religious. Their stability and control are expressed in nonreligious ethical terms. They believe that "all men are created free and equal," or simply approve the adage, "live and let live." It is of no interest to them that the codes of decency in western civilization are all derivations of the Judeo-Christian religion. The ethics may linger even when the faith wanes.

Religion, however, is a large factor in most people's philosophy of life. We have seen that it may be of an ethnocentric order, aiding and abetting a life style marked by prejudice and exclusiveness. Or it may be of a universalistic order, vitally distilling ideals of brotherhood into thought and conduct. Thus we cannot speak sensibly of the relation between religion and prejudice without specifying the sort of religion we mean and the role it plays in the personal life.

NOTES AND REFERENCES

1. W. JAMES. *Varieties of Religious Experience.* New York: Random House, 1902. Modern Library edition, 331.

2. An account of contemporary Protestant sects devoted to vengeance and hate is given by R. L. ROY. *Apostles of Discord.* Boston: Beacon Press, 1953.

3. Quoted from M. HAY. *The Foot of Pride.* Boston: Beacon Press, 1950, 26-32. This author presents an extended history of Catholic treatment of the Jews from earliest times to the present.

4. F. S. LOESCHER. *The Protestant Church and the Negro.* New York: Association Press, 1948.

5. It must not be thought that separate churches for Negro and white communicants are entirely the result of white people's unwillingness to mingle. In many communities, especially in Northern states, Negroes would be genuinely welcomed in white churches. They sometimes prefer their own congregations, however, both because they feel more at ease, and because they wish to give employment to trained Negro clergy. The color bar in churches would disappear more rapidly if white or mixed congregations more often employed qualified Negro clergy.

6. The equivocality can be seen at a glance in the surveys by A. ROSE. *Studies in Reduction of Prejudice.* Chicago: American Council on Race Relations, 1949 (mimeographed); and H. J. Parry. Protestants, Catholics, and prejudice. *International Journal of Opinion and Attitude Research,* 1949, **3**, 205-213.

7. DOROTHY T. SPOERL. Some aspects of prejudice as affected by religion and education. *Journal of Social Psychology,* 1951, **33**, 69-76.

8. G. W. ALLPORT AND B. M. KRAMER. Some roots of prejudice. *Journal of Psychology,* 1946, **22**, 9-39, 27.

9. *Ibid.,* 25.

10. ELSE FRENKEL-BRUNSWIK AND R. N. SANFORD. The anti-Semitic

personality: a research report. In E. SIMMEL (ED.), *Anti-Semitism: A Social Disease.* New York: International Universities Press, 1948, 96-124.

11. *The Acts of the Apostles,* Chapters 10 and 11.

12. A study shows that this complaint against historic religion is one of the chief reasons college students give for their frequent apostasy, especially Jewish students who are particularly alert to the persecutions conducted in the name of religion through many centuries. *Cf.* G. W. ALLPORT, J. M. GILLESPIE, AND JACQUELINE YOUNG. The religion of the post-war college student. *Journal of Psychology,* 1948, **25**, 3-33. It takes broad perspective to see that neither the early prejudice of Jewish-Christians against gentiles, nor of modern Christians against the Jews, affects at bottom the universalistic teaching of either Judaism or Christianity.

13. *Cf.* G. W. ALLPORT. *The Individual and His Religion.* New York: Macmillan, 1950, especially Chapter 3.

14. B. BETTELHEIM AND M. JANOWITZ. Ethnic tolerance: a function of social and personal control. *American Journal of Sociology,* 1949, **55**, 137-145.

Part VIII

REDUCING GROUP TENSIONS

CHAPTER 29

OUGHT THERE TO BE A LAW?

All organizations devoted to the betterment of group relations—
and there are thousands of them—can be classified either as *public*
or as *private* agencies.

The former include so-called Mayor's Committees, Governor's
Committees, or Civic Unity Committees—established in city or
state by executive or by legislative ordinance. Public agencies
likewise include city, state, or federal commissions empowered to
enforce antidiscrimination laws—sometimes all relevant laws, sometimes only some specific laws, such as those dealing with housing,
or fair employment practices. Sometimes a public agency is only
a fact-finding body, an example being the President's Committee on
Civil Rights, whose incisive report in 1947 became a rallying point
for the forces of tolerance.[1] In addition to such public bodies
there are, of course, the basic law-enforcement agencies of the
community, particularly the local and state police whose duty it is to
see that disorder, riots, overt acts of aggression are prevented, and
that all legal protection is afforded to minority groups.

Private agencies are even more numerous in type. They range
from small "race relations" or "good neighbor" committees of
women's clubs, service clubs, or churches, to large-scale national
organizations, such as the Anti-Defamation League, Friends of
Democracy, Inc., National Association for the Advancement of
Colored People, and to coordinating bodies such as the National
Association of Intergroup Relations Officials. Many communities
having public bodies, e.g., a Mayor's Committee, also have private
citizens' committees.

On the whole, public agencies are more conservative than private
agencies because they are continually exposed to pressures from
prejudiced as well as unprejudiced forces within a community.
Private agencies are in a better position to be watchdogs and to
plan and initiate reforms. They are particularly useful as goads
and critics of public bodies in case the latter grow bureaucratic and
inept. But from the point of view of prestige and the enforce-

ment of statutes public bodies have the advantage. In principle, a community needs both types of organization, and there are many instances where the two work harmoniously for a common objective.

In this chapter we are concerned with only one type of public body (lawmaking), and with only one phase of their activity (civil rights legislation). Yet it is well to be aware that governmental remedies are by no means all legislative in character. Executive order can, and has, accomplished a great deal. President Roosevelt's establishment of an emergency Fair Employment Practices Committee in 1941 is a historic case in point. He acted within his delegated powers when he ruled that no federal contract could be granted to a firm that refused on policy to hire members of minority groups. Earlier, Roosevelt had taken a similar step during the depression and required that all public works contracts include nondiscrimination clauses. Negroes, Spanish-Americans, Indians—all depressed groups—benefitted. Executives below the President also use their authority to see that federal housing projects, and other facilities subsidized by the government, are enjoyed equally by all groups. In recent years top authorities in the armed services have issued orders that have gone a long way toward eliminating the traditional segregation among fighting forces.

A Brief History of Legislation[2]

The Constitution, the Bill of Rights, the Fourteenth and Fifteenth Amendments, build a framework of democratic equality for all groups in the American population. But within this framework wide interpretation has reigned.

After the close of the Civil War, Congress passed several laws designed to secure effective equality for the liberated Negro slaves: "to abolish and forever prohibit the system of peonage," to outlaw the Ku Klux Klan, to make it a criminal offense to interfere with the right to vote because of race or color, and even to prohibit discrimination in inns, public conveyances, or other public places. Meanwhile, the defeated and angry South in its various state legislatures was busily engaged in enacting the opposite type of law, commonly called the Black Codes, designed to deny as completely as possible the new-found rights of the liberated race. Only for the short period when federal troops were present in the South during the turbulent Reconstruction era was the Congressional civil rights legislation enforced.

Soon, by a series of events, the South regained its rights to "rule the Negro." The Democratic Congress of 1877 voted to repeal most of the Reconstruction civil rights legislation. The Supreme Court placed exceedingly narrow interpretations upon the Fourteenth and Fifteenth Amendments, leaving their legal implementation largely to individual states. With this encouragement certain states immediately passed segregation laws, and through various subterfuges legally deprived the Negro of his right to vote. Supporting the states' rights point of view was the famous *Plessy v. Ferguson* decision of 1896. In this case the Court accepted the "separate but equal" doctrine under which it was argued that a statute decreeing separation of the races did not in reality deny them equality. The particular decision upheld a Louisiana statute requiring railways to segregate their passengers by color; but the decision carried with it a principle that in effect gave constitutional sanction to all forms of segregation.

Perhaps even more important in restoring the South's rule over the Negro has been the weapon of the filibuster in the Senate. By invoking the right of unlimited debate any Senator opposed to civil rights legislation (usually with the aid of a few like-minded colleagues) can permanently obstruct its passage. So effective is this device that *no civil rights law has been approved by the Senate since 1875.* Nor is there any early prospect of enacting any such law—no matter how large a majority of both Houses of Congress favor it—unless the Senate rules are amended to control filibusters. It is for this reason that proponents of civil rights legislation concentrate attention upon obtaining effective rules of cloture; but even proposals to make such changes in Senate rules elicit filibustering. It is chiefly because of the filibuster that federal laws against poll taxes, lynching, and in favor of equal employment opportunities fail to pass. Time after time the House of Representatives has approved such measures, and they are known to be favored by a majority of Senators, and still they cannot become part of the law of the land.

The stalemate introduced by the Supreme Court decisions and by the filibuster created a reaction in many northern states. They took it upon themselves to legislate in behalf of minority groups. By 1909 eighteen northern states had laws forbidding discrimination in public accommodations. It was not until recent years, however, that a veritable avalanche of civil rights bills descended upon state legislatures. During the year 1949 well over a hundred bills opposing discrimination were introduced. While only a small proportion passed, the yearly accumulation of protective statutes is impressive. Some forbid discrimination in employment, in public housing, in the National Guard. Others eliminate segregation in education, in public facilities, poll tax requirements for voting, or make it a criminal libel to publish antiminority propaganda. At a slower pace, certain southern states have repealed some of their discriminative laws and removed barriers to education and to voting.

The changing temper of the times has not left the Supreme Court unaffected. The tide of its decisions has changed since its nineteenth century pronouncement that "legislation is powerless to eradicate racial instincts." In recent years it has ruled that restrictive covenants in the sale of property cannot be enforced in the courts of the land; that alien land laws (whereby Orientals are barred from owning property) and segregation on conveyances used in interstate transportation are unconstitutional; that institutions of professional training must provide truly equal facilities for the education of all students. Through the insistence upon equality of facilities the Court has a powerful weapon against segregation even if it should not explicitly reverse its *Plessy v. Ferguson* decision. Most states practicing segregation would find the cost of providing two sets of truly equal facilities prohibitive. It is estimated that in the South it would cost one billion dollars to bring the educational opportunities for colored children to an equal level with the white. Thus the Court demand for true equality of provisions would hasten the collapse of the segregation policies because of their economic untenability.

But the moot point is whether the logic of "separate but equal" can stand up at all. Segregation has no root purpose excepting to stamp one group of Americans as inferior to another. More and more attention is being focused upon this issue, and the sentiment against segregation is growing. As we shall see later in this chapter, the problem is now being placed more squarely than ever before the Supreme Court, and its willingness to face it, and perhaps to reverse its *Plessy v. Ferguson* decision, will be a measure of the degree of the social change that is occurring.

Types of Legislation

Broadly speaking, three main classes of legislation protect minority groups: (1) civil rights laws, (2) employment laws, (3) group libel laws.[3] It must, of course, be realized that many laws not *directly* aimed at the protection of minority groups have potentially even greater effects. For example, minimum wage legislation helps to raise the standard of living in a depressed group so that their health and education and self-respect improve, with the further result that they appear more acceptable as associates and neighbors of members of the majority group. Similarly, effective laws against crime might eliminate criminal gangs which are often organized along ethnic lines and sometimes carry their own ethnic prejudices into gang warfare. Antilynching laws have a similar effect.

Civil rights laws include statutes forbidding any public place of amusement, any hotel, restaurant, hospital, public vehicle, library, and the like, to discriminate against a customer because of race, color, creed, or national origin. A large majority of northern and western states have such laws. They are, however, not often enforced, partly because enforcement officials regard them as unimportant, partly because in certain localities prejudiced folkways are strong enough to restrain the official, and partly because people who are discriminated against seldom enter complaints (it is easier to slink away). When public prosecutors do press cases, the fines levied are small, usually $10 to $100, and the prosecutors regard the cases as merely troublesome. Seldom does the law provide for revoking the license of the offender. A hotel operator who excludes a Chinese or Negro may be found guilty and fined a few dollars. He pays, charging the trifling cost to his advertising budget or overhead, and continues his illegal policy.

The constitutionality of such laws is well established, and their spread in popularity at the present time may also betoken a stricter enforcement in the future. It is generally agreed, however, that enforcement requires a commission having the power to investigate complaints, negotiate informally with the offender, educate the offender in the meaning of the law, and, if necessary, have the power to revoke licenses.

Fair educational practices are also the subject of recent legislation. Following the disclosure that certain private schools operating under state charters do in fact exclude minority group members (some medical schools, for example, discriminate against Jewish and Italian applicants), restraining legislation has been passed. Schools are forbidden to seek information concerning the applicant's group membership (through photographs or leading questions); admission is to be on merit alone. A law of this type creates bureaucratic difficulties for many schools that have in fact never practiced discrimination. Yet its proponents believe that it accomplishes a desirable end. Needless to say, states having educational segregation by law do not have statutes of this order.

Fair employment laws: President Roosevelt's executive order establishing a wartime agency to ensure fair employment opportunities seemed to capture the public imagination.[4] Congress retarded the executive order by failing to appropriate sufficient funds for its effective operation, and by failing to pass concurrent legislation that would place penalties upon violators or give the Committee powers to initiate investigations for violation. After the expiration of the wartime agency, Congress failed to establish it by law as a continuing government agency.

But in spite of resistance in Congress, it seems that the FEPC was "an idea whose time had come." Since the passing of the Ives-Quinn law in 1945 in New York, about half of the northern and western states have enacted similar legislation. In many cases cities also have passed FEPC ordinances. Often there are no penalties attached to violation of the law other than uncomfortable sessions with the commission and publicity that might be damaging. So much, however, has been accomplished through conciliation, that the results have been judged highly successful in most places where a tactful enforcement (really "conciliation") commission is at work. Apart from the new job opportunities resulting, the morale of minority groups is raised by the declaration that their rights as working citizens are matters of public concern.

In 1950 *Business Week* sent an inquiry to several large employers in states having a statutory FEPC, asking in effect, "Does it hamper you?" The editors summarized the opinions by saying, "FEPC laws haven't caused near the fuss that opponents predicted. Disgruntled job seekers haven't swamped the commission with complaints. Personal friction hasn't been at all serious. . . . Even those who opposed FEPC aren't actively hostile now." Furthermore, employers seem agreed that the law has not interfered with their basic right to select the most competent workers.[5]

Experience with this type of law has brought a new insight into the handling of prejudice. It has shown how much can be done through persuasion, investigation, publicity. The approach is not one of coercion but rather of conciliation. It turns out that few employers are confirmed in their prejudices; they are merely following what they assume to be accepted folkways. They are cooperative when they are assured that customers, employees, and the law prefer, or at least expect, a condition of no discrimination to prevail.

Now it is true that if employees and customers are *asked* in advance, they often give verbal objections to working with, or being served by, certain minority group members. But it turns out that when equality is practiced, there is little objection. Often there is not even any awareness that change has taken place.

The inconsistency between verbally expressed prejudice and

equalitarian conduct (p. 56) is illustrated by an experiment conducted in a large department store in New York City.[6] A Negro and white clerk worked side by side. The customers served by the Negro were followed into the street and, without knowing that they had been watched in the store, were interviewed. A certain number who had been served by the Negro expressed the sentiment that "they were against being served by Negro clerks." They were then asked if they had ever seen any Negro clerks in department stores. One-fourth said No. Apparently they had either failed to perceive (or to recall) the color of the salesperson who had just served them. Such curious disconnection between verbally expressed prejudice and conduct is instructive. It indicates that in the ordinary stream of living equality will be taken for granted provided only that the issue is not brought into consciousness and verbally articulated.

The same study indicates that in the case of those who recalled having been served by a Negro, prejudice may have been dented by the experience. They said in effect, "Well, it's all right to have Negroes as clerks in certain departments." A person who had been served in the clothing department would approve this arrangement, but say that Negroes ought not to be in more intimate relations as would be required, say, in the food department. But those who had been served by a Negro in the food department tended to say that such placement was acceptable, but that Negroes ought not to work, say, in the clothing department. The prejudice is still held, but it is clearly weakened and on the defensive.

Not only have FEPC laws given little trouble in practice, but they are strategic in the improvement of group relations. They provide jobs at a higher level of income and status than certain minority groups have previously enjoyed. The process fits an important principle of improvement in Negro-white relations stated by Myrdal.[7] He asserts that there is a "rank order of discrimination." Whites, at least southern whites, have greatest opposition to intermarriage, next to social equality; then, in order, to equal use of public facilities, to political equality, to legal equality, and *least* objection to equality in jobs. The Negro's own rank order is almost precisely *reversed*. He craves first and foremost equal job opportunity (because his economic plight is basic to many, if not most, of his troubles). It follows that FEPC legislation, by attacking the issue of discrimination in a way that will give maximum satisfaction to Negroes and minimum dissatisfaction to whites, is psychologically central.

Group libel and incitement laws form a more debatable cluster of legislative remedies.

Legislation aimed at curbing group libel is a logical extension of a legal principle already well established. If a man should publish his opinion that Mr. X is a cheat and a traitor, and if he could not prove his charges, Mr. X might collect handsome damages, especially if his business had been ruined and his prestige in the community damaged. But if the same man publishes his opinion that Japanese or Jewish Americans are all cheats and traitors, Mr. X, who, let us say, is a Japanese-American, may suffer quite as much loss through boycott and scorn, but he has no legal redress. Corporations and voluntary associations (for example, the Knights of Columbus) may successfully sue for libel; but ethnic and racial groups have no protection. Within the past few years a few such statutes have been passed (for example, in Massachusetts), but their enforcement has been virtually nil.

Though reasonable in principle, such laws are difficult to enforce. If they stipulate that malicious intent must be present in the libeler, such intent is hard to prove. And in the present early stage of research on group differences it is not easy to prove conclusively that derogatory statements are false. Furthermore, such laws are unpopular and marginal in their constitutionality, since they seem to abridge the rights of free speech. Public criticism, just and unjust, is part of the tradition of democratic rights, unless it incites to violence. Demagogues, as we saw in Chapter 26, usually halt their tirades short of this point.

Having considered carefully the case for and against group libel legislation, the President's Committee on Civil Rights did not endorse such laws. The remedy for criticism, it felt, is countercriticism, and for talk, more talk, provided that it is open and aboveboard. The Committee did, however, advocate a law making it a federal offense to send anonymous hate literature through the mails. When so serious a battle is on between the forces of bigotry and of civil rights, it seems fair at least that the antagonist identify himself so that he can be answered directly.

All laws to control demagogues run into constitutional barriers. Open breaches of the peace or incitements to violence have always been punished by law. Hence, opponents of special legislation to control the racist rabble-rouser argue that there is no need for it. Proponents argue that there is an insidious effect of demagogy directed against minority groups. The influence is long-lasting, and each tirade is cumulative, until at last a dangerous situation is created. The Supreme

Court is not likely to accept such reasoning, for it operates under the ruling written by Justice Oliver Wendell Holmes in 1919 which declared that restriction of free speech was allowable only when there was "clear and present danger" of violence. Police may interfere only when mob action seems imminent as a result of the demagogue's harangue. Many consider the ruling wise, for if the police were given more latitude they might, under cover of a broad antihate law, suppress criticisms that were uncongenial to them.

The same argument holds for proposals to restrict the use of public property by denying licenses to demagogues whose message is definitely not in the public interest. Such a statute would not stop demagogues speaking on private premises. True, such laws would clearly stipulate that the conscience of democracy must be respected in public places. Yet they too might open the way for capricious administration. The licensing authority might permit certain types of bigots to speak, and might silence others; or, at worst, might under cover of the law deny the privilege of speaking to a political opponent.

While there are many advocates of libel laws, the weight of opinion seems against them. The remedy for prejudiced opinion is not suppression, but rather a free-flowing counter-action by unprejudiced opinion. The same line of argument holds against censorship of films, radio, or press.

Does Legislation Affect Prejudice?

We have noted that the Supreme Court toward the end of the last century justified its conservative decisions on the grounds that the law was powerless to counter "racial instincts." This laissez faire attitude marked much of the social thinking of that period. A leading sociologist of the day, William Graham Sumner, asserted "stateways cannot change folkways." Even today the same view is often heard: "you cannot legislate against prejudice."

The point sounds plausible, but actually it is weak in two respects. First, we can be entirely sure that discriminative laws *increase* prejudice—why, then, should not legislation of the reverse order *diminish* prejudice?

Secondly, legislation is not in fact aimed at prejudice at all, at least not directly. Its intent is to equalize advantages and lessen discrimination. Only as a by-product of the improved conditions do people gain the benefits that come, as we have seen, from equal status contact and from normal acquaintance (Chapter 16). Increasing the skills of minority groups, raising their standard of living, improving their health and education, have similar indirect effects. Further, the establishment of a legal norm creates a public conscience and a standard for expected behavior that check *overt* signs of prejudice. Legislation aims not at controlling prejudice, but only its open expression. But when expression changes, thoughts too, in the long run, are likely to fall into line.

There are, however, certain cogent arguments against the legislative approach. It might, for example, engender a contempt for law and a disregard for it. By and large, Americans are noted for holding their laws lightly. As Myrdal says, "America has become a country where exceedingly much is permitted in practice but at the same time exceedingly much is forbidden by law." [8] Is it wise, therefore, to multiply statutes that will not be obeyed, or that would encounter ignorance and apathy? Even after some years of operation and considerable publicity, most people in New York State do not know that an FEPC law exists. Those who do, and who know also clear cases of discrimination, usually fail to enter complaints or take any steps whatever to invoke the law. This general indifference may be accompanied by the belief that some higher "natural law" gives people the right to hate whom they choose, to separate from people they dislike, and to disregard statutes that interfere. Only busybodies try to legislate morality into other people.

Another point: laws, especially of the puritan type so common in America, attack symptoms, not causes. To force a hotel manager to accept a Filipino guest is not to strike at the roots of his anti-Oriental bias. To force a child to sit next to a Negro child in school does not remove the economic fears that may lie at the bottom of his family's anti-Negro feeling. People are fashioned by deeper forces, not by surface pressure.

Finally, there is a considerable gap between a law "on the books" and a law "in action." Without competent enforcement, any law is a dead letter. It is argued that the low standards of enforcement in the United States make it particularly unwise to legislate in the area of human relations. Such laws are difficult to enforce; they sometimes run counter to public taste, and few people know what the laws are—or care.

Such considerations as these lead some to the view that legislation is the tool least likely to succeed in the diminution of group conflict.

But there are good answers to most of these arguments. While it is true that unless a fairly large percentage of the people are in favor of a law it will not work, yet it is false to say that folkways must always take precedence over stateways. It was the Jim Crow laws in the south that in large part *created* folkways. Similarly, we have seen that FEPC legislation quickly creates new folkways in a factory or department store. Within a very few weeks, Negroes, Mexicans, or Jews are accepted as a matter of course in occupations where for decades they had been excluded.

It is often said that the way must be paved for remedial legislation through education. Up to a point this statement is undoubtedly true. Debate, hearings, and an aroused electorate are all essential. But when the initial work has been done, then the legislation in turn becomes educative. The masses of people do not become converts in advance; rather they are converted by the *fait accompli*. It is a well known psychological fact that most people accept the results of an election or legislation gladly enough after the furore has subsided. Even those who strenuously favored a Democratic candidate for office accept without resentment the Republican who is elected. And those who fought against FEPC or civil rights legislation ordinarily abide by the majority decision if these laws are passed. They allow themselves to be re-educated by the new norm that prevails.

What we are here speaking of is the basic habit of democratic society. After free, and often fierce, debate, citizens bow to the majority will. *They do so with a special kind of willingness if the legislation is in line with their own private consciences.* On this point civil rights legislation has a marked advantage. In Chapter 20 we saw that most Americans have a deep inner conviction that discrimination is wrong and unpatriotic. While their own prejudices may make them squirm and protest in opposition to proposed laws, they may also sigh with relief if the law, in accord with their "better natures," is passed—and enforced. People need and want their consciences bolstered by law, and this is nowhere more true than in the area of group relations.

Actually, in the United States, stateways—at least as expressed in the Constitution—are in advance of folkways. The Constitution is clear in its intentions that total democracy shall prevail. Thus the "official" morality of this country is high, although private morality is in many respects low. The contrast with certain other lands, for example Germany under Hitler, is striking. There the official morality (discrimination, persecution, expropriation of minority groups) was low, and the morality of many private citizens immeasurably higher. But in the United States official morality sets a high ideal. Furthermore, it is expected that the laws of the land shall lead and guide the folkways. Even the violators may approve them in principle. Traffic laws, we know, are often broken, but no one wants to live without them.

While laws do not prevent violations altogether, they certainly act as a restraint. They will deter whoever is deterable. They will not deter the compulsive bigot or demagogue. But neither do laws against arson deter the pyromaniac. Laws, we may say, restrain the middle range of mortals who need them as a mentor in molding their habits.

A final argument in favor of remedial legislation is its ability to break into vicious circles. When group relations are bad, they tend to worsen. Thus, the Negro who is deprived of opportunities for equal employment, equal educational opportunities, equal facilities for health and growth, sinks into an inferior position. He is then regarded as a lower species of mankind and treated with contempt. His opportunities continue, therefore, to deteriorate, and his situation becomes worse. Neither private efforts nor education can break into this aggravated tangle. Only strong, publicly supported legislation can do so. Police powers may be needed to start the spiral of improvement in housing, health, education, and employment.

When discrimination is eliminated, prejudice, as we have said, tends to lessen. The vicious circle begins to reverse itself. The termination of discrimination in employment, housing, and in the armed forces has had the result, we have shown, of creating more friendly ethnic attitudes (Chapter 16). And experience proves that the difficulties of integrating hitherto segregated groups is ordinarily less than anticipated. But it often takes a law, or a strong executive order, to start the process moving. The "principle of cumulation," as Myrdal calls it, holds that raising the Negro plane of living will lower prejudice on the part of the white, which in turn will again raise the Negro plane of living. Benign circles of this order can be established under the initial prompting of law.

To sum up: While it is true that many Americans will not obey laws of which they disapprove strongly, most of them deep inside their consciences do approve civil rights and antidiscrimination legislation. They may approve even while they squeal in protest. Laws in line with one's conscience are likely to be obeyed; when not obeyed they still establish an ethical norm that holds before the individual an image of what his conduct should be. The goad of the law often breaks into a vicious circle so that a process of healing starts to occur. Forces in the individual and in the community that have nothing whatever to do with the law are thus liberated. It is not entirely true that legislation must wait on education—at least not on complete and perfect education, for legislation itself is part of the educative process.

We are not saying that any and every law designed to improve group relations is wise. There are plenty of poorly designed laws. Some of them may be so vague and unworkable that even their educative and conscience-guiding effect is nil. Laws of censorship and suppression are in the long run self-defeating. And while certain laws should perhaps carry stern penalties, it is a generally sound principle that minority group legislation should rely as far as possible on investigation, publicity, persuasion, and conciliation.

There is a special reason why this is true. A prejudiced person is extremely touchy on the subject. A man may accuse himself of prevarication or theft, but seldom of prejudice. We have time and again noted in previous chapters the unconscious forces at work in the prejudiced mind, and the ready defenses and justifications that protect one from insight into his hostilities. It is, therefore, wise to assume that the violator of an antidiscrimination law is unwilling or unable to feel guilt, that he must be allowed to save face, and that a conciliatory approach will gain the desired end better than will punishment.

We have said that laws will, by and large, be obeyed if they are in line with one's conscience, and if they are tactfully administered. We should add an additional condition: they should not be felt to be imposed by an alien will. The South has a legendary resistance to "Yankee interference." Even a law otherwise acceptable may be resisted if it is felt to be a personal (or regional) affront. We are not saying that laws will fail to operate successfully unless they are initiated by one's own legislative representatives, but that the flavor of "alien domination" will probably lessen their effectiveness. Prejudices are not likely to be reduced by laws which, in the manner of their passing, arouse other prejudices.

Legislation and Social Science

In spite of the recent ferment of legislative activity in behalf of minority groups, it is still true that laws to preserve racial *apartheid* occupy greater space in state statute books than do laws that combat discrimination.[9] While the tide seems to be flowing steadily in a new direction it will take a long time for statutory morality in the United States to catch up with Constitutional morality.

In order to understand the situation that exists, it is necessary to take a broadly historical point of view. The suffering and humiliation of the South in the Civil War was a trauma of immeasurable magnitude. Aggressive hostilities were released against the North, against the Negro, and against social change in general —all of which could with some logic be blamed for the intolerable situation. To restore self-esteem it became psychologically necessary to counter the intentions and wishes of the North, and to keep the Negro, if not actually in slavery, at least in a subordinate role.

So intense was this need that even the Supreme Court of the United States felt powerless to resist, and in a series of rulings, culminating in *Plessy v. Ferguson,* virtually capitulated to the South. Seeking to justify its stand, the Court made a series of psychological assumptions which only in subsequent years have been proved false. The assumptions were as follows: (1) Segregation does not stamp the colored race with the badge of inferiority. (2) Legislation is powerless to eradicate "racial instincts" or abolish distinctions based upon physical difference; hence governmental intervention is useless in solving the problems that underlie segregation. (3) If the institution of segregation is left alone, then harmonious relations between races will gradually evolve by a process of mutual adjustment.[10] With the passage of time all of these assumptions have fallen.

The question now arises whether modern social science can be of practical assistance to courts and to legislatures, so that erroneous assumptions concerning the psychological and social consequences of a proposed action might be guarded against. In the nineteenth century this question would have been premature; in the twentieth perhaps it is not. In this volume we have reported scores of recent objective researches that have potential bearing upon social legislation. We are now in a fair position to predict the consequences of segregation and of its abandonment; we know a good deal about the reaction of minority groups who are victimized by discrimination; we understand the impulsive protests against civil rights laws and the reasons why these are generally short-lived. These, and many other findings, represent potential contributions of social science to the clarification and improvement of legal ruling.

Neither the courts nor state and federal legislatures have as yet welcomed the testimony of social science. Granted that science knows relatively little about the successful conduct of human relations, yet some assistance is at hand if wanted. But as yet we have only slender beginnings in the direction of cooperation. One case, involving a Supreme Court decision, may serve to illustrate the present situation.

First it should be pointed out that great resources of skill and money are required to prepare a brief and argue a case before the Supreme Court. An individual by himself is virtually powerless; he can seek redress only if he has the backing of trained lawyers and if his case is financed by a philanthropic individual or agency. Experience shows that best results are obtained by lawyers and organizations who specialize in civil rights issues.[11]

The case we shall report represents the argument prepared by one of these specialized agencies in a recent attempt to invalidate discriminative practices. It is significant for our purposes because several of its central points, and much of its evidence, are derived from social science research in group relations. The argument goes beyond the stock charge that "separate but equal" facilities are not in fact equal.

The brief in question undertook to prove that enforced segregation, even if equal facilities are provided, is in itself discriminatory and hence unconstitutional. Suit was brought by Mr. Henderson, the plaintiff, a Negro, because of the refusal of the Southern Railway Company to serve him in one of its dining cars.[12]

Subsequently the railroad changed its policy so that one out of 13 tables in each diner would be reserved exclusively for Negroes and would be separated by a partition from white diners. The Interstate Commerce Commission held that this rule satisfied the Interstate Commerce Act. That decision was upheld by a District Court. The present brief represents an appeal to the Supreme Court from that decision.

It states clearly that it is not arguing for an enforced commingling of races. No one needs to eat in the presence of a Negro if he does not wish to do so. Private prejudices are one's own business. But enforced segregation denies both colored and white passengers freedom of choice.

The brief then argues that segregation imports, and is designed to import, the inferiority of the Negro race. Everyone understands that enforced segregation is a badge of inferiority. The opinions of many authorities are cited on this point, as well as studies among Negroes which reveal their suffering under this recognized stigma.

The argument of the brief likewise attacks the assumption

upon which the Plessy decision rested, showing evidence that separate facilities in eating, in travel, in standing in line for tickets, all mark the Negro as a lower social caste.

The argument then claims that segregation is harmful to the public interest. Its effects are not confined to the Negro alone. At this point, the results of a social-psychological survey are introduced.[13] Eight hundred forty-nine social scientists who had some special qualifications in the field of race relations were asked their views on enforced segregation; 517 replied. Of these, ninety percent said they believed that it had detrimental effects on the segregated group even if equal facilities were provided; two percent believed it had no harmful effects, and the remaining eight percent did not answer the question or had no opinion. When asked what effects they believed segregation had on the group that enforced it, 83 percent believed them to be detrimental. Among these effects are the anxiety aroused lest the segregated people revolt and get out of hand; likewise the fact that those who enforce segregation become hypocrites in their own eyes, and are forced to live in a world of false slogans and self-deception.

Authorities are cited for the psychiatric judgment that psychosomatic disease is induced by the tensions engendered by segregation and other forms of discrimination.

It is argued further that national welfare is injured by the mutual distrust and ignorance that result from enforced segregation. Experiment and informal opinion agree that normal contacts between races diminish prejudice. The absence of a color line in many countries shows that racial prejudice is neither instinctive nor hereditary, but is probably kept alive by man-made barriers such as segregation.

The brief then steps beyond the domestic plane and points out the undesirable position of the United States on the international scene if the Supreme Court continues to condone segregation.

The Court found for the plaintiff, thus rendering segregation in dining cars in interstate travel illegal. Whether the portion of the argument drawn from social science research played an appreciable part in the Court's decision we cannot say for certain. What is significant is that data from social science investigations were introduced as relevant to the problem.

Summary

Legislation, if enforced, may be a sharp tool in the battle against discrimination. So too may court decisions that invalidate discriminatory legislation left over from the past. Legal action, however, has only an indirect bearing upon the reduction of personal prejudice. It cannot coerce thoughts or instill subjective tolerance. It says, in effect, "your attitudes and prejudices are yours alone, but you may not act them out to a point where they endanger the lives, livelihood, or peace of mind, of groups of American citizens." Law is intended only to control the outward expression of intolerance. But outward action, psychology knows, has an eventual effect upon inner habits of thought and feeling. And for this reason we list legislative action as one of the major methods of reducing, not only public discrimination, but private prejudice as well.

Certain recent developments lead us to believe that social science research in the field of ethnic relations may in the future play a larger part in the shaping of public legislative policy, and therefore indirectly in the reduction of group tensions.

NOTES AND REFERENCES

1. President's Committee on Civil Rights (C. E. WILSON, CHAIRMAN). *To secure these rights.* Washington: U. S. Government Printing Office, 1947.

2. For a fuller account see: *Report on civil rights legislation in the States.* Chicago: American Council on Race Relations, March 1949, **4**, No. 3; also, J. H. BURMA. Race relations and anti-discriminatory legislation. *American Journal of Sociology*, 1951, **56**, 416-423. Especially valuable is W. MASLOW AND J. B. ROBISON, Civil rights legislation and the fight for equality, 1862-1952. *University of Chicago Law Review*, 1953, **20**, 363-413.

3. For a fuller discussion of these three types of legislation see W. MASLOW. The law and race relations. *The Annals of the American Academy of Political and Social Science*, 1946, **244**, 75-81.

4. The majority of people responding to public opinion polls have been found favorable to FEPC. The results are summarized by MASLOW AND ROBISON, *op. cit.*, 396.

5. *Business Week*, February 25, 1950, 114-117. Other evaluations of the operation of FEPC laws are similarly favorable. See M. ROSS. *All Manner of Men.* New York: Harcourt, Brace, 1948.

6. G. SAENGER. *The Social Psychology of Prejudice: Achieving Intercultural Understanding and Cooperation in a Democracy.* New York: Harper, 1953, Chapter 15.

7. G. MYRDAL. *An American Dilemma.* New York: Harper, Vol. 1, 60 ff.

8. *Ibid.*, 17.

9. W. MASLOW AND J. B. ROBISON. *Op. cit.*, 365.

10. T. I. EMERSON. Segregation and the law. *The Nation*, 1950, **170**, 269-271.

11. Prominent among the organizations employing legal methods to defend minority groups are the National Association for the Advancement of Colored People, the American Civil Liberties Union, the Commission for Law and Social Action (of the American Jewish Congress). The increasing activities of such groups are described in an anonymous article entitled, Private attorneys-general: group action in the fight for civil liberties. *Yale Law Journal,* 1949, **58,** 574-598.

12. *Henderson vs. The United States of America, Interstate Commerce Commission and Southern Railway Company.* The description of the case given here is adapted from T. S. KENDLER. Contributions of the psychologist to constitutional law. *American Psychologist,* 1950, **5,** 505-510.

13. Reported by M. DEUTSCHER AND I. CHEIN. The psychological effects of enforced segregation: a survey of social science opinion. *Journal of Psychology,* 1948, **26,** 259-287.

CHAPTER 30

EVALUATION OF PROGRAMS

Our present task is to see how our studies of the causes of prejudice and discrimination can now be applied to remedial programs.

The legislative remedy, discussed in the previous chapter, was examined and approved on the basis of certain scientific considerations. We brought several lines of evidence to converge upon this particular remedial program. Our logic ran somewhat as follows:

In our survey of the sociocultural roots of prejudice (Chapter 14) we noted various aggravating factors present in American society, such as ease of mobility, which sometimes brings a minority group suddenly into an industrial locality. The result is a rapidly growing relative density, and the perception of "threat" by older inhabitants. If through restrictive covenants, segregated schools, or other discriminative practices the minority group is "quarantined" there grow up barriers to communication with attendant suspicion, resentment, and strain. The types of contact that make for lessened prejudice (Chapter 16) become impossible to achieve. Neighbors do not live as neighbors but on guard and defensively.

Now the argument for civil rights legislation rests on the fact that it can change the sociocultural structure in the direction of improving opportunities for equal-status contact in the pursuit of common interests. For example, by outlawing restrictive covenants the Supreme Court makes it somewhat easier for Negroes to disperse themselves in a community and thus avoid the high congestion that leads to the perception of "threat." In the same way, all antidiscrimination legislation helps to dissolve the barriers that segregation imposes, and frees the forces of "equal-status contact" so that they may operate to reduce prejudice and tension.

Still other social science findings are germane to the problem of legislative remedies. Take the question whether prejudiced people will obey antidiscrimination statutes. On this point our discussions of the mental conflict that prejudice arouses in its possessor (Chapter 20) is relevant, as is our discussion of conformity (Chapter 17) and of people's handling of guilt (Chapter 23). It is these findings of social science that led us to predict that antidiscrimination legislation will in principle be accepted and obeyed by the majority of American citizens even though preliminary protest is to be expected.

We need not elaborate the point further. We are saying merely: *Social science tells us that if we wish to reduce prejudice in our society attacks on segregation (legislative or otherwise) are scientifically sound and of high priority.*

But legislative remedies are only one of several possible channels for improving ethnic relations and for changing prejudiced attitudes. The following list—which could be extensively subdivided —suggests others:

> Formal educational methods
> Contact and acquaintance programs
> Group retraining methods
> Mass media
> Exhortation
> Individual therapy

From this list we exclude broad historical and economic changes. While these may be of highest importance, they are too comprehensive to be made the target of any program; or else they are changes that will come about best through legislative action. In the economic field, for example, we have already shown how wage reforms leading to a higher standard of living for minority groups may be expected to enhance their self-respect and diminish defensiveness, while at the same time making for equal-status contact with other elements in the community.

Our list covers fairly well the types of remedial programs that are today employed by the numerous agencies whose goal is to improve group relations within the United States. It is particularly the private agencies that are employing these devices, upon which they spend millions of dollars annually. And these agencies are turning more and more to social science for guidance.

Social science can give aid in two ways. It can, as we have just shown, argue from causes to results. On the basis of a psychological and social analysis of the roots of prejudice, it can with some success predict whether a given mode of operation is likely to succeed or fail. Secondly, it can evaluate in an *ex post facto* manner the results of programs that have been tried.

It is the contribution of social science to the evaluation of programs that we shall now consider.[1]

The Research Approach

Methods for measuring change of attitudes are a recent development. The more we attempt to apply them, the more complexities come to light.[2] The following instance indicates some of the difficulties:

> In 1950 the National Association of Colored Graduate Nurses disbanded after 42 years of independent existence. It did so because Negro nurses were at last welcomed to membership in most local chapters of the American Nurses' Association. Here is an example of attitude change resulting in the termination of one form of segregation.
>
> But to what was it due? Did it come about through the crusading efforts of certain Negro and white nurses? Was the present trend in FEPC legislation, or the tenor of recent Supreme Court decisions, a factor? Did the goodwill and brotherhood propaganda of various national bodies play a part? Or was the change a result of all these and many additional pressures?

Some cause or causes had an effect, but it is not easy to trace the sequence.

The ideal essentials for evaluation research are three in number: (1) There must be first an identifiable program to be evaluated (a course of instruction, a law, a moving picture, a new type of contact between groups). This factor is called the *independent variable*. (2) There must be some measurable indices of change. Attitude scales might be administered before and after the experience, or interviews conducted, or indices of tension within the community computed (for example, the number of group conflicts reported to the police). Such yardsticks are known as the *dependent variable*. (3) Less vital, but still important, is the use of control groups. When the independent variable is applied we should like to prove that the measured change is unquestionably a result of this fact. We can do so best if we have a control group of people (matched for age, intelligence, status) who are not submitted to the impact of the independent variable. If they too (for some mysterious reason) show an equivalent amount of change, then we *cannot* conclude that it was our independent variable that was effective but rather that some other influence was reaching both groups.

The need for a control group is not often realized by investigators. In one survey of 18 evaluations of college programs in intercultural education, it turned out that only four of them had employed controls.[3] It must be admitted that controls are not always effective. Suppose two groups of students are being investigated—one receiving a course of instruction, and the other acting as a control. Now students gossip outside of school. The lessons learned by one group may be passed along informally to the other. In such a case the experimental group contaminates the control.

The desirable design for evaluation research may be summed up in the following scheme:

	Dependent variable	Independent variable	Dependent variable
Experimental Group:	measure of prejudice ⟶	exposure to program ⟶	measure of prejudice
Control Group:	measure of prejudice ⟶	No exposure to program ⟶	measure of prejudice

A problem arises respecting the time when the effects of a program should be evaluated. It is ordinarily easiest to do the evaluating (testing, interviewing, etc.) immediately after the close of the program. But if we detect change then, who knows whether it will endure? And if no change is found, who knows whether the program may not have "sleeper effects" and first show its influence months or even years later? Perhaps the ideal plan is to measure the effects immediately and then again after a lapse of a year.

Enough has been said to show that the field of evaluative research has many obstacles. It is difficult to keep the independent variable uncontaminated; it is hard to devise suitable measures of change; and when the findings are in, one cannot always interpret them with confidence, for all sorts of unwanted variables have intruded themselves into the design. The hurly burly of everyday life in a complex community is very different from a laboratory test tube.

Yet, in spite of these difficulties, there are scores of evaluative studies that pretend to tell how effective some one type of program has been with a specified population.[4] One author who surveyed these studies found himself in despair:

The findings are bewilderingly diverse. Sometimes there is reported a diminution of prejudice, or at least of adverse opinion; sometimes there is no diminution. Sometimes the conclusion is that prejudice is diminished in this respect but not in that; sometimes the relation is reversed. Sometimes one category of students is reported to be more responsive; sometimes another category.[5]

The situation, while complex, is not so hopeless as this author thinks.

Formal Educational Programs

One investigator set herself the task of discovering the effects of the much-publicized Springfield Plan of intercultural education.[6] The Plan (the independent variable) is somewhat broad and flexible and consists of various types of instruction at various grades throughout the child's years in the city's public schools.[7]

The investigator, who teaches in a private college in Springfield, Massachusetts, had the opportunity to study a large number of incoming freshmen who had grown up under the Plan in the city's schools. Available, also, was an even larger number of freshmen who came from outside Springfield and—it is safe to say—did not have as much intercultural training in their background. These non-Springfield students comprised the control groups.

For the dependent variable, the investigator employed the Bogardus Social Distance Scale. The freshmen (764 in all) indicated those ethnic groups that they would not admit to their country, to their neighborhood, to close kinship by marriage, etc.

The results of the study are summarized in Table 13.

Table 13

MEAN SCORE ON THE BOGARDUS SCALE

(The higher the mean score, the higher the degree of prejudice.)

Education	N	Mean	Sigma	Sigma Mean
Educated in Springfield	237	64.76	26.21	1.70
Educated outside Springfield	527	67.60	24.39	1.06

We note that this particular design does not call for a *before* and *after* measure. Hence we cannot prove, as would be desirable, that the young people who took part were equal in prejudice before their educational experience began. If, for example, for some reason the children of Springfield were of a different social composition, or otherwise disposed to grow up with less prejudice than outside children, then the final comparison could not be taken as a measure of the success of the Springfield Plan of intercultural education. There is, however, no reason to suppose that the children in the two samples differed in any such systematic way at the outset.

The author finds that the obtained difference does favor the Springfield school system. Children brought up under the Plan show less social distance than do the others. Statistically, the difference yields a critical ratio of 2.00. While this degree of difference might be the product of chance, it is not likely to be so. And the author points out that the Springfield children spent only part of their school years under the Plan, for it was inaugurated after they were fairly far along in their studies. For this reason, the maximum effect may be achieved only with students of the future.

An interesting sidelight of the study is the fact that, counter to the trend as a whole, Jewish children from Springfield schools showed more intolerance than Jewish students from outside Springfield. The gains were made entirely by Protestants and Catholics. One possible explanation is that the Jewish young people were made overly conscious of the issue of minority groups, and grew more resentful through the succeeding years of elementary and high school.

It is not possible to report all of the available evaluative studies of educational programs. They range widely in type. Some, like the Springfield Plan, are "omnibus," containing many varieties of teaching techniques. Some evaluations are concerned with the impact of special and limited programs. Lloyd Cook has classified the latter under six headings.[8] (1) The "informational approach" imparts knowledge by lectures and textbook teaching. (2) The "vicarious experience approach" employs movies, dramas, fiction, and other devices that invite the student to identify with members of an out-group. (3) The "community study-action approach" calls for field trips, area surveys, work in social agencies or community programs. (4) "Exhibits, festivals, and pageants" encourage a sympathetic regard for the customs of minority groups and our Old World heritage. (5) The "small-group process" applies many principles of group dynamics, including discussion. socioarama, and group retraining. Finally, (6) "individual conference" allows for therapeutic interviewing and counseling.

We are not yet able to say categorically which of these six approaches brings the greatest return. While it is fairly certain that desirable effects appear in approximately two-thirds of the experiments, and ill effects very rarely, we still do not know for sure what methods are most successful. The trend of evidence, as Cook points out, seems to favor *indirect* approaches. By indirect we mean programs that do not specialize in the study of minority groups as such, nor focus upon the phenomena of prejudice as such. The student seems to gain more when he loses himself in community projects, when he participates in realistic situations, and develops, as William James would say, *acquaintance with* the field rather than *knowledge about* the field.

The informational approach. This tentative conclusion clearly puts the informational approach on the defensive. It always has been thought that planting right ideas in the mind would engender right behavior. Many school buildings still display the Socratic motto, *Knowledge Is Virtue.* But the student's readiness to learn facts, it is now pretty well agreed, depends upon the state of his attitudes. Information seldom sticks unless mixed with attitudinal glue. Facts themselves are inhuman; only attitudes are human. Purely factual training often has one of three equally abortive results: it is soon forgotten, or it is distorted in such a way as to rationalize existing attitudes, or the information is allowed to sit in one corner of the mind isolated from the main determinants of living conduct.

This frequent segregation of knowledge from conduct is revealed in a few investigations that have tested both beliefs and attitudes. Intercultural instruction may have the power of correcting erroneous beliefs without appreciably altering attitudes (p. 433). Children may, for example, learn the facts of Negro history without learning tolerance.

Yet there is an argument to be made on the opposite side. Perhaps students may in the short run show no gains or may twist the facts to serve their prejudices. But, in the *long run,* accurate information is probably an ally of improved human relations. To take one example: Myrdal has pointed out that there is no longer any intellectually respectable "race" theory that can justify the position of the Negro in this country. Since people are not wholly irrational, the fact that scientific evidence fails to support the theory of racial inferiority can scarcely fail *gradually* to penetrate into the marrow of their attitudes.

The fundamental premise of intercultural education says in effect, No person knows his own culture who knows only his own culture. A child who grows up to believe that the sun rises and sets on his own in-group, and who views foreigners as strange beings from the outer darkness, is a child lacking perspective on the conditions of his own life. He will never see the American way for what it is—one of many alternative patterns of living that men have invented for their needs. Without intercultural information obtained at school a child cannot acquire this perspective, for most children come from homes and neighborhoods where they have no opportunity to learn about out-groups in an objective way. And so we conclude that the teaching of correct information does not automatically change prejudice; but it may in the long run help.

But, we must ask, may not scientific and factual instruction contain information *unfavorable* to minority groups? Yes, it is conceivable that the incidence of evil traits may be higher in one group than in another (Chapters 6, 7, 9). If so, this information should not be suppressed. If we are going after the truth we must go after the whole of it—not merely after the part that is congenial. Enlightened members of minority groups favor the publication of *all* scientific and factual findings, for they are convinced that when the whole truth is known it will show that most of the common stereotypes and accusations are false. If a small percentage of the accusations prove to be justified, the proper explanations of the findings in terms of adverse conditions under which many minority groups live will improve perspective on the problem and motivate reform. For example, the fact that *some* members of persecuted groups may *sometimes* develop defenses is a fact not to be suppressed but to be faced and sympathetically understood.

How shall we sum up? Mere information, we concede, does not necessarily alter either attitude or action. What is more, its gains, according to available research, seem slighter than those of other educational methods employed. At the same time, there is virtually no evidence that sound factual information does any harm. Perhaps its value may be long delayed, and may consist in driving wedges of doubt and discomfort into the stereotypes of the prejudiced. It seems likely, too, that the greater gains ascribed to other educational (e.g., project) methods require sound factual instruction as underpinning. All in all, we do well to resist the irrational position that invites us to abandon entirely the traditional ideals and methods of formal education. Facts may not be enough, but they still may be indispensable.

Direct versus indirect approaches. A related question arises concerning the merits of focusing attention directly upon intergroup problems. Is it well, for example, for children to discuss the "Negro problem" as such, or is it better for them to approach it through more incidental methods? Some people think that courses in English or geography supply a better context for intercultural studies than courses focused directly on social issues. Why sharpen in the child's mind a sense of conflict? Far better for him to learn the similarities among human groups, and to take for granted the fact that friendly adjustment of the necessary differences is possible.

We cannot be categorical in our decision about this matter. While a child may through indirect methods learn to take cultural pluralism for granted, he may still be perplexed by visible differences in skin color, by the recurrent Jewish holidays, by religious diversity. His education is incomplete unless he understands these matters. Some degree of directness would seem to be required. And with older students there may be even greater value in a direct approach, particularly if through their own experiences they are prepared to face issues head-on.

In an experiment devoted to three modes of teaching at one-week seminars, Rabbi Kagan reports greatest gains by the direct method.[9] To one group of Christian students he taught Old Testament literature, avoiding any mention of Christian-Jewish friction or of present-day problems. In this *indirect* method he merely stressed the positive contribution of Jews to Biblical history. A second group was taught the same subject but with frequent reference to the problem of prejudice, allowing catharsis and a recounting of personal experiences in the class. This *direct* method was most effective. A third group had been taught by the indirect method but the instruction was supplemented by private conferences covering the student's experiences and allowing catharsis. This method he called *focused interview*. Before-and-after tests were administered to all students by a Christian colleague. The author states that the indirect method resulted in no significant change; that the direct method was markedly effective; and that the focused interview likewise yielded positive results. On the whole he favors the direct method. It is important to note that a few extremely anti-Semitic students in the population were unchanged by any of these methods of approach.

It seems probable that the relative success of the direct method in this research may be due to the composition of the group. The students were of high school age and selected for their interest in religious matters. Most of them were thus probably prepared to face ethnic issues frankly and to shift their attitudes in a favorable direction.

We conclude, then, that present evidence on the matter is incomplete. Only in the future can we decide with what groups and under what circumstances direct or indirect methods are to be preferred.

The approach through vicarious experience. Some evidence indicates that films, novels, dramas may be effective, presumably because they induce identification with minority group members. There is indication that this approach may be, for certain children, more effective than the informational or project approach. If this finding stands up in future research, we shall be confronted with an interesting possibility. It may be that strategies of realistic discussion constitute too strong a threat to some people. A milder invitation to identification at the fantasy level may be a more effective first step. Perhaps in the future we shall decide that intercultural programs should *start* with fiction, drama, and films, and move gradually into more realistic methods of training.

Project methods. Most of the remaining methods in intercultural education call for active participation on the part of the student. He makes field trips into the neighborhoods where minorities live; he participates in festivals or community projects with them. He develops an acquaintance with minorities and not merely knowledge about them. Most investigators favor the participation method above all others. It can be adapted to the school program and also for use with adults.

Contact and Acquaintance Programs

The assumption underlying various participation and action programs is that contact and acquaintance make for friendliness. From Chapter 16 we know that this is not always the case. Contact in a hierarchical social system, or between people who equally lack status (poor whites and poor Negroes), or contacts between individuals who perceive one another as threats, are harmful rather than helpful.

The programs we are here discussing, however, strive to bring people of various groups together in a way that enhances mutual respect. It is not easy to do so, for artificiality may easily mar the effort. Lewin has pointed out that many committees on race or community relations do not really engage in common projects of mutual concern. They merely meet to talk about the problem.

Lacking a definite objective goal, such "goodwill" contacts may lead to frustration or even antagonism.[10]

To be maximally effective, contact and acquaintance programs should lead to a sense of equality in social status, should occur in ordinary purposeful pursuits, avoid artificiality, and if possible enjoy the sanction of the community in which they occur. The deeper and more genuine the association, the greater its effect. While it may help somewhat to place members of different ethnic groups side by side on a job, the gain is greater if these members regard themselves as part of a *team*.

Once again we see how important it is to abolish segregation before the optimum conditions of contact and acquaintance can occur. Gandhi, it will be remembered, called for the elimination of untouchability as the *first* point in his program for India. We might well call for it as the first point in a program for America.

Contact and acquaintance programs take many specific forms. The Community Conference or Block Committee is a device successfully tried in Chicago and elsewhere. In it neighbors of different ethnic strains meet for the explicit purpose of improving the region in which they live. In the course of common activity animosities wane and tolerance grows.

A specific technique for accelerating acquaintance has been widely introduced by Rachel Du Bois.[11] The plan, as we saw in Chapter 16, brings together people of diverse ethnic backgrounds in a "neighborhood festival." The leader may start discussion by asking some member to tell about his memories of autumn, of holidays, or of food he enjoyed as a child. The report reminds other participants of equally nostalgic memories, and soon the group is animatedly comparing notes concerning regional and ethnic customs. The distance of the memories, their warmth and frequent humor, lead to a vivid sense of commonality. Group customs and their meaning are seen to be remarkably alike. One member may start a folk song or teach the others a folk dance, and soon a general gaiety prevails. While this technique by itself does not lead to lasting contacts, it is an ice-breaker, and accelerates the process of acquaintance in a community where formerly only barriers may have existed.

While the majority of contact and acquaintance programs have not been evaluated, we know from those that have (several being reported in Chapter 16) that whatever makes for equal-status relationships and for more intimate acquaintance is likely to make for increased tolerance.

What holds for adults in this respect holds also for children.

We have already cited the judgment of several educators that intercultural education in the schools is more effective if it brings about purposive and realistic contacts between the child and various ethnic groups in the community. One well-controlled experiment with first grade children may be cited in this connection.

Trager and Yarrow divided an experimental population of Philadelphia school children into three groups, matched for background and intelligence. One group received a fourteen-session training in intercultural relations according to a carefully prepared curriculum in which community visits, a party in a Negro's home, and other active experiences played a large part. The whole emphasis of the program was to bring the child to see that each occupation, each religion, each race, has a valid part to play in the diversified life of the community.

A second group was instructed also for fourteen sessions on group relations. But the method was very different. It stressed the fact that the American social structure is hierarchical, that deviant groups have "funny customs," and that "the way things are" is, after all, right. While the children in this group were not deliberately indoctrinated with prejudice, their stereotypes were allowed to remain uncorrected, and they were permitted to draw their own inferences from biased teaching materials such as public schools commonly use (e.g., from books depicting Dutch children or Little Black Sambo as given to quaint practices).

The third group of children had no comparable training at all, but spent their time in craft work.

The children's prejudices were measured before and after the seven-week experimental period by the aid of a standard interview and in other ways. It turned out that there was, on the average, a reduction of stereotyping and an increase in tolerance among children in the "cultural pluralism" group, an increase in stereotyping and intolerance among the "status quo" group, and no appreciable change in the control group.

A particularly striking feature of this experiment was the fact that the *same* teachers were used for both styles of pedagogy. Each taught one class by the cultural pluralism approach, and one by the status quo approach. Thus it was not two teachers (one "democratic" and one "authoritarian") whose accomplishments were evaluated, but rather two forms or styles of pedagogy which, with suitable training, a teacher might be expected to master. The experience gained by the teachers from this exacting exercise in role-playing was extremely illuminating to them, converting them to the cultural pluralism approach.[12]

Here we have an interesting example of so-called "action research," i.e., of research based upon a given program installed for the explicit purpose of testing its effectiveness. Its results strengthen our faith in the efficacy of intercultural education of a sort that stresses cultural pluralism and pleasurable contact within the community. It likewise points to the harmful effects of much teaching about group differences that goes on in traditional, status quo school curricula. Finally, in the case of the teachers themselves, it points to changed attitudes that come from role-playing, and from empathizing with two points of view.

Group Retraining

One of the boldest advances of modern social science comes from the invention of role-playing and other techniques that lead to a kind of "forced empathy." The schoolteachers we have just mentioned had a taste of it, but its use forms part of the broader movement known as "retraining"—a specialty of "group dynamics." It has been found that many people are glad to band together in a program that promises to help them improve their skills in human relations. They desire to study techniques of democratic leadership. While they do not join the retraining group expressly to get rid of their prejudices, they may soon learn that it is their own attitudes and biases that are blocking their effectiveness as foremen, teachers, executives.

Unlike the citizen who reads a pamphlet or listens to a sermon, the individual who submits himself to a retraining program is in it up to his eyes. He is required to act out the roles of other people—of employees, of students, of Negro servants; and he learns through such "psychodrama" what it feels like to be in another's shoes. He also gains in insight regarding his own motives, his anxieties, his projections. Sometimes such training programs are supplemented by private sessions with a counselor who helps him further along the road of self-examination. As perspective grows, a deeper understanding of the feelings and thoughts of others develops. Along with such personal involvement comes better conceptualization of the principles of human relations.[13]

Evaluations of this type of training have shown that the gains are greater if social support is maintained. For example, in a study designed to increase skills in community relations work it was found that workers who become isolated in regions where no other members of the training team live tend to be less effective. They become discouraged and overwhelmed by the prejudiced social norms. On the other hand, two or more people who have been retrained and remain together give each other the needed support and carry through their newly acquired insights and skills more effectively.[14]

Not all retraining is of the direct, self-conscious, and self-critical type here described. It may be more objectively centered. An example is the retraining that comes to people who participate in a community self-survey. Volunteers band together to study group relations in their city or region. The experience of designing the study, of framing questions, of conducting interviews, of computing the "discrimination indices" (discovered in housing, employment, schools) is highly educative. The follow-up activities are even more so, for in working to improve the situation uncovered, further gains in knowledge, community skills, and sympathy are bound to result.[15]

Another example of outwardly centered retraining is found in connection with the technique known as "incident control," mentioned in Chapter 20. Its purpose, as in any group retraining, is to break down inhibition and rigidity in several individuals at once, so that they may become more effective in the pursuit of common ends. In this particular case, those who submit to training wish to develop a skill for use in everyday life—skill in offsetting the bigoted remarks that stain our national habits of conversation. What does one say, for example, to a stranger in a public place who has let fall a venomous comment on the Jews that reaches uninvited the ears of many bystanders? Of course there are many situations where propriety says Keep Silent, but there are other situations where silence would lend consent and where, therefore, our sense of justice prompts us to speak up. Research shows that a calm tone of voice, marked by obvious sincerity, and expressing the view that such comments are un-American, has the most favorable effect on bystanders. But it is not easy to summon courage to speak at all, let alone find the right words and control one's voice. Hours of practice under supervision in a group setting are required.[16]

Most of these retraining programs have a marked limitation. They are designed to free the tolerant person of his inhibitions and to provide him with skills if he wants them. It is clear that group retraining cannot be used with people who resist both the method and its objectives. Yet with patience and tact, groups or classes formed for other purposes may be led by easy stages into practicing the techniques of group dynamics.

Furthermore, partial use of these techniques may be used without going the whole way. School children, for example, may easily be led into role-playing.[17] By playing the part of a child in an out-group the juvenile actor may learn through his own organic sensations something of the discomfort and defensiveness engendered by discrimination. A related technique has been employed by Axline, who reports that play therapy in a group of young children resulted in the amelioration of serious racial conflicts within the group.[18] Three or four children, comprising white and colored, are put together in a play situation with dolls and miniature house furnishings. This arrangement offers opportunities for the projection of conflicts and nascent hostility. As the play progresses it is found that accommodation sets in and a genuine readjustment of relationships occurs.

Mass Media

There are grounds for doubting the effectiveness of mass propaganda as a device for controlling prejudices. People whose ears and eyes are bombarded all day with blandishments of special interests tend to develop a propaganda blindness and deafness. And what chance has a mild message of brotherhood when sandwiched in between layers of news reporting war, intrigue, hatred, and crime? What is more, pro-tolerance propaganda is selectively perceived. Those who do not want to admit it to their systems of belief find no trouble in evading it. Usually those who admit it do not need it. But this general pessimism should not block our search for more detailed knowledge. After all, we know that advertising and films have molded our national culture to a considerable degree. May they not profitably be used in the task of remolding it?

Research, though still somewhat meagre, suggests even now certain tentative laws.[19]

(1) While single programs—a film perhaps—show slight effects, several related programs produce effects apparently even greater than could be accounted for in terms of simple summation. This principle of *pyramiding stimulation* is well understood by practical propagandists. Any publicity expert knows that a single program is not enough; there must be a *campaign*.

(2) A second tentative principle concerns the *specificity of effect*. In the spring of 1951 a motion picture theatre in Boston ran the film, *The Sound of Fury*. The picture concluded with the clearly

stated moral that conflicts can be solved only through patience and understanding, not through violence. The audience, deeply moved by the dramatic story, applauded the moral. Later in the same program, a newsreel depicted the late Senator Taft speaking on international relations. He made the identical point that conflict can be solved only through patience and understanding, not through violence. The same audience hissed. What they had learned in one context did not carry over to another. Several researches confirm the point. Opinions may change, but the change tends to be limited to a narrow context and to generalize very little if at all.

(3) A third principle has to do with *attitude regression*. After a period of time opinions tend to slip back toward the original point of view, but not all the way.

(4) This regression, however, is not universal. Studying both the short-run and long-run effect of indoctrination films in the Army, Hovland and his associates found that while attitude regression was common enough, in some people a reverse trend occurred.[20] "Sleeper effects" also came to light. These delayed effects occurred chiefly in "die-hards" who at first resist the message of the film, but later accept it. The sleeper phenomenon is noted especially among well-educated people whose initial opinions are contrary to those held by most other educated people. The authors suggest that latently these individuals have predispositions favoring the propaganda message but must first overcome some inner resistance to it. The moral seems to be that pro-tolerance propaganda reaching people who are ambivalent in their attitudes may have long-range effects, especially among the better educated portions of the population.

(5) Propaganda is more effective when there are no deep-seated resistances. Research shows that people who are "on the fence" are more likely to be affected than those who are deeply committed. We recall here the numerous protective devices that insulate the character-conditioned bigot (Chapter 25).

(6) Propaganda is more effective *when it has a clear field*. The monopoly of propaganda that exists in totalitarian lands forces a monotonous barrage upon the defenseless citizen, and he cannot long maintain his powers of resistance. Counter-propaganda, if it is permitted, throws the individual back upon his own resources of judgment, and frees him from a one-sided view of reality. In the light of this principle it may well be argued that pro-tolerance propaganda is needed—not so much for its positive effects but as an antidote to agitators who work on the other side.

(7) To be effective, propaganda should *allay anxiety*. Bettel-

heim and Janowitz found that propaganda striking at the roots of a person's frame of security tends to be resisted.[21] Appeals geared into existing systems of security are more effective.

(8) A final principle concerns the importance of *prestigeful symbols*. A Kate Smith can sell millions of dollars in war bonds over the radio in a single day. An Eleanor Roosevelt, a Bing Crosby, have prestige for great masses of people. Their espousing of tolerance may win many fence straddlers.

Exhortation

We do not know the effects of preachment, admonishment, or ethical pep talks. Religious leaders have exhorted their followers for centuries to the practice of brotherly love. The cumulated effect seems slight. And yet we cannot be sure that the method is futile. Without such constant admonishment, matters might be much worse than they are.

A reasonable guess might be that exhortation helps strengthen the good intentions of the already converted. And this achievement is not to be scorned, for without religious and ethical reinforcement of their convictions the already converted might not maintain their efforts toward the betterment of group relations. But for the character-conditioned bigot, and for the conformist who finds his social environment too powerful, hortatory eloquence is likely to have small effect.

Individual Therapy

Theoretically, perhaps the best of all methods for changing attitudes is under conditions of individual psychotherapy, for, as we have seen, prejudice is often deeply embedded in the functioning of the entire personality. A distressed individual who seeks the aid of a psychiatrist or counselor is usually desirous of change. He is likely to be ready for a realignment of many of his basic orientations toward life. While it is safe to say that a patient never comes to a therapist for the express purpose of changing his *ethnic* attitudes, still these attitudes may assume a salient role as the course of treatment progresses, and may conceivably be dissolved or restructured along with the patient's other fixed ways of looking at life.

No conclusive study has been made of this hypothesis, although various psychoanalysts have reported their clinical experience.[22] Their experience is particularly cogent since most patients think of psychoanalysis as a "Jewish movement," and this fact alone is almost certain to stir up such anti-Semitic prejudice as may exist. The course of the treatment may be somewhat as follows:

The patient early in his analysis enters into the phase known as "negative transference." He blames the analyst for the suffering that the therapeutic process causes and hates him for his position of dominance and advantage, for being *pro tem* a parent-substitute. Sometimes the analyst is a Jew; even if he is not, the patient thinks of psychoanalysis as a Jewish movement. This circumstance elicits his private anti-Semitic feelings, which more likely than not explode in his outbursts against the analyst. As the treatment progresses, and as the patient gains insight into his whole pattern of values, the anti-Semitism may abate. Indeed, in principle, we should expect that whenever prejudice of any sort intersects with a neurosis, the cure of the neurosis should result in a reduction of the prejudice.

Psychoanalysis is only one mode of treatment. Almost any prolonged interview with a person concerning his personal problems is likely to uncover all major hostilities. In talking about them the patient often gains a new perspective. And if in the course of the treatment he discovers a more generally wholesome and constructive way of life, his prejudice may abate.

An investigator was conducting a long interview with a woman concerning her experience with, and attitudes toward, minority groups. There was no therapeutic intention whatsoever. But in the course of her report the woman told of her anti-Semitic feelings. Reviewing her whole past experience with Jews and with neighborhood anti-Semitism, she gradually gained greatly in self-insight. Finally she exclaimed, "The poor Jews, I guess we blame them for everything, don't we?" Unless she had fixed her attention for a considerable time (about three hours) on this feature of her belief-system, she would not have tracked it down to its sources and placed it in rational perspective in her life.

The frequency of transformations under therapeutic or quasi-therapeutic condition is unknown. More research is needed. But even if this method proves to be the most effective of all methods —and because of its depth and interrelatedness with all portions of the personality, it should be—the proportion of the population reached will always be small.

Catharsis

Experience shows that in certain situations—especially in individual therapy and in group retraining sessions—an explosion of feeling often occurs. When the subject of prejudice comes up for discussion a person who feels his views are under attack or disapproved may need the purging that comes with such explosion.

Catharsis has a quasi-curative effect. It temporarily relieves the tension and may prepare the individual for a change of attitude. It is easier to mend an inner tube after the air has been released. A bit of doggerel expresses the relation between catharsis and tension:

> I was angry with my friend;
> I told my wrath, my wrath did end.
> I was angry with my foe;
> I told it not, my wrath did grow.

It is not true that every expression of hostility has a cathartic effect. Quite the contrary; as we saw in Chapter 22 the display of aggression is not a safety valve, rather it is habit-forming—the more aggression one shows, the more he has. It is only in certain special circumstances that a person who first "blows his top" subsequently becomes willing and able to understand the other side of the argument.

In an eastern city a number of unpleasant instances of ethnic conflict had occurred. Aroused citizens put pressure upon the local police force to introduce a course of instruction dealing with the backgrounds of group antagonism, and the policeman's role in preventing and handling outbreaks.

The police officers who attended this compulsory course were resentful, for the very circumstances under which it was arranged cast reflections upon their competence and fairness. This sense of injustice, together with their own prejudices against certain minority groups, created a condition of tension that made instruction difficult—almost impossible. Whenever an objective point was made concerning Negroes in the community, some police officer would be sure to respond with a story of some vicious Negro who bit him while being arrested.

Every step in the course of instruction encountered stereotypes, caustic anecdotes, and expressions of hostility from the class. None of the instruction seemed to register. It provoked only a torrent of abuse, directed partly to the teacher and partly to the minority groups under discussion. Often the class would complain: "Why does everyone pick on the police?" "We've never had any trouble. Why do we need this course?" "Why don't the Jews mind their business? If they find a dead cat in the ash can they call it anti-Semitism." "The Negro leaders ought to control their people and not set them against the police."

Under such conditions of injured self-esteem it is unlikely that existing prejudice can be changed. No one can be taught who thinks himself under attack.

The course lasted for eight hours. The first six were largely occupied with this type of catharsis. The instructor offered no counterarguments and listened as sympathetically as possible to the hostile outbursts. Gradually a change seemed to occur. For one thing, the class became bored with its own complaining. The attitude at the end seemed to be "We've had our say; now we'll listen to what you have to say on the subject."

Furthermore, there were so many obvious overstatements made in anger that a certain sheepishness crept in. The man who asserted "We've never had any trouble; there is no problem here," soon was telling of several incidents of conflict that he had encountered and as a policeman did not know how to handle. A man who at first railed against Jews tried in later remarks to make amends. In part, catharsis may be effective because one's irrational outburst shocks one's own conscience.

When the immediate tensions had been released, the police officer seemed freer to reconstruct his perception of the total situation. Even while expressing hostility he may be developing private plans for future conduct that will be more acceptable to the community at large. Thus a given official might have been thinking, especially toward the end of the course, somewhat as follows: "Well, I certainly have blown my top. Damn it, I had a right to; it's terrible the way we are picked on. Everybody's got prejudices. But I don't want any trouble in my district. I'd better look out for so and so; he's likely to act up, the way he hates Negroes and Jews. I guess I'll. . . ." and here he begins to construct in imagination a plan for future handling of the problem in his precinct.

It cannot be proved that such mental processes occur during catharsis, but the impression of observers of this particular course of instruction was that during the last two hours, when the antagonism had worn out, the lessons commenced to register and the gain in self-insight was appreciable.[23]

Catharsis alone is not curative. The best that can be said for it is that it prepares the way for a less tense view of the situation. Having had his say, the aggrieved person may be more ready to listen to the other point of view. If his statements have been exaggerated and unfair—as they usually are—the resulting shame modifies his anger and induces a more balanced point of view.

It is not recommended that every program start off by inviting catharsis. To do so would create a negative atmosphere at the outset. When catharsis is needed it will come without special invitation. It is most likely to be needed when people feel that they themselves are under attack. When this situation prevails no progress can be made until catharsis is allowed. With patience, skill, and luck, the leader may then at the right moment guide the catharsis into constructive channels.

NOTES AND REFERENCES

1. Certain portions of the following discussion are drawn from G. W. ALLPORT, *The resolution of intergroup tensions.* New York: National Conference of Christians and Jews, 1953; L. A. COOK (ED.). *College Programs in Intergroup Relations.* Chicago: American Council on Education, 1950; P. A. SOROKIN (ED.). *Forms and Techniques of Altruistic and Spiritual Growth.* Boston: Beacon Press, 1954, Ch. 24.

2. For a technical discussion of the measurement of prejudiced attitudes the reader is referred to MARIE JAHODA, M. DEUTSCH, AND S. W. COOK, *Research Methods in Social Relations: With Special Reference to Prejudice.* New York: Dryden Press, 1951; also, SUSAN DERI, DOROTHY DINNERSTEIN, J. HARDING, AND A. D. PEPITONE. Techniques for the diagnosis and measurement of intergroup attitudes and behavior. *Psychological Bulletin,* 1948, **45**, 248-271.

3. L. A. COOK (ED.). *Op. cit.*

4. Surveys of these evaluational studies have been reported by O. KLINEBERG. *Tensions affecting international understanding: a survey of research.* New York: Social Science Research Council, 1950, Bulletin 62, Chapter 4; R. M. WILLIAMS, JR. *The reduction of intergroup tensions: a survey of research on problems of ethnic, racial, and religious group relations.* New York: Social Science Research Council, 1947, Bulletin 57; A. M. ROSE. *Studies in the reduction of prejudice.* (Mimeographed.) Chicago: American Council on Race Relations, 1947.

5. R. BIERSTEDT. Information and attitudes. In R. M. MACIVER (ED.). *The More Perfect Union.* New York: Macmillan, 1948, Appendix 5.

6. DOROTHY T. SPOERL. Some aspects of prejudice as affected by religion and education. *Journal of Social Psychology,* 1951, **33**, 69-76.

7. J. W. WISE. *The Springfield Plan.* New York: Viking, 1945.

8. See Note #1 above.

9. H. E. KAGAN. *Changing the Attitudes of Christian toward Jew.* New York: Columbia Univ. Press, 1952.

10. K. LEWIN. Research on minority problems. *Technology Review,* 1946, **48**, 163-164, 182-190.

11. RACHEL D. DUBOIS. *Neighbors in Action.* New York: Harper, 1950.

12. HELEN G. TRAGER AND MARIAN R. YARROW. *They Learn What They Live.* New York: Harper, 1952.

13. An elementary exposition of group dynamics is given by S. Chase. *Roads to Agreement.* New York: Harper, 1951, Chapter 9.

14. R. Lippitt. *Training in Community Relations.* New York: Harper, 1949.

15. M. H. Wormser and C. Selltiz. *How to Conduct a Community Self-survey of Civil Rights.* New York: Association Press, 1951.

16. A. F. Citron, I. Chein, and J. Harding. Anti-minority remarks: a problem for action research. *Journal of Abnormal and Social Psychology,* 1950, **45,** 99-126.

17. G. Shaftel and R. F. Shaftel. Report on the use of "practice action level" in the Stanford University project for American ideals. *Sociatry,* 1948, **2,** 243-253.

18. Virginia M. Axline. Play therapy and race conflict in young children. *Journal of Abnormal and Social Psychology,* 1948, **43,** 279-286.

19. A bibliography of research is contained in the monograph by J. T. Klapper. *The Effects of Mass Media.* New York: Columbia University Bureau of Applied Social Research, 1950. (Mimeographed.)

20. C. I. Hovland, et al. *Experiments on Mass Communication.* Princeton: Princeton Univ. Press, 1949.

21. B. Bettelheim and M. Janowitz. Reactions to fascist propaganda: a pilot study. *Public Opinion Quarterly,* 1950, **14,** 53-60.

22. N. W. Ackerman and Marie Jahoda. *Anti-Semitism and Emotional Disorder.* New York: Harper, 1950; R. M. Lowenstein. *Christians and Jews: A Psychoanalytic Study.* New York: International Universities Press, 1950; E. Simmel (Ed.). *Anti-Semitism: A Social Disease.* New York: International Universities Press, 1948.

23. This case is recounted more fully in G. W. Allport. Catharsis and the reduction of prejudice. *Journal of Social Issues,* 1945, **1,** 3-10.

CHAPTER 31

LIMITATIONS AND HORIZONS

SPECIAL OBSTACLES—THE STRUCTURAL ARGUMENT—POSITIVE PRINCIPLES—IMPERATIVES OF INTERCULTURAL EDUCATION—FINAL WORD ON THEORY—FINAL WORD ON VALUES

> . . . We cannot plead that we must wait "until all the facts are in," because we know full well that all the facts never will be in. Nor can we argue that "the facts speak for themselves" and leave it "to the politician and the citizen to draw the practical conclusions." The facts are much too complicated to speak an intelligible language by themselves. They must be organized for practical purposes, that is, under relevant value premises. And no one can do this more adequately than we ourselves.
>
> GUNNAR MYRDAL

In the two previous chapters we have sampled the broad field of remedial programs designed to reduce discrimination or to change attitudes in the direction of greater tolerance. We have commented on these programs both from the point of view of basic research into the causes of discrimination and prejudice and, when evidence was available, in terms of scientific evaluation. Our survey has not been exhaustive, for in recent years programs have mushroomed enormously and scientific interest in these programs has become widespread.[1]

It is only within the past decade that we find an urgent demand for evaluation. The demand itself merits comment. It takes courage for the director of a program or for a board of trustees to submit their activities to impartial judgment. Sometimes the initiative comes from donors, often businessmen, who say in effect, "I'll give money for the program on the condition that you will find out whether my money is well invested." This attitude represents a gain in objectivity and a reduction in the unguided faith and sentimentality that sometimes characterize goodwill activities. We have already commented (Chapter 29) on the way in which social science is beginning to play a part in the area of law; it is even more widely welcomed and sought for in the field of private endeavor. (In passing we wish to call attention to the fact that the evaluative services of social science are in demand not only by intergroup agencies but in connection with programs in education, social work, criminology, therapy, and in other fields where the production of change in attitude is the goal.[2])

While this trend is unquestionably a sign of social and scientific progress, it may also be to some extent self-defeating. The operator may become too dependent on the researcher who, in turn, may not be able to fulfill the large hopes placed in him. The problems of ethnic relations do not fit into neat packages. As we saw in the previous chapter, it is almost impossible to design an evaluative experiment that will take into account the innumerable variables that enter. The roots of the problem are too ramified to justify total reliance upon the excavations of science. As Myrdal says, we cannot "wait until all the facts are in"; Perhaps they never will all be in.

But we can rely on basic and evaluative research to continue and to be increasingly heeded. This encouragement should be kept in mind while we turn to a consideration of various practical and theoretical obstacles that limit the use of research.

Special Obstacles

Anyone who works in the field of intercultural relations knows how often in his community he hears the remark, "There is no problem." Parents, teachers, public officials, police, community leaders seem unaware of the undercurrents of friction and hostility. Until or unless violence breaks out "there is no problem." [3]

We spoke in Chapter 20 of the "mechanism of denial," of the tendency for the ego to defend itself when conflict threatens to upset its equilibrium. The strategy of denial is a quick reflex against disturbing thoughts.

Sometimes the denial is not so deeply bedded, but rests upon sheer habituation to the status quo. People are so accustomed to the prevailing system of caste and discrimination that they think it eternally fixed and entirely satisfactory to all concerned. We have mentioned the finding that most American whites believe that American Negroes are on the whole well satisfied with conditions as they are, an assumption woefully contrary to fact. But even conceding that honest ignorance and sheer habituation account for some of the denial, we must also grant that the deeper mechanism is often at work. We have previously seen that those who are deeply prejudiced are inclined to deny that they are prejudiced. Lacking personal insight, they are unable to take an objective view of conditions in their community. Even a citizen without prejudices of his own is likely to blind himself to injustices and tensions which, if acknowledged, could only upset the even tenor of his life.

One encounters this obstacle widely in school systems, where principals, teachers, and parents often oppose the introduction of intercultural education. Even in communities seething with prejudice we hear, "There is no problem; aren't we all Americans?" "Why put ideas into children's heads?" The attitude reminds us of the resistance shown by many parents, schools, and churches to sex education on the grounds that children might think taboo thoughts (that are surely already in their minds in a muddled fashion).

There are additional obstacles besides apathy and denial. For five years following World War II, the privately supported American Council on Race Relations kept close track of remedial efforts. In its final report it summarizes the principal barriers to progress that it had encountered.[4] In addition to denial, it calls attention to the unbecoming rivalry between competing organizations in the field of group relations. It notes also the unwarranted faith placed in the efficacy of one-factor solutions, in some panacea advocated by an organization specializing in one technique. In particular, it is critical of overemphasis upon mass media and educational programs. It stresses the importance of social structure, for example, pointing out how the traditionally structured system of the South seems to retard all efforts in that region and at the same time imposes a heavy and sodden effect upon the nation as a whole.

Finally, the report calls attention to the tendency of many people, through ignorance or through maliciousness, to identify all advocates of civil rights and all workers in behalf of ethnic relations as "subversive" elements. McCarthyism is a spectre that haunts every worker in the field. While the victim himself sees through the irrationality of the name-calling, most citizens do not. They are led to perceive the worker and his program as vaguely allied to communism. How to combat this irrational overcategorization is a baffling problem. The realistic conflict between east-west ideologies spreads out to include total irrelevancies. We discussed the problem in Chapter 15, but a solution is not easily found.

All of these obstacles are profoundly serious, representing as they do the most firmly entrenched aspects of irrationalism in people and in social systems. But no one has thought that the task of improving group relations is an easy one.

The Structural Argument

The report of the American Council on Race Relations seems pessimistic regarding the effectiveness of single programs. It emphasizes the blanketing impact of social norms that act like an iron curtain of resistance to remedial activities. This important observation merits close scrutiny. It goes to the heart of the whole matter.

The sociologist correctly points out that all of us are confined within one or more social systems. While these systems have some variability, they are not infinitely plastic. Within each system there will be inevitable tensions between groups, due to economic rivalry, crowded housing or transportation facilities, or to traditions of conflict. To meet the strain, the society accords certain groups a superior, and other groups an inferior, position. Custom regulates the distribution of limited privileges, goods, and prestige. Vested interests are pivots within the system, and these in particular resist any attempts at basic change. Further, tradition earmarks certain groups as legitimate scapegoats within the system. Hostility is taken for granted. For example, minor ethnic riots may be tolerated as by-products of the existing strain. Chiefs of police may wink at ethnic gang fights, declaring them normal and natural "kid stuff." To be sure, if the disruption goes too far, the riot squad is called for, or reformers press for legislative relief of the excess tension. But this relief is only sufficient to restore the uneasy equilibrium. If relief went too far it also would destroy the system.

The point of view of the economic determinist is similar (Chapters 13 and 14). He argues that all theories of individual causation are eyewash. A basic structure exists wherein people with higher socioeconomic status cannot, and will not, tolerate equality between laborers, immigrants, Negroes, and other needed peons, and themselves. Prejudice is merely an invention to justify economic self-interest. Until some drastic reform brings true industrial democracy, there can be no effective alteration in the basic social foundations upon which all prejudice rests.

You and I are not normally aware of the extent to which our behavior is constrained and regulated by such features of the social system. We ought not to expect a few detached hours of intercultural education to offset the total press of the environment. People who see a pro-tolerance film will view it as a specific episode and not allow it to threaten the foundations of the system they live in.

The theory holds further that one cannot change segregation, employment customs, or immigration without letting off a chain of effects that would cumulate to produce threatening fractures in the total structure. Each folkway is an ally of every other. If too strong an initial push is allowed it might lead to an acceleration of forces that would destroy the whole system, and therewith our sense of security. Such is the structural view of the sociologist. We discussed this "group norm" theory of prejudice in Chapter 3.

The psychologist, too, it will be recalled, has a structural argument. A prejudiced attitude is not like a cinder in the eye that can be extracted without disturbing the integrity of the organism as a whole. On the contrary, prejudice is often so deeply embedded in character-structure that it cannot be changed unless the entire inner economy of the life is overhauled. Such embeddedness occurs whenever attitudes have "functional significance" for the organism. You cannot expect to change the part without changing the whole. And it is never easy to remake the whole of a personality.

But the psychologist hastens to add that not all attitudes are deeply embedded. A threefold distinction seems helpful.

(1) There is first the individual who keeps his attitudes closely in touch with his own firsthand experience while making allowance for social custom and demand. He manages to adjust attitudes to social reality with little friction while remaining entirely true to his own store of experience. In spite of the social system which surrounds him, his attitudes are flexible. He recognizes clearly when out-groups are unfairly treated, and is friendly to them even in the teeth of an adverse system. Whether he becomes a militant or a mild reformer, or no reformer at all, still his attitudes are strictly his own and not overdetermined by surrounding group norms.

(2) The second class of attitudes, however, are those we have spoken of. They form an internal integration that is self-serving, rigid, sometimes neurotic. Realism is low: the individual neither knows nor cares what the facts are concerning minority groups, nor how harmful in the long run are the discriminatory customs that prevail. The functional significance of these attitudes lies deep, and nothing short of an upheaval in the character structure will change them (Chapter 25).

(3) Finally, and frequently, we find that the ethnic attitudes of many individuals lack internal integration. They are shifting and amorphous, and for the most part are linked to the immediate situation. The person himself may be said to be ambivalent—or, more accurately, multivalent, for, lacking a firm attitude structure, he bends with every pressure. It is with this group that pro-tolerance

appeals may be effective. Pleasant experiences, dramatic lessons, invocations of the American Creed, may be sufficient to provide for the incipient crystallization of a friendly attitude. This type is susceptible to education, to mass media appeals, and to rewarding experience that may start a focus of mental organization where before there was only opportunistic conformity to prevailing prejudice.

We have no way of knowing how numerous each of these types may be. The strictly structural point of view would insist that all of them are affected more than we know by the personal and social systems in which they are set.

Some authors stress the interlocking dependence of both the personal and the social system. They say that one must attack an attitude with due regard to both kinds of systems, which, in combination, hold the attitude embedded in a structural matrix.[5] Newcomb states the case as follows: "Attitudes tend to be persistent (relatively unchanged) when the individual continues to perceive objects in a more or less stable frame of reference."[6] A stable frame of reference may be anchored in the social environment. (All immigrants live on one side of the tracks, all native Americans on the other.) Or it may be an *inner* frame of reference (I am threatened by any alien). Or it may be both. This combined structural view would insist that a shift in the relevant frames of reference must precede change in attitude.

Critique. Whether sociological, psychological, or both, the structural point of view has great merit. It explains why piecemeal efforts are not more effective than they are. It tells us that our problem is stitched into the fabric of social living. It convinces us that the cinder-in-the-eye theory is too simple.

Yet, if we are not careful, the structural view may lead both to false psychology and to false pessimism. It really is not sensible to say that before we change personal attitudes we must change total structure; for in part, at least, the structure is the product of the attitudes of many single people. Change must begin somewhere. Indeed, according to the structural theory, it may start *anywhere,* for every system is to some extent altered by the change in any of its parts. A social or a psychological system is an equilibrium of forces, but it is an unstable equilibrium. The "American dilemma," for example, as Myrdal shows, is a case of such instability. All our official definitions of the social system call for equality, while many (not all) of the informal features of this system call for inequality. There is thus a state of "unstructuredness" in even our most structured systems. And while your personality or mine is certainly a system, can we say that it is impervious to change, or that alteration in the whole must *precede* alteration of parts? Such a view would be absurd.

Granted that America possesses a fairly stable class system wherein ethnic groups have an ascribed status, with prejudice as an accompaniment, still there are also in the American system factors that make for constant change. Americans, for example, seem to have great faith in the changeability of attitudes. The goliath of advertising in this country is erected on this faith; and we are equally confident in the power of education. Our system itself rejects the belief that "you can't change human nature." By and large it repudiates the dictum that "blood will tell." American science, philosophy, social policy incline markedly toward "environmentalism." While this faith may not be entirely justified, the point is that the faith itself is a factor of prime importance. If everyone expects attitudes to change through education, publicity, therapy, then of course they are *more likely* to do so than if no one expects them to change. Our very gusto for change may bring it about, if anything can. A social system does not necessarily retard change; sometimes it encourages it.

Positive Principles

We are not rejecting the structural argument, but rather pointing out that it cannot be used to justify total pessimism. It calls attention forcefully to limitations that exist, but does not deny that new horizons in human relationships are opening.

It is, for example, a perfectly sensible question to ask where, in order to alter social structure or personality structure, change may best begin. In previous chapters we have obtained some, though not final, light on this question. The following principles seem particularly germane.

1. Since the problem is many-sided, there can be no sovereign formula. The wisest thing to do is to attack all fronts simultaneously. If no single attack has large effect, yet many small attacks from many directions can have large cumulative results. They may even give the total system a push that will lead to accelerated change until a new and more agreeable equilibrium is attained.

2. Meliorism should be our guide. People who talk in terms of the ultimate assimilation of all minority groups into one ethnic stock are speaking of a distant Utopia. To be sure, there would be no minority-group problems in a homogeneous society, but it seems probable that in the United States our loss would be greater than our gain. In any case, it is certain that artificial attempts to hasten assimilation will not succeed. We shall improve human re-

lations only by learning to live with racial and cultural pluralism for a long time to come.

3. It is reasonable to expect that our efforts will have some unsettling effects. The attack on a system always has. Thus a person who has been exposed to the intercultural education, to tolerance propaganda, to role-playing, may show greater inconsistency of behavior than before. But from the point of view of attitude change, this state of "unstructuredness" is a necessary stage. A wedge has been driven. While the individual may be more uncomfortable than before, he has at least a chance of recentering his outlook in a more tolerant manner. Investigation shows that people who are aware of, and ashamed of, their prejudices are well on the road to eliminating them.[7]

4. Occasionally there may be a "boomerang effect." Efforts may serve only to stiffen opposition in defense of existing attitudes, or offer people unintended support for their hostile opinions.[8] Such evidence as we have indicates that this effect is relatively slight. It also is a question whether the effect may not be temporary, for any strategy sufficiently effective to arouse defensiveness may at the same time plant seeds of misgiving. It seems probable, too, that "boomerangs" occur chiefly in minds with paranoid trends, where any stimulus, of any type, is absorbed into rigid systems. To be sure, there is the ever-present danger that a given program may be so badly presented that the public cannot understand its intended meaning.[9] But boomerangs in this sense are due merely to ineptitude and to the failure to pretest the program, and are thus avoidable.

5. From what we know of mass media, it seems wise not to expect marked results from this method alone. Relatively few people are in the precise stage of "unstructuredness," and in precisely the right frame of mind, to admit the message. Further, it seems well, on the basis of existing evidence, to focus mass propaganda on specific issues, such, for example, as Fair Employment Practices, rather than upon vague appeals that may not be understood.

6. The teaching and publishing of scientifically sound information concerning the history and characteristics of groups, and about the nature of prejudice, certainly does no harm. Yet it is not the panacea that many educators like to believe. The outpouring of information probably has three benign effects: (a) It sustains the confidence of minorities to see an effort being made to blanket prejudice with truth. (b) It encourages and reinforces tolerant people by integrating their attitudes with knowledge. (c) It tends to undermine the rationalization of bigots. Belief in

the biological inferiority of the Negro, for example, is wavering under the impact of scientific fact; racist doctrines today are on the defensive. Erroneous ideas, Spinoza observed, lead to passion—for they are so confused that no one can use them as a basis for realistic adjustment. Correct and adequate ideas, by contrast, pave the way for a true assessment of life's problems. While not everyone will admit correct ideas when they are offered, it is well to make them available.

7. Action is ordinarily better than mere information. Programs do well therefore to involve the individual in some project, perhaps a community self-survey or a neighborhood festival. When he *does* something, he *becomes* something. The deeper the acquaintance and the more realistic the contacts, the better the results.

By working in the community, for example, the individual may learn that neither his self-esteem nor his attachments are actually threatened by Negro neighbors. He may learn that his own security as a citizen is strengthened when social conditions improve. While preaching and exhortation may play a part in the process, the lesson will not be learned at the verbal level alone. It will be learned in muscle, nerve, and gland best through participation.

8. None of our commonly used methods is likely to work with bigots whose character structure is so inaccessible that it demands the exclusion of out-groups as a condition of life. Yet even for the rigid person there is left the possibility of individual therapy—an expensive method and one that is sure to be resisted; but in principle at least, we need not yet despair completely of the extreme case, especially if tackled young, perhaps in clinics of child guidance, or by wise teachers.

9. While there is no relevant research on the point, it seems likely that ridicule and humor help to prick the pomposity and irrational appeal of rabble-rousers. Laughter is a weapon against bigotry. It too often lies rusty while reformers grow unnecessarily solemn and heavy-handed.

10. Turning now to social programs (the social system), there is first of all considerable agreement that it is wiser to attack segregation and discrimination than to attack prejudice directly. For even if one dents the attitudes of the individual in isolation, he is still confronted by social norms that he cannot surmount. And until segregation is weakened, conditions will not exist that permit equal-status contacts in pursuit of common objectives.

11. It would seem intelligent to take advantage of the vulnerable points where social change is most likely to occur. As Saenger says, "Concentrate on the areas of least resistance." Gains in housing

and economic opportunities are, on the whole, the easiest to achieve. Fortunately, it is these very gains that minorities most urgently desire.

12. Generally speaking, a *fait accompli* that fits in with our democratic creed is accepted with little more than an initial flurry of protest. Cities that introduce Negroes into public jobs find that the change soon ceases to attract attention. Sound legislation is similarly accepted. Official policies once established are hard to revoke. They set models that, once accepted, create habits and conditions favorable to their maintenance.

Administrators, more than they realize, have the power to establish desirable changes by executive order in industry, government, and schools. In 1848 a Negro applied for admission to Harvard College. There were loud protests. Edward Everett, then President, replied, "If this boy passes the examinations he will be admitted and, if the white students choose to withdraw, all the income of the college will be devoted to his education." [10] Needless to say, no one withdrew, and the opposition quickly subsided. The College lost neither income nor prestige, though both at first seemed threatened. Clean-cut administrative decisions that brook no further argument are accepted when such decisions are in keeping with the voice of conscience.

13. The role of the militant reformer must not be forgotten. It is the noisy demands of crusading liberals that have been a decisive factor in many of the gains thus far made. We saw in Chapter 29 how legislative movements are sometimes spearheaded by militant private organizations. It was John Brown, the individualist, who dramatized the plight of the Negro slave, and Harriet Beecher Stowe, the novelist, who fanned the flames of conscience until slavery was abolished. Individuals may be decisive factors in changing even a social system.

These conclusions represent some of the positive principles that derive from research and theory. They are not intended as a complete blueprint—such would be pretentious. The points represent rather certain wedges which if driven with skill might be expected to crack the crust of prejudice and discrimination.

Imperatives of Intercultural Education

Without prolonging our discussion of programs unduly, we wish to call attention once more to the role of the school. We do so partly because of the characteristic faith that Americans have in education, and partly because it is easier to install remedial programs in the school than in the home. School children comprise a vast captive audience; they study what is set before them. While school boards, principals, and teachers may resist the introduction of intercultural education, yet it is increasingly included in the curriculum.

Learning prejudice and learning tolerance are, as we saw in Part V of this volume, subtle and complex processes. The home is undoubtedly more important than the school. And the *atmosphere* of the home is as important, perhaps more important, than the parents' specific teaching concerning minority groups.

It is probably too much to expect teachers to offset the home environment, and yet, as the evaluative studies cited in the previous chapter show, a good deal can be accomplished. The school, like the church and the laws of the land, can set before the child a higher code than is learned at home, and may create a conscience and a healthful conflict even if the prejudiced teachings of the home are not entirely overcome.

As in the home, the atmosphere that surrounds the child at school is exceedingly important. If segregation of the sexes or races prevails, if authoritarianism and hierarchy dominate the system, the child cannot help but learn that power and status are the dominant factors in human relationships. If, on the other hand, the school system is democratic, if the teacher and child are each respected units, the lesson of respect for the person will easily register. As in society at large the *structure* of the pedagogical system will blanket, and may negate, the specific intercultural lessons taught.[11]

We have seen that instruction of the sort that involves the whole child in intercultural activities is probably more effective than merely verbal learning or exhortation. While information is likewise essential, facts stick best when embedded in the soil of interested activity.

Granted these points, the question remains as to what concrete lessons the child or adolescent should learn in the course of his school training. What should be the *content* of intercultural education? Here, as before, we cannot claim that all evidence is in. But we may suggest a few of the imperatives for intergroup education.

The age at which these lessons should be taught need not worry us. If taught in a simple fashion all the points can be made intelligible to younger children and, in a more fully developed way, they can be presented to older students in high school or college. In fact, at different levels of advancement, through "graded lessons," the same content can, and should, be offered year after year.

(1) **Meaning of race.** Various films, filmstrips, and pamphlets are available for school use; these present anthropological facts in

as much detail as the child can absorb. The child should certainly learn the confusion that occurs between genetic and social definitions of race. For example, he should understand that many "colored" people are racially as much Caucasian as Negro, but that a caste definition obscures this biological fact. The misconceptions of racism in its various forms, and the psychology underlying racist myths, can be made clear to older children.

(2) **Customs and their significance in various ethnic groups.** Schools have traditionally taught this lesson, but in a dubious way. Modern exhibits and festivals give a more adequate impression, as do reports in the classroom from children who come from diverse ethnic backgrounds. Especially needed are sympathetic accounts of linguistic and religious backgrounds, with particular reference to the significance of religious holy days. Visits to places of worship in the community help anchor the lesson.

(3) **Nature of group differences.** Less easy to teach, but needed for the purpose of generalizing the two preceding lessons, is a sound understanding of the ways in which human groups differ and do not differ. It is here that fallacious stereotypes can be combatted, likewise "belief in essence." The fact that some differences are merely imaginary, some fall on overlapping normal curves, and some follow a J-curve distribution (Chapter 6), can be taught in a simplified way. A child who understands the precise nature of group differences is less likely to form overbroad categories. The lesson should likewise include a restatement of the role of biological and social factors in producing these differences.

(4) **Nature of tabloid thinking.** Fairly early, children can be made critical of their own too simple categories. They can learn that Foreigner 1 is not the same as Foreigner 2. They can be shown how the law of linguistic precedence in learning (p. 305) creates dangers for them, particularly in the form of derogatory epithets such as "nigger" and "wop." Simple lessons in semantics and in elementary psychology are neither dull nor incomprehensible to children.

(5) **The scapegoating mechanism.** Even a seven-year-old can understand the displacement of guilt and aggression (p. 349). As children grow older they can see the relevance of this principle to the persecution of minority groups throughout the ages. Good teaching may bring the lesson home to the child in such a way that he watches for his own projections and refrains from scapegoating in his personal relationships.

(6) **Traits sometimes resulting from victimization.** The way in which ego defenses develop as a result of persecution is not hard to understand (Chapter 9)—though it is a delicate lesson to teach.

The danger lies in creating a stereotype to the effect that *all* Jews are ambitious and aggressive in order to compensate for their handicaps; or that all Negroes are inclined to sullen hate or petty thieving. The lesson can, however, be taught without primary reference to minority groups. It is essentially a lesson in mental hygiene. Through fiction, to start with, a youngster may learn of the compensations a handicapped (perhaps crippled) child develops. He may go from that point to a discussion of hypothetical cases in class. Through role-playing he may gain insight into the operation of ego defenses. By the age of fourteen the adolescent may be led to see that his own insecurity is due to his lack of firm ground: he is sometimes expected to act like a child, sometimes like an adult. He wants to be an adult, but the conduct of others makes him unsure of whether he belongs to the world of childhood or of adulthood. The teacher may point out that the predicament of the adolescent resembles the permanent uncertainty under which many minority groups have to live. Like adolescents, they sometimes show restlessness, tension, ego defensiveness, which occasionally lead to objectionable behavior. It is far better for the young person to learn the grounds for ego-defensive behavior than for him to be left with the idea that objectionable traits are inherent in certain groups of mankind.

(7) **Facts concerning discrimination and prejudice.** Pupils should not be kept ignorant of the blemishes of the society in which they live. They should know that the American Creed demands more equality than has been achieved. Children should know about the inequalities of housing and educational and job opportunities. They should know how Negroes and other minorities feel about their situation; what it is they especially resent; what hurts their feelings; and what elementary courtesies are in order. Films may be used in this connection, so too the "literature of protest," especially biographical accounts of young American Negroes, such as Richard Wright's *Black Boy*.

(8) **Multiple loyalties are possible.** Schools have always inculcated patriotism, but the terms of allegiance are often narrowly conceived. The fact that loyalty to the nation requires loyalty to all subgroups within the nation is seldom pointed out (see Figure 1, p. 36). We noted in Chapter 25 that the institutional patriot, the superpatriotic nationalist, is more often than not a thoroughgoing bigot. The teaching of exclusive loyalty—whether to nation, school, fraternity, or family—is a method of instilling prejudice. The child may be brought up to see that loyalties are concentric, the larger may contain the smaller, with no exclusion implied (see Figure 2, p. 43).

Final Word on Theory

Are discrimination and prejudice facts of the social structure or of the personality structure? The answer we have given is *Both*. For greater precision we may say that what we call *discrimination* usually has to do with common cultural practices closely linked with the prevailing social system, whereas the term *prejudice* refers especially to the attitudinal structure of a given personality.

While this clarification is helpful, we recognize that the two conditions are simultaneously present and form parts of a single story. And we emphasize once again, as forcefully as possible, that a multiple approach is required. In Chapter 13 we saw that help comes from *historical, sociocultural,* and *situational* analysis, as well as from analysis in terms of *socialization, personality dynamics, phenomenology,* and finally, but not least important, in terms of actual *group differences*. To understand prejudice and its conditions the results of investigations at all these levels must be kept in mind. It is not easy to do so, but there is no other way.

Remedial programs are, broadly considered, of two types: those stressing change in the social structure (e.g., legislation, housing reform, executive fiat), and those stressing change in personal structure (intercultural education, child training, exhortation). But in practice these programs are likely to interlock. Thus to make intercultural education effective, a change in the school system may be required, or an improvement in the practices of mass media will affect both the attitudes of the audience and the policies of the communication system itself. While social science is now in a position to predict with some success the outcome of various single-pointed programs, it is also in a position to advise in favor of a pluralistic approach. Those who wish to improve group relations would do well to engage in a many-pronged attack.

The aim of this volume has been to convince the reader that the problem is truly many-sided. It has aimed likewise to provide a scheme of organization by which the reader may be enabled to keep the many factors in mind. Finally, it has tried to carry the analysis of each major factor deep enough so that solid soil may be prepared for future advances in theory and in remedial practice.

In spite of the boldness of our purpose, we realize that the story we tell will need many corrections in the future, as well as expansion. The sciences of human behavior are still in the infancy of their development. But though we stumble at thresholds, we believe that progress is discernible and that future advances are assured.

Final Word on Values

How can we account for the growing concern of enlightened people with the problem of prejudice, and with the entire subject of irrational human behavior? (Proof of this concern lies in the mounting output of research, theory, and remedial effort.) The answer lies in the threat to democratic values posed by twentieth-century totalitarianism. It was a stuporous error for the western world to believe that democratic ideology, stemming from Judeo-Christian ethics and reinforced by the political creeds of many nations, would of itself gradually overspread the world. Instead of this happening, a frightful retrogression set in. Mankind revealed its weakness: unemployment, hunger, insecurity, the aftermath of war made men a ready prey to demagogues who without compunction brought the democratic ideal down in ruins.

Democracy, we now realize, places a heavy burden upon the personality, sometimes too great to bear. The maturely democratic person must possess subtle virtues and capacities: an ability to think rationally about causes and effects, an ability to form properly differentiated categories in respect to ethnic groups and their traits, a willingness to award freedom to others, and a capacity to employ it constructively for oneself. All these qualities are difficult to achieve and maintain. It is easier to succumb to oversimplification and dogmatism, to repudiate the ambiguities inherent in a democratic society, to demand definiteness, to "escape from freedom."

It is part of the democratic faith that the objective study of the irrational and immature elements in human behavior will help us counteract them. Certain it is that neither Nazi Germany, nor Soviet Russia, nor any other totalitarian land, has permitted science to study unimpeded the psychology of the irrational. Forbidden are researches in public opinion, psychoanalysis, rumor, demagogy, propaganda, prejudice—unless these researches are secretly conducted in the interests of a geopolitical exploitation of men. In the free countries of the world, however, the study of the irrational has speeded up, for our faith still holds that the forces in society and in personality that make for retrogression, ethnocentrism, and hate can be controlled if they are understood.

A few may argue that irrational behavior, including prejudice, is a good thing. We have cited writers, even in western culture, who take this view. Tension, they say, is the very essence of life;

to exist is to struggle, to survive is to conquer. Nature is harsh; men are harsh; to combat prejudice is to court a weakling race. This view, sometimes perversely called Darwinian, is a conceivable position to hold. But it is not common nor ethically acceptable to the values of democracy, which envision equal justice and equal opportunity for the variegated groups of mankind. The search for the roots and remedies of ethnic conflict and prejudice, as represented in this volume, is sustained by a democratic value-orientation. Scientists, like other mortals, cannot help but be motivated by their own personal values.

Value enters the scientific situation at two points. First, it motivates the scientist (or the student) to undertake and sustain his investigations. Second, it directs his final efforts to apply his findings in the service of what he considers to be a desirable social policy. Value does not enter, and therefore cannot distort, the following essential stages of the scientific work. (1) It does not affect the identification or definition of the problem. In Chapter 1 we made clear that prejudice is an existing psychological fact, just as discrimination is an existing social fact. Whether the scientist is for or against prejudice and discrimination cannot alter the fact. Prejudice is not "the invention of liberal intellectuals." It is simply an aspect of mental life that can be studied as objectively as any other. (2) Values do not enter into the process of scientific observation, experimentation, or fact collecting. (On the rare occasions when this does happen the bias of the investigator is detected and rightly reproved.) (3) Values do not enter into the process of generalizing scientific laws (excepting, of course, in the sense that one deems the formation of general laws desirable). It would do a scientist no good to misrepresent his data, or to derive generalizations that are unfounded. If he did so he would merely negate his superordinate value of applying science to the improvement of human relations. (4) Values do not enter into the process of communicating results and theories. Unless there is clear unbiased communication there can be no replication of experiments, no invitation to create a cumulative science that would in the long run achieve the ultimate value in view.

To sum up: The present volume, and the researches it reports, were initiated by the authors' values, which they share with others who hold a democratic ideology; likewise the present volume is written in the hope that the facts and theories presented may contribute to the amelioration of group tensions. At the same time, it claims to be a scientific production as accurate and objective as the present stage of human knowledge allows.

There is one final aspect to the problem of values that we wish to mention. Whereas our goal of reduced tension, increased tolerance, and friendliness is clear enough, we are less clear about the desirable long-range policies in dealing with cultural and racial minorities. Is the amalgamation of all groups a valid ideal, or should we strive to maintain as much diversity and cultural pluralism as possible? For example, *ought* American Indians to preserve their own way of life, or ought they gradually to lose their identity through migration and intermarriage, thus entering into the American melting pot? How about the numerous immigrant groups from Europe, also the Oriental, the Mexican, the Negro?

Those who favor assimilation (a value judgment) point out that when groups completely fuse there is no longer any visible or psychological basis for prejudice. Particularly the less educated portions of a population, who are unable to understand or to value foreign ways, seem to require a homogenization of groups before they can give up their biased thinking. To them unity means conformity.

On the other hand, those favoring cultural pluralism regard it as a great loss (again a value judgment) when ethnic groups discard their distinctive and colorful ways: the cuisine of the Near East, the Italian love of opera, the sage philosophy of the Orient, the art of the Mexican, the tribal lore of the American Indian. When preserved, these ways are of interest and value to the whole nation, and prevent drab standardization in a culture dominated by advertising, canned foods, and sedative television. Yet it is true that at least one large group against which there is prejudice, the American Negro, can scarcely be said to have a distinctive culture, and the cultural pluralist in this case is not very clear regarding the most desirable outcome.

What then is the proper value to hold in this controversy? The question may seem remote and unreal, for the ultimate solution may not be under our voluntary control. Yet in some instances the choice we make now is important. An example is the policy of the federal government respecting the American Indian. The official attitude seems recently to have changed from one encouraging cultural pluralism to one favoring assimilation. The attitude is important because it directs day-by-day policies and immediately affects the lives of those concerned.

While we cannot presume to settle the issue, we may point to what seems a reasonable democratic guideline. For those who wish to assimilate, there should be no artificial barriers placed in their way; for those who wish to maintain ethnic integrity, their efforts should be met with tolerance and appreciation. If such a permissive policy were in force, portions of the Italian, Mexican, Jewish, and colored groups would no doubt lose themselves in the melting pot; others, at least in the foreseeable future, would remain separate and identifiable. Democracy demands that the human personality in its course of development should be allowed to proceed without artificial forces or barricades, so long as this development does not violate the safety and reasonable rights of others. In this way the nation will achieve, at least for a long time to come, a desirable "unity in diversity." What the remote future may hold we cannot foresee.

America, on the whole, has been a staunch defender of the right to be the same or different, although it has fallen short in many of its practices. The question before us is whether progress toward tolerance will continue, or whether, as in many regions of the world, a fatal retrogression will set in. The whole world watches to see whether the democratic ideal in human relationships is viable. Can citizens learn to seek their own welfare and growth not at the expense of their fellow men, but in concert with them? The human family does not yet know the answer, but hopes it will be affirmative.

NOTES AND REFERENCES

1. For a supplementary account of action programs the reader may consult G. SAENGER. *The Social Psychology of Prejudice: Achieving Intercultural Understanding and Cooperation in a Democracy.* New York: Harper, 1953, Chapters 11-16.

2. Representative of recent evaluative researches in these fields are H. W. RIECKEN. *The Volunteer Workcamp: A Psychological Evaluation.* Cambridge: Addison-Wesley, 1952; E. POWERS AND HELEN WITMER. *An Experiment in the Prevention of Delinquency.* New York: Columbia Univ. Press, 1951: L. G. WISPE. Evaluating section teaching methods in the introductory course. *Journal of Educational Research*, 1951, **45**, 161-186.

3. In a survey of many communities one investigator reports that the denial of a problem was almost universally encountered. G. WATSON. *Action for Unity.* New York: Harper, 1947.

4. *The Role of the American Council on Race Relations.* Chicago: American Council on Race Relations, Report, 1950, **5**, 1-4.

5. *Cf.* T. R. VALLANCE. Methodology in propaganda research. *Psychological Bulletin*, 1951, **48**, 32-61.

6. T. M. NEWCOMB. *Social Psychology.* New York: Dryden Press, 1950, 233.

7. *Cf.* G. W. ALLPORT AND B. M. KRAMER. Some roots of prejudice. *Journal of Psychology*, 1946, **22**, 9-39.

8. C. I. HOVLAND, *et al.* *Experiments in Mass Communication.* Princeton: Princeton Univ. Press, 1949, 46-50.

9. E. COOPER AND MARIE JAHODA. The evasion of propaganda: how prejudiced people respond to anti-prejudice propaganda. *Journal of Psychology,* 1947, **23**, 15-25.

10. Quoted by P. R. FROTHINGHAM. *Edward Everett, Orator and Statesman.* Boston: Houghton Mifflin, 1925, 299.

11. T. BRAMELD. *Minority Problems in the Public Schools.* New York: Harper, 1946.

INDEX OF NAMES

INDEX OF SUBJECTS